SIXTH EDITION

FUNDAMENTALS OF ECONOMICS

WILLIAM BOYES
Arizona State University

MICHAEL MELVIN
Arizona State University and BlackRock

SOUTH-WESTERN
CENGAGE Learning

Australia • Brazil • Japan • Korea • Mexico • Singapore • Spain • United Kingdom • United States

SOUTH-WESTERN
CENGAGE Learning

Fundamentals of Economics, Sixth Edition, International Edition
William Boyes and Michael Melvin

Senior Vice President, LRS/Acquisitions & Solutions Planning: Jack W. Calhoun

Editorial Director, Business & Economics: Erin Joyner

Editor-in-Chief: Joe Sabatino

Senior Acquisition Editor: Steve Scoble

Developmental Editor: Elizabeth Lowry

Editorial Assistant: Elizabeth Beiting-Lipps

Senior Brand Manager: Robin LeFevre

Market Development Manager: John Carey

Marketing Coordinator: Ilyssa Harbatkin

Art and Cover Direction, Production Management, and Composition: PreMediaGlobal

Media Editor: Anita Verma

Rights Acquisition Director: Audrey Pettengill

Rights Acquisition Specialist, Text and Images: Deanna Ettinger

Manufacturing Planner: Kevin Kluck

Cover Image: © deliormanli/iStockphoto

International Edition:
ISBN-13: 978-1-285-17610-9
ISBN-10: 1-285-17610-3

Cengage Learning International Offices

Asia
www.cengageasia.com
tel: (65) 6410 1200

Australia/New Zealand
www.cengage.com.au
tel: (61) 3 9685 4111

Brazil
www.cengage.com.br
tel: (55) 11 3665 9900

India
www.cengage.co.in
tel: (91) 11 4364 1111

Latin America
www.cengage.com.mx
tel: (52) 55 1500 6000

UK/Europe/Middle East/Africa
www.cengage.co.uk
tel: (44) 0 1264 332 424

Represented in Canada by Nelson Education, Ltd.
www.nelson.com
tel: (416) 752 9100/(800) 668 0671

Cengage Learning is a leading provider of customized learning solutions with office locations around the globe, including Singapore, the United Kingdom, Australia, Mexico, Brazil, and Japan. Locate your local office at: **www.cengage.com/global**

For product information and free companion resources: **www.cengage.com/international**
Visit your local office: **www.cengage.com/global**
Visit our corporate website: **www.cengage.com**

Printed in the United States of America
1 2 3 4 5 6 7 16 15 14 13 12

To Our Families

W.B. M.M.

BRIEF CONTENTS

CONTENTS

PREFACE

As the title of the first chapter in this text makes clear, economics can be found all around you—in your everyday life, in the decisions you make, and in the news. We invite you to join us as we explore the economic landscape—the concepts and issues that confront us on a daily basis. We will consider important questions such as the following:

- Why are some nations rich while others are dirt poor? (Chapter 1)
- Is competition good for you or should you be protected from it?
- Is income inequality a serious issue? Why do people earn different incomes, and why do different jobs pay different wages? (Chapter 3)
- Should firms seek profits? (Chapter 4)
- What are the benefits of competition? Is a free market system beneficial or costly for society? (Chapter 6)
- Why does the government intervene in the affairs of business? Is such intervention necessary for an economy to function? (Chapter 7)
- Can a free market provide health care or must the government run the health care system? Should illicit drugs be legalized? How does a free market function in the face of discrimination? (Chapter 8)
- How is money traded internationally? (Chapter 10)
- What is a business cycle? (Chapter 11)
- How do banks create money? (Chapter 14)
- What is the Federal Reserve? (Chapter 15)
- Are business cycles related to political elections? (Chapter 16)
- Why do countries restrict international trade? (Chapter 17)
- What is globalization? (Chapter 18)

To help you understand these and other issues, we've tried to boil down economics to its fundamentals—the core concepts. Rather than focusing on formal economic theories, we have chosen to emphasize relevant applications and policy issues.

OUR GOALS IN WRITING THE TEXT

This book is intended for a one-term course in economics, a course that covers the fundamentals of micro- and macroeconomics. The text was written with several objectives in mind. First, one of our goals is to demonstrate the value of economic analysis in explaining daily events. We also want to show how economic analysis can help us understand why individuals, business firms, and even governments behave as they do. To accomplish this, we relate each concept to the individual. For example, we show what *government intervention in free markets* means to you and how money supply affects your paycheck. We believe that the use of real-world examples as illustrations of economic concepts is a more effective approach to learning than the use of hypothetical products, firms, and people as examples.

Second, we want to present the world as a global economic environment and to present the tools you need in order to understand and live in this environment. Whereas other texts ignore or isolate international coverage, we fully integrate a global perspective within our discussion of the traditional fundamentals of economics. Topics such as rich and poor nations, the creation of the European Central Bank, the change in the value of the dollar, issues of the European Union, and the effect of an exchange rate on firms, prices, and employees are all discussed within the context of economic analysis.

A third, overarching goal is to engage students with concepts that are currently meaningful. We want our readers to learn the fundamentals and to develop an economic way of thinking about issues that confront them. We strive to present only the essential topics rather than force readers to delve into abstract topics and become lost in the forest and lose sight of the "trees."

A Focus on Fundamental Questions

Earlier, we introduced some of the important questions considered in the text. These questions, referred to as fundamental questions, provide the organizing framework for the text and its accompanying ancillary package. *Fundamental Questions*, in fact, open and organize each chapter, highlighting the critical issues. Students should preview the chapters with these questions in mind, reading actively for understanding and retention. Each related fundamental question also appears in the margin next to the text discussion and, with brief answers, in the chapter summaries. Finally, fundamental questions are used as the integrating framework for the text and the entire ancillary package. For example, brief paragraph answers to each of the questions are found on the student website.

An Integration of International Issues

As previously noted, the text incorporates a global perspective. In addition to two international chapters—Chapter 17, "Issues in International Trade and Finance," and Chapter 18, "Globalization"—every chapter incorporates global examples to provide a more realistic picture of the economy. Topics include the following:

- Gains from trade (Chapter 1)
- Quotas and bans (Chapter 3)
- Comparative analysis of fiscal policies in different countries (Chapter 13)
- "Global money" and international reserve currencies, including a section on informal financial markets and a *Global Business Insight* box on Islamic banking (Chapter 14)
- Foreign exchange market intervention as part of central bank policy (Chapter 15)
- Business cycles and economic growth issues as important macroeconomic policy issues (Chapter 16)

A Real-World Framework

We have developed a real-world framework that shows how markets work, focusing on competition and the behavior of firms. Instead of becoming bogged down in a theoretical discussion of each market structure model, students learn how businesses behave, compete, create profit, and attempt to sustain profits over time. They learn what business competition means and how it affects their daily lives.

To further connect the text to the real world, we incorporate *Economic Insight* and *Global Business Insight* boxes, which focus on the policies of today's leaders and the business decisions of real companies and governments from around the world. The goal is to help students think critically about news stories and to respond to them with greater insight. Some examples are as follows:

- *Economic Insight:* eBay and Online Markets (Chapter 7)
- *Economic Insight:* Discrimination and Poor Word-Processing Skills (Chapter 8)
- *Economic Insight:* Jobs Moving Offshore (Chapter 3)
- *Economic Insight:* The Value of Homemaker Services (Chapter 10)
- *Global Business Insight:* "Free" Air? (Chapter 1)
- *Global Business Insight:* Price Adjusting Vending Machines (Chapter 4)
- *Global Business Insight:* The IMF and the World Bank (Chapter 17)

CHANGES TO THE SIXTH EDITION

Our objective of making the subject of economics interesting and useful requires constant update of applications and consideration of relevant issues. All data and examples have been updated. Major content has not been changed although all applications and illustrations have been updated. The fifth edition involved major structural changes. In this, the sixth edition, changes deal more with updates and applications than with structural changes.

A COMPLETE TEACHING AND LEARNING SYSTEM

Proven Pedagogical Features

Reviewers and adopters of previous editions have commented very favorably on the learning aids within each chapter. All of these features aim to make learning easier by providing a consistent set of signposts to guide readers along the way.

In-text Referencing System Sections are numbered for easy reference and to reinforce hierarchies of ideas. The numbering system serves as an outline of the chapter, allowing instructors flexibility in assigning reading and making review easy for students.

Fundamental Questions As described earlier, the *Fundamental Questions* provide an organizing framework for the text and ancillary package. They have been carefully reviewed and, in some cases, revised for this edition in order to reflect the essential points for each chapter.

Recaps Briefly listing the main points covered, a *Recap* appears at the end of each major section. Students are able to quickly review what they have just read before going on to the next section.

Now You Try It First introduced in the second edition to help students master some of the analytical techniques introduced in the text, this feature was expanded in the third edition. Now even more of these checkpoint questions provide an opportunity for students to practice a technique when it is first introduced. Answers are provided at the end of the book so that students can immediately check their work and go back to the relevant text discussion if necessary.

Summary The summary at the end of each chapter is organized according to the list of *Fundamental Questions*. It includes a brief synopsis of the discussion, which helps students answer those questions.

End-of-Chapter Exercises A full set of exercises at the end of each chapter provides the student with many additional opportunities for practice—and homework. Answers to these exercises are provided in the *Instructor's Resource Manual* on the instructor website.

Study Guide A study guide is also provided to help test students' chapter knowledge. The answers to the study guide can be found at the back of the book.

A Pedagogically Sound Art Program

Economics can be intimidating, which is why we've incorporated a number of pedagogical devices to help students read and interpret graphs. Annotations on figures point out areas of particular concern or importance. For example, students can see at a glance what parts of the graph illustrate a shortage or a surplus, a change in consumption, or consumer surplus.

A Well-Integrated Ancillary Package

One goal for this revision was to make it easier for students to practice and apply the new information they are learning. Thus, they can review as they read a chapter, review again at the end of a chapter, and go to the student website for additional practice and review questions. Our instructor's materials support this student-centered approach. To foster the development of consistent teaching strategies well integrated with the text, the instructor supplements follow the same pedagogical format as the text, incorporating the *Fundamental Questions* throughout. The instructor supplements are available on instructor's website, located at www.cengagebrain.com.

- **Instructor's Resource Manual** follows the *Fundamental Questions* framework. Each chapter contains a Lecture Outline and Teaching Strategies, Opportunities for Discussion, Answers to End-of-Chapter Exercises, and Internet Exercises. Each chapter also includes an Active-Learning Exercise that instructors can assign as homework or conduct in class.
- **Test Bank**, available in Word format, allows instructors to generate and edit tests easily. The test bank includes over 1,800 questions with a mix of difficulty levels and types—multiple choice, true/false, and essay. All the questions are also referenced according to the in-text numbering system, so instructors can conveniently test down to the paragraph level.
- **PowerPoint Slides** are available in both Lecture and Exhibit formats. Lecture slides contain key lecture points and exhibits from the text. Exhibit slides contain just the exhibits from the text. Instructors can use these PPT offerings as is, or they can edit, delete, and add to them to suit specific class needs.
- **Student Companion Site** provides an extended learning environment for students where materials are carefully developed to complement and supplement each chapter. Students will find numerous opportunities to test their mastery of chapter content—including electronic flashcards, key term crossword puzzles, videos, practice quizzes, and Internet Exercises that are linked to the text. Many of these exercises link students to real data, examples, and resources such as the Federal Trade Commission (Chapter 7), CAFE regulations (Chapter 8), and the Consumer Price Index (Chapter 10).

To access additional course materials, including CourseMate, please visit www.cengagebrain.com. At the CengageBrain.com home page, search for the ISBN of your title (from the back cover of your book) using the search box at the top of the page. This will take you to the product page where these resources can be found.

ACKNOWLEDGMENTS

We are grateful to our friends and colleagues who have so generously given their time, creativity, and insight to help us create and revise this text. In particular, we would like to thank the following people:

Richard Agesa, Marshall University
Philip Baca, New Mexico Military Institute
Diana Bajrami, College of Alameda
Erol Balkan, Hamilton College
Lloyd Beckles, Seminole State College
Charles A. Bennett, Gannon University
R.A. Blewett, St. Lawrence University
John Bockino, Suffolk County Community College
Catherine Broussard, University of Louisiana at Lafayette
Jeff W. Bruns, Bacone College
Giuliana Campanelli Andreopoulos, William Paterson University
Stephanie Campbell, Mineral Area College
Catherine Carey, Western Kentucky University
Carola Conces, University of California, Berkeley
Cynthia Conrad, University of Hartford
Simeon J. Crowther, California State University, Long Beach
Eugene Elander, Plymouth State University
Davis Folsom, University of South Carolina, Beaufort
Paul R. Gowens, Texas State University
Cole Gustafson, North Dakota State University
Arthur J. Janssen, Emporia State University
Vince Marra, University of Delaware
Wade E. Martin, Colorado School of Mines
Constantin Ogloblin, Georgia Southern University
Roger Riefler, University of Nebraska
Michael Rogers, Albany State University
Barbara Ross, Kapi'olani Community College
Lynda Rush, Cal Poly Pomona
Denise L. Stanley, University of Tennessee
Chin-Chyuan Tai, Averett University
Eleanor von Ende, Texas Tech University

We would also like to thank Erik D. Craft from the University of Richmond for his critical eye and detailed feedback during the book's production and Andrea Worrell of ITT Education Services, Inc., for inspiring us to write the text with students like hers in mind.

Finally, we would like to thank Cengage for its excellent work on this edition—specifically, Elizabeth Lowry, Steve Scoble, and Divya Divakaran.

FUNDAMENTALS OF ECONOMICS

iQoncept/Shutterstock.com

PART 1
Markets

CHAPTER 1
Economics and the World Around You

1-1 Why are some countries rich while others are dirt poor?

1-2 What are private property rights?

1-3 What is economic freedom?

1-4 What are opportunity costs?

1-5 What are the gains from trade?

Appendix Working with Graphs

CHAPTER 2
Markets and the Market Process

2-1 How are goods and services allocated?

2-2 How does the market process work?

2-3 What is demand?

2-4 What is supply?

2-5 How is price determined by demand and supply?

2-6 What causes price to change?

CHAPTER 3
The Free Market

3-1 What is the outcome of free markets?

3-2 In a free market system, who determines what is produced?

3-3 Why do different people earn different incomes, and why do different jobs pay different wages?

3-4 When the government intervenes in the market by setting a price floor or price ceiling, what is the result?

3-5 When the government intervenes in the market with a quota, what is the result?

1 Economics and the World Around You

FUNDAMENTAL QUESTIONS

1. Why are some countries rich while others are dirt poor?
2. What are private property rights?
3. What is economic freedom?
4. What are opportunity costs?
5. What are the gains from trade?

PREVIEW

One of the first questions ever considered in the study of economies was why the wealth of nations varies so much. Adam Smith, a Scottish moral philosopher, attempted to describe in his 1776 book *The Wealth of Nations* the conditions that enable a country to become wealthy. Since Smith's time, the topic has not diminished in importance. It is quite amazing to look around the world today and see the huge differences in wealth from one nation to another. A map showing gross domestic product per person (GDP; GDP is the total value of income created in a nation in a year's time) is presented in Figure 1.1. The dark blue countries are the richest, with a per capita GDP exceeding $30,000, followed by lighter blue, turquoise, and so on up to red, the poorest nations, with a per capita GDP ranging from zero to $500.

1 Why are some countries rich while others are dirt poor?

A person in Malawi may have less than $1 a day to live on, while the average person in the United States has more than $40,000 per year. In 1800 it would have been hard to know whether you were living in Latin America, North America, or Europe; standards of living were not very different. By 1900, a differential between wealthy and poor nations was being created and today the differences are huge. According to the United Nations' Food and Agriculture Organization, there are over 800 million people in the world who don't get enough to eat. Thirty percent of children in Malawi are malnourished, and more than two of every ten will die before their fifth birthday.

The United States is rich. Even those in poverty in the United States are in the top 7 percent of all people in the world in terms of wealth. Why haven't all nations progressed like the United States has? Canada is also wealthy, sharing a 2,000-mile border with the United States. Yet, Mexico also shares a 2,000-mile border with the United States, and its standard of living is less than half of the United States'. How can this be? Let's begin our study of economics discussing possible answers to these questions.

FIGURE 1.1 Wealth of Nations

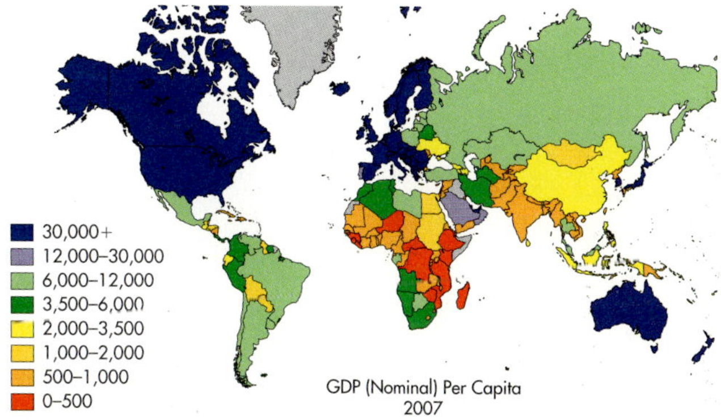

Source: http://data.worldbank.org/indicator/NY.GDP.MKTP.CD/countries?display=map; February 9, 2012.

1. OWNERSHIP

In 1981, about 1,800 families took over a piece of wasteland in San Francisco Solano in the Province of Buenos Aires, Argentina.[1] The occupants were landless citizens organized by a Catholic chapel. The Church and squatters believed the land belonged to the state, so they figured they could simply plop themselves down and enjoy the land. Once situated, the squatters had to resist several attempts of eviction; but eventually, the military government lost track of them.

When the military government was replaced by a democracy, the squatters brought the issue of ownership to the attention of the government, requesting that they be given the land. It was discovered that the land was not state property; the area was composed of different tracts of land, each with a different legal owner. So the Congress of the Province of Buenos Aires ordered the transfer of the land from the original owners to the state in exchange for a monetary compensation. About 60 percent of the land was sold to the government, and these parcels were deeded to the squatters; legal titles secured the property of the parcels. The other original owners refused to give up the land, arguing that the compensation was too low. They contested the government compensation in the Argentine courts, a contest that continued for more than 20 years.

As a result, there are two divisions of land in the occupied region, as illustrated in Figure 1.2: Some of the squatters obtained formal land rights, while others are living in the occupied parcels without paying rent but without legal titles. Although the groups shared the same household characteristics before the ownership and although they lived next to each other for 20 years, the outcome of their ownership arrangements has been dramatically different. Those with title invested in their properties, while those without title did not. The result is that there is a significant difference in the quality of housing on the untitled and titled properties. The titled properties have been upgraded, expanded, and improved. The untitled properties remain run down, deteriorated, crumbling shanties. Not only is the housing different, but those with title behaved differently than those without title: They had fewer children, and the children acquired more education and had better health.

[1] The complete story and some empirical examinations are presented in Sebastian Galiani and Ernesto Schargrodsky, "Property Rights for the Poor: Effects of Land Titling," Coase Institute Working Paper, August 9, 2005.

FIGURE 1.2 Illustration of the Squatter Results in Argentina

Those on the right were given title to the property. Those on the left had no title.

Glow Images, Inc/getty images

Florian Kopp/imagebroker/age fotostock

NOW YOU TRY IT

Explain why those families who acquired title to property behaved differently than those families who had no title. Explain why the houses are of different quality. Explain why those with title had fewer children and more of those children acquired an education.

In 1978 in Xiaogang, Anhui province—the heart of China's rice-growing region—20 families held a secret meeting to find ways to combat starvation. The system that the Communists had in place all over China was leading to a breakdown in food production. Everybody was collectively responsible for tilling the land, and everybody had a share in the land's output. You got your rice share whether you worked hard or not and, as a result, people hardly worked.

The villagers of Xiaogang decided they would divide up the land and farm it individually with each person keeping the output of his own land. They had to keep this arrangement secret out of fear of the Communist authorities. But as rice production in Xiaogang continued to rise, the secret became known. Neighboring villages discovered the secret and implemented their own arrangements. It was not long until the Communist authorities found out. In 1982 the Communist Party decided to allow some individual farming.[2]

The colonies first established in North America—Jamestown and the Virginia colony in 1607 and 1609 respectively—failed miserably. In each case, within a year at least half of the settlers had starved to death. The colonies were established by profit-seeking entities, and the settlers were indentured servants recruited on the streets of London from the homeless and unemployed. The settlers had no financial stake in the outcome of the colony. Working harder or longer was of no benefit to them; having been given free passage to the new world, these settlers were supposed to compensate the Virginia Company through their labor. The investors wanted everything produced to go to a company store and then sent back to England.

When representatives of the government and investors arrived in the colonies to find out why there were problems, it quickly became evident what the basic issue was. People were not working. Why should they? The produce they raised would not keep them alive; instead it had to go to the company store and be shipped back to England. As a result, settlers did not devote their efforts to planting and producing. Once it was realized what the problem was, the solution seemed simple; each settler was given title to a few acres of land, and only a small payment was required from them to provide returns to investors. The colonies prospered from that point on.

2 What are private property rights?

These anecdotes suggest that a primary reason that some nations are rich and others poor is private ownership. It is pretty clear that systems without private ownership don't fare as well as those with such ownership. Look at Figure 1.3 wherein several countries are listed along with their per capita incomes in 1850,

[2] William Easterly, *The White Man's Burden*, p. 108. New York: Penguin Press, 2006.

1900, 1950, and 2000. You can see looking at the red bars, that the incomes do not differ all that much in 1850. But in 2000 (the cross-hatched bars), the differences are staggering. Countries such as India, China, Albania, Hungary, and Poland, where very little private ownership was allowed, did not fare as well as countries where private ownership was allowed. You might note that Hong Kong, which was nothing but a rock without natural resources other than a port, was able to make itself one of the wealthiest "countries" in the world because it was allowed private ownership. (If you have difficulty reading and interpreting charts, you might find the Appendix to Chapter 1 of value.)

In the wealthy nations, when you own something, that something is yours to do with as you want—at least as long as you do not harm others. This seems like such a simple idea. Think about renting a house or renting a car. You don't take care of it in the same way you do when you own the house or own the car. You have no incentive, other than avoiding a fee for damages, because if you spend the time, effort, and money to maintain the house or car or improve it, you get nothing in return. When you own it, you can expect to get something back on any improvements you make.

private property rights: ownership; the right to do anything you want with what you own as long as it does not harm the property of others

This situation is known as **private property rights**. Private property rights mean that people can own things, and they can do what they want pretty much with what they own. Others can neither steal private property nor damage it. In the richest nations, private property rights exist and are enforced. People or governments cannot take your property without just compensation. In the poor nations, either there are no private property rights or what private property rights that do arise are not enforced by government. People can steal or take property and assault you without penalty. Corruption and bribes are necessary to carry out trades or to otherwise use so-called private property.

FIGURE 1.3 Per Capita Income in Several Nations

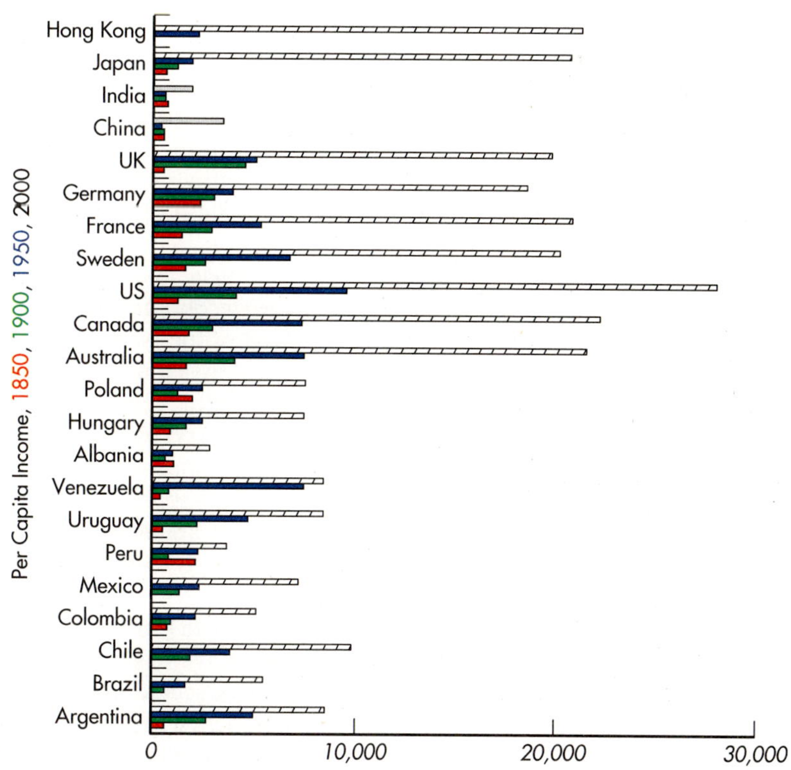

Note: Red is 1850, green 1900, blue 1950, and cross-hatched 2000.
Source: Data come from A. Maddison, The World Economy: Historical Statistics, *OECD*, 2003.

FIGURE 1.4 Per Capita GDP in the United Kingdom

From the beginning of humanity, living standards were barely subsistence at best. This did not improve until the tail end of the 18th century.

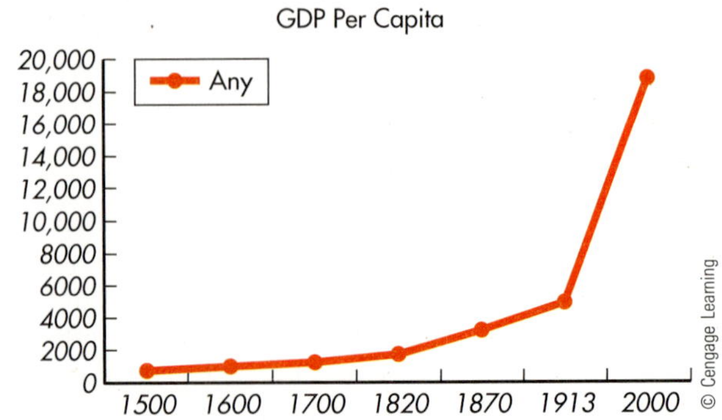

When private property rights are not secure, people are unlikely to be able to sell the things they own or to use them for collateral on a loan or pass them along to family. And they have much less incentive to improve the property because they are not assured of a return on any investments they make.

Until 1800, life was brutal and very short. Expected lifetime was only about 35 in most nations. But something occurred around the turn of the 19th century that led to rapid rises in standards of living in Western nations. Notice in Figure 1.4 how the GDP per capita in the United Kingdom, the world's richest nation at that time, does not begin rising until 1800. What occurred to create the rising standards of living? That is one of the most important questions we ask in economics. And the answer has to do with the private property rights. It was the Industrial Revolution. It is a long story, but the short version of it is that beginning in the 1700s, entrepreneurs finally were secure in knowing that what they invented or created would benefit them, and that they would be able to retain profits and property. This system of private property rights laid the foundation for the Industrial Revolution.

Until just recently in China, everything was owned by government; in Pakistan, no one could be sure that whatever they claimed as theirs would remain theirs; in much of Latin America, the security of private property has not been established over lengthy periods of time. Several times the Mexican government has confiscated private property. Similarly, in other Latin American nations, private property has not been allowed or enforced. For instance, currently the governments of Venezuela and Bolivia have been confiscating what was private property, and their economies are stumbling and heading for serious trouble.

When private property rights are not universal among citizens, or when enforcement is not constant and effective, a nation will not prosper. An abundance of a natural resource such as oil may distort this fact for a while, but the abundance cannot carry over to all citizens unless private property exists. In most oil-producing nations, the oil is owned by government and only a very few benefit from the resource. But when private property rights prevail, nations prosper even without abundant resources. Hong Kong had nothing, no natural resources except a harbor, and it emerged into one of the wealthiest countries in the world in just a few decades. (Hong Kong is not actually a country as it was never independent—part of the British Empire and then China.) The wealthiest nations have a system of private property rights where people can own property and be secure in their ownership. The poorest nations do not.

Look at Figure 1.5, where GDP per capita of the United States and a few Asian nations over time is presented. You can see that China and India did not begin to progress until they began allowing private ownership—about 1990 or so. While China still allows only limited private property, those parts of the economy that have been freed have done very well. In India, private ownership is not only

FIGURE 1.5 Per Capita GDP in the United States, China, India, Japan, and Indonesia

Japan began growing after the United States established a system of private property rights following World War II. China, Indonesia, and India had followed the Soviet Union in adopting communism and government-run economies. When the Soviet Union collapsed in 1989, these countries began moving toward free markets and private property rights.

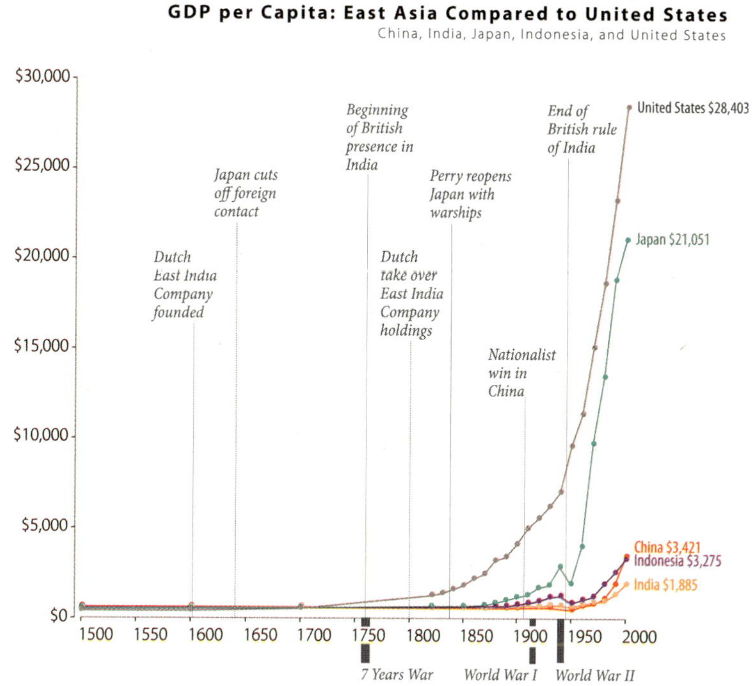

Source: Catherine Mulbrandon, VisualizingEconomics.com.

allowed, but is encouraged. As a result of India's and China's progress, a billion people have risen from dire poverty where life expectancy was less than 35 years to where they are living a decent life, and life expectancy exceeds 72 years.

Private property may seem like something just for the rich, but it is crucial for the poor. If people have no title to property, they cannot rent it to others, subdivide it, sell it, use it for collateral, or pass it on to family. The farmers in Xiaogang who agreed to divide up the land for cultivation could not sell their land or even pass it along to family. Nevertheless, the amount of rice raised on the so-called private plots was significantly greater than when everything was communal, but it could have been so much more had the farmers owned the property.

Private property rights matter. They matter because they create incentives that enable people to improve their standards of living. When you own something, you have the incentive to take care of it, that is, you have the incentive to increase its value and to invest in it. If farmers can raise corn and that corn is theirs, they can take the corn to market and sell it. They will invest in ways to provide better quality and ensure that they have seeds remaining to grow more corn next year. Similarly, when we offer to work, we are taking our own labor, something we own, and exchanging it for pay. The higher the quality of our work, the more valuable we are to our employers and the more we will be paid.

When no one owns something, no one has an incentive to take care of it. Forced to work in shipbuilding factories in Gdansk, Poland, during the communist regime, workers would show up and then loaf. They had no incentives to be productive as they received the same pay no matter what they did. When you own your own labor or property, you have the incentive to make it as valuable as possible because then you can trade for other things you want. When no one owns something, problems arise; for instance, no one owns the fish in the oceans, so no one takes care of them. Overfishing, and in some cases, extinction of species result. The study of economics involves ownership and the problems that arise when there is no ownership or when ownership is common rather than private.

RECAP

1. Private property rights are the rights to do what you want with what you own as long as you do not infringe on the private property rights of others.
2. Private property rights confer ownership. Without ownership, nations do not progress.
3. If you own something you take care of it. If no one owns something or if everyone has common ownership rights to something, no one takes care of that something.

2. ECONOMIC FREEDOM

3

What is economic freedom?

economic freedom: the ability to engage in voluntary trade without interference or restrictions by government or outside parties

If you own something but do not have the right to do what you want with that item, how can you progress? And if an individual cannot progress, how can his nation progress? Economic freedom is important to the success of a nation. **Economic freedom** refers to the degree to which private individuals are able to carry out voluntary exchange. People can buy or sell things without government involvement or without getting the permission of some king or commission. People can work for whom they want at a wage the employer is willing and able to pay.

The *Wall Street Journal* and the Heritage Foundation coauthor an annual measure of economic freedom called the *Index of Economic Freedom*. In an economically free society, individuals are free to work, produce, consume, and invest in any way they please, with that freedom both protected and unconstrained by the state. In economically free societies, governments allow labor, capital, and goods to move freely and refrain from coercion or constraint of liberty beyond the extent necessary to protect and maintain liberty itself. Higher taxes mean less economic freedom, more rules and regulations mean less economic freedom, restrictions on travel mean less economic freedom, restrictions on international trade mean less economic freedom, the paperwork necessary to comply with government rules and regulations means less economic freedom, and so on.

According to the Index of Economic Freedom, the United States slipped in 2012 from the group of countries called "free" to the group of countries called "mostly free" because the role of government in the U.S. economy expanded during 2009–2011. The top 10 economically freest nations are listed in Table 1.1. The United States is only number 10.

2.a. Economic Freedom and Standards of Living

In general, the greater a nation's economic freedom, the higher its standard of living. People in the unfree and repressed economies average less than one-eighth of the income of people in the freest nations, as shown in Figure 1.6.[3]

2.b. Economic Freedom and Quality of Life

You would expect that with a higher standard of living comes better living conditions. There is more money for health care, for better education, for more freedom from diseases and, in general, to support a better and longer life. The Human Development index created by the United Nations rates nations on the basis of quality of life. You can see in Figure 1.7 that, indeed, economic freedom and human development are strongly related. The "free" countries

[3] The average Index of Economic Freedom (IEF) score for a country with GDP growth of over 10% is 10% higher than the IEF score for the countries with GDP growth of 3% or less. These numbers are for 2005. Libya, which had the lowest score where reliable GDP growth figures are available, had a growth rate of 3.5% in a year that the average growth rate was almost 5%. Zimbabwe, which had the second lowest IEF score, had a 6.5% GDP decline.

Table 1.1 2012 Index of Economic Freedom

Each year, the Heritage Foundation and the *Wall Street Journal* calculate the list of the most and least economically free nations.

World Rank	Country	Overall Score	Change From Previous
1	Hong Kong	89.9	0.2
2	Singapore	87.5	0.3
3	Australia	83.1	0.6
4	New Zealand	82.1	−0.2
5	Switzerland	81.1	−0.8
6	Canada	79.9	−0.9
7	Chile	78.3	0.9
8	Mauritius	77.0	0.8
9	Ireland	76.9	−1.8
10	United States	76.3	−1.5

Note: Definition: Free, 80–100; Mostly free, 60–79.9.

Source: http://www.heritage.org/Index/

FIGURE 1.6 Top Ten Highest Standards of Living

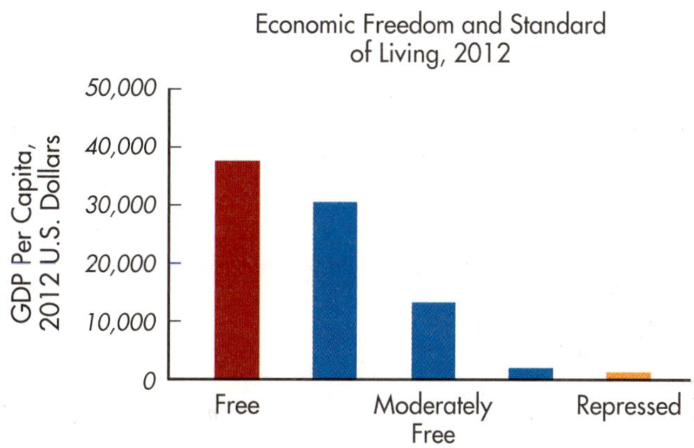

Source: http://www.heritage.org/Index/PDF/2012/Index2012_ExecutiveHighlights.pdf

FIGURE 1.7 Economic Freedom and Human Development

Using the Index of Human Development constructed by the United Nations, we are able to see that economic freedom is strongly related to human development.

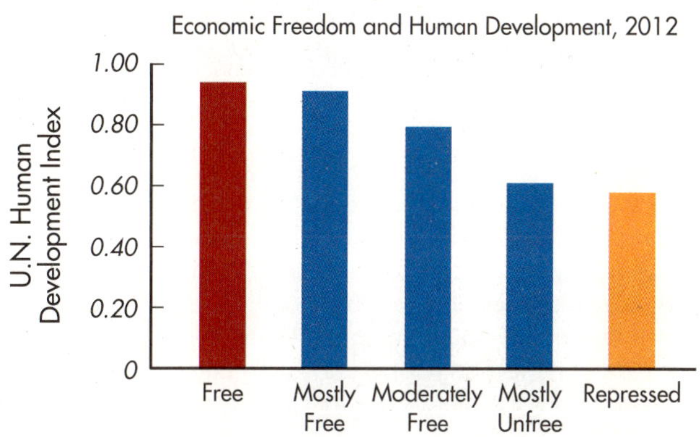

Source: 2011 United Nations Development Report; http://hdr.undp.org/en/; accessed February 9, 2012.

(red bar) have a much higher index of human development than the "repressed" countries (orange bar).

RECAP

1. Economic freedom means you can engage in voluntary transactions without interference or restrictions from government or others.
2. With private property rights and economic freedom, nations progress, standards of living improve, and human development increases.
3. The Index of Economic Freedom is a measure of how much freedom from interference in transactions you voluntarily enter into you have.
4. The higher the index of economic freedom, the higher a nation's standard of living.
5. The Index of Human Development is a measure of the quality of life in a nation.
6. The more economic freedom, the higher is the index of human development.

3. SCARCITY AND OPPORTUNITY COSTS

Why are some countries rich and others poor? The primary reason is that some countries have a system of private property rights and economic freedom and others do not. More economic freedom leads to better conditions for people than less economic freedom. Economic freedom means that the individual and voluntary actions of people dictate what happens in an economy. But, why is ownership necessary? Why can't everyone simply have everything they want? If there was enough of everything that no one would be unable to get what he wants, then ownership would not be necessary. If someone stole something from you, you simply pick up another of that something. The problem is that not everyone can get what they want. There is not enough of anything to satisfy everyone. This is called **scarcity**.

scarcity:
not everyone can get everything he wants

4

What are opportunity costs?

Why are diamonds so expensive while water and air—necessities of life—are nearly free? The reason is that diamonds are relatively scarcer; that is, relative to the available quantities, more diamonds are wanted than water or air. Of course, water is far from free these days. Some people regularly spend over $6 a gallon on bottled drinking water, and most homeowners must pay their local government for tap water. Even air is not always cheap or free, as noted in the Global Business Insight feature: "'Free' Air?"

opportunity costs:
the highest-valued alternative that must be forgone when a choice is made

GLOBAL BUSINESS INSIGHT

Opportunity Costs

A choice is simply a comparison of alternatives. For instance, if you were deciding whether to buy a new car, what would your alternatives be? They would be other makes of automobiles, trucks, even bicycles. They also would be virtually anything else on which the money could be spent. When you choose one thing, the benefits you might get from other things are forgone. Economists refer to the forgone benefits of the next best alternative as **opportunity costs**—the highest-valued alternative that must be forgone when a choice is made.

Opportunity costs are part of every decision and activity. Your opportunity costs of reading this book are whatever else you could be doing—perhaps watching TV, talking with friends, working, or listening to music.

The study of economics begins with *scarcity*. Scarcity refers to the idea that there is not enough of something to satisfy everyone who would like that something. People have unlimited wants—they always want more than they have or can purchase with their incomes. Whether they are wealthy or poor, what they have is never enough. Since people do not have everything they want, they must use their limited time and income to select those things they want most and forgo the rest. The choices they make and the manner in which the choices are made explain much of why the real world is what it is.

3.a. The Opportunity Cost of Going to School

Suppose you decided to attend a school where the tuition and other expenses add up to $4,290 per year. Are these your total costs? If you answer yes, you are ignoring opportunity costs. If instead of going to school you would have chosen to work full-time, then the benefits of full-time employment are part of your opportunity costs. If you could have obtained a position with an annual income of $20,800, the actual cost of school is the $4,290 of direct expenses plus the $20,800 of forgone salary, or $25,090.

Each term you must decide whether to register for school. You could work full-time and not attend school, attend school and not work, or work part-time and attend school. The time you devote to school will decrease as you devote more time to work. You trade off hours spent at work for hours spent in school. If you went to school full-time, you might earn the highest grades. As you work more hours, you gain additional income but might earn lower grades. If this situation occurs, we say that you trade off grades and income.

Societies, like individuals, face scarcities and must make choices, that is, have **trade-offs**. Because resources are scarce, a nation cannot produce as much of everything as it wants. When it produces more health care, it must forgo the production of education, automobiles, or military hardware. When it devotes more of its resources to the military, fewer resources are available to devote to health care, education, or consumer goods.

trade-offs:
what must be given up to acquire something else

3.b. Resources and Income

Some goods are used to produce other goods. For instance, to make chocolate chip cookies we need flour, sugar, chocolate chips, butter, our own labor, and an oven. To distinguish between the ingredients of a good and the good itself, we call the ingredients **resources**. (Resources are also called factors of production and inputs; the terms are interchangeable.) The ingredients of the cookies are the resources, and the cookies are the goods.

As illustrated in Figure 1.8(a), economists have classified resources into three general categories: land, labor, and capital.

1. **Land** includes all natural resources, such as minerals, timber, and water, as well as the land itself.
2. **Labor** refers to the physical and intellectual services of people and includes the training, education, and abilities of the individuals in a society.
3. **Capital** refers to products such as machinery and buildings that are used to produce other goods and services. You will often hear the term *capital* used to describe the financial backing for some project to finance some business. Economists refer to funds used to purchase capital as **financial capital**.

resources:
inputs used to create goods and services

land:
the general category of resources encompassing all natural resources, land, and water

labor:
the general category of resources encompassing all human activity related to the productive process

capital:
the equipment, machines, and buildings used to produce goods and services

financial capital:
the funds used to purchase capital

People obtain income by selling their resources or the use of their resources, as illustrated in Figure 1.8(b). Economists define payment to the owners of land as rent, payment to people who provide labor services as wages, and payment to owners of capital as interest.

Figures 1.8(a) and 1.8(b) are linked because the income that resource owners acquire from selling the use of their resources provides them the ability to buy goods and services. And producers use the money received from selling their goods to pay for the resource services. In Figure 1.8(c), the flows of money are indicated along the outside arrows, and the flows of goods or resource services are indicated along the inside arrows. The resource services flow from resource owners to producers of goods in return for income; the flows of goods go from the producers of the goods to resource owners in return for the money payment for these goods.

FIGURE 1.8 Flow of Resources and Income

Three types of resources are used to produce goods and services: land, labor, and capital. See 1.8(a). The owners of resources are provided income for selling their services. Landowners are paid rent, laborers receive wages, and capital receives interest. See 1.8(b). Figure 1.8(c) links Figures 1.8(a) and 1.8(b). People use their resources to acquire income with which they purchase the goods they want. Producers use the money received from selling the goods to pay for the use of the resources in making goods. Resources and income flow between certain firms and certain resource owners as people allocate their scarce resources to best satisfy their wants.

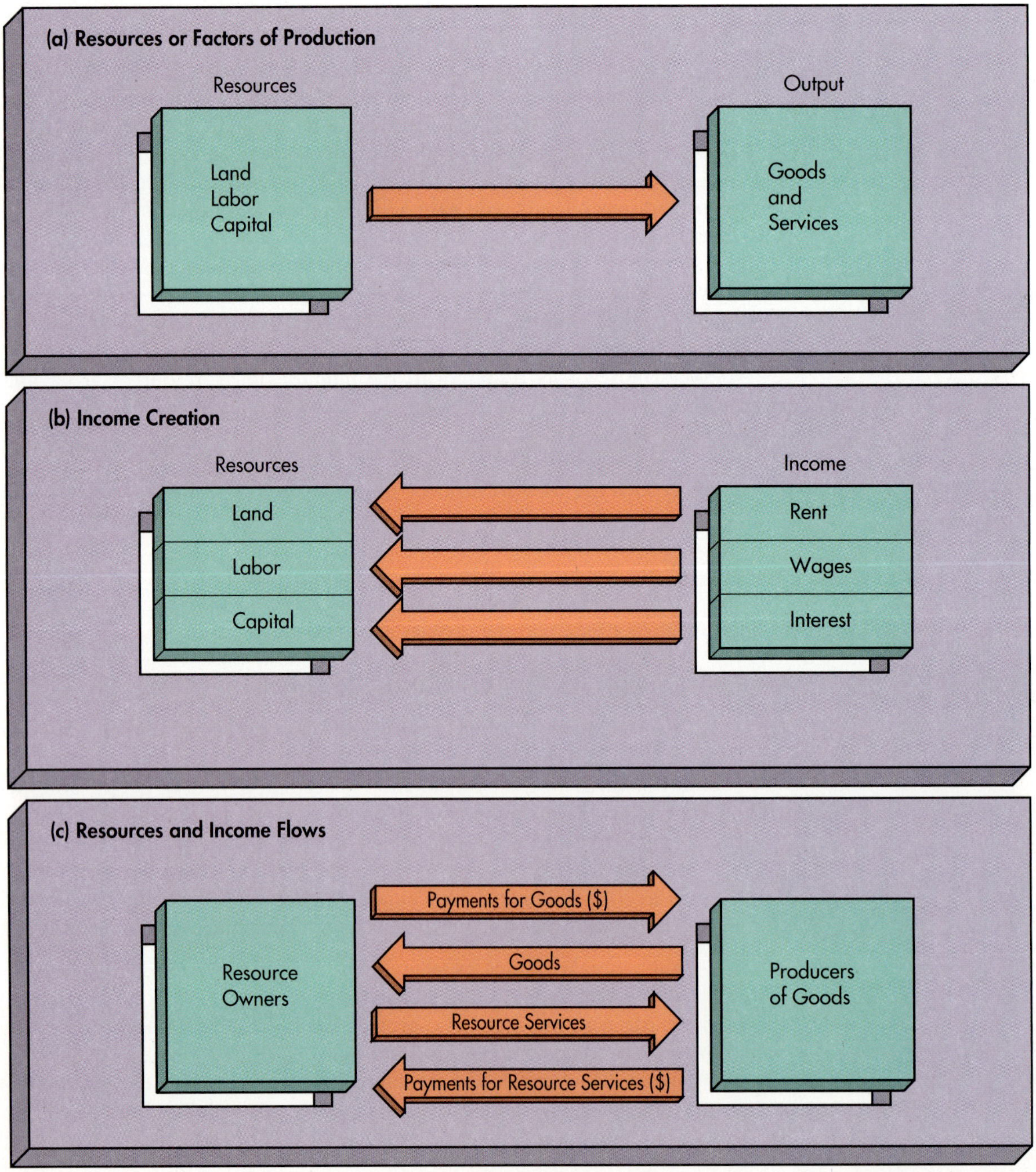

RECAP

1. Scarcity exists when people want more of an item than exists at a zero price.
2. Choices have to be made because of scarcity. People cannot have or do everything they desire all the time. Economics is the study of how people choose to use their scarce resources in an attempt to satisfy their wants.
3. Opportunity costs are the benefits that are forgone due to a choice. When you choose one thing you must give up—forgo—others.
4. Opportunity cost is an individual concept but can be used to demonstrate scarcity and choice for a society as a whole.
5. Goods are produced with resources (also called factors of production and inputs). Economists have classified resources into three categories: land, labor, and capital.
6. Income comes from the ownership of resources.

4. GAINS FROM TRADE

When you walk into your local Starbucks to get a tall mocha frappucino with whip cream, do you wonder who told the people working there to work there or who told the coffee growers to send their coffee beans to this particular Starbucks, or who told the dairy to provide this Starbucks with cream? Probably not. Most of us take all these things for granted. But all of this is exchange; you are trading your money for the drink, for instance. Why do people engage in voluntary trade? People can choose to be self-sufficient—using their resources and producing what they want and need themselves—or they can choose to exchange goods and services with others. By trading, they get more than they can by being self-sufficient.

4.a. Benefits of Trade

Consider a very simple example of the benefits of trade. Suppose two people, Maria and Able, have the ability to carry out two types of tasks, solving math problems and solving economics problems. As shown in Table 1.2, the two tasks take different time and effort from Maria and Able. We will assume that the quality of their work is the same—just the quantity differs. If Maria does nothing but work on math, she is able to solve 10 problems in an hour; and if she does nothing but economics, she is able to solve 10 economics problems in an hour. Her opportunity cost of doing the 10 math problems is the 10 economics problems she could have done. Able, on the other hand, can solve the 10 math problems in an hour but is only able to solve 5 economics problems in that time. Able's opportunity cost of doing the 10 math problems is the 5 economics problems he could have done instead.

Suppose Maria and Able would each like to solve 5 math problems, as shown in Table 1.2. Maria would be able to solve 5 math and 5 economics problems, while Able would be able to solve 5 math and 2.5 economics problems. This is shown in Table 1.3 under "Alone, no trade." Notice that together Maria and Able are able to produce 10 math problems and 7.5 economics problems.

Table 1.2 Choices

Percentage of Resources Devoted to Solving Problems		Maria		Able	
Math	**Economics**	**Math**	**Economics**	**Math**	**Economics**
100	0	10	0	10	0
0	100	0	10	0	5

Table 1.3 Choices and Trade

Trading Situation	Maria's Choices Math	Maria's Choices Economics	Able's Choices Math	Able's Choices Economics	Gain From Trade
Alone, no trade	5	5	5	2.5	None
Trade 1 math problem for 1 economics problem	5	5	5	5	Able 2.5
Trade 2 math problems for 1 economics problem	5	7.5	5	2.5	Maria 2.5

4.b. Specialization and Comparative Advantage

Would it make sense for Maria and Able to exchange answers in order to get more done than if each were to work alone? If so, who will do what? The answer is that the person who sacrifices the fewest economics problems to do math problems does math problems, and the person who sacrifices the fewest math problems to do economics problems does economics problems. In other words, the person with the *lowest opportunity cost* in an activity performs that activity. Even though Maria can do math equally as well as Able and can do economics more efficiently than Able, Able gives up less by specializing in math. Able only has to give up or forgo half an economics problem for each math problem he does, while Maria has to give up one economics problem for each math problem she does. As a result, they will do better having Maria specialize in economics. We say that Able has a **comparative advantage** in math because his opportunity cost in math is lower than Maria's, and Maria has a comparative advantage in economics because her opportunity cost in economics is lower than Able's.

comparative advantage:
the situation where one individual's opportunity cost is relatively lower than another's

NOW YOU TRY IT

Assume that Maria and Able decide to exchange one math answer for three-quarters of an economics answer. Who gains and by how much?

4.c. Gains from Trade

Since Maria, by herself, can do one math problem at the same rate as she can do one economics problem, she will require at least one economics answer from Able to be willing to give him one math answer. Able can solve two math problems for each economics problem, so he will have to get at least half an economics answer from Maria to give her a math answer.

If they should exchange one math answer for one economics answer, then, as shown in row 2 (1:1) of Table 1.3, Maria and Able are each able to get 5 math and 5 economics answers. Although Maria is no better off than if she had done her own work, Able is 2.5 economics answers better off. These additional 2.5 answers are called the **gains from trade**.

gains from trade:
the additional amount one can consume by trading

If, instead of one for one, they agree to exchange two math answers for each economics answer, then, as shown in row 3 (2:1) of Table 1.3, Maria gains 2.5 economics answers, while Able is no better off than if he had done the problems himself. At any rate of exchange between 1:1 and 2:1, both Maria and Able will gain from specializing and exchanging answers.

In virtually every trading situation, both parties gain from voluntary exchange; the amount each party gains—that is, the amount both parties together get that is larger than the sum of what each could have produced without trade—is called the gains from trade.

This simple example illustrates how the real world works. People focus on what they do best and then trade with others. You cook and your roommate cleans; you work on computers and let someone else fix your car; you purchase groceries, letting someone else grow the food. Why do specialization and trade occur? Because people always want more than they currently have, and specializing and then trading enables them to get more than not specializing and not trading.

5

What are the gains from trade?

We have to decide how to use our own scarce resources. We must choose where to devote our energies. Few of us are jacks-of-all-trades. Nations, similarly, have limited amounts of resources and must choose where to devote those resources.

Specializing in those activities that require us to give up the smallest amount of other things—in other words, where we have a comparative advantage—enables us to obtain more than trying to do everything ourselves. A plumber does plumbing and leaves teaching to the teachers. The teacher teaches and leaves electrical work to the electrician.

The same thing occurs among nations. In fact, one of Adam Smith's answers to why some countries are rich was specialization and voluntary trade. Grenada specializes in spice production and leaves manufacturing to the United States. All of this can be shown in an illustration known as the **production possibilities curve (PPC)**. It shows all possible combinations of two products that can be produced with a limited quantity and quality of resources.

Production possibilities curve (PPC): a graphical representation showing the maximum quantity of goods and services that can be produced using limited resources to the fullest extent possible; it shows the maximum output that can be produced using resources fully and efficiently

A nation also has a PPC based on its quantity and quality of resources and its technologies. Consider a nation deciding how much of its resources are to be devoted to national defense and how much to domestic, or nondefense, goods and services. In Figure 1.9, units of defense goods and services are measured on the vertical axis, and units of nondefense goods and services are measured on the horizontal axis.

If all resources are allocated to producing defense goods and services, then 200 million units can be produced, but the production of nondefense goods and services will cease. The combination of 200 million units of defense goods and services and 0 units of nondefense goods and services is point A_1, a point on the vertical axis. At 175 million units of defense goods and services, 75 million units of nondefense goods and services can be produced (point B_1). Point C_1 represents 125 million units of nondefense goods and services and 130 million units of defense goods. Point D_1 represents 150 million units of nondefense goods and services and 70 million units of defense goods and services. Point E_1, a point on the horizontal axis, shows the combination of no production of defense goods and services and total production of nondefense goods and services.

The PPC is a picture of the limitations and trade-offs facing society. The curve shows that more of one type of good can be produced only by reducing the quantity of other types of goods that are produced; it shows that a society has scarce resources.

Suppose a nation produces 130 million units of defense goods and services and 25 million units of nondefense goods and services. That combination, point F_1 in Figure 1.9, lies inside the production possibilities curve. A point lying inside the

FIGURE 1.9 The Production Possibilities Curve

With a limited amount of resources, only certain combinations of defense and nondefense goods and services can be produced. The maximum amounts that can be produced, given various trade-offs, are represented by points A_1 through E_1. Point F_1 lies inside the curve and represents the underutilization of resources. More of one type of good and less of another could be produced, or more of both types could be produced. Point G_1 represents an impossible combination. There are insufficient resources to produce quantities lying beyond the curve.

Combination	Defense Goods and Services (millions of units)	Nondefense Goods and Services (millions of units)
A_1	200	0
B_1	175	75
C_1	130	125
D_1	70	150
E_1	0	160
F_1	130	25
G_1	200	75

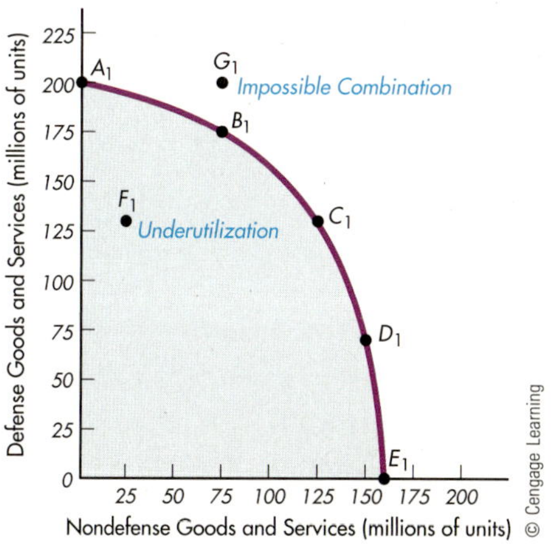

production possibilities curve indicates that resources are not being fully or efficiently used. If the existing work force is employed only 20 hours per week, it is not being fully used. If two workers are used when one would be sufficient—say, two people in each Domino's Pizza delivery car—then resources are not being used efficiently. If there are resources available for use, society can move from point F_1 to a point on the PPC, such as point C_1. The move would gain 100 million units of nondefense goods and services with no loss of defense goods and services.

Point G_1 in Figure 1.9 represents the production of 200 million units of defense goods and services and 75 units of nondefense goods and services. Point G_1, however, represents the use of more resources than are available; it lies outside the production possibilities curve. Unless more resources can be obtained or the quality of resources improved so that the nation can produce more with the same quantity of resources, there is no way the society can currently produce 200 million units of defense goods and 75 million units of nondefense goods.

When two nations, each faced with limited resources and thus each with a different PPC, choose to specialize and trade with each other, each is able to get more than if each chose to be self-sufficient. Trade enables the countries to acquire more than they can produce on their own. In other words, the countries can consume more than they produce—they can move out beyond their PPCs. The gains from trade are shown as the difference between the PPC and a point outside the PPC gained due to voluntary trade, such as illustrated by point G_1 in Figure 1.9.

RECAP

1. Exchange occurs because all parties involved believe the exchange can be beneficial.
2. Opportunity cost is the amount of one good or service that must be given up to obtain one additional unit of another good or service.
3. The rule of specialization is that the individual (firm, region, or nation) will specialize in the activity in which it has the lowest opportunity cost.
4. Specialization and trade enable individuals, firms, and nations to get more than they could without specialization and trade.
5. By specializing in an activity that one does relatively better than other activities, one can trade with others and gain more than if one carried out all activities oneself. This additional amount is referred to as gains from trade.

SUMMARY

Why are some nations rich while others are dirt poor?

1. Ownership and economic freedom are crucial elements of the success of nations.
2. Without ownership, no one has an incentive to work or to improve property or themselves.
3. Without voluntary trade, no one has an incentive to own things or to improve them or themselves.
4. While other factors than ownership and economic freedom may contribute to a country's success, nothing is as important.

What are private property rights?

5. Private property rights mean ownership. You have the right to do what you want with what you own as long as you do not infringe on the private property rights of others.
6. Without ownership, nations do not progress.
7. If you own something you take care of it. If no one owns something or if everyone has common ownership rights to something, no one takes care of that something.

What is economic freedom?

8. Economic freedom means you can engage in voluntary transactions without interference or restrictions from government or others.
9. With private property rights and economic freedom nations progress, standards of living improve, and human development increases.

What are opportunity costs?

10. Economics is the study of how people choose to allocate scarce resources to satisfy their unlimited wants.
11. Scarcity is universal; it applies to anything people would like more of than is available at a zero price. Because of scarcity, choices must be made.
12. Opportunity costs are the forgone opportunities of the next best alternative. Choice means both gaining something and giving up something.
13. When you choose one option, you forgo all others. The benefits of the next best alternative are the opportunity costs of your choice.

What are gains from trade?

14. Comparative advantage is when one person or nation can carry out an activity at less cost than another person or nation.
15. Gains from trade occur when traders specialize according to comparative advantage and trade. The quantity each trader gets above what each could do alone is the gains from trade.

EXERCISES

1. Use economics to explain why diamonds are more expensive than water when water is necessary for survival and diamonds are not.
2. Use economics to explain why people leave tips in the following two cases: (a) at a restaurant they visit often; (b) at a restaurant they visit only once.
3. Use economics to explain why people contribute to charities.
4. In presidential campaigns, candidates always seem to make more promises than they can fulfill: more and better health care; a better environment; only minor reductions in defense; better education; better roads, bridges, sewer systems, and water systems; and so on. What economic concept is ignored by the candidates?
5. What does the old saying "There is no such thing as a free lunch" mean? If someone invites you to a lunch and offers to pay for it, is it free for you?

STUDY GUIDE FOR CHAPTER 1

Key Term Match

Match each term with its correct definition by placing the appropriate letter next to the corresponding number.

A. Private property rights	G. labor
B. scarcity	H. capital
C. opportunity costs	I. comparative advantage
D. tradeoffs	J. specialization
E. resources	K. gains from trade
F. land	L. economic freedom

____ 1. the amount that trading partners benefit beyond the sum of what each could have produced without the trade

____ 2. the physical and intellectual services of people, including the training, education, and abilities of the individuals in a society

____ 3. Land, labor and capital are categories of ____________.

____ 4. products such as machinery and equipment that are used in production

____ 5. everyone can not get everything they want

____ 6. the ability to produce a good or service at a lower opportunity cost than it would cost someone else to produce it

____ 7. all natural resources, such as minerals, timber, and water, as well as the land itself

____ 8. the highest-valued alternative that must be forgone when a choice is made

____ 9. Occurs if economic units produce the goods and services for which they have the lowest opportunity cost, and trade for other items

____ 10. the giving up of one good or activity in order to obtain some other good or activity

____ 11. These exist if people can own things and do pretty much whatever they want to do with the things they own

____ 12. a situation characterized by the ability of individuals to work, produce, consume and invest in any way they please

Quick-Check Quiz

1. Which of the following statements about property rights is false?
   - ☐ a. Owners tend to take better care of their property than renters
   - ☐ b. When property rights are not well defined, resources will tend to be overused.
   - ☐ c. Property rights are more important that abundant resources in raising living standards.
   - ☐ d. The system of property rights laid the foundation for the Industrial Revolution.
   - ☐ e. Only rich nations need to establish and protect property rights.

2. Janine is an accountant who makes $30,000 a year. Robert is a college student who makes $8,000 a year. All other things being equal, who is more likely to stand in a long line to get a cheap concert ticket?
   - ☐ a. Janine; her opportunity cost is lower
   - ☐ b. Janine; her opportunity cost is higher
   - ☐ c. Robert; his opportunity cost is lower
   - ☐ d. Robert; his opportunity cost is higher
   - ☐ e. Janine; because she is better able to afford the cost of the ticket

3. Which of the following should not be considered an opportunity cost of attending college?
   - ☐ a. money spent on living expenses that are the same whether or not you attend college
   - ☐ b. lost salary
   - ☐ c. tuition
   - ☐ d. interest that could have been earned on your money had you put the money into a savings account instead of spending it on tuition
   - ☐ e. opportunities sacrificed in the decision to attend college

4. Exchange among people occurs because
   - ☐ a. everyone involved believes they will gain.
   - ☐ b. one person gains, and the others lose.
   - ☐ c. only one person loses while everyone else gains.
   - ☐ d. people have no other choices.
   - ☐ e. the government requires it.

5. You have an comparative advantage in producing something when you
   - ☐ a. have a higher opportunity cost than someone else.
   - ☐ b. have a special talent.
   - ☐ c. have a lower opportunity cost than someone else.
   - ☐ d. have learned a useful skill.
   - ☐ e. have the same opportunity cost as someone else.

Use the following table to answer study questions 6 through 10.

On a 10-acre farm, one farmer can produce these quantities of corn or wheat in Alpha and Beta.

	Corn	Wheat
Alpha	200	400
Beta	100	300

6. The opportunity cost of corn in Beta is
   - ☐ a. 300 wheat.
   - ☐ b. 1 wheat.
   - ☐ c. 3 wheat.
   - ☐ d. 100 corn.
   - ☐ e. .5 corn.

7. The opportunity cost of corn in Alpha is
   - ☐ a. 400 wheat.
   - ☐ b. 2 wheat.
   - ☐ c. 4 wheat.
   - ☐ d. 100 corn.
   - ☐ e. .5 corn.

8. The opportunity cost of wheat in Beta is
   - ☐ a. .333 corn.
   - ☐ b. 1 wheat.
   - ☐ c. 3 wheat.
   - ☐ d. 300 wheat.
   - ☐ e. .5 corn.

9. The opportunity cost of wheat in Alpha is
   - ☐ a. 400 wheat.
   - ☐ b. 2 wheat.
   - ☐ c. 4 wheat.
   - ☐ d. 100 corn.
   - ☐ e. .5 corn.

10. Which of the following statements is (are) true?
    - ☐ a. Alpha has a comparative advantage in corn, and Beta has a comparative advantage in wheat.
    - ☐ b. Alpha has a comparative advantage in wheat, and Beta has a comparative advantage in corn.
    - ☐ c. Alpha has a comparative advantage in both corn and wheat.
    - ☐ d. Beta has a comparative advantage in both corn and wheat.
    - ☐ e. Neither has a comparative advantage in anything.

11. Vanessa tries to eat a good breakfast every morning. She ranks her favorite breakfasts as follows:
    1. Pancakes,
    2. Waffles

3. Bacon and eggs,
4. Ham and cheese omelet
5. Oat cereal with strawberries.

12. Vanessa had pancakes for breakfast yesterday. What was her opportunity cost?
☐ a. Waffles
☐ b. All the other meals she could have had.
☐ c. The money she paid for the pancakes.
☐ d. Any of the other meals she could have had.
☐ e. Zero-she could have her top choice

Practice Questions and Problems

1. Canada has lagged the United States in its labor productivity performance for the past 25 years. Suppose Canada continues to have poor labor productivity so that the U.S. eventually develops an absolute advantage over Canada in all industries. In this situation, could the U.S. still benefit from trade with Canada? Yes No Defend your answer.
____
____
____
2. Janine decides to buy a ticket to a classical music concert. The ticket costs $10. She spends 30 minutes driving to the ticket office, 60 minutes waiting in line, and 30 minutes eating a snack after buying the ticket. List her opportunity costs of getting the ticket.
____
3. Exchange occurs because ____________ (one person, everyone involved) believes the exchange can be beneficial.
4. It is in your best interest to specialize in the area in which your opportunity costs are ____________ (highest, constant, lowest).
5. The higher the Index of Economic Freedom, the ____________ (higher, lower) a nation's standard of living
6. Chris works at a part-time job that pays $15 per hour. He wants a new shirt to wear next Friday night. He can buy one at the mall for $30, or he can make one (using materials he already has) with five hours of labor.
   a. If Chris makes the shirt himself, how many hours will he spend on making the shirt?
   ____
   b. If Chris works at his job and uses the money to buy a shirt, how many hours of work will it take him to earn the money to buy the shirt?
   ____
   c. What do economists call the three hours Chris saved by working at his job and trading his money for a shirt instead of making it himself?
   ____
7. The following table shows the number of shirts or ties that two tailors, Joe and Harry, can make in one day.

	Shirts	Ties
Joe	1	4
Harry	2	6

   a. Joe's opportunity cost of making one shirt is _______________.
   b. Joe's opportunity cost of making one tie is _______________
   c. Harry's opportunity cost of making one shirt is _______________.
   d. Harry's opportunity cost of making one tie is _______________.
   e. Who has a comparative advantage in making shirts?
   _______________.
   f. Who has a comparative advantage in making ties?
   _______________.
   g. Who should specialize in making ties?
   _______________.
   h. Who should specialize in making shirts?
   _______________.

Exercises and Applications

I Scarce Parking in Wichita?

The following is an excerpt from a Wichita, Kansas, newspaper, the Wichita Eagle:

It's become part of Wichita lore. Folks in these parts are nutty about parking. They want it free. They want it at the front door of wherever they're going. They refuse to look for a parking space anywhere for more than eight or ten seconds. And they think the downtown Wichita parking situation is horrible.

The fact is, there's plenty of parking in the city's core. About 20,000 people work downtown. There are almost 19,000 parking spaces. That nearly 1-to-1 ratio is better than other cities in the region such as Oklahoma City, and it's just as good as Topeka. And the average distance a person has to walk is about a block. That's better than similar-sized cities.

The editorial laments that people don't go downtown for activities because they think they will have trouble parking. Relying on information in the editorial, do you think that parking spaces can be considered a scarce resource in downtown Wichita?

____
____
____

II Resource and Income Flows

Complete the figure below.

III Opportunity Costs

Mr. Safi and Mr. Nohr are neighbors. Mr. Safi makes $200 an hour as a consultant while Mr. Nohr makes $10 an hour as an aerobics instructor. The men are complaining that the grass on their lawns has grown so fast due to recent rainy weather that it is hard to keep their lawns looking nice. Mr. Nohr mows his lawn himself. Mr. Safi comments that he hires a neighbor's child to cut his grass "because it is too expensive for me to cut it myself." Explain Mr. Safi's comment.

____

____

____

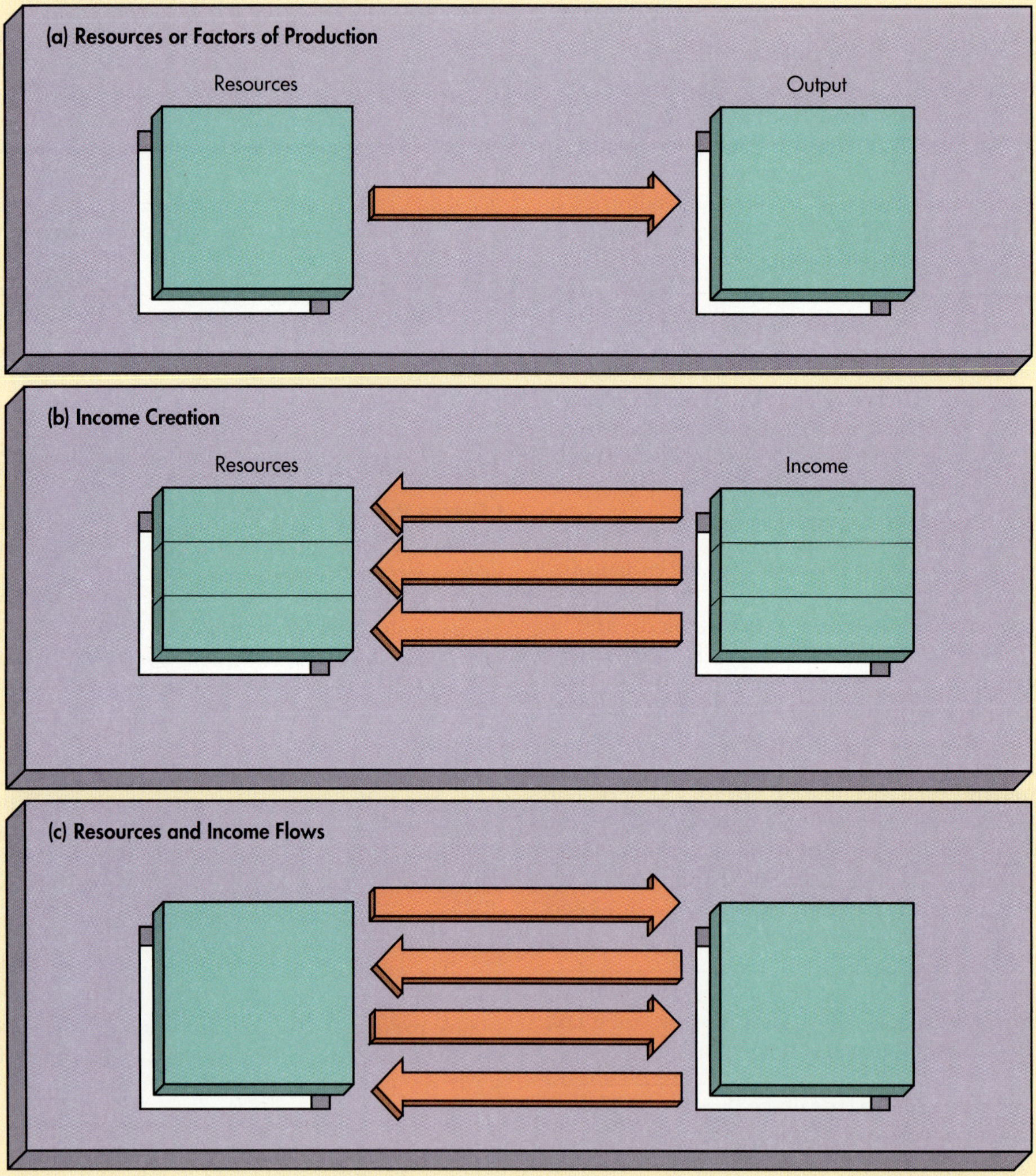

APPENDIX TO CHAPTER 1

WORKING WITH GRAPHS

1. READING AND CONSTRUCTING GRAPHS

It is important to understand how the axes (the horizontal and vertical lines) are used and what they measure. Let's begin with the horizontal axis, the line running across the page in a horizontal direction. Notice in Figure 1.1(a) that the line is divided into equal segments. Each point on the line represents a quantity, or the value of the variable being measured. For example, each segment could represent 10 years or 10,000 pounds of diamonds or some other value. Whatever is measured, the value increases from left to right, beginning with negative values, going on to zero, which is called the origin, and then moving on to positive numbers.

A number line in the vertical direction can be constructed as well, also shown in Figure 1.1(a). Zero is the origin, and the numbers increase from bottom to top. Like the horizontal axis, the vertical axis is divided into equal

FIGURE 1.1 The Axes, the Coordinate System, and the Positive Quadrant

Figure 1.1(a) shows the vertical and horizontal axes. The horizontal axis has an origin, measured as zero, in the middle. Negative numbers are to the left of zero, positive numbers to the right. The vertical axis also has an origin in the middle. Positive numbers are above the origin; negative numbers are below. The horizontal and vertical axes together show the entire coordinate system. Positive numbers are in quadrant I, negative numbers in quadrant III, and combinations of negative and positive numbers in quadrants II and IV.

Figure 1.1(b) shows only the positive quadrant. Because most economic data are positive, often only the upper right quadrant, the positive quadrant, of the coordinate system is used.

(a) The Coordinate System **(b) The Positive Quadrant**

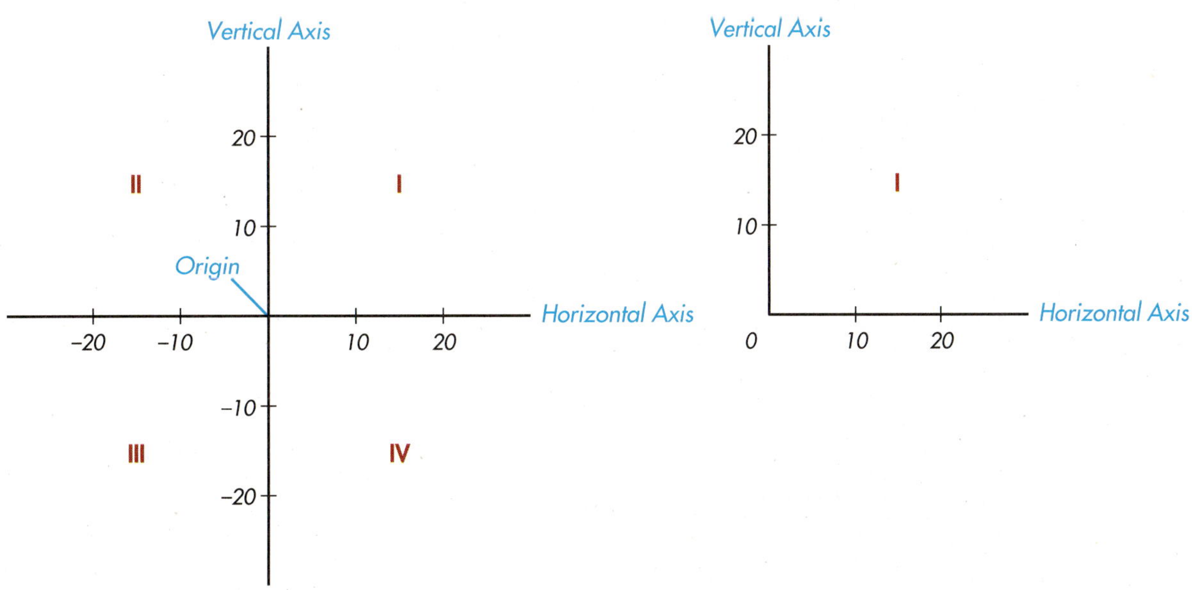

segments; the distance between 0 and 10 is the same as the distance between 0 and 210, between 10 and 20, and so on.

Putting the horizontal and vertical lines together lets us express relationships between two variables graphically. The axes cross, or intersect, at their origins, as shown in Figure 1.1(a). From the common origin, movements to the right and up, in the area—called a quadrant—marked I, are combinations of positive numbers; movements to the left and down, in quadrant III, are combinations of negative numbers; movements to the right and down, in quadrant IV, are negative values on the vertical axis and positive values on the horizontal axis; and movements to the left and up, in quadrant II, are positive values on the vertical axis and negative values on the horizontal axis.

Economic data are typically positive numbers: the unemployment rate, the inflation rate, the price of something, the quantity of something produced or sold, and so on. Because economic data are usually positive numbers, the only part of the coordinate system that usually comes into play in economics is the upper right portion, quadrant I. That is why economists may simply sketch a vertical line down to the origin and then extend a horizontal line out to the right, as shown in Figure 1.1(b). When data are negative, the other quadrants of the coordinate system may be used.

1.a. Constructing a Graph from a Table

Now that you are familiar with the axes, that is, the coordinate system, you are ready to construct a graph using the data in the table in Figure 1.2. The table lists a series of possible price levels for a personal computer (PC) and the corresponding number of PCs people choose to purchase. The data are only hypothetical; they are not drawn from actual cases.

The information given in the table is graphed in Figure 1.2. We begin by marking off and labeling the axes. The vertical axis is the list of possible price levels. We begin at zero and move up the axis at equal increments of $1,000.

FIGURE 1.2 Prices and Quantities Purchased

The information given in the table is graphed below. We begin by marking off and labeling the axes. The vertical axis is the list of possible price levels. The horizontal axis is the number of PCs purchased. Beginning at zero, the axes are marked at equal increments of 1,000. According to the information presented in the table, if the price level is $10,000, no PCs are purchased. The combination of $10,000 and 0 PCs is point A on the graph. At a price of $9,000, there are 1,000 PCs purchased. This is point B. The final step in constructing a line graph is to connect the points that are plotted. When the points are connected, the straight line slanting downward shows the relationship between the price of PCs and the number of PCs purchased.

Point	Price per PC (thousands of dollars)	Number of PCs Purchased (thousands)
A	10	0
B	9	1
C	8	2
D	7	3
E	6	4
F	5	5
G	4	6
H	3	7
I	2	8
J	1	9
K	0	10

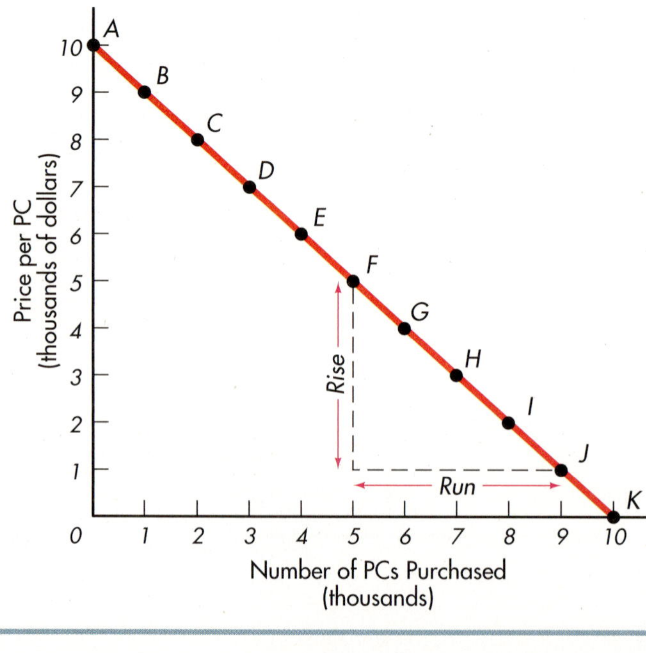

The horizontal axis is the number of PCs sold. We begin at zero and move out the axis at equal increments of 1,000 PCs. According to the information presented in the table, if the price is $10,000, no one buys a PC. The combination of $10,000 and 0 PCs is point *A* on the graph. To plot this point, find the quantity zero on the horizontal axis (it is at the origin), and then move up the vertical axis from zero to a price level of $10,000. (Note that we have measured the units in the table and on the graph in thousands.) At a price of $9,000, there are 1,000 PCs purchased. To plot the combination of $9,000 and 1,000 PCs, find 1,000 units on the horizontal axis and then measure up from there to a price of $9,000. This is point *B*. Point *C* represents a price of $8,000 and 2,000 PCs. Point *D* represents a price of $7,000 and 3,000 PCs. Each combination of price and PCs purchased listed in the table is plotted in Figure 1.2.

The final step in constructing a line graph is to connect the points that are plotted. When the points are connected, the straight line slanting downward from left to right in Figure 1.2 is obtained. It shows the relationship between the price of PCs and the number of PCs purchased.

1.b. Interpreting Points on a Graph

Let's use Figure 1.2 to demonstrate how points on a graph may be interpreted. Suppose the current price of a PC is $6,000. Are you able to tell how many PCs are being purchased at this price? By tracing that price level from the vertical axis over to the curve and then down to the horizontal axis, you find that 4,000 PCs are purchased. You can also find what happens to the number purchased if the price falls from $6,000 to $5,000. By tracing the price from $5,000 to the curve and then down to the horizontal axis, you discover that 5,000 PCs are purchased. Thus, according to the graph, a decrease in the price from $6,000 to $5,000 results in 1,000 more PCs being purchased.

1.c. Shifts of Curves

Graphs can be used to illustrate the effects of a change in a variable not represented on the graph. For instance, the curve drawn in Figure 1.2 shows the relationship between the price of PCs and the number of PCs purchased. When this curve was drawn, the only two variables that were allowed to change were the price and the number of computers. However, it is likely that people's incomes determine their reaction to the price of computers as well. An increase in income would enable more people to purchase computers. Thus, at every price more computers would be purchased. How would this be represented? As an outward shift of the curve, from points *A*, *B*, *C*, etc., to *A*9, *B*9, *C*9, and so on, as shown in Figure 1.3.

Following the shift of the curve, we can see that more PCs are purchased at each price than was the case prior to the income increase. For instance, at a price of $8,000 the increased income allows 4,000 PCs to be purchased rather than 2,000. The important point to note is that if some variable that influences the relationship shown in a curve or line graph changes, then the entire curve or line changes; that is, it shifts.

As we have seen, graphs can be used to illustrate the effects of a change in a variable not explicitly shown on the graph. For instance, if a nation obtains more resources, points outside its current production possibilities curve become attainable. Suppose a country discovers new sources of oil within its borders and is able to greatly increase its production of oil. Greater oil supplies would enable the country to increase production of all types of goods and services.

Figure 1.4 shows the production possibilities curve before (PPC_1) and after (PPC_2) the discovery of oil. Curve PPC_1 is based on the data given in the table in Figure 1.8. Curve PPC_2 is based on the data given in the table in Figure 1.9, which shows the increase in the production of goods and services that results from the increase in oil supplies. The first combination of goods and services on PPC_2, point A_2, is 220 million units of defense goods and 0 units of nondefense goods. The second point, B_2, is a combination of 200 million units of defense goods and 75 million

FIGURE 1.3 Shift of Curve

An increase in income allows more people to purchase PCs at each price. At a price of $8,000, for instance, 4,000 PCs are purchased, rather than 2,000.

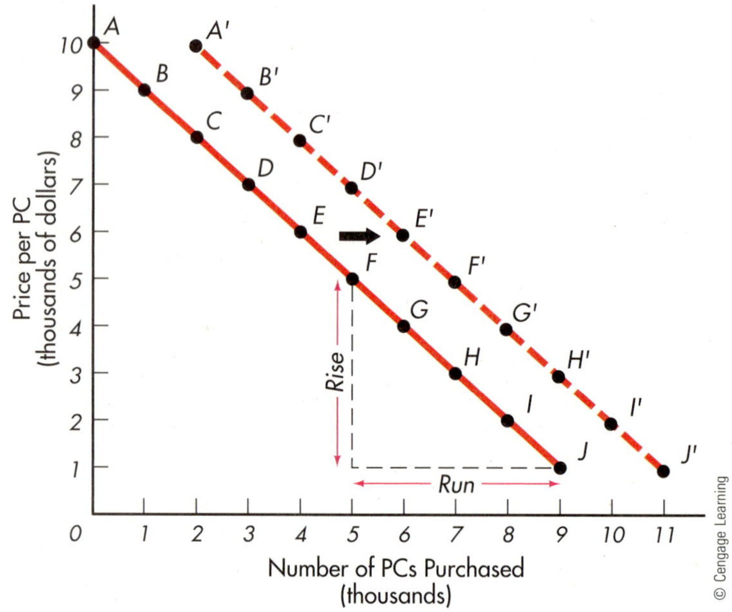

FIGURE 1.4 A Shift of the Production Possibilities Curve

Whenever everything else is not constant, the curve shifts. In this case, an increase in the quantity of a resource enables the society to produce more of both types of goods. The curve shifts out, away from the origin.

Combination	Defense Goods and Services (millions of units)	Nondefense Goods and Services (millions of units)
A_1	200	0
B_1	175	75
C_1	130	125
D_1	70	150
E_1	0	160
F_1	130	25
G_1	200	75

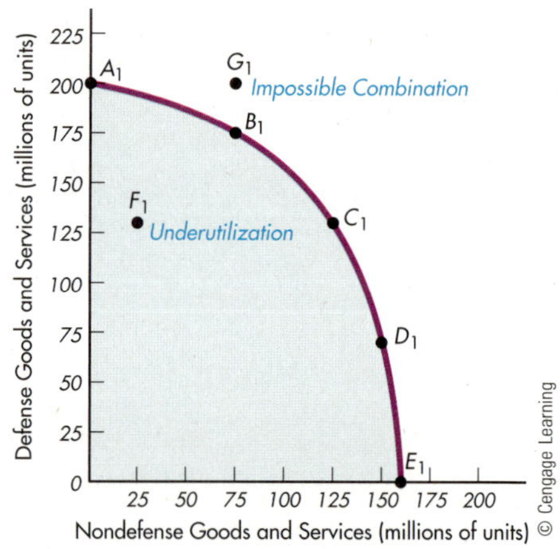

units of nondefense goods. Points C_2 through F_2 are the combinations shown in the table of Figure 1.5. Connecting these points yields the bowed-out curve, PPC_2. Because of the availability of new supplies of oil, the nation is able to increase the production of all goods, as shown by the shift from PPC_1 to PPC_2. A comparison of the two curves shows that more goods and services for both defense and nondefense are possible along PPC_2 than along PPC_1.

The outward shift of the PPC can be the result of an increase in the quantity of resources, but it also can occur because the quality of resources improves. For instance, a technological breakthrough could conceivably improve the way that communication occurs, thereby requiring fewer people and machines and less time to produce the same quantity and quality of goods. The work force could become more literate, thereby requiring less time to produce the same quantity and quality of goods. Any one of these quality improvements in resources could lead to an outward shift of the PPC.

SUMMARY

1. Most economic data are positive numbers, so often only the upper right quadrant of the coordinate system is used in economics.
2. Curves illustrate the relationship between two variables.
3. Curves are drawn assuming that nothing that might affect the relationship between two variables changes. When one such change occurs, the curves shift.

EXERCISES

1. Plot the data listed in the table below.
   a. Measure price along the vertical axis and quantity along the horizontal axis and plot the first two columns.
   b. Show what quantity is sold when the price is $550.
   c. Directly below the graph in part a, plot the data in columns 2 and 3. In this graph, measure quantity on the horizontal axis and total revenue on the vertical axis.
   d. What is total revenue when the price is $550? Will total revenue increase or decrease when the price is lowered?

Price ($)	Quantity Sold	Total Revenue
1,000	200	200,000
900	400	360,000
800	600	480,000
700	800	560,000
600	1,000	600,000
500	1,200	600,000
400	1,400	560,000
300	1,600	480,000
200	1,800	360,000
100	2,000	200,000

2. Listed below are the production possibility curves for two countries producing health care and food. If they devote all resources to health care, Haiti can care for 1,000 people a month, while Cuba can care for 500. If they split their resources 50–50, Haiti can care for 500 people and produce 7 tons of food, while Cuba can care for 250 and produce 3 tons of food. Putting all resources into food, Haiti can produce 10 tons, while Cuba can produce 7.
   a. Plot Haiti's and Cuba's production possibility curves.
   b. Can you see any possible gains from trade that might occur? ______________.
   c. What would Haiti specialize in? What would Cuba specialize in?

GLOBAL BUSINESS INSIGHT

"Free" Air?

Although air might be what we describe as a free good, quality, breathable air is not free in many places in the world. In fact, breathable air is becoming a luxury in many places. Consider the Opus Hotel in Vancouver, British Columbia. It is the first North American hotel to offer hand-held oxygen dispensers in every room. These oxygen canisters are small enough to fit into a purse or briefcase and hold enough air for 12 minutes of breathing time. Breathing oxygen is said to increase energy, improve cognitive performance, and reduce the effects of hangovers.

An oxygen bar where you can inhale 95 percent pure O_2 is the latest craze to hit Dublin, Ireland, and other large cities around the world. Sniffing concentrated, flavored oxygen is a big hit in the United States.

Although these "luxury" purchases of oxygen are increasing, less-developed countries find their sales of oxygen to be more a matter of necessity. In Mexico City, clean, breathable air is hard to find. In this city of 20 million people and more than 3 million cars, dust, lead, and chemicals make the air unsafe to breathe more than 300 days a year. Beijing is no different.

Percentage of Effort Devoted to Health Care	Haiti		Cuba	
	Health Care	Food	Health Care	Food
100	1,000	0	500	0
50	500	7	250	3
0	0	10	0	7

3. Plot the PPC given by the following data.

Combination	Health Care	All Other Goods
A	0	100
B	25	90
C	50	70
D	75	40
E	100	0

a. Calculate the opportunity cost of each combination compared to the combination before. Compare *A* to *B*, *B* to *C*, *C* to *D*, and *D* to *E*.

b. Suppose a second nation has the following PPC. Plot the PPC. Are you able to define which nation has a comparative advantage in which activity?

Combination	Health Care	All Other Goods
A	0	50
B	20	40
C	40	25
D	60	5
E	65	0

2 Markets and the Market Process

FUNDAMENTAL QUESTIONS

1. How are goods and services allocated?
2. How does the market process work?
3. What is demand?
4. What is supply?
5. How is price determined by demand and supply?
6. What causes price to change?

PREVIEW

People (and firms and nations) can get more if they specialize in certain activities and then trade with one another to acquire the goods and services they desire. But how are the specialized producers to get together or to know who specializes in what? We could allow the government to decide, or we could rely on first-come, first-served, or even simply luck. Typically it is the market mechanism—buyers and sellers interacting via prices—we rely on to ensure that gains from trade occur. To see why, consider the following situation and then carry out the exercise.

I. At a sightseeing point, reachable only after a strenuous hike, a firm has established a stand where bottled water is sold. The water, carried in by the employees of the firm, is sold to thirsty hikers in six-ounce bottles. The price is $1 per bottle. Typically only 100 bottles of the water are sold each day. On a particularly hot day, 200 hikers want to buy at least one bottle of water. Indicate what you think of each of the following means of distributing the water to the hikers:

1. Increasing the price until the quantity of water bottles hikers are willing and able to purchase exactly equals the number of water bottles available for sale
   a. agree completely
   b. agree with slight reservation
   c. disagree
   d. strongly disagree
   e. totally unacceptable
2. Selling the water for $1 per bottle on a first-come, first-served basis
   a. agree completely
   b. agree with slight reservation
   c. disagree
   d. strongly disagree
   e. totally unacceptable

3. Having the local authority (government) buy the water for $1 per bottle and distribute it according to its own judgment
   a. agree completely
   b. agree with slight reservation
   c. disagree
   d. strongly disagree
   e. totally unacceptable
4. Selling the water at $1 per bottle following a random selection procedure or lottery
   a. agree completely
   b. agree with slight reservation
   c. disagree
   d. strongly disagree
   e. totally unacceptable

The following is a similar situation but involves a different product.

II. A physician has been providing medical services at a fee of $100 per patient and typically sees 30 patients per day. One day the flu bug has been so vicious that the number of patients attempting to visit the physician exceeds 60. Indicate what you think of each of the following means of distributing the physician's services to the sick patients:

1. Raising the price until the number of patients the doctor sees is exactly equal to those patients willing and able to pay the doctor's fee
   a. agree completely
   b. agree with slight reservation
   c. disagree
   d. strongly disagree
   e. totally unacceptable
2. Selling the services at $100 per patient on a first-come, first-served basis
   a. agree completely
   b. agree with slight reservation
   c. disagree
   d. strongly disagree
   e. totally unacceptable
3. The local authority's (government's) paying the physician $100 per patient and choosing who is to receive the services according to its own judgment
   a. agree completely
   b. agree with slight reservation
   c. disagree
   d. strongly disagree
   e. totally unacceptable

4. Selling the physician's services for $100 per patient following a random selection procedure or lottery
   a. agree completely
   b. agree with slight reservation
   c. disagree
   d. strongly disagree
   e. totally unacceptable

III. There are many more people needing a kidney transplant than there are kidneys available. Indicate what you think of each of the following ways of determining who gets the kidneys:
   1. Potential recipients' buying the kidneys from donors, paying a price sufficient to equalize the number of kidneys needed and the number provided
      a. agree completely
      b. agree with slight reservation
      c. disagree
      d. strongly disagree
      e. totally unacceptable
   2. Allocating the kidneys on a first-come, first-served basis
      a. agree completely
      b. agree with slight reservation
      c. disagree
      d. strongly disagree
      e. totally unacceptable
   3. The government's deciding who gets the kidneys
      a. agree completely
      b. agree with slight reservation
      c. disagree
      d. strongly disagree
      e. totally unacceptable
   4. Providing the kidneys according to a random procedure such as a lottery
      a. agree completely
      b. agree with slight reservation
      c. disagree
      d. strongly disagree
      e. totally unacceptable

With the market system, this bakery must provide baked goods that have high value to others. If it does not, consumers may switch to an alternate source of baked goods.

Denis Raev/iStockphoto.com

1. ALLOCATION MECHANISMS

1

How are goods and services allocated?

How did you respond to the alternative choices? You had the choice among four allocation mechanisms for the scarce goods and services: market; first-come, first-served; government; and random. Did you notice that no matter which allocation mechanism is used, someone gets the good or service and someone doesn't? With the market system, it is those who are least willing or able to pay who must do without. Under the first-come, first-served system, it is those who arrive later who do without. Under the government scheme, it is those not in favor or those who do not match up with the government's rules who do without. And with a random procedure, it is those who do not have the lucky ticket or correct number who are left out.

Since each allocation mechanism is in a sense unfair, how do we decide which to use? One way might be the incentives each creates. Suppose, just as a thought experiment, that everything—and we mean everything—in a society were allocated using a single allocation mechanism.

With the first-come, first-served allocation scheme, the incentive is to be first. You would have no reason to improve the quality of your products or to increase the value of your resources. Your only incentive would be to be first. Supply would not increase. Why would anyone produce when all everyone wants is to be first? As a result, growth and standards of living would not rise. A society based on first-come, first-served would die a quick death.

The government scheme provides an incentive either to be a member of government and thus help determine the allocation rules or to perform according to government dictates. There are no incentives to improve production and efficiency or quantities supplied and, therefore, no reason for the economy to grow. We've seen how this system fared with the collapse of the Soviet Union.

The random allocation provides no incentives at all—simply hope that manna from heaven will fall on you.

With the market system, the incentive is to acquire purchasing ability (to obtain income and wealth). This means you must provide goods that have high value to others or resources that have high value to producers. For example, you can enhance your worth as an employee by acquiring education or training, which increases the value of the resources you own.

The market system also provides incentives for quantities of scarce goods to increase. In the case of the water stand in the first scenario, if the price of the water increases and the owner of the water stand is earning significant profits, others may carry or truck water to the top of the hill and sell it to thirsty hikers, and the amount of water available thus increases. In the case of the doctor in the second scenario, other doctors may think that opening an office near the first might be a way to earn more, and the amount of physician services available increases. Since the market system creates the incentive for the amount supplied to increase, economies grow and expand and standards of living improve. The market system also ensures that resources are allocated to where they are most highly valued. If the price of an item rises, consumers may switch over to another item or another good or service that can serve about the same purpose. When consumers switch, production of the alternative good rises and thus resources used in its production must increase as well. The resources then flow from the now lower-valued use to the new higher-valued use.

1.a. **Efficiency**

efficiency:
the measure of how well an allocation system satisfies people's wants and needs

Economists evaluate the outcome of an economic system in terms of **efficiency**. Efficiency is a measure of how well a system satisfies people's wants and needs. An efficient system occurs when people get what they want and are willing to pay for at the lowest possible costs, and resources are used in their highest-valued use. In contrast, an inefficient allocation is wasteful; better use of the available resources would allow more or better goods and services to be provided.

A system of markets and prices is generally the most efficient means of coordinating and organizing activities. Why? Because it takes fewer resources to work than any other system. Individuals offer to sell goods and services at various prices, and other individuals offer to buy goods and services at various prices. Without having anyone coordinating the buyers and sellers, the market determines a price for each traded good at which the quantities that people are willing and able to sell are equal to the quantities that people are willing and able to buy. This price informs buyers and sellers as to what they must give up to acquire a unit of the good (i.e., their opportunity costs) and thereby lets them know whether their activities have value and in which activities they should specialize.

Day in and day out, without any conscious central direction, the market system induces people to employ their talents and resources where these resources and talents have the highest value. People do not have to be fooled, cajoled, or forced to do their parts in a well-functioning market system, but instead they pursue their own objectives as they see fit. Workers, attempting to maximize their own individual happiness and well-being, select the training, careers, and jobs where their talents and energy are most valuable. Producers, pursuing only private profits, develop the goods and services on which consumers put the highest value and produce these goods and services at the lowest possible costs. Owners of resources, seeking only to increase their own wealth, deploy these assets in socially desirable ways.

Does this behavior on the part of people lead to greed and selfishness? By saying that markets organize activities and allocate resources, are economists saying people should just do what they want irrespective of what their behavior does to others? The answer is no. Economists assume that people are self-interested, not mean-spirited and selfish. Someone like Mother Teresa, who spent her life in the ghettos of India serving the poorest of the poor, would be described as self-interested. She gained satisfaction from sacrificing and helping others. Greed can do good if directed appropriately. The entrepreneur is greedy for success. The scientist is greedy for new knowledge. The artist is greedy for creativity. This type of greed can serve society well. Interacting in free markets enables these people to pursue self-interests without harming others. But what about someone who is greedy for someone else's money or car and steals it? This is not a voluntary market transaction. This type of behavior is what economists call a violation of private property rights. When what people own is not secure and can be taken by others, a free market system does not work. When behavior that harms someone else occurs, then the victim's private property rights have been violated. Economists say that voluntary exchange with secure private property rights is essential for a free market. When these do not exist, something other than the market will be used to allocate scarce resources.

1.b. Alternatives to Market Allocation

The price, or market, system is the predominant allocation mechanism in most industrial societies today because it is generally the most efficient. Yet not all exchanges take place through the market system. Many medical services are provided on a first-come, first-served basis. Classes in schools are often allocated on a first-come, first-served basis. The use of highways or roadways is typically first-come, first-served. Governments allocate many goods: radio and television broadcast bands, land use (zoning), rights-of-way at intersections, and many others. Even luck—random allocation—plays a part in the allocation of some items such as concert tickets, lottery winnings, and other contest prizes. If the market system is such an efficient mechanism, why is it not universally relied on? One reason is that for some products people do not like the outcome of the market system. They don't think it is fair, or they think some other way to allocate the scarce goods and services would be preferable. A second reason is that the market system may not be the most efficient allocation mechanism in some circumstances. A third reason is that in some circumstances, the market may simply not be able to function. We will talk about each of these after we have discussed how markets allocate scarce goods, services, and resources.

RECAP

1. Allocation mechanisms are the means used to distribute scarce goods and resources. Common allocation mechanisms are first-come, first-served; government; random; and the market system.
2. The outcome of an exchange system is evaluated on the basis of efficiency. An efficient allocation of resources is one in which resources are allocated so that no one can be made better off without harming someone else.
3. The price or market system is relied on for most exchanges because it is generally the most efficient. It creates incentives that lead to growth and improvements in standards of living.

2. HOW MARKETS FUNCTION

2 How does the market process work?

When the Mazda Miata was introduced in the United States in 1990, the little sports roadster was an especially desired product in southern California. As shown in Figure 2.1, the suggested retail price was $13,996, the price at which it was selling in Detroit. In Los Angeles, the purchase price was nearly $25,000.

Several entrepreneurs recognized the profit potential in the $10,000 price differential and sent hundreds of students to Detroit to pick up Miatas and drive them back to Los Angeles. Within a reasonably short time, the price differential between Detroit and Los Angeles was reduced. The increased sales in Detroit drove the price there up, while the increased number of Miatas being sold in Los Angeles reduced the price there. The price differential continued to decline until it was less than the cost of shipping the cars from Detroit to Los Angeles. This story of the Mazda Miata illustrates how markets work to allocate scarce goods,

When first introduced, the Mazda Miata was in such demand in Los Angeles that the price rose significantly higher than in other cities. Because of this high demand, the market worked to allocate more of this scarce good to Los Angeles, where the car had the highest value.

FIGURE 2.1 Arbitrage

The Mazda Miata was initially selling for nearly $25,000 in Los Angeles and $14,000 in Detroit. People purchased the car in Detroit and sold it in Los Angeles, thereby driving the prices closer together.

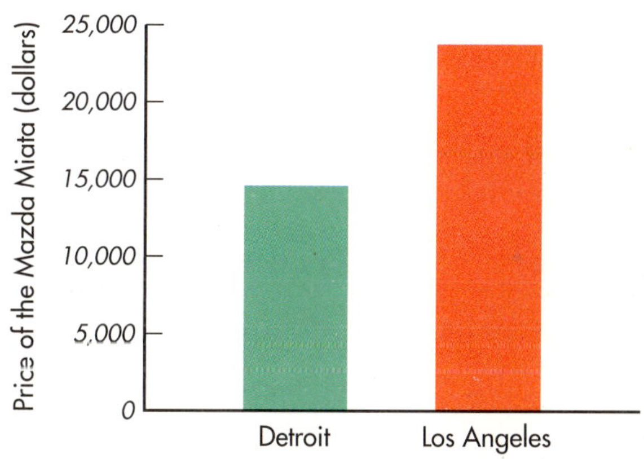

services, and resources. A product is purchased where its price is low and sold where its price is high. As a result, resources devoted to that product flow to where they have the highest value. The same type of situation occurred with the introduction of the Mini Cooper in 2001. The car was an especially hot item in California, so people purchased the car in Chicago or New York, where there was less demand, and had the cars shipped to California.

Suppose an electronics firm is inefficient, its employees surly, and its products not displayed well. To attempt to earn a profit, the firm charges more than the efficiently run firm down the street. Where do customers go? Obviously, they seek out the best deal and go to the efficient firm. The more efficient store has to get more supplies, hire more employees, acquire more space, and so on. The inefficient store lays off employees and sells used equipment and supplies. In short, the resources flow from where they are not as highly valued to where they are more highly valued.

The market process tends to ensure that the goods and services consumers want are provided at the lowest possible price, that resources are used where they are most highly valued, and that inefficient firms and inefficiency in general do not last.

Why does the market process work? For a very simple reason. People are looking for the best deal—the highest quality products at the lowest prices. So when an opportunity for a "best deal" arises, people respond to it by purchasing where the price is low and selling where the price is high.

A market consists of demand (buyers) and supply (sellers). In the rest of this chapter we will look at the market process in more detail by examining demand, then supply, and then putting the two together.

RECAP

1. A market need not be a specific location. A market exists when buyers and sellers interact to buy and sell a specific product.
2. The market process refers to the buying and selling of a good and the resulting allocation of resources to their highest-valued uses.

3. DEMAND

3

What is demand?

The demand for a good or service is based on the behavior of the buyers of that good or service. **Demand** is a relationship between the price of the good or service and the quantity of that good or service people are willing and able to buy. That relationship is such a strong one that it is referred to as a law—the law of demand.

demand:
the amount of a product that people are willing and able to purchase at every possible price

law of demand:
an inverse relationship between price and quantity demanded

3.a. The Law of Demand

The law of demand states that:

1. the quantity of a well-defined good or service
2. that people are willing and able to purchase
3. during a particular period of time
4. decreases as the price of that good or service rises and increases as the price falls
5. everything else held constant.

The first phrase ensures that we are referring to the same item, that we are not mixing different goods. A Rolex watch is different from a Timex watch; Polo brand golf shirts are different goods than generic brand golf shirts; Mercedes-Benz automobiles are different goods than Yugo automobiles.

The second phrase indicates that people must not only want to purchase some good; they must also be able to purchase that good in order for their wants to be counted as part of demand. For example, Sue would love to buy a membership to the Paradise Valley Country Club, but because a membership costs $55,000, she is not able to purchase a membership. Though willing, she is not able. At a price of $5,000, however, she is willing and able to purchase a membership.

The third phrase points out that the demand for any good is defined for a specific period of time. Without reference to a time period, a demand relationship would not make any sense. For instance, the statement that "at a price of $3 per Happy Meal, 13 million Happy Meals are demanded" provides no useful information. Are the 13 million meals sold in one week or one year? Think of demand as a rate of purchase at each possible price over a period of time—two per month, one per day, and so on.

The fourth phrase points out that price and quantity demanded move in opposite directions; that is, as the price rises, the quantity demanded falls, and as the price falls, the quantity demanded rises.

The final phrase, "everything else held constant," ensures that things or events that affect demand other than price do not change. The demand for a good or service depends on the price of that good or service but also on income, tastes, prices of related goods and services, expectations, and the number of buyers. If any one of these changes, demand changes.

3.b. **The Demand Schedule**

demand schedule: a table listing the quantity demanded at each price

A **demand schedule** is a table or list of prices and the corresponding quantities demanded for a particular good or service. Consider the demand for access time to online games. Console games made their debut in the 1970s, but it has been in the first decade of this century in which the growth of online games or interactive console games have really exploded. There are different formats and ways to download games and access networks, but let us deal with a simple setting wherein you can purchase access to a network featuring games such as World of Warcraft on a weekly basis. The table in Figure 2.2 is a demand schedule for hours of access to the games. It shows the number of hours per week that a consumer named Bob would be willing and able to buy at each price during a month, everything else held constant. As the price of the access time gets higher relative to the prices of other goods, Bob would be willing and able to purchase fewer access hours.

At a price of $5 per hour, Bob indicates that he will purchase only 10 hours during the week. At a price of $4, Bob tells us that he will purchase 20 hours during the week. As the price drops from $5 to $4 to $3 to $2 and to $1, Bob is willing and able to purchase more access time. At a price of $1, Bob would purchase 50 hours of access for the week.

3.c. **The Demand Curve**

demand curve: a graph showing the law of demand

A **demand curve** is a graph of the demand schedule. The demand curve shown in Figure 2.2 is plotted from the information given in the demand schedule. The price per hour of access time (price per unit) is measured on the vertical axis, and the number of hours of access per week (quantity per unit of time) is measured on the horizontal axis. The demand curve slopes downward because of the inverse relationship between the price and the quantity that Bob is willing and able to purchase. Point *A* in Figure 2.2 corresponds to combination *A* in the table: a pricc of $5 and 10 hours per week demanded. Similarly, points *B*, *C*, *D*, and *E* in

FIGURE 2.2 Bob's Demand Schedule and Demand Curve for Hours of Access per Week

The number of hours of access to online games that Bob is willing and able to buy at each price during the week is listed in the table, or demand schedule. The demand curve is derived from the combinations given in the demand schedule. The price–quantity combination of $5 per hour and 10 hours is point *A*. The combination of $4 per hour and 20 hours is point *B*. Each combination is plotted, and the points are connected to form the demand curve.

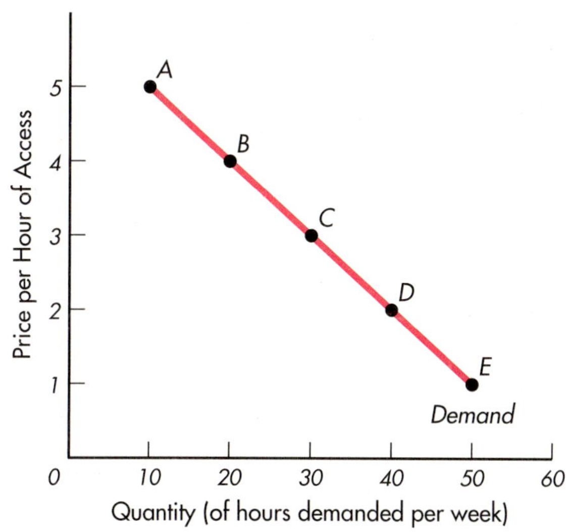

Combination	Price per Hour (constant quality units)	Quantity Demanded per Week (constant quality units)
A	$5	10
B	$4	20
C	$3	30
D	$2	40
E	$1	50

Figure 2.2 represent the corresponding combinations in the table. The line connecting these points is Bob's demand curve for hours of access to a network game.

All demand curves slope down because of the law of demand: As price falls, quantity demanded increases. The demand curves for bread, electricity, automobiles, colleges, labor services, health care, and any other good or service you can think of slope down. You might be saying to yourself, "That's not true. When the price of some rock concerts goes up, more people want to attend the concert. As the ticket price goes up, going to the concert becomes more prestigious, and the quantity demanded actually rises." To avoid confusion in such circumstances, we say "everything else held constant." With this statement, we are assuming that tastes don't change and that, therefore, the goods *cannot* become more prestigious as the price changes. Similarly, we do not allow the quality or the brand name of a product to change as we define the demand schedule or demand curve. We concentrate on the one quality or the one brand; so when we say that the price of a good has risen, we are talking about a good that is identical at all prices.

3.d. From Individual Demand Curves to a Market Curve

Bob's demand curve for hours of access to a network game is plotted in Figure 2.2. Unless Bob is the only person who plays the game, his demand curve is not the total or market demand curve. **Market demand** is derived by adding up the quantities that everyone is willing and able to purchase at each price—the sum of all individual demands. The market demand curve is the horizontal sum of all individual demand curves of all consumers in the market. The table in Figure 2.3 lists the demand schedules of three individuals, Bob, Maria, and Liu. If these three were the only consumers in the market, then the market demand would be the sum of their individual demands, shown as the last column of the table.

market demand: the sum of the individual demands

When speaking of the demand curve or demand schedule, we are using constant quality units. The quality of a good does not change as the price changes along a demand curve.

NOW YOU TRY IT

Using the demand schedule for two individuals, Andrea and Rene, compute the market demand if these two are the only consumers.

Price	$10	$8	$6	$4
Quantity Andrea is willing and able to purchase	5	7	8	9
Quantity Rene is willing and able to purchase	3	4	6	7

Bob's, Maria's, and Liu's demand schedules are plotted as individual demand curves in Figure 2.3(a). In Figure 2.3(b), their individual demand curves have been added together to obtain the market demand curve for hours of access per week to a network game. (Notice that we add in a horizontal direction—that is, we add the quantities at each price, not the prices at each quantity.) At a price of $5, we add the quantity that Bob would be willing and able to buy, 10, to the quantity that Maria would be willing and able buy, 5, to the quantity that Liu would be willing and able buy, 15, to get the market quantity demanded of 30. At a price of $4, we add the quantities that each of the consumers is willing and able to buy to get the total quantity demanded of 48. At all prices, then, we add the quantities demanded by each individual consumer to get the total, or market quantity, demanded.

3.e. Changes in Demand and Changes in Quantity Demanded

When one of the **determinants of demand**—income, tastes, prices of related goods, expectations, or number of buyers—is allowed to change, the demand for a good or service changes as well. What does it mean to say that demand changes? Demand is the entire demand schedule, or demand curve. When we say that demand changes, we are referring to a change in the **quantities demanded** at each and every price.

determinants of demand: things that influence demand other than the price

quantity demanded: the amount of a product that people are willing and able to purchase at a specific price

A change in demand is represented by a shift of the demand curve.

FIGURE 2.3 The Market Demand Schedule and Demand Curve

The market is defined to consist of three individuals: Bob, Maria, and Liu. Their demand schedules are listed in the table and plotted as the individual demand curves shown in Figure 2.3(a). By adding the quantities that each demands at every price, we obtain the market demand curve shown in Figure 2.3(b). At a price of $1, we add Bob's quantity demanded of 50 to Maria's quantity demanded of 25 to Liu's quantity demanded of 27 to obtain the market quantity demanded of 102. At a price of $2, we add Bob's 40 to Maria's 20 to Liu's 24 to obtain the market quantity demanded of 84. To obtain the market demand curve, for every price we sum the quantities demanded by each market participant.

(a) Individual Demand Curves

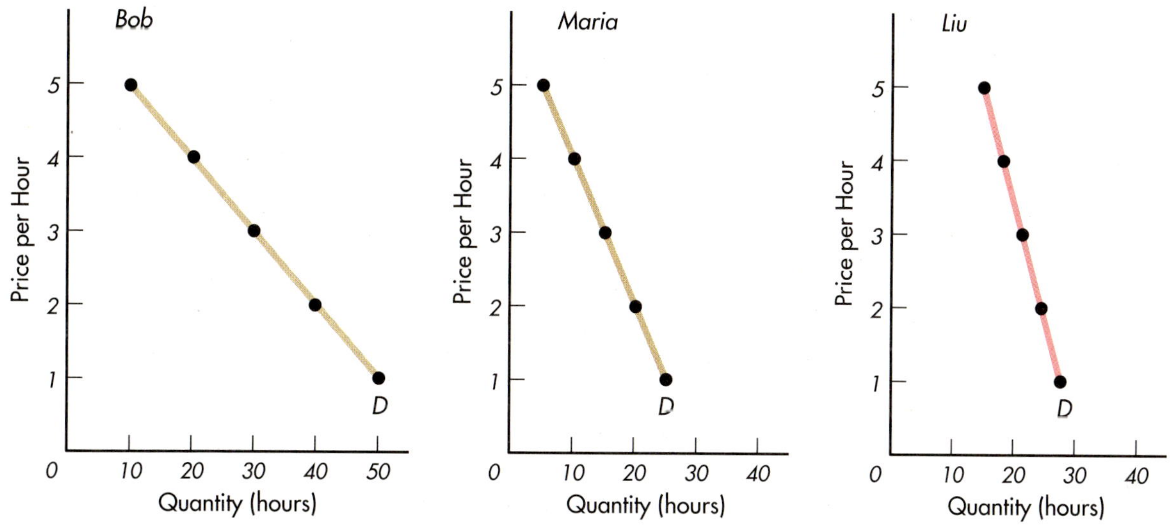

(b) Market Demand Curve

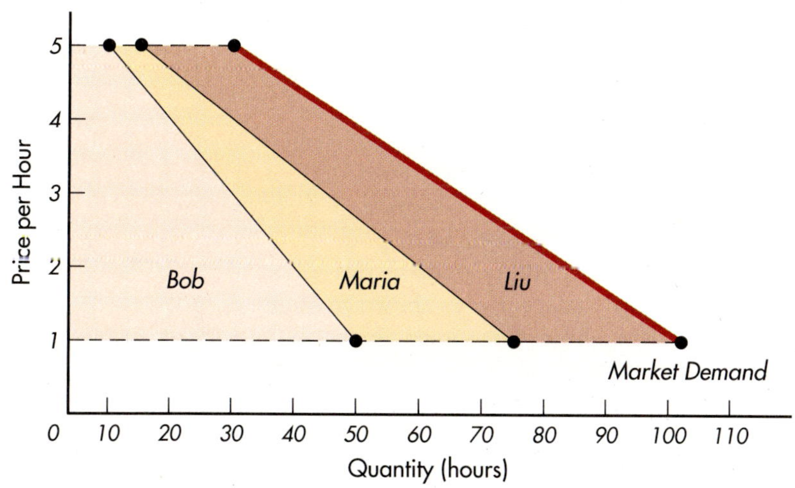

Price per Hour	Quantities Demanded per Year by Bob	Maria	Liu	Market Quantity Demanded
$5	10 +	5 +	15 =	30
$4	20	10	18	48
$3	30	15	21	66
$2	40	20	24	84
$1	50	25	27	102

For example, if Bob's income rises, then he is willing and able to purchase more access time for the network game. At each and every price, the number of hours of access time that Bob is willing and able to buy each week rises. An increase in demand is expressed by a rightward shift of the demand curve, such as shown in Figure 2.4(a) in the move from D_1 to D_2. Conversely, if Bob's income declines, then he would be willing and able to purchase less access time. This decrease in demand is expressed as a leftward shift of the demand curve, as shown in Figure 2.4(b) in the move from D_1 to D_2.

A change in quantity demanded is represented by a movement along one demand curve.

FIGURE 2.4 An Increase and a Decrease in Demand

In Figure 2.4(a), an increase in demand occurs due to an increase in income. The consumer is willing and able to purchase more at every price. This change is expressed as a rightward shift of the demand curve from D_1 to D_2. Figure 2.4(b) shows a decrease in demand due to a decrease in income. The consumer is willing to purchase less at every price. This is illustrated as a leftward shift of demand from D_1 to D_2.

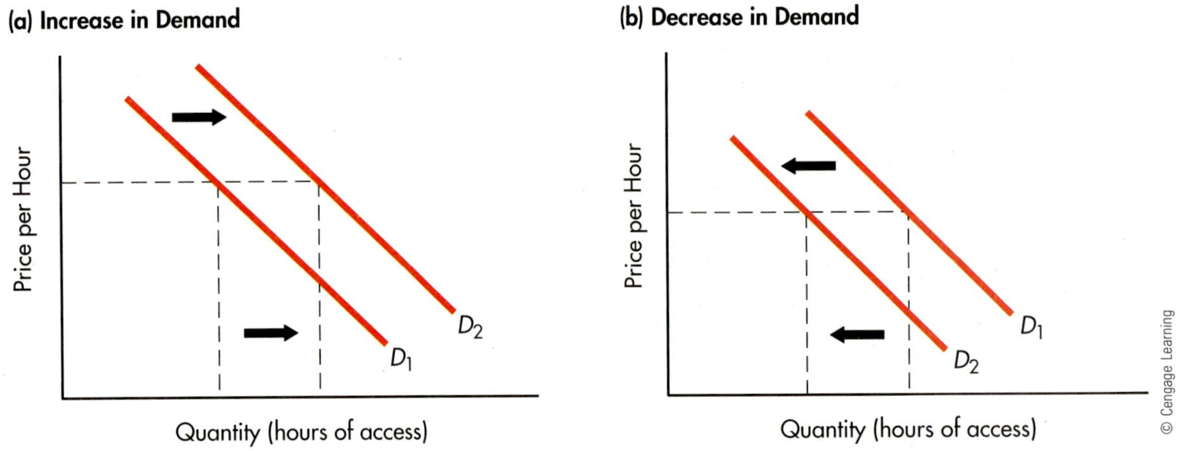

When the price of a good or service is the only factor that changes, the quantity demanded changes, but the demand curve does not shift. Instead, as the price of the access time is decreased (increased), everything else held constant, the quantity that people are willing and able to purchase increases (decreases). This change is merely a movement from one point on the demand curve to another point on the same demand curve, not a shift of the demand curve. A *change in the quantity demanded* is the phrase that economists use to describe the change in the quantities of a particular good or service that people are willing and able to purchase as the price of that good or service changes. A change in the quantity demanded, from point *A* to point *B* on the demand curve, is shown in Figure 2.5(b). Compare this to a change in demand illustrated by the shift of the entire curve as shown in Figure 2.5(a).

The demand curve shifts when income, tastes, prices of related goods, expectations, or the number of buyers changes. Let's consider how each of these determinants of demand affects the demand curve.

normal goods: as income rises, quantity demanded rises

inferior goods: as income rises, quantity demanded falls

3.e.1. **Income** The demand for any good or service depends on income. For most goods and services, the higher someone's income is, everything else the same, the more that person can purchase at any given price. These are called **normal goods**. The increase in Bob's income causes his demand to increase. This change is shown in Figure 2.5(a) by the shift to the right from the curve labeled D_1 to the curve labeled D_2. Increased income means a greater ability to purchase goods and services. At every price, more hours of access time are demanded along curve D_2 than along curve D_1; this is an increase in demand.

For some goods and services, however, the amount demanded declines as income rises, everything else the same. The reason could be that these are goods or services that people use only when their incomes are declining—such as bankruptcy services. In addition, people might not like the good or service as well as they like a more expensive good or service, so when their income rises, they purchase the more expensive items. These types of items are called **inferior goods**.

FIGURE 2.5 A Change in Demand and a Change in the Quantity Demanded

According to the table, Bob's demand for access time has increased by 5 hours at each price. In Figure 2.5(a), this change is shown as a shift of the demand curve from D_1 to D_2. Figure 2.5 (b) shows a change in the quantity demanded. The change in quantity demanded is an increase in the quantity that consumers are willing and able to purchase at a lower price. It is shown as a movement along the demand curve from point *A* to point *B*.

Price per Hour	Quantities Demanded per Week: Before	After
$5	10	15
$4	20	25
$3	30	35
$2	40	45
$1	50	55

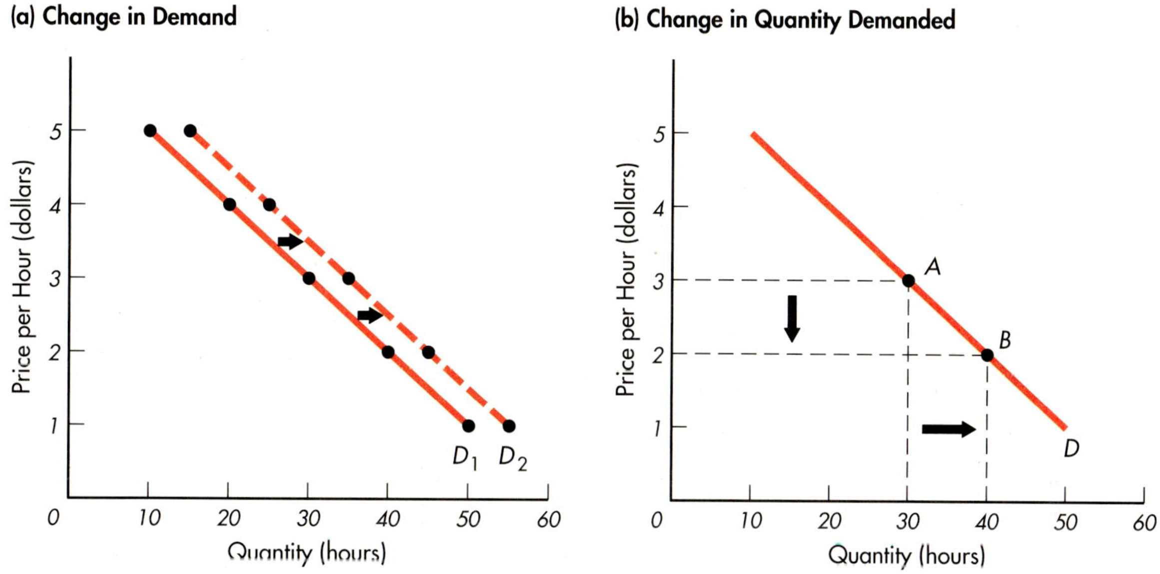

3.e.2. **Tastes** The demand for any good or service depends on individuals' tastes and preferences. When the iPod came out in 2000, it became an instant success. The Sony Walkman lost market share and essentially disappeared. Tastes changed toward the more mobile and, more important, the more powerful iPod. Thousands of songs could be stored on an iPod, whereas the Walkman was constrained by the size of the CD. The iPhone incorporates the iPod into a mobile phone, and it too has been a huge success. Consumers no longer demand the old fixed-line phones but instead want more capabilities in their mobile phones and MP3 devices; their tastes have changed.

substitute goods: items that can be used in place of each other; as the price of one rises, demand for the other rises

3.e.3. **Prices of Related Goods and Services** Goods and services may be related in two ways. **Substitute goods** can be used in place of each other, so that as the cost of one rises, everything else the same, people will buy more of the other. Bread and crackers, BMWs and Acuras, movie downloads and theater movies, universities and community colleges, electricity and natural gas, time used to access network games and time used for other activities are, more or less, pairs of substitutes. As the price of entertainment venues rises, everything else held constant, the demand for access time for network games will rise; the demand curve for access time will shift to the right.

complementary goods: items that are used together; as the price of one rises, demand for the other falls

Complementary goods are goods that are used together, and so as the price of one rises, everything else the same, consumers buy less of it but also buy less of the complementary good. Bread and margarine, beer and peanuts, cameras and film, shoes and socks, CDs and CD players, a computer or game board and access to network games, and iPods and iTunes are examples of pairs of complementary goods. As the price of a machine on which to play network games rises, people purchase less access time to those network games. The demand curve for a complementary good shifts to the left when the price of the related good increases.

3.e.4. **Expectations** Expectations about future events can have an effect on demand today. People make purchases today because they expect their income level to be a certain amount in the future, or because they expect the price of certain items to be higher in the future. You might buy running shoes today if you expect the price of those shoes to be higher tomorrow. You might buy your airline ticket home now rather than wait until semester break if you expect the price to be higher next month.

3.e.5. **Number of Buyers** Market demand consists of the sum of the demands of all individuals. The more individuals there are with income to spend, the greater the market demand is likely to be. For example, the populations of Florida and Arizona are much larger during the winter than they are during the summer. The demand for any particular good or service in Arizona and Florida rises (the demand curve shifts to the right) during the winter and falls (the demand curve shifts to the left) during the summer.

RECAP

1. According to the law of demand, as the price of any good or service rises (falls), the quantity demanded of that good or service falls (rises), during a specific period of time, everything else held constant.
2. A demand schedule is a listing of the quantity demanded at each price.
3. The demand curve is a downward-sloping line plotted using the values in the demand schedule.
4. Market demand is the sum of all individual demands.
5. Demand changes when one of the determinants of demand changes. A demand change is illustrated as a shift of the demand curve.
6. The determinants of demand are income, tastes, prices of related goods and services, expectations, and number of buyers.
7. The quantity demanded changes when the price of the good or service changes. This is a change from one point on the demand curve to another point on the same demand curve.

4. SUPPLY

4

What is supply?

Why do students get discounts at movie theaters? Demand *and* supply. Why do restaurants offer early bird specials? Demand *and* supply. Why is the price of hotel accommodations in Phoenix higher in the winter than in the summer? Demand *and* supply. Why is the price of beef higher in Japan than in the United States? Demand *and* supply. Both demand and supply determine price; neither demand nor supply alone determines price. We now discuss supply.

4.a. The Law of Supply

supply: the quantities suppliers are willing and able to supply at each price

quantity supplied: the amount supplied at any specific price

law of supply: as the price rises, the quantity supplied rises and vice versa

Just as demand is the relation between the price and the quantity demanded of a good or service, supply is the relation between the price and the quantity supplied. **Supply** is the amount of the good or service that producers are willing and able to offer for sale at each possible price during a period of time, everything else held constant. **Quantity supplied** is the amount of the good or service that producers are willing and able to offer for sale at a *specific* price during a period of time, everything else held constant. According to the **law of supply**, as the price of a good or service rises, the quantity supplied rises, and vice versa.

The formal statement of the law of supply consists of five phrases:

1. The quantity of a well-defined good or service that
2. producers are willing and able to offer for sale
3. during a particular period of time
4. increases as the price of the good or service increases and decreases as the price decreases,
5. everything else held constant.

determinants of supply: those factors that affect supply other than price

The first phrase is the same as the first phrase in the law of demand. The second phrase indicates that producers must not only *want* to offer the product for sale but be *able* to offer the product. The third phrase points out that the quantities producers will offer for sale depend on the period of time being considered. The fourth phrase points out that more will be supplied at higher than at lower prices. The final phrase ensures that the **determinants of supply** do not change. The determinants of supply are those factors other than the price of the good or service that influence the willingness and ability of producers to offer their goods and services for sale—the prices of resources used to produce the product, technology and productivity, expectations of producers, the number of producers in the market, and the prices of related goods and services. If any one of these should change, supply changes.

4.b. The Supply Schedule and Supply Curve

supply schedule: a list of prices and corresponding quantities supplied

supply curve: a plot of the supply schedule

A **supply schedule** is a table or list of the prices and the corresponding quantities supplied of a good or service. The table in Figure 2.6 presents a single firm's supply schedule for access to network games. (We will assume that three firms offer access to the same network games.) The schedule lists the quantities that each firm is willing and able to supply at each price, everything else held constant. As the price increases, the firm is willing and able to offer more access time to the network games.

A **supply curve** is a graph of the supply schedule. Figure 2.6 shows Aber's supply curve of access time to the network games. The price and quantity combinations given in the supply schedule correspond to the points on the curve. For instance, combination *A* in the table corresponds to point *A* on the curve; combination *B* in the table corresponds to point *B* on the curve, and so on for each price–quantity combination.

The supply curve slopes upward. This means that a supplier is willing and able to offer more for sale at higher prices than it is at lower prices. This should make sense—if prices rise, everything else held constant, the supplier will earn more profits. Higher profits create the incentive for the supplier to offer more for sale.

4.c. From Individual Supply Curves to the Market Supply

To derive market supply, the quantities that each producer supplies at each price are added together, just as the quantities demanded by each consumer are added

FIGURE 2.6 Aber's Supply Schedule and Supply Curve of Access Time to Network Games

The quantity that Aber is willing and able to offer for sale at each price is listed in the supply schedule and shown on the supply curve. At point *A*, the price is $5 per hour and the quantity supplied is 60 hours. The combination of $4 per hour and 50 hours is point *B*. Each price–quantity combination is plotted, and the points are connected to form the supply curve.

Combination	Price per Hour (constant quality units)	Quantity Supplied per Week (constant quality units)
A	$5	60
B	$4	50
C	$3	40
D	$2	30
E	$1	20

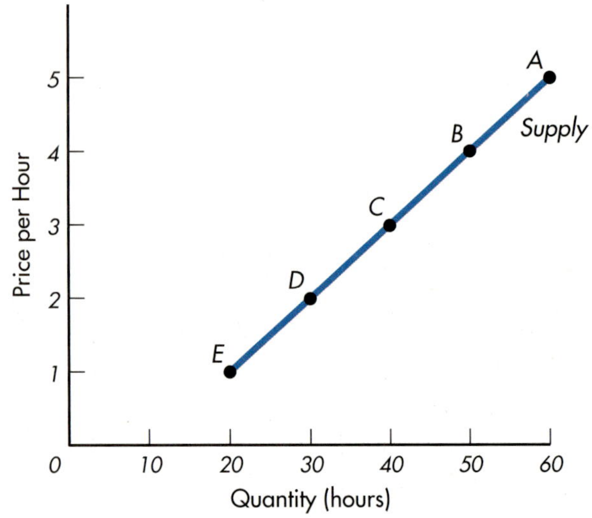

together to get market demand. The table in Figure 2.7 lists the supply schedules of three firms that sell access to network games: Aber, Broadband, and Courage. The supply schedules are plotted in Figure 2.7(a). Then in Figure 2.7(b) the individual supply curves have been added together (in a horizontal direction) to obtain the market supply curve. At a price of $5, the quantity supplied by Aber is 60, the quantity supplied by Broadband is 30, and the quantity supplied by Courage is 12. This means a total quantity supplied in the market of 102. At a price of $4, the quantities supplied are 50, 25, and 9, for a total market quantity supplied of 84. The market supply schedule is the last column in the table. The graph of the price and quantity combinations listed in this column is the market supply curve. The market supply curve slopes up because each of the individual supply curves has a positive slope. The market supply curve tells us that the quantity supplied in the market increases as the price rises.

4.d. Changes in Supply and Changes in Quantity Supplied

When we draw the supply curve, we allow only the price and quantity supplied of the good or service that we are discussing to change. Everything else that might affect supply is assumed not to change. If any of the determinants of supply—the prices of resources used to produce the product, technology and productivity, expectations of producers, the number of producers in the market, and the prices of related goods and services—changes, the supply schedule changes and the supply curve shifts.

A change in the quantity supplied is a movement along the supply curve. A change in the supply is a shift of the supply curve.

4.d.1. Prices of Resources If labor costs rise, higher prices will be necessary to induce each store to offer as many hours of access as it did before the cost of the resource rose. The higher cost of resources causes a decrease in supply,

FIGURE 2.7 The Market Supply Schedule and Curve of Access Time to Network Games

The market supply is derived by summing the quantities that each supplier is willing and able to offer for sale at each price. In this example, there are three producers: The supply schedules of each are listed in the table and plotted as the individual supply curves shown in Figure 2.7(a). By adding the quantities supplied at each price, we obtain the market supply curve shown in Figure 2.7(b). For instance, at a price of $5, Aber offers 60 units, Broadband 30 units, and Courage 12 units, for a market supply quantity of 102. The market supply curve reflects the quantities that each producer is able and willing to supply at each price.

Quantities Supplied per Year by							
Price per Hour	Aber		Broadband		Courage		Market Quantity Demanded
$5	60	+	30	+	12	=	102
$4	50		25		9		84
$3	40		20		6		66
$2	30		15		3		48
$1	20		10		0		30

(a) Individual Supply Curves

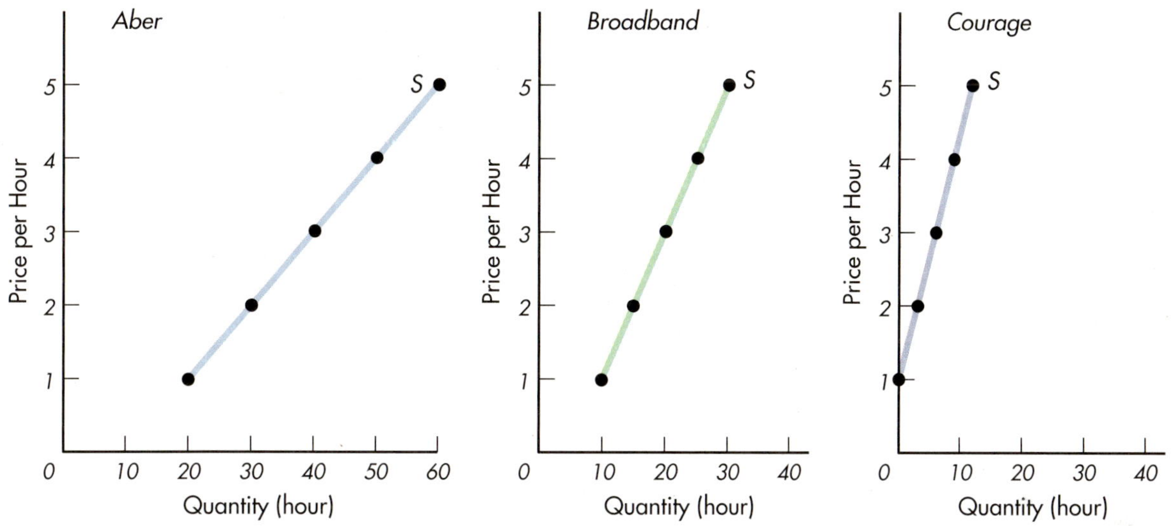

(b) Market Supply Curve

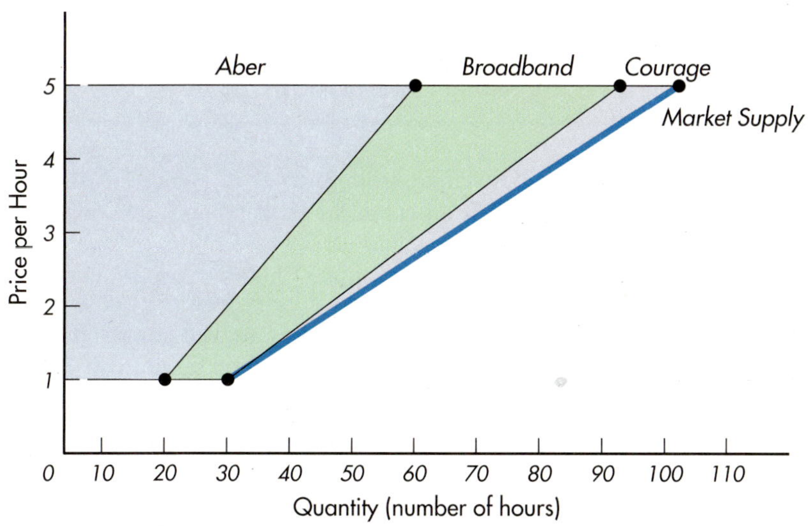

FIGURE 2.8 A Shift of the Supply Curve

Figure 2.8(a) shows a decrease in supply and the shift of the supply curve to the left, from S_1 to S_2. The decrease is caused by a change in one of the determinants of access time to network games—an increase in the price of labor. Because of the increased price of labor, producers are willing and able to offer fewer access hours at each price than they were before the cost of labor rose. Supply curve S_2 shows that at a price of $3 per hour of access, suppliers will offer 57 hours. That is 9 hours less than the 66 hours at $3 per access hour indicated by supply curve S_1. Conversely, to offer a given quantity, producers must receive a higher price per access hour than they previously were getting: $3.50 per hour for 66 hours (on supply curve S_2) instead of $3 per hour (on supply curve S_1).

Figure 2.8(b) shows an increase in supply. A technological improvement or an increase in productivity causes the supply curve to shift to the right, from S_1 to S_2. At each price, a higher quantity is offered for sale. At a price of $3, 66 hours were offered, but with the shift of the supply curve, the quantity of hours for sale at $3 apiece increases to 84. Conversely, producers can reduce prices for a given quantity—for example, charging $2 per hour for 66 hours.

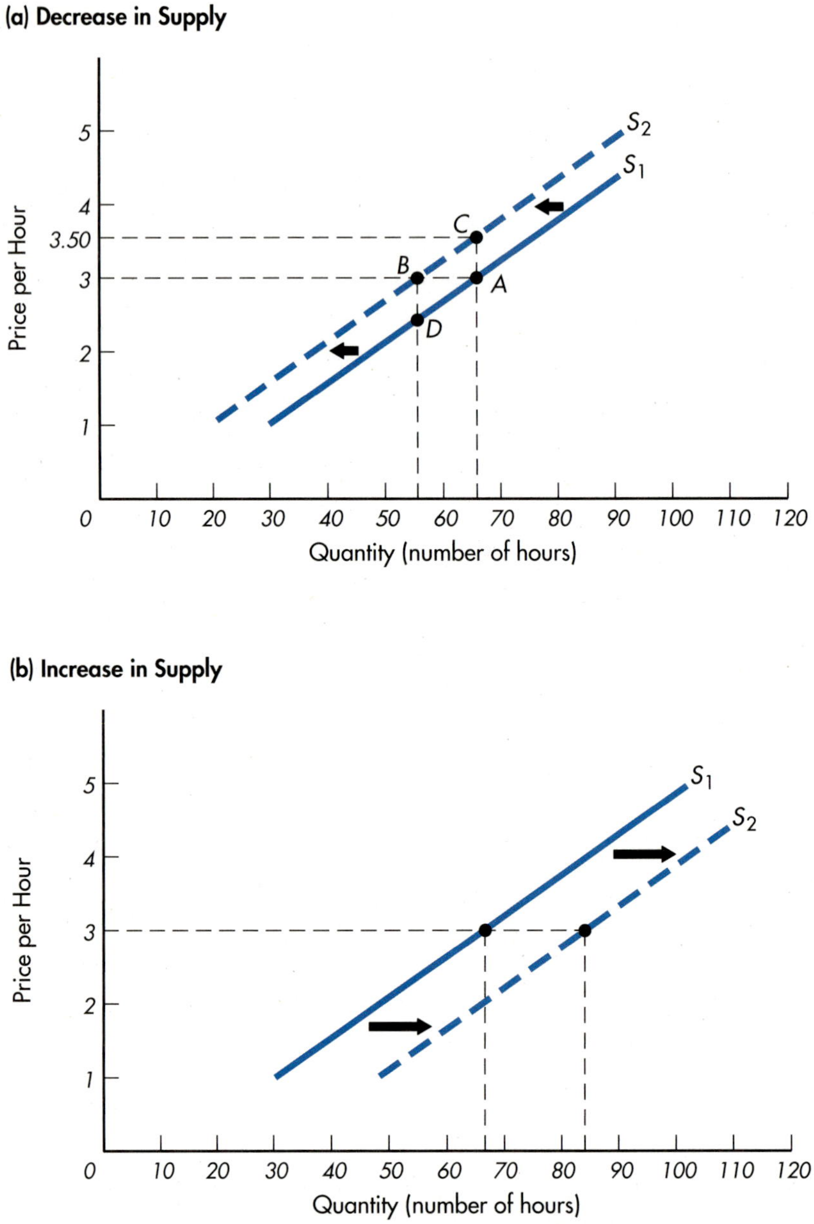

meaning a leftward shift of the supply curve, from S_1 to S_2 in Figure 2.8(a). Compare point B on curve S_2 with point A on curve S_1. Both points correspond to a price of $3, but along curve S_1, sellers are willing to offer 66 hours of access time, whereas curve S_2 indicates that sellers will offer only 57 hours of access time.

4.d.2. **Technology and Productivity** If resources are used more efficiently in the production of a good or service, more of that good or service can be supplied for the same cost, or the original quantity supplied can be produced for a lower cost. As a result, the supply curve shifts to the right, as in Figure 2.8(b).

The move from horse-drawn plows to tractors or from mainframe computers to personal computers meant that each worker was able to produce more. The increase in output produced by each unit of a resource is called a *productivity increase*. **Productivity** is defined as the quantity of output produced per unit of resource. Improvements in technology cause productivity increases, which lead to an increase in supply.

productivity:
total output per unit of input

4.d.3. **Expectations of Suppliers** Sellers may choose to alter the quantity offered for sale today because of a change in expectations regarding the determinants of supply. A supply curve illustrates the quantities that suppliers are willing and able to supply at every possible price. If suppliers expect that something is going to occur to resource supplies or the cost of resources, then they may alter the quantities that they are willing and able to supply at every possible price. The key point is that the supply curve will shift if producers expect something to occur that will alter their anticipated profits at every possible price, not just a change in one price. For instance, the expectation that demand will decline in the future does not lead to a shift of the supply curve; it leads instead to a decline in quantity supplied, because the new demand curve (the expected lower demand) would intersect the supply curve at a lower price and a smaller output level.

4.d.4. **Number of Suppliers** When more people decide to supply a good or service, the market supply increases. More is offered for sale at each and every price, causing a rightward shift of the supply curve.

4.d.5. **Prices of Related Goods or Services** The opportunity cost of producing and selling any good or service is the forgone opportunity to produce any other good or service. If the price of an alternative good changes, then the opportunity cost of producing a particular good changes. This could cause the supply curve to change. For instance, if McDonald's can offer hamburgers or salads with equal ease, an increase in the price of salads could lead the manager to offer more salads and fewer hamburgers. The supply curve of salads would shift to the right, and the supply curve of hamburgers would shift to the left.

A *change in supply* occurs when the quantity supplied at each and every price changes or there is a shift in the supply curve—like the shift from S_1 to S_2 in Figure 2.9(a). A change in one of the determinants of supply brings about a change in supply.

When only the price changes, a greater or smaller quantity is supplied. This is shown as a movement along the supply curve, not as a shift of the curve. A change in price is said to cause a *change in the quantity supplied.* An increase in quantity supplied is shown in the move from point *A* to point *B* on the supply curve of Figure 2.9(b).

FIGURE 2.9 A Change in Supply and a Change in the Quantity Supplied

In Figure 2.9(a), the quantities that producers are willing and able to offer for sale at every price decrease, causing a leftward shift of the supply curve from S_1 to S_2. In Figure 2.9(b), the quantities that producers are willing and able to offer for sale increase, because of an increase in the price of the good, causing a movement along the supply curve from point *A* to point *B*.

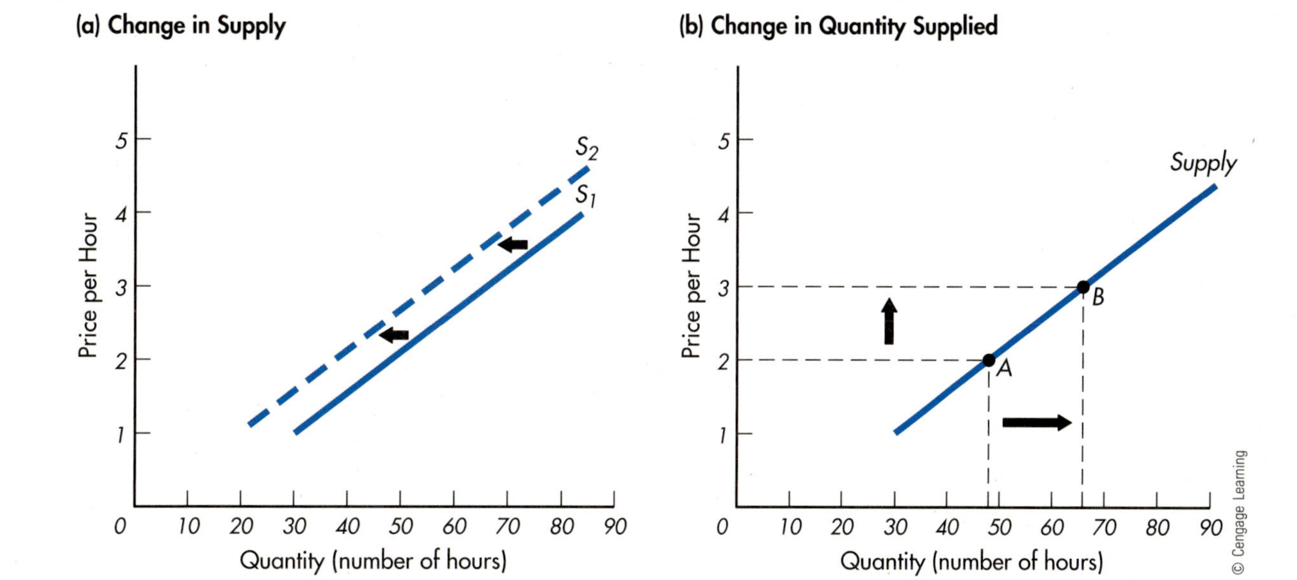

RECAP

1. According to the law of supply, the quantity supplied of any good or service is directly related to the price of the good or service during a specific period of time, everything else held constant.
2. Market supply is found by adding together the quantities supplied at each price by every producer in the market.
3. Supply changes if the prices of relevant resources change, if technology or productivity changes, if producers' expectations change, if the number of producers changes, or if the prices of related goods and services change.
4. Changes in supply are reflected in shifts of the supply curve. Changes in the quantity supplied are reflected in movements along the supply curve.

5. EQUILIBRIUM: PUTTING DEMAND AND SUPPLY TOGETHER

5

How is price determined by demand and supply?

The demand curve shows the quantity of a good or service that buyers are willing and able to purchase at each price. The supply curve shows the quantity that producers are willing and able to offer for sale at each price. Only where the two curves intersect is the quantity supplied equal to the quantity demanded. This intersection is the point of **equilibrium**.

equilibrium:
the price and quantity at which quantity demanded equals quantity supplied

5.a. Determination of Equilibrium

Figure 2.10 brings together the market demand and market supply curves for access hours to network games. The supply and demand schedules are listed in

FIGURE 2.10 Equilibrium

Equilibrium is established at the point where the quantity that suppliers are willing and able to offer for sale is the same as the quantity that buyers are willing and able to purchase. Here, equilibrium occurs at the price of $3 per hour of access to network games and the quantity of 66 hours of access per week. It is shown as point e, at the intersection of the demand and supply curves. At prices above $3, the quantity supplied is greater than the quantity demanded, and the result is a surplus. At prices below $3, the quantity supplied is less than the quantity demanded, and the result is a shortage. The area shaded tan shows all prices at which there is a surplus—where quantity supplied is greater than the quantity demanded. The amount of the surplus is measured in a horizontal direction at each price. The area shaded blue represents all prices at which a shortage exists—where the quantity demanded is greater than the quantity supplied. The amount of the shortage is measured in a horizontal direction at each price.

Price per Hour	Quantity Demanded per Week	Quantity Supplied per Week	Status
$5	30	102	Surplus of 72
$4	48	84	Surplus of 36
$3	66	66	Equilibrium
$2	84	48	Shortage of 36
$1	102	30	Shortage of 72

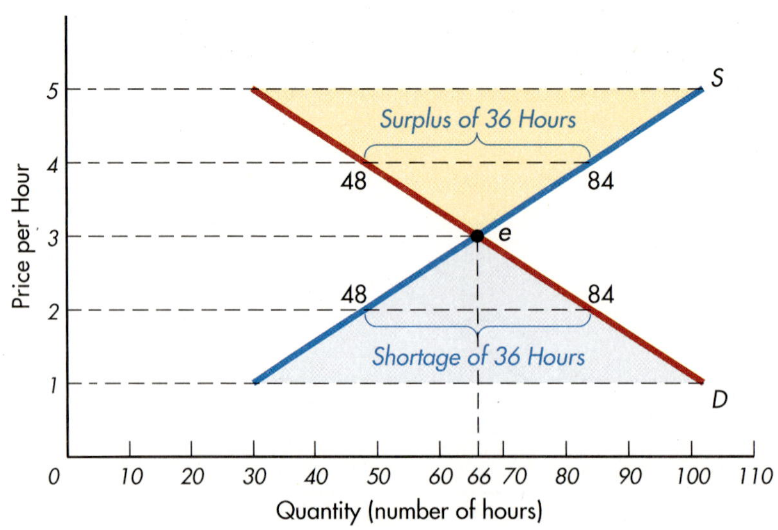

disequilibrium:
a price level at which quantities demanded and supplied are not the same

surplus:
the quantity demanded is less than the quantity supplied

shortage:
the quantity demanded is greater than the quantity supplied

the table, and the curves are plotted in the graph in Figure 2.10. Notice that the curves intersect at only one point, labeled *e*, a price of $3 and a quantity of 66. The intersection point is the equilibrium price, the only price at which the quantity demanded and quantity supplied are the same. You can see that at any other price, the quantity demanded and quantity supplied are not the same. This is called **disequilibrium**.

Whenever the price is greater than the equilibrium price, a **surplus** arises. For example, at $4, the quantity of hours of access demanded is 48, and the quantity supplied is 84. Thus, at $4 per hour, there is a surplus of 36 hours—that is, 36 hours supplied are not purchased. Conversely, whenever the price is below the equilibrium price, the quantity demanded is greater than the quantity supplied and there is a **shortage**. For instance, if the price is $2 per hour of access, consumers will want and be able to pay for more hours of access than are available. As shown in the table in Figure 2.10, the quantity demanded at a price of $2 is 84, but the quantity supplied is only 48. There is a shortage of 36 hours of access at the price of $2.

Neither a surplus nor a shortage will exist for long if the price of the product is free to change. Suppliers who are stuck with hours of access not being purchased will lower the price and reduce the quantities they are offering for sale in order to eliminate a surplus. Conversely, suppliers who cannot supply enough hours to meet demand and who have consumers on hold or losing connection will raise the price to eliminate a shortage. Surpluses lead to decreases in the price and the quantity supplied and increases in the quantity demanded. Shortages lead to increases in the price and the quantity supplied and decreases in the quantity demanded.

A shortage exists only when the quantity that people are willing and able to purchase at a particular price is more than the quantity supplied *at that price*. Scarcity occurs when more is wanted at a zero price than is available.

NOW YOU TRY IT

Using the information provided below, find the equilibrium price and quantity. Then show the equilibrium on a graph of demand and supply curves.

Price	$1,200	$1,000	$800
Quantity Demanded	400	800	1,200
Quantity Supplied	1,000	800	600

Note that a shortage is not the same thing as scarcity.

5.b. Changes in the Equilibrium Price: Demand Shifts

Equilibrium is the combination of price and quantity at which the quantities demanded and supplied are the same. Once an equilibrium is achieved, there is no incentive for suppliers or consumers to move away from it. An equilibrium price changes only when demand and/or supply changes—that is, when the determinants of demand or the determinants of supply change.

Let's consider a change in demand and what it means for the equilibrium price. Suppose that experiments on rats show that playing network games causes brain damage. As a result, a large segment of the human population decides not to purchase access time to the games. Suppliers experience a decrease in the number of customers willing and able to pay for access, as shown in Figure 2.11 by a leftward shift of the demand curve, from curve D_1 to curve D_2.

Once the demand curve has shifted, the original equilibrium price of $3 per hour of access per week at point e_1 is no longer the equilibrium. At a price of $3, the quantity supplied is still 66, but the quantity demanded has declined to 48 (look at the demand curve D_2 at a price of $3). There is, therefore, a surplus of 18 hours of access time per week at the price of $3.

FIGURE 2.11 The Effects of a Shift of the Demand Curve

The initial equilibrium price ($3 per hour of access time) and quantity (66 hours of access time) are established at point e_1, where the initial demand and supply curves intersect. A change in the tastes for access hours to the network games causes demand to decrease, and the demand curve shifts to the left. At $3 per hour of access, the initial quantity supplied, 66 hours, is now greater than the quantity demanded, 48 hours. The surplus of 18 hours causes suppliers to reduce the amount of hours of access offered and to lower the price. The market reaches a new equilibrium, at point e_2, $2.50 per hour and 57 hours per week.

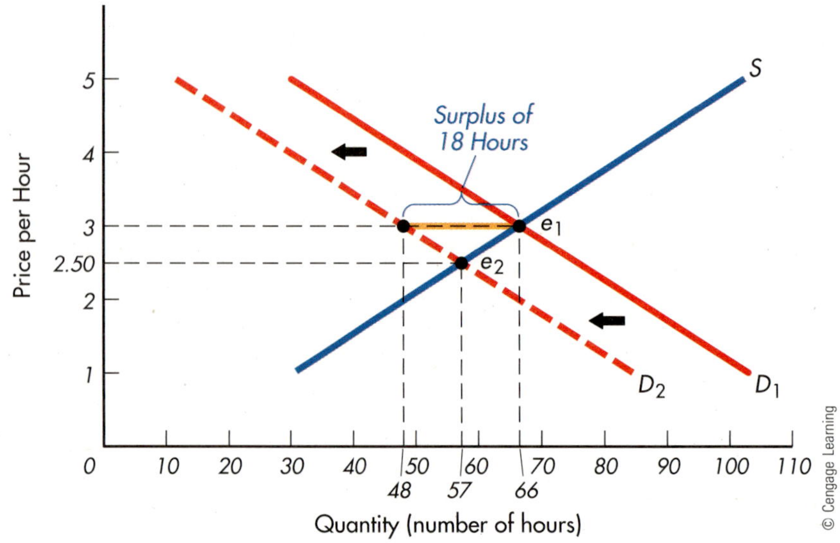

With a surplus comes downward pressure on the price. This downward pressure occurs because producers acquire fewer hours of access for purchase and reduce the price in an attempt to sell those hours not being used. Suppliers continue reducing the price and the quantity available until consumers purchase all the hours that the sellers have available, or until a new equilibrium is established. That new equilibrium occurs at point e_2 with a price of $2.50 and a quantity of 57.

The decrease in demand is represented by the leftward shift of the demand curve. A decrease in demand results in a lower equilibrium price and a lower equilibrium quantity as long as there is no change in supply. Conversely, an increase in demand would be represented as a rightward shift of the demand curve and would result in a higher equilibrium price and a higher equilibrium quantity as long as there is no change in supply.

5.c. **Changes in the Equilibrium Price: Supply Shifts**

The equilibrium price and quantity may be altered by a change in supply as well. If the price of relevant resources, technology and productivity, the expectations of suppliers, the number of suppliers, or the prices of related products change, supply changes.

Let's consider an example. Suppose a tax is imposed on all Internet access and that this tax increases the cost for the network game suppliers to provide access time. This is represented by a leftward shift of the supply curve in Figure 2.12.

The leftward shift of the supply curve, from curve S_1 to curve S_2, leads to a new equilibrium price and quantity. At the original equilibrium price of $3 at point e_1, 66 hours of access are supplied. After the shift in the supply curve, 48 hours are

NOW YOU TRY IT

Using the following data, determine the equilibrium price and quantity. Then, using Quantity Supplied (2), find the equilibrium price and quantity. Use a diagram to illustrate what occurred.

Price	$10	$9	$8	$7	$6
	$5	$4	$3	$2	$1
Quantity Supplied	200	180	160	140	120
	100	80	60	40	20
Quantity Demanded	10	50	85	100	120
	140	160	170	175	178
Quantity Supplied (2)	240	220	200	180	160
	140	120	100	80	60

FIGURE 2.12 The Effects of a Shift of the Supply Curve

The initial equilibrium price and quantity are \$3 and 66 hours, at point e_1. When the Internet tax is imposed, suppliers' costs have risen, and so they are willing and able to offer fewer hours for sale at each price. The result is a leftward (upward) shift of the supply curve, from S_1 to S_2. At the old price of \$3, the quantity demanded is still 66, but the quantity supplied falls to 48. The shortage is 18 hours of access time. The shortage leads to a new equilibrium, e_2, the intersection between curves S_2 and D, which is \$3.50 per hour of access time and 57 hours of access time.

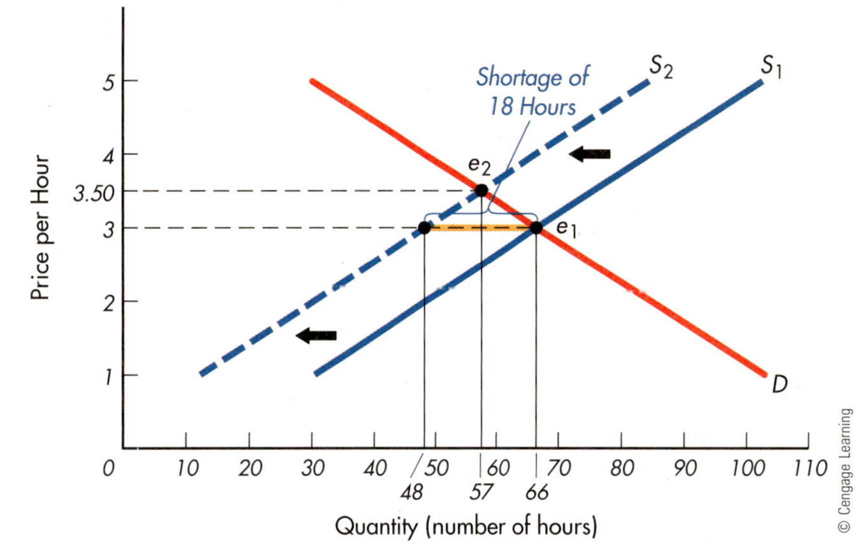

supplied at a price of \$3 per hour, and there is a shortage of 18 hours per week. The shortage puts upward pressure on price. As the price rises, consumers decrease the quantities that they are willing and able to purchase, and suppliers increase the quantities that they are willing and able to supply. Eventually, a new equilibrium price and quantity is established at \$3.50 and 57 hours of access each week at point e_2.

The decrease in supply is represented by the leftward shift of the supply curve. A decrease in supply with no change in demand results in a higher price and a lower quantity. Conversely, an increase in supply would be represented as a rightward shift of the supply curve. An increase in supply with no change in demand would result in a lower price and a higher quantity.

RECAP

1. Equilibrium occurs when the quantity demanded and the quantity supplied are equal: it is the price–quantity combination where the demand and supply curves intersect.
2. A price that is above the equilibrium price creates a surplus. Producers are willing and able to offer more for sale than buyers are willing and able to purchase.
3. A price that is below the equilibrium price leads to a shortage. Buyers are willing and able to purchase more than producers are willing and able to offer for sale.
4. When demand changes, price and quantity change in the same direction. Both rise as demand increases, and both fall as demand decreases.
5. When supply changes, price and quantity change but not in the same direction. When supply increases, price falls and quantity rises. When supply decreases, price rises and quantity falls.

SUMMARY

How are goods and services allocated?

1. The allocation of scarce goods, services, and resources can be carried out in any number of ways. The market mechanism is one possible allocation mechanism.
2. The market mechanism is the most efficient allocation mechanism in most instances.
3. There are cases in which the market mechanism is not used because people do not like the result of the market allocation.
4. There are cases in which the market mechanism is not used because the market mechanism is not the most efficient.

How does a market process work?

5. The market process refers to the interaction between buyers and sellers and how the market goes about allocating scarce resources.

What is demand?

6. Demand is the quantities that buyers are willing and able to buy at alternative prices.
7. The quantity demanded is the amount buyers are willing and able to buy at a specific price.
8. The law of demand states that as the price of a well-defined commodity rises (falls), the quantity demanded during a given period of time will fall (rise), everything else held constant.
9. Demand will change when one of the determinants of demand changes; that is, when income, tastes, prices of related goods and services, expectations, or number of buyers change. A demand change is illustrated as a shift of the demand curve.

What is supply?

10. Supply is the quantities that sellers will offer for sale at alternative prices.
11. The quantity supplied is the amount sellers offer for sale at one price.
12. The law of supply states that as the price of a well-defined commodity rises (falls), the quantity supplied during a given period of time will rise (fall), everything else held constant.
13. Supply changes when one of the determinants of supply changes; that is, when prices of resources, technology and productivity, expectations of producers, number of producers, or prices of related goods or services (in production) change. A supply change is illustrated as a shift of the supply curve.

How is price determined by demand and supply?

14. Equilibrium is the price at which the quantity buyers are willing and able to buy equals the quantity sellers are willing and able to sell.
15. A price that is higher than equilibrium means that buyers are willing and able to buy less than sellers are willing and able to supply. This will force sellers to reduce the price.

16. A price that is lower than equilibrium means that buyers are willing and able to buy more than sellers are willing and able to supply. This will force sellers to raise the price.
17. Together, demand and supply determine the equilibrium price and quantity.

What causes price to change?

18. A price that is above equilibrium creates a surplus, which leads to a lower price.
19. A price that is below equilibrium creates a shortage, which leads to a higher price.
20. A change in demand or a change in supply (a shift of either curve) will cause the equilibrium price and quantity to change.

EXERCISES

1. Illustrate each of the following events using a demand and supply diagram for bananas.
   a. Reports surface that imported bananas are infected with a deadly virus.
   b. Consumers' incomes drop.
   c. The price of bananas rises.
   d. The price of oranges falls.
   e. Consumers expect the price of bananas to decrease in the future.
2. Answer true or false, and if the statement is false, change it to make it true. Illustrate your answers on a demand and supply graph.
   a. An increase in demand is represented by a movement up the demand curve.
   b. An increase in supply is represented by a movement up the supply curve.
   c. An increase in demand without any changes in supply will cause the price to rise.
   d. An increase in supply without any changes in demand will cause the price to rise.
3. Using the following schedule, define the equilibrium price and quantity. Plot the demand and supply curves and show the equilibrium price and quantity.

Price	Quantity Demanded	Quantity Supplied
$1	500	100
2	400	120
3	350	150
4	320	200
5	300	300
6	275	410
7	260	500
8	230	650
9	200	800
10	150	975

4. A severe drought in California has resulted in a nearly 30 percent reduction in the quantity of citrus grown and produced there. Explain what effect this event might have on the Florida citrus market.
5. The prices of the Ralph Lauren Polo line of clothing are considerably higher than comparable quality lines. Yet it sells more than a JCPenney brand line of clothing. Does this violate the law of demand?
6. In December, the price of Christmas trees rises, and the quantity of trees sold rises. Is this a violation of the law of demand?
7. Evaluate the following statement: "The demand for U.S. oranges has increased because the quantity of U.S. oranges demanded in Japan has risen."
8. The federal government requires that all foods display information about fat content and other ingredients on food packages. The displays have to be verified by independent laboratories. The price of an evaluation of a food product could run as much as $20,000. What impact do you think this law will have on the market for meat?
9. Draw a downward-sloping demand curve and an upward-sloping supply curve for orange juice. Show what happens in each of the following cases:
   a. A freeze in Florida kills 30 percent of the oranges.
   b. A technological breakthrough has enabled Idaho to grow oranges.
   c. The supply of oranges from Mexico has been banned. The Mexican oranges accounted for about 15 percent of the market.
10. Explain what it means when the supply of television sets rises. Explain what it means when the quantity supplied of television sets rises. Explain how the price of television sets could rise, and yet the supply of television sets not change.

STUDY GUIDE FOR CHAPTER 2

Key Term Match

Match each term with its correct definition by placing the appropriate letter next to the corresponding number.

A. efficiency
B. demand
C. law of demand
D. demand schedule
E. demand curve
F. market demand
G. quantity demanded
H. determinants of demand
I. substitute goods
J. complementary goods
K. supply
L. law of supply
M. determinants of supply
N. supply schedule
O. supply curve
P. equilibrium
Q. surplus
R. shortage

____ 1. a graph showing the law of demand

____ 2. items that can be used in place of each other; as the price of one rises, demand for the other rises

____ 3. the quantities suppliers are willing and able to supply at each price

____ 4. a plot of the supply schedule

____ 5. a relationship between the price of a good or service and the quantity of that good or service people are willing and able to buy

____ 6. the price and quantity at which demand equals supply

____ 7. the quantity of a well-defined good or service that people are willing and able to purchase during a particular period of time decreases as the price of that good or service rises and increases as the price falls, everything else held constant

____ 8. as the price rises, the quantity supplied rises, and vice versa

____ 9. things that influence demand other than price

____ 10. a list of prices and corresponding quantities supplied

____ 11. items that are used together; as the price of one rises, demand for the other falls

____ 12. when the quantity demanded is less than the quantity supplied

____ 13. a table listing the quantity demanded at each price

____ 14. the sum of individual demands

____ 15. when the quantity demanded is greater than the quantity supplied

____ 16. factors other than price that affect supply

____ 17. a measure of how well an economic system satisfies people's wants and needs

____ 18. the amount of a product that people are willing and able to purchase at a specific price

Quick-Check Quiz

1. Consider the market for powdered hot chocolate mixes. What will happen in the market for powdered hot chocolate mixes if prices for key commodities (like cocoa) rise?
   - ☐ a. The demand for powdered hot chocolate mixes will increase, causing the equilibrium price and quantity to increase.
   - ☐ b. The demand for powdered hot chocolate mixes will decrease, causing the equilibrium price and quantity to decrease.
   - ☐ c. The supply of powdered hot chocolate mixes will increase, causing the equilibrium price to decrease and the equilibrium quantity to increase.
   - ☐ d. The supply of powdered hot chocolate mixes will decrease, causing the equilibrium price to increase and the equilibrium quantity to decrease.
   - ☐ e. The supply of powdered hot chocolate mixes will decrease, causing the equilibrium price and quantity to increase

2. Which of the following would cause an increase in the demand for eggs?
   - ☐ a. The price of eggs drops.
   - ☐ b. The price of bacon rises.
   - ☐ c. A government report indicates that eating eggs three times a week increases the chances of having a heart attack.
   - ☐ d. A decrease in the cost of chicken feed makes eggs less costly to produce.
   - ☐ e. None of the above would increase the demand for eggs.

3. If the price of barley, an ingredient in beer, increases,
   - ☐ a. the demand for beer will increase.
   - ☐ b. the demand for beer will not change.
   - ☐ c. the demand for beer will decrease.
   - ☐ d. the quantity of beer demanded will increase.
   - ☐ e. Both a and d are correct.

4. The Nook e-reader and the Kindle are devices that can be used to read e-books. What would you expect to happen in the market for Kindles if its competitor Barnes and Noble cut the price on its Nook e-reader?
   - ☐ a. The demand for Kindles will increase, causing the equilibrium price and quantity to increase.
   - ☐ b. The demand for Kindles will decrease, causing the equilibrium price and quantity to decrease.
   - ☐ c. The supply of Kindles will increase, causing the equilibrium price to decrease and the equilibrium quantity to increase.
   - ☐ d. The supply of Kindles will decrease, causing the equilibrium price to increase and the equilibrium quantity to decrease.
   - ☐ e. The supply of Kindles will decrease, causing the equilibrium price and quantity to increase

5. Japanese producers of a type of microchip offered such low prices that U.S. producers of the chip were driven out of business. As the number of producers decreased,
   - ☐ a. the market supply of microchips increased—that is, the supply curve shifted to the right.
   - ☐ b. the market supply of microchips increased—that is, the supply curve shifted to the left.
   - ☐ c. the market supply of microchips decreased—that is, the supply curve shifted to the right.
   - ☐ d. the market supply of microchips decreased—that is, the supply curve shifted to the left.
   - ☐ e. there was no change in the supply of microchips. (This event is represented by a movement from one point to another on the same supply curve.)

6. Consider the market for milk. Suppose that dairy workers form a union and receive a $3 per hour wage increase. What will happen now?
   - ☐ a. The demand for milk will increase, causing the equilibrium price and quantity to increase.
   - ☐ b. The demand for milk will decrease, causing the equilibrium price and quantity to decrease
   - ☐ c. The supply of milk will decrease, causing the equilibrium price to increase and the equilibrium quantity to decrease.
   - ☐ d. The supply of milk will increase, causing the equilibrium price to decrease and the equilibrium quantity to increase.
   - ☐ e. The demand for milk will increase and the supply of milk will decrease, causing the equilibrium price to increase and the equilibrium quantity to increase.

7. Medical research from South Africa indicates that vitamin A may be useful in treating measles. If the research can be substantiated, the
   - ☐ a. supply of vitamin A will increase, causing equilibrium price and quantity to increase.
   - ☐ b. supply of vitamin A will increase, causing equilibrium price to fall and quantity to increase.
   - ☐ c. demand for vitamin A will increase, causing equilibrium price and quantity to increase.
   - ☐ d. demand for vitamin A will increase, causing equilibrium price to rise and quantity to fall.
   - ☐ e. supply of vitamin A will increase, causing equilibrium price to rise and quantity to fall.

8. An increase in demand
   - ☐ a. shifts the demand curve to the left.
   - ☐ b. causes an increase in equilibrium price.
   - ☐ c. causes a decrease in equilibrium price.
   - ☐ d. causes a decrease in equilibrium quantity.
   - ☐ e. does not affect equilibrium quantity.

9. Which of the following is *not* a determinant of demand?
   - ☐ a. income
   - ☐ b. tastes
   - ☐ c. prices of resources
   - ☐ d. prices of complements
   - ☐ e. consumers' expectations

10. Which of the following is *not* a determinant of supply?
    - ☐ a. prices of resources
    - ☐ b. technology and productivity
    - ☐ c. prices of complements
    - ☐ d. producers' expectations
    - ☐ e. the number of producers

Practice Questions and Problems

1. Write the type of allocation method each example represents. Choose from the following: random allocation; market allocation; first-come, first-served allocation; or government allocation.
   a. ______________ Winning a lottery
   b. ______________ The high bidder at an auction gets a valuable painting.
   c. ______________ The mayor of a city decides who will be hired.
   d. ______________ Students at Big Football U. can park on campus without charge, but there aren't enough parking spaces for all students.

2. List five determinants of demand.
____
____
____

3. An increase in income __________ (increases, decreases) the __________ (demand, quantity demanded) for haircuts.
4. Many Americans have decreased their consumption of beef and switched to chicken in the belief that eating chicken instead of beef lowers cholesterol. This change in tastes has __________ (increased, decreased) the __________ (demand, quantity demanded) for beef and __________ (increased, decreased) the __________ (demand, quantity demanded) for chicken.
5. If a crisis in the Middle East causes people to expect the price of gasoline to increase in the future, then demand for gasoline today will __________ (increase, not change, decrease).
6. If the price of Pepsi increases, the demand for Coke and other substitutes will __________ (increase, not change, decrease).
7. List five determinants of supply.
____
____
____

8. Suppose that a crisis in the Middle East cuts off the supply of oil from Saudi Arabia. If S_1 is the original market supply of oil, draw another supply curve, S_2, on the graph to show the effect of Saudi Arabia's departure from the market. The __________ (quantity supplied, supply) has __________ (increased, decreased).

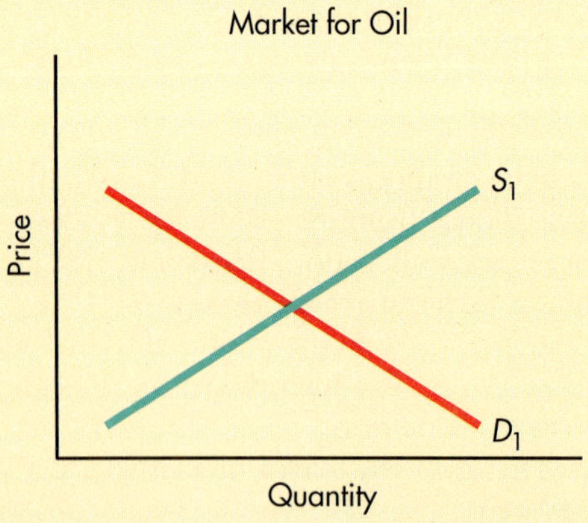

9. If the price of tomato sauce increases, the __________ (supply, quantity supplied) of pizza will __________ (increase, decrease).
10. A new process for producing microchips is discovered that will decrease the cost of production by 10 percent. The supply of microchips will __________ (increase, decrease, not change), which means the supply curve will __________ (shift to the right, shift to the left, not change).
11. A paper manufacturer can produce notebook paper or wedding invitations. If the price of wedding invitations skyrockets, we can expect the supply of __________ (notebook paper, wedding invitations) to __________ (increase, decrease).
12. Shortages lead to a(n) __________ (increase, decrease) in price and quantity supplied and to a(n) __________ (increase, decrease) in quantity demanded.
13. Surpluses lead to a(n) __________ (increase, decrease) in price and quantity supplied and to a(n) __________ (increase, decrease) in quantity demanded.
14. If design changes in the construction of milk cartons cause the cost of production to decrease, we can expect the __________ (demand for, supply of) cartons to __________ (increase, decrease), the equilibrium price to __________ (increase, decrease), and the equilibrium quantity to __________ (increase, decrease).
15. The following graph shows the market for corn. The equilibrium price is __________, and the equilibrium quantity is __________. If the price of corn is \$14, the quantity demanded will be __________ and the quantity supplied will be __________. A __________ (shortage/surplus) of __________ units will develop, causing the price and quantity supplied to __________, and the quantity demanded to __________. __________. If the price is \$4, the quantity demanded will be __________ and the quantity supplied will be __________. A __________ (shortage/surplus) of __________ units will develop, causing the price and quantity supplied to __________, and the quantity demanded to __________.

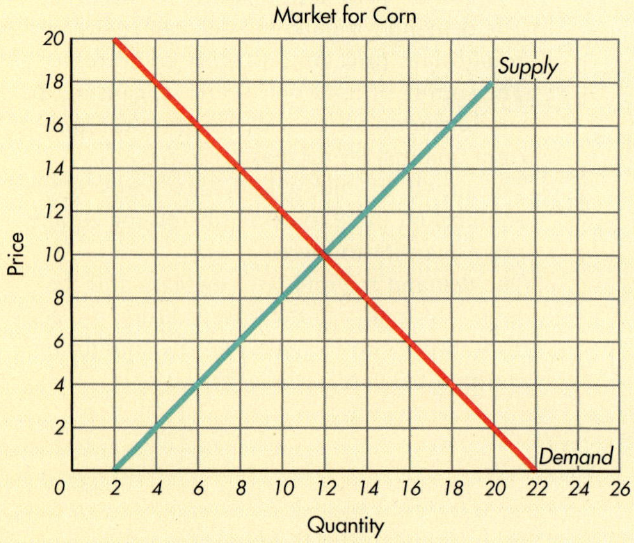

Use the following table to answer questions 16 through 19.

Price	Quantity Demanded	Quantity Supplied
$0	24	0
1	20	2
2	16	4
3	12	6
4	8	8
5	4	10
6	0	12

16. The equilibrium price is ____________.
17. The equilibrium quantity is ____________.
18. If the price is $2, a ____________ of ____________ units will develop, causing the price to ____________.
19. If the price is $5, a ____________ of ____________ units will develop, causing the price to ____________.

Exercises and Applications

I The Market for Battery-Operated Dancing Flowers

For each event listed below, indicate whether it affects the demand or supply of battery-operated dancing flowers and the direction (increase or decrease) of the change. Also indicate what will happen to equilibrium price and quantity. Remember, the determinants of demand are income, tastes, prices of related goods or services, consumers' expectations, and the number of buyers. The determinants of supply are prices of resources, changes in technology or productivity, producers' expectations, number of producers, and prices of related goods or services (goods that are substitutes or complements in production).

a. There is a change in tastes toward battery-operated dancing gorillas.
b. The price of plastic falls.
c. A technological breakthrough makes it cheaper to produce plastic flowers.
d. Consumers' incomes rise.
e. The price of battery-operated dancing gorillas rises.
f. The price of plastic for making flowers skyrockets.
g. A fire destroys a major production facility for dancing flowers.
h. Consumers expect lower prices for dancing flowers in the future.

	Demand	Supply	Price	Quantity
a.	______	______	______	______
b.	______	______	______	______
c.	______	______	______	______
d.	______	______	______	______
e.	______	______	______	______
f.	______	______	______	______
g.	______	______	______	______
h.	______	______	______	______

3 The Free Market

FUNDAMENTAL QUESTIONS

1. What is the outcome of free markets?
2. In a free market system, who determines what is produced?
3. Why do different people earn different incomes, and why do different jobs pay different wages?
4. When the government intervenes in the market by setting a price floor or price ceiling, what is the result?
5. When the government intervenes in the market with a quota, what is the result?

PREVIEW

It is the incentives created by allocation mechanisms that make the market system "better" than the others. A system of markets and prices is generally the most *efficient* means of coordinating and organizing activities, where "efficiency" means you get the same amount at a lower cost. Individuals offer to sell goods and services at various prices, and other individuals offer to buy goods and services at various prices. Without anyone coordinating the buyers and sellers, the market determines a price for each traded good and quantities at which people are willing and able to buy. And the market does this using fewer resources than other allocation mechanisms.

In his television special *Greed*,[1] John Stossel wonders how beef gets to New York from the farms in Iowa. Economist Walt Williams responds: "If it was all compassion and caring about your fellow man, I feel sorry for New Yorkers in terms of beef. Not a single cow would end up in New York." Somehow the right amount of beef makes its way from a field in Iowa to a restaurant in Manhattan. Similarly, a neighborhood flower vendor sets out exactly what her customers want every morning even though the plants may come from halfway around the world; the baker has the bread his customers prefer; the chef has the exact ingredients to prepare the meals desired by patrons. An economy involves billions of transactions every day that take place without any central planning or government dictates.

1
What is the outcome of free markets?

We have the things we desire when we desire them because of the market. We can purchase nearly anything 24 hours a day from the comfort of our own homes. Not only are the goods we purchase much better than the same type of goods were just a few years ago, but we are able to purchase more of them. We see this improvement in constantly rising standards of living in

[1] ABC News, Home Video, *Greed*, by John Stossel, March 11, 1999.

In the market system, beef makes its way from a farm in Iowa to a table in a New York restaurant through hundreds of transactions made by individuals pursuing their own self-interests.

nearly every aspect of life: Life expectancy has nearly doubled in a century, for example, and diseases such as polio, tuberculosis, typhoid, and whooping cough have been almost wiped out.

These changes have occurred because the market encourages people to do what they do best and to improve themselves. And everyone acting to improve and increase their own living standards leads to a thriving and ever-improving standard of living for society. It is the result of the free or unfettered market.

1. THE UNFETTERED MARKET

A market is free or unfettered if nothing interferes with people entering into voluntary transactions. In an unfettered market, you can purchase what you want and are able to pay for from anyone you want. The government doesn't tell you who you have to purchase from, or what price you will pay.

It was stated in Chapter 2 that specialization according to comparative advantage can generate more output than being self-sufficient. Of course, specialization means you are not producing all the things you need to survive, let alone to prosper. So to get what you want, you must exchange what you produce for those things you actually want, which requires some form of coordination. In a market system, that coordination is carried out not by some centralized bureaucrat but by individuals pursuing their self-interests. The farmer raises cattle in order to sell the cattle and be able then to purchase whatever else the farmer wants. The butcher packages and sells the beef so he can have money to purchase a car, house, and so on. The truck driver delivers the beef so he can earn the money necessary to purchase whatever he desires.

The supermarket sells the beef to customers. The beef makes its way from Iowa to New York via hundreds if not hundreds of thousands of transactions wherein individuals are seeking not beef, but something else.

Prices inform buyers what they must give up to acquire a unit of the good, and prices let suppliers know whether their activities have value. Day in and day out, without any conscious central direction, the price system induces people to employ their talents and resources in the most effective manner.

People do not have to be fooled or forced to do their part in a market system but instead pursue their own objectives as they see fit. Workers, attempting to maximize their own individual happiness and well-being, select the training, careers, and jobs where their talents and energy are most valuable. Producers, pursuing only private profits, develop the goods and services on which consumers put the highest value and produce these goods and services at the lowest possible costs. Owners of resources and capital assets, seeking only to increase their own wealth, deploy these assets in socially desirable ways.

This scenario sounds good, but it can't possibly be true, can it? Don't many people have no choice but to work in terrible conditions, or what, in less-developed countries, is called a sweatshop? It might seem that poor people who have been exploited by the market system suffer more than they would without it. However, appearances are deceiving; they are actually better off. If people take jobs in unpleasant, low-wage facilities voluntarily, they do so because it is the best employment option they have. What would happen if every sweatshop in the less-developed nations were eliminated, and wages and working conditions improved to match the standards in wealthy nations? Every person who had a job in those facilities would be unemployed.[2]

When trade is not voluntary, it is a different matter. When people are forced to work in occupations not of their choosing, when citizens are forced through threat of violence to pay tribute or taxes, then the trade is not making people better off. People engage in voluntary trade or exchange because they are able to get more for less—to make themselves better off. In fact, one of the principles of economics is that people try to make themselves as well off as possible.

2

In a free market system, who determines what is produced?

1.a. The Market Process: Price and Quantity Adjustment

As we discussed in Chapter 2, when the Mazda Miata was introduced in the United States in 1990, the little sports roadster was an especially desired product in southern California. Its suggested retail price was $13,996, the price at which it was selling in Detroit. In Los Angeles, however, the purchase price was nearly $25,000. The identical product, the Miata, was selling for different prices in different markets—the Detroit auto market and the Los Angeles auto market. Mazda had somehow totally misread the market for the Miata and supplied too many in Detroit and too few in Los Angeles.

In Figure 3.1 there are two markets shown, the market for Miatas in Los Angeles and the market for Miatas in Detroit. In Los Angeles there are many people and many highways. In addition, the weather is quite good for cruising in a convertible. In Detroit, there are fewer people, fewer highways, and the

[2] The Independent Institute found that the typical sweatshop worker is paid above the national average (for workers) in six of the nine countries for which they compiled data. See Benjamin Powell and David Skarbek, "Sweatshops and Third World Living Standards: Are the Jobs Worth the Sweat?" Working Paper 53, September 27, 2004, www.independent.org/pdf/working_papers/ 53_sweatshop.pdf.

FIGURE 3.1 Comparison of Miata Prices in Los Angeles and Detroit Using Demand and Supply Curves

Demand for the sports car is higher relative to supply in Los Angeles because of the weather, the number of highways, and the number of drivers. In Detroit, the weather is not often appropriate for a convertible. There are fewer people and fewer highways in Detroit than in Los Angeles. The result is a higher price in Los Angeles than in Detroit.

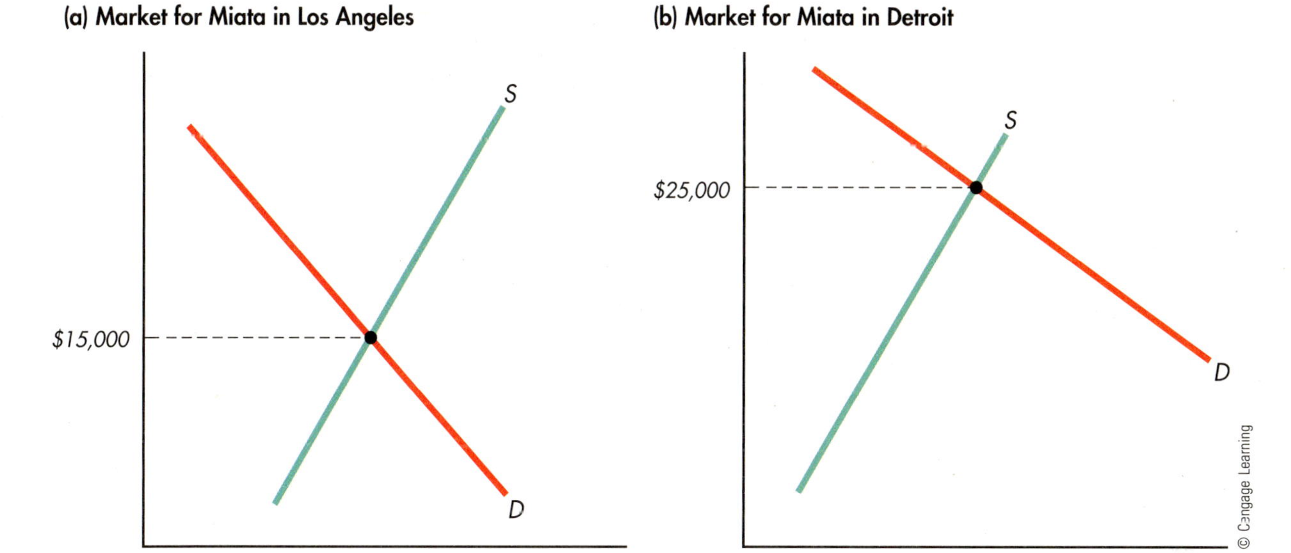

weather is not so conducive to the enjoyment of a convertible. As a result, the demand relative to supply in Los Angeles, seen in Figure 3.1(a), is much higher than that in Detroit, which is shown in Figure 3.1(b). The price differential was almost $10,000.

The price differential was so large that people could purchase the car in Detroit, drive it to Los Angeles, sell it there as used, and still make a nice profit. So hordes of people descended on Detroit to purchase the sports car. The increased sales in Detroit drove the price up there, shown as an outward shift of the demand curve in the Detroit market, shown in Figure 3.2(b). The Miatas brought to Los Angeles increased the supply of Miatas in southern California, shown by an outward shift of the supply curve in Figure 3.2(a). The price differential between the two cities declined as the price in Detroit rose and the price in Los Angeles fell. The price in Detroit and the price in Los Angeles moved closer and closer as demand continued to rise in Detroit and supply continued to rise in Los Angeles. The prices and quantities of the cars in the two cities stopped changing once there was no chance to make a profit by buying a car in Detroit and selling it in Los Angeles.

The process of buying identical products in one market and selling them in another at virtually the same time is referred to as **arbitrage**. Arbitrage is the market process in operation. It ensures that resources are allocated to their highest-valued uses—that inefficient transactions, inefficient organizations, and inefficiency of any sort wither away. Arbitrage is a search for gains. By buying in a low-priced market and selling in a higher-priced market, you come away with a gain or a profit.

The search for profit is the market in action. What would occur if resources were not used efficiently—that is, in their highest-valued use—by a firm?

FIGURE 3.2 Shift of Demand and Supply Curves of Figure 3.1

People purchased Miatas in Detroit for the sole purpose of selling them in Los Angeles. The demand curve in the Detroit market in Figure 3.2(b) shifted out. The supply curve of Miatas in the Los Angeles market shifted out in Figure 3.2(a). The price differential for the identical item in Detroit and Los Angeles declined. It would continue to decline until it was not possible to earn a profit buying the car in Detroit and selling it in Los Angeles.

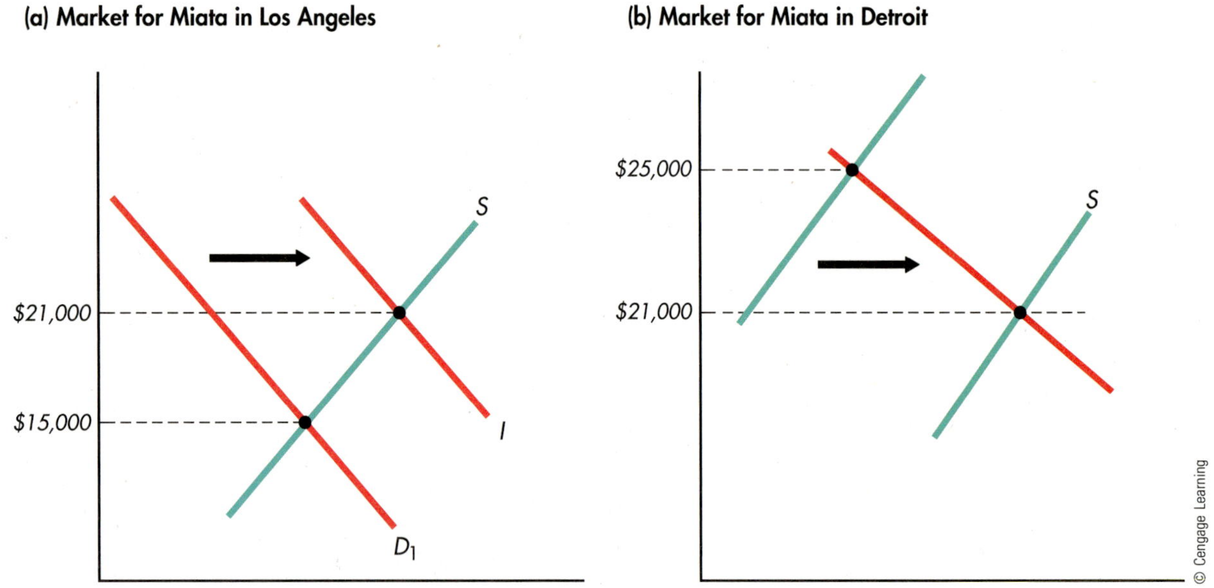

That firm could not stay in business. For instance, when Walmart enters a community, it offers products at much lower prices than the mom-and-pop stores that exist in the community. Customers buy from Walmart rather than from the existing stores. The mom-and-pop stores must offer low prices as well, but they can't unless they become as efficient as Walmart. In communities where the mom-and-pop stores fail to match Walmart's prices, many end up going out of business. The resources previously employed in the small businesses are let go and must find uses in other endeavors.

Why does the free market work this way? It stems from the basic assumption that individuals want to make themselves as well off as possible. So people will try to sell the use of their resources for the highest value possible. If an opportunity exists for earning more, will the resources remain where they are? No. Because people want to make themselves as well off as possible, they are always looking for ways to create greater returns—higher pay, better investments, higher rents. This is why the Miatas moved from Detroit to Los Angeles.

When people are free to enter into voluntary transactions and when firms must compete for business, the market outcome is good for all participants. Resources are used where they have the highest value (and thus resource owners become more wealthy), and the goods and services people want and are able to pay for are provided at the lowest possible prices.

3

Why do different people earn different incomes, and why do different jobs pay different wages?

1.b. The Unfettered Labor Market

Older workers tend to earn higher wages than younger workers, males earn more than females, whites earn more than African Americans and Latinos, and unionized workers earn more than nonunionized workers. Why? Is it because the free market is not working?

The labor market consists of the demand for labor and the supply of labor. In an unfettered market, people voluntarily agree to work at a job of their choosing and for an employer of their choosing, and employers hire who they want for each job. Employers have to make a profit to remain in business, so their demand for labor depends on how much value workers provide to the firm.

How many workers does a firm hire? Those employees who bring in at least as much revenue for the firm as they cost in would be valuable to the firm; they would be hired. The higher the price of labor (the more it costs the firm), the less labor the firm will demand. Thus, the labor demand curve slopes down.

The labor supply comes from households. People decide whether to work and how many hours to work at each possible wage. The higher the hourly wage, the more hours people are willing and able to work. In addition, some people who would not be willing to work at a low wage may decide to enter the labor force if the wage gets high enough. This means that the labor supply curve slopes up.

The labor demand and labor supply curves are shown in Figure 3.3. The intersection of the labor demand and labor supply curves determines the equilibrium wage (W_e) and the quantity of hours people work at this wage (Q_e).

The labor market pictured in Figure 3.3 suggests that as long as workers are the same and as long as jobs and employers are identical, there will be one equilibrium wage. In fact, workers are not the same, jobs are not the same, and wages are definitely not the same. College-educated people tend to earn more than people with only a high school education, and people with a high school education tend to earn more than those with only a grammar school education. Riskier jobs tend to pay more than less risky jobs. There is, in reality, a labor market for each type of worker and each type of job.

GLOBAL ECONOMIC INSIGHT

Jobs Moving Offshore

In 2005, the U.S. Department of Labor estimated, based on trends noted in 2003 and 2004, that 3.3 million jobs would be moved out of the United States by 2015.

Type	2005	2015
Business	61,252	348,028
Computer	108,991	472,632
Management	37,477	288,281
Architecture	32,202	184,347
Office	295,034	1,659,310
All Other	52,636	367,615
Total	**587,592**	**3,320,213**

Resources flow to where they have the highest value. If the resources cannot flow—for example, if workers in China or India cannot move to the United States—then the uses of the resources will go to where the costs are lowest; in other words, the jobs flow to the workers. The movement of resources occurs within a country just as it does among countries. The accompanying graph shows how the U.S. economy has shifted from manufacturing to services over the past several decades. An economy in which voluntary trade occurs will see a constant shift of uses of resources. As it does, jobs will disappear in some uses and increase in others. The buggy whip manufacturers disappeared as the auto appeared; the slide rule manufacturers disappeared as the calculator and then the PC appeared. In each case, workers displaced by the changes were hurt; the new jobs created benefited those who had acquired the skills necessary to get one of the newly created jobs.

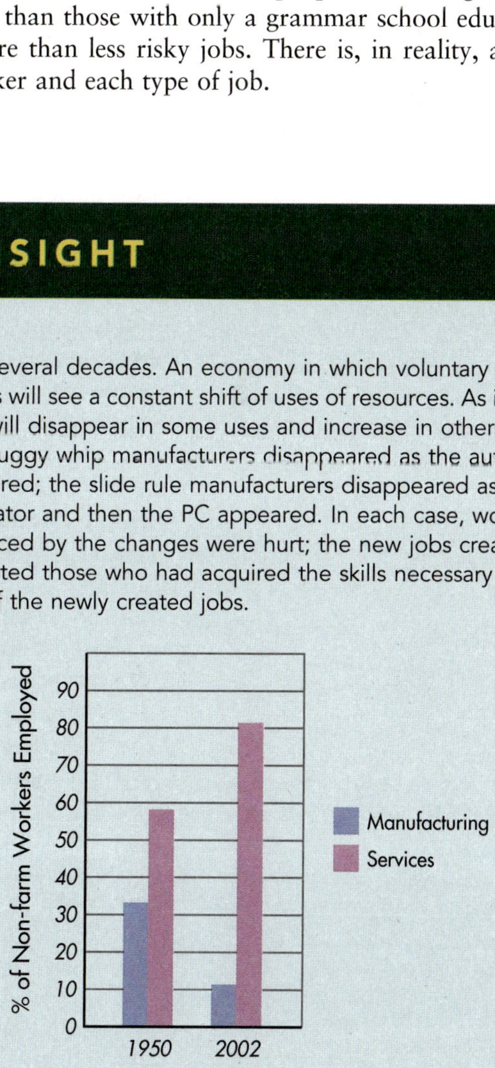

FIGURE 3.3 Labor Market Equilibrium

If all workers are identical to firms—that is, if a firm doesn't care whether it hires Bob, Raj, Keiko, or Allie—and if all firms and jobs are the same to workers—that is, if a worker doesn't care whether a job is with IBM or Ted's Hot Dog Stand—then one demand curve and one supply curve define the labor market. The intersection of the two curves is the labor market equilibrium at which the wage rate is determined.

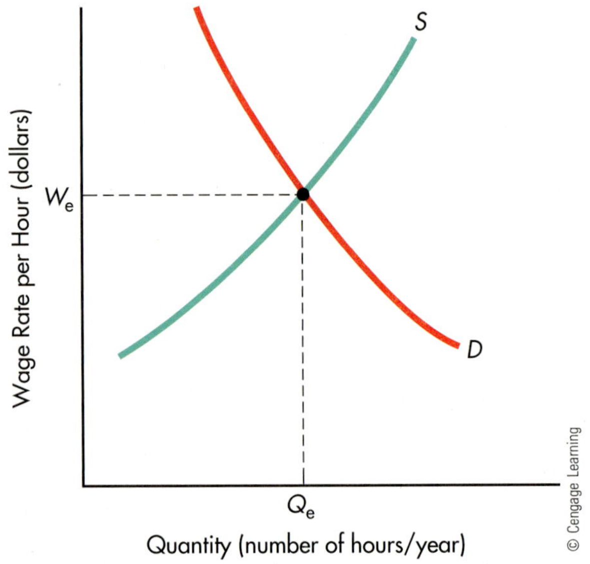

Some jobs are quite unpleasant because they are located in undesirable locations or are dangerous or unhealthy. How does a firm get someone to take a dangerous or unhealthy job? By paying them more. People choose to work in unpleasant occupations because they earn more money. Workers mine coal, clean sewers, and weld steel beams 50 stories off the ground because, compared to alternative jobs for which they could qualify, these jobs pay well.

In Figure 3.4, two labor markets are represented: one for a risky occupation and one for a less risky occupation. Each market is free or unfettered—in other words, people can freely choose to work in either one. At each wage rate, fewer people are willing and able to work in the risky occupation than in the less risky occupation. Thus, if the demand curves were identical, the supply curve of the risky occupation would be above (to the left of) the supply curve of the less risky occupation. Fewer people are willing to take the riskier job than the less risky job if the riskier job pays the same as the less risky job. As a result, the equilibrium wage rate in the risky occupation, \$60 per hour, is higher than the equilibrium wage rate in the less risky occupation, \$35 per hour. The difference between the wage in the risky occupation and the wage in the less risky is an equilibrium differential—the compensation a worker receives for undertaking the greater risk. Unlike the case of the Miata sports car selling at different prices in Los Angeles and Detroit, where the cars were transferred from Detroit to Los Angeles, this price differential will not attract more workers from the less risky occupation to the risky one. This wage difference is an equilibrium differential—the amount needed to offset the additional risk.

Commercial deep-sea divers are exposed to the dangers of drowning and several physiological disorders as a result of compression and decompression. They choose this job because they earn about 90 percent more than the average high school graduate. Coal miners in West Virginia and in Wales in the United Kingdom are exposed to coal dust, black lung disease, and cave-ins. They choose to work in the mines because the pay is twice what they could earn elsewhere. Wage differentials ensure that deep-sea diving jobs, coal-mining jobs, and other risky occupations are filled.

NOW YOU TRY IT

A PA (physician's assistant) earns about \$65,000 per year, whereas a physician earns \$200,000 per year. Explain the difference in salaries.

FIGURE 3.4 Compensating Wage Differential

Figure 3.4(a) shows the market for a risky occupation. Figure 3.4(b) shows the market for a less risky occupation. At each wage rate, fewer people are willing and able to work in the risky occupation than in the less risky occupation. Thus, the supply curve of the risky occupation is higher (supply is less) than the supply curve of the less risky occupation. As a result, the wage ($60 per hour) in the risky occupation is higher than the wage ($35 per hour) in the less risky occupation. The differential ($60 – $35 = $25) is an equilibrium differential—the amount necessary to induce enough people to fill the jobs. If the differential were any higher, more people would flow to the risky occupation, driving wages there down and wages in the less risky occupation up. If the differential were any lower, shortages would prevail in the risky occupation, driving wages there up.

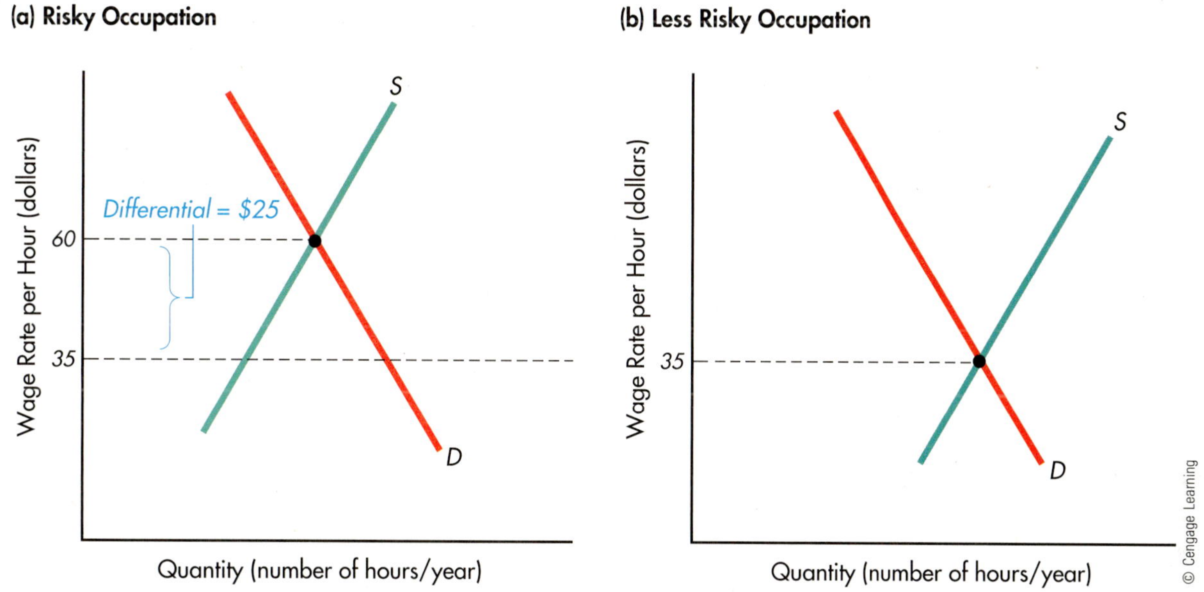

compensating wage differential: wage differences due to different risks or job characteristics

Any characteristic that distinguishes one job from another may result in a **compensating wage differential**. A job that requires a great deal of travel and time away from home usually pays more than a comparable job without the travel requirements because most people find extensive travel and time away from home to be costly. If people were indifferent to travel, there would be no wage differential. Notice that the differential is caused by people's voluntary actions, not by law or other types of coercion.

People differ with respect to their tastes for risky jobs, but they also differ with respect to their training and abilities. These differences influence the level of wages for two reasons: (1) skilled workers are more valuable to most firms than unskilled workers and (2) the supply of skilled workers is smaller than the supply of unskilled workers because it takes time and money to acquire training and education. These things mean that skilled labor will earn higher wages than less skilled labor. For instance, in Figure 3.5, the skilled-labor market results in a wage of $35 per hour, whereas the unskilled-labor market results in a wage of $8 per hour. The difference exists because the demand for skilled labor relative to the supply of skilled labor is greater than the demand for unskilled labor relative to the supply of unskilled labor.

RECAP

1. In a free market buyers and sellers voluntarily interact without any interference. No one is coerced to buy or sell.
2. The market price is established where demand and supply are equal.
3. In a market free from interference, resources are allocated to where their use has the highest value simply by the actions of buyers and sellers. This action, seeking of profit, is called arbitrage.

FIGURE 3.5 Skilled and Unskilled Labor

Two labor markets are pictured. Figure 3.5(a) shows the market for skilled labor. Figure 3.5(b) shows the market for unskilled labor. The smaller supply in the skilled-labor market results in a higher wage there.

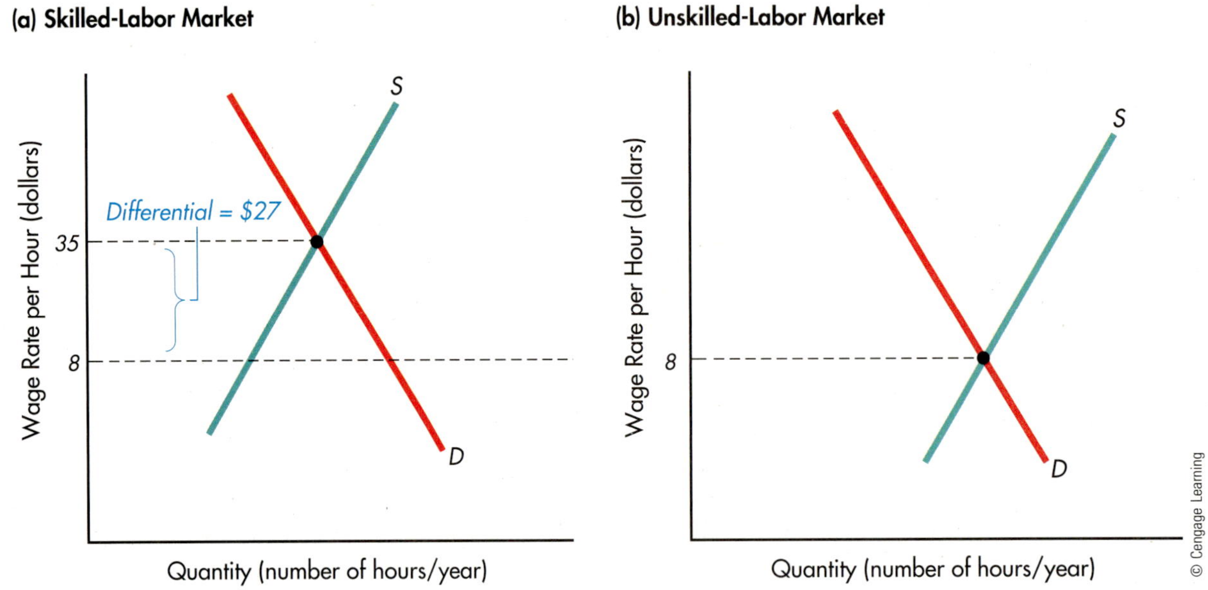

4. In a free market, consumers determine what is produced. Consumers wanted the Miata in Los Angeles, and the cars were moved there. Consumers of labor (employers) want and acquire skilled workers; employers offering risky jobs want and acquire workers willing to accept those risks.
5. The wage rate and the quantities of workers employed in any free labor market are determined by the voluntary exchanges between employers and employees. This is illustrated graphically as the intersection of the labor demand and labor supply curves.
6. In reality, there are many different labor markets—markets for skilled versus unskilled labor, markets for dangerous versus non-dangerous jobs, and so on.
7. An equilibrium wage differential or compensating wage differential exists when the equilibrium wage in two different labor markets is different.

Free markets automatically allocate scarce goods and resources to where they have the highest value. People choose to work in high-risk or low-risk jobs, depending on their desires, and employers seeking more skilled workers voluntarily pay more to acquire those types of workers. No one is coerced to do what they don't want to do. Instead, interactions between buyers and sellers will determine a price at which demand equals supply.

2. MARKET INTERVENTIONS

The search for profit is the market in action—it is competition. Competition drives out inefficiency and ensures that resources are allocated to their highest-valued uses.

People oppose Walmart opening stores in their neighborhood because the local neighborhood stores are driven out of business. Walmart seems to be the ultimate nightmare for small, neighborhood shops.[3] However, this nightmare is competition in operation; it is progress. We can look back and see the amazing technological breakthroughs of the past 300 years, bringing to the public the steam engine; spinning wheel; telephone; and vaccines against measles, mumps, polio, and other diseases. Yet those advances eradicated whole industries—telegraph operators, blacksmiths, and bloodletters. In 1900 half of all Americans worked in farming or ranching; today less than 2 percent of the population is involved in these industries.

Although entire industries have been destroyed by competition, many more have been created. We have more and better foodstuffs, even though fewer people work on the farm. The people who would have been farming had things not changed are instead designing computer software, playing professional sports, and producing movies. This process of resources moving to where their value is the greatest as a result of competition is called **creative destruction.**

Creative destruction is a tremendous positive force in the long run—the problem is that in the short run people lose jobs and ways of life. When a steel plant in Gary, Indiana closes, hundreds of workers are idled. They can't pay their mortgages, buy groceries, or send their kids to school. A few years later many will have left Gary for other cities and jobs; others will have taken jobs with new companies moving into the area; and others will have retired. For some it is extremely difficult and sad. But in the long run, more wealth is created, better products are provided, and standards of living rise.

Why does competition work this way? It stems from the basic assumption that individuals want to make themselves as well off as possible. So people will try to sell the use of their resources for the highest value possible. Given a choice among occupations, people will choose the one that provides them the best quality of life. If that particular occupation no longer provides the best quality of life, people will move, or acquire training, or pursue other occupations. Similarly, people will rent their land according to the highest-valued use for that land, and they will put their savings/investments into those activities that they expect to generate the greatest return for any given risk. If nothing changed, then the resources would remain where they are, doing exactly what they are doing. But because people want to make themselves as well off as possible, they are always looking for ways to create greater returns—higher pay, better investments, higher rents. They come up with better ways of doing things. Bill Gates devised a computer operating system for the PC; Intel came up with faster computer chips; Walmart created an inventory control system that enabled it to sell items for less than other retailers could. These innovations occurred because of competition—people are continually looking for ways to excel, to earn more, and live better.

Competition drives prices ever closer to the costs of production. If it costs \$.70 to produce a cup of coffee and you sell it for \$1.50, someone is going to come along and sell it for \$1. Then someone else will sell it for \$.90. Eventually, it will be selling for something very near \$.70. Competition requires that resources be used as efficiently as possible. Anyone not being as efficient as possible will not last long in the market. If you can't produce coffee for \$.90, you will not be in business when the price drops below \$.90.

Moreover, being efficient at one point in time does not mean you will remain there forever. Just look at the performance of firms over time. You not only have to build a better mousetrap, but you have to continually improve it. There is no resting on one's laurels when competition is prevalent. In 2006 and 2007, Walmart stumbled as other retailers were able to introduce comparable

[3] Andrea M. Dean and Russell S. Sobel, in "Has Wal-Mart Buried Mom and Pop?" (*Regulation*, Spring 2008, pp. 38–45), argue that "... Wal-Mart has had no significant impact on the overall size and growth of U.S. small business activity" (p. 45).

efficiencies and match the low prices. It is very difficult for a firm to sustain its success over many years.

The free competitive market provides a kind of consumer heaven. We get what we want, when we want it, and at the lowest possible prices. Yet, at the same time, it seems like a problem for sellers. Prices are driven down lower and lower as rivals attempt to solicit customers. As long as a rival can begin selling what you are selling, you are limited in what you can earn. To earn more than what the free competitive market would allow, a business has to acquire some way to limit the competition they face. Although coffee costs about $.70 per cup, Starbucks charges $1.65 for a small (or "tall") cup of coffee. Starbucks charges more than most other coffee shops and makes good money while charging more; it does this because it has acquired a sort of **monopoly** in that it is the only seller of Starbucks brand coffee.

monopoly: one supplier of a good or service

How is a firm able to maintain its monopoly—that is, to limit competition? Starbucks has done it by creating a well-known name and reputation. People know they will get the same taste and ambience no matter which Starbucks they enter. Coca-Cola has done it by convincing people that its combination of corn syrup and water is different from any other combination; it is Coke, not just soda. A **brand name** is a form of monopoly—a market niche in which competition is limited. A firm with a strong brand name can charge more for the same item than a firm with a generic name. In these cases, consumers choose to purchase from these companies. Consumers are not forced or required to purchase from them but choose to do so and to pay high prices because they perceive a benefit.

brand name: a way to differentiate similar products from each other

A more formidable barrier to competition is the government. Government can grant monopolies and impose regulations, restrictions, market controls, and on and on, all to alter or restrict competition. The market cannot work to create the incentives necessary to raise standards of living or to solve shortages and surpluses if economic freedom does not prevail.

In a free market, it is simply demanders and suppliers who, through their purchasing and selling decisions, determine how much is produced and at what prices. In many cases in the real world, governments intervene in free markets. In the rest of this chapter we compare the free market with a market in which the government has intervened. In Chapter 6 we will look at how firms limit competition and impede the functioning of the free market.

2.a. Price Floor: Minimum Wage

price floor: a specific level below which price is not allowed to fall

A **minimum wage** is a government policy that requires firms to pay wages that equal or exceed the specified level. The federal minimum wage in the United States is currently $7.25 per hour. Individual states may specify their own minimum wage if the wage exceeds the federal level. Figure 3.6 shows the relationship between the state minimum wage and the federal level.

In a free labor market, a worker's wage is determined by the value he or she contributes to the firm. A minimum wage set above the equilibrium wage creates a labor surplus (unemployment). In Figure 3.7, setting the minimum wage (W_M) at $7.25, above the equilibrium wage (W) of $4, creates a labor surplus of $Q_S - Q_D$. In other words, all the people willing and able to work at $7.25 are unable to get jobs. At the $7.25 per hour wage, line Q_S shows how many people are willing and able to work, but only Q_D are able to find jobs. A surplus of $Q_S - Q_D$ workers is created. Notice also that employment falls from the equilibrium level of Q_e to Q_D.

Who is most affected by the surplus? Those who have the least value to the firm. Studies show that a minimum wage adversely affects teenagers and other low-skilled workers, causing increased unemployment in these groups. A 10 percent increase in the minimum wage is estimated to result in a 1 to 3 percent decrease in teenage employment. The increase in the minimum wage

FIGURE 3.6 Minimum Wage Laws in the States, July 1, 2010

Minimum wage and overtime premium pay standards applicable to nonsupervisory, nonfarm, private sector employment under state and federal laws.

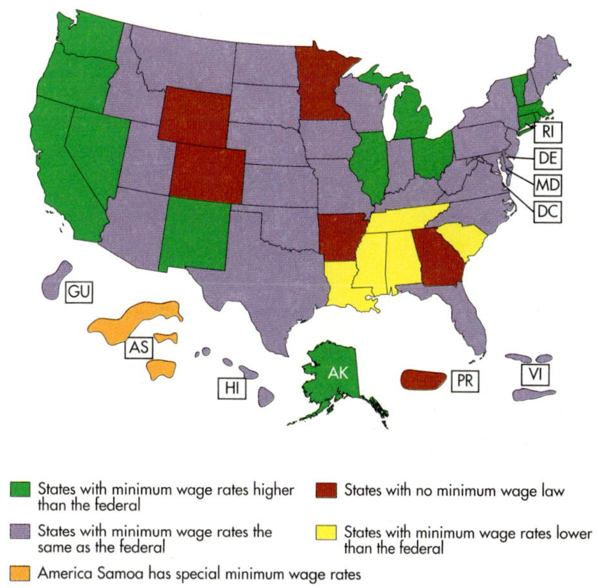

Note: Where federal and state laws have different minimum wage rates, the higher standard applies.

Source: United States Department of Labor (www.dol.gov/whd/minwage/america.htm).

FIGURE 3.7 Minimum Wage

The imposition of a minimum wage reduces the number of jobs offered to workers and reduces the employment of workers.

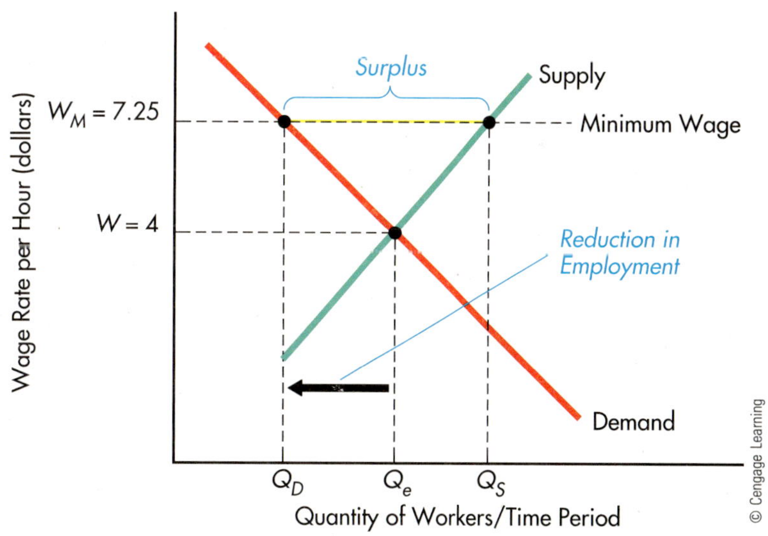

from \$4.35 to \$5.15 per hour was an 18 percent increase. This caused somewhere between a 1.8 to 5.4 percent reduction in teenage employment. Going to \$7.25 has even a larger effect on teen unemployment. Currently unemployment for those between the ages of 16 and 19 exceeds 60 percent.

Government interference in a free market leads to distortions. In the case of the minimum wage, the distortion is large-scale unemployment among teens.

Whenever a price floor is set, a surplus arises, whether it is a surplus of people willing and able to work, or a surplus of a good or service.

2.b. Price Ceilings: The Market for Rental Housing

4

When the government intervenes in the market by setting a price floor or price ceiling, what is the result?

price ceiling: a specific level above which price is not allowed to rise

Equilibrium in a free market is established by the voluntary interaction of buyers and sellers; the market price and the quantity produced and sold are defined at the point where the demand and supply curves intersect. In the previous section, we saw that a price floor causes surpluses. What will be the result of a maximum price, a **price ceiling**? A price ceiling is the situation in which a price is not allowed to rise to its equilibrium level. Los Angeles, San Francisco, and New York are among more than 125 U.S. cities that have rent controls. A rent control law places a ceiling on the rents that landlords can charge for apartments. Figure 3.8 is a demand and supply graph representing the market for apartments in New York. The equilibrium price is $3,000 per month. The government has set a price of $1,500 per month as the maximum that can be charged. The price ceiling is shown by the yellow line. At the rent control price of $1,500 per month, 3,000 apartments are available, but consumers want 6,000 apartments. There is a shortage of 3,000 apartments.

The shortage means that not everyone willing and able to rent the apartments will be allowed to. Since the price is not allowed to ration the apartments, something else will have to. It may be that those willing and able to stand in line the longest will get the apartments. Perhaps bribing an important official might be the way to get an apartment. Perhaps relatives of officials or important citizens will get the apartments. Whenever a price ceiling exists, a shortage results, and some rationing device other than price will arise.

Had the government set the rent control price at $4,000 per month, the price ceiling would not have had an effect. Since the equilibrium is $3,000 a month, the price would not have risen to $4,000. Only if the price ceiling is below the equilibrium price will it be an effective price ceiling.

NOW YOU TRY IT

Using the following data, indicate what would happen if a price ceiling of $3 was imposed. What would happen if the price ceiling was raised to $7?

Price	$10	9	8	7	6	5	4	3	2	1
Quantity Demanded	5	10	15	20	25	30	35	40	45	50
Quantity Supplied	50	45	40	35	30	25	20	15	10	5

FIGURE 3.8 Rent Controls

A demand and supply graph representing the market for apartments in New York City is shown. The equilibrium price is $3,000 a month. The government has set a price ceiling of $1,500 a month. The government's price ceiling is shown by the solid yellow line. At the government's price, 3,000 apartments are available, but consumers want 6,000. There is a shortage of 3,000 apartments.

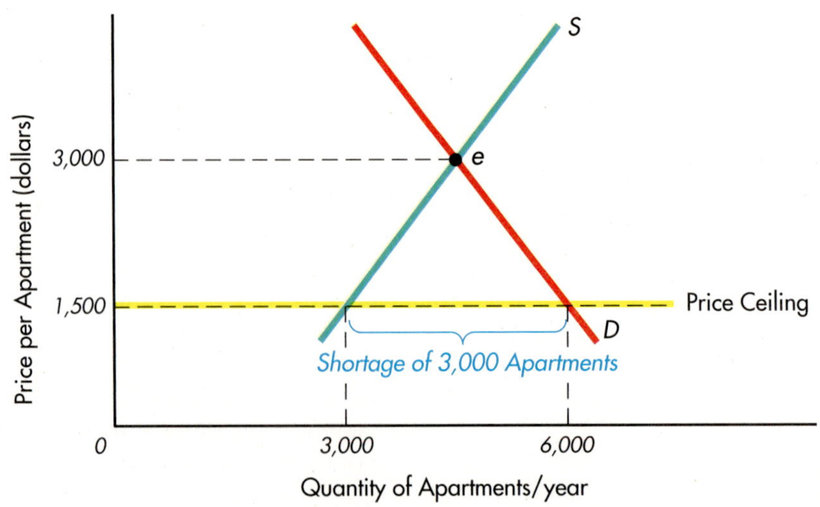

Ivan Barta/Alamy Limited

Rent control laws, like those in more than 125 U.S. cities, set apartment prices below market demand, causing a shortage of apartments. Under rent control, apartments must be rationed by some means other than price.

Price ceilings are not uncommon features in the United States or in other economies. China had a severe housing shortage for 30 years because the price of housing was kept below equilibrium. Faced with unhappy citizens and realizing the cause of the shortage, officials began to lift the restrictions on housing prices in 1985. The shortage has diminished. In the former Soviet Union, prices on all goods and services were defined by the government. For most consumer items, the price was set below equilibrium; shortages existed. The long lines of people waiting to purchase food or clothing were the result of the price ceilings on all goods and services. In the United States, price ceilings on all goods and services have been imposed at times. During World War I and World War II and during the Nixon administration of the early 1970s, wage and price controls were imposed. These were price ceilings on goods and services. As a result of the ceilings, people were unable to purchase many of the products they desired. The Organization of Petroleum Exporting Countries (OPEC) restricted the quantity of oil produced in the early 1970s and drove the price up considerably. The U.S. government responded by placing a price ceiling on gasoline. The result was long lines at gas stations—shortages of gasoline.

2.c. Quotas

5

When the government intervenes in the market with a quota, what is the result?

quota:
a limit on the amount of a good that may be imported

A **quota** allows only a limited quantity to be brought into the country. For instance, most nations have quotas on migration—only certain numbers of people can enter a country each year. Most nations also place quotas on some products. It is common to have quotas on agricultural products. For instance, the United States limits the amount of sugar that other nations may sell in the United States.

To illustrate the effects of a quota, the U.S. market for sugar is shown in Figure 3.9. The supply of sugar in the United States consists of the quantities supplied by U.S. producers plus the quantities sent to the United States from other nations. In Figure 3.9, if there were no restrictions on price or quantity, the U.S. price would equal the world price of sugar, P_w. Now, what occurs when the United States places a quota on the sugar other nations can sell in the United States? A quota means less sugar will be supplied in the United States since other nations are restricted from shipping their sugar to the United States. The supply is less, so the supply curve shifts in. The smaller supply means a higher price. The more restrictive the quota—that is, the less the amount the

FIGURE 3.9 The Effects of a Quota on the U.S. Market for Sugar

Without restrictions on price or quantity, the U.S. price would equal the world price of sugar, P_w. When the United States places a quota on the sugar other nations can sell in the United States, the supply curve shifts in, since it is just the amount U.S. producers can supply plus the quota amount from the rest of the world. The U.S. sugar price is higher.

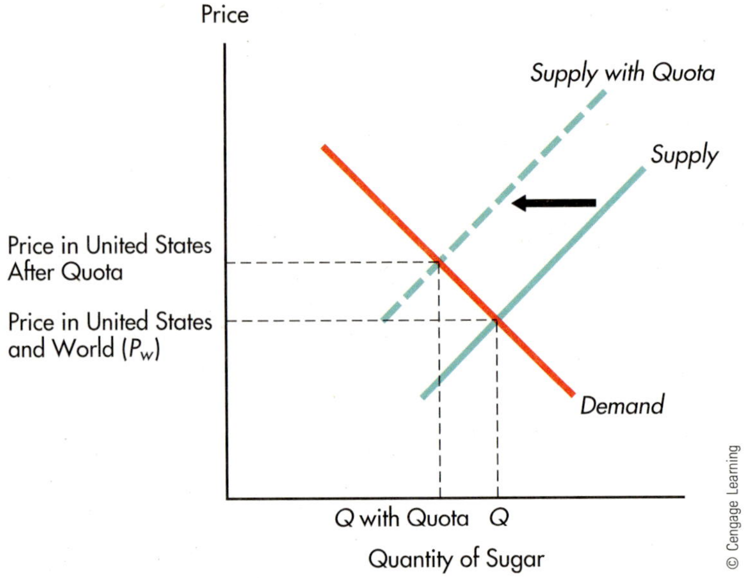

NOW YOU TRY IT

The government limits how much sugar other countries export to the United States. Illustrate what would happen to the price of sugar in the United States if the quota was decreased. What would a reduction in the amount of sugar exported to the United States do to the world price of sugar?

quota allows to be shipped to the United States—the higher the U.S. price will be. The U.S. price is higher than the world price.

2.d. Bans: The Ban on Trans Fats

When something is outlawed, made illegal, it is banned or prohibited. For instance, many cities across the United States have banned smoking in public buildings, restaurants, or other places. A **ban** means there is no transaction of that item allowed. In 2007, city and state legislators started looking at trans fats as something to legislate out of existence. Trans fats are formed when liquid oils are made into solid fats with ingredients such as partially hydrogenated vegetable oil, which is used for frying and baking. Trans fats are favored because of their long shelf life, and they turn up in processed foods such as cookies, pizza dough, and crackers, and in premade blends such as pancake and hot chocolate mixes. The Food and Drug Administration estimates that the average American eats 4.7 pounds of trans fats each year. Trans fats have been found to be unhealthy, leading to heart disease. Some have claimed that trans fats contribute to tens of thousands of cases of heart disease each year.

In 2007, New York City became the first U.S. city to ban the use of trans fats in restaurants. The restaurants weren't able to simply substitute one ingredient for another. They had to overhaul recipes, change nationwide supply operations, and try to convince customers that the new French fries and doughnuts would taste just as good as the originals.

If the ban eliminates the product altogether, then we don't need to look at the market for trans fats—it has disappeared. But what happens to the market for a food product that uses trans fats, such as French fries?

The demand for and supply of French fries, as well as the equilibrium price and quantity, are shown in Figure 3.10. What effect does the ban on trans fats have on this market? The restaurants have higher costs—finding new

FIGURE 3.10 A Ban on Trans Fats

The ban on a certain type of cooking oil can affect the market for products that use this cooking oil. It raises the cost (reduces supply) and may alter demand (change tastes). The result of the ban is a higher price and a lower quantity.

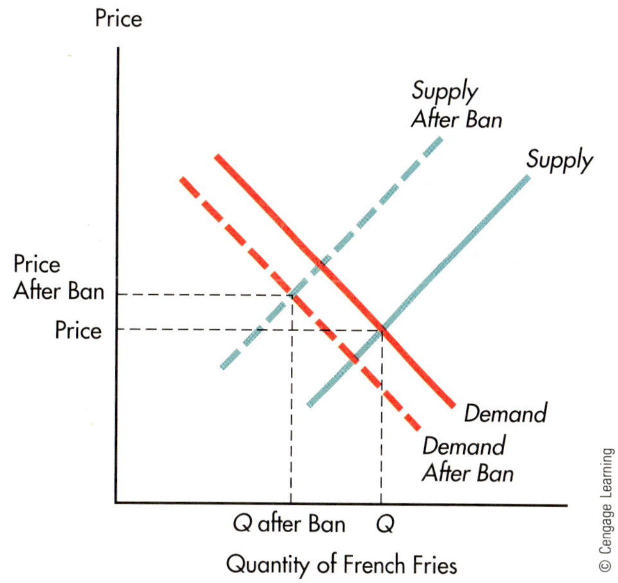

cooking oils that have the same taste and quality as those that create trans fats is expensive. This means that suppliers will offer any given quantity of French fries only at a higher price. The supply curve shifts in to "Supply After Ban." Consumers, also, may react to the ban. They may not like the French fries as much after the ban. If this is the case, the demand would shift in to "Demand After Ban." There is a possibility that demand might not shift in by much or might actually shift out slightly if, as a result of being somewhat more healthy, some consumers purchase more French fries than they did when the fries were made with trans fats. The result, in this case, would be that the price of fries would be a little higher and the quantity of fries produced and sold a little less.

RECAP

1. Government interference in markets distorts the market. The price and/or quantity does not adjust so that demand and supply are equal. Instead, shortages or surpluses will exist.
2. A minimum wage is a government policy requiring firms to pay at least that wage—a wage that is above the equilibrium wage. A limit on how low a price can go.
3. A price ceiling is a price set below the market price. Price ceilings lead to shortages. Rent controls are price ceilings—rent cannot exceed some level which is less than what would occur in a free market.
4. A quota is a limit on the quantity of a good that can be supplied in a market. It leads to a higher price than would occur in a free market.
5. A ban is a prohibition of the sale and consumption of a good or service. If effective, a ban may eliminate the market for the banned substance but raise the costs of other goods and services that relied on the banned substance.

SUMMARY

What is the outcome of a free market?

1. In a free market, consumers get what they want and are willing to buy at the lowest possible costs, and resources are used where they have the highest value.

In a free market system, who determines what is produced?

2. In a free market, it is the consumers who decide what is produced. If the consumers switch their preferences from one item to another, producers will provide what the consumers are willing and able to pay for.

Why do different people earn different incomes, and why do different jobs pay different wages?

3. The labor market consists of the demand for and supply of labor.
4. The wage rate and the quantities of workers employed are determined by the equilibrium between labor demand and labor supply.
5. In reality, there are many different labor markets—markets for skilled versus unskilled labor, markets for dangerous versus non-dangerous jobs, and so on.
6. An equilibrium wage differential or compensating wage differential exists when the equilibrium wage in two different labor markets is different.

When the government intervenes in the market by setting a price floor or price ceiling, what is the result?

7. A price ceiling is a limit on how high the price can be. If it is set below the equilibrium price, it creates a shortage.
8. A price floor is a limit on how low the price can be. If it is set above the equilibrium price, it creates a surplus.

When the government restricts the quantity that can be sold, what occurs?

9. The name for such a restriction is quota.
10. A quota raises the price of the goods or service on which the quota has been placed.

What is the effect of a ban on a good, service, or resource?

11. A ban is a prohibition against the purchase or sale of a good or service. If effective, the market for that good or service is eliminated.
12. Goods or services that used the banned item as an ingredient will have to be altered to use substitutes. The ban raises the cost of the good or service.

EXERCISES

1. Using the schedule below, define the equilibrium price and quantity. Describe the situation at a price of $10. What will occur? Describe the situation at a price of $2. What will occur?

Price	Quantity Demanded	Quantity Supplied
$0	500	100
2	400	120
3	350	150
4	320	200
5	300	300
6	275	410
7	260	500
8	230	650
9	200	800
10	150	975

2. Suppose the government imposed a minimum price of $7 in the schedule of exercise 1. What would occur? Illustrate.
3. Using the data from exercise 1, indicate what the price would have to be to represent an effective price ceiling. Point out the surplus or shortage that results. Illustrate a price floor and provide an example of a price floor.
4. A common feature of skiing is waiting in lift lines. Does the existence of lift lines mean that the price is not working to allocate the scarce resource? If so, what should be done about it?
5. Many restaurants don't take reservations. You simply arrive and wait your turn. If you arrive at 7:30 in the evening, you have at least an hour wait. Notwithstanding that fact, a few people arrive, speak quietly with the maitre d', hand him some money, and are promptly seated. At some restaurants that

do take reservations, there is a month-long wait for a Saturday evening, three weeks for a Friday evening, two weeks for Tuesday through Thursday, and virtually no wait for Sunday or Monday evening. How do you explain these events using demand and supply?

6. Give an example of a compensating wage differential in your community. What does it mean?
7. Using demand and supply, illustrate the effects of a quota imposed by the Canadian government on U.S. wheat. Show the U.S. wheat market and the Canadian wheat market.
8. Using demand and supply, illustrate the effects of a ban on the use of steroids on the market for steroids. If people go to baseball games to see home runs, what will the ban do to the baseball market?

STUDY GUIDE FOR CHAPTER 3

Key Term Match

Match each term with its correct definition by placing the appropriate letter next to the corresponding number.

A. compensating wage differential
B. subsidy
C. price ceiling
D. price floor
E. tariff
F. quota
G. ban

____ 1. a situation in which the price is not allowed to rise above a certain level

____ 2. wage differences that make up for the higher risk or poorer working conditions of one job over another

____ 3. a tax on exports or imports

____ 4. payments made by government to encourage the production or purchase of a good

____ 5. a situation in which the price is not allowed to decrease below a certain level

____ 6. A limit on the amount of a good that may be imported

____ 7. a situation where buying or selling something is illegal

Quick-Check Quiz

1. What would happen in the market for rental housing in New York City if rent controls were abolished?
   - ☐ a. The demand for rental housing would decrease.
   - ☐ b. The supply of rental housing would increase
   - ☐ c. Neither the demand nor the supply of rental housing would change, but the market price and quantity would rise.
   - ☐ d. The demand for rental housing would decrease, but the supply of rental housing would increase.
   - ☐ e. The demand for rental housing would increase, but the supply of rental housing would decrease.
2. A decrease in demand results in a ____________ causing the equilibrium price to ____________ and the equilibrium quantity to ____________.
   - ☐ a. shortage; increase; increase
   - ☐ b. surplus; decrease; increase
   - ☐ c. shortage; increase; decrease
   - ☐ d. surplus; decrease; decrease
   - ☐ e. surplus; increase; decrease
3. The change in tastes away from low-fat meals initially resulted in a(n)
   - ☐ a. decrease in the demand for low-fat meals.
   - ☐ b. increase in the supply of low-fat meals.
   - ☐ c. increase in the quantity supplied of low-fat meals.
   - ☐ d. decrease in the quantity supplied of low-fat meals.
   - ☐ e. increase in the supply of low-carb foods.
4. Which of the following statements is false?
   - ☐ a. The demand for labor slopes down.
   - ☐ b. The supply of labor slopes up.
   - ☐ c. Younger workers earn higher wages than older workers.
   - ☐ d. Riskier jobs pay more than less risky jobs.
   - ☐ e. Males earn more than females.
5. Which statement is true?
   - ☐ a. The supply of workers in a less risky occupation is less than the supply of workers in a risky occupation.
   - ☐ b. The supply of workers in a less risky occupation is greater than the supply of workers in a risky occupation.
   - ☐ c. Firms will employ more people or hire people to work more hours as the wage rate increases.
   - ☐ d. Equilibrium-compensating wage differentials attract more workers from the less risky occupations to the risky ones.
   - ☐ e. The lower the hourly wage, the more hours that people are willing and able to work.
6. Which of the following caused the demand for health care to increase in recent years?
   - ☐ a. The percentage of elderly in the population is greater than before.
   - ☐ b. The cost of medical care has increased.
   - ☐ c. Government programs enable many people to get medical care without having to pay for it.
   - ☐ d. All of the above caused the demand for health care to increase in recent years.

☐ e. Only *a* and *c* are reasons for the increase in the demand for health care in recent years.

7. A price ceiling
   ☐ a. is a minimum price.
   ☐ b. will cause a shortage if the ceiling is set above the equilibrium price.
   ☐ c. will cause a shortage if the ceiling is set below the equilibrium price.
   ☐ d. will cause a surplus if the ceiling is set above the equilibrium price.
   ☐ e. will cause a surplus if the ceiling is set below the equilibrium price.

8. A price floor
   ☐ a. is a maximum price.
   ☐ b. will cause a shortage if the floor is set above the equilibrium price.
   ☐ c. will cause a shortage if the floor is set below the equilibrium price.
   ☐ d. will cause a surplus if the floor is set above the equilibrium price.
   ☐ e. will cause a surplus if the floor is set below the equilibrium price.

9. If a price ceiling is set above the equilibrium price,
   ☐ a. a shortage will occur.
   ☐ b. a surplus will occur.
   ☐ c. the demand for the good or service will increase.
   ☐ d. the supply for the good or service will increase.
   ☐ e. the equilibrium price and quantity will prevail.

Practice Questions and Problems

1. In the market system, the ____________ ultimately determines what is to be produced.
2. Any characteristic that distinguishes one job from another may result in a ____________.
3. Business firms respond to changes in consumers' tastes because they want to make ____________.
4. When the demand for a good or service changes, resources move from an activity in which their value is relatively ____________ to an activity in which their value is relatively ____________.
5. In any labor market, the wage rate and number of jobs depend on the ____________ and ____________ curves for labor.
6. ____________ (Business firms, Households) demand labor.
7. ____________ (Business firms, Households) supply labor.
8. The demand for labor slopes ____________, showing that the higher the price of labor, the ____________ (more, less) labor the firm will demand.
9. The supply of labor slopes ____________, showing that the higher the hourly wage, the ____________ hours people are willing to work.
10. Health care expenditures have increased so much because the ____________ for health care services has increased relative to the ____________.
11. ____________ and ____________ are government programs that pay for medical services.
12. The emergence of Medicare and Medicaid in 1966 caused the ____________ (demand, supply) for health care services to ____________ (increase, decrease).
13. Because Medicare and Medicaid reduce the cost of purchasing health care, they are examples of ____________.
14. A price ceiling will cause a shortage only if it is set ____________ (above, equal to, below) the equilibrium price.
15. A price floor will cause a surplus only if it is set ____________ (above, equal to, below) the equilibrium price.
16. A price ceiling will have no effect if it is set ____________ (above, equal to, below) the equilibrium price.
17. If the U.S. government imposed a quota on Toyota automobiles, it would ____________ (limit, expand) the ____________ (quantity, price) of Toyota automobiles that could be sold in the United States. The quota would have the effect of ____________ (increasing, reducing) the ____________ (demand for, supply of) automobiles offered for sale in the United States.
18. A tariff is a tax on goods imported into a country. If the U.S. government decided to impose a tariff on foreign-made televisions sold in the United States, you could predict that the tariff would ____________ (increase, decrease) the cost of foreign-made televisions, which would ____________ (increase, decrease) the ____________ (demand, supply) of foreign-made televisions, in turn ____________ (increasing, decreasing) the price of foreign-made televisions and (increasing, decreasing) the quantity of televisions brought into the United States.
19. A ban on the use of copper in housing construction would have the effect of ____________ (increasing, decreasing) the price of copper. If nothing works as well as copper or can be used at the same cost as copper for housing construction, then the ban would have the effect of ____________ (increasing decreasing) the cost of housing.)

Exercises and Applications

I Price Controls and Medical Care

As the price of health care rises, politicians may consider price controls on certain medical procedures to keep costs down.

1. Would the price controls take the form of a price ceiling or a price floor? ____________

2. What do you think would happen in the market for these medical procedures if price controls were adopted?

II A Solution for High Gasoline Prices?

A state senator recently suggested a way to lower the price of gas: Cap how much companies can raise gasoline prices. The senator proposed a bill that called for the wholesale price of gas to be capped for one year in his state. The senator wanted to help struggling businesses and families in the wake of the recent recession. An analyst who opposed the measure suggested that people in that state would need to start buying bicycles if the legislation passed.

a. Does the senator's cap constitute a price ceiling or price floor?
b. Why does the senator's opponent think people in that state will need bicycles if the legislation passes?

PART 2
Consumers, Firms, and Social Issues

CHAPTER 4
The Firm and the Consumer

4-1 How do firms make money?

4-2 What happens to sales when the price of a good or service changes?

CHAPTER 5
Costs and Profit Maximization

5-1 What is the relationship between costs and output in the short run?

5-2 What is economic profit?

5-3 Why is profit maximized when $MR = MC$?

CHAPTER 6
Competition

6-1 What are the benefits of competition?

6-2 What is creative destruction?

6-3 What does free entry and competition mean?

6-4 What are barriers to entry?

6-5 Is there a difference in behavior when there are just a few competitors as compared to when there are lots of competitors?

CHAPTER 7
Business, Society, and the Government

7-1 What are the benefits from free markets?

7-2 Why don't people like market allocation?

7-3 What is antitrust policy?

7-4 What is the purpose of regulation?

7-5 What is "too big to fail"?

7-6 What are market failures?

7-7 How might market failures be corrected?

7-8 What are government failures?

CHAPTER 8
Government Intervention versus Free Markets

8-1 What is a free market?

8-2 What is the main reason many economists do not believe in or trust the free market?

8-3 Can a free market provide health care, or is a government-run health care system necessary?

8-4 Is the free market able to handle environmental accidents?

8-5 Would a free market for drugs be better for society than the war on drugs?

8-6 Can discrimination occur in a free market?

4 The Firm and the Consumer

FUNDAMENTAL QUESTIONS

1. How do firms make money?
2. What happens to sales when the price of a good or service changes?

PREVIEW

In previous chapters, we have examined buyers and sellers as a whole and how they interact in markets. Let's now look more closely at the interaction between buyers and sellers by examining a single firm. A single firm exists as an umbrella over many individual exchanges—exchanges between an accountant and a salesman, a manager and a line worker, and so on. The firm combines all these individual transactions into one entity—the firm—because it is more efficient than if each were a separate entity. The employee does a job, and the manager supervises many employees. If each employee and manager were a separate entity, each would have to negotiate, contract, and determine a price at which each exchange would occur. The firm minimizes all these transactions.

What is the purpose of a firm? One principle of economics is that people are self-interested. Each wants more, a higher quality, and so on, at a lower cost. Thus, the owners of a business want that business to make a profit—to sell enough products at a high enough price that the firm can pay its costs and then be able to provide the owners with what is left. The employees of the firm want the firm to earn enough to pay them a good wage. The people who have lent money to the firm want the firm to earn enough to pay back the loans and interest. In short, the firm attempts to maximize profit.

Profit is defined as total revenue less total cost. Where does revenue come from? What are costs? How does the firm maximize profit? We answer these questions in this and the next chapter.

1. REVENUE

1

How do firms make money?

total revenue:
price times quantity sold ($P \times Q$)

Firms earn revenue by selling goods and services to consumers. **Total revenue** is the price a product sells for multiplied by the number of units of the product that is sold ($P \times Q$). How does a firm know the price to charge and the quantity to produce and offer for sale? It must know what the demand for its goods and services is. Demand is a relationship between price and quantity; demand tells the firm how much it could sell at each price. Thus, the firm would know what its revenue would be at each price if it knew what the demand for its goods and services was.

1.a. Total, Average, and Marginal Revenue

Let's use the table in Figure 4.1 to discuss revenue for a bicycle store. Column 1 is the total quantity (Q) of bikes sold. Column 2 is price (P). If the price is $1,700, 1 bike is sold. To sell 2 bikes, the store has to lower the price to $1,600. If the price is $1,500, 3 bikes are sold, and so on.

Total revenue (TR) is found by multiplying the quantity of bikes sold by the price each bike is sold for. If only 1 bike is to be sold, the price is $1,700, and total revenue is $1,700. If 2 bikes are to be sold, the store must lower the price to $1,600 apiece, and total revenue is $3,200. If 3 bikes are to be sold, then the price must be lowered to $1,500 apiece, and total revenue is $4,500.

average revenue (AR):
per-unit revenue, total revenue divided by quantity

$$AR = \frac{TR}{Q} = \frac{P \times Q}{Q}$$

Columns 4 and 5 present two very useful pieces of information: average and marginal revenues. **Average revenue (AR)** is the per-unit revenue, the total revenue divided by the total number of bikes sold. Average revenue is listed in column 4. For the first bike, total revenue is $1,700, and average revenue is $1,700. For 2 bikes, total revenue is $3,200, and average revenue is $1,600. For 3 bikes, total revenue is $4,500, and average revenue is $1,500.

You might have noticed that average revenue is just price: Compare columns 2 and 4 and you'll see that they are the same. So demand is average revenue.

FIGURE 4.1 Average and Marginal Revenue

The average-revenue (demand) and marginal-revenue curves are plotted here. As price declines, per-unit revenue (the average revenue) declines. The downward-sloping marginal-revenue curve lies below the average-revenue curve.

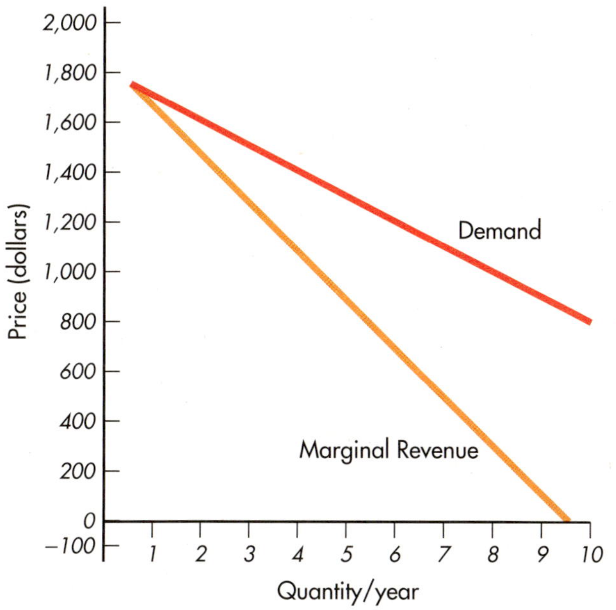

(1) Total Quantity (Q)	(2) Price (P)	(3) Total Revenue (TR)	(4) Average Revenue (AR)	(5) Marginal Revenue (MR)
1	$1,700	$1,700	$1,700	$1,700
2	1,600	3,200	1,600	1,500
3	1,500	4,500	1,500	1,300
4	1,400	5,600	1,400	1,100
5	1,300	6,500	1,300	900
6	1,200	7,200	1,200	700
7	1,100	7,700	1,100	500
8	1,000	8,000	1,000	300
9	900	8,100	900	100
10	800	8,000	800	−100

marginal revenue (*MR*): incremental revenue, change in total revenue divided by change in quantity

$$MR = \frac{\text{change in } TR}{\text{change in } Q}$$

Marginal revenue (*MR*) is the incremental revenue, the additional revenue from selling one more unit of output. Marginal revenue is listed in column 5. The marginal revenue of the first bike sold is the *change* in revenue that the firm receives for increasing its sales from 0 to 1 unit. When sold, the first bike brings in $1,700 in revenue, so the marginal revenue is $1,700. The marginal revenue of the second bike sold is the *change* in revenue that the firm receives for increasing its sales from 1 to 2 bikes. The second bike brings in an additional $1,500 in revenue, so the marginal revenue of the second bike is $1,500. The third bike brings in an additional $1,300 in revenue, so the marginal revenue of the third bike is $1,300.

NOW YOU TRY IT

If the price of a good or service is $10 per unit no matter how many units are sold, calculate average total revenue and marginal revenue at each quantity.

You may have wondered why a firm would care about its average or marginal revenue. The average-revenue curve is the same as the demand curve, showing the quantity demanded at each price. Marginal revenue helps the firm determine the price to charge and the quantity to offer for sale.

The average- and marginal-revenue schedules are plotted in Figure 4.1. The average-revenue (demand) curve slopes down, indicating that as the price declines, the per-unit revenue declines. The marginal-revenue curve also slopes down. It is steeper than the average-revenue curve and lies below it.

RECAP

1. Total revenue is the quantity sold multiplied by the price at which each unit is sold.
2. Average revenue (per-unit revenue) is the total revenue divided by the number of units sold.
3. Marginal revenue is the incremental revenue, the additional revenue obtained by selling one more unit of output.
4. Average revenue is the same as price.

2. HOW DOES A FIRM LEARN ABOUT ITS DEMAND?

Demand provides a great deal of information to a business and is something the firm has to know about. There are several ways in which a business can learn about the demand for its goods and services. One approach, which you have probably run across, is a survey. Polling organizations are hired by firms to ask consumers questions about demand. You may see the surveys conducted in malls where passersby are asked a series of questions about a product, or you may get a phone call—usually at dinnertime—from a telemarketer.

Another type of survey is called the focus group. A focus group usually consists of several randomly chosen shoppers who are paid to spend a few minutes completing questionnaires or answering questions.

Another approach to obtaining information about demand is to use actual experience. A firm that has been in business for a period of time can use its actual experience to map out its demand—comparing past prices and quantities demanded, levels of income, number of customers, changes in the season, and so on. A new firm might have to rely on the experiences of other firms by using the prices and quantities demanded of a firm with a similar product that has been in business for a period of time. A firm offering a new product might do a test trial, introducing the product in just one city. A test trial allows the firm to learn about the relationship between price and quantity demanded before it introduces the product nationwide.

Many firms have instituted information retrieval or inventory control systems that record demand information on a continuous basis. Walmart was one of the first firms to implement such a system. Scanners at checkout registers record data about every transaction, which are analyzed at the corporate headquarters. The system is used to keep track of sales and prices and to automatically order more inventory.

2.a. **Example: Demand for Auto Safety**

In the late 1980s, when auto companies were trying to decide whether to introduce air bags, they wondered how the bags would affect demand. For instance, GM argued that people would not pay more for a car with an air bag. The auto companies turned to consumer surveys to estimate the demand for the safety features. On the basis of a poll of 200 large fleet buyers, GM found that 33 percent were willing to buy the air bag only if the cost was $50 or less, an additional 28 percent were willing to pay as much as $100, and 19 percent more were willing to pay up to $150. Only 20 percent were willing to pay more than $200 for the air-bag option. As a result, GM offered the air bags on only 20 percent of its models.

Ford, on the other hand, conducted a market experiment by introducing the air bags on one model but not on a similar model to see how consumers would respond. The higher price on the air-bag model did not affect sales as much as the GM survey indicated. As a result, Ford introduced the air bags on more models than GM did.

2.b. **Example: Demand for Oranges**

Researchers from the University of Florida examined the competition between California and Florida Valencia oranges. The researchers arranged for nine supermarkets in Grand Rapids, Michigan, to vary the prices charged for Florida and California Valencia oranges daily for 31 days. More than 9,250 dozen oranges were sold during the time period. The researchers found that people preferred the Florida oranges but were very sensitive to price differences. A small price increase would cause consumers to purchase California rather than Florida Valencia oranges.

2.c. **Example: Location in Store Displays**

Researchers from Arizona State University and Harvard University investigated whether it made a difference in product sales whether the product was located near the front of the store in a display by itself or placed on shelves with other products. The researchers set up various displays and then introduced a select group of customers to the displays. The focus groups—the groups of potential

Researchers discovered that demand is higher when a product is displayed by itself near the front of a store and lower when it is displayed on shelves with other products.

customers—indicated that they would purchase more of the product when it was placed in a display by itself and the display was located near the front of the store than when it was located on shelves mixed in with other products.

RECAP

1. Firms utilize several methods to gather information about their customers—that is, to learn about demand.
2. Surveys, opinion polls, telemarketing, and focus groups all provide information related to what people say they will do in various circumstances.
3. Actual data based on experience may be used to infer information about demand.
4. Instantaneous information such as that provided by scanning devices connected to computers can provide useful information about demand.

3. KNOWING THE CUSTOMER

We've talked about how demand provides useful information to a business about revenue. But we've only touched the surface. Demand provides a great deal more information about revenue than we've discussed to this point.

Suppose you are in charge of setting the price of McDonald's Big Mac. McDonald's has been losing market share to other fast food operations. You have correctly reasoned that you should lower the price of the Big Mac to increase sales. The problem is that you don't know how much to lower it. Should the price be \$.99 or \$.85 or \$.55? The answer depends on how consumers respond to the price change. Economists have devised a measure of how much consumers alter their purchases in response to price changes. This measure is called the price elasticity of demand.

3.a. The Price Elasticity of Demand

price elasticity of demand: the percentage change in quantity demanded divided by the percentage change in price

The **price elasticity of demand** is a measure of the magnitude by which consumers alter the quantity of some product they purchase in response to a change in the price of that product. The more price-elastic demand is, the more responsive consumers are to a price change—that is, the more consumers will adjust their purchases of a product when the price of that product changes. Conversely, the less price-elastic demand is, the less responsive consumers are to a price change.

The price elasticity of demand is defined as the percentage change in the quantity demanded of a product divided by the percentage change in the price of that product.

$$e_d = \frac{\text{percentage change in quantity demanded}}{\text{percentage change in price}}$$

elastic: percent change in quantity demanded greater than percent change in price

unit elastic: price elasticity = −1

inelastic: percent change in quantity demanded less than percent change in price

Demand can be **elastic**, **unit elastic**, or **inelastic**. Demand is said to be elastic when the percentage change in price is less than the percentage change in quantity demanded. For instance, if the quantity of videotapes that are rented falls by 3 percent whenever the price of a videotape rental rises by 1 percent, the price elasticity of demand for videotape rentals is −3 and demand is elastic.

When the price elasticity of demand is −1, demand is said to be unit elastic. For example, if the price of private education rises by 1 percent and the quantity of private education purchased falls by about 1 percent, the price elasticity of demand is −1.

Demand is said to be inelastic when a 1 percent rise in price brings forth a smaller than 1 percent decline in quantity demanded. For example, if the price

NOW YOU TRY IT

What is the price elasticity of demand if the percentage change in quantity demanded is 5 when price change is 20 percent? What is price elasticity of demand if percentage change in quantity demanded is 20 when the price change is 5 percent?

perfectly elastic: infinite price elasticity

perfectly inelastic: zero price elasticity

2 What happens to sales when the price of a good or service changes?

of gasoline rises by 1 percent and the quantity of gasoline purchased falls by 0.2 percent, the price elasticity of demand is −0.2.

3.a.1. **Price Elasticity and Shape of the Demand Curve** The shape of a demand curve depends on the price elasticity of demand. A **perfectly elastic** demand curve is a horizontal line that shows that consumers can purchase any quantity they want at the single price (P_1) shown in Figure 4.2(a). An example of a perfectly elastic demand might be the demand for disk drives in PCs. There are quite a few disk drive manufacturers, and PC manufacturers do not care which drive they install in their machines; consumers have no idea which disk drive company produced their drives. As a result, if the price of one brand of disk drives is increased, the PC manufacturers are likely to move to another brand of disk drive. A perfectly elastic demand means that even the smallest price change will cause consumers to change their consumption by a huge amount—in fact, by totally switching purchases to the producer with the lowest prices.

A **perfectly inelastic** demand curve is a vertical line, illustrating the idea that consumers cannot or will not change the quantity of a product they purchase when the price of the product is changed. Perhaps insulin to a diabetic person is a reasonably vivid example of a product whose demand is perfectly inelastic. The diabetic would pay almost any price to get the quantity (Q_1) needed to remain healthy. Figure 4.2(b) shows a perfectly inelastic demand curve.

In between the two extreme shapes of demand curves are the demand curves for most products. Figure 4.2(c) illustrates two demand curves. One is a relatively flat line (D_2), and the other is a relatively steep line (D_1). The curve D_2 is said to be more price-elastic than D_1.

FIGURE 4.2

Figure 4.2(a) Perfectly Elastic Demand

The quantity demanded varies from zero to infinity at the one price. Demand is so sensitive to price that even an infinitesimal change leads to a total change in quantity demanded.

Figure 4.2(b) Perfectly Inelastic Demand

The quantity demanded is the same no matter what the price. Demand is completely insensitive to price.

Figure 4.2(c) Alternative Demand Curves

The curves D_1 and D_2 represent straight, downward-sloping demand curves. The curve D_2 is said to be more elastic than D_1 because at every single price the elasticity of demand is higher at D_2 than at D_1.

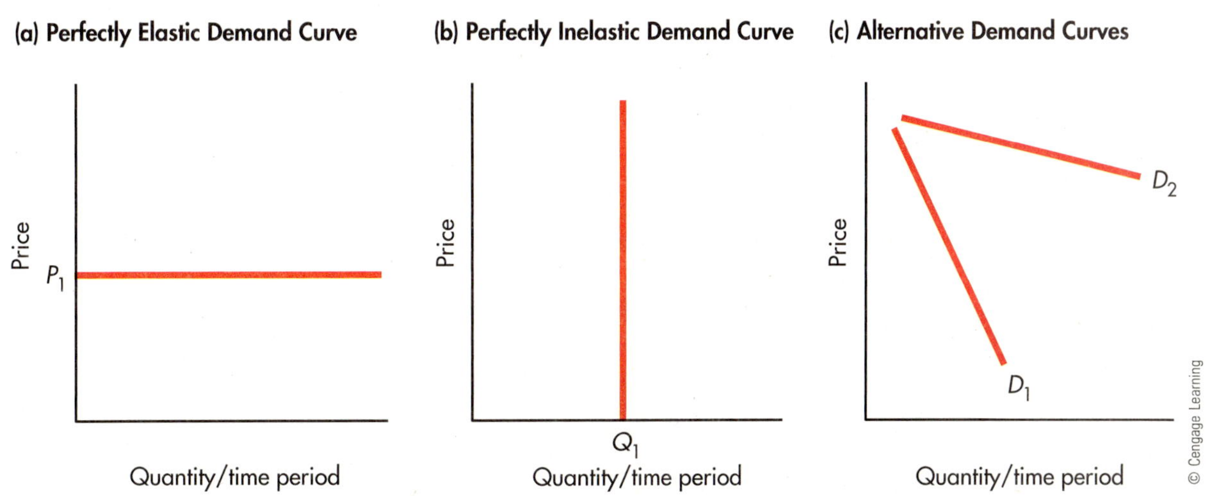

3.b. Price Elasticity and Revenue

Why is the price elasticity of demand an important piece of information? It tells us how consumers will react to a price change. This means it also tells us what will happen to revenue as the price is increased or decreased.

The price elasticity of demand tells us whether a price change will increase or decrease revenue. We know that total revenue (TR) is the price of a product multiplied by the quantity sold: $TR = P \times Q$. We also know that when the price goes up, the quantity demanded declines, and vice versa. So whether total revenue increases or decreases when the price changes depends on which changes more, the price or the quantity demanded.

NOW YOU TRY IT

If the price elasticity of demand for movies at the local theater is 1.4, how could the movie theater increase its revenue?

If P rises by 10 percent and Q falls by more than 10 percent, then total revenue declines as a result of the price rise. If P rises by 10 percent and Q falls by less than 10 percent, then total revenue rises as a result of the price rise. If P increases by 10 percent and Q falls by 10 percent, total revenue does not change as the price changes. *Thus, total revenue increases as price is increased if demand is inelastic, decreases as price is increased if demand is elastic, and does not change as price is increased if demand is unit elastic.*

For example, if the price elasticity of demand for gasoline is −0.2, then a 10 percent increase in price—say, from $1.20 per gallon to $1.32 per gallon—will result in a decline of quantity demanded by only 2 percent. Thus, total revenue will rise. As long as demand is inelastic, increasing the price raises revenue.

On the other hand, if the price elasticity of demand is −2.0, such as is the case for video rentals, then a 10 percent increase in price—say, from $1.99 to $2.19—will lead to a 20 percent reduction in quantity demanded. This means that total revenue will decline. As long as demand is elastic, increasing the price reduces revenue.

Total revenue and price move in opposite directions when demand is elastic and in the same direction when demand is inelastic. When demand is elastic, a price rise leads to a decline in total revenue and a price decrease causes total revenue to rise. When demand is inelastic, a price rise leads to an increase in total revenue and a price decline leads to a decrease in total revenue. Thus, to increase revenue, a firm will increase price when demand is inelastic and reduce price when demand is elastic.

3.b.1. Price Discrimination

The relationship between the price elasticity of demand and revenue explains many things we observe in the real world.

Not all consumers respond in the same way to a change in the price of a product. For instance, the demand for airline service by the business traveler is different from the demand by the tourist. The business traveler typically is on a tighter schedule than the tourist, so the tourist has many more flying options than the business traveler. This means that the demand by the business traveler is less price-elastic than the demand by the tourist.

The airline can increase revenue by increasing price to the business traveler and lowering it to the tourist. (Increase price to increase revenue if demand is price-inelastic; decrease price to increase revenue if demand is price-elastic.) It is for this reason that you find airlines offering substantial discounts for staying over a Saturday night or for purchasing tickets several weeks in advance. These policies, called **price discrimination**, distinguish the tourist from the business traveler.

price discrimination: different prices charged to different customers

Price discrimination is a way to increase revenue by separating customers into groups according to the price elasticity of demand. Movie theaters separate customers into different groups—children, senior citizens, and others. Senior citizens' demand for movies has a higher price elasticity than the rest of the population's demand for movies. Thus, the movie theater discriminates by charging a higher price to the rest of the population than it does to senior citizens. Children's demand for movies also has a higher price elasticity, partly because their parents have to attend the movie with them, which raises the amount spent and thus the sensitivity to price.

Warehouse-type stores, such as Costco and Sam's Club, cater to customers who are willing to purchase larger quantities of a product to get a lower price. Their demand for certain products has a higher price elasticity than that of consumers who are not willing to purchase in large quantities. In this case, firms lower their prices for large quantities of goods to attract the type of customer who cares less about ambiance or service than about lower prices.

NOW YOU TRY IT

Golf courses often charge tourists more than residents and charge more during good weather months than during bad weather months. Why?

3.c. Determinants of Price Elasticity

If you are going to use the price elasticity of demand to set the price on any good, you have to know what things influence that elasticity. In general:

1. The more substitutes there are for a product, the higher the price elasticity of demand.
2. The greater the importance of the product in the consumer's total budget, the higher the price elasticity of demand.
3. The longer the time period under consideration, the higher the price elasticity of demand.

Consumers who can easily switch from one product to another without losing quality or some other attribute associated with the original product will be very sensitive to a price change. Their demand will be very elastic. I don't care what type of rice I eat. As a consequence, when I go to the store, I buy the lowest priced rice. If the price of that brand of rice should rise even a little bit, I would purchase what would then be the lowest priced rice. If there were just one type of rice, I couldn't simply switch from one brand to another. I would have to decide whether to switch to potatoes or pasta or simply do without. In this case, I would not be quite as price sensitive.

A senior citizen discount is offered at movie theaters because senior citizens typically have many more substitutes than working people do for their recreational dollar. The seniors have more time to seek out alternative entertainment and to attend movies at different times. In contrast, working people are more limited as to when they can attend a movie. Similarly, business travelers have few substitutes for the times they need to travel; they have to take the airline at that time. As a result, their demands for airline seats are relatively inelastic. But vacationers typically are more flexible and thus are more price sensitive.

Vacationers tend to have more flexibility than do business travelers in the days and times they choose to travel. Their demand for airline seats is relatively elastic.

© Baerbel Schmidt/Stone+/Getty Images

When there are fewer close substitutes for a product, the firm can increase the price without losing significant business and revenue. It is for this reason that firms attempt to create brand names and customer loyalty. Increasing brand name recognition and customer loyalty toward that brand means that fewer close substitutes exist and thus that the price elasticity of demand is lower. It is because of brand name recognition that Coca-Cola is priced higher than Safeway brand cola and Bayer aspirin is priced higher than Walgreen's aspirin.

The greater the portion of the consumer's budget a good constitutes, the more price-elastic is the demand for the good. Because a new car and a European vacation are quite expensive, even a small percentage change in their prices can take a significant portion of a household's income. As a result, a 1 percent increase in price may cause many households to delay the purchase of a car or vacation. Coffee, on the other hand, accounts for such a small portion of a household's total weekly expenditures that a large percentage increase in the price of coffee will probably have little effect on the quantity of coffee purchased. The demand for vacations is usually more price-elastic than the demand for coffee.

The longer the period under consideration, the more price-elastic is the demand for any product. The demand for most goods and services over a short period of time—say, a few hours or a few days—is less price-elastic. However, over a period of a year or several years, the demand for most products will be more price-elastic. For instance, the demand for gasoline is almost perfectly inelastic over a period of a month. No good substitutes are available in so brief a period. Over a 10-year period, however, the demand for gasoline is much more price-elastic. The additional time allows consumers to alter their behavior to make better use of gasoline and to find substitutes for gasoline.

RECAP

1. The price elasticity of demand is a measure of how sensitive consumers are to price changes. An elastic demand is one for which a 1 percent change in price leads to a greater than 1 percent change in the quantity demanded. An inelastic demand is one for which a 1 percent change in price leads to a less than 1 percent change in quantity demanded.
2. When demand is elastic, a 1 percent price decrease will lead to a greater than 1 percent increase in the quantity demanded. This means that total revenue rises when the price is decreased in the elastic region of demand.
3. When demand is inelastic, a 1 percent decrease in price leads to a smaller than 1 percent increase in quantity demanded. As a result, total revenue declines whenever price is decreased in the inelastic region of a demand curve.

GLOBAL BUSINESS INSIGHT

Price Adjusting Vending Machines

The Coca-Cola Company tested a vending machine that can automatically raise prices for its drinks during hot weather. A temperature sensor and a computer chip altered the required change you needed to insert into the machine to get your can of Coke. The idea is based on price elasticity. If you want a Coke when it is hot outside, you will pay more than if you purchase it when it is cool. The reason is that consumers are less sensitive to a price increase when it is hot—they are thirstier. In cool weather, they aren't as thirsty and figure they can wait to get a soda. Coca-Cola also considered adjusting prices based on the demand at a specific machine. Prices could be discounted at a vending machine in a building during the evening or when there is less traffic. Reactions to the heat-sensitive Coke machine were not enthusiastic in the United States, but such machines are in operation in Japan.

4. Price discrimination is a pricing strategy, whereby different customers are charged different prices for identical products. Price discrimination is based on different consumers having different price elasticities of demand. The customers with the higher price elasticities are charged lower prices than those with lower price elasticities.
5. The determinants of the price elasticity of demand include the availability of substitutes, the cost of the good or service relative to income, and the time period being considered.

4. WHAT'S TO COME?

Once a firm has information about the demand for its goods and services, it is part of the way toward knowing the price to charge and the quantities to produce and offer to sell in order to earn a profit. From demand, a firm can determine revenue. But can it make a profit? To know this, a firm must have both demand information and cost information. We'll turn to cost information in Chapter 5.

What did you decide about the Big Mac? Are you lowering the price? How much?

SUMMARY

How do firms make money?

1. Total revenue is price multiplied by quantity sold.
2. Marginal revenue is the incremental revenue that comes from increasing or decreasing the quantity of a good or service that is sold.
3. Average revenue is per-unit revenue. It is the same thing as demand.
4. Marginal revenue is less than average revenue. The marginal-revenue curve lies below the average-revenue (demand) curve.

What happens to sales when the price of a good or service changes?

5. The price elasticity of demand is a measure of the responsiveness of consumers to changes in price. It is defined as the percentage change in the quantity demanded of a good divided by the percentage change in the price of the good.
6. Demand is price-elastic when the percentage change in price is less than the percentage change in quantity demanded; it is price-inelastic when the percentage change in price is less than the percentage change in quantity demanded; it is unit elastic when the price elasticity is -1.
7. The price elasticity of demand is always a negative number because of the law of demand; when price goes up, quantity demanded goes down, and vice versa. If demand is price-elastic, total revenue and price changes move in opposite directions. An increase in price causes a decrease in total revenue, and vice versa. If demand is inelastic, then price changes and total revenue move in the same direction.
8. Firms use price elasticity to set prices. In some cases, a firm will charge different prices to different sets of customers for an identical product. This is called price discrimination.
9. The greater the number of close substitutes, the greater the price elasticity of demand.
10. The greater the proportion of a household's budget a good constitutes, the greater the household's price elasticity of demand for that good.
11. The demand for most products over a longer time period has a greater price elasticity than the same product demand over a short time period.

EXERCISES

1. Use the table below to complete the following exercise. Plot the price and quantity data. Indicate the price elasticity value at each price. What happens to the elasticity value as you move down the demand curve?

Price	% Change in Price	Quantity Demanded	% Change in Quantity
$5		100	
10	100	80	220
15	66	60	225
20	33	40	233
25	25	20	250
30	20	0	2,100

2. Below the demand curve plotted in exercise 1, plot the total-revenue curve, measuring total revenue on the vertical axis and quantity on the horizontal axis.
3. What would a 10 percent increase in the price of movie tickets mean for the revenue of a movie theater if the price elasticity of demand was, in turn, −0.1, −0.5, −1.0, and −5.0?
4. Suppose the price elasticity of demand for movies by teenagers is −0.2 and that by adults is −2.0. What policy would the movie theater implement to increase total revenue?
5. Explain why senior citizens often obtain special price discounts.
6. Using the following data, calculate total, average, and marginal revenues:

Price	Quantity Sold
$100	200
90	250
80	300
70	350
60	400
50	450
40	500
30	550
20	600

7. In recent years, U.S. car manufacturers have charged lower car prices in western states in an effort to offset the competition by the Japanese cars. This two-tier pricing scheme has upset many car dealers in the eastern states. Many have called it discriminatory and illegal. Can you provide another explanation for the two-tier pricing scheme?

STUDY GUIDE FOR CHAPTER 4

Key Term Match

Match each term with its correct definition by placing the appropriate letter next to the corresponding number.

A. total revenue
B. average revenue (*AR*)
C. marginal revenue (*MR*)
D. price elasticity of demand
E. elastic
F. Unit-elastic demand inelastic
G. inelastic
H. perfectly elastic demand
I. perfectly inelastic demand
J. price discrimination

____ 1. incremental revenue, change in total revenue divided by change in quantity

____ 2. percentage change in price smaller than percentage change in quantity

____ 3. price multiplied by quantity sold

____ 4. percentage change in price greater than percentage change in quantity demanded

____ 5. zero price elasticity

____ 6. price elasticity equal to −1

____ 7. per-unit revenue, total revenue divided by quantity

____ 8. different prices charged to different customers

____ 9. infinite price elasticity

____ 10. the percentage change in quantity demanded divided by the percentage change in price

Quick-Check Quiz

1. One day while you are in a shopping mall, someone comes up to you and asks you questions about a product. What is the firm that is paying someone to ask the questions probably trying to get information about?
   - ☐ a. its supply
   - ☐ b. its demand
   - ☐ c. its production costs
   - ☐ d. the quality of its management
   - ☐ e. its negative revenue
2. What method for learning about demand for a product can only be used by a firm that has been making the product for a period of time?
   - ☐ a. shopping mall surveys
   - ☐ b. telephone surveys
   - ☐ c. the firm's actual experience
   - ☐ d. doing a test trial in one or two cities
   - ☐ e. using focus groups

3. When price elasticity is greater than 1, total revenue increases if price
   - ☐ a. decreases.
   - ☐ b. increases.
   - ☐ c. holds constant.

4. A business knows that it has two sets of customers, one of which has a much more elastic demand than the other. If the business uses price discrimination, which set of customers should receive a lower price?
   - ☐ a. Both sets should receive the same price.
   - ☐ b. It doesn't matter to the business which gets a lower price.
   - ☐ c. The set with the more price elastic demand should receive a lower price.
   - ☐ d. The set with the less elastic demand should receive a lower price.

5. The price elasticity of demand for a product is largest when there
   - ☐ a. are no good substitutes for the product.
   - ☐ b. is only one good substitute for the product.
   - ☐ c. are two or three good substitutes for the product.
   - ☐ d. are many good substitutes for the product.

6. The price elasticity of demand for a product is largest when the
   - ☐ a. product constitutes a large portion of the consumer's budget.
   - ☐ b. product constitutes a small portion of the consumer's budget.
   - ☐ c. time period under consideration is very short.

7. The price elasticity of demand for a product is largest when the
   - ☐ a. time period under consideration is long.
   - ☐ b. time period under consideration is very short.
   - ☐ c. product constitutes a small portion of the consumer's budget.

8. Suppose you are the city manager of a small midwestern city. Your city-owned bus system is losing money, and you have to find a way to take in more revenue. Your staff recommends raising bus fares, but bus riders argue that reducing bus fares to attract new riders would increase revenue. You conclude that
   - ☐ a. your staff thinks that the demand for bus service is elastic whereas the bus riders think that demand is inelastic.
   - ☐ b. your staff thinks that the demand for bus service is inelastic whereas the bus riders think that demand is elastic.
   - ☐ c. both your staff and the bus riders think that the demand for bus service is elastic.
   - ☐ d. both your staff and the bus riders think that the demand for bus service is inelastic.
   - ☐ e. both your staff and the bus riders think that the demand for bus service is unit elastic.

9. People have many choices regarding the clothing they buy. As a result, the demand for a particular item of clothing is likely to be ____________ over the relevant price range.
   - ☐ a. elastic
   - ☐ b. inelastic
   - ☐ c. unit elastic
   - ☐ d. perfectly inelastic.
   - ☐ e. There is not enough information to determine the elasticity of demand for clothing.

Practice Questions and Problems

1. The equation for calculating total revenue is
   ____
2. The equation for calculating average revenue is
   ____
3. The equation for calculating marginal revenue is
   ____
4. Incremental revenue is another term for
   ____
5. Average revenue is the same as
   ____
6. Use the following demand schedule to calculate total revenue, average revenue, and marginal revenue.

Price	Quantity	Total Revenue	Average Revenue	Marginal Revenue
$10	1	______	______	______
9	2	______	______	______
8	3	______	______	______
7	4	______	______	______

7. The equation used to calculate the price elasticity of demand is

$$e_d = \frac{\text{percentage change in } \_\_\_\_\_\_}{\text{percentage change in } \_\_\_\_\_\_}$$

8. Use the following demand schedule to calculate total revenue, average revenue, and marginal revenue.

Price	Quantity	Total Revenue	Average Revenue	Marginal Revenue
$5	1	______	______	______
5	2	______	______	______
5	3	______	______	______
5	4	______	______	______

How does the relationship between price and marginal revenue differ between problem 6 and problem 8?

____

____

9. Use the following demand schedule to calculate total revenue, average revenue, and marginal revenue.

Be careful doing this one—remember the exact definition of marginal revenue.

Price	Quantity	Total Revenue	Average Revenue	Marginal Revenue
$20	100	______	______	______
18	200	______	______	______
16	300	______	______	______
14	400	______	______	______

10. If a 5 percent change in the price of movies causes a 10 percent change in the number of movie tickets sold, e_d equals ______________ and demand is ______________ (elastic, inelastic, unit elastic).
11. If a 6 percent change in the price of coffee causes a 3 percent change in the quantity of coffee bought, e_d equals ______________ and demand is ______________ (elastic, inelastic, unit elastic).
12. If a 2 percent change in the price of wine causes a 2 percent change in the number of bottles of wine bought, e_d ______________ equals and demand is ______________ (elastic, inelastic, unit elastic).
13. If a 5 percent change in the price of heroin causes no change in the amount of heroin bought, e_d equals ______________ and demand is ______________ (perfectly elastic, perfectly inelastic).
14. Complete the following table.

Demand Elasticity	Price Change	Effect on Total Revenue (Increase, Decrease, Unchanged)
Elastic	Increase	______________
Elastic	Decrease	______________
Inelastic	Increase	______________
Inelastic	Decrease	______________
Unit elastic	Increase	______________
Unit elastic	Decrease	______________

15. A product with ______________ (many, few) good substitutes would have a more elastic demand than a product with ______________ (many, few) good substitutes.
16. The demand for ______________ (new cars, all new cars) is likely to be ______________ (more, less) elastic than the demand for new Chevrolet cars.
17. A product that takes a ______________ (large, small) portion of a consumer's budget has a more elastic demand than a product that takes a ______________ (large, small) portion.
18. When consumers have a ______________ (long, short) time to react to price changes, demand is more elastic than when consumers have a ______________ (long, short) period of time to react.

Exercises and Applications

I Taxing Gasoline to Reduce Pollution

According to the law of demand, taxes that increase the price of a product are expected to reduce consumption of the product. Five years ago, British Columbia imposed a carbon tax on gasoline.. The tax raised the price of gasoline by about 4.4%. A government official said gasoline consumption in the province decreased by 3% as a result of the tax. For simplicity, assume that all of this decrease was indeed caused by the price of gasoline increasing $.06 as a result of the tax increase. Use this information to answer the following questions.

1. In British Columbia, the demand elasticity for gasoline over this price range is ______________. (Round to 2 decimal places). Demand for this product is ______________ (elastic, inelastic).
2. Use the determinants of demand elasticity discussed in Section 3 of the chapter to explain why you would expect the demand for gasoline to be elastic or inelastic.

   ____

   ____
3. British Columbia was hoping the carbon tax would decrease the use of carbon fuels and therefore improve air quality. Given the elasticity of demand for gasoline, would this relatively small increase in the price dramatically decrease the consumption of gasoline?

II Price Discrimination in Airline Fares

Southwest Airlines touts an application called DING. The potential buyer downloads the application to his or her phone or computer, and it sends an alert when exclusive, limited-time-only airfare deals are available. The deals are only available through DING. The logic is that customers who are willing to go through a lot of trouble or inconvenience to get a deal are demonstrating their price sensitivity.

1. Will the main customers for Southwest's discounted tickets via its DING application be people whose demand for air travel is elastic or inelastic?

   ____

   ____

   ____
2. Does Southwest think the demand for airline tickets for vacation travel is elastic, inelastic, or unit elastic? Explain your answer.

   ____

   ____

   ____

3. Southwest makes it difficult to get the discounted tickets by making the discounts available only for a limited time and only via the DING ap,, Given what you know about the elasticity of demand for business travelers and vacation travelers, Southwest must think that ____________ (business, vacation) travelers will be the main customers using its DING application.

You can find further practice tests in the Online Quiz at: www.cengagebrain.com

5

Costs and Profit Maximization

FUNDAMENTAL QUESTIONS

1. What is the relationship between costs and output in the short run?
2. What is economic profit?
3. Why is profit maximized when *MR* = *MC*?

PREVIEW

We would all enjoy getting the things we purchase at lower prices. But a firm can't supply goods and services for very long if it can't sell them for at least what it costs the firm to supply them. A firm hires labor; purchases or leases equipment, buildings, and land; and acquires raw materials. What it pays for these resources are the firm's costs. The firm must decide how many resources it needs and then what is the least costly way to acquire and use these resources. Once the firm figures out its costs, it can compare the costs with the revenues to see if it can make a profit.

In this chapter, we first discuss costs, and then we combine costs and revenue to see how the firm earns a profit.

1. COSTS

The costs of producing and selling goods and services are the costs of the resources used (i.e., the costs of land, labor, and capital). Total cost is $C \times Q$—the cost of each quantity of output supplied multiplied by the quantity supplied.

What happens to costs as the quantity of output rises? Since more resources are required to sell more output, it would seem logical that costs would rise as the quantity of output rises. This is the case; costs do rise as output rises, but each unit increase in output does not increase costs by the same amount. As output rises unit by unit, costs rise relatively slowly at first but then increase more and more rapidly. The reason is that at first one additional resource can do a lot. For example, hiring another employee can allow the firm to deal with several more customers. But eventually it takes an increasing amount of additional resources to increase output by another unit. With too many salespeople, each customer has to wait until his or her salesperson can get access to a cash register, for example.

1.a. Total, Average, and Marginal Costs

average total costs (*ATC*): per-unit costs, total costs divided by quantity

$$ATC = \frac{TC}{Q}$$

Let's use the table in Figure 5.1 to discuss costs for the same bicycle store from Chapter 4. The costs for the bicycle firm, Pacific Bikes, to sell bicycles each week are shown. Column 1 lists the total quantity (Q) of output—the number of bikes offered for sale each week. Column 2 lists the total costs (TC) of providing each output level; it is the total cost schedule.

Column 3 lists **average total costs (*ATC*)**. Average total costs are derived by dividing the total costs by the quantity of output—in this case, the number

FIGURE 5.1 Average Total and Marginal Costs

The curves for average total and marginal costs in the short run are U-shaped. Every firm, no matter what it does and no matter what its size, has cost curves that look like those shown here. For every firm, as output rises, per-unit and incremental costs initially fall but eventually rise.

(1) Total Output (Q)	(2) Total Cost (TC)	(3) Average Total Cost (ATC)	(4) Marginal Cost (MC)
0	$1,000	—	—
1	2,000	$2,000	$1,000
2	2,800	1,400	800
3	3,500	1,167	700
4	4,000	1,000	500
5	4,500	900	500
6	5,200	867	700
7	6,000	857	800
8	7,000	875	1,000
9	9,000	1,000	2,000

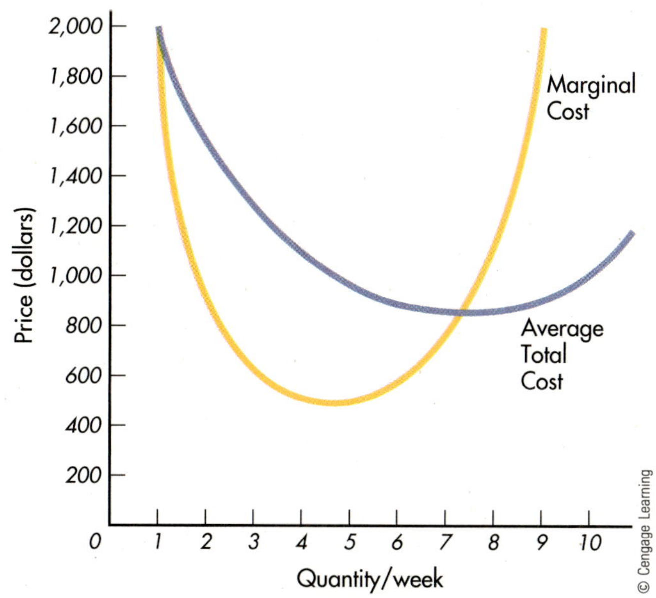

of bicycles. Average total costs inform the manager what the costs of producing each unit of output are.

marginal costs (*MC*): incremental costs, change in total costs divided by change in quantity

$$MC = \frac{\text{change in } TC}{\text{change in } Q}$$

Marginal costs (*MC*), the additional costs that come from selling an additional unit of output, are listed in column 4. Marginal costs are the incremental costs, the change in costs resulting from a small decline or increase in output. Marginal costs inform the manager whether the last unit of output offered for sale increased costs by a huge amount, a small amount, or not at all.

NOW YOU TRY IT

Using the data, calculate average total cost and marginal cost at each quantity.

Quantity	100	200	300	400	500	600
Total Cost	$2,000	$2,900	$3,700	$4,400	$5,000	$6,200

The average and marginal cost schedules are plotted in the graph in Figure 5.1. The *ATC* curve declines until 7 bicycles and then rises. The *MC* curve begins below the *ATC* curve and declines until 4 bicycles, stays the same for the 5th, and then begins to climb. The *MC* curve passes through the *ATC* curve at the minimum point of the *ATC* curve.

1.b. The Long Run and the Short Run: Why Are the Short-Run Cost Curves U-Shaped?

1 What is the relationship between costs and output in the short run?

Both the curves for average and marginal costs are described as U-shaped; as output rises, per-unit and incremental costs initially fall but eventually rise. The shapes of these curves are quite important because every firm, no matter what it does and no matter what its size, has cost curves that look like those in Figure 5.1 in the short run. The **short run** is a period of time just short enough so that at least one of the resources can't be changed. How long is this? It depends on the type of business. An airline may have year-long leases on equipment and year-long contracts with employees. In such a case, the short run would be anything less than one year. A basket weaver may have no leases and may be able to alter all of its resources within a week's time. In this case, the short run would be anything less than one week.

short run: a period of time just short enough so that at least one resource is fixed

It is important to distinguish between the short run and the long run. The **long run** is a period of time just long enough so that everything can be changed. In the short run, the firm has fewer options. It cannot expand or contract its entire operation. It can change only some of its resources, the resources referred to as variable. For instance, for the bike shop, the number of employees can be changed quite readily, probably within a day or two. But it would take a long time to change the size of the building and the number of cash registers, display areas, and repair stations. It is this fact that gives us the U-shaped cost curves. To understand why, let's look more closely at the operations of the bicycle shop.

long run: period of time just long enough so that everything can be changed

The number of bicycles that can be assembled or repaired and then offered for sale during one week is shown in Table 5.1. One employee can put together and

Table 5.1 Output with Different Combinations of Resources

Number of Employees	Capital (number of repair stations and cash registers) 1	2	3	4	5	6	7
0	0	0	0	0	0	0	0
1	3	10	25	34	41	40	39
2	6	25	36	45	52	53	50
3	10	36	48	57	61	62	61
4	13	44	58	64	69	70	69
5	13	50	65	71	76	77	77
6	11	54	70	76	80	82	84
7	10	55	72	79	82	85	89
8	8	54	68	80	83	86	90

ZUMA Press/Newscom

The number of employees in this bike store is a variable resource, whereas the building space is limited and is therefore a fixed resource.

sell 3 bicycles if the bike store has 1 station for assembling the bikes, 10 bicycles if the bike store has 2 repair stations, 25 bicycles if the bike store has 3 stations, and so on. With a second employee, output is increased with each quantity of repair stations: 2 employees and 1 repair station now generate 6 bicycles, and so on.

In the long run every possible combination is an option for the firm. But suppose that Pacific Bikes had previously constructed 1 repair station and cannot change the number for at least a year. The firm is operating in the short run because it cannot change the size of the building or the number of repair stations. In this case, the number of repair stations is the fixed resource. The options open to Pacific Bikes in the short run are only those under column 1. Pacific Bikes can vary the number of employees but not the number of repair stations in the short run.

As the first units of the variable resource (employees) are hired, each additional employee can prepare and sell many bicycles. But after a time, there are too many employees in the store ("too many chefs stirring the broth"), and each additional employee adds only a little to total bicycles offered for sale. If the employees must stand around waiting for tools or room to work on the bikes, then an additional employee will allow few, if any, additional bicycles to be repaired or assembled and sold. Eventually, adding another employee may actually detract from the productivity of the existing employees as they bump into each other and mix their tools up. The limited capacity of the fixed resources—the number of repair stations, repair stands, cash registers, and building space—causes the efficiency of the variable resource—the employees—to decline.

1.b.1. The Law of Diminishing Marginal Returns

This relationship between quantities of a variable resource and quantities of output is called the **law of diminishing marginal returns**. According to the law of diminishing marginal returns, when successive equal amounts of a variable resource are combined with a fixed amount of another resource, output will initially increase rapidly, then increase more slowly, and eventually decline. By looking at Table 5.1, you can see the law of diminishing marginal returns at each quantity of repair stations. When the number of employees for any given quantity of repair stations is increased, output will rise rapidly at first but then more slowly. Similarly, if the number of employees is fixed and the number of repair stations is variable, the law of diminishing marginal returns also applies. With 1 employee, for instance, as the number of repair stations is increased, output rises from 3 to 10 to 25 to

law of diminishing marginal returns: as the quantity of a variable resource is increased while fixed resources do not change, output initially rises rapidly, then more slowly, and eventually may decline

NOW YOU TRY IT

Explain how adding more and more air bags to automobiles illustrates the law of diminishing marginal returns.

34, and so on. The first increases are large, but output rises less rapidly and eventually declines as the number of repair stations is increased.

Diminishing marginal returns is not unique to the bicycle industry. In every instance in which increasing amounts of one resource are combined with fixed amounts of other resources, the additional output initially increases but eventually decreases. A classic example is pouring increasing amounts of water on a potted plant. Initially, the water helps the plant grow. Eventually, the water drowns the plant.

The law of diminishing marginal returns also applies to studying. During the first hour you study a subject, you probably get a great deal of information. During the second hour you may also learn a large amount of new material, but eventually another hour of studying will provide no benefits and could be counterproductive.

Every firm (and every individual and nation as well) is faced with the law of diminishing marginal returns. The law is, in fact, a physical property, something that is inescapable. It is important in economics because it defines the relationship between costs and output in the short run for every firm no matter what the firm does, no matter how large the firm is, no matter where the firm is located. For every firm, as it increases the amount of a variable resource it uses along with a fixed resource, the firm is able to get a great deal of additional output initially, but eventually the additional output increases more slowly and may actually decline. And since the firm has to pay for each employee or each unit of variable resource, its costs rise slowly at first as output increases, but then they rise more and more rapidly as output rises. This fact gives us the U shape of the average-, total-, and marginal-cost curves.

RECAP

1. Average total costs (*ATC*) are total costs divided by the total quantity of the good offered for sale (*Q*). **Average total costs are per-unit costs.**

$$ATC = \frac{\text{total costs}}{\text{quantity of output}}$$

2. Marginal costs (*MC*) are the incremental costs that come from producing one more or one less unit of output:

$$MC = \frac{\text{change in total costs}}{\text{change in quantity of output}}$$

3. The short run is a period of time just short enough so that at least one of the resources is fixed. The long run is a period of time just long enough so that everything can be changed.
4. The law of diminishing marginal returns applies only to the short run as variable resources are combined with a fixed resource.
5. According to the law of diminishing marginal returns, as successive units of a variable resource are added to the fixed resources, the additional output will initially rise but will eventually decline.
6. Diminishing marginal returns occur because the efficiency of variable resources depends on the quantity of the fixed resources.
7. The law of diminishing marginal returns results in the U-shaped curves of average total and marginal costs.

2. MAXIMIZING PROFIT

Suppose I open a coffee shop at a nice location near the school. I purchase beans and equipment and rent the building. I set up a nice surround-sound system, have comfortable seating installed, and subscribe to wireless Internet and provide it to customers. Once these costs are factored in, I figure that it costs me $.70 to supply a cup of coffee. But that $.70 does not pay me anything for the money I used to start the coffee shop or for the time I devote to working in the shop. I figure that it takes $.10 per cup to compensate me for the money I put into the business to get it started and for the time I put into the business each day. I sell the cup of coffee for $1.50, so I am enjoying a profit of $1.50 − $.80 = $.70 on each cup of coffee. The profit is great; I am doing better than I could expect to do in any other business. But that profit also looks great to others. It is not very difficult to do what I am doing; as a result, someone else locates nearby and begins offering coffee for $1.40. Then still another begins selling coffee at $1.20 per cup. The process of people entering the business continues until the price is driven down to where it just covers all costs, $.80. At $.80 per cup, no one has an incentive to enter and bid prices lower.

This is the process of competition. A business starts, earns profits that exceed all costs, including the costs of the owner's time and investments, which attracts competitors. The competitors bid the price down until there is no more incentive for new businesses to start. That process may take place over several years—such as the competition arising against the iPhone—or it may take place almost immediately—such as with the corner gyro shop.

2.a. Economic Profit

2
What is economic profit?

Why would the price be bid down to $.80, rather than $.70 or $1.00? If the price of the coffee was bid down to $.70, it would mean that the owner was not being fully compensated for the money or time he put into the company. This says he would be better off doing something else. For instance, suppose $50,000 is required to start the business and suppose that the owner could earn 5 percent using the money elsewhere. Then, rather than investing in the company, the owner could have earned 5 percent on the $50,000, or $2,500 per year, by putting the money in a savings account or some other investment. Not earning that $2,500 is a cost, an opportunity cost of the owner's money. Similarly, if the owner gave up a job where he earned $60,000 a year to work in the coffee shop, then that is a cost, an opportunity cost. The coffee shop needs to pay the owner $60,000 to fully compensate him for his time. If he could only get $40,000, the owner would actually be taking a loss of $20,000. He would be pulling out $40,000 but could have been getting $60,000 at his old job. **Economic profit** is total revenue less all *opportunity costs*, including the owner's time and money.

economic profit: revenue less all costs, including the opportunity cost of the owner's capital

2.a.1. Zero Economic Profit

Suppose the coffee shop ends up selling coffee for $.80 per cup. The owner is being fully compensated, including getting paid exactly what he could have gotten paid doing something else. When revenue is equal to total opportunity costs, economic profit is zero. **Zero economic profit** says that all opportunity costs are being paid. "Zero" doesn't sound good, but it is in reality as good as it gets—there is no alternative that will do better. The owners have no reason to sell their equity or to get out of the business. Similarly, there is no incentive for new competitors to enter the business. (We will explain in a moment why zero economic profit is actually "normal" accounting profit.)

zero economic profit: revenue just pays all opportunity costs

2.a.2. Positive Economic Profit

If the price of the coffee is $1 per cup, it would mean that the firm is covering all opportunity costs and has $.20 per cup left over. The coffee shop would be earning **positive economic profit**. The owner is not only getting more than 5 percent on his $50,000 investment, but he is also taking more than $60,000 out of the business. The owner is earning more than his opportunity costs. This sends a signal to others that perhaps they too could earn more than their costs. More competitors would enter the business, increasing supply and driving price down.

positive economic profit: revenue exceeds all opportunity costs

2.a.3. Negative Economic Profit

When a firm does not earn enough revenue to pay all of its opportunity costs, we say the firm is earning **negative economic profit**. Negative economic profit means that the resources used in the business would have a higher value in another use. A firm that continues to earn a negative economic profit will eventually go out of business.

negative economic profit: revenue does not pay for all opportunity costs

2.a.4. **Normal Profit** When firms can enter a business and freely compete with existing businesses, economic profit will eventually be driven to zero. Be sure you realize that zero economic profit means the firm is earning a profit; the owners could not do better going into another business or working for someone else and earning a salary. Accountants refer to zero economic profit as **normal profit** because it is the accounting profit that can be earned once competition has occurred. It is the return owners can expect to earn once competition has driven price to its lowest possible level.

normal profit: zero economic profit

RECAP

1. Economic profit is *total revenue – total opportunity costs.*
2. Total costs = cost of land + cost of labor + cost of capital (debt + equity).
3. Economic profit can be positive, zero, or negative.
4. Positive economic profit means that revenue exceeds all opportunity costs. Owners could not do better investing in any other business. Other investors look at the possibility of also doing better than what they are currently doing and enter the business.
5. Negative economic profit means that revenue is less than total opportunity costs. Owners would be better off using their resources in some other way.
6. Zero economic profit means that revenue is equal to total opportunity costs.
7. The accounting name for zero economic profit is normal profit.

3. THE PROFIT-MAXIMIZING RULE: *MR* = *MC*

3

Why is profit maximized when *MR* = *MC*?

The goal of a for-profit firm is to earn the most profit it can, to maximize profit. The firm has to select a price to charge and determine how much it needs to sell in order to maximize profit. How does it do this? The economic rule defining what to do is a basic one, no different from the way you decide how much to eat for lunch. You eat another bite as long as that bite gives you more enjoyment than misery. When you have eaten enough that one more bite would actually cause you more misery than enjoyment, you stop eating. A firm attempting to maximize profit will sell one more unit of its goods or services as long as the additional revenue obtained exceeds the additional cost of supplying and selling that last unit of a good or service.

3.a. Graphical Derivation of the *MR* = *MC* Rule

Profit is maximized at the price and quantity at which *MR* = *MC*. Marginal costs are the additional costs of producing one more unit of output. Marginal revenue is the additional revenue obtained from selling one more unit of output. If the production of one more unit of output increases costs less than it increases revenue—that is, if marginal costs are less than marginal revenue—then producing (and selling) that unit of output will increase profit. Conversely, if the production of one more unit of output costs more than the revenue obtained from the sale of that unit, then producing that unit of output will decrease profit. *When marginal revenue is greater than marginal cost, producing more will increase profit. Conversely, when marginal revenue is less than marginal cost, producing more will decrease profit. Thus, profit is at a maximum when marginal revenue equals marginal cost: MR = MC.*

Consider Figure 5.2, in which the curves of average total and marginal cost from Figure 5.1 are drawn along with the curves of demand and marginal revenue from Chapter 4. Figure 5.2 illustrates the fundamental decisions made by all business managers and owners. The profit-maximizing rule, *MR* = *MC*, is

A firm attempting to maximize its profits is much like a person who decides to stop eating at the point where taking one more bite will cause more misery than enjoyment.

fixed costs:
costs of fixed resources; costs that do not change as output changes

variable costs:
costs that vary as output varies

illustrated in the table of Figure 5.2, which lists output, total revenue, total costs, marginal revenue, marginal cost, and profit for Pacific Bikes. The first column is the total quantity (*Q*) of bikes sold. Column 2 is the price (*P*) of each bike. Column 3 is the total revenue (*TR*) generated by selling each quantity. Column 4 is average revenue (*AR*) (which is the same as demand)—total revenue divided by quantity. Column 5 lists marginal revenue (*MR*)—the change in total revenue that comes with the sale of an additional bike.

Total costs (*TC*) are listed in column 6. You might note that costs are $1,000 even when no bikes are sold. Costs that have to be paid even when production is zero are called **fixed costs**. Fixed costs are items such as the lease on the building and the payment on the loans used to construct repair stations. Other costs, referred to as **variable costs**, change as output changes. Variable costs include the costs of employees, electricity, water, and materials—items that change as quantity changes.

Average total cost (*ATC*) is listed in column 7; it is total cost divided by quantity. Marginal cost (*MC*), the additional cost of selling an additional bike, is listed in column 8. The marginal cost of the first bike is the additional cost of offering the first bike for sale, $1,000; the marginal cost of the second bike is the increase in costs that results from offering a second bike for sale, $800. Total profit, the difference between total revenue and total costs ($TR - TC$), is listed in the last column.

The first bike costs an additional $1,000 to sell; the marginal cost (additional cost) of the first bike is $1,000. When sold, the bike brings in $1,700 in revenue, so the marginal revenue is $1,700. Since marginal revenue is greater than marginal cost, the firm is better off selling that first bike than not selling it.

The second bike costs an additional $800 (column 8) to sell and brings in an additional $1,500 (column 5) in revenue when sold. With the second bike, marginal revenue exceeds marginal cost. Thus, the firm is better off producing two bikes than none or one.

Profit continues to rise until the sixth bike is sold. The marginal cost of selling the seventh bike is $800, and the marginal revenue is $500. Thus, marginal cost is greater than marginal revenue. Profit declines if the seventh bike is sold. The firm can maximize profit by selling six bikes, the quantity at which marginal revenue and marginal cost are equal.

We can easily find the profit-maximizing price and quantity in Figure 5.2. Profit is maximized at the point at which $MR = MC$. The quantity the firm should sell to maximize profit is given by dropping a line down to the horizontal axis from the $MR = MC$ point, a quantity of $Q^* = 6$. The price that the firm should charge to sell this quantity is given by extending the vertical line from the $MR = MC$ point up to the demand curve. The demand curve tells us how much consumers are willing and able to pay for the quantity Q^*.Then we draw a horizontal line over to the vertical axis, the price axis, at $P^* = \$1{,}200$.

Total revenue is given by the rectangle $06CP^*$. The total cost is found by multiplying average total cost by quantity. We draw a vertical line from $Q^* = 6$ up to the average-total-cost curve; it intersects at point *D*. This gives us the per-unit costs of selling six bikes. We then draw a horizontal line over to the vertical axis; this represents multiplying *ATC* by $Q^* = 6$. The resulting rectangle $06D\$867$ is the total cost. Total profit, then, is the difference between total revenue and total cost. Total profit is given by the rectangle $\$867DCP^*$.

NOW YOU TRY IT

Using Figure 5.2, find the profit-maximizing output level if price is a constant $800 no matter how many units are sold.

FIGURE 5.2 Revenue, Costs, and Profit

When marginal revenue is greater than marginal cost, there is less output and some profit that could be earned is not. When marginal revenue is less than marginal cost, there is more output and profit is reduced.

(1) Total Output (Q)	(2) Price (P)	(3) Total Revenue (TR)	(4) Average Revenue (AR)	(5) Marginal Revenue (MR)	(6) Total Cost (TC)	(7) Average Total Cost (ATC)	(8) Marginal Cost (MC)	(9) Total Profit (TR – TC)	
0	0	0	0	0	$1,000	—	—	–$1,000	
1	$1,700	1,700	1,700	1,700	2,000	$2,000	$1,000	–300	
2	1,600	3,200	1,600	1,500	2,800	1,400	800	400	
3	1,500	4,500	1,500	1,300	3,500	1,167	700	1,000	
4	1,400	5,600	1,400	1,100	4,000	1,000	500	1,600	
5	1,300	6,500	1,300	900	4,500	900	500	2,000	
6	1,200	7,200	1,200	700	5,200	867	700	2,000	Profit Maximum
7	1,100	7,700	1,100	500	6,000	857	800	1,700	
8	1,000	8,000	1,000	300	7,000	875	1,000	1,000	
9	900	8,100	900	100	9,000	1,000	2,000	–900	

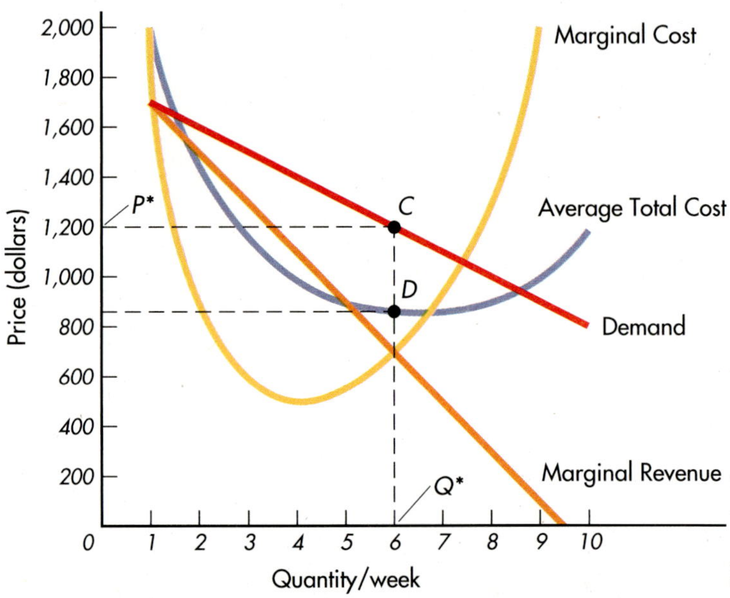

Figure 5.2 provides a great deal of information about business behavior. The demand curve may be different (steeper or flatter) depending on the price elasticity of demand, or the position of the cost curves might be different depending on cost conditions; but irrespective, profit is maximized when $MR = MC$. Every decision a manager or owner makes comes down to comparing marginal revenue and marginal cost. Should the firm increase advertising expenditures? If the *MR* from doing so is greater than the *MC*, then yes. Should the firm hire another employee? If the *MR* from doing so exceeds the *MC*, then yes. This decision-making approach shouldn't be any surprise to you. It is how you make decisions as well. You compare your marginal revenue (your additional benefits) of doing something to your marginal costs. If your marginal

NOW YOU TRY IT

Substitute the following into Figure 5.2 and calculate marginal revenue and marginal cost.

Quantity	Price
0	$2,400
1	2,300
2	2,200
3	2,100
4	2,000
5	1,900
6	1,800
7	1,700
8	1,600
9	1,500

revenue exceeds your marginal cost, you do it. Nike's familiar slogan, "Just Do It," might be restated as "If *MR* exceeds *MC*, then do it."

3.b. What Have We Learned?

We have covered a great deal of territory. We have learned how firms select the price to charge and quantity to sell to maximize profit. A firm will supply the quantity and charge a price given by the point at which *MR* = *MC*. Marginal revenue depends on demand—that is, on consumers. The firm must know what the consumer likes and what prices the consumer is willing and able to pay. It must supply its goods and services at those prices if it is to maximize its profit.

For-profit firms behave in this way to maximize profit, and therefore they sell a quantity and set a price determined by the point at which *MR* = *MC*. So if we know marginal revenue and marginal cost, determining the quantity to sell and the price to charge is trivial. The problem is that marginal revenue and marginal cost are typically not known. All opportunity costs are not reported in accounting statements. Moreover, accountants allocate costs among activities or across departments; they do not calculate the *incremental* cost of producing one more unit or the *incremental* revenue from selling one more unit. As a result, it is often said that marginal cost and marginal revenue are not really useful. Why, then, do we pay so much attention to the rule *MR* = *MC*?

Although accountants do not provide marginal cost information and although executives may say they pay no attention to marginal cost or marginal revenue, these concepts are critical aspects of their decision making. Consider, for instance, how an airline decides to price its services. The price of seats varies considerably depending on the time one flies, whether a Saturday night stay occurs, and when one purchases a ticket. Often an airline flying with some empty seats will sell the seats at the last moment very inexpensively. In fact, the price of the seat is often below the average cost of flying the plane. The average total cost (per passenger cost) for Southwest Airlines is about $.07 per mile. Yet Southwest will often sell some of its seats on distances of 1,000 miles for $25. Why? Because $25 is significantly more than $0. The marginal cost of adding one more passenger is nearly zero. Thus, the additional (marginal) revenue of the seat, $25, is greater than the marginal cost. The executives of Southwest know that they are better off selling the seat than not selling it. They know this not because they have calculated marginal revenue and marginal cost but because they know they make more profit by doing so. The profit-maximizing rule, *MR* = *MC*, may not be on executives' lips or in their manuals, but it does describe their behavior. They set price *as if* they were calculating *MR* and *MC*. They decide to allocate resources to a project *as if* they were calculating *MR* and *MC* of that project.

RECAP

1. The profit-maximizing rule is to produce the quantity at which marginal revenue equals marginal cost, *MR* = *MC*, and to sell that quantity at the price given by demand.

SUMMARY

What is the relationship between costs and output in the short run?

1. The short run is a period of time just short enough so that the quantity of at least one of the resources cannot be altered.
2. Average total costs are the costs per unit of output—total costs divided by the quantity of output sold.

3. As quantity rises, total costs rise. Initially, as quantity rises, total costs rise slowly. Eventually, as quantity rises, total costs rise more and more rapidly. This means that average total costs fall initially as output is increased but eventually rise.
4. According to the law of diminishing marginal returns, when successive equal amounts of a variable resource are combined with a fixed amount of another resource, the additional output will initially rise but will eventually decline.
5. The U shape of short-run, average-total-cost curves is due to the law of diminishing marginal returns.
6. The objective of firms is to make a profit. The difference between sales, or the value of output, and the input costs (including the opportunity costs) is called economic profit.

What is economic profit?

7. Economists take into account all opportunity costs. Profit is total revenue less all costs including the return to owners necessary to keep them from investing elsewhere.
8. Normal accounting profit is a zero economic profit. Positive economic profit occurs when revenue is greater than all opportunity costs. Negative economic profit occurs when revenue is less than total opportunity costs.

Why is profit maximized when $MR = MC$?

9. Profit is maximized at the output level at which total revenue exceeds total costs by the greatest amount, at the point at which $MR = MC$.
10. The supply rule for all firms is to supply the quantity at which the firm's marginal revenue and marginal costs are equal and to charge a price given by the demand curve at that quantity.

EXERCISES

1. Use the table below and find average total costs and marginal costs.

Output	Costs	ATC	MC
0	$100	$____	$____
1	175	____	____
2	225	____	____
3	255	____	____
4	300	____	____
5	400	____	____

2. Use the completed table for exercises a and b.
   a. Plot each of the cost curves.
   b. At what quantity of output do marginal costs equal average total costs?
3. Describe the relation between marginal and average total costs.
4. In the following figure, if the firm has average total costs ATC_1, which rectangle measures total profit? If the firm has average costs ATC_2, what is total profit?

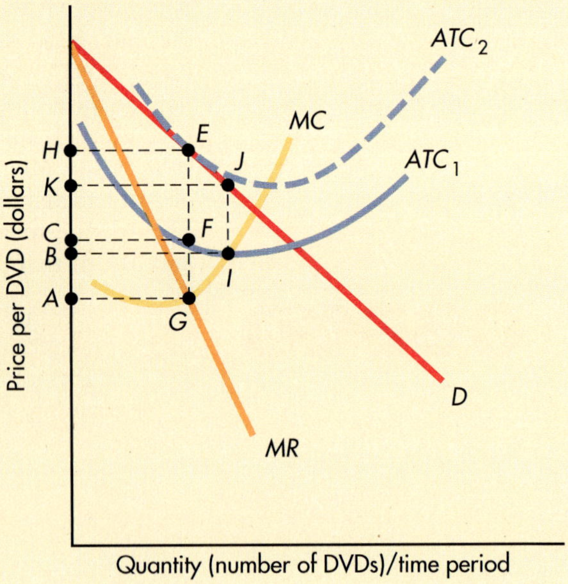

5. Using the following demand schedule, compute marginal and average revenue:

Price	$100	$95	$88	$80	$70	$55	$40	$22
Quantity	1	2	3	4	5	6	7	8

6. Suppose the marginal costs of producing the good in exercise 5 is a constant $10 per unit of output. What quantity of output will the firm sell?
7. What follows is some accounting information for each of the firms shown. Can you tell which firm is the most successful? Explain.

	Boeing	Goodyear	Liz Claiborne	Circuit City
Sales	$5,601	$423	$622	$1,767
Profits	$254	$26.9	$56.2	$31.6

8. Explain why a firm will be unable to earn positive economic profit in the long run if other firms can freely enter and compete with the existing firm. Explain why that firm will not earn negative economic profit in the long run.
9. Can accounting profit be positive if economic profit is negative? Can accounting profit be negative and economic profit positive? Explain.
10. Use the following information to calculate accounting profit and economic profit:

Sales	$100
Employee expenses	40
Inventory expenses	20
Value of owner's labor in any other enterprise	40

STUDY GUIDE FOR CHAPTER 5

Key Term Match

Match each term with its correct definition by placing the appropriate letter next to the corresponding number.

A. average total costs (*ATC*)
B. marginal costs (*MC*)
C. short run
D. long run
E. law of diminishing marginal returns
F. economic profit
G. zero economic profit
H. positive economic profit
I. negative economic profit
J. normal profit
K. fixed costs
L. variable costs

____ 1. revenue larger than all costs

____ 2. costs that have to be paid even when production is zero

____ 3. per-unit cost; total cost divided by the total output

____ 4. revenue less all costs

____ 5. the additional cost of producing one more unit of output

____ 6. a period of time short enough so that the quantities of at least one of the resources cannot be varied

____ 7. profit that occurs when total revenue is greater than total opportunity costs

____ 8. profit that occurs when total revenue equals total opportunity costs

____ 9. costs that change relative to output

____ 10. declining marginal increases in output attributed to combining equal additional amounts of a variable resource with a fixed amount of another resource

____ 11. a period of time in which everything can be changed

____ 12. A situation in which total revenue is less than all opportunity costs.

Quick-Check Quiz

1. According to the law of diminishing marginal returns, as successive units of a variable resource are added to some fixed resources, the additional output will
   - ☐ a. initially rise but will eventually decline.
   - ☐ b. initially decline but will eventually rise.
   - ☐ c. continually rise.
   - ☐ d. continually decline.
   - ☐ e. remain constant.

2. The primary objective of business firms is to
   - ☐ a. sell as much as possible.
   - ☐ b. keep their total costs to the minimum.
   - ☐ c. keep their marginal costs to the minimum.
   - ☐ d. maximize profit.
   - ☐ e. pay their employees more than other workers earn.

3. A firm is getting normal profit when
   - ☐ a. revenue just pays all opportunity costs.
   - ☐ b. it has a zero economic profit.
   - ☐ c. revenue just pays the cost of all resources except capital.
   - ☐ d. all of the above are true.
   - ☐ e. only a and b are true.

4. A firm can increase its profit by producing another unit of output when
   - ☐ a. total revenue is more than total cost.
   - ☐ b. total revenue is less than total cost.
   - ☐ c. total revenue is equal to total cost.
   - ☐ d. marginal revenue is more than marginal cost.
   - ☐ e. marginal revenue is less than marginal cost.

5. Miss Andrea's Dance Studio is considering offering an additional ballet class for adult students 21 years of age or older. The market rate is \$10 per student per class. Miss Andrea can teach the class herself or pay another teacher \$20 per class. She doesn't think her utility or insurance costs will change as a result of offering this class. No other costs matter. If she doesn't offer the ballet class, Miss Andrea can rent her studio space to a ballroom dancing instructor who will pay her \$30 per hour for using the space. How many students must Miss Andrea have in the new ballet class to make it worthwhile to offer the class?
   - ☐ a. 1 or more students
   - ☐ b. 2 or more students
   - ☐ c. 3 or more students
   - ☐ d. 4 or more students
   - ☐ e. 5 or more students

Practice Questions and Problems

1. You calculate marginal costs (*MC*) by using this equation: ____________.
2. The short run is a period of time just short enough so that ____________ of the resources is ____________.
3. Diminishing marginal returns happen in any type of business firm because the efficiency of variable resources depends on the ____________ of the ____________.
4. Use the following total cost table for Joe's Gourmet Hamburgers to calculate Joe's *ATC* and *MC*. Then plot the *TC* curve on graph (a) below, and plot the *ATC* and *MC* curves on graph (b).

Burgers	TC	ATC	MC
0	\$5.50	\$ ____	\$ ____
1	9.00	____	____
2	10.00	____	____
3	10.50	____	____
4	11.50	____	____
5	13.00	____	____
6	15.00	____	____
7	17.50	____	____
8	20.50	____	____
9	24.00	____	____
10	28.00	____	____

(a) Total Costs

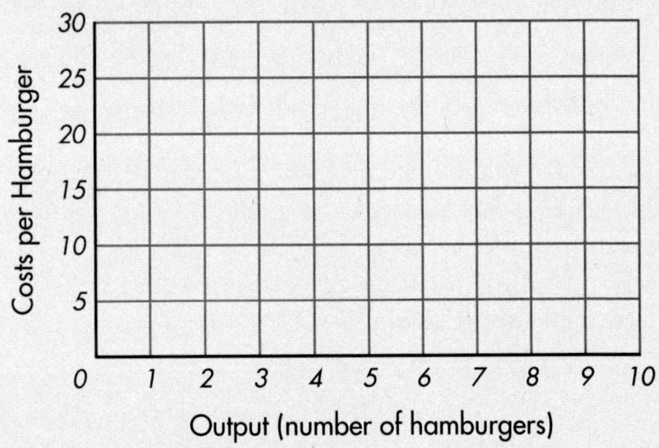

(b) Unit Costs

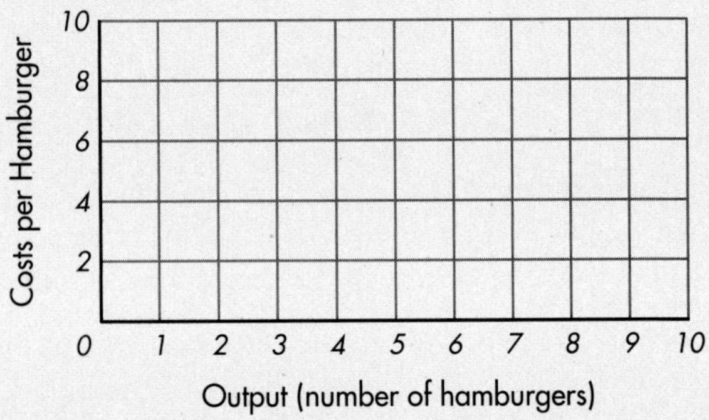

5. The *ATC* and *MC* curves are shaped like the letter ____________.
6. If the marginal cost is greater than the average total cost, the average total cost will ____________ (rise, not change, fall).
7. Fill in the blanks on the following questions.
   a. If Joe's Gourmet Hamburgers and other similar restaurants are currently receiving a ____________ (negative, positive, zero) economic profit, other people are likely to open similar restaurants.
   b. If Joe's Gourmet Hamburgers and other similar restaurants are currently receiving a ____________ (negative, positive, zero) economic profit, other people are *not* likely to want to open similar restaurants.
8. Last year, the accountant for Joe's Gourmet Hamburgers gave Joe the following information:

Revenues	\$200,000
Labor costs	140,000
Land costs	10,000
Debt costs	20,000
Equity costs	50,000

   a. Joe's economic profit was ____________.
   b. Joe received a ____________ (negative, positive, zero) economic profit.

c. Based on Joe's results, other people are _____________ (likely, unlikely) to open new restaurants like Joe's.
d. How much more revenue does Joe need to receive a normal profit, assuming his costs don't change? _____________.

9. If the marginal revenue from selling another unit of output is _____________ (more, less) than the marginal cost, the firm should produce another unit.
10. You have opened a coffee shop near the campus. You have a special attribute in that your coffee tastes better than that offered by other shops. You have costs that come to $.80 per cup you sell, and you sell the coffee at $1.50 per cup. If your special attribute can be readily copied, you will soon find that the price you sell the coffee at will be _____________. At that point you will be earning a _____________ profit. On the other hand, if your special attribute is a secret, much like Coca-Cola's syrup formula, you will find that your price per cup will _____________ over time and you will earn _____________ profit.
11. When a firm earns more than enough revenue to pay all of the costs, including the opportunity costs of owners and/or investors, then we can expect others to _____________. If it is relatively easy for others to enter a business and begin competing with the profitable firm, then we know that economic profit will be driven to _____________ by competition. If the profitable firm has or does something that creates the profit that others cannot easily mimic, then economic profit will be _____________. Only when that special something can be mimicked or replaced will economic profit be driven to _____________. If the government provides a license to operate the business, which only the profitable business has been able to get, then we expect the profitable firm to earn a positive economic profit for how long? _____________.

Exercises and Applications

I Profit Maximization and Pollution Reduction

The ideas of profit maximization and of comparing marginal revenue and marginal cost to find the profit-maximizing output level can be useful even for organizations that are not involved in profit maximization. All organizations need to find the most effective ways of reaching their goals.

Suppose you are the head of the Environmental Protection Agency (EPA), and you have to decide how much, if any, pollution a particular water treatment plant should be allowed to produce. Right now, the plant produces 4 tons of pollutants per day. The plant is owned by the federal government, so any cleanup costs will be paid through taxes. Let's assume that the EPA knows what the benefits and costs (in dollars) are from reducing pollution by various amounts. Using the benefits and costs in the following table, find the amount of pollution reduction that provides people with the biggest "profit." Profit in this case is the net value people get from pollution reduction: the total benefits minus the total costs.

Pollution Improvement: Tons Reduced per Day	Marginal Benefits	Marginal Costs
1	$ 10 million	$ 1 million
2	5 million	4 million
3	2 million	10 million
4	1 million	30 million

1. The plant should reduce pollution by _____________ tons per day.
2. Explain why you chose this amount.
____
____
____

6 Competition

FUNDAMENTAL QUESTIONS

1. What are the benefits of competition?
2. What is creative destruction?
3. What does free entry and competition mean?
4. What are barriers to entry?
5. Is there a difference in behavior when there are just a few competitors as compared to when there are lots of competitors?

PREVIEW

In Chapter 5, we started with a situation in which a coffee shop is opened at a nice location near the school. The total costs—the opportunity costs of land, labor, and capital—add up to $.80 a cup. Initially the price is set at $1.50, so the coffee shop experiences a very nice profit of $.70. The profit is great, but it also looks great to others; as a result, someone else locates nearby and begins offering coffee for $1.40. Then still another begins selling it at $1.20. The process of people entering the business continues until the price is driven down to where it just covers all costs, $.80. This story illustrates the process of competition. A business starts, earns profits that exceed all costs, including even the costs of the owner's time and investments, and this attracts competitors. But what occurs if rivals cannot enter the business or can enter but cannot duplicate perfectly what the first firm does? In this chapter, we examine answers to these questions.

1. COMPETITION AND ENTRY

1 What are the benefits of competition?

Competition occurs in many ways. Walmart is able to offer lower prices because of its economies of scale. Nordstrom does not attempt to offer the lowest prices. Instead, it focuses on service. Sharper Image attempts to be the first to offer a product—charging a higher price than other stores will when the product is more widely available. Apple focuses on innovation, attempting to offer products or features that others don't have. Each of these forms of competition is intended to do the same thing: to earn a positive economic profit. But no matter on which basis competition occurs, if others can do the same thing, economic profit will be driven to zero (accounting profit will be driven to its normal level). If another department store could match Nordstrom's products and service but do so at a lower price, consumers would abandon Nordstrom and shop at the other store. This would drive Nordstrom's profits down until they were at the normal or zero economic profit level. If iPods can be replaced with another company's MP3, then Apple's profit will be driven to the normal level.

No matter the form of competition, competition benefits individuals. Consumers are able to get the goods and services they desire and are willing to pay for at the lowest possible prices (at zero economic profit). In addition, resources are used in their highest-valued activities. If resources used to produce transistor radios are no longer valuable in that activity, they will be reallocated to other uses, say building iPods.

2 What is creative destruction?

Competition benefits society by providing the goods and services consumers are willing and able to buy, by providing these at the lowest possible cost and by ensuring that resources are allocated to their highest-valued use. What does it mean to say resources are allocated to their highest-valued use? Do you know what a vacuum tube is—or was? It was the amplifying device that allowed televisions and radios to work. But it was large and cumbersome. The use of transistors instead of vacuum tubes meant that televisions and radios could be much smaller and require far less power to operate. The typical portable radio of the 1950s was about the size and weight of a lunchbox and contained several heavy (and nonrechargeable) batteries. By comparison, the "transistor" could fit in a pocket and weighed half a pound or less and was powered by standard flashlight batteries or a single compact 9-volt battery. The resources that had been used in vacuum tube manufacture, distribution, use, and sale were left without uses. They were either discarded or recycled to be used in another activity.

AP Photo/Paul Sakuma

Competition ensures that resources are allocated to their highest-valued use, like producing iPods instead of vacuum tubes.

The transistor radio barely remains in existence; try finding one in Best Buy or Target or anywhere else. It has been replaced by MP3 devices such as the iPod. People want to listen to the music they desire rather than listening to the talk or music offered by a radio station. Resources that were used in manufacturing vacuum tubes were left without tasks once consumers switched to the transistors. Resources used in transistor radios are being left without tasks as people switch to the MP3s. This means that some land previously used for buildings, equipment, and retail stores that sold transistor radios will be left without use. Some employees will be left without jobs. Over time, some of these resources and employees will find uses in other activities, where they have more value than they would in the transistor business. This process of the destruction of old, inefficient activities is called **creative destruction**. Competition is the engine of creative destruction.

creative destruction: the process of competition whereby old, inefficient, or obsolete goods, services, and resources are driven out of business as new or efficient technologies and goods and services arise

In 1900, 47 percent of the U.S. labor force were employed in agriculture. Today, only 3 percent are employed in agriculture. Yet, more agriculture is produced today than in 1900, and 44 percent (the 47% in 1900 that were in agriculture less the 3% in agriculture today) of the labor force are not unemployed. What occurred? Where did all these people go? Competition drove resource owners to seek activities where the resources had higher value. People left the farm to find employment in the city.

Creative destruction typically takes time and can be a difficult, even cruel process. It takes time for the competition to make some occupations and some goods and services obsolete. And it takes time for resource owners to find new ways to increase the value of their resources. People without a job on the farm typically cannot find jobs in manufacturing the next day. Training and education are often necessary for people to be ready for a new occupation. A man working in a steel mill for 30 years doing the same thing day after day is suddenly out of a job when the steel mill closes due to competition from steel around the world. This is sad for the man and his family. It is difficult for them and for those who sell the family food, clothing, and other goods and services. Over time, however, the replacement of the steel mill makes society better off. Steel becomes less expensive, which means cars, trucks, trains, planes, and buildings are less expensive. Since consumers spend less on these things and on the goods and services that use these things, they have more income to spend on other things. Kindles and iPads are invented, and people have the money to buy them. Resources have been reallocated from the steel mills to the manufacture of cars, trucks, trains, planes, Kindles, and iPads. Society's incomes and standards of living have risen. But families that have to go through the experience of losing jobs and incomes as creative destruction works its way may never recover. This aspect of competition causes many people to dislike competition and many nations to restrict or regulate competition. In many cases, creative destruction is not allowed to occur. What then happens?

3

What does free entry and competition mean?

The results of competition will be different depending on whether rivals can enter the business. If entry is free, then the profit will attract competitors. More competitors mean more supply, which results in a lower price. If entry is not free, then the results depend on how rivals try to compete.

1.a. **Commodities and Differentiation**

When entry is free and rivals can duplicate identically what each other does, the price will be bid down until there is no more incentive for new businesses to enter. At this point, the product, the coffee, has been turned into what is called a **commodity**. If the coffee is a commodity, then one cup of coffee from one shop is no different than a cup from another shop, and there are lots of sellers of coffee. Economists refer to a situation where there are lots of sellers of a commodity product as **perfect competition**. With perfect competition, every product is identical and all sell for the same price—the opportunity cost.

commodity: goods perceived to be identical no matter who supplies them

perfect competition: a market structure characterized by such a large number of firms that no one firm has an effect on the market

Now consider a slightly different scenario. The first coffee shop has created a special attribute that others find difficult to copy. The atmosphere or ambience of the shop and the special drinks—double, mocha, macchiato, with caramel and whipped cream on top—provide the original shop an attribute that customers value. In fact, they think that this attribute is worth \$.10 on each cup of coffee. So what happens when the shop opens and sets a price of \$1.50? It is earning a huge profit, \$.70 per cup. Others enter and open up coffee shops. The price drops because there are more suppliers. The original coffee shop begins to lose business once the other shops are offering their coffee at a price below \$1.40. As rivals continue entering, the price is driven down further, eventually resting at \$.80 a cup. While rivals are selling the coffee at \$.80, the original coffee shop is able to retain its sales by lowering the price to \$.90. The first is able to earn positive economic profit because of the value of its special attribute, if the cost of supplying its coffee is no different from the cost to the other shops. And as long as that attribute is valued by consumers, the shop will be able to earn positive economic profit.

Recently, a magazine surveyed coffee drinkers and found that more liked McDonald's coffee and Dunkin' Donuts coffee than Starbucks coffee. Yet Starbucks charges \$1.75 for a cup and McDonald's and Dunkin' Donuts only about \$ 1.20. Why? Because Starbucks sells not just the coffee, but the entire experience of going to a Starbucks shop. And until McDonald's or some other coffee sellers come up with a way to take away the value that consumers place on the entire Starbucks experience, Starbucks will be able to earn those positive economic profits.

differentiated: a good, service, or firm that consumers believe to be somewhat unique

Economists say that Starbucks has **differentiated** its product. Differentiation means there are substitutes, but consumers place a premium on the

ECONOMIC INSIGHT

The American Girls Phenomenon

For many years, the parents of daughters complained about the dearth of toys available for girls. Other than Barbie, what was there? Then came the American Girls, a collection of historical dolls made by Pleasant Company, each with a series of books describing each girl's place in history. Girls love the dolls; nearly 4 million of them were sold in the past 11 years. In addition to the dolls, the Pleasant Company sells clothes, accessories, furniture, craft kits, and even matching clothes in real-girl sizes.

The Pleasant Company dolls were so successful that competitors began to offer their own collections, each with a distinct twist. Like the American Girls, the dolls are sold exclusively by mail order, and each comes with its own predetermined, fantasy history. There's Global Friends, which spins stories about girls from different cultures. Just Pretend offers Laurel the Woodfairy with her own trellis and lute and Alissa the Princess with an armoire and a throne. My Twinn dolls are custom-made to match photographs of their owners, down to the shape of their eyebrows and placement of freckles. Savannah and her friends from Storybook Heirlooms each have a distinct personality.

Many of these dolls are sized just differently enough so that their expensive clothes won't fit on dolls from rival collections. The 18-inch American Girls dolls, for example, are too chubby to fit into the clothes made for the more svelte 18-inch Magic Attic Club dolls. The Little Women dolls are 16 inches tall. My Twinn is 23 inches. Global Friends dolls are only 14 inches.

The economic profit of these doll companies seems to have been driven to zero and, as a result, additional companies are not entering the market. American Girls and Mattel's Barbie control more than 40 percent of the U.S. market. Barbie's annual sales of almost \$900 million are more than three times larger than those of Pleasant Company's American Girls, which in turn overshadow the sales of its competitors.

The doll story illustrates the market process. For years, there was only Barbie—a doll with dimensions that no real person could achieve and which focused on no intellectual aspects. Then an entrepreneur (Pleasant Company) comes up with a new product—American Girls dolls and the whole package of highly readable, fictionalized history books, clothes, and accessories—and is very successful. Other entrepreneurs see the success and want to get in on the good thing. They begin copycat companies, but to be successful, they have to be slightly different. In this case, the dolls are different sizes and have different stories than those of the American Girls. The success of Pleasant Company attracted new resources to the market—new companies. New companies with different approaches continued to enter the doll market until the potential for success looked no better than that for other industries, and the market topped out.

differentiated product. To the consumer, a Starbucks coffee is a different entity than a McDonald's coffee. Economists refer to a market in which there are many smaller firms with differentiated products as **monopolistic competition**. The coffee shop with the special attribute is in monopolistic competition; what occurs is that over time the special attribute loses value as rivals are able to mimic it or come up with better alternatives.

monopolistic competition: a market structure characterized by a large number of firms, easy entry, and differentiated products

The difference is what consumers value—what they pay extra for.

1.b. Monopoly

Consider yet another scenario. Suppose the university has decided to allow only one coffee shop to locate on the campus. This coffee shop is the only seller of coffee in the vicinity of the campus. It has a **monopoly**. It can set a price of $1.50 and not fear that competitors will enter and begin taking away sales because the university does not allow entry to occur. The coffee shop earns a profit of $.70 per cup. It has to pay the university in return for giving the firm a monopoly, but as long as its profit is greater than zero, it is better off than if it did not have the monopoly. Moreover, since rivals cannot enter and compete with the monopoly, the firm can earn positive economic profit for as long as it is the sole supplier.

monopoly: a market structure in which there is just one firm, and entry by other firms is not possible

Table 6.1 summarizes the three different types of markets. Notice that with free entry, competition drives economic profits to zero. But when entry is not free, such as in the monopoly case, profits are competed down to zero only if the monopoly disappears.

1.c. Competition and the Shape of Demand Curves

The initial coffee shop has a demand for its coffee that looks like the one illustrated in Figure 6.1(a). As the price of the coffee is lowered, the quantity sold increases. The firm determines it could maximize its profit by setting the price at $1.50 per cup and selling 1,000 cups a day, as shown by the point where $MR = MC$. If there are no restrictions on entry, the profit made by the shop will attract competitors.

As competitors open their shops, they provide more substitutes for consumers and take business away from the original shop. Demand becomes more elastic as more substitutes become available. The demand curve shifts in and rotates so that it becomes flatter and flatter, as shown in Figure 6.1(b).

If the coffee shop has created a unique or special attribute that consumers are willing to pay for, then the firm is able to earn positive economic profit. This is shown in Figure 6.1(b) by the price of $.90 per cup. But unless entry is forbidden, rivals will continue to attack the first firm, eventually driving the value of the attribute to zero. If the value of the attribute disappears, then the coffee is a commodity, and every firm offers the exact same thing at the exact same price. This is illustrated by a demand curve that is perfectly flat (perfectly elastic), as shown in Figure 6.1(c).

Figure 6.1(c) shows the demand for a single coffee shop once the coffee has become a commodity. The demand curve is horizontal, illustrating the idea that the individual shop has no ability to set a price above $.80 per cup. If a firm

Table 6.1 Summary of Competition

Type of Market	Entry Condition	Economic Profit After Entry
Perfect competition (commodity)	Easy (free)	Zero
Monopolistic competition	Differentiation	Positive until value of differentiation disappears
Monopoly	No entry	Positive as long as monopoly exists

FIGURE 6.1 The Coffee Shop

Figure 6.1(a)

The coffee shop creates a unique experience and determines the profit-maximizing price to be $1.50 per cup of coffee. This exceeds total costs of $.80 per cup, creating an economic profit of $.70 per cup.

Figure 6.1(b)

As rivals enter and compete with the initial coffee shop, the price is bid down. The shop lowers the price until it is receiving its opportunity costs, $.80 per cup, plus the value consumers place on its special attribute, $.10 per cup.

Figure 6.1(c)

As the value of the special attribute is eroded, the product becomes a commodity. The coffee and experience offered by the initial shop are not valued any differently than the coffee and experience offered by a different shop. The price is driven down to just equal opportunity costs. Economic profit is zero.

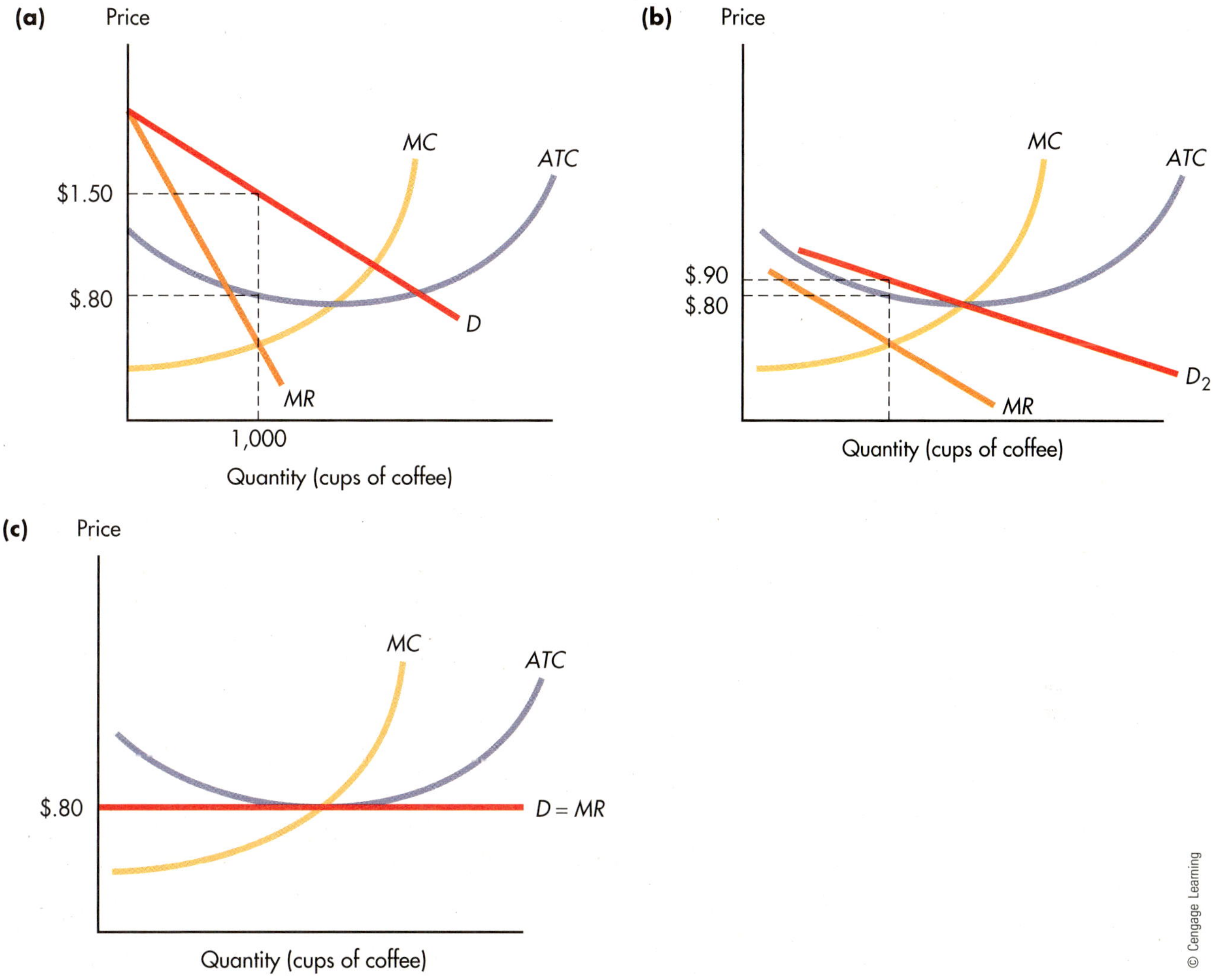

price taker: a firm in a perfectly competitive market structure

does set a higher price, consumers go elsewhere (their demand is price elastic), and no one buys anything at the higher-priced shop. For this reason, individual sellers in a commodity market are called **price takers**. They have to sell their good or service at the same price as everyone else in the market, the lowest possible price, which is equal to total costs.

The only decision a commodity seller has to make is how much to sell. A commodity seller can sell as little or as much as it chooses, at the market price. It will sell nothing at a higher price, and it has no incentive to sell at a lower price.

Table 6.2 Summary of Demand Curves and Competition

Type of Market	Shape of Demand Curve	Relationship of Price and $MR = MC$
Perfect competition (commodity)	Horizontal	$P = MR = MC$
Monopolistic competition	Sloping down	$P > MR = MC$
Monopoly	Sloping down	$P > MR = MC$

The coffee shop can sell one cup for \$.80, two cups for \$.80 apiece, and so on, for \$.80 apiece. Each additional cup of coffee sold brings in \$.80 of additional revenue (marginal revenue). The demand and marginal-revenue curves are the same horizontal line. The quantity that the seller chooses to supply is the quantity that will maximize profit, and that is the quantity where $MR = D = MC$.

Table 6.2 summarizes the perfectly competitive, monopolistically competitive, and monopoly markets. Notice that with free entry (perfect competition), the demand curve is horizontal because there are absolutely no differences among firms. In addition, competition drives price down until it equals marginal cost. If products are differentiated and the differentiation has value, then the demand curve slopes down. Competition drives price down but for as long as consumers value the differences among products and firms, price will be higher than marginal cost. When the differences lose value, demand becomes horizontal and price is driven down to marginal cost. When there is only one firm, then the demand curve slopes down and there is no competitor, so price is not driven down.

RECAP

1. Creative destruction is a term given to the process of competition whereby old, inefficient, or obsolete goods, services, and resources are driven out of business as new or more efficient technologies and goods and services arise.
2. When entry is easy or free and competitors can offer an identical product, no firm can earn positive economic profit.
3. A commodity is a product that is identical no matter who sells it. A cup of coffee from one seller is no different, in the consumer's mind, than a cup from a different seller. This type of market is called perfect competition.
4. When a firm can create a special attribute that other firms cannot copy identically, the firm can earn positive economic profits as long as consumers place a value on that special attribute. Economists refer to this situation as monopolistic competition. A monopoly is a sole supplier—that is, the only supplier of a good or service. If a firm has a monopoly, the firm can earn positive economic profit as long as the monopoly prohibits entry.
5. The market demand curve for a good or service will slope downward, illustrating the idea that as the price of the good or service is lowered, the quantity demanded will rise. The fewer substitutes there are, the more price inelastic demand is. As more and more competitors enter the business, consumers have more and more choices. As a result, demand for any single seller's good or service will become more price elastic, and the demand curve will become flatter and flatter. In perfect competition, the single firm's demand curve is horizontal.
6. The demand curve for the seller of a commodity—that is, the demand for a good or service offered by a single seller in a perfectly competitive market—will be perfectly elastic or horizontal.

2. CREATING BARRIERS TO ENTRY

4

What are barriers to entry?

What have we learned to this point? One concept is that positive economic profit will not last long if a seller simply does the same thing others do. As more and more sellers do the same thing, the demand curve becomes flatter and flatter. Over time, the only way that positive economic profit will continue to be earned is if others cannot copy the unique activity or product that creates the profit. Barriers to entry—that is, restriction on the ability of rivals to open new firms in competition with the incumbent firm—is the only way the incumbent can earn positive economic profit for a long period of time. By creating a special attribute that the other coffee shops could not create, the original shop is much like a monopoly—the sole supplier of a specific good or service. The difference between monopolistic competition and a monopoly is that rivals will keep attacking the special attribute by doing similar things or by innovating, thereby eventually eroding the value of the special attribute. With a monopoly, entry does not occur.

By obtaining the right from the authorities to have the only coffee shop near the university, the coffee shop is able to earn positive economic profit. The existence of economic profit will continue to attract rivals. But as long as they are not allowed to compete, the monopoly firm will be able to earn economic profit.

Clearly, for the firm and its owners, having a monopoly is better than being a price taker. If you owned the coffee shop, you would try to find ways to restrict or block entry by rivals. You might create a brand name that has value—in other words, it is a special attribute that consumers are willing and able to pay for. You might find ways to raise the cost to rivals of entering the business. You might agree to work with one or two rivals to keep others out of the market. You might even seek the government's help in restricting entry.

2.a. Brand Names

A well-known company can have a real advantage over newcomers. Aspirin might simply be aspirin, but Bayer aspirin is much more expensive than generic aspirin. Why? Because of the brand name. To many people, the brand name is a signal of quality or reliability.

Consider the case of a sidewalk vendor who sells neckties on the streets of a large city. If such a "firm" tells customers that it will guarantee the quality of its ties, customers will certainly question the validity of the guarantee since if the firm decides to go out of business, it can do so instantaneously. It has no headquarters, no brand name, no costly capital equipment, and no loyal customers to worry about. A firm with no obvious stake in the future has a difficult time persuading potential customers it will make good on its promises. In contrast, a firm that has devoted significant resources to items that have no liquidation value, such as advertising campaigns or physical structures such as the McDonald's golden arches, is not as likely to pick up and leave at a moment's notice.

2.b. Sunk Costs

sunk cost: cost that cannot be recouped

If the costs of entering a business are high, and if the costs are sunk, then firms are likely to be more reluctant to enter an industry. A **sunk cost** is an expenditure that cannot be recouped. What a firm spends on advertising can't be recouped. The firm cannot sell the advertising to another firm. A firm that builds a sign or golden arches cannot then sell that sign or those arches to another firm. Sunk costs can serve as effective barriers to entry since they tell a potential new firm that it has to throw just as much money away on similar sunk expenditures if it is going to compete. If, to compete with Microsoft, firms must also have interests in a film studio, then the costs to enter Microsoft's business will have risen considerably. If, to compete with Nike, a firm has to spend twice as much enlisting endorsements and on advertising, firms may be reluctant to enter the athletic shoe market.

McDonald's has devoted significant resources to items that have no liquidation value, like the golden arches, in order to establish its brand name.

Rob Broek/iStockphoto.com

2.c. Unique Resources

If all firms in a market have the same resources and capabilities, no strategy for earning economic profit is available to one firm that would not also be available to all other firms in the market. Any strategy that confers advantage could be immediately imitated by any other firm. However, if a firm has a unique resource, that resource may serve as a barrier to entry. A single family owned the only mine that produced desiccant clay. For years, this clay was the only material that could meet certain necessary standards for inhibiting the accumulation of humidity in packaging. But, of course eventually firms found substitutes for the desiccant clay.

De Beers controlled about 80 percent of the diamonds in the world when the Russian economy was tightly controlled by the government. De Beers had a unique resource—acquisition and distribution of diamonds. With the breakdown of the Soviet empire, De Beers has had to fear a flood of diamonds and a reduction in the uniqueness of its resource.

Microsoft has hired as many of the best scientists as it can. This stock of top scientists is expected to allow Microsoft to maintain its advantage in the software market. These scientists are a unique resource. Google has successfully garnered many of the top scientists in its competition with Microsoft.

2.d. Firm Size and Economies of Scale

An important barrier to entry can be the size of the firm relative to the market. If a firm must be large in order to enter an industry, then the costs of being large may be too much, and entry may be very difficult, if not impossible. In this case, a firm already in the industry may be able to earn positive economic profit. Size can be an advantage when it produces economies of scale.

Remember the distinction between the short run and the long run? The short run is a period of time just short enough so that at least one of the resources cannot be changed. The relationship between output and costs *in the short run* is explained by the law of diminishing marginal returns. In the long run, everything is variable. This means that the law of diminishing marginal returns does not apply. The relationship between output and costs *in the long run* is defined by whether there are economies or diseconomies of scale.

economies of scale: the decreases in per-unit costs when all resources are increased

The term **economies of scale** means that as the size of a firm increases (all of its resources are increased), its per-unit costs decline. If economies of scale exist, a larger firm can produce a product at a lower per-unit cost than a smaller firm can. This means that a new entrant would have to enter as a big firm in order to compete with existing firms.

Economies of scale can arise because a larger size allows more specialization—for example, an employee can focus on one activity rather than trying to do several different things. Economies of scale also can result because larger machines are more efficient than smaller ones—for example, large blast furnaces produce many more tons of steel than the smaller, open-hearth furnaces in the same amount of time and for about the same cost.

However, larger size does not automatically improve efficiency. The specialization that comes with large size often requires the addition of specialized managers. A 10 percent increase in the number of employees may require an increase greater than 10 percent in the number of managers. A manager to supervise the other managers is needed. Paperwork increases. Meetings are held more often. The amount of time and labor that are not devoted to producing output increases. It may become increasingly difficult for the CEO to coordinate the activities of each division head and for the division heads to communicate with one another. Larger machines are not always more efficient than smaller ones. A larger building may not allow more efficient production than a smaller building. When increasing size leads to higher per-unit costs, we say that there are **diseconomies of scale**.

diseconomies of scale: the increases in per-unit costs when all resources are increased

NOW YOU TRY IT

Sketch the long-run average total cost curve when a firm experiences economies of scale from zero output to an output quantity of 1 million per day and then diseconomies of scale for output quantities greater than 1 million.

It might seem that a large firm would always have an advantage over smaller firms if there are economies of scale. In fact, it would seem that the market would have to be just one firm—a monopoly—since the largest firm would be able to drive the others out of business. But appearances can be deceiving.

Most industries experience both economies and diseconomies of scale. Consider the fresh cookie industry. The cookie manufacturer Mrs. Fields trains all of its store managers at its headquarters in Park City, Utah. The training is referred to as Cookie College. By spreading the cost of Cookie College over more than 700 outlets, Mrs. Fields is able to achieve economies of scale. However, the company faces some diseconomies because the cookie dough is produced at one location and distributed to the outlets in premixed packages. The dough factory can be large, but the distribution of dough produces diseconomies of scale that worsen as outlets are opened farther and farther away from the factory.

When long-run costs are characterized by economies of scale for smaller sizes and then by diseconomies of scale for larger sizes, the larger firm may or may not have a cost advantage over the smaller firm. It depends on demand. If demand is very large, then the firm will produce only an amount that allows it to experience economies of scale. Once diseconomies of scale begin—that is, once per-unit costs begin to rise—the firm will not produce any more. In this case, the very large firm would not have an advantage over the small firm. When demand is sufficient only for a firm to experience economies of scale, then the larger firm has an advantage over the smaller firm. When demand is so large that a firm would experience diseconomies of scale trying to supply all of demand, then the large firm does not have an advantage over a small firm. When only diseconomies of scale occur, small firms have an advantage over larger firms.

Diseconomies of scale typically arise because of the growth of bureaucracy. It takes more supervisors to manage an increasing number of employees. It requires more meetings for the increased number of supervisors to communicate. All these increased nonproductive activities lead to rising per-unit costs as the size of the firm increases.

RECAP

1. A firm will attempt to slow down the onslaught of competitors when the firm earns a positive economic profit. Anything that can restrict entry is called a barrier to entry.
2. A firm will be able to earn a positive economic profit if it can create a special attribute that other firms cannot easily mimic and that consumers value. Brand name is the term given to such special attributes.
3. A sunk cost is a cost that cannot be recouped. If the incumbent firm can impose sunk costs as a condition to entry, firms may be inhibited from entering.
4. If a firm has a unique resource needed in the operation of the firm, then other firms may not be able to enter the business until a substitute can be found.
5. Economic profit induces entry and new competition, which drives economic profit to zero unless there are barriers.
6. The long run is a period just long enough so that all resources are variable; there are no fixed resources.
7. Economies of scale occur when the per-unit costs decline as all resources (the size of the firm) increase in the long run.
8. If an industry is characterized by economies of scale, then the large firm can produce at lower per-unit costs than the small firm can. To enter this industry, a firm must be large.
9. Whether economies of scale give a cost advantage to a large firm depends on the extent of the market. If demand is sufficiently large so that a large firm can realize economies of scale, then firm size is a distinct advantage.
10. Diseconomies of scale occur when, as the size of the firm increases, the per-unit costs rise.

3. NUMBER OF FIRMS: OLIGOPOLY

5

Is there a difference in behavior when there are just a few competitors as compared to when there are lots of competitors?

In many industries there are just a few large firms that dominate the market. Microsoft, Google, and Apple dominate operating software; Airbus and Boeing dominate aircraft building; there are just a few major airlines and a few auto producers. In Mexico, only two or three companies provide goods and services in areas such as finance, telecommunications, broadcasting, and retailing. And in Poland, a candidate for finance minister argued that the country's current economic problems are due to the dominance of just one or a few firms in the fuel sectors and the financial markets. When a few firms dominate a market, an oligopoly is said to exist. *Oligopoly* is a market structure characterized by (1) few firms, (2) either standardized or differentiated products, and (3) difficult entry. Oligopoly may take many forms. It may consist of one dominant firm coexisting with many smaller firms or a group of giant firms that dominate the industry. Whatever the number of firms, the characteristic that describes oligopoly is *interdependence*—that is, an individual firm in an oligopoly does not decide what to do without considering what the other firms in the industry will do. When a large firm in an oligopoly changes its behavior, the demand curves of the other firms are affected significantly. For this reason, it is often difficult to draw a simple demand curve for an oligopoly firm. Instead, we describe the behaviors that occur in ways other than by drawing demand curves.

In perfectly competitive markets, what one firm does affects each of the other firms so slightly that each firm essentially ignores the others. Each firm in an oligopoly, however, must watch the actions of the other firms closely because the actions of one can dramatically affect the others. This interdependence among firms leads to actions not found in the other market structures.

Oligopolies may result from government intervention or from cost conditions. The roots of Mexico's oligopolies reach back to the 1950s and 1960s, when the government funded private businesses and closed the domestic market to international competition. During that era, the government created a culture in which the state supported companies—government officials forced mergers to create larger companies, and later helped their friends who headed those companies. Large companies owned by powerful dynasties such as the mining company Grupo Mexico, the transportation company TMM, and Bancomer, the country's biggest bank, date from this period. The close relationship between business and government is known as "crony capitalism." In Russia, crony capitalism dominated after the fall of the Soviet Empire in 1990. Former government officials, red directors and oligarchs, grabbed assets and took control of former state-owned enterprises such as mining, oil, and utilities.

It is not just developing nations or former communist nations whose governments create oligopolies. In Japan, businesses require government approval for many actions, including entering a new business. For instance, from the early 1990s through 2005, the government allowed only three phone companies—NTT DoCoMo Inc., KDDI Corp., and Vodafone KK—to offer services, although it is now widening the market to allow six new firms to enter the business. In the European Union (EU), the large monopolies and oligopolies created by national governments had to restructure so they could do business in the entire EU.

Oligopoly can arise as the result of economies of scale. Since the cost per unit of output declines as a firm gets larger, only the larger firms can remain in business. A small business cannot offer goods and services at prices as low as a larger business can. Thus, the number of companies is determined by the size of the market—where the market demand curve intersects the long-run average total cost curve. Whereas in a monopoly or a government-created oligopoly, competition may be very limited or nonexistent, in an oligopoly that is not supported by the government, the firms must constantly innovate and seek other barriers to entry. Cutthroat competition—competition through innovation, patents, and other means—is often the companion of oligopoly.

3.a. Oligopoly and Competition

Competition does not just mean that firms lower their prices. In the real world, we observe as much competition through innovation as we do through price. In computer hardware and software, for example, firms race to see which will be the first to come out with a new product or which can obtain the patent on an innovation. Consumers are constantly being presented with upgrades and improvements to existing products as well as brand new products. Pharmaceutical companies race to create new drugs. They don't compete on price, but rather on innovation. With oligopolies, competition usually occurs with something other than price. As long as entry is not barred, profit will be competed away just as in monopolistic competition. But if entry is barred, the firms in an oligopoly can earn an economic profit.

Often, the competitive behavior of oligopolies looks much like a card game—bridge or poker, for instance—where strategies are designed depending on the cards the players are dealt. Underbidding, overbidding, bluffing, deceit, and other strategies are used. In fact, the analogy between games and firm behavior is so strong that economists and mathematicians developed the field of **game theory** to apply to certain types of economic behavior.

game theory:
a description of oligopolistic behavior as a series of strategic moves and countermoves

3.b. The Dilemma: Game Theory

Consider the situation in which two firms that dominate a market must decide whether to devote additional resources to advertising. When a firm in any given industry advertises its product, its demand increases for two reasons. First, people who had not used that type of product before learn about it, and some will buy it. Second, other people who already consume a different brand of the

FIGURE 6.2 Dilemma: Dominant Strategy Game

Figure 6.2 illustrates the dominant strategy game. The dominant strategy for firm A is to advertise. No matter what firm B does, firm A is better off advertising. If firm B does not advertise, firm A earns 80 not advertising and 100 advertising. If firm B does advertise, firm A earns 40 not advertising and 70 advertising. Similarly, firm B is better off advertising no matter what firm A does. Both A and B have dominant strategies—advertise.

		Firm A: Advertise	Firm A: Not Advertise
Firm B	Advertise	Firm A 70 Firm B 80	Firm A 40 Firm B 100
	Not Advertise	Firm A 100 Firm B 50	Firm A 80 Firm B 90

same product may switch brands. The first effect boosts sales for the industry as a whole, whereas the second redistributes existing sales within the industry.

Assume that Figure 6.2 illustrates the possible actions that two firms might take and the results of those actions. The top left rectangle represents the payoffs, or results, if both A and B advertise; the bottom left is the payoffs when A advertises but B does not; the top right is the payoffs when B advertises but A does not; and the bottom right is the payoffs if neither advertises. If firm A can earn higher profits by advertising than by not advertising, whether or not firm B advertises, then firm A will surely advertise. This is referred to as a **dominant strategy**—a strategy that produces the best results no matter what strategy the opposing player follows.

dominant strategy: a strategy that produces best results no matter what strategy the opposing firm follows

Firm A compares the left side of the matrix to the right side and sees that it earns more by advertising, no matter what firm B does. If B advertises and A advertises, then A earns 70, but if B advertises and A does not advertise, it earns 40. If B does not advertise, then A earns 100 by advertising and only 80 by not advertising. The dominant strategy for firm A is to advertise. And according to Figure 6.2, the dominant strategy for firm B is also to advertise. Firm B will earn 80 by advertising and 50 by not advertising if A advertises, and will earn 100 by advertising but only 90 by not advertising if A does not advertise. But notice that both firms would be better off if neither advertised; firm A would earn 80 instead of 70, and firm B would earn 90 instead of 80. Yet the firms cannot afford to *not* advertise because they would lose more if the other firm advertised and they didn't. This situation is known as the prisoners' dilemma; see the Economic Insight "The Prisoners' Dilemma" for a more complete description of why it has this name.

This situation is exactly what cigarette producers faced in the 1960s. None of the cigarette manufacturers wanted to do much advertising. Yet strategic behavior suggested that they must. Firm A advertises, so firm B must also do so. Then each firm ups the advertising ante, and the firms are in an advertising war. How can this expensive advertising competition be controlled? Each firm alone has no incentive to do it, since unilateral action will mean a significant loss of market share. The two parties have fallen into a prisoners' dilemma. This is a remarkable result—that individually rational action results in both persons being made worse off in terms of their own self-interested purposes. Yet there are many interactions in the modern world that seem very much like this prisoners' dilemma—for example, arms races, road congestion, and the depletion of fisheries.

3.c. Repeated Games

Notice that in the prisoners' dilemma, the two parties interacted only once. Repetition of the interactions leads to quite different results. In addition, notice that in the prisoners' dilemma games, no communication between the parties is allowed. If they could communicate and commit themselves to coordinated strategies, a different outcome would result. In fact, what occurred with the cigarette companies and their advertising dilemma is that the companies faced with expenditure increases on advertising time after time lobbied to have the government pass a law banning cigarette advertising. A ban on cigarette advertising on television has been in effect since January 1, 1971. The ban was intended by the government as a means to reduce cigarette smoking and was supported by many different groups. Yet who did this ban really benefit?

The lack of communication in the prisoners' dilemma games is an artificial situation. The firms don't have to simply wait to see what the other does—they can sit down and talk it out. Acting jointly allows firms to earn more profits than they would if they acted independently or against each other. To avoid the destructiveness of strategic behavior, the few firms in an oligopoly may collude, or come to some agreement about price and output levels. These agreements would provide the members of the oligopoly with higher profits, but it is illegal to collude.

ECONOMIC INSIGHT

The Prisoners' Dilemma

Two people have been arrested for a crime, but the evidence against them is weak. The sheriff keeps the prisoners separated and offers each of them a special deal: If the prisoner confesses, that prisoner can go free as long as only he confesses, and the other prisoner will get 10 or more years in prison. However, if both prisoners confess, each will receive a reduced sentence of two years in jail. The prisoners know that if neither confesses, they will be cleared of all but a minor charge and will serve only two days in jail. The problem is that they do not know what deal the other is being offered, nor whether the other will take the deal.

The options available to the two prisoners are shown in the four cells of the figure. Prisoner B's options are shown in the horizontal direction, and prisoner A's are shown in the vertical direction. In the upper left cell is the result if both prisoners confess. In the lower left cell is the result if prisoner A does not confess but prisoner B does; in the upper right cell is the result of prisoner A's confessing but prisoner B's not confessing; and in the lower right cell is the result when neither prisoner confesses. The dominant strategy for both prisoners is to confess and receive two years of jail time.

If the prisoners had been loyal to each other, each would have received a much smaller penalty. Because both chose to confess, each is worse off than he or she would have been if he or she had known what the other was doing. Yet in the context of the interdependence of the decisions, each made the best choice.

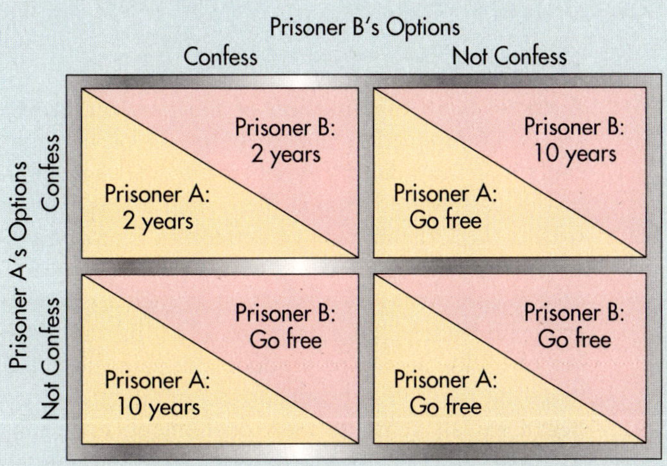

Can firms cooperate to avoid being in a prisoners' dilemma and also avoid colluding? Suppose you are talking on the telephone with a business associate and the connection is broken. Do you call your associate or do you wait for her to call you? If you call, you might get only a busy signal because she is also calling. If you wait, neither of you might call. What is best for you depends on what your associate does, and vice versa. There are two possible results. These are called **Nash equilibria**, named after the economist John Nash (featured in the movie *A Beautiful Mind*) and his solution to this problem. A Nash equilibrium occurs where there is not a dominant strategy. In this case, the equilibrium could be that you call and she does not; or she calls and you do not. Even though there are two Nash equilibria, the problem is that without some rule of behavior, you may end up with a busy signal or no call. You could prevent this problem by announcing at the beginning of each phone conversation who will call if the connection is broken. Of course, this is very inefficient. No one wants to make such an announcement at the beginning of each call. What arises then is an efficient way to move toward the Nash equilibrium, called a **convention**. A typical convention is that the person who called originally calls again.

Nash equilibria: no player can be made better off by changing unilaterally

convention: an institution procedure increasing efficiency

One way for firms to communicate without illegally colluding is to allow one firm to be the leader in changes in price or advertising activities and then for rivals to follow that leader. A manager of one firm does not call up a manager of a rival firm and say, "Follow my lead." The firms just learn over time that one firm will act as a leader. Then when the leader makes a change, the others duplicate what the leader has done. This enables all firms to know exactly what their rivals will do. It avoids the prisoners' dilemma situation where excessive expenditures are made on advertising or other activities. This type of oligopoly is called a *leadership oligopoly*. If it is price changes that take place, then it is called a *price-leadership oligopoly*.

The steel industry in the 1960s is an example of a dominant-firm price-leadership oligopoly. For many years, steel producers allowed U.S. Steel to set prices for the entire industry. The cooperation of the steel companies led to higher profits than would have occurred with rivalry. However, the absence of rivalry is said to be one reason for the decline of the steel industry in the United States. Price leadership removed the need for the steel companies to compete by maintaining and upgrading their equipment and materials and by developing new technologies. As a result, foreign firms that chose not to behave as price followers emerged as more sophisticated producers of steel than U.S. firms.

For many years, airlines also relied on a price leader. In many cases, the price leader was not the dominant airline, but instead was one of the weaker or new airlines. In recent years, however, airlines have communicated less through a price leader and more through their computerized reservation systems. As a result, the Department of Justice forced competing airlines not to use the same reservation system.

3.d. Cartel

A **cartel** is an organization of independent firms whose purpose is to control and limit production and to maintain or increase prices and profits. A cartel can result from either formal or informal agreement among members. Like collusion, cartels are illegal in the United States. The cartel most people are familiar with is the Organization of Petroleum Exporting Countries (OPEC), a group of nations rather than a group of independent firms. During the 1970s, OPEC was able to coordinate oil production in such a way that it drove the market price of crude oil from $1.10 a barrel to $32 a barrel. For nearly eight years, each member of OPEC agreed to produce a certain, limited amount of crude oil as designated by the OPEC production committee. Then in the early 1980s, the cartel began to fall apart as individual members began to cheat on the agreement. Members began to produce more than their allocation in an attempt to increase profit. As each member of the cartel did this, the price of oil fell from about

cartel: an organization of independent firms whose purpose is to control and limit production and maintain or increase prices and profits; an organization of independent producers that dictates the quantities produced by each member of the organization

$30 per barrel to $12 per barrel in 1988. (Today the price is nearly $100 per barrel because of the cartel and the increased demand for oil.)

Production quotas for different firms or different nations are not easy to maintain. Most cartels do not last very long because their members cheat on the agreements. If each producer thinks that it can increase its own production, and thus its profits, without affecting what the other producers do, all producers end up producing more than their assigned amounts; the price of the product declines, and the cartel falls apart. If they compete, price is driven down to where it just covers opportunity costs. If they agree to keep price high and split the profits, they are both better off. An agreement not to reduce prices is called **collusion**. In order for collusion to be effective, each firm has to offer less for sale than each would have in competition. In the coffee shop example from earlier in this chapter, the initial coffee shop sold 1,000 cups a day at a price of $1.50 per cup and earned a positive economic profit of $.70 per cup. Free entry drove the price down to $.80 per cup from the initial price of $1.50 as the total supply of coffee rose. Suppose the coffee shops decided to cooperate with each other and agreed not to sell at lower prices. By doing this, each shop could earn some positive economic profit. But to keep the price high, each shop will have to supply less than each would in competition. For instance, if two shops agreed to share the market, each would set a price of $1.50 and offer 500 cups of coffee. If there were three, four, or five firms, the agreement to keep price high and share the market would mean each shop would be able to supply less. If successful, though, the competitors together become more like a monopoly, reducing the quantity supplied and keeping the price high.

collusion: the practice by rivals to limit competition by agreeing not to lower prices or to work together to limit entry by others

But when there are lots of firms, it is much more difficult to collude than when there are just a few firms because there is a strong incentive for firms to cheat on their agreements. If one coffee shop lowers its price, it may earn more profits than the other members of the cartel. If a cartel is to work, a way to stop cheaters, to penalize them, must be found. In most cartels, the strongest member takes over and polices it. In OPEC, it is Saudi Arabia that serves as police. When a member does not adhere to the prescribed quantity, Saudi Arabia opens its valves and floods the market with petroleum. Saudi Arabia can do this because it is the nation with the largest supply of petroleum. The flooded market means a lower price and thus lower profits for all countries. Among the drug cartels of Colombia and Mexico, one family polices the agreement; cheaters typically end up dead. Without a policing authority, a cartel will fall apart.

Even though cartels are generally illegal in the United States, a few have been sanctioned by the government. The National Collegiate Athletic Association (NCAA) is a cartel of colleges and universities. It sets rules of behavior and enforces those rules through a governing board. Member schools are placed on probation or their programs are dismantled if they violate the agreement. The citrus cartel, composed of citrus growers in California and Arizona, enforces its actions through its governing board. Sunkist Growers Inc., a cooperative of many growers, represents more than half of the California and Arizona citrus producers and also plays an important role in enforcing the rules of the cartel.

3.e. Facilitating Practices

Actions by firms can contribute to cooperation and collusion even though the firms do not formally agree to cooperate. Such actions are called **facilitating practices**. Pricing policies can give the impression that firms are explicitly fixing prices, or cooperating, when in fact they are merely following the same strategies. For instance, the use of **cost-plus or markup pricing** tends to lead to similar or identical pricing behavior among rival firms. If firms set prices by determining the average cost of an item and adding a fixed markup to the cost, they are engaging in cost-plus pricing. If all firms face essentially the same costs, then all firms will set essentially the same prices. If costs decrease, then

facilitating practices: actions by oligopolistic firms that can contribute to cooperation and collusion even though the firms do not formally agree to cooperate; actions that lead to cooperation among rivals

cost-plus or markup pricing: a pricing policy whereby a firm computes its average cost of producing a product and then sets the price at some percentage above this cost; a price set by adding an amount to the per-unit cost of producing and supplying a good or service

all firms will lower prices by the same amount and at virtually the same time. Such pricing behavior is common in the grocery business.

Another practice that leads to implicit cooperation is the most-favored-customer policy. Often, the time between purchase and delivery of a product is quite long. To avoid the possibility that customer A purchases a product at one price and then learns that customer B purchased the product at a lower price or benefited from product features that were unavailable to customer A, a producer will guarantee that customer A will receive the lowest price and all features for a certain period of time. Customer A is thus a **most-favored customer (MFC)**.

most-favored customer (MFC): a customer who receives a guarantee of the lowest price and all product features for a certain period of time; a commitment that the customer will receive a lower price if anyone else receives a lower price

The MFC policy actually gives firms an incentive not to lower prices, even in the face of reduced demand. A firm that lowers the price of its product must then give rebates to all MFCs, which forces all other firms with MFC policies to do the same. In addition, the MFC policy allows a firm to collect information on what its rivals are doing. Customers will return products for a rebate when another firm offers the same product for a lower price.

An MFC policy discourages price decreases because it requires producers to lower prices retroactively with rebates. If all rivals provide all buyers with MFC clauses, a high price is likely to be stabilized in the industry.

RECAP

1. Oligopoly is a market structure in which there are so few firms that each must take into account what the others do, entry is difficult, and either undifferentiated or differentiated products are produced.
2. An oligopoly may come into being because government allows only a few firms to control or dominate an industry, or it may arise as a result of economies of scale.
3. Interdependence and strategic behavior characterize oligopoly.
4. The prisoners' dilemma shows how firm interactions can result in an outcome that is not the best for the competing firms.
5. Oligopolistic firms have incentives to cooperate. In a price-leadership oligopoly, one firm determines the price and quantity, knowing that all other firms will follow suit. The price leader is usually the dominant firm in the industry.
6. Collusion, or making a secret cooperative agreement, is illegal in the United States. Cartels, also illegal in the United States, rest on explicit cooperation achieved through formal agreement.
7. The incentive for cartel members to cheat typically leads to the collapse of the cartel. To minimize cheating, one member must police the others.
8. Facilitating practices implicitly encourage cooperation in an industry.

SUMMARY

What are the benefits of competition?

1. Competition drives price to the lowest possible level, where opportunity costs are paid and economic profit is zero.
2. Competition ensures resources are used where their value is highest.
3. Competition drives inefficient and obsolete activities out of existence.

What is creative destruction?

4. Competition means that firms have to offer what consumers want at prices they are willing and able to pay. Firms that are wasteful or inefficient and

firms that offer obsolete products will be driven out of business. In other words, businesses and industries are destroyed by competition as new ones are created.

5. Creative destruction is part of the process of creating benefits for society. It also means that some members of society will be harmed by competition. Resources used in the activities that are obsolete or inefficient will be displaced.

What does free entry and competition mean?

6. With free entry and competition, firms will earn zero economic profit.
7. Positive economic profit attracts rivals who bid the price down until firms are able to pay for opportunity costs but nothing more. This type of market is referred to as a commodity market and called perfect competition.
8. When a firm offers something unique or different, the demand curve for its good or service slopes downward. If the firm earns a positive economic profit and rivals can open businesses that offer the same thing, then the demand curve for the first firm shifts in and flattens out, or becomes more elastic. If competition results in the firms offering identical goods and services, then the demand curve for any one firm is horizontal, perfectly elastic.

What are barriers to entry?

9. If a firm is able to create a special attribute, some way to differentiate its product that consumers value, then entry and competition will not necessarily drive economic profit to zero. If consumers place a value on the attribute that other firms cannot compete with, then the firm is able to earn positive economic profit as long as consumers continue to value that special attribute.
10. If a firm is the only firm selling a product without close substitutes, it is called a monopoly.
11. A market in which firms offer similar but not identical products and can begin a business easily is called monopolistic competition.
12. If entry is easy, it is not possible for a firm to earn positive economic profit in the long run. If a firm earns a positive profit, others see that the firm is earning more than the owners' opportunity costs and want to get in on the good thing as well. More firms enter the business, compete with the first, and drive profit to zero.
13. If entry is difficult, a firm can earn a positive economic profit for as long as entry does not occur.

Is there a difference in behavior when there are just a few competitors as compared to when there are lots of competitors?

14. An oligopoly is a market dominated by just a few firms. Firms are interdependent, meaning that what one does significantly affects rivals. Because of this interdependence, it is often not possible to illustrate a firm's demand using a simple demand curve. Instead, game theory and other approaches are used to illustrate the interaction of consumers and firms in an oligopoly.
15. Oligopolies can arise from government interference in business and/or from economies of scale.
16. Collusion and cartels, both illegal in the United States, are forms of interaction that can arise from oligopolies.
17. Economies of scale occur when the costs per unit of output decline as all resources (the size of the firm) increase—that is, as output rises.

18. In an industry or business that has economies of scale, the larger firms can produce more cheaply than the smaller firms. As a result, the larger firms can sell at a price that is lower than what the smaller firms can.

EXERCISES

1. Using a single industry, contrast and compare perfect competition and monopoly. For instance, using the coffee shop example, explain how its behavior might differ if it had many rivals who would and could copy whatever it does, or if it had no rivals.
2. Which would you think best characterizes the following businesses—a commodity market, a market with differentiation, or a monopoly?
   a. airlines
   b. fast food
   c. computer chips
   d. corn
   e. diamonds
3. A monopolist has no rivals. Yet it cannot simply set an exorbitantly high price. Do you agree with this statement? Explain.
4. Complete the following table.

Output	Price	Total Costs	Total Revenue ($P \times Q$)
1	$5	$10	______
2	5	12	______
3	5	15	______
4	5	19	______
5	5	24	______
6	5	30	______
7	5	45	______

5. Explain why firms advertise.
6. Give 10 examples of differentiated goods or services. Explain what differentiates them.
7. Why will a firm choose to produce where $MR = MC$? Why not choose a quantity where $MR > MC$?
8. Use the information in the table of question 4 to calculate total revenue, marginal revenue, and marginal costs. Indicate the profit-maximizing level of output. What market structure is this firm operating in? What would change if the structure were monopolistic competition?
9. Draw a perfectly elastic demand curve on top of a standard U-shaped, average-total-cost curve. Now add in the marginal cost and marginal revenue curves. Find the profit-maximizing point, $MR = MC$. Indicate the firm's total revenue and total costs.
10. Describe profit maximization in terms of marginal revenue and marginal costs.
11. Using demand curves, illustrate the effect of product differentiation on haircutters.
12. Why might society prefer a situation in which entry can occur to a situation in which entry is restricted?
13. Under what circumstances would a large size provide an advantage to a firm? How could it serve as a barrier to entry?
14. You and your rival must simultaneously decide what price to advertise in the weekly newspaper. If you each charge a low price, you each earn zero profits. If you each charge a high price, you each earn profits of $3. If you charge different prices, the one charging the higher price loses $5 and the one charging the lower price makes $5.
    a. Find the equilibrium when there are no repeated transactions.
    b. Now suppose there are repeated transactions. How would that change the results?
15. The South American cocaine industry consists of several "families" that obtain the raw material, refine it, and then ship it to the United States. It is not a difficult business to enter, particularly on the retail end where drug dealers sell the drug to consumers in the United States. What would you predict would happen to the economic profits of the drug dealer? Suppose the families in South America form a cartel. What is the result of the cartel?

STUDY GUIDE FOR CHAPTER 6

Key Term Match

Match each term with its correct definition by placing the appropriate letter next to the corresponding number.

A. commodity
B. perfect competition
C. differentiated
D. monopolistic competition
E. monopoly
F. price takers
G. collusion
H. cartel
I. cost-plus or markup pricing
J. sunk cost
K. economies of scale
L. diseconomies of scale
M. creative destruction
N. facilitating practices
O. most-favored customer (MFC)
P. game theory
Q. Nash equilibria
R. convention
S. dominant strategy

___ 1. a market structure characterized by a large number of firms, easy entry, and differentiated products

___ 2. a good, service, or firm that consumers believe to be somewhat unique

___ 3. a description of oligopolistic behavior as a series of strategic moves and countermoves

___ 4. a market structure characterized by such a large number of firms that no one firm has an effect on the market

___ 5. old, inefficient activities driven out of business by competition

___ 6. no player can be made better off by changing unilaterally

___ 7. cost that cannot be recouped

___ 8. a market structure in which there is just one firm, and entry by other firms is not possible

___ 9. the decreases in per-unit costs when all resources are increased

___ 10. an institution procedure increasing efficiency

___ 11. the increases in per-unit costs when all resources are increased

___ 12. goods perceived to be identical no matter who supplies them

___ 13. an organization of independent producers that dictates the quantities produced by each member of the organization

___ 14. actions that lead to cooperation among rivals

___ 15. a strategy that produces better results no matter what strategy the opposing firm follows

___ 16. a price set by adding an amount to the per-unit cost of producing and supplying a good or service

___ 17. a commitment that the customer will receive a lower price if anyone else receives a lower price

___ 18. rivals agree not to compete with each other

___ 19. a firm in a perfectly competitive market structure

Quick-Check Quiz

1. Which of the following market characteristics are *not* used to define market structures?
   - ☐ a. the number of firms in the market
   - ☐ b. the ease of entry into the market by new competitors
   - ☐ c. the percentage of the firm's income that is paid in taxes
   - ☐ d. the type of product produced (identical or differentiated)
   - ☐ e. all of the above characteristics are used to define market structures

2. Regardless of market structure, a firm maximizes its profits by producing the quantity of output at which
   - ☐ a. $P = MR$.
   - ☐ b. $P = MC$.
   - ☐ c. $MR = MC$.
   - ☐ d. $MC = D$.
   - ☐ e. $D = MR$.

3. When the owner of a firm is getting zero economic profit,
   - ☐ a. the owner should exit that market in the short run.
   - ☐ b. the owner should exit that market in the long run.
   - ☐ c. the owner cannot make any more money by exiting the market and doing something else with her resources.
   - ☐ d. the owner is not receiving any income from owning the firm.
   - ☐ e. the owner is getting rich.

4. In which market structures do firms receive just a normal profit in the long run?
   - ☐ a. monopoly and perfect competition
   - ☐ b. monopolistic competition and perfect competition
   - ☐ c. monopoly and monopolistic competition
   - ☐ d. monopoly and oligopoly
   - ☐ e. monopolistic competition and oligopoly

5. What is the most important determinant of whether or not firms receive economic profits in the long run?
   - ☐ a. how easy it is for new firms to enter the market
   - ☐ b. the size of the firms in a market
   - ☐ c. the size of the market overall
   - ☐ d. the amount of taxes firm owners pay
   - ☐ e. the amount of taxes the firm's customers pay

6. Collusion refers to a situation where
   - ☐ a. rivals agree to lower prices as much as possible.
   - ☐ b. rivals refuse to deal with each other.
   - ☐ c. rivals agree not to reduce prices.
   - ☐ d. rivals form an organization to help with advertising.
   - ☐ e. rivals merge to become one big firm.

7. In game theory, a strategy that produces the best results no matter what strategy the opposing player follows is called
   - ☐ a. a dominant strategy
   - ☐ b. a Nash equilibrium
   - ☐ c. a paramount strategy.

☐ d. a facilitating practice.
☐ e. a prisoners' dilemma.

8. Entry by new firms drives
☐ a. profits to their maximum.
☐ b. normal profits to zero.
☐ c. profits to their minimum.
☐ d. economic profits to their maximum.
☐ e. economic profits to zero.

9. If there are economies of scale, then
☐ a. a larger firm can produce a product at a lower cost than a small firm can.
☐ b. a larger firm can produce a product at a higher cost than a small firm can.
☐ c. a larger firm can produce a product at the same cost that a small firm can.
☐ d. small firms make more profits than large firms.
☐ e. small firms make the same profits as large firms.

Practice Questions and Problems

1. ______________ competition is the market structure in which ______________ (many, few, one) firms are producing a(n) ______________ (identical, differentiated) product, and entry is ______________ (easy, difficult, impossible).
2. ______________ competition is the market structure in which ______________ (many, few, one) firms are producing ______________ a(n) (identical, differentiated) product, and entry is ______________ (easy, difficult, impossible).
3. Which type of market is also called a commodity market? ______________
4. In the short run, new firms ______________ (do, do not) have time to enter a market. In the long run, new firms (do, do not) have time to enter a market.
5. The existing firms in a perfectly competitive market are currently receiving economic profits. In the long run, firms will ______________ (enter, exit) the market, driving the market price ______________ (up, down) and economic profits (up, down). This will continue until firms are receiving ______________ profits.
6. The existing firms in a perfectly competitive market are currently receiving economic losses. In the long run, firms will ______________ (enter, exit) the market, driving the market price ______________ (up, down) and economic profits ______________ (up, down). This will continue until firms are receiving ______________ profits.
7. In monopolistic competition, firms that earn ______________ (economic profits, economic losses, normal profits) in the long run will not remain in business.
8. If entry into a market is restricted, consumer surplus will become ______________ (larger, smaller) than if entry is not restricted.
9. The following graph shows a market with free entry, with price and quantity determined by the point where demand and supply cross. Mark the area of consumer surplus with horizontal lines.

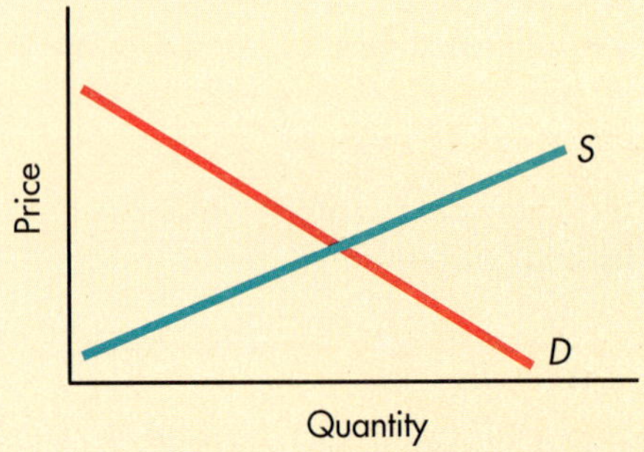

10. A firm will have a ______________ (lower, higher) price elasticity of demand if customers believe its product is better than its competitors' products than it would if customers believe its product is the same as its competitors' products.
11. List two ways that a firm can create barriers to entry.
____
____
12. Aluminum is extracted from a mineral called bauxite. Before World War II, the Aluminum Company of America owned many bauxite deposits and tried to buy new deposits as they were discovered. Use the concepts discussed in this chapter to explain why Alcoa bought all that bauxite.
____
____
____
13. Economies of scale exist when average costs ______________ (increase, decrease, remain the same) as the size of the firm increases.
14. Diseconomies of scale exist when average costs ______________ (increase, decrease, remain the same) as the size of the firm increases.
15. Explain why economies of scale can be a barrier to entry.

Exercises and Applications

I Is Advertising Profitable?

Joe's Gourmet Hamburgers is thinking about using advertising to differentiate its burgers from all the other burgers in town. An advertising agency has developed a campaign that will add $5 per hour to Joe's costs. The agency also estimated the increases in demand it expects Joe's Gourmet Hamburgers to get from the campaign.

1. The following table shows Joe's Gourmet Hamburgers' current demand and costs.

Quantity Sold/Hour	*ATC*	*MC*	*P*	*MR*
1	$26.50	$12.50	$12.00	$12.00
2	16.25	6.00	11.00	10.00
3	11.50	2.00	10.00	8.00
4	9.25	2.50	9.00	6.00
5	8.00	3.00	8.00	4.00
6	7.25	3.50	7.00	2.00
7	6.79	4.00	6.00	0
8	6.50	4.50	5.00	2.00

a. Joe's current profit-maximizing quantity is ____________ hamburgers.

b. His current profit-maximizing price is ____________.

c. At this quantity and price, Joe's economic profit would be ____________.

2. The following table shows the agency's estimates of Joe's demand and costs after the advertising campaign.

Quantity Sold/Hour	*ATC*	*MC*	*P*	*MR*
1	$31.50	$12.50	$15.00	$15.00
2	18.75	6.00	13.75	12.50
3	13.17	2.00	12.50	10.00
4	10.50	2.50	11.25	7.50
5	9.00	3.00	10.00	5.00
6	8.08	3.50	8.75	2.50
7	7.50	4.00	7.50	0
8	7.13	4.50	6.25	2.50

a. Joe's profit-maximizing quantity here is ____________ hamburgers.

b. His profit-maximizing price is ____________.

c. At this quantity and price, Joe's economic profit would be ____________.

II. Away With the Old! In with the New!

Apple caused quite a stir when the company stopped putting floppy disk drives on its computers. Many consumers were angry that they could not retrieve information stored on their floppy disks. The company defended this move by saying that floppy disks were becoming obsolete, and that consumers would abandon floppy disks for flash drives, which were smaller and could hold more information.

a. The process by which older, less efficient technologies, like floppy disks, are replaced by newer, more efficient technologies, like flash drives, is called ____________.

b. What are other recent examples of creative destruction? (Hint: Try an Internet search for obsolete products that are still manufactured to get ideas.)

III. The Stability of Cartels

Cartels usually break up because members have an incentive to cheat. If members can cheat without being detected, they are more likely to do so and the cartel will eventually break up. If it is easy for members of the cartel to monitor each other's behavior to prevent cheating, the cartel will last longer. Use your intuition to choose the conditions that make cartels **more** stable:

a. Few firms versus many firms in the industry

b. Homogeneous versus heterogeneous products

c. Similar cost structures versus different cost structures

7 Business, Society, and the Government

FUNDAMENTAL QUESTIONS

1. What are the benefits from free markets?
2. Why don't people like market allocation?
3. What is antitrust policy?
4. What is the purpose of regulation?
5. What is "too big to fail"?
6. What are market failures?
7. How might market failures be corrected?
8. What are government failures?

PREVIEW

Before the late 19th century, government comprised a very small percentage of gross domestic product in most Western countries—typically, no more than 5 percent. But with the 20th century came the growth of governments across the Western world, which has continued to the point now where government expenditures are 40 or 50 percent of gross domestic product. Given the benefits of the free market, why has government grown? In this chapter, we provide some answers to that question.

1. THE BENEFITS OF COMPETITION REVIEWED

1

What are the benefits from free markets?

Economists like to illustrate the benefits of competition by comparing the results of a commodity market with the results of a monopoly. As we have seen, when entry can occur, no firm can get away with anything. Any time consumers don't like a product or a service, they can switch to another firm. Any time a firm earns positive economic profit, other firms will copy that firm and eventually drive the price down to its lowest possible level.

A simple way to illustrate the benefits of competition is to look at a demand and supply diagram. The demand for coffee is the sum of all the consumer demands for coffee at all the coffee shops in existence. A demand curve shows the price that buyers are willing and able to pay for each quantity of a good or service. When the market is a commodity market and free entry has driven prices to where they just cover opportunity costs, then consumers have to pay only the equilibrium price and sellers can sell only at the equilibrium price. Notice in Figure 7.1 that although a consumer would be willing and able to pay P_m for a cup of coffee, she only pays the market price, P_{fe}. The triangle ABP_{fe} measures how much savings consumers get by paying the equilibrium price rather than what they would be willing and able to pay. This is called **consumer surplus**.

consumer surplus: the difference between what the consumer is willing to pay for a unit of a good and the price that the consumer actually has to pay; the difference between what consumers would be willing to pay and what they have to pay to purchase some item

What happens to consumer surplus when there is no competition? Without competition, the coffee seller is a monopoly, and a monopoly firm can charge a higher price by selling a lower quantity of output. Notice in Figure 7.2, which is essentially the same as Figure 7.1, that the higher price (P_m) means less is sold (Q_m). This means that consumer surplus is reduced from ABP_{fe} to ACP_m. The consumer surplus, indicated by the rectangle $P_{fe}ECP_m$, is taken from the consumer and collected by the monopoly. The consumer surplus that was indicated by the triangle *CEB* is simply lost, collected by neither the consumers nor the firm. This loss carries the name **deadweight loss**.

deadweight loss: the reduction of consumer surplus without a corresponding increase in monopoly profit when a perfectly competitive firm is monopolized

Deadweight loss is a measure of the benefits society gains from competition that disappear when competition is limited or restricted. The greater the barriers to entry, the more economic profit the firm can earn, the longer the firm can continue to earn positive economic profit, and the fewer the benefits that the consumer gains. It is entry and competition that generate the benefits of the market system. It is restrictions to entry that transfer consumer surplus to producers and create deadweight losses.

FIGURE 7.1 Consumer Surplus

The demand curve shows the quantities that consumers are willing and able to pay for the good or service. The market price, P_{fe}, is determined by rivals competing with each other and the price being bid down until it just matches opportunity costs per unit of output. Although some consumers would be willing and able to purchase some quantities at prices higher than the market price, they don't have to. They only have to pay the market price. Consumers thus get a bonus from competition, the area indicated by the triangle ABP_{fe}. This is consumer surplus.

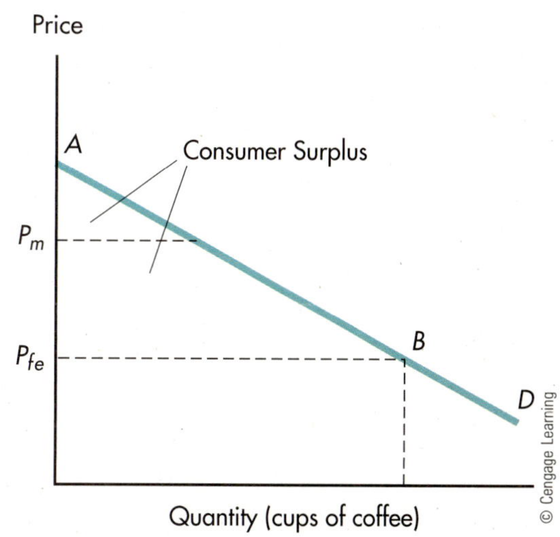

FIGURE 7.2 Monopoly and Consumer Surplus

Without competition, the firm can charge a higher price by reducing the quantity it sells, price P_m and quantity Q_m. The consumer surplus is reduced to the triangle AP_mC. The rectangle $P_mCE P_{fe}$, which was consumer surplus, is now taken by the monopolist. The triangle CEB, which was consumer surplus, is just wasted, going to neither consumer nor seller.

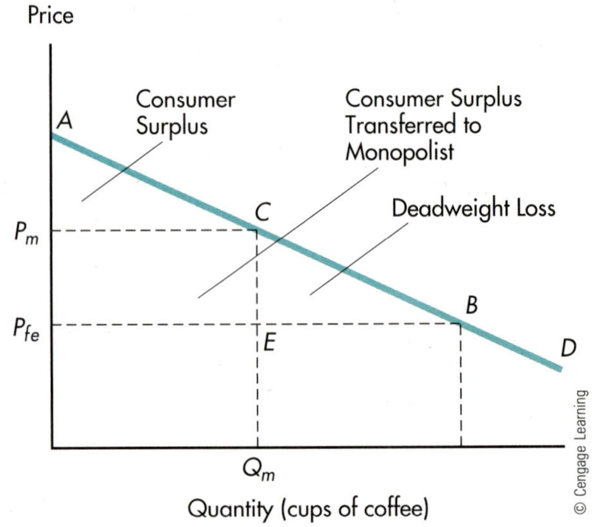

The market system is generally the most efficient allocation mechanism—it best satisfies people's wants and needs and raises their standards of living. Without anyone dictating what buyers and sellers do, the market determines a price for each traded good at which the quantities that people are willing and able to sell are equal to the quantities that people are willing and able to buy. Day in and day out, the market system induces people to employ their talents and resources where they have the highest value. People do not have to be fooled, cajoled, or forced to do their parts in the market system. Instead, they pursue their own self-interests and, in so doing, generate the most good for society.

In Chapter 6, we learned more about how the market system works. Firms acquire resources and then organize and coordinate the resources to create and offer for sale various goods and services. The value that consumers place on these goods and services must be more than the value they place on the individual resources alone or else the firm will cease to exist. When a firm's goods and services have more value than the opportunity cost of the resources used to create and sell the goods and services, then rivals will begin to compete with that firm. In other words, when economic profit is negative, the firm will cease to exist; when economic profit is positive, the sharks will attack. Rivals will enter and compete. People will get the goods and services they want at the lowest possible prices, and resources will be used where their value is highest.

RECAP

1. Consumer surplus is a measure of the benefits consumers get from competition and free entry. It is the difference between the market price and the price consumers would be willing and able to pay for a good or service.
2. Without competition, consumer surplus is reduced because the seller is able to charge a higher price and offer a smaller quantity of a good or service for sale.
3. Deadweight loss is a measure of the benefits that would result from competition and free entry when entry is limited or restricted.

2. GOVERNMENT INVOLVEMENT IN THE MARKET

Governments build highways and provide medical insurance, welfare, border security, schools, and education. Government tells power companies what prices they can charge for electricity and cable suppliers what prices they may charge for cable service; government specifies which radio station broadcasts on which frequency, which airline can fly to which city, and so on. Many goods and services are allocated by a first-come first-served system—for example, medical care, classes at schools, access to highways, airline flights, and tickets to concerts or athletic events. If the market system is such an efficient and beneficial mechanism, why is it not universally relied on? The answer is either that people don't like the results of competition or that the market does not work very well in certain situations.

2 Why don't people like market allocation?

2.a. Disagreement with the Market Outcome

The result of competition is not always happy and cheery—this is why it is called *creative destruction*. Some people are displaced from jobs and others experience a loss of income as their resources become replaced. Those who are willing and able to pay for something get that something while those not willing or not able do without. These facts may cause people to oppose or dislike market allocation, claiming that it is not fair.

The questionnaire in the preview to Chapter 2 gives an indication of the attitudes people have toward market outcomes. In Figure 7.3, the allocation mechanisms *price*, *first-come first-served*, *government*, and *random* are listed across the horizontal axis for two types of goods and services, non-health related and health related. The vertical axis shows the percentage of people responding to the questionnaire in various locations throughout the United States who stated that they agreed with the use of the allocation mechanism in each circumstance. The percentage of people who agree with the market (price) for non-health items is about 50 percent, whereas it is only about 20 percent for the health-related goods and services. The percentage that agree with the

FIGURE 7.3 Agreement with Allocation Mechanisms

The vertical axis shows the percentage of people who agreed with the use of the allocation mechanism in each circumstance. The horizontal axis lists the four allocation mechanisms considered. (Percentages need not equal 100, since someone could choose the same answer for more than one question.)

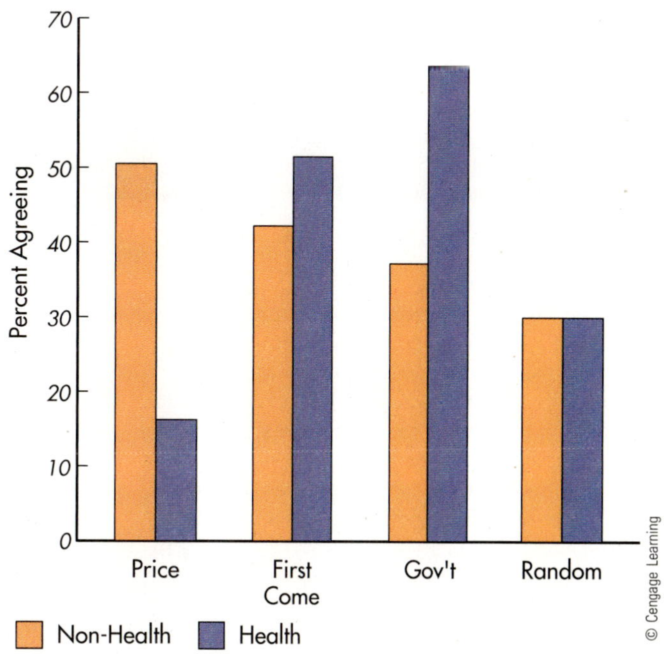

government is about 40 percent for non-health items and nearly 70 percent for health-related items. The percentages agreeing with first-come first-served or with random allocation mechanisms are between the percentages favoring the market or the government.

It is clear that many people do not like the outcome of markets, especially concerning life and death issues. When people do not like an outcome, they may call on the government to change the outcome. Politicians will do what voters elect to have done. So, one reason that the government intervenes in markets or replaces the market entirely and serves as the allocation mechanism is the attitude of the general public about market allocation.

2.b. **Monopolization and Antitrust**

3 What is antitrust policy?

Another reason that government intervenes in the market process is to enhance competition or, as some people say, to create a level playing field. The objective of a business is to earn the largest economic profit possible. The goal of a business is not to benefit society, although free markets and competition result in that. The goal is to earn profit, to restrict competition, limit entry, and charge consumers higher prices. If a firm could monopolize a market and become the only supplier, then it could restrict supply, raise price, and earn more profit.

monopolization of a market: market dominance by one firm gained unfairly

The government attempts to limit business practices that restrict competition by defining certain business practices to be illegal. Antitrust laws are designed to prevent what is called the **monopolization of a market**—the attempt to unfairly restrict or bar entry by rivals. The problem is how to tell if an action unfairly restricts entry. It is straightforward to state that collusion and cartels are illegal. But is an agreement by Apple and book publishers to not sell ebooks below a certain price competitive or anticompetitive? Is a low price competitive or anticompetitive if it drives some firms out of business? Does Walmart use unfair practices to compete against the small mom-and-pop stores in towns where Walmart decides to locate? Is Apple acting unfairly by not making iPods compatible with other MP3 player systems? Is the merger of two big office stores a way for the stores to experience economies of scale and thus be more efficient, or is it a way to dominate the market and behave like a monopolist? These and many other controversial issues often are the central features of lawsuits and antitrust laws. **Antitrust** refers to the laws that restrict "trusts"—large dominant firms—from behaving anticompetitively.

antitrust: laws that restrict large dominant firms from behaving anticompetitively

ECONOMIC INSIGHT

eBay and Online Markets

Internet auctions are attracting increasing numbers of buyers and sellers. The most well-known company in this online market arena is eBay, founded in 1995. On any given day, there are millions of items listed across thousands of categories. Sellers list an item for a small fee, and buyers bid for that item. The auctions typically last three or four days, and at the end of the auction time, the high bidder receives the item. eBay is far from the only company offering online auctions. The biggest growth area for online auctions is that between businesses. Auto companies purchase supplies through online auctions; John Deere and other manufacturers purchase supplies through online auctions. New business-to-business auctions are being created every day. The online auctions focus most attention on price; customers view or read about the product and the product's features and then offer a price. The result is that prices are driven to their lowest possible level—much like the model of perfect competition.

What does the online auction mean for businesses wedded to buildings and face-to-face contact with customers? When Walmart located in a small town, the local businesses were hard-pressed to compete with it. They could not offer the variety or the low prices that Walmart offered. In town after town, local businesses attempted to keep Walmart from entering. Think about what an online auction could do. eBay is a rival to virtually every store in your city or neighborhood, and there is no way to keep eBay from entering.

In the 1960s, computers were sold or leased as complete systems, combinations of central processing units and peripherals—tape drives, disk drives, programs, and other components. A Control Data disk drive did not provide direct competition for an IBM disk drive because the Control Data unit would not work with the IBM central processing unit and software. In the late 1960s, several companies developed tape and disk drives that were compatible with the IBM units. This development allowed the companies to sell the peripherals in direct competition with IBM, forcing IBM to respond to competition on each piece of equipment as well as on the entire system. IBM's ability to control price and output in the peripherals market was reduced, but because the peripheral companies could not produce a compatible central processing unit, IBM retained the ability to control price and output in the systems market. So IBM dropped the price of its peripherals to the point at which the other firms could not compete and retained its higher price on the central processing unit. It was taken to court for its actions. After several years and millions of dollars, IBM won the right to continue its actions. By that time, IBM-compatible peripherals were being manufactured by several companies.

NOW YOU TRY IT

What is the difference between monopoly and monopolization?

There are about 400 long-distance telephone companies operating in the United States today. This was not always the case. Prior to 1984, the long-distance market was controlled by a single firm, AT&T, and that firm was regulated by the government. The government dictated telephone rates and service. In 1984, the government decreed that AT&T had to be broken into what is now AT&T (the long-distance company) and seven local calling companies, known today as The Regional Bell Operating Companies. The long-distance market was deregulated. The government allowed any firm that wanted to offer long distance to enter the market and offer the service. The government gave up trying to dictate rates and service. As a result, hundreds of new companies entered the market, and long-distance prices have declined by about 70 percent.

During the 1980s, 1990s, and early 2000s, Microsoft was under government scrutiny because of the claim that the operating system owned by Microsoft was so dominant that it allowed Microsoft to charge much higher prices than would occur in a competitive market with free entry. During the 1990s, the argument against Microsoft was that the company required computer

GLOBAL BUSINESS INSIGHT

Dumping

Dumping means that a firm sells its products for less than its cost of production or, in other words, sells at a loss. Why would a firm sell at a loss? One reason could be that a firm would sell in one market at a loss so that it could run other firms out of that market and then control the market. Of course, this strategy would be a success only if the firm could keep others from entering that market after it takes control. Thus, dumping is a difficult thing to carry out. What appears to be dumping can often merely be price discrimination. A firm charges a lower price in another country than it does for the same product in its home country. This would be a perfectly logical strategy if the consumers in the home country have a lower price elasticity of demand than consumers in the foreign country. In this case, the firm would increase revenue by setting a higher price in the home country and a lower one in the foreign country. This pricing strategy would be no different than charging senior citizens lower prices for movie tickets than the general population is charged.

This is not to say that there are no legitimate cases of dumping, but many cases involve government subsidies and taxes rather than competition among firms. One case of dumping occurred with sugar produced in the European Union (EU) and sold in China. The EU provides subsidies and protection to sugar producers, who then can sell their sugar at prices that are below production costs. China pointed out that the average production cost of sugar in Guangxi is 2,230 yuan per ton, as compared to 5,623 yuan per ton in the EU. But when the EU provides a subsidy of 4,127 per ton, the EU sugar exporters can sell for as low as 1,429 yuan and as high as 2,230 yuan and drive Chinese sugar producers out of the market. The result of the dumping is that sugar prices in China have dropped by 35 percent, and the amount of sugar produced in China has declined significantly.

manufacturers and retailers to include its Internet browser with each personal computer, thereby precluding other firms such as Netscape from competing in the market. During the 2000s, Microsoft was accused of unfairly bundling or combining its software in an attempt to restrict competition. In 2002, Microsoft agreed to license its technology so that other producers could produce equipment that would seamlessly communicate with Windows. In 2003, several nations undertook antitrust action against Microsoft, and others followed in 2004.

The government also scrutinizes the price strategies of large firms. The government has been involved in several cases of predatory pricing. It is argued that a firm will sell a product below its costs to try to drive another firm out of business for the sole purpose of then raising the price to excessive levels later. Predatory pricing has proven to be a difficult case for the government to win. Not only must the firm sell below its own cost, but it must then create significant barriers to entry if it is to raise its price to "excessive" levels. Without the barriers to entry, once the predatory firm earns positive economic profit, other firms will enter and again compete with the predatory firm.

Price discrimination comes under international scrutiny on a regular basis. The World Trade Organization, the international agency involved in business behavior, has examined many cases in which an industry in one country accuses competitors in another country of dumping. For instance, U.S. industries have filed claims of dumping against South African manufacturers of steel plate; against German, Italian, and French winemakers; against Japanese manufacturers of semiconductors; against Singapore; and against 19 steel-producing nations. Many companies from other countries have accused U.S. firms of dumping.

4

What is the purpose of regulation?

regulation: the control of some aspect of business by the government

natural monopolies: when economies of scale lead to just one firm

2.c. Economic Regulation

Antitrust laws set rules of behavior for large firms. In many industries, the government does more than simply set the rules of behavior. Often it intervenes in the operation of the business, dictating the price that can be charged or the areas that can be or have to be served. In some cases, the government actually pays for and produces the good or service—public education, for instance. These types of intervention are referred to as **regulation**.

The government has regulated some industries because of the argument that the industries are **natural monopolies**. A natural monopoly is one that would arise because the industry consists only of economies of scale. With economies of scale, the largest firm could set a price below which any smaller firm would need to charge to stay in business. The market would have just one firm—a monopoly. For many years following the Industrial Revolution, it was argued that the railroads were natural monopolies. Thus, the government has been involved in the railroad industry for more than 100 years. Electric utilities have been regulated because of the argument that they are natural monopolies, as have airlines. The argument for regulating airlines was to create orderly growth and to avoid a natural monopoly. From the mid-1930s to the mid-1970s, the Civil Aeronautics Authority (CAA) and its successor, the Civil Aeronautics Board (CAB), controlled entry into the airline industry. Each airline was restricted to specific routes. For example, United Airlines was authorized to serve north–south routes on the West Coast, and Delta and Eastern served such routes on the East Coast.

5

What is "too big to fail"?

2.d. Crises: Too Big To Fail

The immediate cause of the 2006–2010 economic crisis was the bursting of the U.S. housing bubble, which peaked in 2006. High default rates on what are called "subprime" loans and adjustable rate mortgages (ARMs) began to increase quickly thereafter. A subprime loan is a loan made to individuals with a high risk of default. An ARM is a loan that has a low initial interest rate, but the interest rate is adjusted every so often, depending on market conditions.

An increase in loan packaging, marketing, and incentives, such as easy initial terms and a long-term trend of rising housing prices, encouraged borrowers to assume difficult mortgages in the belief they would be able to quickly refinance at more favorable terms. However, once interest rates began to rise and housing prices started to drop moderately in 2006 and 2007, borrowers were unable to make their payments. Defaults and foreclosure activity increased dramatically as easy initial terms expired, home prices failed to go up as anticipated, and ARM interest rates reset higher. As housing prices declined, major global financial institutions that had borrowed and invested heavily in mortgage-related assets reported significant losses.

Between 1997 and 2006, the price of the typical American house had increased by 124 percent, a rate significantly higher than at any other time during the previous several decades. But the housing bubble popped, and by September 2008 average U.S. housing prices had declined by over 20 percent from their mid-2006 peak. During 2007, lenders began foreclosure proceedings on nearly 1.3 million properties, a 79 percent increase over 2006. Foreclosures increased to 2.3 million in 2008, an 81 percent increase from 2007. By September 2008, 14.4 percent of all U.S. mortgages outstanding were either delinquent or in foreclosure. Initially the companies most affected were those directly involved in home construction and mortgage lending, such as Northern Rock and Countrywide Financial. But over 100 mortgage lenders went bankrupt during 2007 and 2008.

Then came the "too-big-to-fail" firms. Concerns that investment bank Bear Stearns would collapse in March 2008 resulted in its fire sale to JPMorgan Chase, forced by the Federal Reserve and the Treasury. Several other institutions either were acquired under duress or were subject to government takeover. These included Lehman Brothers, Merrill Lynch, Fannie Mae, Freddie Mac, Washington Mutual, Wachovia, and AIG. The list of bailouts and takeovers is shown in Table 7.1.

The private companies mentioned above were not the only ones in trouble, nor were they the only ones who received bailouts. In September 2008, the

High default rates on subprime loans and ARMs led to the bursting of the U.S. housing bubble, which was the immediate cause of the 2006–2010 economic crisis.

Andy Dean Photography/Shutterstock.com

Table 7.1 Bailouts and Other Expenditures in Reaction to "Too Big To Fail"

American International Group	$182 billion
Asset Guarantee Program*	$12.5 billion
Auto Supplier Support Program	$5 billion
Automotive Industry Financing Program	$80.1 billion
Total Federal Funds	$6.4 trillion

*Asset Guarantee Program comprises Citigroup ($5 billion) and Bank of America ($7.5 billion).

Note: Figures as of November 16, 2009.

Sources: CNN Money.com (http://money.cnn.com/news/storysupplement/economy/bailouttracker/index.html), May 29, 2010, Federal Reserve, Treasury, FDIC, CBO, White House.

government-sponsored mortgage companies Fannie Mae and Freddie Mac were put into conservatorship by the Federal Housing Finance Agency (FHFA). This meant the government would manage the enterprises directly. As of January 2010, the seizure of Fannie Mae and Freddie Mac has cost taxpayers $121 billion.

As a result of the financial crash, the government has taken over several firms, developed regulations for others, and bailed out others, all in the name of "too big to fail." What does too big to fail mean? Typically, the term is used to describe a firm whose failure would cause a major ripple effect throughout the economy, causing other firms to fail and increasing unemployment. Then the argument follows that if such a firm were to be close to failing, the government would have to take it over or bail it out in order to prevent the ripples from becoming tsunamis.

Many people who support the idea of too big to fail think that sheer size alone doesn't mean that a firm is too big to fail. Instead, it is the firm's interconnectedness with the rest of the economy—or what is known as "systemic risk"—that matters. Bear Stearns and Lehman Brothers, it is argued, were comparatively small and raised relatively little concern by themselves, but because of their interconnectedness, their failures shocked the entire financial system. So when other financial firms looked as if they were going to collapse, the government took some over, bailed out others, and allowed a few to enter bankruptcy. Similarly, when General Motors and Chrysler looked like they were ready to collapse, it was argued that the ripple effects would be too large—that the companies were too big to fail—so the government took over General Motors and provided huge loans to Chrysler.

Does the idea of a firm's being too big to fail make sense? Do government bailouts solve potential problems? Many people argue that if firms are too big to fail, then they shouldn't exist. Some argue that firms should be limited in size. Others believe that government intervention is not necessary and leads to further, more problematic issues. The capitalist system works because firms that are not efficient go out of business.

moral hazard: a situation where imperfect information provides an incentive for a consumer or producer to change behavior after agreeing to a specific behavior

One of the problems with the government's bailing out of too-big-to-fail firms is called **moral hazard**. Moral hazard occurs when a participant in an activity agrees to a certain behavior with other participants but then changes behavior to the detriment of the other participants. For instance, suppose you get a good driver discount on your auto insurance and then drive more recklessly. This would be moral hazard behavior. If the government has a too-big-to-fail policy, then it is implicitly guaranteeing the survival of large firms. But, because of the government's implicit guarantee of their survival, firms considered too big to fail have more incentive to undertake high-risk activities. They reason that rewards would benefit the corporation and its shareholders, while catastrophic losses would be borne by taxpayers (i.e., through a government bailout).

RECAP

1. The free market creates benefits for consumers—called consumer surplus. It is the amount that consumers would be willing and able to pay for goods and services less the amount they actually pay.
2. Interference with the free market creates distortions and wastes. This is called deadweight loss.
3. The free market leads to creative destruction. Many people do not like this aspect of free markets and so call on government to minimize the "destructive" part of creative destruction.
4. The government sets rules of business behavior with antitrust laws. It is illegal to form cartels or to collude. Other practices often have to be decided in courts or by the Justice Department or the Federal Trade Commission. The idea of antitrust is that it is an attempt to prevent monopolization of a market.
5. In some cases, the government dictates what price firms can charge, the quantity they have to supply, and other aspects of business. This is called economic regulation.
6. The 2006–2010 financial and housing collapse led to large-scale government takeovers, bailouts, and loans to private businesses.
7. Bailouts create potential moral hazard problems whereby companies considered too big to fail don't attempt to minimize risk and take precautions, like companies without potential bailouts would.

3. MARKET FAILURES

The market may not work efficiently or allocate resources to their highest-valued uses in some circumstances. For instance, highways become littered with garbage because no one has to pay for littering and no one owns the roads. Roads become congested because no one owns the roads and no one pays to use the highway. Air becomes polluted because no one owns the air and no one pays for emitting pollutants. Animals and plants become endangered because no one owns them. These problems are referred to as market failures. A market failure occurs whenever people don't get what they want and are willing and able to pay for at the lowest possible prices, and resources are not allocated to their highest-valued use.

6

What are market failures?

3.a. Externalities

The decision to purchase an SUV affects others. The emissions for an SUV are larger than those for a small car or a hybrid battery–gasoline car. In addition, if a collision between an SUV and a small car occurs, the inhabitants of the SUV are much less likely to be injured. Yet the effects on pollution or the environment created by those emissions that affect everyone are not the responsibility of the SUV owners. The SUV owners don't have to compensate the small car owners for putting their lives at risk nor pay for the additional pollution. The problem is that people who are not voluntarily part of the transaction to purchase the SUV have to bear these costs—you or me or anyone who does not own an SUV.

externalities: a cost or benefit created by a transaction that is not paid for or enjoyed by those carrying out the transaction

Because the people who are not part of the decision to purchase and drive the SUV must bear the costs of that transaction, these costs are called **externalities**. The problem created by externalities is that the price of the private transaction does not reflect all the costs of the items involved in that transaction. If it did, the price of SUVs would be higher and fewer would be purchased. This means that *too many* SUVs are driven and *too much* pollution created. "Too many" and "too much" refer to the quantities that would occur if there were no external costs. So, the market is not working to allocate resources to their highest-valued uses. Too many are being used in creating and selling SUVs and too few in other activities.

The market for SUVs is illustrated in Figure 7.4. The demand for SUVs is D, and the supply is S_p. The "p" represents the private costs to the owner. This does not include the costs created by the SUV in terms of risk to smaller vehicles or increased emissions. The equilibrium quantity and price are depicted as Q_p and P_p. If the external costs were included in the cost of supplying the SUV, then the supply would be S_s. As a result, the quantity purchased would be less (Q_s rather than Q_p) and the price would be higher (P_s rather than P_p).

McDonald's sells its drinks in plastic or Styrofoam cups. Customers discard the cups, often simply throwing them out of the car window. Neither McDonald's nor the customers pay for cleaning up the trash. Society as a whole has to pay the costs of cleaning up the trash; those who threw the trash out the window and the McDonald's restaurant that put the food and drinks in the containers pay no more than anyone else.

Externalities can be positive or negative. If they are negative, they impose costs on others; if they are positive, they grant benefits to others. There are 1.5 million cars stolen in the United States each year. An antitheft device called LoJack was first introduced in Boston in 1986 and is now available in most major metropolitan areas. Usually sold to new car purchasers by car dealers for a one-time fee of about $600, the LoJack system involves a small radio transmitter that is hidden in the car. If the car is reported stolen, the police activate the transmitter by remote control with high-tech equipment provided by the company. About 95 percent of stolen vehicles equipped with LoJack are recovered. By leading police directly to stolen cars, LoJack helps them to shut down "chop shops" that dismantle vehicles for resale of parts. Professional car thieves have no way of knowing whether a car is armed with LoJack. As a result, it is estimated that one auto theft is eliminated annually for every three LoJack systems that are installed. Thus, the benefit to society in terms of less overall auto theft—benefits such as lower insurance costs—exceeds the benefit to the individual owners who install the LoJack system. Society benefits by the sum of the benefits each owner who installs a LoJack system receives and the reduced insurance costs everyone receives.

FIGURE 7.4 Negative Externality

The demand for SUVs is D, and the supply is S_p. The externality represents higher costs than are reflected in the supply. If the externality was internalized, then the supply would be S_s, price would be higher (P_s rather than P_p), and the quantity sold smaller (Q_s rather than Q_p).

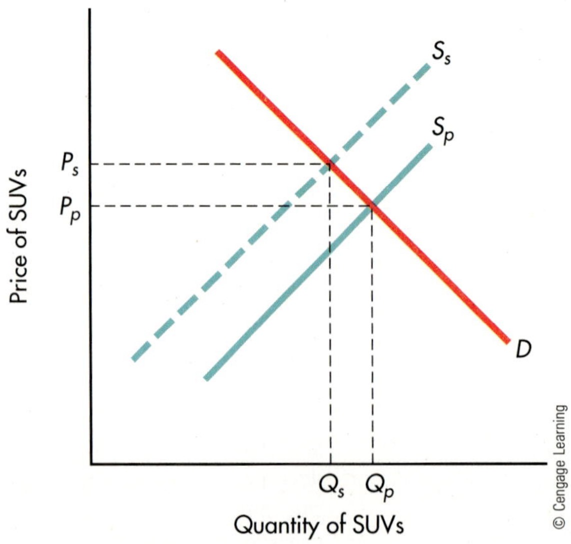

Another positive externality is created by vaccination programs, such as those for the flu. It takes time to get a shot. It often costs and often hurts, so many people choose not to get the vaccine. As long as many other people get the vaccine, then someone who doesn't is less likely to come down with the flu. Those who do not get the vaccine benefit from those who do get the vaccination.

Externalities refer to situations in which not all costs or benefits are included in a transaction. In other words, people not involved in a transaction receive a benefit or a cost from the transaction. If not all costs and benefits are included in a transaction, then resources may not be allocated to their highest-valued uses. In the case of a negative externality, more resources go into the activity than if the external cost was accounted for. For instance, more Styrofoam cups are produced and sold than if McDonald's and/or customers had to pay the additional cost of cleanup for the discarded cups. In the case of a positive externality, not enough resources go into the activity. For instance, if all of the benefits of the LoJack system were provided only to the individual buyers, the buyers would receive a lower price and more LoJack systems would be installed.

Some activities have both positive and negative externalities. Smoking is claimed to be one such activity. Secondhand cigarette smoke is an irritant and bothers some people a great deal—a negative externality. The American Lung Association says that the average smoker dies seven years earlier than the average nonsmoker. This might be viewed as a positive externality in that these people won't live long enough to enjoy social security or receive society-provided health care. Nonsmokers get to share the funds left by smokers.

Every activity has associated positive and/or negative externalities. A simple action such as purchasing milk at a grocery store has many externalities associated with it. By standing in the grocery line, you impose costs on others who have to wait for you to make your transaction. Also, by purchasing the milk you are expressing to the store your desire for the store to carry that brand of milk; this benefits others who also want to have the milk available. Every innovation and invention creates jobs and new industries. These are positive externalities. At the same time, the innovation and invention replace now obsolete jobs and industries, thereby driving them out of business. These are negative externalities.

Are all of these externalities distortions of the market—that is, inefficient uses of resources? If you love gardening and thus create a beautifully landscaped front lawn that provides benefits to people just passing by, will you stop doing the gardening because the people passing by don't pay you for the benefits they receive? Although a positive externality is created, it is not sufficient to alter the amount of gardening that occurs.

private property rights: the right to claim ownership of an item

internalized: a situation when what was an external cost is paid for by the parties creating the cost

Nobel Laureate Ronald Coase did not necessarily see externalities as market failures. He saw the problem as one of **private property rights** (ownership). If private property rights are well defined, then the externality often can be resolved through private negotiation. Consider how Coase might describe the following situation. One neighbor, Bob, liked to play his music late into the night. Another neighbor, Rosa, was an early-to-bed, early-to-rise person. The music was an externality to Rosa. If Bob owned the right to play the music, Rosa would have to work something out, perhaps by improving soundproofing in her house or paying Bob not to play the music. If Rosa owned the right to quiet, then Bob would have to play the music less loudly or pay Rosa to allow him to play it loudly. In either case, once someone has the property right, the externality is solved; it is said to have been **internalized**.

3.b. Common Ownership

Common ownership is another case where the market is not able to efficiently allocate goods and services, as illustrated in this simple story about four people named Everybody, Somebody, Anybody, and Nobody. There was an important job to be done, and Everybody was sure that Somebody would do it. Anybody could have done it, but Nobody did it. Somebody got angry about that because it was Everybody's job. Everybody thought Anybody could do it. But Nobody realized that Everybody wouldn't do it. The end result was that Everybody blamed Somebody when Nobody did what Anybody could have. When nobody owns something, nobody takes care of it. When somebody owns something, somebody takes care of it. When everybody owns something, nobody takes care of it.

Chickens and cows are not on the endangered-species list, but elephants and rhinos are. Why? No one owns the elephants and rhinos. The result is that they are *overutilized*—they are becoming extinct. In most nations with elephants, large national parks have been created in which hunting is forbidden. But even in the face of these bans on hunting, the reduction in the number of elephants has continued in most of the African nations. Government allocation of resources by creating common ownership does not solve the problems of common ownership. In contrast to the common ownership strategy, the governments of Botswana, Zimbabwe, and South Africa created private property rights by allowing individuals to own elephants. These elephant farmers ensure that the elephants breed and reproduce so that they can be sold for their tusks, for hunting in special hunting parks, or to zoos in developed nations. This has led to a revival of the elephant population in these nations.

Common ownership or lack of private property rights means the market cannot work. If you don't own something, you can't sell or trade it. The creation of private property rights creates the ownership necessary for markets to function.

3.c. Some Goods Don't Fit the Market: Public Goods

public goods:
a good that is not excludable and is not rivalrous

free rider:
a consumer or producer who enjoys a good or service without paying for it

If something is available for you to use and you don't have to pay for it, why would you pay? That's the problem with what economists call **public goods**: People can get these goods without paying for them. When goods are public, an individual has an incentive to be a **free rider**—a consumer or producer who enjoys the benefits of a good or service without paying for that good or service. As an example, suppose that national defense was not provided by the government and paid for with tax money; instead, you would not be protected by the armed forces unless you paid a fee. A problem would arise because national defense is a public good; you would be protected whether or not you paid for it as long as others paid. Of course, because each person has an incentive not to pay for it, few will voluntarily do so, and so the good may not be provided, or, if it is provided, the quantity produced will be "too small" from society's viewpoint—that is, from what would have occurred had private property rights been well defined.

Public goods have two properties that provide problems for markets. The first property is called *nonrivalry* in consumption; the second is called *nonexcludability*. An example of a nonexcludable public good is national defense—if one person in an area receives it, all do. Television broadcasts are an example of a nonrivalrous good. When one person views a television show, the signal to others does not diminish.

Since one person's purchases are automatically available to all (in the nonexcludable case), there is a temptation to *free-ride* on others' contributions. If free-riding is extensive, no one has an incentive to offer a good for sale. This may explain why national defense is a function for government. If the government did not provide it, no one would.

3.d. What We Don't Know Can Hurt Us: Asymmetric Information

Imagine you see a car with a "for sale" sign on the corner. You contact the owner, ask about the car, drive it, and decide to purchase it. A month later the car fails to work, and you find out it is not repairable. You have been taken.

Because of such a risk, if you ever purchase a used car, you won't pay much for it. In general, because people don't know much about the used cars offered by private individuals, those cars command very low prices. This means that anyone wanting to sell a used car in premium condition is not going to get what the car is really worth. High-quality used cars are traded in or transferred among friends and family. As a result, the only used cars in the market are *lemons*.

adverse selection: a situation where a lack of information causes low-quality items to dominate a market and high-quality items to be driven out of the market

This is called an **adverse selection** problem—bad quality drives good quality out of the market. Adverse selection arises because buyers and sellers possess different information—what is called asymmetrical information. When asymmetrical information exists, the market may not efficiently allocate goods and services to their highest valued use.

Another example of asymmetrical information often suggested exists in lending markets. Lending institutions do not know whether a potential borrower is a good risk or not. So to be sure to cover risks and expenses, the lender increases the interest rate on the loans provided. As the interest rate is increased, low-risk borrowers drop out of the market. It is the high-risk borrowers who remain in the market. The lender is in a quandary; if the interest rate is lowered, all borrowers—low and high risk—seek loans. If the lender increases the interest rate, low-risk borrowers drop out of the market, leaving just the high-risk borrowers.

Both moral hazard and adverse selection occur because of asymmetric information. Remember the moral hazard problem? Suppose you purchase a new car; you drive safely until you get insurance. Once you have insurance, you drive recklessly because if anything happens, your new car is covered. This change in your behavior is called moral hazard. If the insurance company has no information about your driving behavior after selling insurance to you, the company is unable to charge you what would be commensurate with your riskier behavior.

Asymmetric information can create problems for markets. If the bank cannot know whether people applying for a loan are high or low risk, it may not find it worthwhile to provide loans. If the company cannot judge whether you will change behavior in an adverse way once you get the insurance, it may not offer insurance.

Buying a used car from an individual is a case of asymmetric information, because the buyer does not know much about the car being offered for sale.

JGI/Jamie Grill/Jupiter Images

7

How might market failures be corrected?

3.e. Market Problems and the Government

Private property rights are necessary for a market to exist and work. When private property rights are not defined or are ambiguous, goods and services may not be allocated to where they have the highest value. In such situations, there are incentives for a solution to be devised.

Private negotiation between affected parties could solve or internalize an externality problem. Private property rights would have to be well defined, and negotiation would have to be possible. Similarly, the common ownership problem could be resolved by creating and assigning private property rights. The assignment of rights might not be very easy, however. For instance, it could be difficult to identify the relevant parties, bring them together to negotiate, establish the terms, and then enforce the agreement. With just two parties, Bob and Rosa, there was no problem getting together and discussing the issue. But consider the difficulty of getting every SUV owner to meet and agree on proper ways to solve the problems of pollution and the risk of injury in collisions.

People often call on the government to reduce externality problems. One approach that the government uses is to impose a tax or to provide a subsidy for those creating the externality. Consider the SUVs again. If the government imposed a tax on SUVs, based on the amount of pollution the firm created, buyers would have to consider the extra cost when deciding whether to purchase the vehicle. The tax is a way in which the government can force the polluter to *internalize* the externality—that is, to pay for it rather than have society pay for it. The tax would reduce the quantity of SUVs purchased and internalize the costs of the externalities. In other words, SUV buyers would pay for the increased costs that owning an SUV creates for others.

In the case of a positive externality, the government might provide a subsidy rather than impose a tax. Suppose each person getting an inoculation is given some money. More people would be willing to be inoculated. The subsidy induces buyers to increase the quantities that they are willing and able to buy at each price.

The problem with taxes and subsidies is that those setting the taxes and subsidies (the government, in most cases) must guess at what level the tax or subsidy must be set. A tax that is too high will create an inefficiency of too little production; a tax that is not high enough will do the opposite.

The government could simply outlaw SUVs or, in the case of the positive externality of vaccines, it might mandate that all children under the age of six be inoculated. But the command approach increases costs to society. It leads to too few SUVs or to too many people being inoculated.

In some cases, the government imposes a command and then attempts to create a market to meet that command. For instance, the government defines the quantity of pollutants it will allow in a particular area. Permits that enable the owners of the permits to pollute are then issued. For example, if the target pollution level in the Los Angeles basin is 400 billion pounds of particulates per day, the government could issue a total of 400 permits, each permitting the emission of 1 billion pounds of particulates per day. Then the government could sell the permits. Demanders, typically the polluting firms, would purchase the permits, allowing them to pollute up to the amount specified by the permits they own. If a firm purchased 20 permits, it could emit up to 20 billion particulates per day. If that firm implemented a cleaner technology or for some other reason did not use all of its permits, it could sell them to other firms. The resulting price would be an equilibrium—where traders are comparing the cost of purchasing permits to the costs of implementing cleaner technologies.

If the amount of pollution allowed is reduced, then fewer permits are issued. Demanders bid for the now fewer pollution permits, and drive the price of the permits up. As the price rises, some firms will decide not to purchase the permits but instead to purchase new pollution abatement equipment or to reduce the amount of pollutants they produce.

NOW YOU TRY IT

An immunization that prevents cancer is now available. It protects against human papillomavirus (HPV) infection, which is responsible for virtually all cases of uterine cervical cancer. HPV is the only known virus that is the sole cause of a specific cancer. The Centers for Disease Control and Prevention recommends immunization for all girls 11 to 12 years old, before the age women become sexually active. The vaccine is licensed by the FDA for women and girls ages 9 to 26 and is also recommended by the CDC for women who are already sexually active or who have Pap smear abnormalities. Research continues on the immunization of males. Controversial legislation has been introduced in some states to create a school requirement for inoculation of sixth-grade girls. If it becomes law, can it be explained as a government solution to a market failure problem? Explain.

The higher price gives firms an incentive to adopt more efficient pollution abatement equipment. The permit market may enable outsiders to influence the total amount of pollution created. If anyone can purchase permits, you might purchase permits simply as a way to make money. If you expect the price of the permits to rise in the future, you might purchase the permits now, hoping to sell them later. If the price does rise, the owners of the permits will be able to sell them for a gain. Special interest groups might purchase permits in order to control the quantity of pollution. Environmental groups, such as the Nature Conservancy and the Sierra Club, have purchased permits and taken them out of circulation. In this way, they reduce the total number of permits in circulation and thus reduce the total amount of pollution permitted.

social regulation: government regulation of health, safety, the environment, and employment policies

3.e.1. **Social Regulation** Although economists debate the costs and benefits of regulation, the amount of regulation has grown steadily since the Great Depression. Most of this growth has been due to what is called **social regulation**, rather than economic regulation. Social regulation is concerned with the conditions under which goods and services are produced and the impact of these goods on the public. The following government agencies are concerned with social regulation:

- **The Occupational Safety and Health Administration** (OSHA), which protects workers against injuries and illnesses associated with their jobs.
- **The Consumer Product Safety Commission** (CPSC), which specifies minimum standards for the safety of products.
- **The Food and Drug Administration** (FDA), which oversees the safety and effectiveness of food, drugs, and cosmetics.
- **The Equal Employment Opportunity Commission** (EEOC), which focuses on the hiring, promotion, and discharge of workers.
- **The Environmental Protection Agency** (EPA), which controls air, water, and noise pollution.

The government has become increasingly involved with health and safety in the workplace, the human resource policies of business (e.g., compensation, pensions, harassment, evaluation, stress, and so on), and the environmental consequences of business activities.

Most of the arguments made in support of social regulation are based on the idea that the regulation will aid the public. Over 10,000 workers die in job-related accidents in the United States each year. Air pollution is a problem in many cities, leading to cancer and other diseases, which in turn means increased demands on health care agencies. Hundreds of children are killed each year as a result of poorly designed toys. Unfair discharges from jobs, discrimination, and sexual harassment occur. Many people argue that without government regulation, these events would be much more serious and would impose tremendous costs on society.

There are costs to the regulation, however. It is expensive to administer the agencies and enforce the rules and regulations. The annual administrative costs of federal regulatory activities exceed $15 billion. The costs to businesses of complying with the rules and regulations have been estimated to exceed $300 billion per year. Complying with environmental regulations alone costs businesses more than $200 billion per year.

Added to the direct costs of regulations are the opportunity costs. For instance, the lengthy process for approving new biotechnology has stymied advances in agriculture. Regulatory restrictions on the telecommunications industry have resulted in the fact that the United States lagged behind Japan in the development of fiber optics and high-definition television. The total cost imposed on the U.S. economy from federal government regulations is estimated to be more than $600 billion a year, or $6,000 per household.

Are the regulations worth the costs? To answer this question, we need to compare the costs and benefits of each regulation. But this can be a difficult proposition. It may require us to answer this question: How much is a life worth? Simply asking the question offends many people. But answering the question is what economists think is necessary if regulation is to benefit not only special interest groups. To economists, life is worth what people are willing to pay to stay alive. Of course, that differs from person to person, but the values could be used to place limits on what regulations to implement. For instance, by using the extra pay that people require to take dangerous jobs or by calculating the total value of expenditures on smoke detectors and safer cars, estimates of how much people value life could be made. Although the estimates vary widely, none exceed $10 million. Some economists thus argue that any regulation costing more than $10 million per life saved should not be implemented. For instance, rules on unvented space heaters save lives for just $130,000 each, whereas regulations on asbestos removal exceed $100 million per life saved. According to a comparison of costs and benefits, the first rule should be implemented, but the second should not.

NOW YOU TRY IT

Which of the following regulations would be implemented based on a cost-benefit calculation?

Grain dust	saves 4 lives per year at a cost of $5.3 million per life
Copper smelters	save .06 life per year at a cost of $26 million per life saved
Formaldehyde	saves .01 life per year at a cost of $72 billion per life saved

The cost-benefit test for regulation would limit regulations designed to benefit a very few at the cost of many. However, the cost-benefit test also should include the opportunity costs implied by interfering with the free market, according to many economists. If seatbelts and antilock braking systems are desired by the public, won't the public voluntarily pay the price to have these safety systems? Why, then, is regulation necessary unless it is to benefit some special interest group?

8

What are government failures?

3.e.2. **Is Government Necessary?** When so-called market failures exist, is it necessary to have the government serve as the allocating mechanism? Private actions can resolve market failure problems in many cases. Building large stadiums around baseball or football fields restricts the viewing of the games from outside the stadiums—you have to purchase a ticket to see the contest. Without the stadiums, the games would be available for anyone to watch—for free—and no one would pay to watch.

Asymmetric information issues may also be resolved by the proper definition of private property rights. Adverse selection and moral hazard problems are primarily problems of ambiguous ownership of property rights. Who owns the information that is necessary, and how is that information to be provided in the market? When moral hazard or adverse selection exists, there may be an opportunity for someone to profit from providing information. CARFAX provides the history of a car for a fee. Equifax and other credit agencies provide individual credit histories for a fee. These firms illustrate that the market can often solve what is called a market failure problem. When the missing information can be privately provided, the market failure problem disappears.

Sometimes a moral hazard problem can be reduced by having the person or firm creating the hazard and the person or firm being taken advantage of share in the costs. This is one reason insurance companies require a deductible and banks and other lending institutions require a down payment—so that the company and the customer share in the expenses and risks. You are more likely to drive carefully and safeguard your health if you have to pay some of the costs of an accident or illness. Similarly, if you must pay a copayment, you are less likely to behave in a way that causes you to bear a large number of such copayments.

Although turning to the government to solve market problems might make sense theoretically, it can have practical problems. We have discussed several possible types of market failure. For each, there are usually two types of solutions.

In one, the government is only minimally involved. In the other, the government does everything. For instance, if the government can assign private property rights to an externality problem, the problem can be solved privately. But if private property rights cannot be assigned, then the government may have to command businesses and individuals to behave in specific ways. Similarly, a public good might be provided privately and financed by government, or the government might have to provide it and pay for it.

Because the government is so involved in these market failure issues, we have to evaluate how efficiently the government can do the job. Whereas it is one thing to argue that a market failure cannot be resolved privately, it is quite another to argue that the inefficiency created by the failure is worse than the inefficiency of having the government try to solve the problem. At least, this is what James Buchanan, who received the 1986 Nobel Prize in economics, argues.

Inefficiencies with government allocation often arise not because legislators are incompetent or ignorant, but because of problems with individual incentives. Consider, for instance, a senator from Arizona who wants to reduce government spending, so he votes "no" on all spending bills. The result is that Arizona residents do not get federal government money to build highways and bridges, while the residents of those states with senators who aren't as conscientious as the Arizona senator receive federal government dollars for their bridges and roads.

The behavior of the senators is similar to the situation facing a group of diners who are going to split the bill for dinner equally. Herb and nine friends are having dinner at Chimichangas in Phoenix. To simplify the task of paying for their meal, they have agreed in advance to split the cost of their meal equally, with each paying one-tenth of the total check. Herb recognizes that if he orders more expensive items than the others, he will be gaining at the expense of his nine friends. So he orders appetizers, the most expensive entree, and the most exorbitant dessert and drinks. The problem is that each of his nine friends recognizes the same thing. Each orders far more than he would if he were dining alone. As a result, the total bill rises.

Legislators will support one another's special or so-called pork-barrel programs, causing total government spending to rise significantly. Consider a voter in a congressional district that contains one one-hundredth of the country's taxpayers. Suppose that district's representative is able to deliver a public project that generates benefits of $100 million for the district, but costs the government $150 million. Because the district's share of the tax bill for the project will be only a fraction of the total cost of the project, residents of the district are millions of dollars better off with the project than without it. And that explains why so many voters favor legislators who have a successful record of "bringing home the bacon."

Why would legislator A support such a project in legislator B's home district? After all, B's project will cause A's constituents' taxes to rise by a small amount, while they get absolutely no benefit. The answer is that if A does not support B's project, then B will not support A's. The practice of legislators supporting one another's projects is called **logrolling**.

logrolling:
legislators support one another's projects in order to ensure support for their own

A primary cause of inefficiency in government is that the gains from government projects are often concentrated in the hands of a few beneficiaries, while the costs are spread among many. This means that the beneficiaries have an incentive to organize and lobby in favor of their projects. For example, in the 1990s, the Cosmetology Association in many states lobbied the state legislators to require more stringent licensing requirements for manicurists. The reason for the lobbying was the number of new spas and salons that were being established by immigrants. These spas were driving prices down; some of them were offering manicures for $10 rather than the $25 charged at the established spas. If manicurists were required to go to school for six months, the number of new spas that would open for business would decline, and prices at established spas could be upheld. The laws benefited the existing cosmetologists at the expense of new upstart manicurists. Although the Cosmetology Association was willing to devote resources to its lobbying effort, no group opposed the legislation.

Who gains with government intervention, and who loses? There is a debate among economists over this issue. On one side, it is argued that without the government's monitoring and limiting of the behavior of large firms, markets would be dominated by one or a few firms, and consumer surplus would be minimal. On the other side, it is argued that the government intervenes not to improve efficiency but to provide benefits to special interest groups. Opponents of regulation argue that the natural monopoly and chaos arguments are not valid. They point out that most government regulation has been undertaken to protect special interests—the railroad barons, for example. When trucking became a direct competitor to the railroad, the government placed the trucking industry under regulation. Trucking was regulated not because it was a natural monopoly but because years of regulation had put railroads at a disadvantage relative to trucking.

Every transaction creates externalities. Which does the government choose to regulate? Many argue that the answer depends on who has most effectively lobbied the government. In 2010, an oil derrick 50 miles out to sea blew up, and the oil well associated with the derrick, more than a mile below the surface, started pumping millions of barrels of oil into the Gulf of Mexico. It is the worst oil disaster in history. British Petroleum (BP) owned the well and was responsible for stopping the gushing oil and for cleaning up the disaster afterward. The U.S. government was responsible for regulating the drilling and issuing permits. Who was responsible for the externality? Some argue that it was BP because their emergency measures failed to work. Others say it was the Obama administration because it did not regulate the drilling tightly enough. But the primary issue is why the well was drilled five miles out to sea and a mile below the surface, when it would have been a relatively easy and quick fix had the same accident occurred on land. What special interest groups benefited from forcing the drilling so far offshore?

RECAP

1. Often when the outcome of a market exchange is not favorable to specific individuals or groups, these individuals or groups attempt to change the allocation system to something other than the market system.
2. The market may be less efficient than other allocation mechanisms in certain circumstances. These are referred to as market failures.
3. Market failures include externalities, public goods, and asymmetric information. In these cases, the ownership or private property rights are not well defined.
4. When private transactions create costs or benefits that are not borne by the participants in that transaction, an externality occurs. Externalities may be negative or positive.
5. When something is not owned, it is called a common or public good. Public goods have two properties that provide problems for markets. The first property is called nonrivalry in consumption; the second is called nonexcludability.
6. When buyers and sellers have different amounts of knowledge about their private transactions, there is an asymmetric information problem. Adverse selection occurs when the asymmetric information forces the high-quality good or service out of the market. Moral hazard occurs when behavior is changed once an agreement has been made relying on pre-agreement behavior.
7. Market failures mean that either too many or too few resources are allocated to goods and services; resources are not allocated to their highest-valued uses.

8. When individuals or groups do not like market outcomes and/or when market outcomes are not efficient, a government allocation is instituted.
9. Having the government resolve market failure problems may impose greater costs on society than if the government did not try to resolve the problems, owing to government inefficiency.
10. Government inefficiencies result from the legislative process, from the incentives of politicians, and from benefits being allocated to special interests.
11. Which is worse, market failure or government failure? Some support government solutions and others market solutions.
12. The type of solution to implement or whether to implement an intervention in the market depends on a cost-benefit calculation.

SUMMARY

What are the benefits from free markets?

1. The market allocates resources to their highest-valued use. In the market, those willing and able to pay for a good or service get the good or service; those not willing or not able are left without.

Why don't people like market allocation?

2. Creative destruction means some people and some resources get displaced, thrown out of jobs, or left out of activities.
3. The market may fail to allocate resources to their highest-value use in certain circumstances.

What is antitrust policy?

4. A monopoly charges a higher price and sells a lower quantity than a market with competition and free entry. This allows the monopolist to earn a positive economic profit.
5. Antitrust policy is the attempt by government to restrict firms from monopolizing a market.
6. Antitrust law is the government's attempt to minimize the negative impacts of cartels, collusion, and other unfair business practices on society. Cartels and collusion are illegal. Other practices are scrutinized by the Justice Department and Federal Trade Commission and are the subject of lawsuits.

What is the purpose of regulation?

7. The purpose of regulation is to limit the power of natural monopolies.

What is "too big to fail"?

8. By "too big to fail," people mean that should a firm collapse, it will affect the entire economy or global economy.
9. Government policy to protect those considered too big to fail leads to moral hazard and other problems.

What are market failures?

10. A market failure occurs when the market does not allocate resources to their highest-valued use.
11. An externality occurs when some costs or benefits created by a private transaction are not accounted for in the private transaction.

12. A public good is a good or service that is not excludable and is not rivalrous. Common ownership means anyone can have access to the item commonly owned. As a result, no one has an incentive to pay for it or to take care of it.
13. Asymmetric information means that buyers and sellers have different amounts of information about a private transaction. This can lead to adverse selection, where bad quality drives good quality out of the market. It can also lead to moral hazard, where people change their behavior and behave in a certain way after an agreement has been made.

How might market failures be corrected?

14. One solution to market failure is to clearly define private property rights.
15. One solution to market failure is for the government to intervene with a tax or a subsidy.
16. One solution to market failure is for government to dictate what behavior is allowed.
17. One solution to market failure is for government to define private property rights, specify quantities, and turn allocation over to a market.

What are government failures?

18. Legislators may participate in logrolling in order to get benefits for constituents and get elected. Logrolling is the practice of trading votes—I vote for your bill if you vote for mine.
19. Government decisions may be determined by special interest groups rather than what is best for the economy or society as a whole.

EXERCISES

1. Suppose the Disney Company was experiencing above-normal profits. What would you predict would happen over time?
2. Explain why a proposed merger between Staples and Office Max was not allowed by the Department of Justice.
3. How would you derive the demand for milk at the local grocery store? How would you derive the demand for tuna? How would you derive the demand for national defense?
4. The government is considering the adoption of a higher standard of success in tests for pharmaceuticals that will be sold in the United States. Suppose the benefits of the regulation were 1,000 lives saved per year. Would you support adoption of the regulation? Explain.
5. Smokers impose negative externalities on nonsmokers. Suppose the airspace in a restaurant is a resource owned by the restaurant owner.
   a. How would the owner respond to the negative externality caused by smokers?
   b. Suppose smokers own the airspace. How would that change matters?
   c. If the government gives ownership of the air to nonsmokers, would that change matters?
   d. What does a ban on smoking in the restaurant do?
6. Discuss the argument that education should be subsidized because it creates a positive externality.
7. Why is national defense called a public good?
8. Explain why the number of elephants and rhinos is declining in nations where the animals are housed on national parks and rising in nations where the animals are privately owned and farmed by individuals.
9. Explain what it means to be "too big to fail."

STUDY GUIDE FOR CHAPTER 7

Key Term Match

Match each term with its correct definition by placing the appropriate letter next to the corresponding number.

A. monopolization of a market
B. antitrust
C. regulation
D. natural monopolies
E. externalities
F. private property rights
G. internalized
H. public goods
I. free rider
J. adverse selection
K. moral hazard
L. social regulation
M. logrolling
N. consumer surplus
O. deadweight loss

____ 1. a cost or benefit created by a transaction that is not paid for or enjoyed by those carrying out the transaction

____ 2. the control of some aspect of business by government

____ 3. the right to claim ownership of an item

____ 4. market dominance by one firm that is gained unfairly

____ 5. the difference between what the consumer is willing to pay for a unit of a good and the price that the consumer actually has to pay; the difference between what consumers would be willing to pay and what they have to pay to purchase some item

____ 6. a situation where what was an external cost is paid for by the parties creating the cost

____ 7. a good that is not excludable and is not rivalrous

____ 8. laws that restrict large dominant firms from behaving anticompetitively

____ 9. a consumer or producer who enjoys a good without paying for it

____ 10. the reduction of consumer surplus without a corresponding increase in monopoly profit when a perfectly competitive firm is monopolized

____ 11. a situation where a lack of information causes low-quality items to dominate a market and high-quality items to be driven out of the market

____ 12. a situation where imperfect information provides an incentive for a consumer or producer to change behavior after agreeing to a specific behavior

____ 13. when economies of scale lead to just one firm

____ 14. legislators support one another's projects to ensure support for their own projects

____ 15. government regulation of health, safety, the environment, and employment policies

Quick-Check Quiz

1. The benefits that come from an exchange in a market are
   - ☐ a. deadweight loss minus consumer surplus.
   - ☐ b. producer surplus plus consumer surplus.
   - ☐ c. consumer surplus minus deadweight loss.
   - ☐ d. only deadweight loss.
   - ☐ e. consumer surplus plus deadweight loss.

2. Government intervenes in the market for which of the following reasons?
   - ☐ a. to prevent monopolization of a market
   - ☐ b. to prevent collusion
   - ☐ c. to prevent price fixing
   - ☐ d. to reduce issues associated with creative destruction
   - ☐ e. all of the above are possible reasons government might intervene in markets

3. The decision to enter a freeway creates
   - ☐ a. an externality in that it affects others on the freeway.
   - ☐ b. an internality in that it affects others on the freeway.
   - ☐ c. a moral hazard in that no one knows why the person is on the freeway.
   - ☐ d. adverse selection because only the worst drivers will be on the freeway.
   - ☐ e. no ill effects.

4. When nobody owns something, ____________ takes care of it. When someone owns something, ____________ takes care of it. When everyone owns something, ____________ takes care of it.
   - ☐ a. nobody; everybody; somebody
   - ☐ b. nobody; somebody; nobody
   - ☐ c. nobody; everybody; nobody
   - ☐ d. somebody; nobody; everybody
   - ☐ e. somebody; nobody; somebody

5. When people can enjoy a good or service without paying for the good or service, we say that the person consuming the good or service is
   - ☐ a. a moral hazard.
   - ☐ b. a public good.
   - ☐ c. a free rider.
   - ☐ d. an adverse selection.
   - ☐ e. a negative externality.

6. The government often intervenes to solve market failure problems. But the government may have failures of its own. Which of the following could be described as a government failure?
   - ☐ a. inefficiencies due to incentives of individuals in government
   - ☐ b. using votes to allocate goods and services rather than markets
   - ☐ c. adverse selection
   - ☐ d. moral hazard
   - ☐ e. natural monopolies
7. Monopolization of a market can be illegal when
   - ☐ a. the monopoly is gained unfairly.
   - ☐ b. consumers receive benefits from the monopoly.
   - ☐ c. the monopolist benefits from economies of scale.
   - ☐ d. the monopolist makes political contributions.
   - ☐ e. the government grants the monopoly.
8. Secondhand smoke has led antismoking crusaders to pass smoking bans. We could describe secondhand smoke as
   - ☐ a. a cost of legislation.
   - ☐ b. a benefit to smokers.
   - ☐ c. a negative externality.
   - ☐ d. a public good.
   - ☐ e. a positive externality.
9. By providing bailouts to firms called "too big to fail," which of the following potential problems is created?
   - ☐ a. logrolling
   - ☐ b. externality
   - ☐ c. moral hazard
   - ☐ d. firms that are too small
   - ☐ e. public good

Practice Questions and Problems

1. Some teenagers engage in behaviors that result in increased costs for their parents: leaving lights on when they leave the house, turning on air conditioning without closing the windows, driving over the speed limit in the family car, etc. The teenagers do not have an incentive to change these behaviors if the parents are the ones to bear the cost. The problem the parents face is called ______________.
2. Competition results in inefficient and obsolete goods and resources being replaced. This process is called ______________.
3. People will call on the government to allocate goods and services when they ______________ (do, don't) like the results of market allocation.
4. The objective of businesses is to ______________.
5. In comparison with perfect competition, a monopolist ______________ quantity supplied and ______________ price.
6. The set of laws intended to create a level playing field—that is, to prevent the unfair monopolization of a market—is called ______________.
7. A natural monopoly would be a firm operating in a business for which ______________ (economies, diseconomies) of scale exist throughout the entire market. This would enable a larger firm to be ______________ (more, less) efficient than a smaller firm and thus be able to charge a ______________ (higher, lower) price than the smaller firm.
8. When the government pays for and provides a good or service or dictates the prices and quantities firms can charge and must sell, we say that the firms are ______________.
9. When you drive your car, the fuel is burned and exhaust created. The exhaust is expelled from the engine and into the air. The cost of the emission is not paid by you—it is instead paid for by innocent bystanders. This situation is referred to as a(n) ______________. If the problem is solved, we say that the cost has been ______________.
10. One solution to some market failures is to assign ownership or ______________. When this is possible, it allows the affected parties to negotiate a solution. This was the idea of what economist?
11. Chickens and cows are not on the endangered species list but the black rhino is. Why?
12. A market-based solution to an externality problem requires that what exists? (Think of the example of pollution and pollution permits.) ______________
13. During the last few decades ______________ (regulation, social regulation) has been out of favor but ______________ (regulation, social regulation) has grown.
14. The government regulates many activities and imposes rules of behavior on many businesses. To determine whether the regulations are worth the costs, it is necessary to carry out a comparison of ______________ and ______________.
15. Suppose that a new law limiting the use of greenhouse gases is being considered. It is estimated that the law will cost $900 billion per year, or $100 million per life saved. What would the value of life have to be for this law to make economic sense? ______________
16. When private property rights are ill-defined, ______________ (too much, too little) of a resource is consumed.
17. When positive externalities exist, ______________ (too much, too little) of a good is consumed or produced.

Exercises and Applications

I The Pelzman Effect

University of Chicago professor Sam Pelzman's research suggests that when the government enacts stricter safety regulations, people respond by engaging in more risky behaviors, which then offsets some of the effect of the regulations. For example, automatic lane departure correction technology automatically returns a car to its lane if the car drifts out of it. The Pelzman effect implies that if cars were required to have this technology, drivers might feel safe enough to drive home after an evening of drinking. The Pelzman effect is a variant of what economic concept discussed in this chapter? ____________

II Halloween Street

Broadview Street in Wichita, Kansas is known locally as Halloween Street. Many homeowners on this street put up very elaborate Halloween decorations. Huge throngs of people come to view the decorations in the week before Halloween, causing traffic jams on this residential street. People who walk to the street to view the decorations often tramp across residents' lawns as they walk from house to house. You are a homeowner on Broadview St. Your religious views do not include an appreciation for Halloween, so you do not put up Halloween decorations and are appalled at the ones your neighbors have put up. For you, your neighbors'decorations are an example of a ____________.

You can find further practice tests in the Online Quiz at: www.cengagebrain.com

8 Government Intervention

FUNDAMENTAL QUESTIONS

1. What is a free market?
2. What is the main reason many economists do not believe in or trust the free market?
3. Can a free market provide health care, or is a government-run health care system necessary?
4. Is the free market able to handle environmental accidents?
5. Will a free market for drugs be better for society than the war on drugs?
6. Can discrimination occur in a free market?

PREVIEW

It is often claimed by economists that there is essential agreement in the profession on almost everything. Well, if that was ever the case, it is not now. There are several schools of economic thought—Chicago free market economists, Keynesian economists, Austrian economists, Marxists, and others. In this chapter, we consider the division between economists who argue that free unfettered markets will work best for society and economists who argue that you can't trust the market, that government and experts must control and guide the economy.

You can see the division among economists in the following remark by Paul Samuelson.

> *"And today we see how utterly mistaken was the Milton Friedman notion that a market system can regulate itself. We see how silly the Ronald Reagan slogan was that government is the problem, not the solution. This prevailing ideology of the last few decades has now been reversed. Everyone understands now, on the contrary, that there can be no solution without government."*[1]

Milton Friedman, 1912–2006; American winner of the Nobel Prize for Economics in 1976.

Milton Friedman was the son of an immigrant merchant who died when Milton was 15. Friedman obtained his BA in

---

[1] Paul Samuelson, "Don't Expect Recovery Before 2012—With 8% Inflation," interview by Nathan Gardels, *New Perspectives Quarterly*, 27 (Spring 2009).

economics at Rutgers in 1932, his MA from the University of Chicago in 1933, and his PhD from Columbia University in 1946, by which time he was Professor of Economics at the University of Chicago. In 1988, he was awarded the Presidential Medal of Freedom and the National Medal of Science. In addition to his scientific work, Friedman also wrote extensively on public policy, always with a primary emphasis on the preservation and extension of individual freedom. His most important books in this field are (with Rose D. Friedman) *Capitalism and Freedom* (University of Chicago Press, 1962); *Bright Promises, Dismal Performance* (Thomas Horton and Daughters, 1983), which consists mostly of reprints of columns he wrote for *Newsweek* from 1966 to 1983; (with Rose D. Friedman) *Free to Choose* (Harcourt Brace Jovanovich, 1980), which complements a 10-part television series of the same name shown over the Public Broadcasting Service (PBS) network in early 1980; and (with Rose D. Friedman) *Tyranny of the Status Quo* (Harcourt Brace Jovanovich, 1984), which complements a three-part television series of the same name, shown over PBS in early 1984.

Rick Friedman/WpN/PhotoShot, Inc.

Paul Samuelson, 1915–2009.

One of the 20th century's most influential economists, Paul Samuelson, improved the quality of mathematical analysis in his field, formalized several branches of economic science, and helped popularize Keynesian economics in America. He was the first American to win the Nobel Prize for Economics, honored in 1970. Samuelson's magnum opus, which did more than any other single book to spread the mathematical revolution in economics, is *Foundations of Economic Analysis*. Based on his Harvard PhD dissertation, the book shows how virtually all economic behavior can be understood as maximizing or minimizing subject to a constraint.

1. ARGUMENTS OVER THE BENEFICENCE OF MARKETS

1

What is a free market?

The market system is generally the most efficient allocation system—it best satisfies people's wants and needs and raises their standards of living. Without anyone dictating what buyers and sellers do, the market determines a price for each traded good at which the quantities that people are willing and able to sell are equal to the quantities that people are willing and able to buy. Day in and day out, the market system induces people to employ their talents and resources where they have the highest value. People do not have to be fooled, cajoled, or forced to do their parts in the market system. Instead, they pursue their own self-interests and, in so doing, generate the most good for society.

In Chapters 6 and 7, we learned that firms acquire resources and then organize and coordinate the resources to create and offer for sale various goods and services. The value that consumers place on these goods and services must be more than the value they place on the individual resources alone or else the firm would cease to exist. When a firm's goods and services have more value than the opportunity cost of the resources used to create and sell the goods and services, then rivals will begin to compete with that firm. In other words, when economic profit is negative, the firm will cease to exist; when economic profit is positive, the sharks will attack. Rivals will enter and compete. People will get the goods and services they want at the lowest possible prices and resources will be used where their value is highest.

1.a. What Is Wrong with Free Markets?

In Figure 8.1 a free, competitive market is illustrated. The price P_1 and quantity Q_1 represent the result of competition, the lowest possible price and quantity that people want and are able to pay for. This price and quantity result from resources being used where they are most valued. As stated in Chapter 6, if another department store could match Nordstrom's products and service but do so at a lower price, consumers would abandon Nordstrom and shop at the other store. This would drive Nordstrom's profits down until they were at the normal or zero economic profit level. If iPods can be replaced with another company's MP3 player at lower prices and/or higher quality, then Apple's profit will be driven to the normal level. Thus, P_1 and Q_1 are the points where consumers are currently happy with what they are getting and prices are as low as possible.

When competition is limited and entry restricted, then Figure 8.1 is changed. With total entry restrictions, the entire market is converted into a single firm, the monopolist (or a cartel of firms acting as a monopolist). The firm maximizes profit by restricting quantity to Q_2 and raising price to P_2. Restrictions on competition and entry harm the consumer by reducing quantity and raising price.

But even so, it is argued, a free market causes too many problems. For instance, in Figure 8.2, a free market is hit by a sudden reduction in demand caused by any number of things, such as speculative activities, unexpected resource changes, or some other crisis. The free market adjusts to the demand reduction when firms exit business and price and quantity are reduced (P_2 and Q_2).

2

What is the main reason many economists do not believe in or trust the free market?

Here is the crux of the argument between free market economists and non–free market economists—the speed with which a free unfettered competitive market adjusts to changes. Critics of the free market argue that the adjustment from the first equilibrium to the second takes too much time.

FIGURE 8.1 The Controversy over Free Markets

In a perfectly competitive market, P_1 and Q_1 represent the competitive price and quantity. When entry is restricted and the market is monopolized, output is reduced to Q_2 and price is increased to P_2, the profit-maximizing price and quantity (where $MR = MC$ or S).

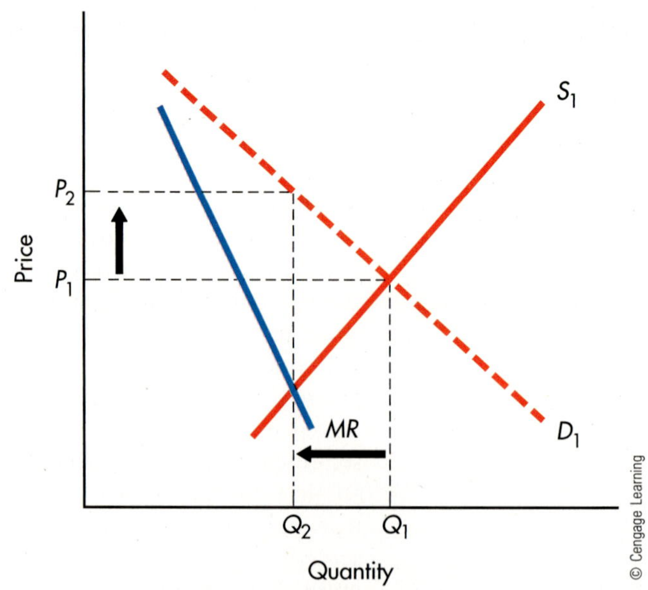

FIGURE 8.2 Free Market Hit by a Crisis

The free market reacts to a sudden demand decrease when some firms exit business and others reduce output. The result is an adjustment to P_2 and Q_2, the new lowest possible price and quantity people want and are willing to pay for. The problem in the market arises when the adjustment from P_1 and Q_1 to P_2 and Q_2 occur only after a considerable period of time.

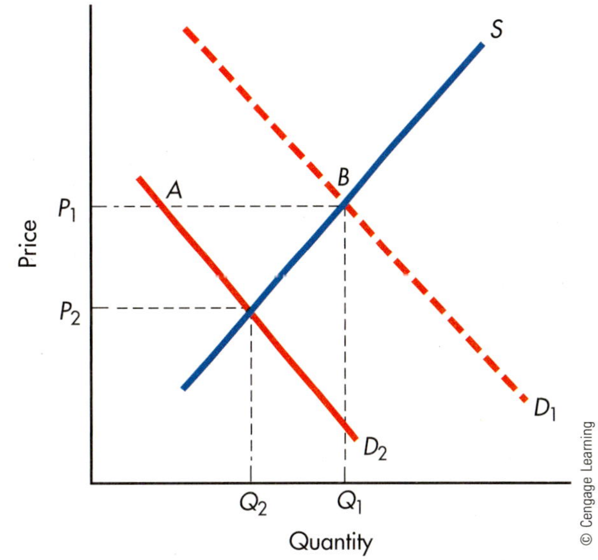

A slow adjustment of the market means resources will be unemployed and inventories will stock up on shelves for awhile. If demand decreases but price and quantity do not immediately follow, then a surplus will occur (*A* to *B* in Figure 8.2). If the market is wheat, then a surplus of wheat will exist; wheat will lie dying in the field. If this market is cars, then excess inventories of cars will exist; cars will pile up on dealer lots. And, if the market is the labor market, then there is a surplus of labor; unemployment rises.

John Maynard Keynes, the leading economist of the 1930s, captured this criticism of free markets with the following statement:

> The long run is a misleading guide to current affairs. In the long run we are all dead.[2]

Free market economists argue that markets will adjust to a demand shock without government intervention. Under this view, when something like the Great Depression in 1930 or the financial collapse in 2006–2008 occurs, the free market response would be to do nothing, because in the long run the markets would solve the problem, the price of labor would fall to P_2, more firms would hire, people would return to work, and the economy would return to full employment.

However, Keynes said this was madness—in the depth of a recession, why not try to do something about it, rather than leave it to market forces? In the long run, the recession may end, but the long run could be 10, 15, or more years. Keynes wanted to try to solve the depression immediately, rather than wait 10 or 15 years, or however long the "long run" was.

This viewpoint is the basis of many of the arguments between free market economists and the Keynesian or non–free market economists. *It simply takes too long for the market to work things out. People, central planners, and governments can do it better.* The counter argument is that while we might be dead in the long run, our children and grandchildren won't be. So we should do what is best for the economy in the long run, and that is to leave markets alone. By intervening in free markets, inefficiencies arise that slow the growth of the economy and harm future generations. In the end, intervening in the functioning of free markets just makes the situation worse and creates additional problems.

[2] Keynes, *Tract on Monetary Reform* (1923), Ch. 3.

Let us look at a few issues where the debate over free markets and government control has raged for years. Many people claim that the free market fails when it comes to health care, to the environment, and to labor markets. Let's delve into these issues to see whether the free market is able to deal with them.

2. HEALTH ECONOMICS

3

Can a free market provide health care, or is a government-run health care system necessary?

Spending for health care in the United States exceeds $2 trillion. Health care expenditures, only 5.9 percent of GDP in 1965, exceed 16 percent of GDP today. Health care spending varies tremendously among groups in the U.S. population. Only 1 percent of people account for almost 30 percent of total health care expenditures, 5 percent account for 55 percent of all health care expenditures, and the healthiest 50 percent of the population account for only 4 percent of expenditures. The elderly are the major users of health care, whereas the young are the smallest users.

2.a. Quality of Health Care

Critics of the current U.S. health care system argue that even though per capita spending on health care in the United States exceeds that of every other nation, U.S. health care is not as good as that found in other nations. Out of the 193 member states of the World Health Organization, the United States ranked first in per capita health care expenditures, but 31st in life expectancy (78-year average life span) and 152nd in infant mortality rate (6 deaths per 1,000 infants during the first year after birth).

Others argue that many of these measures are misleading. For instance, although Cuba has an infant mortality rate of 7.3 deaths per 1,000 live births, the mortality of children in Cuba in the age group from 1 to 4 years is 11.8, significantly higher than that in the United States. Moreover, measures differ from country to country. The United States counts all births as live if they show any sign of life, regardless of prematurity or size. This includes what many other countries report as stillbirths and don't include as infant deaths. In most other countries, the death of an infant born less than 30 centimeters in length is not counted as a live birth. This threshold effectively excludes many very low–birth weight babies, such as those weighing less than 2.2 pounds. Yet close to one-third of all infant deaths recorded in the United States are among infants weighing 2.2 pounds or less. If these very low–birth weight infants were reclassified in the United States as "stillborn" rather than "live births," the U.S. infant mortality rate would be near the best in the world.[3]

Supporters of U.S. health care also point out that life expectancy is a poor choice of measure of the quality of health care. Life expectancy is a function of lifestyle more than health care. In the United States, deaths from automobile accidents and murder lower life expectancy much more than in other developed nations. If adjusted for murder and automobile accidental deaths, the U.S. life expectancy would rival most other countries.

Most Americans rate the nation's health care as no better than average when compared with health care in other industrialized countries. Just 15 percent say health care in this country is the "best in the world," whereas 27 percent rate it as "below average." There are stark political divisions in opinions about how the health care system compares with those in other industrialized countries. Republicans say U.S. health care is either the best in the

[3] "Twenty Myths about Single-Payer Health Insurance: International Evidence on the Effects of National Health Insurance in Countries Around the World," by John C. Goodman and Devon M. Herrick, National Center for Policy Analysis (http://debate-central.ncpa.org/topics/2002/book2.pdf), June 5, 2010.

world (28 percent) or above average (29 percent). Democrats largely take the opposite view, with nearly seven in ten saying U.S. health care is either average (35 percent) or below average (34 percent).[4]

2.b. The Right to Health Care

Much of the debate between free market economists and non–free market economists over health care lies whether health care is a right. Those who believe it is a right argue that everyone should have the opportunity to receive quality health care. Those who do not think it is a right, say that the free market should determine health care just as the market does for any good or service. With a free market system, only those willing and able to purchase health care will get health care.

The competitive free market does not ensure that everyone gets health care. It would ensure that the health care provided is done so at the lowest possible price for the quality and quantity people want and are able to purchase. But health care, like most any other good or service, is scarce. The idea of scarcity is that there is not enough of something to meet everyone's wants and needs. In a free market system, it would seem that some would get left out.

In a 2004 survey, 77 percent of Americans say health care should be a right, with 47 percent strongly agreeing and 28 percent agreeing somewhat.[5] Those who believe health care should be a right cite the following two reasons:

1. All Americans should have a right to health care because the Declaration of Independence states that all men have the unalienable right to "life," which entails having the health care needed to preserve life.
2. Health care is a right for all Americans because the preamble of the U.S. Constitution states its purpose is to "promote the general welfare" of the people. Just as all Americans have the right to an education, they should have the right to health care because they both "promote the general welfare."

Other people, who believe health care is *not* a right, cite the following two reasons:

1. Health care should not be a right because it is inconsistent with the Declaration of Independence, which guarantees the right to "pursue" happiness, not the right to happiness or free medical services.
2. Health care should not be considered a right because the preamble of the U.S. Constitution states that its purpose is to "promote" the general welfare, not to provide it.[6]

Having a right to health care means guaranteeing health care for everyone. The free market surely does not provide everyone with health care. So if health care is provided in a free market, what should be done with those left out, those unable to purchase care? This is a major part of the debate that has gone on in the United States for decades. Many argue that since health care is a right, the government must provide it. Government-provided health care for everyone is called universal health care with a single payer—the government. Franklin D. Roosevelt attempted to introduce universal care back in 1932, and virtually every Democratic administration since has introduced a bill to enact some form or first step to universal care.

---

[4] "Few See U.S. Health Care as 'Best in the World'," Pew Research Center (http://pewresearch.org/pubs/1293/health-care-public-gives-lukewarm-rating-to-american-system), June 6, 2010.

[5] "Nation's Health Care System Ill, 2004 Survey Finds," Kellogg Foundation (http://healthcare.procon.org/sourcefiles/KelloggSurvery2004.pdf).

[6] Right to HealthCare ProCon.Org (http://healthcare.procon.org/), June 5, 2010.

2.c. Do the Laws of Economics Apply to Health Care?

Many people claim that the laws of economics do not apply to health care. They argue that health care is different from other goods and services. Let's look at this claim.

Is health care a scarce good? The answer is a clear yes; at a zero price, more people want health care than there is health care available—the definition of a scarce good. Scarcity means that choices must be made, that there is an opportunity cost for choosing to purchase the scarce good. The choice is made on the basis of rational self-interest. In a free market, people could choose to purchase as much health care and the kind and quality of health care as they want depending on their ability to pay. This is no different from food—people can choose to purchase as much and the quality and type of food as they want, depending on their ability to pay. These principles of economics suggest that health care is an economic good and is subject to the laws of economics.

The demand curve for health care looks like any other demand curve; it slopes down because the higher the price, the lower the quantity demanded. The demand curve is probably quite inelastic, but it does slope downward. There also is a standard-looking supply curve. Physicians, hospitals, and medical firms offer an increasing quantity of health care for sale as the price rises. The demand and supply curves look no different from the curves representing a market in any other economic good.

In Figure 8.3, the price for health care is the level at which the demand and supply curves intersect, the point of equilibrium. At price P_1, the quantity of health care demanded is equal to the quantity supplied. Those people who are willing and able to pay price P_1 (all those lying along the demand curve from A to B) get the medical care. Those who are not willing and able to pay the price (all those lying along the demand curve from B to C) do not get the care.

2.c.1. The Health Care Market Is Not Free The problems that arise in the health care market are due not to a repeal of the laws of economics, but instead to interference in the market. People believe that they and others have an inalienable right to medical care, that it is not right to ignore those people making up the demand curve from B to C on D_1. As a result, government programs such as Medicare and Medicaid have been created. These programs, along with private insurance programs, mean that most of the payments for medical care are made by third parties. The *third-party payment system* allows many of those who would not otherwise be willing and able to purchase health care, those lying along the demand curve from B to C, to be able to purchase the care. This shifts the demand curve out, which drives health care costs up, as shown by the shift from D_1 to D_2 in Figure 8.3.

The government and private insurance programs thus face ever-rising health care costs. Each new equilibrium means that some are unable to afford the care; if their demand is covered, the demand curve shifts out again, to D_3. This continues as long as someone is willing and able to pay the price. That someone has been the government, principally through Medicare, and private employers through employee benefit plans. The result has been double-digit price increases for health care for over a decade.

2.c.2. Why Does Competition Not Drive Price Down? When the Mazda Miata was first introduced in the United States, the price in Southern California exceeded the price in Detroit by about 25 percent, with the result being that the supply of Miatas in Southern California rose as Miatas in Detroit were shipped out. This lowered the prices of the cars in Southern California. When housing prices rose faster than inflation or prices of other assets, the

FIGURE 8.3 Do Laws of Economics Apply to Health Care?

The price of health care is the level at which the demand and supply curves intersect, the point of equilibrium. At price P_1, the quantity of health care demanded is equal to the quantity supplied. Those people who are willing and able to pay price P_1 (all those lying along demand curve D_1 from *A* to *B*) get the health care. Those who are not willing and able to pay the price (all those lying along the demand curve from *B* to *C*) do not get the health care. The third-party payment system allows many who would not otherwise be willing and able to purchase health care (those lying along the demand curve from *B* to *C*) to be able to purchase the care. This shifts the demand curve out and drives health care costs up, as shown by the shift in the demand curve from D_1 to D_2.

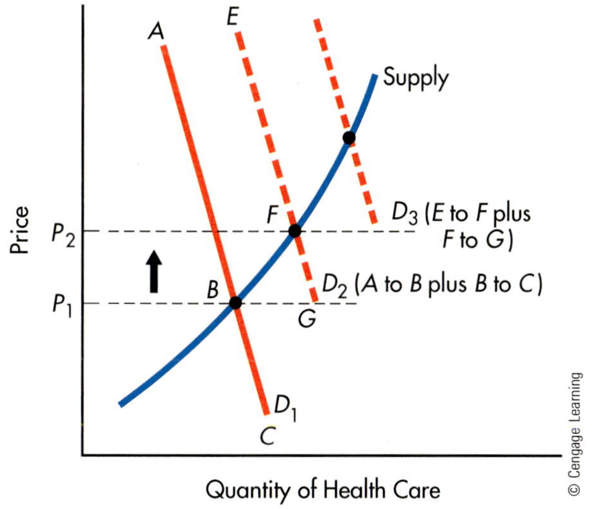

quantity of houses on the market rose, thereby slowing the increase in prices. In general, when the price in one sector rises relative to other sectors, resources flow to where they are most highly valued. If prices of energy rise faster than prices elsewhere in the economy, then there is a profit opportunity for suppliers of energy. The potential of profit induces suppliers to enter the energy sector, so supply rises, slowing the price increases. This is the way the market works—competition drives resources to those uses where they are most highly valued and thus ensures that prices in one area of a free market system are not continually rising faster than those in another sector. In the case of health care, demand and supply have caused prices to rise significantly faster than inflation or prices in other sectors of the economy. In a free market, we would expect resources to flow into health care and reduce the differential between its prices and prices elsewhere. Why is this not happening?

There are three primary reasons that health care costs in the United States continue to rise faster than costs in other sectors of the economy. One is the restrictions on entry. The American Medical Association (AMA) restricts the supply of physicians. The AMA limits who can give prescriptions to only its members; a few years ago, pharmacists were responsible for dispensing drugs. The government (Food and Drug Administration [FDA]) restricts entry of drugs to the U.S. marketplace. The Medicare system (government) restricts the movement of resources from one area in the health care market to another. In addition, health insurance is regulated on a state-by-state basis. This restricts the possibility of someone buying a less expensive policy from an insurer in another state and thus restricts competition. In sum, restrictions do not allow the market to work to allocate goods and services and resources to where they have the highest value. The market for health care is far from a free, unregulated market. The restrictions and regulations inhibit the entry and exit of firms and inhibit the effect of competition on prices.

2.d. Health Insurance

Of the $2 trillion spent on health care in the United States, private health insurance accounts for 40 percent. Private direct payments account for only 15 percent. Direct payments are out-of-pocket payments made by individuals, including copayments and deductibles. Government spending on health care constitutes 45 percent of the total; the federal government pays about 70 percent of this 45 percent. Medicare, the largest publicly sponsored health care program, funds health care services for about 40 million aged and disabled enrollees. The Medicare program pays for 20 percent of all national health expenditures and is rising due to part D, the drug benefit plan enacted in 2006. Medicaid, a jointly funded federal and state program, finances 16 percent of health care, covering the costs of medical care for poor families, the neediest elderly, and persons who are eligible for social security disability benefits.

The main issue in health care is actually health insurance not health care. Health care is available to everyone—those without insurance can obtain care at emergency rooms of hospitals. But, people using the emergency rooms are utilizing one of the most costly methods of obtaining health care. Figuring out what is wrong with the insurance market and repairing it would be much more efficient.

Approximately 30 to 35 million people did not have health insurance as of 2009. Many of these were young healthy people who chose not to purchase insurance, but many were either people with preexisting conditions who were unable to get insurance or people without jobs.

Health insurance in the United States is employer based, meaning that most people obtain health insurance through their employers. The reason that health insurance is employer based is that during World War II, the government placed wage and price controls on the economy. Since businesses were unable to attract employees by offering higher wages, they turned to offering benefits, particularly health insurance. Then in 1947 Congress provided tax benefits to firms offering health insurance. This incentive ensured that the employer-based health system would remain in force.

The fact that health insurance is provided by employers means those without jobs, or those working for small firms that do not offer health insurance, may not have insurance. Moreover, if you lose a job, you lose your insurance. Then if you get ill and while ill find another job, you are not provided with the employer-based health insurance for at least several months. You are excluded because you have a preexisting condition. If you have a job and insurance and then get ill, you may not leave the job to take another better job because you will lose insurance and not be able to get it at the new job because of your preexisting condition. The employer-based health care system is very inefficient. Resources are not free to move to where they have the highest value, wages are lower than they would be if no insurance was provided by employers, and people do not choose which kind and how much health insurance to purchase.

2.d.1. Third-Party Payer

"Third party" means someone other than the supplier or demander is paying for the good or service. Third-party payment systems are typically inefficient because the actual buyers and sellers don't react to prices. Neither the buyer nor the seller has an incentive to seek lower cost options or to forgo some treatment or test. Excess doctor visits and excessive tests occur because consumers don't bear the costs.

When you purchase almost any good or service, you pay for it. You have to decide whether that good or service is more valuable to you than anything else that money could be used for. Consider, for example, Lasik eye surgery and plastic surgery. If you decide to have Lasik eye surgery to improve your vision or to have plastic surgery to change some aspect of your body, you cannot use insurance coverage. As a result, you must decide what is the best use of your own money. Also, suppliers must compete for your business—you can't simply show up with your insurance card. As a result, these are the only two areas of medicine where prices have fallen and quality has risen. Moreover, Lasik eye surgery has the highest patient satisfaction ratings of any surgery, it has gotten better over time and . . . *Lasik eye surgery has fallen in price.* In 1998, the average price of Lasik eye surgery was about $2,200 per eye; in 2004, the average price was $1,350, and it continued to fall until about 2006. The average price in 2012 is about $1,000, but this cost includes new technologies and higher quality surgery.[7]

2.e. What Causes Health Care Costs To Rise?

Rising costs or expenditures mean that the demand for health care has risen relative to the supply (see Figure 8.4). The initial demand for health care is D_1, and the supply of medical health care is S_1. The intersection determines the price of health care, P_1, and the total expenditures, P_1 times Q_1. An increase in demand relative to supply is shown as an outward shift of the demand curve, from D_1 to D_2. As a result, the price of health care rises, from P_1 to P_2, as do the total expenditures on health care, from P_1 times Q_1 to P_2 times Q_2. What accounts for the rising demand relative to supply? Health care costs have risen because the demand for health care has risen relative to supply.

2.e.1. Demand Increase: The Aging Population

The elderly consume four times as much health care per capita as the rest of the population. About 90 percent of the expenditures for nursing home care are for persons 65 or over, a group that constitutes only 12 percent of the population. Those 65 or older account for 35 percent of hospital expenditures. And the older the population, the greater the spending. Per capita spending on personal health care for those 85 years of age or over is 2.5 times that for people aged 65 to 69 years. For hospital care, per capita consumption is twice as great for those aged 85 or over compared to those aged 65 to 69; for nursing home care, it is 23 times as great.

2.e.2. Demand Increase: The Financing Mechanism

For demand to increase, the aged must be both *willing* to buy medical care and *able* to pay for it. The emergence of Medicare and Medicaid in 1966 gave many more elderly

FIGURE 8.4 The Market for Health Care: A Demand Shift

The demand for and supply of health care determine the price of health care (P_1) and the total expenditures ($P_1 \times Q_1$). Rising health care expenditures may be due to increased demand. A larger demand (D_2) means a higher price and a greater total quantity of expenditures ($P_2 \times Q_2$).

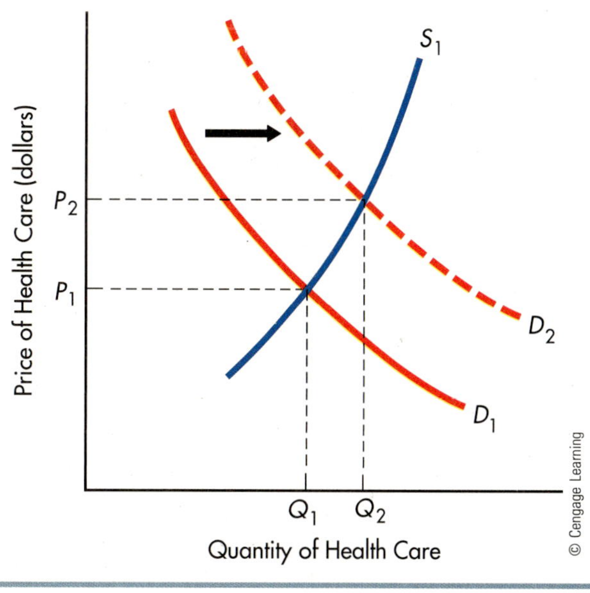

7 "Cost of LASIK and Other Corrective Eye Surgery," by Liz Segre, with updates by Marilyn Haddrill; reviewed by Robert L. Epstein, MD, in All About Vision (http://www.allaboutvision.com/visionsurgery/cost.htm), June 4, 2010.

the ability. Medicare covers the cost of the first 100 days of hospital or nursing home care for the elderly and disabled, providing benefits to 32 million people. Medicare also, since 2006, provides prescription drug benefits. Like social security, Medicare is funded by payroll taxes (taxes taken out of paychecks before the checks are received) and is available on the basis of age (or disability), *not* need. By contrast, Medicaid helps only the neediest people, including many elderly people whose Medicare benefits have run out. As a result, Medicaid is the program that is most associated with long-term health care (such as for people living in nursing homes).

The effect of the Medicare and Medicaid programs has been to increase the demand for services and to decrease the price elasticity of demand because individuals do not pay for much of their health care. Private sources pay for about 55 percent of personal health care for the population as a whole, and Medicare and Medicaid pick up most of the remainder. Private sources, however, pay for 74 percent of care for people under age 65. For the elderly, the private share of spending is only 15 percent for hospital care, 36 percent for physicians' services, and 58 percent for nursing home care. Medicaid spending for those 85 or over is seven times the spending for people aged 65 to 69 and three times greater than the spending for people aged 75 to 79. This difference is attributable to the heavy concentration of Medicaid money in nursing home care, which those 85 or over use much more than others. Medicare spending for the oldest group is double that for the 65 to 69 age group.

2.e.3. **Demand Increase: New Technologies**

New medical technologies provide the very sick with increased opportunities for treatment. Everyone wants the latest technology to be used when their life or the lives of their loved ones are at stake.

2.e.4. **Supply**

Even if the demand curve for health care were not shifting out, the cost of health care could be forced up by a leftward shift of the supply curve, as shown in Figure 8.5. The supply curve shifts up, from S_1 to S_2, if the cost of producing medical care is rising—that is, if resource prices are rising or if diseconomies of scale are being experienced.

Hospitals The original function of hospitals was to provide the poor with a place to die. Not until the 20th century could wealthy individuals who were sick find more comfort, cleanliness, and service in a hospital than in their own

FIGURE 8.5 The Market for Health Care: A Supply Shift

The rising cost of health care may be caused by an increase in the costs of supplying health care. The supply curve shifts up from S_1 to S_2, and the price of health care rises from P_1 to P_2.

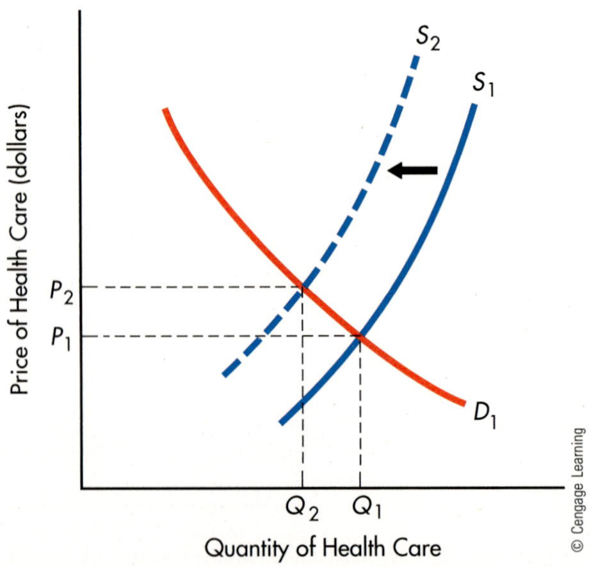

homes. As technological changes in medicine occurred, the function of the hospital changed: The hospital became the doctor's workshop.

The cost of hospital care is attributable in large part to the way in which current operations and capital purchases are financed. Only a small fraction of the cost of hospital care is paid directly by patients; the bulk comes from *third parties*, of which the government is the most important.

Physicians Physicians affect the cost of medical health care not only through their impact on the operation of the hospital, but also through their fees. Expenditures on physicians' services rose more rapidly than any other health care expenditure category in the 1980s and 1990s. Is the increased cost of physicians due to a shortage of doctors? The answer is not necessarily yes. From 1966 to 1997, the supply of physicians increased 100 percent, whereas the U.S. population increased about 25 percent. As a result, the number of active physicians per 100,000 people increased substantially, from 169 in 1975 to 240 in 1997, and it has remained near that level since 1997.

The factors that have led to rising physicians' fees include an increase in demand relative to the supply of certain types of physicians, the ability of physicians to restrict price competition, and the payment system. The number of physicians per population has risen in many areas of the country. Yet because the AMA restricts advertising by physicians, consumers are unable to obtain complete information about prices or professional quality, and physicians are less likely to compete through advertising or lower prices. Moreover, the restrictions on advertising enable established physicians to keep new, entering physicians from competing for their customers.

The payment system influences both physicians' fees and the supply of physicians. Over 31 percent of all physicians' fees are set by the government. More than 75 percent are set by third-party providers. Physicians are reimbursed on the basis of procedures and according to specialty. A gynecologist would have to examine 275 women a week to achieve the income earned by a cardiac surgeon doing two operations per week. More than 60 percent of all physicians in the United States are specialists. The payment system has induced more physicians to specialize in certain areas than would have occurred otherwise.

The costs of doing business have risen for physicians. For instance, the cost of malpractice insurance has increased about 25 percent a year during the past two decades. Although only about 1 percent of health care expenditures can be directly attributed to malpractice suits, there are some implicit costs associated with the fear of such suits. This fear has caused an increase in both the number of tests ordered by physicians and the quantity of medical equipment purchased by them.

Prescription Drugs The fastest-growing health expenditure category since 1995 has been prescription medicines. Prescription drug expenditures grew by an annual average of 15 percent during this period. Again, looking at the demand for and supply of prescription drugs explains the increase. Medicare has increased the ability to buy drugs. In addition, the existence of new drugs raises the demand for drugs as people seek better medicines and previously unavailable cures for diseases. On the supply side, the cost of producing a new drug has risen dramatically; on average, it costs a company more than 1 billion dollars to bring a new drug to the market.

Part of the high and rising production cost is caused by government restrictions regarding which drugs can be placed on the market in the United States. The only way a company can sell a new drug or medical device in the United States is to get permission from the FDA, and the FDA is increasingly reluctant to give this permission. It has a very strong incentive to keep unsafe products off the market, even if in doing so it may block beneficial new products. As a result, the FDA has made it increasingly difficult to bring a new drug to market. The time required to bring a new drug to market, including preclinical testing, clinical development, and regulatory review, has increased from a low of 6.3 years in 1963–1965 to 16.1 years. This delay means that the percentage of drugs that are available first in the United States is low. Although more than 60 percent of biopharmaceutical products approved in the United States, Europe, or Japan originated in the United States, less than 18 percent were first marketed in the United States.

2.f. **Reforming Health Care: Toward a Free Market or a Government System?**

A few changes in the market for health insurance would eliminate most of the problems the United States is experiencing. First, it is necessary to get rid of the third-party payer system. Individuals must be responsible for their health care expenditures. Just like with any other good or service, the consumer must weigh costs and benefits in deciding whether to buy more. Those requiring aid or those on Medicare could be given vouchers so they too would be able to control their health care dollars. With a voucher, consumers could choose any health plan on the market. If they could keep any funds left over, they would have an incentive to use expenditures wisely.

Second, the employer-based system needs to be replaced. Congress needs to give consumers who purchase their own coverage the same tax break as workers with job-based coverage. Leveling the playing field—whether with tax credits, a standard deduction for health insurance, or large health savings accounts—would boost purchases of non–job-based coverage. Third, the state health insurance regulations that prevent people from purchasing health plans available in other states should be eliminated so that insurers have to compete for business. Similarly, the restrictions on doctors competing across state lines should be eliminated. Giving clinicians the freedom to practice medicine across state lines would eliminate barriers for retail clinics and economical health plans. Although these changes might not eliminate all problems, they would reduce the inefficiencies in the current health care system.

The Obama Administration chose not to make these relatively simple changes and instead moved the system toward a government-run system with the enactment of the Patient Protection and Affordable Care Act (PPACA) on March 23, 2010. Instead of moving toward the free market, the choice was to move toward central planning and government control. One fundamental and controversial part of the Act was a mandate requiring everyone to purchase insurance. This mandate has been attacked as being unconstitutional because the government cannot force people to purchase something. In June 2012, the Supreme Court rendered its decision. Four justices declared the entire law unconstitutional, including the mandate. Four justices declared the law constitutional. The deciding vote was rendered by Chief Justice John Roberts who rewrote the law, declaring the "mandate" was actually a tax and thus constitutional due to the constitution's taxing clause. As a result, the law is to be implemented unless repealed by a vote from Congress, which is not vetoed by the President.

RECAP

1. The health care and health insurance system in the United States has not been a free market system at least since the 1930s.
2. Government intervention on the basis that health care is a right has created an inefficient and costly system.
3. The demand for medical care has risen at a very rapid rate. One reason for the increase is the introduction of Medicare and Medicaid and private insurance plans that make demand relatively inelastic. Consumers do not have to choose whether to use their own money for health care or for something else. The third-party payment system removes the role of price in the market.

4. The third-party payment system and the large role of government in financing health care have driven up the cost of providing medical care. The way the government programs pay physicians has led to higher rates of return in certain specialties and lower rates for general practice, and thus have drawn an increasing number of physicians to those specialties and away from general practice. In addition, physicians are paid on the basis of procedures or tests rather than by results.
5. The laws of economics do apply to the medical arena. They just have not been allowed to operate. If the free market did work in the health care arena, some would get health care and some would not. Thus, if the general population wants health care treated as a right, some method of efficiently financing health care to those unable to purchase it must be found.

3. THE OIL SPILL

4

Is the free market able to handle environmental accidents?

The question of whether man has caused climate change, or whether climate change is just part of a natural cycle of the sun, is at the center of the debate over global warming. Is climate change caused by the free market? Can the free market ensure that man-made greenhouse gases don't harm the environment, or must that be left to government? To examine answers to these questions, we must look at the markets for natural resources.

3.a. The Market for Natural Resources

renewable resources: resources that can renew themselves

nonrenewable resources: resources that cannot replenish themselves

The term "natural resources" refers to two types of resources—**renewable resources** and **nonrenewable resources**. Renewable resources are the trees, plants, and animals that can reproduce. Nonrenewable resources are resources that can be used only once and cannot be replaced, such as coal, natural gas, and oil.

Let's consider nonrenewable natural resources first. Only a fixed amount of oil or coal exists, so the more that is used in any given year, the less remains for future use. As some of the resource is used today, less is available next year. This concept is shown in Figure 8.6. The vertical line along the right side of the figure illustrates the idea that there is a fixed amount of the resource. Although there is a fixed amount in total, at any given time there is a varying amount depending on the price of the resource. For example, supply curve $S_{present}$ represents the quantity that resource owners are willing to extract and offer for sale during any particular year. As the price rises, more is extracted now, leaving less available in the future. This causes the supply curve of the resource in the future to shift up, as shown in Figure 8.6 by the move from $S_{present}$ to S_{future}. The shift occurs because the cost of acquiring or extracting the resource rises as the amount of the resource in existence falls. For instance, in the late 1800s, oil became an important resource. At first, it was extracted with small pumps that gathered up the oil seeping out of the ground. Once that extremely accessible source was gone, wells had to be dug. Over time, wells had to be deeper and be placed in progressively more difficult terrain. From land, to the ocean off California, to the rugged waters off Alaska, to the wicked North Sea, the search for oil has progressed. Each progression is more difficult and thus more costly.

The demand for a nonrenewable natural resource is determined in the same way as the demand for any other resource. Demand is the value of that resource to the firm and to consumers at each price—what the resource contributes to the firm's revenue and consumers' enjoyment.

Equilibrium occurs in the market for a nonrenewable natural resource when the demand for and supply of that resource are equal, as shown in Figure 8.6 at

FIGURE 8.6 The Market for Nonrenewable Resources

Supply curve $S_{present}$ represents the quantity that resource owners are willing to extract and offer for sale during any particular year. As the price rises, more is extracted now, leaving less available in the future, $S_{present}$ to S_{future}. The demand for a nonrenewable natural resource depends on what the resource contributes to the firm's revenue and consumers' enjoyment. Equilibrium occurs in the market for a nonrenewable natural resource when the demand and supply curves intersect.

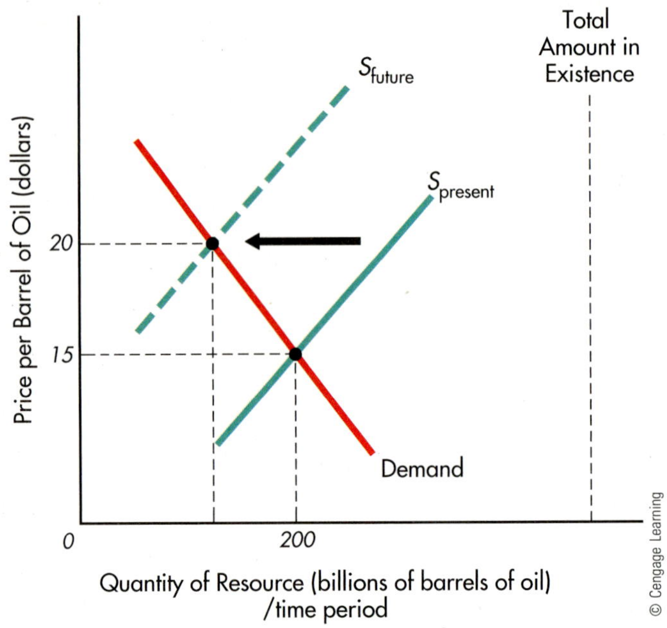

$15 and 200 billion barrels. The equilibrium price, $15, and equilibrium quantity, 200 billion barrels, represent the price and quantity today. Extracting and selling the equilibrium quantity of 200 billion barrels today reduces the quantity available in the future by 200 billion barrels. This means that extracting the resource tomorrow is probably going to be more costly than extracting it today. Thus, the supply curve for the resource in the future (S_{future}) lies above the supply curve for the present ($S_{present}$) if any of the resource is being consumed today. With a higher supply curve and the same demand, the price is higher, $20 rather than $15. Thus, the price in the future is likely to be higher than the price today if some of the resource is extracted and sold today.

The resource owner must decide whether to extract and sell the resource today or leave it in the ground for future use. Suppose that by extracting and selling the oil that lies below someone's land today, the landowner can make a profit of $10 per barrel after all costs have been paid. With that $10 the owner could buy stocks or bonds, put the money into a savings account, or use it to acquire education or marketable skills. If the owner could earn 10 percent doing one of these alternatives, then, in essence, the owner would realize $11 one year from now from the $10 profit obtained today. Should the oil be extracted today? The answer depends on how much profit the resource owner expects to earn on the oil one year from now, which depends on the price of oil and the cost of extraction one year from now. The high price would also induce people to search for alternatives—to invent new technologies that do not use petroleum, for example.

You can probably understand why economists argue that it is unlikely the world will ever run out of nonrenewable resources. As the total amount of oil or any other nonrenewable resource in existence is reduced, its price in the future will rise. It will continue rising as the supply dwindles until it is so high that no one would extract the oil, thus saving it for the future.

Renewable natural resources are different from nonrenewable resources in the sense that renewable (nonexhaustible) natural resources can be used repeatedly without depleting the amount available for future use. Plants and animals can replenish themselves if there are enough members of a species available to reproduce. The problem is not that there is a fixed quantity of a renewable natural resource but that it will be consumed too rapidly for it to reproduce. The role of the market for renewable resources is to determine a price at which the quantity of the resource used is just sufficient to enable the resource to renew itself at a rate that best satisfies society's wants. For instance, the rate at which trees are harvested depends on comparing the rate at which the value of the forests increases over time and the rate that could be earned by razing the forests, selling the trees, and placing the money into another activity today. A large harvest one year means fewer trees available in the future and a longer time for renewal to occur. This would suggest a lower price for the trees today and a higher price in the future, which would induce some tree owners to hold off harvesting their trees.

The markets for nonrenewable and renewable resources operate to ensure that current and future wants are satisfied in the least costly manner and that resources are used in their highest-valued alternative now and in the future. When a nonrenewable resource is being rapidly depleted, its future price rises so that less of the resource is used today. When a renewable resource is being used at a rate that does not allow the resource to replenish itself, the future price rises so that less of the resource is used today.

The markets for natural resources can allocate resources to their highest-valued uses as long as private property rights are well defined and enforced. Problems arise when private property rights are not well defined and enforced.

Consider the British Petroleum (BP) oil well in the Gulf of Mexico that exploded and then began spewing oil in 2010. Every day, thousands of gallons of oil flowed out of the well, which was five miles offshore and a mile under sea level, and caused enormous damage to the coastline. The crude oil killed wildlife, ruined fishing industries, and discouraged families from using the beach, thereby harming tourist-based businesses.

A major problem with the 2010 accident in the Gulf of Mexico is that government intervention in the market had forced BP to move 50 miles out to sea and attempt to extract oil from a well one mile under the sea level. So when the accident did occur, it was much more difficult to plug the hole and stop the gushing oil than if the oil well had been on land or in shallow waters.

Can government control and regulation do better than the free market when it comes to protecting the environment? Not unless the government were to simply eliminate all oil drilling anywhere; government regulation is what forced BP to drill for oil 50 miles out to sea.

Opponents of free markets might argue that the BP oil spill is an example of a negative externality and that an externality is a *market failure*—meaning that the free market cannot work in such cases. In this case, the speed of adjustment of the free market is not at the core of the argument among free market economists and those who favor government intervention; instead, the issue is whether externalities are market failures. Remember that the definition of a market failure is that the market does not allocate resources to their highest-valued use.

Economic profit is a signal; it indicates whether more resources will be allocated to an activity and whether existing resources in an activity will flow to another use. Suppose it costs me $.70 to produce a cup of coffee and I sell that cup of coffee for $1.50. I am earning a positive economic profit, which means I am earning more than my opportunity costs. Others, seeing that I am profitable, think they might also do better switching over from what they currently are doing to sell coffee. This competition drives the price down. Now, what would happen if the coffee's roasting process sent out a noxious smell that sickened people walking by? In that case, I am creating a negative externality. I don't pay for the sickness that the roasting of beans causes, and I don't charge my customers extra to pay for it. Therefore, the price of my coffee does not take into account all costs—the price is lower than it should be. For society as a whole, too much coffee is roasted and consumed. This is, by definition, a market failure. Consider what would happen if the noxious odor is disliked enough that people refuse to purchase my coffee until I get the emissions under control. If enough people did this, I would "internalize" the externality so that I did not lose my entire business. My costs would rise, and I might raise the price a little. The higher price would mean fewer beans are roasted and consumed. In this case, the market did eventually deal with the externality and forced it to be internalized.

The market can deal with an externality over time if private property rights are well defined. Clearly my roasting process caused the illness; I owned the emissions. Similarly, BP owns the oil that gushed out of the blown well in the Gulf of Mexico. It will have to pay for damages the oil creates. But not everything affected by the oil spill is owned. Will BP compensate someone for the wildlife killed by the sludge and the businesses harmed as a result of the spill or will the government have to impose some type of cost on BP? BP did set up a fund to compensate those harmed by the spill. BP was also fined by the government and investigations continue on exactly who was at fault in causing the spill.

RECAP

1. Nonrenewable natural resources are natural resources whose supply is fixed. Renewable natural resources are natural resources that can be replenished.
2. The gap between the equilibrium price today and the equilibrium price at some point in the future generates a rate of return on resources. When that rate of return exceeds what is currently available elsewhere, then the resource is not extracted or used. When that return is less than what can be earned elsewhere, the resource is extracted and sold.
3. Under ideal economic conditions, the harvest rate of renewable resources is such that the amount used meets society's demands and allows the resources to reproduce.
4. Is the free market able to deal with externalities? If private property rights can be assigned, then it is likely the market can force the internalization of the externality.
5. In cases where private property rights cannot be assigned, the free market will have difficulty solving an externality problem.

4. ILLICIT DRUGS

5

Will drug legalization be better than the war on drugs?

The market for illicit or illegal drugs is complicated, large, and a very interesting illustration of how markets function. Worldwide trade in illicit drugs constitutes 4 percent of total world trade, as much as textiles and steel. The biggest share of the trade occurs in the United States. Americans spend nearly \$60 billion a year on illegal drugs—\$38 billion on cocaine, \$10 billion on heroin, \$7 billion on marijuana, and \$3 billion on other illegal drugs—about 60 percent of all illicit drugs consumed in the world.

4.a. The Suppliers

Figure 8.7 illustrates the demand, cost, and profit conditions of a supplier of illicit drugs. The supplier's costs include harvesting and refining the drug, transporting it to the drug dealers in the United States, paying employees, and securing the weapons and bribes necessary to carry out the business. Those costs are shown as the average-total-cost and marginal-cost curves. The supplier will maximize profit by determining the quantity at which $MR=MC$ and then setting a price to sell that amount. The resulting quantity is Q, and the price is P.

The supplier is earning a positive economic profit, so other suppliers want to get in on the business. The ease or difficulty of entry depends on the type of

FIGURE 8.7 The Market for Illicit Drugs

The market demand consists of the demand of all users, addicts as well as casual users. The supplier of the drugs finds the quantity, *Q*, at which *MR* = *MC* and sets the price at the demand for the quantity, *P*.

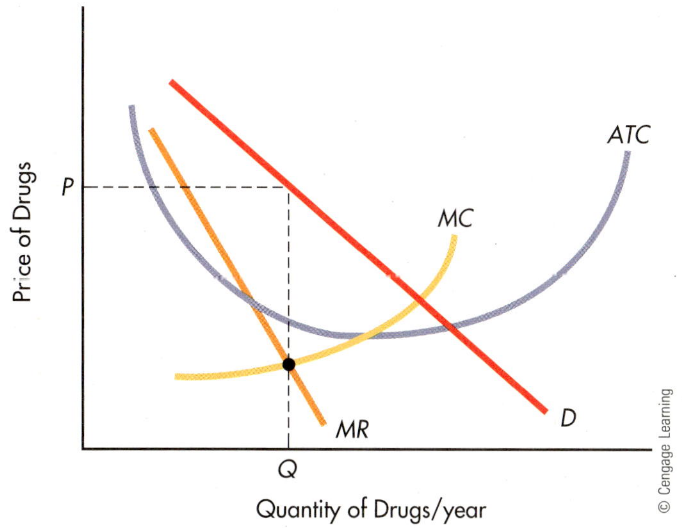

illicit drug. It is not difficult to enter the market for so-called designer drugs such as amphetamines and crystal ice. A few over-the-counter chemicals and an abandoned building are sufficient to manufacture the drugs. The markets for cocaine and heroin are more difficult to enter. A supplier must have access to the resources (coca and poppies) as well as the refining facilities and transportation and distribution channels to get the product to the market.

Since there are few suppliers in the cocaine and heroin markets, what each one does affects the others. If one attempts to increase its market area, the others respond. If one lowers the price, the others respond. In situations in which there are just a few suppliers, the suppliers often decide it is better to cooperate than to engage in cutthroat competition. Thus, drug cartels have been formed, such as Medellin, Sinaloa, Belarussa, and so forth. The cartels assign territories to members and dictate quantities and prices.

As with most cartels, there is an enforcer ensuring that other members follow the rules. In the Organization of Petroleum Exporting Countries (OPEC), Saudi Arabia serves as the enforcer. Whenever one of the member nations decides to increase oil production above its quota, Saudi Arabia will open its facilities and flood the market with oil. The cheating nation ends up with lower revenues than if it had remained within its quota. In the National College Athletic Association (NCAA), whenever a school athletic department cheats, the NCAA administration penalizes it with forfeiture of prize money and sanctions.

The enforcer in the drug cartel literally destroys the errant supplier; drive-by shootings, bombings, and so on, are the ways in which the cartel's enforcer ensures that cheating by members of the cartel won't occur.

As with all profit-maximizing firms, drug suppliers want to alter the demand curves for their products, making them more price inelastic and shifting them out. Since the demand by the hard-core user is very price inelastic already, the suppliers focus on the novice or first time user's demand. Their demand is very elastic—they will only "try" the drug if the price is very low. By offering discounts, higher quality drugs, and even free samples, the suppliers hope to change the price elasticity of demand.

The suppliers would also like to reduce their costs. The primary cost of the drug suppliers is the cost of avoiding having products confiscated, employees arrested, and facilities destroyed. Suppliers attempt to reduce the probability of such costs by bribing or, in some cases, assassinating officials.

Although operating in an illegal market means there are costs of avoiding detection, would the existing suppliers like to see drugs legalized? The answer is a resounding *no*. Legalization would reduce the costs of entry to potential new suppliers and drive down economic profits.

4.b. The War on Drugs

Throughout the ages, governments have chosen to ban products and activities. In Egypt in the 1500s, coffee was banned. Tobacco was banned in Russia and the Ottoman Empire in the 1700s. The United States banned the sale and use of alcohol in the 1920s. Opiates and cocaine were banned in the United States in 1914; marijuana was banned in 1937. The United States has devoted enormous resources to the attempt to control illicit drugs, without much apparent success. The federal government currently spends about $30 billion per year on what is called "the war on drugs." State and local governments spend another $20 billion each year. In addition, nearly 50 percent of all arrests and incarcerations are related to the drug war. Yet consumption of drugs has increased over the past 20 years.

The government's war on drugs focuses primarily on the supply side of the market. Most economists agree that the war on drugs has raised the cost of supplying and selling drugs. Some costs are not increased—drug suppliers, for example, do not pay income taxes or social security taxes, nor do they obey minimum wage laws or other labor regulations. Nevertheless, the net effect of prohibition is to increase the costs of supplying the good or service. Who pays these higher costs? Because the buyer wants the drugs almost as much at a very high price as at a low price (price inelasticity of demand), the supplier just adds the extra costs to the price. In other words, the costs are passed on from supplier to buyer. In Figure 8.8, the extreme case of a perfectly inelastic demand is illustrated. The *MC* curve shifts up to reflect the increased costs imposed on the suppliers by the war on drugs. But the supplier simply increases the price, from P_1 to P_2. The price increase fully reflects the increased costs.

FIGURE 8.8 A Perfectly Inelastic Demand and the War on Drugs

The supplier can pass along costs to the consumer in terms of a higher price. In the case of a perfectly inelastic demand, the price increase is equal to the increased costs caused by the war on drugs.

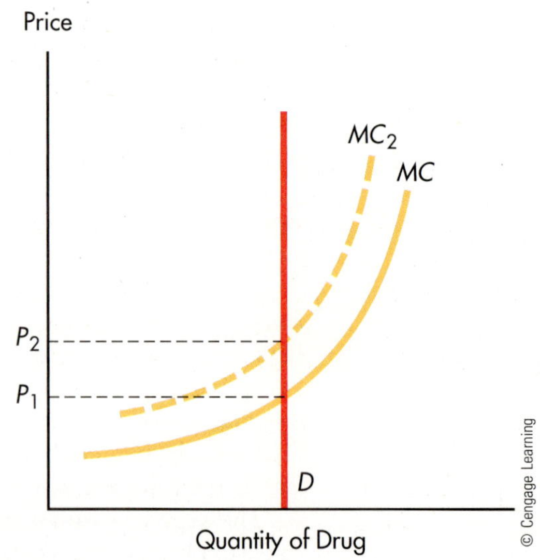

The more elastic the demand, the less can be passed along to consumers in terms of a higher price. If, for example, demand was perfectly elastic, then none of the increased costs could be passed along to consumers as a higher price.

Why is it so difficult to eliminate a good or service? It is because of the price elasticity of demand. When demand is inelastic, prohibition drives up prices but does not reduce the quantity demanded. Banning something with an elastic demand would be much easier. In fact, if demand was very elastic, a ban could drive the product out of existence. Raising the suppliers' costs results in a reduction in profits since suppliers cannot raise price and continue selling about the same amount. Buyers are not willing and able to pay a higher price for the banned item. So if economic profit is driven down to where it is negative, suppliers would stop supplying.

The ban on illicit drugs leads to a higher price. This means that drug users have to look for a way of getting the same result at a lower cost. During alcohol prohibition (1920–1933), the United States changed from a nation that consumed mostly beer and wine to one that consumed primarily bourbon and gin. Consumers wanted to consume alcohol, but the illegality of it drove prices up. The higher prices caused consumers to look for forms of alcohol that were less costly. Since bourbon and gin had about 40 percent alcohol and beer and wine less than 10 percent, bourbon and gin were better buys. In addition, the supply of beer and wine was reduced more than that of so-called hard liquor. Suppliers found it more profitable to deal in the most potent form of liquor possible. Why risk smuggling a keg of beer when a case of whiskey brought higher profits at a lower risk of being found out by authorities? The same thing has occurred with illicit drugs. In drug-producing countries such as Peru and Afghanistan, people use illicit drug crops in their natural form (chewing coca leaves and smoking raw opium), which is far less powerful than the processed forms in which the drugs are available in the Western countries.

NOW YOU TRY IT

Using Figure 8.5, illustrate a case where demand is perfectly elastic. Show how price will not rise when costs rise.

Suppliers begin supplying ever more potent forms of the banned substance because their profit per unit of output is higher. In addition, because purchases of the banned substance are illegal, buyers have no way to verify the quality of the product they are buying. When you purchase aspirin, you know the brand name of the supplier—Bayer, for instance. Cocaine users don't know whether the fellow on the street corner is reliable or even if he will be there tomorrow. As a result, the supplier may "cut" his drugs with impurities or substances that increase profit. These may lead to bad reactions or even death. In fact, many so-called overdoses appear to be negative reactions to impurities in the drugs.

Illicit drugs are typically supplied by a monopoly or a cartel acting like a monopoly. Each drug dealer is a member of the cartel. As such, they are told how much they can sell, where they can sell it, and the price they must charge. Although drug dealers might make money by selling their prescribed drugs at prescribed prices, each also thinks that he or she could do better selling even more or selling at a higher price. So, quite often, the drug dealers try to push a few more drugs, move to a better location, or charge a slightly higher price.

These practices create problems for the cartel. If one drug dealer gets away with the behavior, others may try to do the same thing. If the practices become widespread, the cartel would dissolve, and economic profits would be driven down as competition and entry occur. So the cartel ensures that members don't cheat. Gang killings and turf battles are typically the cartel's enforcers making sure that the dealers don't cheat on the cartel.

Some consumers are unable to pay the higher prices for the drugs. But desiring the drugs or being addicted to them means the consumers must obtain money. One way to do this is through crime. As prohibition occurs and becomes more stringent, crimes of property and theft rise.

4.c. The Free Market: Legalizing Drugs

Nobel economist Milton Friedman argued as long ago as 1972 that legalizing drugs would simultaneously reduce the amount of crime and raise the quality of law enforcement. Yet the idea never gathered much support, probably because of the fear that legalization would lower prices and cause more people to try drugs. For instance, it's estimated that cocaine sells for 10 to 40 times its free market price, so the drug would be much less expensive if legalized.

What does the lower price do to consumption? It depends on the price elasticity of demand. Although demand for illicit drugs is highly inelastic, it is not perfectly inelastic. This means that lower prices for drugs would encourage some additional consumption. How much more would depend on how inelastic demand is. The demand for marijuana is probably more price elastic than the demand for heroin or cocaine, because marijuana is viewed as being less addictive and less harmful. Legalization of marijuana would lead to lower prices and additional consumption. It would also lead to fewer people being incarcerated due to selling or buying marijuana and, obviously, significantly lower enforcement costs. Legalization of cocaine and heroin would probably lead to some additional consumption but less so than in the case of marijuana.

Legalization means that using, buying, or selling a legal drug is all right. It is no different than using, buying, or selling tobacco, or alcohol, or soda. Decriminalization means that using, buying, or selling an illegal drug carries no criminal penalty. There are no test cases for complete legalization of illicit drugs but there are for decriminalization of such drugs.

In 2001, Portugal became the first European country to officially abolish all criminal penalties for personal possession of drugs, including marijuana, cocaine, heroin, and methamphetamine. Under Portugal's new regime, people found guilty of possessing small amounts of drugs are sent to a panel consisting of a psychologist, social worker, and legal adviser for appropriate treatment (which may be refused without criminal punishment), instead of jail. Many critics of this policy claimed that it would lead to increased drug usage. But, a study in 2009 found that in the five years after personal possession was decriminalized, illegal drug use among teens in Portugal declined and rates of new HIV infections caused by sharing of dirty needles dropped, while the number of people seeking treatment for drug addiction more than doubled.[8]

RECAP

1. The market for some illicit drugs is difficult to enter. Suppliers have formed cartels and restricted entry.
2. The demand for illicit drugs is inelastic.
3. Increasing the costs of supplying drugs causes the suppliers to increase the price. Because demand is inelastic, the suppliers' profits remain high, and drug users pay the increased costs in terms of a higher price.
4. Prohibition has increased costs, led to more potent forms of drugs in use, and caused increased levels of crime.
5. Legalization of drugs would lead to lower costs and reduce the ill effects of illegal markets. Coupled with a tax, the level of consumption following legalization would not increase.
6. The market for illegal drugs is easy to enter. As a result, economic profit is driven to zero by competition. Drug prohibition can make entry more difficult and enable suppliers to earn positive economic profits.

[8] White Paper, April 2, 2009, *Drug Decriminalization in Portugal: Lessons for Creating Fair and Successful Drug Policies*, by Glenn Greenwald.

5. DISCRIMINATION

6

Can discrimination occur in a free market?

discrimination: the practice of treating people differently in a market, based on a characteristic having nothing to do with that market

Discrimination is the practice of treating different people differently in a market, based on some characteristic that has nothing to do with the market. In the labor market, discrimination occurs when someone or some group receives favorable treatment for a reason that has nothing to do with that person's or group's job performance.

5.a. Can Discrimination Exist in a Free Market?

Discrimination on the basis of characteristics that have nothing to do with one's job performance is costly in a market in which entry is easy. Suppose, for instance, that customers preferred to be served by only a certain kind of individual. Customers would then have to be willing to pay higher prices to be served by the preferred group. This concept is illustrated in Figure 8.9.

The firm can supply the good by using the services of any employee, along cost curve MC_A. The firm can also use the preferred employees, but then the cost of supplying the good is higher (MC_P). Those customers who want the product but only if served by the preferred group must pay P_P, whereas those customers choosing to be served by anyone pay only P_A.

Discrimination requires paying a premium to associate or not to associate with certain groups. As we know, any firm not using resources efficiently will be driven out of the market if entry is easy. When entry is easy, higher costs due to discrimination could drive the discriminating firm out of the market. If customers are not willing to pay the premium (the difference between P_P and P_A), then the firm cannot discriminate.

If a firm has erected strict barriers to entry, then the discrimination may not be costly. A monopoly or even a government agency that does not have to compete with another firm could get away with using resources less efficiently. Managers, employees, and even customers of monopolies or government agencies may be able to discriminate without having more efficient firms drive them out of the market. Indeed, studies have shown that most discrimination takes place in government agencies, firms that do business with the government, and regulated monopolies.

5.b. Statistical Discrimination

Discrimination may occur because of a lack of information rather than a taste for or against certain groups. For instance, employers must try to predict the

FIGURE 8.9 Discrimination

The demand by customers for a product is *D*. The supplier has a marginal cost of MC_P to supply the good if the employee is a member of the preferred group and MC_A if the employee is not a member of the preferred group.

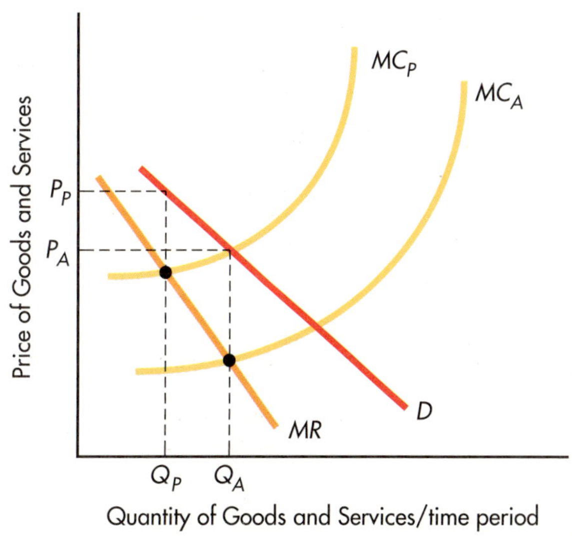

potential value of job applicants to the firm, but rarely do they know what a worker's actual value will be. Often, the only information available when they hire someone is information that may be imperfectly related to value in general and may not apply to a particular person at all. Using characteristics such as education, experience, age, and test scores as the basis for selecting among job applicants may keep some very good people from getting a job and may result in hiring some unproductive people.

Suppose two types of workers apply for a word-processing job—those who can process 80 words per minute and those who can process only 40 words per minute. The problem is that these actual productivities are unknown to the employer. The employer can observe only the results of a five-minute word-processing test given to all applicants. How can the employer decide who is lucky or unlucky on the test and who can actually process 80 words per minute? Suppose the employer discovers that applicants from a particular vocational college, the AAA School, are taught to perform well on preemployment tests, but their average overall performance as employees is less than that of the rest of the applicants—some do well and some do not. The employer might decide to reject all applicants from AAA because the good and bad ones can't be differentiated. Is the employer discriminating against AAA? The answer is yes. The employer is **statistically discriminating**. Statistical discrimination can cause a systematic preference for one group over another at the expense of some individuals in the group.

statistically discriminating: using characteristics that apply to a group, although not to all individual members of that group, as an allocation device

What is the effect of a ban on statistical discrimination? It would raise the firm's costs. The firm would either have to collect information about each applicant or risk hiring some of the lower-quality word processors. Since costs rise, profits fall. This would induce the firm to reduce its output and to reduce the number of resources used, including labor.

So would a ban on statistical discrimination be a good law even if it raises costs and creates job losses? The answer is determined by comparing the costs and benefits to society of allowing statistical discrimination versus the costs and benefits to society of outlawing statistical discrimination.

RECAP

1. Discrimination is costly in a market economy when entry into markets is easy.
2. Statistical discrimination occurs due to a lack of information. When the characteristics of a group are imposed on each member of that group whether they apply or not, statistical discrimination occurs.

ECONOMIC INSIGHT

Discrimination and Poor Word-Processing Skills

In 2007, Adrian Zachariasewycz filed suit against the law firm Morris, Nichols, Arsht & Tunnell, as well as the University of Michigan Law School. Zachariasewycz claimed that Morris, Nichols fired him unlawfully during his summer associateship and that the firing both defamed him and violated his due process rights. In the claim brought against the law school, it was alleged that Michigan's grading system discriminated against him and other students because of poor typing skills. The complaint read: "Certain exams taken by [plaintiff] that required students to be skilled touch-typists in order to produce a competitive response resulted in borderline failing grades by virtue of the low volume of prose [plaintiff] could type in the time allotted as compared with other students." The lawsuit asked for an unspecified amount of money damages.

SUMMARY

What is a free market?

1. A free competitive market is one in which entry is easy and prices and other information are well known.
2. A free market is not interfered with by government.

What is the main reason many economists do not believe in or trust the free market?

3. The free market adjusts to demand and supply changes, but the time it takes to adjust is what concerns many economists.
4. John Maynard Keynes captured the debate with his statement that "in the long run we are all dead."

Can a free market provide health care or is a government-run health care system necessary?

5. A free market can handle health care just as it handles any other good or service, but the current health care market is far from a free market.
6. The free market means some people get the good or service and some don't. Care is not distributed equally. But with health care being scarce, no allocation system will ensure everyone gets equal health care.
7. The government interventions such as Medicare and Medicaid have led to rapidly rising health care costs.
8. Health care costs have also risen because of the way health insurance is provided. An employer-based system creates inefficiencies—for example, those without jobs do not have insurance, and those with preconditions have difficulty finding insurance.
9. The third-party payer system—where neither buyer nor seller pays for health care—creates inefficiencies. Buyers do not care how much health care costs, and sellers provide services on the basis of reimbursement rates, not on consumer costs.

Is the free market able to handle environmental accidents?

10. Environmental issues occur in the markets for resources.
11. Renewable resources are resources that can replenish themselves.
12. Nonrenewable resources are resources whose total amount in existence is limited.
13. The market for resources determines prices at which the rate of use of renewable resources allows the resources to replenish and limits the rate at which the nonrenewable resources are consumed.
14. A free resource market would not necessarily guarantee that accidents and environmental disasters would never occur. However, without government interventions and restrictions in the market, it is likely fewer accidents would occur.
15. Most environmental problems are the result of private property rights not being well defined. When no one owns something, no one takes care of it.
16. When an externality occurs, either too much or too little is consumed or produced relative to the quantities that would occur if all costs and benefits were included.
17. If the costs of the externalities can be internalized, the socially desired level of emissions will result. The market will minimize externalities if private property rights are well defined so that the creators of externalities are forced to internalize the externalities.

18. Global environmental problems are more difficult to resolve than domestic ones because of the lack of property rights. When no one government owns the resource being damaged by an externality, then the externality cannot be resolved by any one government.

Will a free market for drugs be better than the war on drugs?

19. Banning or prohibiting items for which consumers have a price-elastic demand is relatively easy. People just switch to a close substitute. Banning items for which demand is price inelastic is another matter. Consumers don't have substitutes, so they continue attempting to purchase the banned item.
20. The war on drugs has raised the cost of supplying and selling drugs. Yet because demand is price inelastic, consumption has not decreased much. Costs are passed along to consumers, who pay higher prices but consume nearly as much.
21. The war on drugs results in suppliers offering ever more potent forms of the drugs. In addition, the incentive to maintain quality of the drugs is reduced as suppliers seek additional profits.
22. Crime rises as suppliers compete for turf and sales and consumers look for resources with which to purchase the drugs.
23. Legalization of drugs would reduce crime and lower the prices of drugs, possibly leading to increased consumption.

Does discrimination make economic sense?

24. Discrimination occurs when some factor not related to an individual's value to the firm affects the wage rate that person receives.
25. Discrimination is costly to those who discriminate and should not last in a market economy, at least when entry is easy.
26. Statistical discrimination is the result of imperfect information and can occur as long as information is imperfect.

EXERCISES

1. What is a free market? Why do governments interfere with the operation of free markets?
2. Why have expenditures on medical care risen more rapidly than expenditures on any other goods and services?
3. Why are there more medical specialists and fewer general practitioners in the United States now than was the case 50 years ago?
4. What is a third-party payer? How does that affect the cost of health care?
5. Explain what is meant by the term *discrimination*. Explain what statistical discrimination is.
6. Why do economists say that discrimination is inherently inefficient and therefore will not occur in general?
7. Use the following table to answer these four questions:
   a. What are the external costs per unit of output?
   b. What level of output will be produced?
   c. What level of output should be produced to achieve economic efficiency?
   d. What is the value to society of correcting the externality?

Quantity	Marginal Costs (*MC*)	Marginal Social Costs (*MSC*)	Marginal Revenue (*MR*)
1	$ 2	$ 4	$ 12
2	4	6	10
3	6	8	8
4	8	10	6
5	10	12	4

8. If, in exercise 7, the *MC* and *MSC* columns were reversed, you would have an example of what? Would too much or too little of the good be produced?

9. Overfishing refers to catching fish at a rate that does not allow the fish to repopulate. What is the fundamental problem associated with overfishing of the oceans? What might lead to underfishing?

10. Compare a ban on trans fats to a ban on cocaine. What do the markets look like? How are they different? Which ban would be easier to enforce? Explain.

STUDY GUIDE FOR CHAPTER 8

Key Term Match

Match each term with its correct definition by placing the appropriate letter next to the corresponding number.

A. renewable resources
B. nonrenewable resources
C. discrimination
D. statistically discriminating
E. Third party payer

____ 1. resources that can replenish themselves

____ 2. the practice of treating people differently in a market which is based on a characteristic having nothing to do with that market

____ 3. Someone other than the demander or the supplier is paying for the good or service

____ 4. using characteristics that apply to a group, although not to all individual members of that group, as an allocation device

____ 5. resources that cannot replenish themselves

Quick-Check Quiz

1. Which of the following would reduce health care costs?
   - ☐ a. Requiring everyone to buy health insurance.
   - ☐ b. Getting rid of the third party payment system
   - ☐ c. Restricting the flow of prescription drugs from other countries
   - ☐ d. Requiring Medicare and Medicaid to cover more services
   - ☐ e. Prohibiting physicians from advertising the cost of their services

2. Which of the following statements is true?
   - ☐ a. Suppliers of illicit drugs would like to see these drugs legalized because their costs would decrease.
   - ☐ b. The markets for cocaine and heroin have barriers to entry.
   - ☐ c. If illicit drugs were legalized, the drug cartels would make higher profits.
   - ☐ d. The government's policy of eliminating drug "factories" and confiscating supplies addresses the differences between addicts and experimental users.
   - ☐ e. Designer drugs are extremely difficult to manufacture.

Practice Questions and Problems

1. ______________ means that someone other than the demander or supplier is paying for the good or service.
2. Keynesians believe that the time that free markets take to adjust to market conditions is ______________ (relatively short, too long).
3. The market can deal with an externality over time if ______________ are well defined.
4. The demand for illicit drugs by hard-core users is price ______________ (elastic, inelastic).
5. The lower the price elasticity of demand, the ______________ (easier, tougher) it is to ban illegal drugs.
6. Legalizing drugs would ______________ (increase, decrease) the costs of production and ______________ (increase, decrease) the profits made by drug cartels.
7. The U.S. antidrug effort consists of trying to reduce the ______________ (supply of, demand for) illegal drugs.
8. When drug dealers' costs rise, they pass these costs to consumers if demand is ______________ (elastic, inelastic).
9. Discrimination based on personal prejudice is usually ______________ (costly, profitable) for a firm.
10. When entry is ______________ (easy, difficult), having higher costs due to discrimination may drive a firm out of the market.

Exercises and Applications

I Creative Destruction

During the years 2008–2010 the economy experienced a serious crisis; demand declined, as did income and output. A debate raged among economists as to whether the government should increase spending and bail out failing companies, or whether the economy should be left alone to eventually adjust back to growth and full employment.

1. Suppose the state of the economy is represented by the following graph where demand and supply (D_1 and S_1) represent the total demand in the economy for goods and services and the total supply of those goods and services.
   a. The market equilibrium shows that quantity of output is ______________ and the overall price level is ______________.
   b. Using the ideas presented in this chapter, explain what occurs as demand decreases.

____

____

____

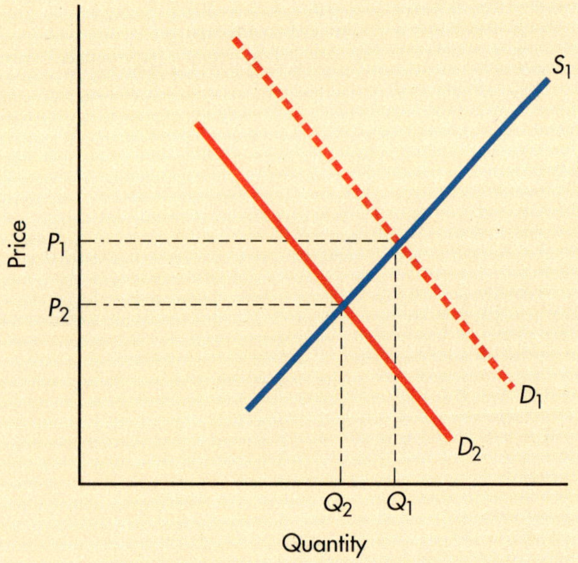

2. If the economy is left alone, what occurs? What does the new equilibrium represent, full employment or unemployment? If the government increases spending, what occurs?

____

____

____

3. One of the most useful characteristics of a market economy is that price changes signal changes in the relative scarcity of different products and resources and encourage people to respond to those changes. Can you think of any ways in which labor markets, by setting salaries based on comparable worth, can do the same thing without having math teachers receiving higher salaries than English teachers?

____

____

____

II Drug Prohibition and Drug Addiction

In the text it was noted that in drug-producing countries such as Peru and Afghanistan, people use illicit drug crops in their natural form (e.g., chewing coca leaves and smoking raw opium), which is far less powerful than the processed forms in which the drugs are available in Western countries. Why are the drugs shipped to Western countries so much more powerful than the drugs found in the drug-producing countries?

____

____

____

III Insurance and Health Care Costs

The United States relies on a third-party payment system whereby individuals and employers purchase insurance that allows patients to receive health care services that are in turn paid for by insurance providers. For the elderly and disabled, the government assumes the role of the insurer, using funds from payroll taxes from current workers to pay medical providers for care provided to those currently enrolled in Medicare, Medicaid, and other public health care programs.

The purpose of insurance, whether public or private, is to spread catastrophic risks over a large pool of individuals. Automobile insurance provides an excellent example. When was the last time you submitted a claim to your auto insurer asking to be reimbursed for an oil change or a tire rotation? Never. But that begs the question, why do you have auto insurance? For most of us, the answer is to cover the cost of a new car if we total our current one or to cover the expense (both property and medical) of the other party if we are involved in a multivehicle crash.

1. For the sake of argument, let's assume that auto insurance *did* pay for routine maintenance. How would this affect your behavior?

____

____

2. What would this change do to the demand for automobile maintenance? What would happen to the prices of automobile maintenance?

____

____

____

____

You can find further practice tests in the Online Quiz at: www.cengagebrain.com

iDoncept/Shutterstock.com

PART 3
The National and Global Economies

CHAPTER 9
An Overview of the National and International Economies

9-1 What is a household, and what is household income and spending?

9-2 What is a business firm, and what is business spending?

9-3 How does the international sector affect the economy?

9-4 What does government do?

9-5 How do the three private sectors—households, businesses, and the international sector—interact in the economy?

9-6 How does the government interact with the other sectors of the economy?

CHAPTER 10
Macroeconomic Measures

10-1 How is the total output of an economy measured?

10-2 What is the difference between nominal and real GDP?

10-3 What is the purpose of a price index?

10-4 How is money traded internationally?

10-5 How do nations record their transactions with the rest of the world?

CHAPTER 11
Unemployment, Inflation, and Business Cycles

11-1 What is a business cycle?

11-2 How is the unemployment rate defined and measured?

11-3 What is the cost of unemployed resources?

11-4 What is inflation?

11-5 Why is inflation a problem?

CHAPTER 12
Macroeconomic Equilibrium: Aggregate Demand and Supply

12-1 What is aggregate demand?

12-2 What causes the aggregate demand curve to shift?

12-3 What is aggregate supply?

12-4 Why does the short-run aggregate supply curve become steeper as real GDP increases?

12-5 Why is the long-run aggregate supply curve vertical?

12-6 What causes the aggregate supply curve to shift?

12-7 What determines the equilibrium price level and real GDP?

CHAPTER 13
Fiscal Policy

13-1 How can fiscal policy eliminate a GDP gap?

13-2 How has U.S. fiscal policy changed over time?

13-3 What are the effects of budget deficits?

13-4 How does fiscal policy differ across countries?

CHAPTER 14
Money and Banking

14-1 What is money?

14-2 How is the U.S. money supply defined?

14-3 How do countries pay for international transactions?

14-4 Why are banks considered intermediaries?

14-5 How does international banking differ from domestic banking?

14-6 How do banks create money?

9
An Overview of the National and International Economies

FUNDAMENTAL QUESTIONS

1. What is a household, and what is household income and spending?
2. What is a business firm, and what is business spending?
3. How does the international sector affect the economy?
4. What does government do?
5. How do the three private sectors—households, businesses, and the international sector—interact in the economy?
6. How does the government interact with the other sectors of the economy?

PREVIEW

You decide to buy a new Toyota, so you go to a Toyota dealer and exchange money for the car. The Toyota dealer has rented land and buildings and hired workers in order to make cars available to you and other members of the public. The employees earn income paid by the Toyota dealer and then use their incomes to buy food from the grocery store. This transaction generates revenue for the grocery store, which hires workers and pays them incomes that they then use to buy groceries and Toyotas. Your expenditure for the Toyota is part of a circular flow. Revenue is received by the Toyota dealer, who pays employees, who, in turn, buy goods and services.

Of course, the story is complicated by the fact that the Toyota is originally manufactured and purchased in Japan and then shipped to the United States before it can be sold by the local Toyota dealer. Your purchase of the Toyota creates revenue for the local dealer as well as for the manufacturer in Japan, which pays Japanese autoworkers to produce Toyotas. Furthermore, when you buy your Toyota, you must pay a tax to the government, which uses tax revenues to pay for police protection, national defense, the legal system, and other services. Many people in different areas of the economy are involved.

An economy is made up of individual buyers and sellers. Economists could discuss the neighborhood economy that surrounds your university, the economy of the city of Chicago, or the economy of the state of Massachusetts. But typically it is the national economy, the economy of the United States, that is the center of their attention. To clarify the operation of the national economy, economists usually group individual buyers and sellers into sectors: households, businesses, government, and the international sector. Since the U.S. economy affects, and is affected by, the rest of the world, to understand how the economy functions, we must include the international sector. In this chapter, we examine basic data and information on each individual sector and examine how the sectors interact.

1. HOUSEHOLDS

household: one or more persons who occupy a unit of housing

A **household** consists of one or more persons who occupy a unit of housing. The unit of housing may be a house, an apartment, or even a single room, as long as it constitutes separate living quarters. A household may consist of related family members, such as a father, mother, and children, or it may comprise unrelated individuals, such as three college students sharing an apartment. The person in whose name the house or apartment is owned or rented is called the *householder*.

1.a. Number of Households and Household Income

1

What is a household, and what is household income and spending?

There are about 120 million households in the United States. The breakdown of households by age of householder is shown in Figure 9.1. Householders in the age ranges of 35–44 and 45–54 years old make up the largest number of households. Householders between 45 and 54 years old have the largest median income. The *median* is the middle value—half of the households in an age group have an income higher than the median, and half have an income lower than the median. Figure 9.1 shows that households in which the householder is between 45 and 54 years old have a median income of about $64,000, substantially higher than the median incomes of other age groups. Typically, workers in this age group are at the peak of their earning power. Younger households are gaining experience and training; older households include retired workers.

Thirty-three percent of all households are two-person households. The stereotypical household of husband, wife, and two children accounts for only 14 percent of all households. There are relatively few large households in the United States. Of the more than 117 million households in the country, only about 1 percent have seven or more persons.

1.b. Household Spending

consumption: household spending

Household spending is called **consumption**. Householders consume housing, transportation, food, entertainment, and other goods and services. Household spending (also called *consumer spending*) is the largest component of total spending in the economy—rising to about $10.7 trillion in 2011.

FIGURE 9.1 Age of Householder, Number of Households, and Median Household Income in the United States

The figure reveals that householders aged 35 to 44 make up the largest number of households, and householders aged 45 to 54 earn the highest median annual income.

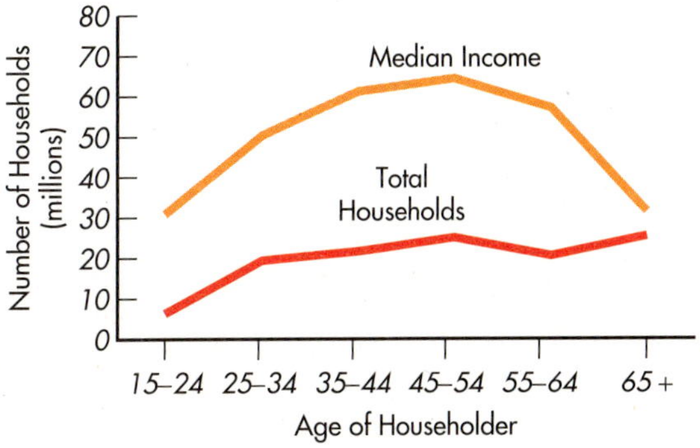

Source: U.S. Department of Commerce, *Current Population Survey, 2012* (http://www.census.gov).

The stereotypical household of husband, wife, and two children accounts for only 14 percent of all households.

RECAP

1. A household consists of one or more persons who occupy a unit of housing.
2. An apartment or house is rented or owned by a householder.
3. As a group, householders between the ages of 45 and 54 have the highest median incomes.
4. Household spending is called consumption.

2. BUSINESS FIRMS

A business firm is a business organization controlled by a single management. The firm's business may be conducted at more than one location. The terms *company*, *enterprise*, and *business* are used interchangeably with *firm*.

2.a. Forms of Business Organizations

2

What is a business firm, and what is business spending?

Firms are organized as sole proprietorships, partnerships, or corporations. A sole proprietorship is a business owned by one person. This type of firm may be a one-person operation or a large enterprise with many employees. In either case, the owner receives all the profits and is responsible for all the debts incurred by the business. There is no separation between the owner and the firm in that the owner has unlimited liability for the firm's debts, and profits are taxed at the owner's individual income tax rate. However, the owner also has sole control over business decisions.

A partnership is a business owned by two or more partners who share both the profits of the business and responsibility for the firm's losses. The partners could be individuals, estates, or other businesses. Partners owning a firm have unlimited liability for firm debts and are taxed at individual tax rates.

State law allows the formation of corporations. A corporation is a business whose identity in the eyes of the law is distinct from the identity of its owners. A corporation is an economic entity that, like a person, can own property and borrow money in its own name. The owners of a corporation are shareholders. If a corporation cannot pay its debts, creditors cannot seek payment from the shareholders' personal wealth. The corporation itself is responsible for all its actions. The shareholders' liability is limited to the value of the stock they own. Corporations are taxed at corporate income tax rates. In many corporations there are many shareholders who exercise no control over the firm. A separation of ownership and control may occur when the professional managers of the firm are different individuals from those who own large amounts of stock.

multinational business: a firm that owns and operates producing units in foreign countries

Many firms are global in their operations even though they may have been founded and may be owned by residents of a single country. Firms typically first enter the international market by selling products to foreign countries. As revenues from these sales increase, the firms realize advantages by locating subsidiaries in foreign countries. A **multinational business** is a firm that owns and operates producing units in foreign countries. The best-known U.S. corporations are multinational firms. Ford, IBM, PepsiCo, and McDonald's all own operating units in many different countries. Ford Motor Company, for instance, is the parent firm of sales organizations and assembly plants located around the world. As transportation and communication technologies progress, multinational business activity will grow.

2.b. Business Statistics

There are far more sole proprietorships than partnerships or corporations in the United States. The great majority of sole proprietorships are small businesses, with revenues under $25,000 a year. Similarly, more than half of all partnerships also have revenues under $25,000 a year, but only about a quarter of the corporations are in this category.

Approximately two-thirds of sole proprietorships earn less than $25,000 per year, but they account for less than 10 percent of the revenue earned by proprietorships. The less than 1 percent of proprietorships with revenue of $1 million or more account for about 20 percent. Even more striking are the figures for partnerships and corporations. The 5 percent of partnerships with the largest revenue account for almost 90 percent of total partnership revenue. In the case of corporations, the lowest 25 percent of revenue firms account for less than 0.1 percent of total corporate revenue, while the top 25 percent of corporations account for more than 90 percent of corporate revenue.

Big business is important in the United States. There are many small firms, but large firms and corporations account for the greatest share of business revenue. Although there are only about one-third as many corporations as sole proprietorships, corporations have more than 15 times the revenue of sole proprietorships.

2.c. Firms Around the World

Big business is a dominant force in the United States. Many people believe that because the United States is the world's largest economy, U.S. firms are the largest in the world. Figure 9.2 shows that this is not entirely true. Of the 10 largest corporations in the world (measured by sales), only three are based in the United States. Big business is not just a U.S. phenomenon.

2.d. Business Spending

investment: spending on capital goods to be used in producing goods and services

Investment is the expenditure by business firms for capital goods—such as machines, tools, and buildings—that will be used to produce goods and services. The economic meaning of *investment* is different from the everyday meaning, "a financial transaction such as buying bonds or stocks." In economics, the term *investment* refers to business spending for capital goods.

FIGURE 9.2 The World's Ten Largest Public Companies

As shown in the chart, large firms are not just a U.S. phenomenon.

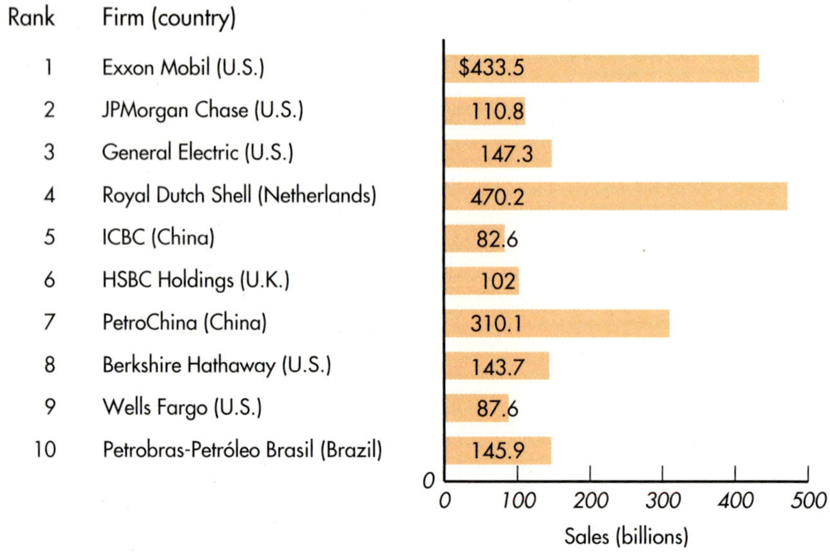

Source: "The Forbes 2000" (http://www.forbes.com/global2000/).

Investment spending in 2011 was $1,916 billion, an amount equal to roughly one-sixth of consumption, or household spending. Investment increases unevenly, actually falling at times and then rising very rapidly. Even though investment spending is much smaller than consumption, the wide swings in investment spending mean that business expenditures are an important factor in determining the economic health of the nation.

RECAP

1. Business firms may be organized as sole proprietorships, partnerships, or corporations.
2. Large corporations account for the largest fraction of total business revenue.
3. Business investment spending fluctuates widely over time.

3. THE INTERNATIONAL SECTOR

3 **How does the international sector affect the economy?**

Today, foreign buyers and sellers have a significant effect on economic conditions in the United States, and developments in the rest of the world often influence U.S. buyers and sellers. For instance, exchange rate changes can affect the demand for and supply of U.S. goods and services.

3.a. Types of Countries

The nations of the world may be divided into two categories: industrial countries and developing countries. Developing countries greatly outnumber industrial countries (see Figure 9.3). The World Bank (an international organization that makes loans to developing countries) groups countries according to per capita income (income per person). Low-income economies are those with per capita incomes of $1,005 or less. Lower-middle-income economies have per capita incomes of $1,006 to $3,975. Upper-middle-income economies have per capita incomes of $3,976 to $12,275. High-income economies—oil exporters and industrial market economies—have per capita incomes of greater than $12,275. Some countries are not members of the World Bank and so are not categorized, and information about a few small countries is so limited that the World Bank is unable to classify them.

FIGURE 9.3 World Economic Development

The colors on the map identify low-income, middle-income, and high-income economies. Countries have been placed in each group on the basis of GNP per capita and, in some instances, other distinguishing economic characteristics.

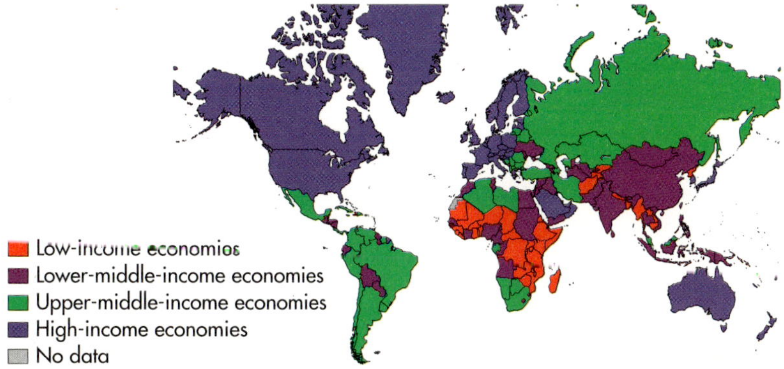

Source: World Bank (http://www.worldbank.org).

It is readily apparent from Figure 9.3 that low-income economies are heavily concentrated in Africa, whereas lower-middle-income economies are heavily concentrated in Asia. Countries in these regions have a low profile in U.S. trade, although they may receive aid from the United States. U.S. trade is concentrated with its neighbors Canada and Mexico, along with the major industrial powers.

3.a.1. **The Industrial Countries** The richest industrial market economies are listed in the bar chart in Figure 9.4. The countries listed in Figure 9.4 are among the wealthiest countries in the world. Not appearing on the list are high-income, oil-exporting nations such as Libya, Saudi Arabia, Kuwait, and the United Arab Emirates, which are still considered to be developing.

The economies of the industrial nations are highly interdependent. As conditions change in one nation, business firms and individuals looking for the best return or interest rate on their funds may shift large sums of money from one country to others. As they do, economic conditions in one country spread to other countries. As a result, the industrial countries, particularly major economic powers such as the United States, Germany, and Japan, are forced to pay close attention to each other's economic policies.

3.a.2. **The Developing Countries** Referring back to Figure 9.3, we see that the developing countries (sometimes referred to as the less-developed countries, or LDCs) are classified as low or middle income. These countries differ greatly in terms of the provision of basic human needs to the average citizen. A major way that such countries can raise living standards is by selling goods to the rest of the world.

The United States tends to buy, or *import*, primary products such as agricultural produce and minerals from developing countries. Products that a country buys from another country are called **imports**. The United States tends to sell, or *export*, manufactured goods to developing countries. Products that a country sells to another country are called **exports**. The United States is the largest producer and exporter of grains and other agricultural output in the world. The efficiency of U.S. farming relative to farming in much of the rest of the world gives the United States a comparative advantage in many agricultural products.

imports:
products that a country buys from other countries

exports:
products that a country sells to other countries

3.b. International Sector Spending

Economic activity between the United States and the rest of the world includes U.S. spending on foreign goods and foreign spending on U.S. goods. Figure 9.5 shows how U.S. exports and imports are spread over different countries. Trade with the industrial countries of Western Europe, Canada, and Japan accounts for about half of total U.S. trade. Trade with neighbors Mexico and Canada accounts for about 32 percent of exports and 26 percent of imports.

FIGURE 9.4 The Industrial Market Economies

The bar chart lists some of the wealthiest countries in the world. Ironically, high-income, oil-exporting countries such as Libya, Saudi Arabia, Kuwait, and the United Arab Emirates do not appear on the list because they are still considered to be developing.

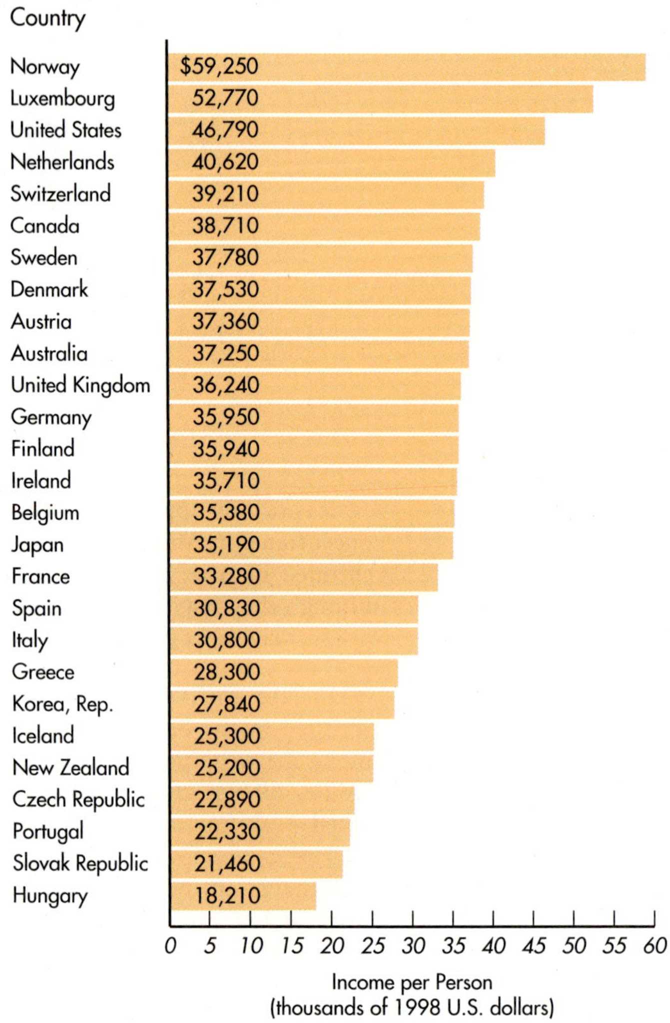

Source: World Bank, *World Development Report, 2010.*

trade surplus: the situation that exists when imports are less than exports

trade deficit: the situation that exists when imports exceed exports

net exports: the difference between the value of exports and the value of imports

When exports exceed imports, a **trade surplus** exists. When imports exceed exports, a **trade deficit** exists. Figure 9.5 shows that the United States imports much more than it exports.

The term **net exports** refers to the difference between the value of exports and the value of imports: net exports equals exports minus imports. Positive net exports represent trade surpluses; negative net exports represent trade deficits. In 2011, U.S. net exports were −$727 billion.

RECAP

1. The majority of U.S. trade is with the industrial market economies.
2. Exports are products sold to foreign countries; imports are products bought from foreign countries.
3. Exports minus imports equals net exports.
4. Positive net exports signal a trade surplus; negative net exports signal a trade deficit.

FIGURE 9.5 Direction of U.S. Trade

This chart shows that a trade deficit exists for the United States, since U.S. imports greatly exceed U.S. exports. The chart also shows that trade with neighbors Mexico and Canada accounts for about 32 percent of U.S. exports and 26 percent of U.S. imports.

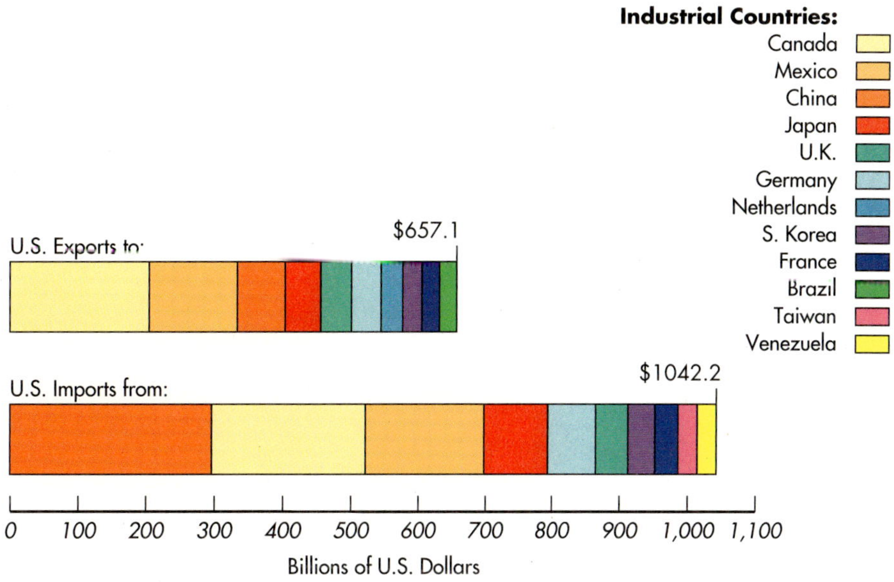

Source: *U.S. Census Foreign Trade Statistics, 2011* (www.census.gov/foreign-trade).

4. OVERVIEW OF THE U.S. GOVERNMENT

4 What does government do?

When Americans think of government policies, rules, and regulations, they typically think of Washington, DC, because their economic lives are regulated and shaped more by policies made there than by policies made at the state and local levels.

Who actually is involved in economic policymaking? Important government institutions that shape U.S. economic policy are listed in Table 9.1. This list is far from inclusive, but it does include the agencies with the broadest powers and greatest influence. Economic policy involves macroeconomic issues like government spending and control of the money supply and microeconomic issues aimed at providing public goods like police and military protection and correcting problems such as pollution.

4.a. Government Policy

The government has been given many functions in the economy. These include providing some goods, regulating some firm behaviors, and promoting competition via laws restricting the ability of business firms to engage in certain practices.

monetary policy: policy directed toward the control of money and credit

Federal Reserve: the central bank of the United States

Most attention is given to the government's monetary and fiscal policies. **Monetary policy** is policy directed toward the control of money and credit. The major player in this policy arena is the Federal Reserve, commonly called "the Fed." The **Federal Reserve** is the central bank of the United States. It serves as a banker for the U.S. government and regulates the U.S. money supply.

The Federal Reserve System is run by a seven-member Board of Governors. The most important member of the board is the chairman, who is appointed by the president for a term of four years. The board meets regularly (10 to 12 times a year) with a group of high-level officials to review the current economic situation and set policy for the growth of U.S. money and credit. The Federal Reserve exercises a great deal of influence on U.S. economic policy.

Table 9.1 U.S. Government Economic Policymakers and Related Agencies

Institution	Role
Fiscal Policymakers	
President	Provides leadership in formulating fiscal policy
Congress	Sets government spending and taxes and passes laws related to economic conduct
Monetary Policymaker	
Federal Reserve	Controls money supply and credit conditions
Related Agencies	
Council of Economic Advisers	Monitors the economy and advises the president
Office of Management and Budget	Prepares and analyzes the federal budget
Treasury Department	Administers the financial affairs of the federal government
Commerce Department	Administers federal policy regulating industry
Justice Department	Enforces legal setting of business
Comptroller of the Currency	Oversees national banks
International Trade Commission	Investigates unfair international trade practices
Federal Trade Commission	Administers laws related to fair business practices and competition

fiscal policy:
policy directed toward government spending and taxation

Fiscal policy, the other area of macroeconomic policy, is policy directed toward government spending and taxation. In the United States, fiscal policy is determined by laws that are passed by Congress and signed by the president. The relative roles of the legislative and executive branches in shaping fiscal policy vary with the political climate, but usually it is the president who initiates major policy changes. Presidents rely on key advisers for fiscal policy information. These advisers include cabinet officers such as the Secretary of the Treasury and the Secretary of State as well as the Director of the Office of Management and Budget. In addition, the president has a Council of Economic Advisers made up of three economists—usually a chair, a macroeconomist, and a microeconomist—who, together with their staff, monitor and interpret economic developments for the president. The degree of influence wielded by these advisers depends on their personal relationship with the president.

4.b. Government Spending

Federal, state, and local government spending for goods and services between 1960 and 2011 is shown in Figure 9.6. Except during times of war in the 1940s and 1950s, federal expenditures were roughly similar in size to state and local expenditures until 1970. Since 1970, state and local spending has been growing more rapidly than federal spending.

Combined government spending on goods and services is larger than investment spending but much smaller than consumption. In 2011, combined government spending on consumption was $2,547 billion.

transfer payments:
income transferred from one citizen who is earning income to another citizen who may not be

Besides government expenditures on goods and services, government also serves as an intermediary, taking money from taxpayers with higher incomes and transferring this income to those with lower incomes. Such **transfer payments** are a part of total government expenditures, so the total government budget is

The Federal Reserve in Washington, DC

much larger than the expenditures on goods and services reported in Figure 9.6. In 2011, total expenditures by federal, state, and local governments for goods and services were $2,547 billion. In this same year, transfer payments paid by all levels of government were $2,371 billion.

The magnitude of federal government spending relative to federal government revenue from taxes has been a major issue in recent U.S. national

FIGURE 9.6 Federal, State, and Local Government Expenditures for Goods and Services

In the 1950s and early 1960s, federal government spending was above state and local government spending. In 1971, state and local expenditures rose above federal spending and have remained higher ever since.

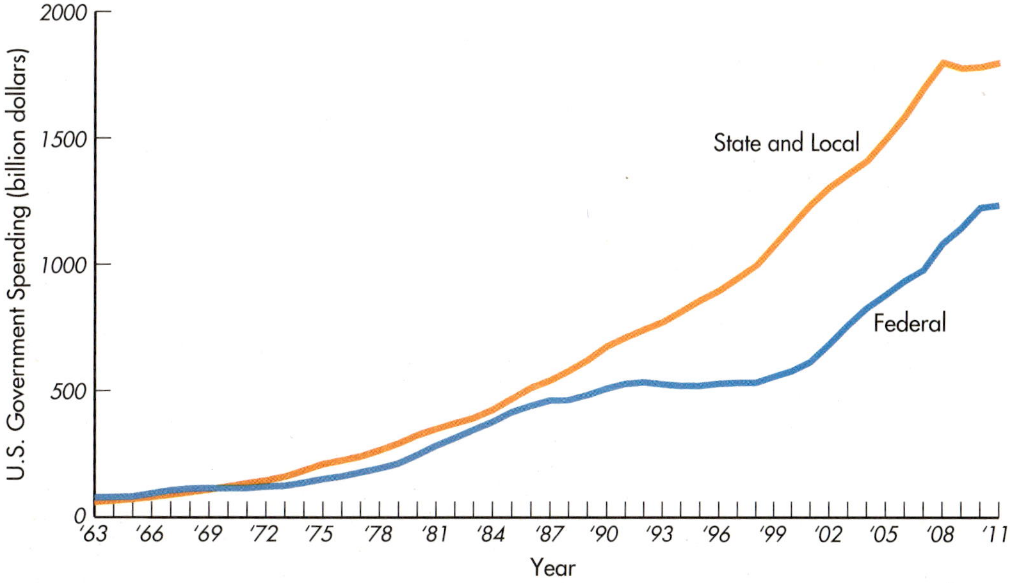

Source: Data are from the *Economic Report of the President, 2012.*

FIGURE 9.7 U.S. Federal Budget Deficits

The budget deficit is equal to the excess of government spending over tax revenue. If taxes are greater than government spending, a budget surplus (shown as a negative deficit) exists. The United States has generally run a budget deficit since 1960. Starting in 1998, a budget surplus appeared for four years.

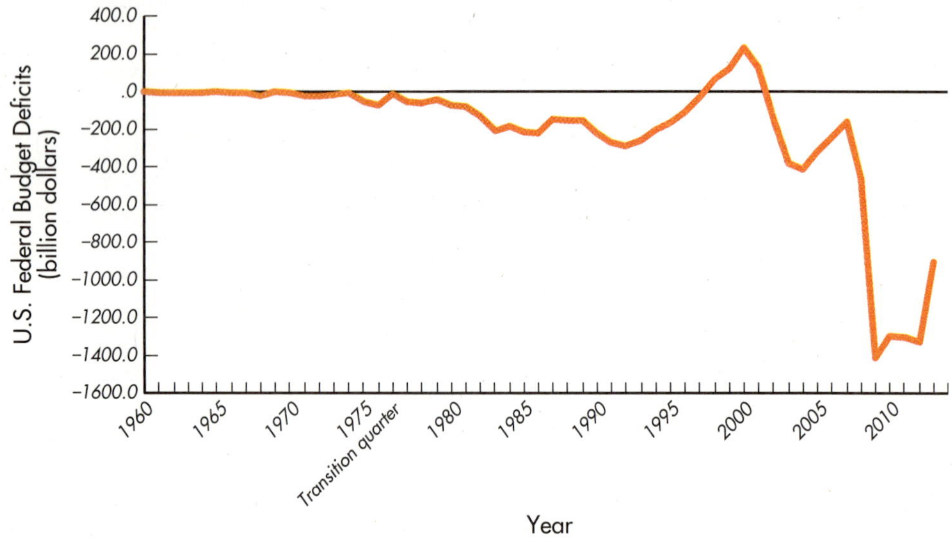

Note. Year 2012 and 2013 are estimates.

Source: Data are from the *Economic Report of the President, 2012.*

budget surplus: the excess that results when government spending is less than revenue

budget deficit: the shortage that results when government spending is greater than revenue

elections. Figure 9.7 shows that the federal budget was roughly balanced until the early 1970s. The budget is a measure of spending and revenue. A balanced budget occurs when federal spending is approximately equal to federal revenue. This was the case through the 1950s and 1960s. If federal government spending is less than tax revenue, a **budget surplus** exists. Until 1998, the last time the U.S. government had a budget surplus was in 1969. By the early 1980s, federal government spending was much larger than revenue, so a large **budget deficit** existed. The federal budget deficit grew very rapidly to well over $200 billion by the early 1990s. When spending is greater than revenue, the excess spending must be covered by borrowing, and this borrowing can have effects on investment and consumption as well as on economic relationships with other countries. In the late 1990s, the budget deficit dropped rapidly as strong economic growth generated tax revenues that grew more rapidly than expenditures, and a surplus was realized by 1998. However, by 2002, the budget had returned to a deficit.

RECAP

1. The microeconomic functions of government focus on issues aimed at providing public goods such as police and military protection and correcting problems such as pollution.
2. Macroeconomic policy attempts to control the economy through monetary and fiscal policies.
3. The Federal Reserve conducts monetary policy. Congress and the president formulate fiscal policy.
4. Government spending is larger than investment spending but much smaller than consumption spending.
5. When government spending exceeds tax revenue, a budget deficit exists. When government spending is less than tax revenue, a budget surplus exists.

5. LINKING THE SECTORS

private sector:
households, businesses, and the international sector

public sector:
the government

Now that we have an idea of the size and structure of each **private sector**—households, businesses, and the international sector—and the government, also known as the **public sector**, let's discuss how the sectors interact.

5.a. The Private Sector

Households own all the basic resources, or factors of production, in the economy. Household members own land and provide labor, and they are the entrepreneurs, stockholders, proprietors, and partners who own business firms.

Households and businesses interact with each other by means of buying and selling. Businesses employ the services of resources in order to produce goods and services. Business firms pay households for their services of resources.

Households sell their resource services to businesses in exchange for money payments. The flow of resource services from households to businesses is shown by the blue arrow beneath the sectors of households, government, and firms shown in Figure 9.8. The flow of money payments from firms to households is shown by the gold arrow under Resource Services. Households use the money payments to buy goods and services from firms. These money payments are the firms' revenues. The flow of money payments from households to firms is shown by the gold arrow near the top of the diagram. The flow of goods and services from firms to households is shown by the blue arrow under Payments for Goods and Services. There is, therefore, a flow of money and goods and services from one sector to the other. The payments made by one sector are the receipts taken in by the other sector. Money, goods, and services flow from households to firms and back to households in a circular flow.

5

How do the three private sectors—households, businesses, and the international sector—interact in the economy?

Households do not spend all of the money they receive. They save some fraction of their income. In Figure 9.8, we see that household saving is deposited in financial intermediaries such as banks, credit unions, and savings and loan firms. A financial intermediary accepts deposits from savers and makes loans to borrowers. The money that is saved by the households reenters the economy in the form of investment spending as business firms borrow for expansion of their productive capacity.

circular flow diagram:
a model showing the flow of output and income from one sector of the economy to another

To simplify this **circular flow diagram**, let's assume that households are not directly engaged in international trade and that only business firms are buying and selling goods and services across international borders. This assumption is not far from the truth for the industrial countries and for many developing countries. We typically buy a foreign-made product from a local business firm rather than directly from the foreign producer.

The lines Net Exports and Payments for Net Exports connect firms and foreign countries in Figure 9.8. Notice that neither line has an arrow indicating the direction of flow as do the other lines in the diagram. The reason is that net exports of the home country may be either positive (a trade surplus) or negative (a trade deficit). When net exports are positive, there is a net flow of goods from the firms of the home country to foreign countries and a net flow of money from foreign countries to the firms of the home country. When net exports are negative, the opposite occurs. A trade deficit involves a net flow of goods from foreign countries to the firms of the home country and a net flow of money from firms in the home country to foreign countries. If exports and imports are equal, net exports are zero because the value of exports is offset by the value of imports.

6

How does the government interact with the other sectors of the economy?

5.b. The Public Sector

Governments at the federal, state, and local levels interact with both households and firms. Because the government employs factors of production to produce government services, households receive payments from the government in exchange for the services of the factors of production. The flow of resource services from households to government is illustrated by the blue arrow from households to government in Figure 9.8. The flow of money from government to households is shown by the gold arrow from government to households. We assume that government, like a household, does not trade directly with foreign countries but obtains foreign goods from domestic firms that do trade with the rest of the world.

Households pay taxes to support the provision of government services, such as national defense, education, and police and fire protection. In a sense, then, the household sector is purchasing goods and services from the government as well as from private businesses. The flow of tax payments from households and

FIGURE 9.8 The Circular Flow: Households, Firms, Government, and Foreign Countries

The diagram assumes that households and government are not directly engaged in international trade. Domestic firms trade with firms in foreign countries. The government sector buys resource services from households and goods and services from firms. This government spending represents income for the households and revenue for the firms. The government uses the resource services and goods and services to provide government services for households and firms. Households and firms pay taxes to the government to finance government expenditures.

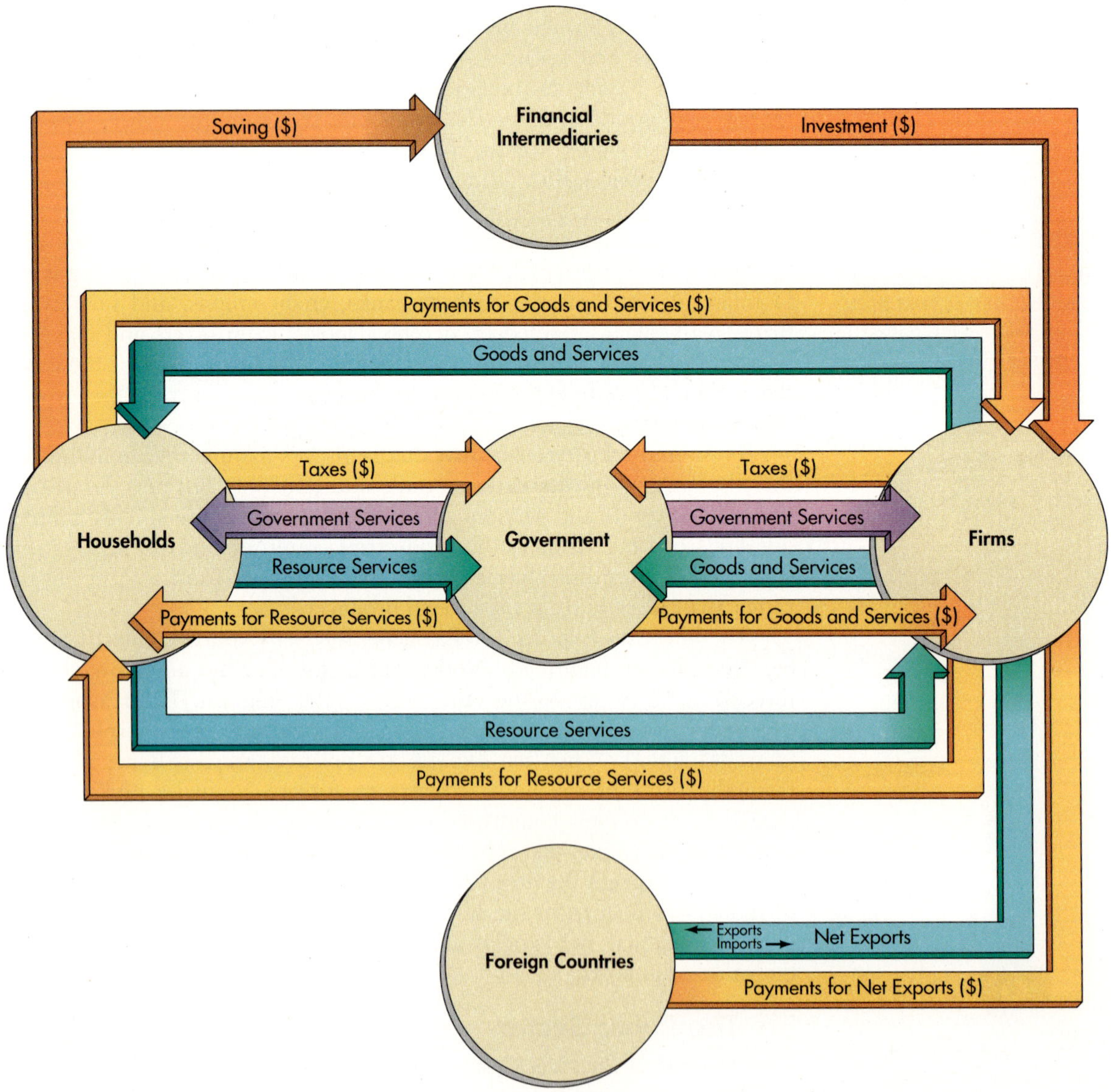

firms to government is illustrated by the gold arrows from households and firms to government, and the flow of government services to households and firms is illustrated by the purple arrows coming from government.

The addition of government brings significant changes to the model. Households have an additional place to sell their resources for income, and businesses have an additional market for goods and services. The value of private production no longer equals the value of household income. Households receive income from government in exchange for providing resource services to government. The total value of output in the economy is equal to the total income received, but government is included as a source of income and a producer of services.

RECAP

1. The circular flow diagram illustrates how the main sectors of the economy fit together.
2. Government interacts with both households and firms. Households receive government services and pay taxes; they provide resource services and receive income. Firms sell goods and services to government and receive income.
3. The circular flow diagram shows that the value of output is equal to income.

SUMMARY

What is a household, and what is household income and spending?

1. A household consists of one or more persons who occupy a unit of housing.
2. Household spending is called consumption and is the largest component of spending in the economy.

What is a business firm, and what is business spending?

3. A business firm is a business organization controlled by a single management.
4. Businesses may be organized as sole proprietorships, partnerships, or corporations.
5. Business investment spending—the expenditure by business firms for capital goods—fluctuates a great deal over time.

How does the international sector affect the economy?

6. The international trade of the United States occurs predominantly with the other industrial economies.
7. Exports are products sold to the rest of the world. Imports are products bought from the rest of the world.
8. Exports minus imports equal net exports. Positive net exports mean that exports are greater than imports and a trade surplus exists. Negative net exports mean that imports exceed exports and a trade deficit exists.

What does government do?

9. The government carries out microeconomic and macroeconomic activities. The microeconomic activities involve providing public goods and correcting market failures. The macroeconomic activities attempt to control the economy through monetary and fiscal policies.

10. In the United States, monetary policy is the province of the Federal Reserve, and fiscal policy is up to the Congress and the president.

How do the three private sectors—households, businesses, and the international sector—interact in the economy?

11. Money, goods, and services flow from households to firms and back in a circular flow.
12. Some household income is not spent but instead is saved in financial intermediaries from which firms borrow for expansion of their productive capacity.
13. The circular flow diagram assumes that households are not directly engaged in international trade but, rather, that only business firms buy and sell goods and services across international borders.

How does the government interact with the other sectors of the economy?

14. The circular flow diagram illustrates interactions among all sectors of the economy—households, businesses, the international sector, and the public sector.

EXERCISES

1. Is a family a household? Is a household a family?
2. Which sector (household, business, or international) spends the most? Which sector spends the least? Which sector, because of volatility, has importance greater than is warranted by its size?
3. What does it mean if net exports are positive?
4. Why does the value of output always equal the income received by the resources that produced the output?
5. Total spending in the economy is equal to consumption plus investment plus government spending plus net exports. If households want to save and thus do not use all of their income for consumption, what will happen to total spending? Because total spending in the economy is equal to total income and output, what will happen to the output of goods and services if households want to save more?
6. People sometimes argue that imports should be limited by government policy. Suppose a government quota on the quantity of imports causes net exports to rise. Using the circular flow diagram as a guide, explain why total expenditures and national output may rise after the quota is imposed. Who is likely to benefit from the quota? Who will be hurt?
7. Draw the circular flow diagram linking households, business firms, and the international sector. Use the diagram to explain the effects of a decision by the household sector to increase saving.
8. Suppose there are three countries in the world. Country A exports $22 million worth of goods to country B and $10 million worth of goods to country C; country B exports $6 million worth of goods to country A and $12 million worth of goods to country C; and country C exports $8 million worth of goods to country A and $2 million worth of goods to country B.
   a. What are the net exports of countries A, B, and C?
   b. Which country is running a trade deficit? A trade surplus?
9. There are many more sole proprietorships than corporations or partnerships. Why are there so many sole proprietorships? Why is the revenue of the average sole proprietorship less than that of the typical corporation?
10. Using the circular flow diagram, illustrate the effects of an increase in taxes imposed on the household sector.

STUDY GUIDE FOR CHAPTER 9

Key Term Match

Match each key term with its correct definition by placing the appropriate letter next to the corresponding numbers.

A. household
B. consumption
C. multinational business
D. investment
E. imports
F. exports
G. trade surplus
H. trade deficit
I. net exports
J. monetary policy
K. Federal Reserve
L. fiscal policy
M. transfer payments
N. budget surplus
O. budget deficit
P. private sector
Q. public sector
R. circular flow diagram

___ 1. spending by businesses on capital goods to be used in producing goods and services

___ 2. products that a country buys from other countries

___ 3. the shortage that results when government spending is greater than revenue

___ 4. the situation that exists when imports exceed exports

___ 5. policy directed toward government spending and taxation

___ 6. a firm that owns and operates producing units in foreign countries

___ 7. the excess that results when government spending is less than revenue

___ 8. the situation that exists when imports are less than exports

___ 9. income transferred from one citizen who is earning income to another citizen who may not be

___ 10. the difference between the value of exports and the value of imports

___ 11. a model showing the flow of output and income from one sector of the economy to another

___ 12. one or more persons who occupy a unit of housing

___ 13. households, businesses, and the international sector

___ 14. household spending

___ 15. the central bank of the United States

___ 16. the government

___ 17. products that a country sells to other countries

___ 18. policy directed toward the control of money and credit

Quick-Check Quiz

1. Householders ______________ years old have the largest median annual income.
   - ☐ a. 15 to 24
   - ☐ b. 25 to 34
   - ☐ c. 45 to 54
   - ☐ d. 55 to 64
   - ☐ e. over 64

2. Household spending, or consumption, is the ______________ component of total spending in the economy.
   - ☐ a. largest
   - ☐ b. second largest
   - ☐ c. third largest
   - ☐ d. fourth largest
   - ☐ e. smallest

3. Which of the following is *not* a component of household spending?
   - ☐ a. capital goods
   - ☐ b. housing
   - ☐ c. transportation
   - ☐ d. food
   - ☐ e. entertainment

4. In ______________ the owner(s) of the business is (are) responsible for all the debts incurred by the business and may have to pay those debts from his/her (their) personal wealth.
   - ☐ a. a sole proprietorship
   - ☐ b. a partnership
   - ☐ c. a corporation
   - ☐ d. sole proprietorships and partnerships
   - ☐ e. sole proprietorships, partnerships, and corporations

5. ____________ are the most common form of business organization, but ____________ account for the largest share of total revenues.
   - ☐ a. Sole proprietorships; partnerships
   - ☐ b. Sole proprietorships; corporations
   - ☐ c. Partnerships; corporations
   - ☐ d. Corporations; sole proprietorships
   - ☐ e. Partnerships; sole proprietorships

6. U.S. trade is concentrated with
   - ☐ a. major industrial powers.
   - ☐ b. developing countries.
   - ☐ c. Canada and Mexico.
   - ☐ d. oil exporters.
   - ☐ e. a and c.

7. Low-income countries are concentrated heavily in
   - ☐ a. Central America.
   - ☐ b. South America.
   - ☐ c. North America.
   - ☐ d. Africa.
   - ☐ e. Western Europe.

8. Combined government spending on goods and services is larger than ____________ but smaller than ____________.
   - ☐ a. consumption; net exports
   - ☐ b. consumption; investment
   - ☐ c. net exports; investment
   - ☐ d. investment; net exports
   - ☐ e. investment; consumption

9. Which of the following is a macroeconomic function of government?
   - ☐ a. provision of military protection
   - ☐ b. promotion of competition
   - ☐ c. determining the level of government spending and taxation
   - ☐ d. provision of police protection
   - ☐ e. correction of pollution problems

10. The ____________ is (are) responsible for fiscal policy, and the ____________ is (are) responsible for monetary policy.
    - ☐ a. Federal Reserve; Congress
    - ☐ b. Federal Reserve; Congress and the president
    - ☐ c. Congress; Federal Reserve
    - ☐ d. Congress and the president; Federal Reserve
    - ☐ e. Congress; Federal Reserve and the president

Practice Questions and Problems

1. The largest component of total spending in the economy is ____________ spending.
2. Householders in the age ranges of _____ and _____ years old make up the largest number of households.
3. ____________ account for the largest percentage of business revenue.
4. The ____________ is an international organization that makes loans to developing countries.
5. The wide swings in this type of spending make it an important factor in determining the economic health of a nation: ____________.
6. ____________ (Industrial/Developing) countries greatly outnumber ____________ (industrial/developing) countries.
7. The World Bank groups countries according to ____________.
8. List three microeconomic functions of government.
   ____
   ____
9. What is the purpose of the circular flow diagram?
10. The circular flow diagram shows that the value of ____________ is equal to income.

Exercises and Applications

I The Circular Flow Diagram

Use the following diagram to see whether you understand how the three sectors of the economy are linked together. In the blanks below, fill in the appropriate labels. Money flows are represented by gold and orange lines. Flows of physical goods and services are represented by blue and purple lines.

a. ______________________________
b. ______________________________
c. ______________________________
d. ______________________________
e. ______________________________
f. ______________________________
g. ______________________________
h. ______________________________
i. ______________________________
j. ______________________________
k. ______________________________
l. ______________________________
m. ______________________________
n. ______________________________
o. ______________________________
p. ______________________________

You can find further practice tests in the Online Quiz at: www.cengagebrain.com

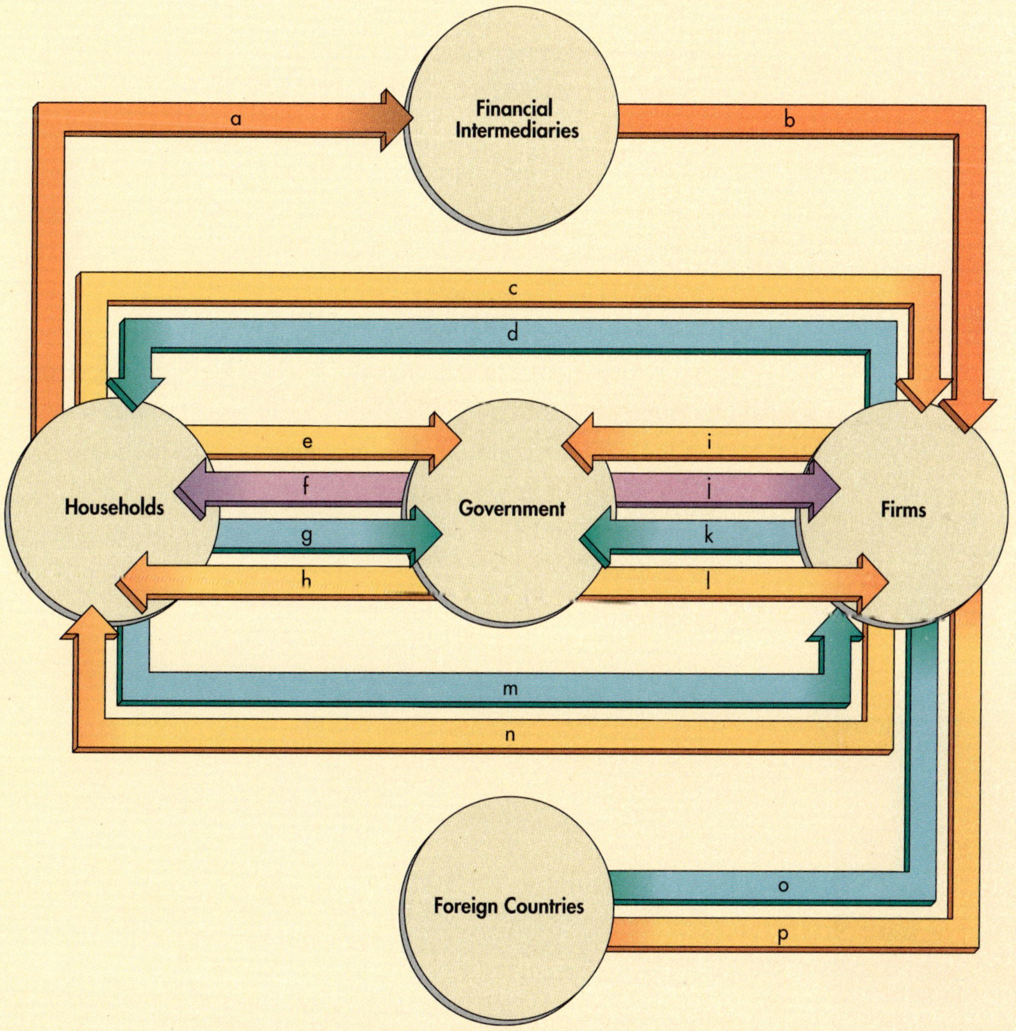

10 Macroeconomic Measures

FUNDAMENTAL QUESTIONS

1. How is the total output of an economy measured?
2. What is the difference between nominal and real GDP?
3. What is the purpose of a price index?
4. How is money traded internationally?
5. How do nations record their transactions with the rest of the world?

PREVIEW

Just as we use degrees of temperature on a thermometer as a measure of a person's health, we must use economic data to analyze the health of an economy. Since we prefer more goods and services to less, we need a good way to measure how much is produced to see whether the economy is providing more goods and services over time and, if so, how much more. Since we like prices to rise slower rather than faster, we need a good way to monitor how prices change in the economy. Since we trade goods, services, and money with the rest of the world, we need good measures of how much is traded and what things cost. In this chapter, we will learn how economists measure things such as output and inflation. We will also find out how trade with the rest of the world is counted. This will allow a solid foundation on which future chapters will build as we use this information in further analysis of business conditions both at home and abroad.

1. MEASURES OF OUTPUT AND INCOME

1

How is the total output of an economy measured?

national income accounting: the framework that summarizes and categorizes productive activity in an economy over a specific period of time, typically a year

In this chapter we discuss gross domestic product (GDP), real GDP, and other measures of national productive activity by making use of the **national income accounting** system used by all countries. National income accounting provides a framework for discussing macroeconomics. It measures the output of an entire economy as well as the flows between sectors. It summarizes the level of production in an economy over a specific period of time, typically a year. In practice, the process *estimates* the amount of activity that occurs. It is beyond the capability of government officials to count every transaction that takes place in a modern economy. Still, national income accounting generates useful and fairly accurate measures of economic activity in most countries, especially wealthy industrial countries that have comprehensive accounting systems.

1.a. Gross Domestic Product

Modern economies produce an amazing variety of goods and services. To measure an economy's total production, economists combine the quantities of oranges, golf balls, automobiles, and all the other goods and services produced into a single measure of output. Of course, simply adding up the number of things produced—the number of oranges, golf balls, and automobiles—does not reveal the *value* of what is being produced. If a nation produces 1 million more oranges and 1 million fewer automobiles this year than it did last year, the total number of things produced remains the same. But because automobiles are much more valuable than oranges, the value of output has dropped substantially. Prices reflect the value of goods and services in the market, so economists use the money value of things to create a measure of total output, a measure that is more meaningful than the sum of units produced.

gross domestic product (GDP): the market value of all final goods and services produced in a year within a country

The most common measure of a nation's output is GDP. **Gross domestic product (GDP)** is the market value of all final goods and services produced in a year within a country's borders. A closer look at three parts of this definition—*market value*, *final goods and services*, and *produced in a year*—will make clear what the GDP does and does not include.

ECONOMIC INSIGHT

The Value of Homemaker Services

One way GDP underestimates the total value of a nation's output is by failing to record nonmarket production. A prime example is the work homemakers do. Of course, people are not paid for their work around the house, so it is difficult to measure the value of their output. But notice that we say *difficult*, not *impossible*. Economists can use several methods to assign value to homemaker services.

One is an opportunity cost approach. This approach measures the value of a homemaker's services by the forgone market salary the homemaker could have earned if he or she worked full-time outside the home. The rationale is that society loses the output the homemaker would have produced in the market job in order to gain the output the homemaker produces in the home.

Another alternative is to estimate what it would cost to hire workers to produce the goods and services that the homemaker produces. For example, what would it cost to hire someone to prepare meals, iron, clean, and take care of the household? It has been estimated that the average homemaker spends almost 8 hours a day, 7 days a week, on household work. This amounts to over 50 hours a week. At a rate of $20 an hour, the value of the homemaker's services is over $1,000 a week.

Whichever method we use, two things are clear. The value of homemaker services to the household and the economy is substantial. And by failing to account for those services, the GDP substantially underestimates the value of the nation's output.

Market Value The *market value* of final goods and services is their value at market price. The process of determining market value is straightforward when prices are known and transactions are observable. However, there are cases when prices are not known and transactions are not observable. For instance, illegal drug transactions are not reported to the government; this means they are not included in GDP statistics. In fact, almost any activity that is not traded in a market is not included. For example, production that takes place in households, such as homemakers' services (as discussed in the Economic Insight "The Value of Homemaker Services"), is not counted, nor are unreported barter and cash transactions. For instance, if a lawyer has a sick dog and a veterinarian needs some legal advice, by trading services and not reporting the activity to the tax authorities, each can avoid taxation on the income that would have been reported had they sold their services to each other. If the value of a transaction is not recorded as taxable income, it generally does not appear in the GDP. There are some exceptions, however. Contributions toward GDP are estimated for *in-kind wages*, or nonmonetary compensation such as room and board. Values of GDP also are assigned to the output consumed by a producer—for example, the home consumption of crops by a farmer.

Final Goods and Services The second part of the definition of GDP limits the measure to *final goods and services*, the goods and services available to the ultimate consumer. This limitation avoids double counting. Suppose a retail store sells a shirt to a consumer for $20. The value of the shirt in the GDP is $20. But the shirt is made of cotton that has been grown by a farmer, woven at a mill, and cut and sewn by a manufacturer. What would happen if we counted the value of the shirt at each of these stages of the production process? We would overstate the market value of the shirt.

intermediate goods: goods that are used as inputs in the production of final goods and services

Intermediate goods are goods that are used in the production of a final product. For instance, the ingredients for a meal are intermediate goods to a restaurant. Similarly, the cotton and the cloth are intermediate goods in the production of the shirt. The stages of production of the $20 shirt are shown in Figure 10.1. The value-of-output axis measures the value of the product at each

FIGURE 10.1 Stages of Production and Value Added in Shirt Manufacturing

A cotton farmer sells cotton to a textile mill for $1, adding $1 to the value of the final shirt. The textile mill sells cloth to a shirt manufacturer for $5, adding $4 to the value of the final shirt. The manufacturer sells the shirt wholesale to the retail store for $12, adding $7 to the value of the final shirt. The retail store sells the final shirt to a consumer for $20, adding $8 to the value of the final shirt. The sum of the prices received at each stage of production equals $38, which is greater than the price of the final shirt. The sum of the value added at each stage of production equals $20, which equals the market value of the shirt.

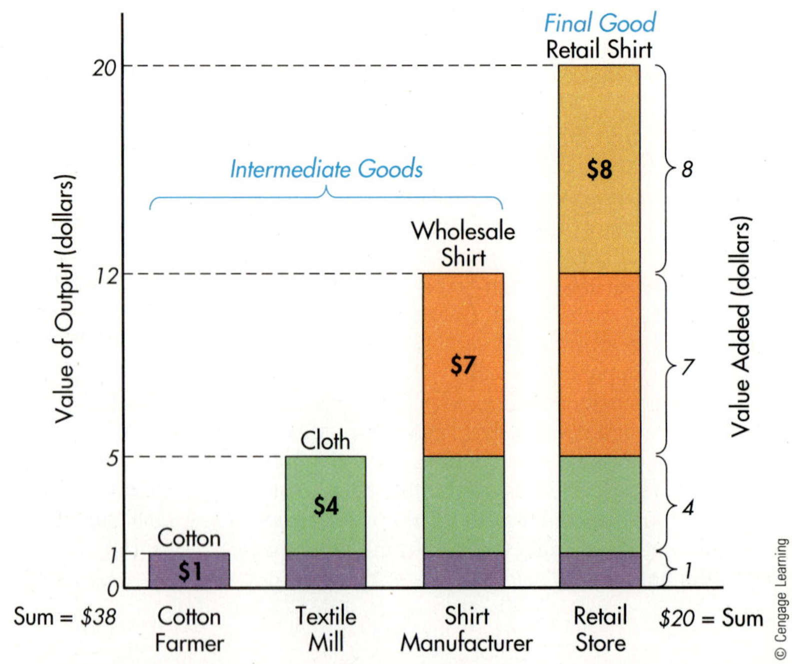

stage. The cotton produced by the farmer sells for $1. The cloth woven by the textile mill sells for $5. The shirt manufacturer sells the shirt wholesale to the retail store for $12. The retail store sells the shirt—the final good—to the ultimate consumer for $20.

Remember that GDP is based on the market value of final goods and services. In our example, the market value of the shirt is $20. That price already includes the value of the intermediate goods that were used to produce the shirt. If we add to it the value of output at every stage of production, we would be counting the value of the intermediate goods twice, and we would be overstating the GDP.

value added:
the difference between the value of the output and the value of the intermediate goods used in the production of that output

It is possible to compute GDP by computing the **value added** at each stage of production. Value added is the difference between the value of the output and the value of the intermediate goods used in the production of that output. In Figure 10.1, the value added by each stage of production is listed at the right. The farmer adds $1 to the value of the shirt. The mill takes the cotton worth $1 and produces cloth worth $5, adding $4 to the value of the shirt. The manufacturer uses $5 worth of cloth to produce a shirt it sells for $12, so the manufacturer adds $7 to the shirt's value. Finally, the retail store adds $8 to the value of the shirt—it pays the manufacturer $12 for the shirt and sells it to the consumer for $20. The sum of the value added at each stage of production is $20. The total value added, then, is equal to the market value of the final product.

Economists can compute GDP using two methods: the final goods and services method uses the market value of the final good or service; the value-added method uses the value added at each stage of production. Both methods count the value of intermediate goods only once. This is an important distinction: GDP is based not on the market value of *all* goods and services but on the market value of all *final* goods and services.

Produced in a Year The GDP measures the value of output *produced in a year*. The value of goods produced last year is counted in last year's GDP; the value of goods produced this year is counted in this year's GDP. The year of production, not the year of sale, determines allocation to GDP. Although the value of last year's goods is not counted in this year's GDP, the value of services involved in the sale is. This year's GDP does not include the value of a house built last year, but it does include the value of the real estate broker's fee; it

The market value of these shirts includes the value of the intermediate goods that were used to produce the shirts.

VikOl/Shutterstock

does not include the value of a used car, but it does include the income earned by the used car dealer in the sale of that car.

inventory: the stock of unsold goods held by a firm

To determine the value of goods produced in a year but not sold in that year, economists calculate changes in inventory. **Inventory** is a firm's stock of unsold goods. If a shirt that is produced this year remains on the retail store's shelf at the end of the year, it increases the value of the store's inventory. A $20 shirt increases that value by $20. Changes in inventory allow economists to count goods in the year in which they are produced whether or not they are sold.

Changes in inventory can be planned or unplanned. A store may want a cushion above expected sales (*planned inventory changes*), or it may not be able to sell all the goods it expected to sell when it placed the order (*unplanned inventory changes*). For instance, suppose Jeremy owns a surfboard shop, and he always wants to keep 10 surfboards above what he expects to sell. This is done so that in case business is surprisingly good, he does not have to turn away customers to his competitors and lose those sales. At the beginning of the year, Jeremy has 10 surfboards and then builds as many new boards during the year as he expects to sell. Jeremy *plans* on having an inventory at the end of the year of 10 surfboards. Suppose Jeremy expects to sell 100 surfboards during the year, so he builds 100 new boards. If business is surprisingly poor so that Jeremy sells only 80 surfboards, how do we count the 20 new boards that he made but did not sell? We count the change in his inventory. He started the year with 10 surfboards and ends the year with 20 more unsold boards for a year-end inventory of 30. The change in inventory of 20 (equal to the ending inventory of 30 minus the starting inventory of 10) represents output that is counted in GDP. In Jeremy's case, the inventory change is unplanned since he expected to sell the 20 extra surfboards that he has in his shop at the end of the year. But whether the inventory change is planned or unplanned, changes in inventory will count output that is produced but not sold in a given year.

1.a.1. **GDP as Output** The GDP is a measure of the market value of a nation's total output in a year. Remember that economists divide the economy into four sectors: households, businesses, government, and the international sector. The total value of economic activity equals the sum of the output produced in each sector. Since GDP counts the output produced in the United States, U.S. GDP is produced in business firms, households, and government located within the boundaries of the United States. Not unexpectedly in a capitalist country, privately owned businesses account for the largest percentage of output: In the United States, 76 percent of the GDP is produced by private firms. Government produces 12 percent of the GDP, and households 12 percent.

In terms of output, GDP is the value of final goods and services produced by domestic households, businesses, and government units. If some of the firms producing in the United States are foreign owned, their output produced in the United States is counted in U.S. GDP.

1.a.2. **GDP as Expenditures** Here we look at GDP in terms of what each sector pays for goods and services it purchases. The dollar value of total expenditures—the sum of the amount each sector spends on final goods and services—equals the dollar value of output. Household spending is called *consumption*. Households spend income on goods and services to be consumed. Business spending is called *investment*. Investment is spending on capital goods that will be used to produce other goods and services. The two other components of total spending are *government spending* and *net exports*. Net exports are the value of *exports* (goods and services sold to the rest of the world) minus the value of *imports* (goods and services bought from the rest of the world).

$$\text{GDP} = \text{consumption} + \text{investment} + \text{government spending} + \text{net exports}$$

Or, in the shorter form commonly used by economists,

$$GDP = C + I + G + X$$

where X is net exports.

Consumption, or household spending, accounts for 71 percent of national expenditures. Government spending represents 18 percent of expenditures, and business investment 14 percent. Net exports are negative (-3 percent); this means that imports exceed exports. To determine total national expenditures on *domestic* output, the value of imports, spending on foreign output, is subtracted from total expenditures.

1.a.3. GDP as Income The total value of output can be calculated by adding up the expenditures of each sector. And because one sector's expenditures are another's income, the total value of output also can be computed by adding up the income of all sectors.

Business firms use factors of production to produce goods and services. The income earned by factors of production is classified as wages, interest, rent, and profits. *Wages* are payments to labor, including fringe benefits, social security contributions, and retirement payments. *Interest* is the net interest paid by businesses to households plus the net interest received from foreigners (the interest they pay us minus the interest we pay them). *Rent* is income earned from selling the use of real property (houses, shops, farms). Finally, *profits* are the sum of corporate profits plus proprietors' income (income from sole proprietorships and partnerships).

In terms of income, wages account for 51 percent of the GDP. Interest and corporate profits account for 7 percent and 11 percent of the GDP, respectively. Proprietors' income accounts for 8 percent. Rent (2 percent) is very small in comparison. *Net factor income from abroad* is income received from U.S.-owned resources located in other countries minus income paid to foreign-owned resources located in the United States. Since U.S. GDP refers only to income earned within U.S. borders, we must deduct this kind of income to arrive at GDP (0.1 percent).

capital consumption allowance: the estimated value of depreciation plus the value of accidental damage to capital stock

depreciation: a reduction in value of capital goods over time due to their use in production

The GDP also includes two income categories that we have not discussed: capital consumption allowance and indirect business taxes. **Capital consumption allowance** is not a money payment to a factor of production; it is the estimated value of capital goods used up or worn out in production plus the value of accidental damage to capital goods. The value of accidental damage is relatively small, so it is common to hear economists refer to capital consumption allowance as **depreciation**. Machines and other capital goods wear out over time. The reduction in the value of capital stock due to its being used up or worn out over time is called depreciation. A depreciating capital good loses value each year of its useful life until its value is zero.

Even though capital consumption allowance does not represent income received by a factor of production, it must be accounted for in GDP as income. Otherwise the value of GDP measured as output would be higher than the value of GDP measured as income. Depreciation is a kind of resource payment, part of the total payment to the owners of capital. All of the income categories—wages, interest, rent, profits, and capital consumption allowance—are expenses incurred in the production of output.

indirect business taxes: taxes that are collected by businesses for a government agency

Indirect business taxes, such as capital consumption allowances, are not payments to a factor of production. They are taxes collected by businesses that then are turned over to the government. Both excise taxes and sales taxes are forms of indirect business taxes.

For example, suppose a motel room in Florida costs \$80 a night. A consumer would be charged \$90. Of that \$90, the motel receives \$80 as the value of the service sold; the other \$10 is an excise tax. The motel cannot keep the \$10; it must turn it over to the state government. (In effect, the motel is acting as the government's tax collector.) The consumer spends \$90; the motel earns \$80. To balance expenditures and income, we have to allocate the \$10 difference to indirect business taxes.

To summarize, GDP measured as income includes the four payments to the factors of production: wages, interest, rent, and profits. These income items represent expenses incurred in the production of GDP. From these we must subtract net factor income from abroad in order for the total to sum to GDP. Along with these payments are two non-income items: capital consumption allowance and indirect business taxes.

GDP = wages + interest + rent + profits − net factor income from abroad + capital consumption allowance + indirect business taxes

GDP is the total value of output produced in a year, the total value of expenditures made to purchase that output, and the total value of income received by the factors of production. Because all three are measures of the same thing—GDP—all must be equal.

1.b. Other Measures of Output and Income

GDP is the most common measure of a nation's output, but it is not the only measure. Economists rely on a number of others in analyzing the performance of components of an economy.

gross national product (GNP): gross domestic product plus receipts of factor income from the rest of the world minus payments of factor income to the rest of the world

1.b.1. Gross National Product (GNP)

GNP equals GDP plus receipts of factor income from the rest of the world minus payments of factor income to the rest of the world. If we add to GDP the value of income earned by U.S. residents from factors of production located outside the United States and subtract the value of income earned by foreign residents from factors of production located inside the United States, we have a measure of the value of output produced by U.S.-owned resources—GNP.

Figure 10.2 shows the national income accounts in the United States in 2011. The figure begins with the GDP and then shows the calculations necessary to obtain the GNP and other measures of national output. In 2011, the U.S. GNP was $15,339.5 billion.

net national product (NNP): gross national product minus capital consumption allowance

1.b.2. Net National Product (NNP)

NNP equals GNP minus capital consumption allowance. The NNP measures the value of goods and services produced in a year less the value of capital goods that became obsolete or were used up during the year. Because the NNP includes only net additions to a nation's capital, it is a better measure of the expansion or contraction of current output than is GNP. Remember how we defined GDP in terms of expenditures in section 1.a.2:

GDP = consumption + investment + government spending + net exports

gross investment: total investment, including investment expenditures required to replace capital goods consumed in current production

net investment: gross investment minus capital consumption allowance

The investment measure in GDP (and GNP) is called **gross investment**. Gross investment is total investment, which includes investment expenditures required to replace capital goods consumed in current production. The NNP does not include investment expenditures required to replace worn-out capital goods; it includes only net investment. **Net investment** is equal to gross investment minus capital consumption allowance. Net investment measures business spending over and above that required to replace worn-out capital goods.

Figure 10.2 shows that in 2011, the U.S. NNP was $13,389.4 billion. This means that the U.S. economy produced well over $13 trillion worth of goods and services above those required to replace capital stock that had depreciated. $1,950 billion in capital was "worn out" in 2011.

national income (NI): net national product minus indirect business taxes

1.b.3. National Income (NI)

NI equals the NNP minus statistical discrepancy. The statistical discrepancy captures small adjustments from NNP that do not represent incomes earned in production. NI captures the costs of the factors of production used in producing output.

FIGURE 10.2 U.S. National Income Accounts, 2011 (billion dollars)

Gross domestic product plus receipts of factor income from the rest of the world minus payments of factor income to the rest of the world equals gross national product. Gross national product minus capital consumption allowance equals net national product. Net national product minus indirect business taxes equals national income. National income plus income currently received but not earned (transfer payments, personal interest, dividend income) minus income currently earned but not received (corporate profits, net interest, social security taxes) equals personal income. Personal income minus personal taxes equals disposable personal income.

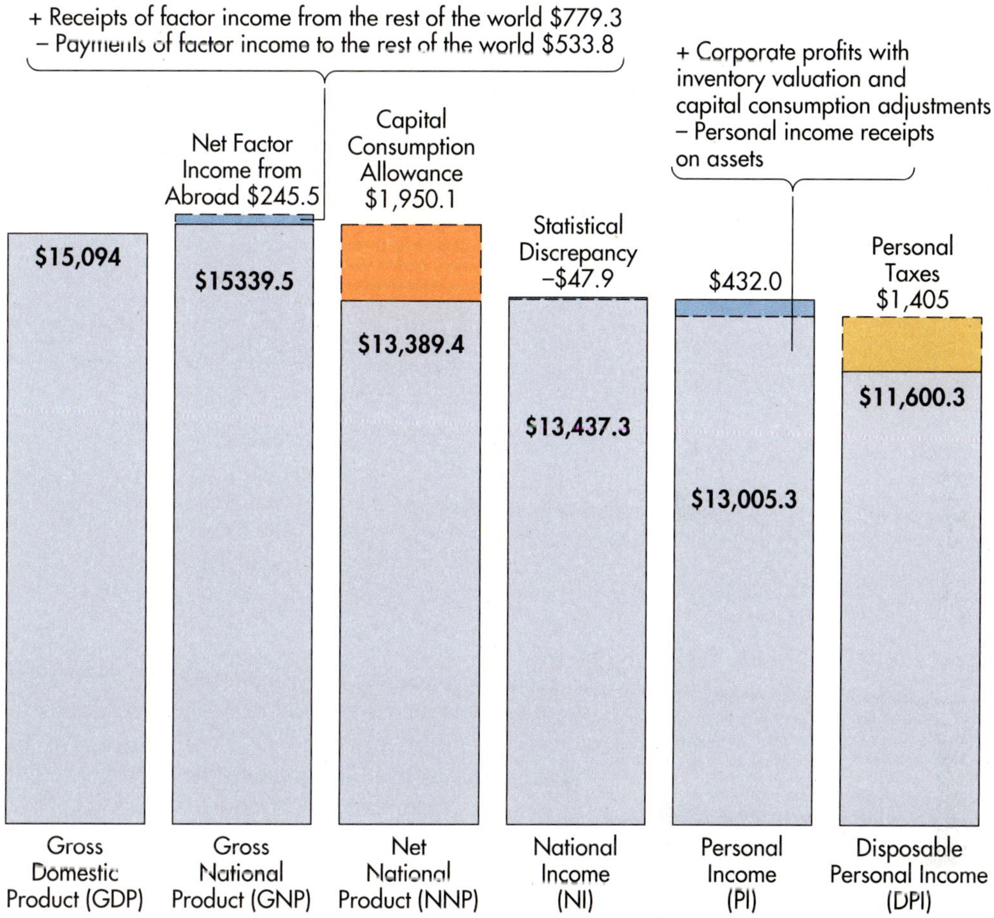

Source: U.S. Department of Commerce, Bureau of Economic Analysis (www.bea.gov).

personal income (PI): national income plus income currently received but not earned, minus income currently earned but not received

1.b.4. **Personal Income (PI)** PI is national income adjusted for income that is received but not earned in the current year and income that is earned but not received in the current year. Social security and welfare benefits are examples of income that is received but not earned in the current year. As you learned in Chapter 9, they are called transfer payments. An example of income that is currently earned but not received is profits that are retained by a corporation to finance current needs rather than paid out to stockholders. Another is social security (FICA) taxes, which are deducted from workers' paychecks.

disposable personal income (DPI): personal income minus personal taxes

1.b.5. **Disposable Personal Income (DPI)** DPI equals personal income minus personal taxes—income taxes, excise and real estate taxes on personal property, and other personal taxes. The DPI is the income that individuals have at their disposal for spending or saving. The sum of consumption spending plus saving must equal disposable personal income.

RECAP

1. Gross domestic product (GDP) is the market value of all final goods and services produced in an economy in a year.
2. GDP can be calculated by summing the market value of all final goods and services produced in a year, by summing the value added at each stage of production, by adding total expenditures on goods and services (GDP = consumption + investment + government spending + net exports), and by using the total income earned in the production of goods and services (GDP = wages + interest + rent + profits), subtracting net factor income from abroad, and adding depreciation and indirect business taxes.
3. Other measures of output and income include gross national product (GNP), net national product (NNP), national income (NI), personal income (PI), and disposable personal income (DPI).

National Income Accounts

GDP = consumption + investment + government spending + net exports

GNP = GDP + receipts of factor income from the rest of the world − payments of factor income to the rest of the world

NNP = GNP − capital consumption allowance

NI = NNP − statistical discrepancy

PI = NI − income earned but not received + income received but not earned

DPI = PI − personal taxes

2. NOMINAL AND REAL MEASURES

The GDP is the market value of all final goods and services produced within a country in a year. Value is measured in money terms, so the U.S. GDP is reported in dollars, the German GDP in euros, the Mexican GDP in pesos, and so on. Market value is the product of two elements: the money price and the quantity produced.

NOW YOU TRY IT

Use the following information to find the value of:

a. GDP
b. GNP
c. NNP
d. NI
e. PI
f. DPI

Consumption	$600
Gross investment	$100
Government spending	$200
Net exports	$100
Income earned but not received	$20
Income received but not earned	$30
Personal taxes	$200
Capital consumption allowance	$230
Receipts of factor income from the rest of the world	$50
Payments of factor income to the rest of the world	$50
Indirect business taxes	$90

2.a. Nominal and Real GDP

Nominal GDP measures output in terms of its current dollar value. **Real GDP** is adjusted for changing price levels. In 1980, the nominal U.S. GDP was $2,788 billion; in 2011, it was $15,094 billion—an increase of 441 percent. Does this mean that the United States produced 441 percent more goods and services in 2011 than it did in 1980? If the numbers reported are for nominal GDP, we cannot be sure. Nominal GDP cannot tell us whether the economy produced more goods and services because nominal GDP changes when prices change *and* when quantity changes.

Real GDP measures output in constant prices. This allows economists to identify the changes in actual production of final goods and services: Real GDP measures the quantity of goods and services produced after eliminating the influence of price changes contained in nominal GDP. In 1980, real GDP in the United States was $5,839 billion; in 2011, it was $13,315 billion, an increase of 128 percent. The 441 percent increase in

Table 10.1 Exchange Rates
May 16, 2012

	Currency per US$	US$ per Currency
Australian Dollar	1.00589	0.994144
Canadian Dollar	1.00738	0.992674
Chinese Yuan	6.32179	0.158183
Euro	0.785053	1.2738
Japanese Yen	80.4914	0.0124237
Mexican Peso	13.805	0.0724375
New Zealand Dollar	1.30327	0.767301
Singapore Dollar	1.26676	0.789416
Swiss Franc	0.942927	1.06053
United Kingdom Pound	**0.6458**	**1.5484**

Let's go back to comparing the price of the Canadian shirt in Seattle and Vancouver. The symbol for the U.S. dollar is \$. The symbol for the Canadian dollar is C\$. The shirt sells for \$20 in Seattle and C\$25 in Vancouver. Suppose the exchange rate between the U.S. dollar and the Canadian dollar is .8. This means that C\$1 costs \$.80.

To find the domestic currency value of a foreign currency price, multiply the foreign currency price by the exchange rate:

$$\text{Domestic currency value} = \text{foreign currency price} \times \text{exchange rate}$$

In our example, the U.S. dollar is the domestic currency:

$$\text{U.S. dollar value} = \text{C\$}25 \times 0.8 = \$20$$

If we multiply the price of the shirt in Canadian dollars (C\$25) by the exchange rate (0.8), we find the U.S. dollar value (\$20). After adjusting for the exchange rate, then, we can see that the shirt sells for the same price when the price is measured in a single currency.

4.b. Exchange Rate Changes and International Trade

Because exchange rates determine the domestic currency value of foreign goods, changes in those rates affect the demand for and supply of goods traded internationally. Suppose the price of the shirt in Seattle and in Vancouver remains the same, but the exchange rate changes from .8 to .9 U.S. dollars per Canadian dollar. What happens? The U.S. dollar price of the shirt in Vancouver increases. At the new rate, the shirt that sells for C\$25 in Vancouver costs a U.S. buyer \$22.50 (C\$25 × 0.9).

A rise in the value of a currency is called *appreciation*. In our example, as the exchange rate moves from \$.8 = C\$1 to \$.9 = C\$1, the Canadian dollar appreciates against the U.S. dollar. As a country's currency appreciates, international demand for its products falls, other things equal.

Suppose the exchange rate in our example moves from \$.8 = C\$1 to \$.7 = C\$1. Now the shirt that sells for C\$25 in Vancouver costs a U.S. buyer \$17.50 (C\$25 × 0.7). In this case, the Canadian dollar has *depreciated* in value relative to the U.S. dollar. As a country's currency depreciates, its goods sell for lower prices in other countries and the demand for its products increases, other things remaining equal.

When the Canadian dollar is appreciating against the U.S. dollar, the U.S. dollar must be depreciating against the Canadian dollar. For instance, when the exchange rate between the U.S. dollar and the Canadian dollar moves from \$.8 = C\$1 to \$.9 = C\$1, the reciprocal exchange rate—the rate between the Canadian dollar and the U.S. dollar—moves from C\$1.25 = \$1 (1/0.8 = 1.25) to C\$1.11 = \$1 (1/0.9 = 1.11). At the same time that Canadian goods are becoming more expensive to U.S. buyers, U.S. goods are becoming cheaper to Canadian buyers.

RECAP

1. The foreign exchange market is a global market in which currencies of different countries, largely bank deposits, are bought and sold.
2. An exchange rate is the price of one country's money in terms of another's.
3. Foreign demand for domestic goods decreases as the domestic currency appreciates and increases as the domestic currency depreciates.

5. THE BALANCE OF PAYMENTS

5 How do nations record their transactions with the rest of the world?

The U.S. economy does not operate in a vacuum. It affects and is affected by the economies of other nations. This point was brought home to Americans in recent years as newspaper headlines announced the latest trade deficit, and politicians denounced foreign countries for running trade surpluses against the United States. It seemed as if everywhere there was talk of the balance of payments.

The **balance of payments** is a record of a country's trade in goods, services, and financial assets with the rest of the world. This record is divided into categories, or accounts, that summarize the nation's international economic transactions. For example, one category measures transactions in merchandise; another measures transactions involving financial assets (bank deposits, bonds, stocks, loans). These accounts distinguish between private transactions (by individuals and businesses) and official transactions (by governments). Balance of payments data are reported quarterly for most developed countries.

5.a. Balance of Payments Accounts

current account: the sum of the merchandise, services, investment income, and unilateral transfers accounts in the balance of payments

balance of trade: the balance on the merchandise account in a nation's balance of payments

The balance of payments uses several different accounts to classify transactions (see Table 10.2). The **current account** is the sum of the balances in the merchandise, services, investment income, and unilateral transfers accounts.

Merchandise This account records all transactions involving goods. U.S. exports of goods bring money into the country for U.S. exporters. U.S. imports of foreign goods require payments to foreign sellers. When exports exceed imports, the merchandise account shows a surplus. When imports exceed exports, the account shows a deficit. The balance on the merchandise account is frequently referred to as the **balance of trade**.

Table 10.2 Simplified U.S. Balance of Payments, 2011 (millions of dollars)

Account	Net Balance
Merchandise	\$ – 738,292
Services	\$178,336
Investment income	\$221,065
Unilateral transfers	\$ – 134,550
Current account	\$ – 473,440
Financial account	\$394,137
Statistical discrepancy	\$80,464

Source: Data from Bureau of Economic Analysis (http://www.bea.gov).

In 2011, the merchandise account in the U.S. balance of payments showed a deficit of $\$-738{,}292$ million. In other words, the United States bought more goods from other nations than it sold to them.

Services This account measures trade involving services. It includes travel and tourism, royalties, transportation costs, and insurance premiums. In 2011, the balance on the services account was a $178,336 million surplus.

Investment Income The income earned from investments in foreign countries brings money into the United States; the income paid on foreign-owned investments in the United States takes money out of the United States. Investment income is the return on a special kind of service: It is the value of services provided by capital in foreign countries. In 2011, there was a surplus of $221,065 million in the investment income account.

Unilateral Transfers In a unilateral transfer, one party gives something but gets nothing in return. Gifts and retirement pensions are forms of unilateral transfers. For instance, if a farmworker in El Centro, California, sends money to his family in Guaymas, Mexico, this is a unilateral transfer from the United States to Mexico. In 2011, that unilateral transfers balance was a deficit of $134,550.

The current account is a useful measure of international transactions because it contains all of the activities involving goods and services. The **financial account** is where trade involving financial assets and international investment is recorded. In 2011, the current account showed a deficit of $473,440 million. This means that U.S. imports of merchandise, services, investment income, and unilateral transfers were $473,440 million greater than exports of these items.

financial account: the record in the balance of payments of the flow of financial assets into and out of a country

If we draw a line in the balance of payments under the current account, then all entries below the line relate to financing the movement of merchandise, services, investment income, and unilateral transfers into and out of the country. Financial account transactions include bank deposits, purchases of stocks and bonds, loans, land purchases, and purchases of business firms. Inflows of money associated with the U.S. financial account reflect foreign purchases of U.S. financial assets or real property such as land and buildings; outflows of money reflect U.S. purchases of foreign financial assets and real property. In 2011, the U.S. financial account showed a surplus of $394,137 million.

The *statistical discrepancy account*, the last account listed in Table 10.2, could be called "omissions and errors." Government cannot accurately measure all transactions that take place. Some international shipments of goods and services go uncounted or are miscounted, as are some international flows of capital. The statistical discrepancy account is used to correct these omissions and errors. In 2011, measured deficits exceeded measured surpluses, so the statistical discrepancy was $80,464 million.

Over all of the balance of payments accounts, the sum of surplus accounts must equal the sum of deficit accounts. The bottom line—the *net balance*—must be zero. It cannot show a surplus or a deficit. When people talk about a surplus or a deficit in the balance of payments, they actually are talking about a surplus or a deficit in one of the balance of payments accounts. The balance of payments itself, by definition, is always in balance.

5.b. The Current Account and the Financial Account

The current account reflects the movement of goods and services into and out of a country. The financial account reflects the flow of financial assets into and out of a country. In Table 10.2, the current account shows a deficit balance of $473,440 million. Remember that the balance of payments must *balance*. If there is a deficit in the current account, there must be a surplus in the financial account that offsets that deficit.

What is important here is not the bookkeeping process, the concept that the balance of payments must balance, but rather the meaning of deficits and surpluses in the current and financial accounts. These deficits and surpluses tell us whether a country is a net borrower from or lender to the rest of the world. A deficit in the current account means that a country is running a net surplus in its financial account. And it signals that a country is a net borrower from the rest of the world. A country that is running a current account deficit must borrow from abroad an amount sufficient to finance that deficit. A financial account surplus is achieved by selling more bonds and other debts of the domestic country to the rest of the world than the country buys from the rest of the world.

Figure 10.5 shows the current account balance in the United States. The United States experienced large current account deficits in the 1980s and then again in the late 1990s and 2000s. Such deficits indicate that the United States consumed more than it produced. Remember that in section 1.a.2 of this chapter, GDP is equal to total expenditures, or $GDP = C + I + G + X$, where X is net exports. A country with a current account deficit will have negative net exports. Rewriting the total spending equation as $X = GDP - C - I - G$, a negative X means that domestic spending, $C + I + G$, must be greater than domestic production, GDP. This means that the United States sold financial assets and borrowed large amounts of money from foreign residents to finance its current account deficits. This large foreign borrowing made the United States the largest debtor in the world. A *net debtor* owes more to the rest of the world

FIGURE 10.5 The U.S. Current Account Balance

The current account of the balance of payments is the sum of the balances in the merchandise, services, investment income, and unilateral transfers accounts. The United States experienced large current account deficits in the 1980s and much larger deficits more recently.

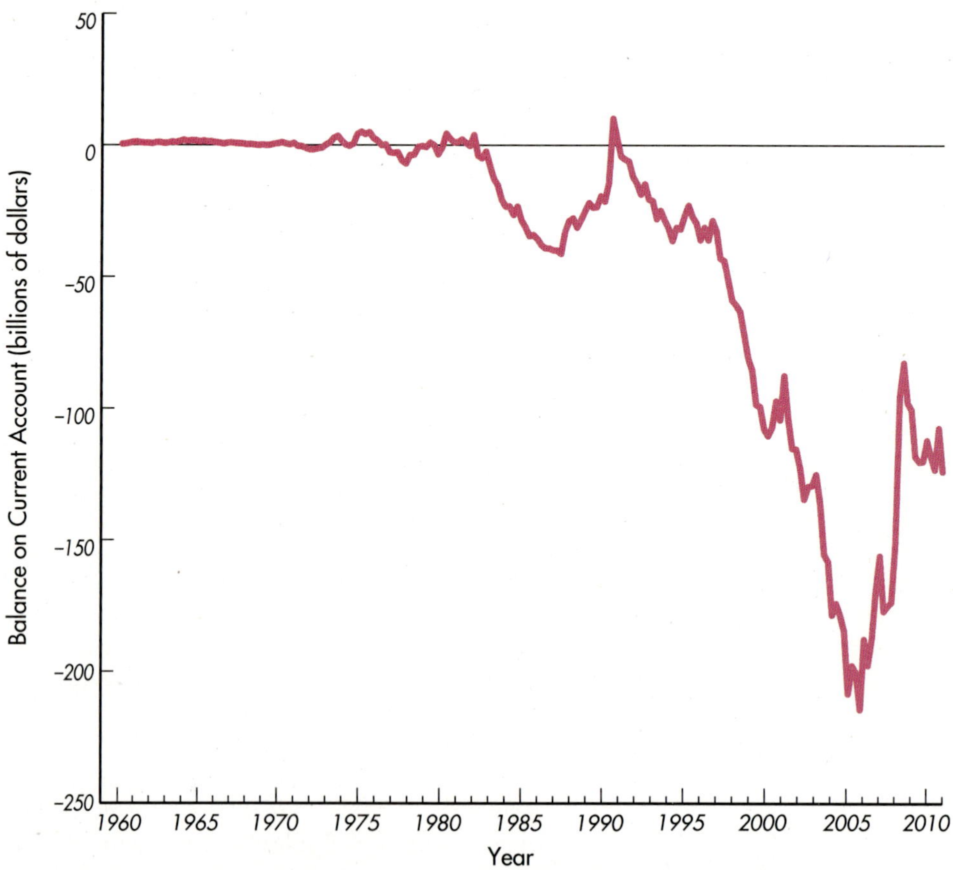

Source: U.S. Department of Commerce, Bureau of Economic Analysis (www.bea.gov).

than it is owed; a *net creditor* is owed more than it owes. The United States was an international net creditor from the end of World War I until the mid-1980s. The country financed its large current account deficits in the 1980s by borrowing from the rest of the world. As a result of this accumulated borrowing, in 1985 the United States became an international net debtor for the first time in almost 70 years. Since that time, the net debtor status of the United States has grown steadily.

RECAP

1. The balance of payments is a record of a nation's international transactions.
2. The current account is the sum of the balances in the merchandise, services, investment income, and unilateral transfers accounts.
3. A surplus exists when money inflows exceed outflows; a deficit exists when money inflows are less than outflows.
4. The financial account is where the transactions necessary to finance the movement of merchandise, services, investment income, and unilateral transfers into and out of the country are recorded.
5. The net balance in the balance of payments must be zero.
6. A deficit in the current account must be offset by a surplus in the financial account. It also indicates that the nation is a net borrower.

SUMMARY

How is the total output of an economy measured?

1. National income accounting is the system economists use to measure both the output of an economy and the flows between sectors of that economy.
2. Gross domestic product (GDP) is the market value of all final goods and services produced in a year in a country.
3. The GDP also equals the value added at each stage of production.
4. The GDP as output equals the sum of the output of households, business firms, and government within the country.
5. The GDP as expenditures equals the sum of consumption plus investment plus government spending plus net exports.
6. The GDP as income equals the sum of wages, interest, rent, profits, proprietors' income, capital consumption allowance, and indirect business taxes less net factor income from abroad.
7. Other measures of national output include gross national product (GNP), net national product (NNP), national income (NI), personal income (PI), and disposable personal income (DPI).

What is the difference between nominal and real GDP?

8. Nominal GDP measures output in terms of its current dollar values including the effects of price changes; real GDP measures output after eliminating the effects of price changes.

What is the purpose of a price index?

9. A price index measures the average level of prices across an economy.
10. Total expenditures on final goods and services equal total income.

How is money traded internationally?

11. Foreign exchange is currency and bank deposits that are denominated in foreign currency.

12. The foreign exchange market is a global market in which people trade one currency for another.
13. Exchange rates, the price of one country's money in terms of another country's money, are necessary to compare prices quoted in different currencies.
14. The value of a good in a domestic currency equals the foreign currency price times the exchange rate.
15. When a domestic currency appreciates, domestic goods become more expensive to foreigners, and foreign goods become cheaper to domestic residents.
16. When a domestic currency depreciates, domestic goods become cheaper to foreigners, and foreign goods become more expensive to domestic residents.

How do nations record their transactions with the rest of the world?

17. The balance of payments is a record of a nation's transactions with the rest of the world.
18. The current account is the sum of the balances in the merchandise, services, investment income, and unilateral transfers accounts.
19. The financial account reflects the transactions necessary to finance the movement of merchandise, services, investment income, and unilateral transfers into and out of the country.
20. A deficit in the current account must be offset by a surplus in the financial account.

EXERCISES

1. The following table lists the stages required in the production of a personal computer. What is the value of the computer in the GDP?

Stage	Value Added
Components manufacture	$ 60
Assembly	250
Wholesaler	540
Retailer	1,500

2. What is the difference between GDP and each of the following?
   a. gross national product
   b. net national product
   c. national income
   d. personal income
   e. disposable personal income

Use the following national income accounting information to do exercises 3–7:

Stage	Value Added
Consumption	$400
Imports	10
Net investment	20
Government purchases	100
Exports	20
Capital consumption allowance	20
Statistical discrepancy	5
Receipts of factor income from the rest of the world	12
Payments of factor income to the rest of the world	10

3. What is the GDP for this economy?
4. What is the GNP for this economy?
5. What is the NNP for this economy?
6. What is the national income for this economy?
7. What is the gross investment in this economy?
8. Why has nominal GDP increased faster than real GDP in the United States over time? What would it mean if an economy had real GDP increasing faster than nominal GDP?
9. If a surfboard is produced this year but not sold until next year, how is it counted in this year's GDP and not next year's?
10. What is the price of 1 U.S. dollar in terms of each of the following currencies, given the following exchange rates?
    a. 1 European euro = $.95
    b. 1 Chinese yuan = $.12
    c. 1 Israeli shekel = $.30
    d. 1 Kuwaiti dinar = $3.20
11. A bicycle manufactured in the United States costs $150. Using the exchange rates listed in Table 10.1,

what would the bicycle cost in the currency of each of the following countries?
   a. Australia
   b. Britain
   c. Canada
12. The U.S. dollar price of a Swedish krona changes from $.1572 to $.1730.
   a. Has the dollar depreciated or appreciated against the krona?
   b. Has the krona appreciated or depreciated against the dollar?

Use the information in the following table on Mexico's international transactions to do exercises 13–15 (the amounts are the U.S. dollar values in millions):

Merchandise imports	$96,000
Merchandise exports	89,469
Services exports	10,901
Services imports	10,819
Investment income receipts	4,032
Investment income payments	17,099
Unilateral transfers	4,531

13. What is the balance of trade?
14. What is the current account?
15. Did Mexico become a larger international net debtor during this period?
16. If the U.S. dollar appreciated against the euro, what would you expect to happen to U.S. net exports with Germany?
17. Suppose the U.S. dollar price of a British pound is $1.50; the dollar price of a euro is $.90; a hotel room in London, England, costs 120 British pounds; and a comparable hotel room in Hanover, Germany, costs 220 euros.
   a. Which hotel room is cheaper to a U.S. tourist?
   b. What is the exchange rate between the euro and the British pound?
18. Use the national income accounting definition $GDP = C + I + G + X$ to explain what a current account deficit (negative net exports) means in terms of domestic spending, production, and borrowing.

STUDY GUIDE FOR CHAPTER 10

Key Term Match

Match each term with its correct definition by placing the appropriate letter next to the corresponding number.

A. national income accounting
B. gross domestic product (GDP)
C. intermediate goods
D. value added
E. inventory
F. capital consumption allowance
G. depreciation
H. indirect business taxes
I. gross national product (GNP)
J. net national product (NNP)
K. gross investment
L. net investment
M. national income
N. personal income
O. disposable personal income
P. nominal GDP
Q. real GDP
R. price index
S. base year
T. GDP price index (GDPPI)
U. consumer price index
V. cost of living adjustments (COLAs)
W. producer price index (PPI)
X. foreign exchange
Y. foreign exchange market
Z. balance of payments
AA. current account
BB. balance of trade
CC. financial account

____ 1. the difference between the value of the output and the value of the intermediate goods used in the production of that output

____ 2. taxes that are collected by businesses for a government agency

____ 3. a measure of the average price level in an economy

____ 4. the stock of unsold goods held by a firm

____ 5. national income plus income currently received but not earned, minus income currently earned but not received

____ 6. a reduction in value of capital goods over time due to their use in production

____ 7. gross domestic product plus receipts of factor income from the rest of the world minus payments of factor income to the rest of the world

____ 8. currency and bank deposits that are denominated in foreign money

____ 9. the sum of the merchandise, services, investment income, and unilateral transfers accounts in the balance of payments

____ 10. the market value of all final goods and services produced in a year within a country

____ 11. a measure of the quantity of final goods and services produced, obtained by eliminating the influence of price changes from the nominal GDP statistics

____ 12. a measure of the average price of goods and services purchased by the typical household

____ 13. gross national product minus capital consumption allowance

____ 14. a global market in which people trade one currency for another

____ 15. a measure of national output based on the current prices of goods and services

____ 16. total investment, including investment expenditures required to replace capital goods consumed in current production

____ 17. the balance on the merchandise account in a nation's balance of payments

____ 18. a record of a country's trade in goods, services, and financial assets with the rest of the world

____ 19. net national product minus indirect business taxes

____ 20. the year against which other years are measured

____ 21. the framework that summarizes and categorizes productive activity in an economy over a specific period of time, typically a year

____ 22. an increase in wages that is designed to match increases in the prices of items purchased by the typical household

____ 23. the estimated value of depreciation plus the value of accidental damage to capital stock

____ 24. the record in the balance of payments of the flow of financial assets into and out of a country

____ 25. goods that are used as inputs in the production of final goods and services

____ 26. gross investment minus capital consumption allowance

____ 27. personal income minus personal taxes

____ 28. a broad measure of the prices of goods and services included in the gross domestic product

____ 29. a measure of average prices received by producers

Quick-Check Quiz

1. Which of the following is counted in GDP?
   - ☐ a. the value of homemaker services
   - ☐ b. estimated illegal drug transactions
   - ☐ c. the value of oil used in the production of gasoline
   - ☐ d. estimated in-kind wages
   - ☐ e. the sale of a used automatic dishwasher

2. A price index equal to 90 in a given year
   - ☐ a. indicates that prices were lower than prices in the base year.
   - ☐ b. indicates that the year in question was a year previous to the base year.
   - ☐ c. indicates that prices were 10 percent higher than prices in the base year.
   - ☐ d. is inaccurate—price indexes cannot be lower than 100.
   - ☐ e. indicates that real GDP was lower than GDP in the base year.

3. Social security payments are tied to the
   - ☐ a. GDP price index.
   - ☐ b. wholesale price index.
   - ☐ c. CPI.
   - ☐ d. nominal GDP.
   - ☐ e. PPI.

4. The foreign exchange market, like the New York Stock Exchange, is located in a specific building in New York City. ________________ (true or false?)

5. In August, 2012, U.S. Disposable Personal Income had risen for seven months in a row. This was a ________________ (negative/positive) sign for the U.S. economy, since consumption expenditures account for about ________________ % of GDP.

6. If the U.S. dollar drops to 1.2535 euros from 1.2564 euros, then the dollar has
   - ☐ a. appreciated against the euro, and the prices of European cars will increase in the United States.
   - ☐ b. appreciated against the euro, and the prices of European cars will decrease in the United States.
   - ☐ c. depreciated against the euro, and the prices of European cars will increase in the United States.
   - ☐ d. depreciated against the euro, and the prices of European cars will decrease in the United States.
   - ☐ e. depreciated against the euro, and the prices of American cars will increase in Europe.

7. If a Japanese investor bought the Epic Center office building in Wichita, Kansas, the transaction would be recorded as a ____________ in the ____________ account.
   - ☐ a. credit; current
   - ☐ b. credit; financial
   - ☐ c. debit; current
   - ☐ d. debit; financial
   - ☐ e. credit; investment income

8. A country with a deficit in its current account
   - ☐ a. exports more goods and services than it imports.
   - ☐ b. is running a deficit in its financial account.
   - ☐ c. is a net lender to the rest of the world.
   - ☐ d. is a net borrower from the rest of the world.
   - ☐ e. is running a surplus in its merchandise account.

9. You hear on the news that in the next few months, the dollar is expected to change from $1=.976 Swiss francs to $1=.9593 Swiss francs.
   - ☐ a. The dollar is expected to ____________ (appreciate, depreciate) against the franc.
   - ☐ b. Swiss goods will be ____________ (more expensive, cheaper) in the United States.
   - ☐ c. As a result of the change in exchange rates, U.S. exports to Switzerland will ____________ (increase, decrease), all other things being equal.
   - ☐ d. Your company, located in the U.S. is planning to make a big purchase of Swiss products. Other relevant conditions are forecasted to remain stable. If you think the currency exchange forecast is accurate, you should ____________ (wait a few months to make the purchase, buy as soon as possible)

10. You read in the paper that the producer price index (PPI) has risen. In the future, you can expect the consumer price index (CPI) to ____________ (rise, fall). If your income does not change, your future purchasing power will ____________ (rise / not change, fall).

Practice Questions and Problems

1. List the three factors of production and the name of the payments each factor receives. What additional three items must be figured in to find gross domestic product?

   ____

   ____

   ____

2. A lei maker buys flowers from a nursery for $130. She makes 50 leis from the flowers and sells each lei for $3.99. What is the value added for the lei maker?

   ____

3. A Kansas farmer sells wheat to a craftsperson to make into decorative ornaments. The farmer sells his wheat to the craftsperson for $300. The craftsperson adds labor, valued at $200, and some ribbons, valued at $50, and produces 110 ornaments. What is the final market value of each ornament?
4. Unplanned inventory ____________ (is, is not) included in the GDP.
5. Write the formulas for the following:

   Gross domestic product as expenditures (GDP):

   ____

   Gross domestic product as income (GDP):

   ____

   Gross national product (GNP):

   ____

   Net national product (NNP):

   ____

   National income (NI):

   ____

   Personal income (PI):

   ____

   Disposable personal income (DPI):

   ____

6. Use the following information to calculate GDP, GNP, NNP, and NI. All figures are in billions of dollars.

Capital consumption allowance	328
Profits	124
Rents	6
Interest	264
Net factor income from abroad	43
Wages and salaries	1,803
Personal taxes	398
Proprietor's income	248
Indirect business taxes	273

GNP ____________ GDP ____________

NNP ____________ NI ____________

7. The following table shows nominal GDP and the implicit GDP deflator for three years. Use this information to calculate the real GDP and to answer the following questions. Round to a whole number.

Year	Nominal GDP	Implicit GDP Deflator	Real GDP
1	206	98	______
2	216	100	______
3	228	115	______

   a. Which year is the base year? ____________
   b. Prices in year 3 were ____________ (higher, lower) than prices in the base year.
   c. During year 3, nominal GDP ____________ (increased, did not change, decreased).
8. Why isn't nominal GDP a good measure of the strength or weakness of the economy? What measure would be better? ____________.
9. If the price index in the current year is 212, then prices have ____________ (increased, not changed, decreased) by ____________ percent from the base year.
10. What is the price of one U.S. dollar given the following exchange rates?
    a. 1 Canadian dollar = $.86610
    b. 1 euro = $.8707
    c. 1 Japanese yen = $.00677
    d. 1 British pound = $1.8155
11. A digital camera manufactured in the United States costs $150. Using the exchange rates listed in the following table, what would the camera cost in each of the following countries?

Country	U.S. Dollar Equivalent	Currency per U.S. Dollar
Euro area (euro)	.8707	1.1485
Pakistan (rupee)	.0463	21.61
Philippines (peso)	.04413	22.66

    a. Euro area ____________
    b. Pakistan ____________
    c. Philippines ____________

Exercises and Applications

I Understanding Price Indexes

Suppose the economy of Strandasville produces only four goods: CDs, pizza, desk chairs, and sweaters. The following tables show the dollar value of output for three different years.

Year	Number of CDs	Price per CD	Number of Pizzas	Price per Pizza
1	1,000	$5	8,000	$6.00
2	1,000	$6	8,000	$6.60
3	4,000	$7	10,000	$6.80

Year	Number of Desk Chairs	Price per Chair	Number of Sweaters	Price per Sweater
1	3,000	$20	5,000	$20
2	3,000	$25	5,000	$18
3	3,500	$25	4,900	$15

1. Calculate the total dollar value of output for year 1, year 2, and year 3.
   ____
   ____
   ____
2. The dollar value of output in year 2 is higher than the dollar value of output in year 1
   a. entirely because of price changes.
   b. entirely because of output changes.
   c. because of both price and output changes.
3. The dollar value of output in year 3 is higher than the dollar value of output in year 2
   a. entirely because of price changes.
   b. entirely because of output changes.
   c. because of both price and output changes.

II The Balance of Payments as an Indicator

A surplus in the merchandise account means that a nation is exporting more goods than it is importing. This is often interpreted as a sign that a nation's producers can produce at a lower cost than their foreign counterparts. A trade deficit may indicate that a nation's producers are less efficient than their foreign counterparts.

Interpret these statements in terms of what you have read about the United States as the world's largest debtor nation. Can you explain why many analysts view the U.S. balance of payments accounts with concern in recent years?

____
____
____

III The Balance of Payments and Exchange Rates

If U.S. residents lend and invest less in foreign countries than foreigners lend and invest in the United States, the financial account will be in surplus. If U.S. purchases of foreign stocks and bonds exceed foreign purchases of U.S. stocks and bonds, then more funds are leaving the country than entering it, and the financial account will be in deficit. Pretend that you are willing to sell your DVD player to a French resident. Would you prefer to be paid in U.S. dollars or in euros? Since you can't easily spend euros in this country, you would prefer to be paid in U.S. dollars. Therefore, if the French buy more U.S. goods and services, they will need dollars to pay for them, and the dollar will appreciate against the euro. Similarly, if U.S. investors demand more French bonds and stocks, the euro will appreciate.

What impact will a financial account surplus have on domestic currency? If U.S. federal budget deficits continue, what will be the impact on the dollar?

____

____

You can find further practice tests in the Online Quiz at: www.cengagebrain.com

11 Unemployment, Inflation, and Business Cycles

FUNDAMENTAL QUESTIONS

1. What is a business cycle?
2. How is the unemployment rate defined and measured?
3. What is the cost of unemployed resources?
4. What is inflation?
5. Why is inflation a problem?

PREVIEW

If you were graduating from college today, what would your job prospects be? In 1932, they would have been bleak. A large number of people were out of work (about one in four workers), and a large number of firms had laid off workers or gone out of business. If you were graduating from school in Spain in 2012, the unemployment rate was 24 percent and the prospects for new graduates were dim. In fact, many workers were looking to foreign countries to find jobs since there were so few jobs at home. At any time, job opportunities depend not only on the individual's ability and experience but also on the current state of the economy.

All economies have cycles of activity: periods of expansion, when output and employment increase, followed by periods of contraction, when output and employment decrease. For instance, during the expansionary period of the 1990s, fewer than 5 percent of U.S. workers had no job by 1997. But during the period of contraction of 2008–2009, 10 percent of U.S. workers had no job. When the economy is growing, the demand for goods and services tends to increase. To produce those goods and services, firms hire more workers. Economic expansion also has an impact on inflation. As the demand for goods and services goes up, the prices of those goods and services also tend to rise. By the late 1990s, following several years of economic growth, consumer prices in the United States were rising by about 3 percent a year. During periods of contraction, as more people are out of work, demand for goods and services tends to fall, and there is less pressure for rising prices. During the period of the Great Depression in the 1930s in the United States, consumer prices fell by more than 5 percent in 1933. Both price increases and the fraction of workers without jobs are affected by business cycles in fairly regular ways. But their effects on individual standards of living, income, and purchasing power are much less predictable.

Why do certain events move in tandem? What are the links between unemployment and inflation? What causes the business cycle to behave as it does? What effect does government activity have on the business cycle and on unemployment and inflation? Who is harmed by rising unemployment and inflation? Who benefits? Macroeconomics attempts to answer all of these questions.

1. BUSINESS CYCLES

1

What is a business cycle?

In this chapter we describe the business cycle and examine measures of unemployment and inflation. We talk about the ways in which the business cycle, unemployment, and inflation are related. And we describe their effects on the participants in the economy.

The most widely used measure of a nation's output is gross domestic product. When we examine the value of real GDP over time, we find periods in which it rises and other periods in which it falls.

1.a. Definitions

business cycle:
pattern of rising real GDP followed by falling real GDP

This pattern—real GDP rising, then falling—is called a **business cycle**. The pattern occurs over and over again, but as Figure 11.1 shows, the pattern over time is anything but regular. Historically the duration of business cycles and the rate at which real GDP rises or falls (indicated by the steepness of the line in Figure 11.1) vary considerably.

recession:
a period in which real GDP falls

Figure 11.1 clearly shows that the U.S. economy has experienced up-and-down swings in the years since 1959. Still, real GDP has grown at an average rate of approximately 3 percent per year. Although it is important to recognize that periods of economic growth, or prosperity, are followed by periods of contraction, or **recession**, it is also important to recognize the presence of long-term economic growth; despite the presence of periodic recessions, in the long run the economy produces more goods and services. The long-run growth in the economy depends on the growth in productive resources, such as land, labor, and capital, along with technological advances. Technological change increases the productivity of resources so that output increases even with a fixed amount of inputs. In recent years there has been concern about the growth rate of U.S. productivity and its effect on the long-run growth potential of the economy.

FIGURE 11.1 U.S. Real GDP

The shaded areas represent periods of economic contraction (recession). The table lists the dates of business-cycle peaks and troughs. The peak dates indicate when contractions began; the trough dates, when expansions began.

Peaks	Troughs
April 1960	February 1961
December 1969	November 1970
November 1973	March 1975
January 1980	July 1980
July 1981	November 1982
July 1990	March 1991
March 2001	November 2001
December 2007	June 2009

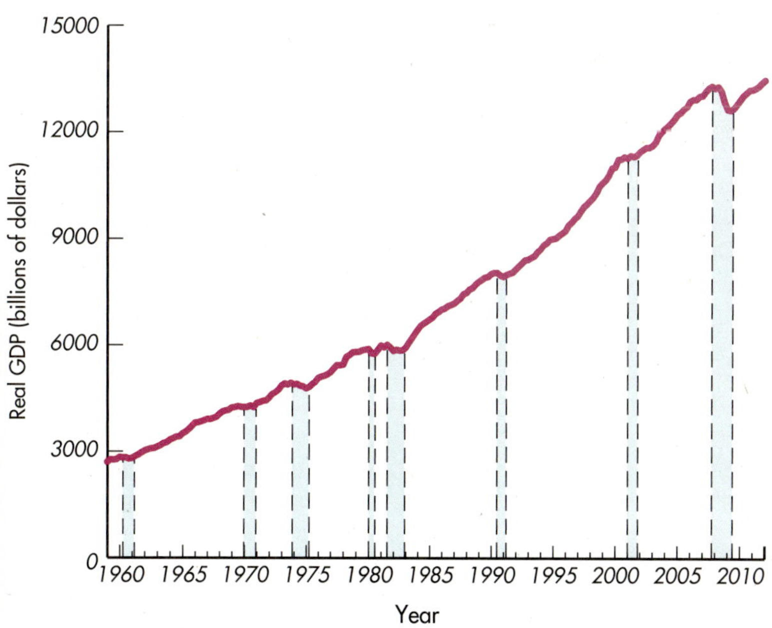

Source: Bureau of Economic Analysis (www.bea.gov).

FIGURE 11.2 The Business Cycle

The business cycle contains four phases: the expansion (boom), when real GDP is increasing; the peak, which marks the end of an expansion and the beginning of a contraction; the contraction (recession), when real GDP is falling; and the trough, which marks the end of a contraction and the beginning of an expansion.

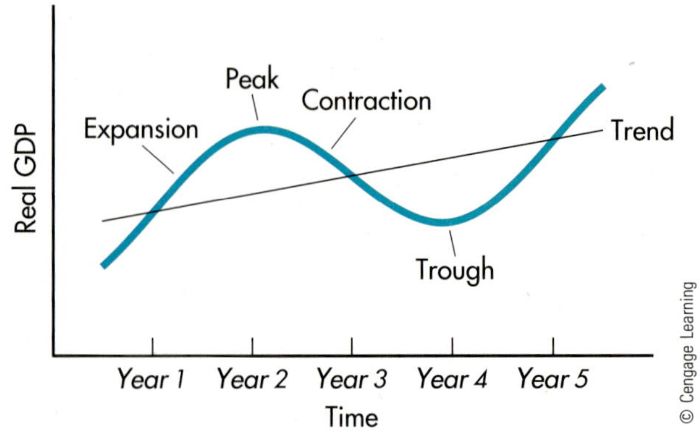

Figure 11.2 shows how real GDP behaves over a hypothetical business cycle and identifies the stages of the cycle. The vertical axis on the graph measures the level of real GDP; the horizontal axis measures time in years. In year 1, real GDP is growing; the economy is in the *expansion* phase, or *boom* period, of the business cycle. Growth continues until the *peak* is reached, in year 2. Real GDP begins to fall during the *contraction* phase of the cycle, which continues until year 4. The *trough* marks the end of the contraction and the start of a new expansion. Even though the economy is subject to periodic ups and downs, real GDP, the measure of a nation's output, has risen over the long term, as illustrated by the upward-sloping line labeled *Trend*.

If an economy is growing over time, why do economists worry about business cycles? Economists try to understand the causes of business cycles so that they can learn to moderate or avoid recessions and their harmful effects on standards of living.

1.b. **Historical Record**

The official dating of recessions in the United States is the responsibility of the National Bureau of Economic Research (NBER), an independent research organization. The NBER defines a recession as "a period of significant decline in total output, income, employment, and trade, usually lasting from six months to a year, and marked by widespread contractions in many sectors of the economy." People sometimes say that a recession is defined by two consecutive quarters of declining real GDP. This informal idea of what constitutes a recession seems consistent with the past recessions experienced by the United States—every recession through the 1990s has had at least two quarters of falling real GDP. However, this is not the official definition of a recession. The business cycle dating committee of the NBER generally focuses on monthly data. Close attention is paid to the following monthly data series: employment, real personal income less transfer payments, the volume of sales of the manufacturing and wholesale–retail sectors adjusted for price changes, and industrial production. The focus is not on real GDP since it is only measured quarterly and does not permit the identification of the month in which business cycle turning points occur. The NBER has identified the shaded areas in the graph in Figure 11.1 as recessions and the unshaded areas as expansions. Recessions are periods between cyclical peaks and the troughs that follow them. Expansions are periods between cyclical troughs and the peaks that follow them. There have been 13 recessions since 1929. The most severe was the Great Depression. It occurred between 1929 and 1933, and national

depression: a severe, prolonged economic contraction

output fell by 25 percent. A **depression** is a prolonged period of severe economic contraction. The fact that people refer to "the Depression" when speaking about the recession that began in 1929 indicates the severity of that contraction relative to others in recent experience. There was widespread suffering during the Depression. Many people were jobless and homeless, and many firms went bankrupt. The most recent recession began in December 2007 and ended in June 2009. This was the most severe downturn since the Great Depression. In fact, some have referred to this latest recession as the "Great Recession" due to the magnitude and duration of the slowdown in business activity. In fact, even though the recession was dated as having ended in 2009, the number of workers without a job remained high for years after the recession officially ended as the growth of the economy was positive but weak.

1.c. Indicators

We have been talking about the business cycle in terms of real GDP. There are a number of other variables that move in a fairly regular manner over the business cycle. The Department of Commerce classifies these variables in three

The Great Depression left many jobless and homeless, like these men waiting in line for a free meal at a New York municipal lodging house.

AP PHOTOS

Table 11.1 Indicators of the Business Cycle

Leading Indicators	Coincident Indicators	Lagging Indicators
Average workweek	Payroll employment	Labor cost per unit of output
Unemployment claims	Industrial production	Inventories to sales ratio
Manufacturers' new orders	Personal income	Unemployment duration
Stock prices	Manufacturing and trade sales	Consumer credit to personal income ratio
New plant and equipment orders		Outstanding commercial loans
New building permits		Prime interest rate
Delivery times of goods		Inflation rate for services
Interest rate spread		
Money supply		
Consumer expectations		

categories—leading indicators, coincident indicators, and lagging indicators—depending on whether they move up or down before, at the same time as, or following a change in real GDP (see Table 11.1).

leading indicator: a variable that changes before real output changes

Leading indicators generally change before real GDP changes. As a result, economists use them to forecast changes in output. Looking at Table 11.1, it is easy to see how some of these leading indicators could be used to forecast future output. For instance, new building permits signal new construction. If the number of new permits issued goes up, economists can expect the amount of new construction to increase. Similarly, if manufacturers receive more new orders, economists can expect more goods to be produced.

Leading indicators are not infallible, however. The link between them and future output can be tenuous. For example, leading indicators may fall one month and rise the next while real output rises steadily. Economists want to see several consecutive months of a new direction in the leading indicators before forecasting a change in output. Short-run movements in the indicators can be very misleading.

coincident indicator: a variable that changes at the same time that real output changes

Coincident indicators are economic variables that tend to change at the same time real output changes. For example, as real output increases, economists expect to see employment and sales rise. The coincident indicators listed in Table 11.1 have demonstrated a strong tendency over time to change along with changes in real GDP.

lagging indicator: a variable that changes after real output changes

The final group of variables listed in Table 11.1, **lagging indicators**, do not change their value until after the value of real GDP has changed. For instance, as output increases, jobs are created and more workers are hired. It makes sense, then, to expect the duration of unemployment (the average time workers are unemployed) to fall. The duration of unemployment is a lagging indicator. Similarly, the inflation rate for services (which measures how prices change for such things as dry cleaners, veterinarians, and other services) tends to change after real GDP changes. Lagging indicators are used along with leading and coincident indicators to identify the peaks and troughs in business cycles.

RECAP

1. The business cycle is a recurring pattern of rising and falling real GDP.
2. Although all economies move through periods of expansion and contraction, the duration of expansion and recession varies.
3. Real GDP is not the only variable affected by business cycles; leading, lagging, and coincident indicators also show the effects of economic expansion and contraction.

2. UNEMPLOYMENT

2

How is the unemployment rate defined and measured?

Recurring periods of prosperity and recession are reflected in the nation's labor markets. In fact, this is what makes understanding the business cycle so important. If business cycles signified only a little more or a little less profit for businesses, governments would not be so anxious to forecast or to control their swings. It is the human costs of lost jobs and incomes—the inability to maintain standards of living—that make an understanding of business cycles and of the factors that affect unemployment so important.

2.a. Definition and Measurement

unemployment rate: the percentage of the labor force that is not working

The **unemployment rate** is the percentage of the labor force that is not working. The rate is calculated by dividing the number of people who are unemployed by the number of people in the labor force:

$$\text{Unemployment rate} = \frac{\text{number unemployed}}{\text{number in labor force}}$$

This ratio seems simple enough, but there are several subtle issues at work here. First, the unemployment rate does not measure the percentage of the total population that is not working; it measures the percentage of the *labor force* that is not working. Who is in the labor force? Obviously, everybody who is employed is part of the labor force. But only some of those who are not currently employed are counted in the labor force.

The Bureau of Labor Statistics of the Department of Labor compiles labor data each month based on an extensive survey of U.S. households. All U.S. residents are potential members of the labor force. The Labor Department arrives at the size of the actual labor force by using this formula:

$$\begin{aligned}\text{Labor force} = {} & \text{all U.S. residents} - \text{residents under 16 years of age} \\ & - \text{institutionalized adults} - \text{adults not looking for work}\end{aligned}$$

NOW YOU TRY IT

A survey has been taken of 1,000 people in a neighborhood. It is found that 800 people are working full time. Of the 200 not working, 100 are housewives or househusbands, 50 are actively looking for a job, 20 are retired, and 30 are under 16 years of age. Using the definition of the unemployment rate and labor force, answer the following questions:

1. What is the size of the neighborhood labor force?
2. What is the neighborhood unemployment rate?

So the labor force includes those adults (an adult being 16 or older) currently employed or actively seeking work. It is relatively simple to see to it that children and institutionalized adults (e.g., those in prison or long-term care facilities) are not counted in the labor force. It is more difficult to identify and accurately measure adults who are not actively looking for work.

A person is actively seeking work if he or she is available to work, has looked for work in the past four weeks, is waiting for a recall after being laid off, or is starting a job within 30 days. Those who are not working and who meet these criteria are considered unemployed.

2.b. Interpreting the Unemployment Rate

Is the unemployment rate an accurate measure? The fact that the rate does not include those who are not actively looking for work is not necessarily a failing. Many people who are not actively looking for work—homemakers, older citizens, and students, for example—have made a decision to do housework, to retire, or to stay in school. These people rightly are not counted among the unemployed.

discouraged workers: workers who have stopped looking for work because they believe no one will offer them a job

But there are people missing from the unemployment statistics who are not working and are not looking for work, yet would take a job if one was offered. **Discouraged workers** have looked for work in the past year but have given up looking for work because they believe that no one will hire them. These individuals are ignored by the official unemployment rate even though they are able to work and may have spent a long time looking for work. Estimates of the number of discouraged workers indicate that in 2011, about 3.3 million people were not counted in the labor force yet claimed that they were available for work. Of this group, 989,000 people were considered to be discouraged workers. In this case, the reported unemployment rate underestimates the true burden of unemployment in the economy because it ignores discouraged workers.

underemployment: the employment of workers in jobs that do not utilize their productive potential

Discouraged workers are one source of hidden unemployment; underemployment is another. **Underemployment** is the underutilization of workers—employment in tasks that do not fully utilize their productive potential—including part-time workers who prefer full-time employment. Even if every worker has a job, substantial underemployment leaves the economy producing less than its potential GDP.

The effect of discouraged workers and underemployment is an unemployment rate that understates actual unemployment. In contrast, the effect of the *underground economy* is a rate that overstates actual unemployment. A sizable component of the officially unemployed is actually working. The unemployed construction worker who plays in a band at night may not report that activity because he or she wants to avoid paying taxes on his or her earnings as a musician. This person is officially unemployed but has a source of income. Many officially unemployed individuals have an alternative source of income. This means that official statistics overstate the true magnitude of unemployment. The larger the underground economy, the greater this overstatement (see the Economic Insight "The Underground Economy").

We have identified two factors, discouraged workers and underemployment, that cause the official unemployment rate to underestimate true unemployment. Another factor, the underground economy, causes the official rate to overestimate the true rate of unemployment. There is no reason to expect these factors to cancel one another out, and there is no way to know for sure which is most important. The point is to remember what the official data on unemployment do and do not measure.

2.c. Types of Unemployment

Economists have identified four basic types of unemployment:

- **Seasonal unemployment** A product of regular, recurring changes in the hiring needs of certain industries on a monthly or seasonal basis.
- **Frictional unemployment** A product of the short-term movement of workers between jobs and of first-time job seekers.

ECONOMIC INSIGHT

The Underground Economy

Official unemployment data, like national income data, do not include activity in the underground economy. Obviously, drug dealers and prostitutes do not report their earnings. Nor do many of the people who supplement their unemployment benefits with part-time jobs. In addition, people such as the waiter who reports a small fraction of his actual tips and the housecleaning person who requests payment in cash in order to avoid reporting taxable income are also part of the underground economy.

Because activity in the underground economy goes unreported, there is no exact way to determine its size. Estimates range from 5 to 33 percent of the gross domestic product. With the GDP at $14.5 trillion, this places the value of underground activity between $73 billion and $4.7 trillion.

We will never know the true size of the underground economy, but evidence suggests that it is growing. That evidence has to do with cash. The vast majority of people working in the underground economy are paid in cash. One indicator of the growth of that economy, then, is the rise in currency over time relative to checking accounts. Also, per capita holdings of $100 bills have increased substantially. Certainly, much of the demand for $100 bills is a product of inflation (as the prices of goods and services go up, it is easier to pay for them in larger-denomination bills). But there is also a substantial rise in real holdings of $100 bills as well.

The underground economy forces us to interpret government statistics carefully. We must remember the following:

- Official income statistics understate the true national income.
- Official unemployment data overestimate true unemployment.
- When the underground economy grows more rapidly than the rest of the economy, the true rate of growth is higher than reported.

- **Structural unemployment** A product of technological change and other changes in the structure of the economy.
- **Cyclical unemployment** A product of business-cycle fluctuations.

In certain industries, labor needs fluctuate throughout the year. When local crops are harvested, farms need lots of workers; the rest of the year, they do not. (Migrant farm workers move from one region to another, following the harvests, to avoid seasonal unemployment.) Ski resort towns like Park City, Utah, are booming during the ski season, when employment peaks, but need fewer workers during the rest of the year. In the nation as a whole, the Christmas season is a time of peak employment and low unemployment rates. To avoid confusing seasonal fluctuations in unemployment with other sources of unemployment, unemployment data are seasonally adjusted.

Frictional and structural unemployment exist in any dynamic economy. In terms of individual workers, frictional unemployment is short term in nature. Workers quit one job and soon find another; students graduate and soon find a job. This kind of unemployment cannot be eliminated in a free society. In fact, it is a sign of efficiency in an economy when workers try to increase their income or improve their working conditions by leaving one job for another. Frictional unemployment is often called *search unemployment* because workers take time to search for a job after quitting a job or leaving school.

Frictional unemployment is short term; structural unemployment, on the other hand, can be long term. Workers who are displaced by technological change (e.g., assembly-line workers who have been replaced by machines) or by a permanent reduction in the demand for an industry's output (e.g., cigar makers who have been laid off because of a decrease in demand for tobacco) may not have the necessary skills to maintain their level of income in another industry. Rather than accept a much lower salary, these workers tend to prolong their job search. Eventually, they adjust their expectations to the realities of the job market, or they enter the pool of discouraged workers.

Structural unemployment is very difficult for those who are unemployed. But for society as a whole, the technological advances that cause structural unemployment raise living standards by giving consumers a greater variety of goods at a lower cost.

Cyclical unemployment is a result of the business cycle. As a recession occurs, cyclical unemployment increases, and as growth occurs, cyclical unemployment decreases. It is also a primary focus of macroeconomic policy. Economists believe that a greater understanding of business cycles and their causes may enable them to find ways to smooth out those cycles and swings in unemployment. Much of the analysis in future chapters is related to macroeconomic policy aimed at minimizing business-cycle fluctuations. In addition to macroeconomic policy aimed at moderating cyclical unemployment, other policy measures—for example, job training and counseling—are used to reduce frictional and structural unemployment.

2.d. **Costs of Unemployment**

3

What is the cost of unemployed resources?

The cost of being unemployed is more than the obvious loss of income and status suffered by the individual who is not working. In a broader sense, society as a whole loses when resources are unemployed. Unemployed workers produce no output. So an economy with unemployment will operate inside its production possibilities curve rather than on the curve. Economists measure this lost output in terms of the *GDP gap*:

$$\text{GDP gap} = \text{potential real GDP} - \text{actual real GDP}$$

potential real GDP: the output produced at the natural rate of unemployment

natural rate of unemployment: the unemployment rate that would exist in the absence of cyclical unemployment

Potential real GDP is the level of output produced when nonlabor resources are fully utilized and unemployment is at its natural rate. The **natural rate of unemployment** is the unemployment rate that would exist in the absence of cyclical unemployment, so it includes seasonal, frictional, and structural unemployment. The natural rate of unemployment is not fixed; it can change over time. For instance, some economists believe that the natural rate of unemployment has risen in recent decades, a product of the influx of baby boomers and women into the labor force. As more workers move into the labor force (begin looking for jobs), frictional unemployment increases, raising the natural rate of unemployment. The natural rate of unemployment is sometimes called the *non-accelerating-inflation rate of unemployment*, or NAIRU—the idea being that there would be upward pressure on wages and prices in a "tight" labor market when the unemployment rate fell below the NAIRU.

Potential real GDP measures what we are capable of producing at the natural rate of unemployment. If we compute potential real GDP and then subtract actual real GDP, we have a measure of the output lost as a result of unemployment, or the cost of unemployment.

Potential and real GDP and the gap between them is shown in Figure 11.3(a). The gap widens during recessions and narrows during expansions. As the gap widens (as the output not produced increases), there are fewer goods and services available, and living standards are lower than they would be at the natural

FIGURE 11.3 The GDP Gap

The GDP gap is the difference between what the economy can produce at the natural rate of unemployment (potential GDP) and actual output (actual GDP). When the unemployment rate is higher than the natural rate, actual GDP is less than potential GDP. The gap between potential and actual GDP is a cost associated with unemployment. Recession years are shaded to highlight how the gap widens around recessions.

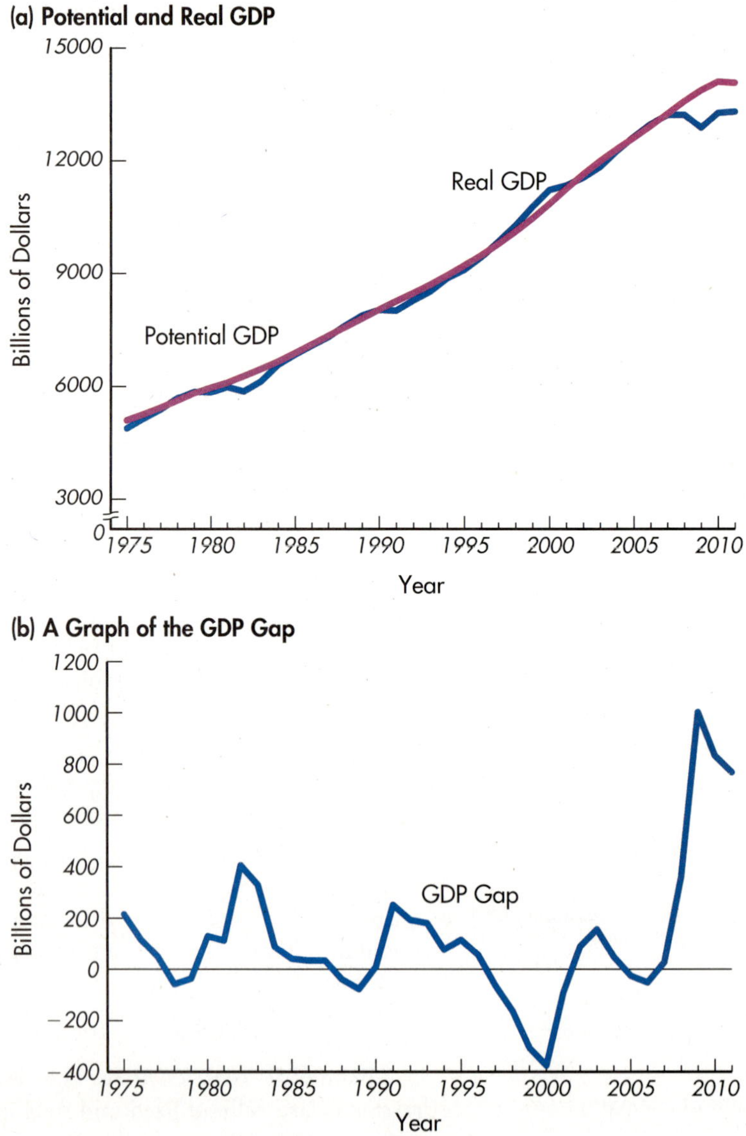

Source: Federal Reserve Bank of St. Louis; http://research.stlouisfed.org.

rate of unemployment. Figure 11.3(b) is a graph of the gap between potential and real GDP, taken from Figure 11.3(a). One can see that the expansion of the 1990s eliminated the GDP gap by 1997.

In the past, economists used the term *full employment* rather than *natural rate of unemployment*. Today, the term *full employment* is rarely used because it may be interpreted as implying a zero unemployment rate. If frictional and structural unemployment are always present, zero unemployment is impossible; there must always be unemployed resources in an economy. *Natural rate of unemployment* describes the labor market when the economy is producing what it realistically can produce in the absence of cyclical unemployment.

What is the value of the natural rate of unemployment in the United States? In the 1950s and 1960s, economists generally agreed on 4 percent. By the 1970s, that agreed-on rate had gone up to 5 percent. In the early 1980s, many economists placed the natural rate of unemployment in the United States at 6 to 7 percent. By the late 1980s, some had revised their thinking, placing the rate back at 5 percent. In fact, economists do not know exactly what the natural rate of unemployment is. Over time it varies within a range from around 4 percent to around 7 percent. It will also vary across countries, as labor markets and macroeconomic policies differ.

2.e. The Record of Unemployment

Unemployment rates in the United States from 1951 to 2011 are listed in Table 11.2. Over this period, the unemployment rate for all workers reached a low of 2.8 percent in 1953 and a high of 9.6 percent in 1982 and 1983. While the table does not show 2009, in October 2009, the unemployment rate reached 10.1 percent. U.S. labor faced the toughest employment situation since the Great Depression of the 1930s. Table 11.2 shows some general trends in the incidence of unemployment across different demographic groups:

- **In early years, the unemployment rate for women is higher than it is for men.** Several factors may be at work here. First, during this period, a

Table 11.2 Unemployment Rates in the United States

	Unemployment Rate, Civilian Workers*						
	All Civilian					Both Sexes	
Year	Workers	Males	Females	16–19 Years	White	Black	Hispanic
1951	3.3	2.8	4.4	8.2	3.1	—	—
1955	4.4	4.2	4.9	11.0	3.9	—	—
1959	5.5	5.2	5.9	14.6	4.8	—	—
1963	5.7	5.2	6.5	17.2	5.0	—	—
1967	3.8	3.1	5.2	12.9	3.4	—	—
1971	5.9	5.3	6.9	16.9	5.4	—	—
1975	8.5	7.9	9.3	19.9	7.8	14.8	12.2
1979	5.8	5.1	6.8	16.1	5.1	12.3	8.3
1983	9.6	9.9	9.2	22.4	8.4	19.5	13.7
1987	6.2	6.2	6.2	16.9	5.3	13.0	8.3
1991	6.8	7.2	6.4	18.7	6.1	12.5	10.0
1995	5.6	5.6	5.6	17.3	4.9	10.4	9.3
1999	4.2	4.1	4.3	13.9	3.7	8.0	6.4
2003	6.0	6.3	5.7	17.5	5.2	10.8	7.7
2007	4.6	4.7	4.5	15.7	4.1	8.3	5.6
2011	8.9	9.4	8.5	24.4	7.9	15.8	11.5

*Unemployed as a percentage of the civilian labor force in the group specified.

Source: U.S. Department of Labor: Bureau of Labor Statistics.

large number of women entered the labor force for the first time. Second, discrimination against women in the workplace limited job opportunities for them, particularly early in this period. Finally, a large number of women move out of the labor force on temporary maternity leaves. In the recession beginning in 2007, male unemployment rose relative to that for females as employment in manufacturing fell relative to employment in services—and men are more heavily represented in manufacturing industries.

- **Teenagers have the highest unemployment rates in the economy.** This makes sense because teenagers are the least-skilled segment of the labor force.
- **Whites have lower unemployment rates than nonwhites.** Discrimination plays a role here. To the extent that discrimination extends beyond hiring practices and job opportunities for minority workers to the education that is necessary to prepare students to enter the workforce, minority workers will have fewer opportunities for employment. The quality of education provided in many schools with large minority populations may not be as good as that provided in schools with large white populations. Equal opportunity programs and legislation are aimed at rectifying this inequality.

Although exact comparisons across countries are difficult to make because countries measure unemployment in different ways, it is interesting to look at the reported unemployment rates of different countries. Table 11.3 lists unemployment rates for seven major industrial nations. The rates have been adjusted to match as closely as possible the U.S. definition of unemployment. For instance, the official Italian unemployment data include people who have not looked for work in the past 30 days. The data for Italy in Table 11.3 have been adjusted to remove these people. If the data had not been adjusted, the Italian unemployment rates would be roughly twice as high as those listed.

Countries not only define unemployment differently; they also use different methods to count the unemployed. All major European countries except Sweden use a national unemployment register to identify the unemployed. Only those people who register for unemployment benefits are considered unemployed. A problem with this method is that it excludes those who have not registered because they are not entitled to benefits, and it includes those who receive benefits but would not take a job if one was offered. Other countries—among them

Table 11.3 Unemployment Rates in Major Industrial Countries

	Civilian Unemployment Rate (In Percentages)						
Year	**United States**	**Canada**	**France**	**Italy**	**Japan**	**United Kingdom**	**Germany**
1960	5.5	6.5	1.5	3.7	1.7	2.2	1.1
1965	4.5	3.6	1.6	3.5	1.2	2.1	.3
1970	4.9	5.7	2.5	3.2	1.2	3.1	.5
1975	8.5	6.9	4.1	3.4	1.9	4.6	3.4
1980	7.1	7.5	6.4	4.4	2.0	7.0	2.9
1985	7.2	10.5	10.4	6.0	2.6	11.2	7.5
1990	5.5	8.1	9.2	7.0	2.1	6.9	5.0
1995	5.6	9.5	11.7	12.0	3.2	8.8	6.5
2000	4.0	5.7	9.6	10.6	4.7	5.5	8.3
2005	5.1	6.0	10.1	8.1	4.5	4.8	11.2
2010	9.6	7.1	9.4	8.6	4.8	7.9	7.2

Source: *Economic Report of the President, 2012* (Washington, DC: U.S. Government Printing Office, 2012).

the United States, Canada, Sweden, and Japan—conduct monthly surveys of households to estimate the unemployment rate. Surveys allow more comprehensive analysis of unemployment and its causes than the use of a register does. The Organization for Economic Cooperation and Development, an organization created to foster international economic cooperation, compared annual surveys of the labor force in Europe with the official register of unemployment data and found that only 80 to 85 percent of those surveyed as unemployed were registered in Germany, France, and the United Kingdom. In Italy, only 63 percent of those surveyed as unemployed were registered.

Knowing their limitations, we can still identify some important trends from the data in Table 11.3. Through the 1960s and early 1970s, European unemployment rates generally were lower than U.S. and Canadian rates. Over the next decade, European unemployment rates increased substantially, as did the rates in North America. But in the mid-1980s, while U.S. unemployment began to fall, European unemployment remained high. The issue of high unemployment rates in Europe has become a major topic of discussion at international summit meetings. The Global Business Insight "High Unemployment in Europe" discusses this issue further. Japanese unemployment rates, like those in Europe, were much lower than U.S. and Canadian rates in the 1960s and 1970s. However, although Japanese rates remained much lower in the 1980s and 1990s, by 2000 a prolonged economic slowdown in Japan had led to rising unemployment.

RECAP

1. The unemployment rate is the number of people unemployed as a percentage of the labor force.
2. To be in the labor force, one must either have or be looking for a job.
3. By its failure to include discouraged workers and the output lost because of underemployment, the unemployment rate understates real unemployment in the United States.
4. By its failure to include activity in the underground economy, the U.S. unemployment rate overstates actual unemployment.
5. Unemployment data are adjusted to eliminate seasonal fluctuations.
6. Frictional and structural unemployment are always present in a dynamic economy.
7. Cyclical unemployment is a product of recession; it can be moderated by controlling the period of contraction in the business cycle.
8. Economists measure the cost of unemployment in terms of lost output.
9. Unemployment data show that teenagers have the highest unemployment rates in the economy, and that nonwhites have higher unemployment rates than whites.

3. INFLATION

4

What is inflation?

inflation:
a sustained rise in the average level of prices

Inflation is a sustained rise in the average level of prices. Notice the word *sustained*. Inflation does not mean a short-term increase in prices; it means prices are rising over a prolonged period of time. Inflation is measured by the percentage change in the price level. The inflation rate in the United States was 3.2 percent in 2011. This means that the level of prices increased 2.9 percent over the year.

3.a. Absolute Versus Relative Price Changes

In the modern economy, over any given period, some prices rise faster than others. To evaluate the rate of inflation in a country, then, economists must know what is happening to prices on average. Here it is important to distinguish between *absolute* and *relative* price changes.

GLOBAL BUSINESS INSIGHT

High Unemployment in Europe

The data in Table 11.3 indicate that European countries tend to have higher unemployment rates than other industrial countries. This is not true of all European countries, but it is certainly true for the biggest: France, Germany, Italy, and Spain. One factor that contributes to the higher unemployment rates in these countries is government policy with regard to the labor market. Countries that have policies that encourage unemployment should be expected to have more unemployed workers. In a recent speech, a British scholar gave his analysis of why Europe has such high unemployment. One story he told illustrates how government policy aimed at protecting citizens against unemployment can create the very unemployment that is the cause for concern. In Italy, laws require parents to support their adult children who do not work, even if the children are entirely capable of working. The story goes as follows:

The Italian Court of Cessation ruled that a professor at Naples University, separated from his family, must continue to pay his 30-year-old son €775 per month until he can find himself suitable employment. This despite the fact that the son owns a house and possesses an investment trust fund worth €450,000. The judges said that an adult son who refused work that did not reflect his training, abilities, and personal interests could not be held to blame. In particular the judges said[,] "You cannot blame a young person, particularly from a well-off family, who refuses a job that does not fit his aspirations." By contrast, under U.K. law, a separated father would only have to support his children until they completed full-time education (Stephen Nickell, 2002).

The government requirement that parents support unemployed adult children encourages the children to remain unemployed.

Among men of prime working age (age 25–54), there are more who are inactive and not participating in the labor force than there are unemployed. The majority of these men are receiving benefits from the government, claiming disability or illness. In the 1970s, there were many fewer disabled or ill workers as a fraction of the population. But as social benefits were increased, and the eligibility rules were relaxed, the number claiming to suffer from such problems also increased. The unfortunate truth of human nature is that as you provide better support for those who truly need help, there will be more and more who do not truly need it yet will claim a need. The experience of Denmark is instructive in this regard. Denmark has generous unemployment benefits. But in the 1990s, Danish eligibility requirements were tightened, creating greater incentives for the unemployed to look for work. Danish unemployment rates fell dramatically as a result.

Another effect of government policy is related to a person's loss of job skills while unemployed. Unemployment benefits in Europe are relatively high and can last a long time. Unemployment benefits in the United States are relatively low and have a shorter duration. Given just these facts, one would expect more European unemployment since the unemployed would be out of work for a longer time in Europe than in the United States. If people are not working for a prolonged time, they are more likely to find their work skills deteriorating, so they are less likely to be attractive candidates for jobs if and when they do look for work. Therefore, a longer duration of unemployment benefits, meant to protect workers who lose their jobs, will also contribute to more workers' job skills appearing to be inadequate to employers when the workers do apply for employment.

Other factors contributing to higher unemployment rates in some countries are the restrictions on the ability of firms to terminate workers and the requirement that firms pay high separation costs to workers who are fired. The more difficult it is for firms to adjust their labor force in the face of economic fluctuations, the less likely firms are to hire new workers. If you own a business and your sales increase, you are more likely to hire extra employees to meet the increased demand for your product. However, you cannot be sure that your sales will remain higher permanently, so you would be very conservative about hiring new workers if you would have to pay terminated workers a large amount of money if sales fell and you needed to lay off some of your employees. Such labor market rigidities, aimed at protecting workers from losing jobs, create incentives against hiring so that those who would like to work cannot get hired.

The lesson learned from large European countries is that government policies aimed at protecting workers from unemployment may create a bigger unemployment problem. Then the costs imposed on the economy in terms of taxes and reduced labor market flexibility may exceed the benefits to those who keep their jobs or receive unemployment compensation because of the programs.

Sources: Stephen Nickell, "A Picture of European Unemployment: Success and Failure," speech given to CESifo Conference in Munich, December 2002; and Lars Ljungqvist and Thomas Sargent, "The European Unemployment Dilemma," Journal of Political Economy, 1998.

Let's look at an example using the prices of fish and beef:

	Year 1	Year 2
1 pound of fish	$1	$2
1 pound of beef	$2	$4

In year 1, beef is twice as expensive as fish. This is the price of beef *relative* to fish. In year 2, beef is still twice as expensive as fish. The relative prices have not changed between years 1 and 2. What has changed? The prices of both beef and fish have doubled. The *absolute* levels of all prices have gone up, but because they have increased by the same percentage, the relative prices are unchanged.

Inflation measures changes in absolute prices. In our example, all prices doubled, so the inflation rate is 100 percent. There was a 100 percent increase in the prices of beef and fish. Inflation does not proceed evenly through the economy. Prices of some goods rise faster than others, which means that relative prices are changing at the same time that absolute prices are rising. The measured inflation rate records the *average* change in absolute prices.

3.b. Effects of Inflation

To understand the effects of inflation, you have to understand what happens to the value of money in an inflationary period. The real value of money is what it can buy—in other words, its *purchasing power.*

$$\text{Real value of \$1} = \frac{\$1}{\text{price level}}$$

4. WHY IS INFLATION A PROBLEM?

The higher the price level, the lower the real value (or *purchasing power*) of the dollar. For instance, suppose an economy had only one good—milk. If a glass of milk sold for $.50, then one dollar would buy two glasses of milk. If the price of milk rose to $1, then a dollar would only buy one glass of milk. The purchasing power, or real value, of money falls as prices rise.

Table 11.4 lists the real value of the dollar in selected years from 1946 to 2011. The price level in each year is measured relative to the average level of prices over the 1982–1984 period. For instance, the 1946 value, 0.195, means that prices in 1946 were, on average, only 19.5 percent of prices in the 1982–1984 period. Notice that as prices go up, the purchasing power of the dollar falls. In 1946, a dollar bought five times more than a dollar bought in the early 1980s. The value 5.13 means that one could buy 5.13 times more goods and services with a dollar in 1946 than one could in 1982–1984.

Prices have risen steadily in recent decades. By 2011, they had gone up more than 100 percent above the average level of prices in the 1982–1984 period. Consequently, the purchasing power of a 2011 dollar was lower. In 2011, $1 bought just 44 percent of the goods and services that one could buy with a dollar in 1982–1984.

If prices and nominal income rise by the same percentage, it might seem that inflation is not a problem. It doesn't matter whether it takes twice as many dollars now to buy fish and beef as it did before if we have twice as many dollars in income available to buy the products. Obviously, inflation is very much a problem when a household's nominal income rises at a slower rate than prices. Inflation hurts those households whose income does not keep up with the prices of the goods they buy.

In the 1970s in the United States, the rate of inflation rose to near-record levels. Many workers believed that their incomes were lagging behind the rate of inflation, so they negotiated cost-of-living raises in their wage contracts. The typical cost-of-living raise ties salary to changes in the consumer price index. If

Table 11.4 The Real Value of a Dollar

Year	Average Price Level*	Purchasing Power of a Dollar†
1946	0.195	5.13
1950	0.241	4.15
1954	0.269	3.72
1958	0.289	3.46
1962	0.302	3.31
1966	0.324	3.09
1970	0.388	2.58
1974	0.493	2.03
1978	0.652	1.53
1982	0.965	1.04
1986	1.096	0.91
1990	1.307	0.77
1994	1.482	0.67
1998	1.630	0.61
2002	1.800	0.56
2006	2.016	0.50
2010	2.181	0.46
2011	2.249	0.44

*Measured by the consumer price index; U.S. Department of Labor, Bureau of Labor Statistics (http://data.bls.gov/).
†Calculated by taking the reciprocal of the consumer price index (1/CPI).

the CPI rises 8 percent over a year, workers receive an 8 percent raise plus compensation for experience or productivity increases. As the U.S. rate of inflation fell during the 1980s, concern about cost-of-living raises subsided as well.

It is important to distinguish between expected and unexpected inflation. *Unexpectedly high inflation* redistributes income away from those who receive fixed incomes (e.g., creditors who receive debt repayments of a fixed amount of dollars per month) toward those who make fixed expenditures (e.g., debtors who make fixed debt repayments per month). For example, consider a simple loan agreement.

Maria borrows $100 from Al, promising to repay the loan in one year at 10 percent interest. In one year, Maria will pay Al $110—principal of $100 plus interest of $10 (10 percent of $100, or $10).

When Maria and Al agree to the terms of the loan, they do so with some expected rate of inflation in mind. Suppose they both expect 5 percent inflation over the year. In one year it will take 5 percent more money to buy goods than it does now. Al will need $105 to buy what $100 buys today. Because Al will receive $110 for the principal and interest on the loan, he will gain purchasing power. However, if the inflation rate over the year turns out to be surprisingly high—say, 15 percent—then Al will need $115 to buy what $100 buys today. He will lose purchasing power if he makes a loan at a 10 percent rate of interest.

nominal interest rate: the observed interest rate in the market

real interest rate: the nominal interest rate minus the rate of inflation

Economists distinguish between nominal and real interest rates when analyzing economic behavior. The **nominal interest rate** is the observed interest rate in the market and includes the effect of inflation. The **real interest rate** is the nominal interest rate minus the rate of inflation:

$$\text{Real interest rate} = \text{nominal interest rate} - \text{rate of inflation}$$

If Al charges Maria 10 percent nominal interest, and the inflation rate is 5 percent, the real interest rate is 5 percent ($10 - 5 = 5$ percent). This means that Al will earn a positive real return from the loan. However, if the inflation rate is 10 percent, the real return from a nominal interest rate of 10 percent is zero (10 − 10 = 0). The interest Al will receive from the loan will just compensate him for the rise in prices; he will not realize an increase in purchasing power. If the inflation rate is higher than the nominal interest rate, then the real interest rate is negative; the lender will lose purchasing power by making the loan.

Now you can see how unexpected inflation redistributes income. Borrowers and creditors agree to loan terms on the basis of what they *expect* the rate of inflation to be over the period of the loan. If the *actual* rate of inflation turns out to be different from what was expected, then the real interest rate paid by the borrower and received by the lender will be different from what was expected. If Al and Maria both expect a 5 percent inflation rate and agree to a 10 percent nominal interest rate for the loan, then they both expect a real interest rate of 5 percent (10 − 5 = 5 percent) to be paid on the loan. If the actual inflation rate turns out to be greater than 5 percent, then the real interest rate will be less than expected. Maria will get to borrow Al's money at a lower real cost than she expected, and Al will earn a lower real return than he expected. Unexpectedly high inflation hurts creditors and benefits borrowers because it lowers real interest rates.

Figure 11.4 shows the real interest rates on U.S. Treasury bills. You can see a pronounced pattern in the graph. In the late 1970s, there was a period of negative real interest rates, followed by high positive real rates in the 1980s. The evidence suggests that nominal interest rates did not rise fast enough in the 1970s to offset high inflation. This was a time of severe strain on many creditors, including savings and loan associations and banks. These firms had lent funds at fixed nominal rates of interest. When those rates of interest turned out to be lower than the rate of inflation, the financial institutions suffered significant losses. In the early 1980s, the inflation rate dropped sharply. Because

FIGURE 11.4 The Real Interest Rate on U.S. Treasury Bills

The real interest rate is the difference between the nominal rate (the rate actually observed) and the rate of inflation over the life of the bond. The figure shows the real interest rate in June and December for each year. For instance, in the first observation for June 1970, a six-month Treasury bill paid the holder 6.91 percent interest. This is the nominal rate of interest. To find the real rate of interest on the bond, we subtract the rate of inflation that existed over the six months of the bond's life (June to December 1970), which was 5.17 percent. The difference between the nominal interest rate (6.91 percent) and the rate of inflation (5.17 percent) is the real interest rate, 1.74 percent. Notice that real interest rates were negative during most of the 1970s and then turned highly positive (by historical standards) in the early 1980s.

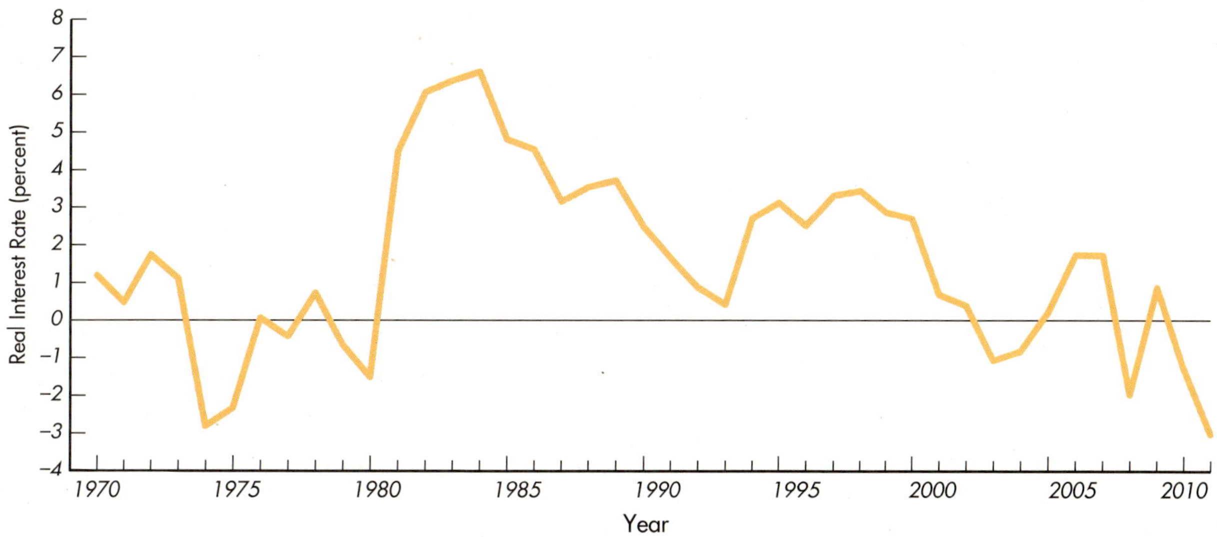

Source: Board of Governors of the Federal Reserve System.

nominal interest rates did not drop nearly as fast as the rate of inflation, real interest rates were high. In this period many debtors were hurt by the high costs of borrowing to finance business or household expenditures.

Real interest rates have been negative again in recent years, but unlike in the 1970s, inflation has not been high. Negative real interest rates can also result from low nominal interest rates and moderate inflation, as was the case in 2010 and 2011. Nominal interest rates, which cannot be negative, were near the "zero lower bound."

Unexpected inflation affects more than the two parties to a loan. Any contract calling for fixed payments over some long-term period changes in value as the rate of inflation changes. For instance, a long-term contract that provides union members with 5 percent raises each year for five years gives the workers more purchasing power if inflation is low than if it is high. Similarly, a contract that sells a product at a fixed price over a long-term period will change in value as inflation changes. Suppose a lumber company promises to supply a builder with lumber at a fixed price for a two-year period. If the rate of inflation in one year turns out to be higher than expected, the lumber company will end up selling the lumber for less profit than it had planned. Inflation raises costs to the lumber company. Usually the company would raise its prices to compensate for higher costs. Because the company contracted to sell its goods at a fixed price to the builder, however, the builder benefits at the lumber company's expense. Again, unexpectedly high inflation redistributes real income or purchasing power away from those receiving fixed payments to those making fixed payments.

One response to the effects of unexpected inflation is to allow prices, wages, or interest rates to vary with the rate of inflation. Labor sometimes negotiates cost-of-living adjustments as part of new wage contracts. Financial institutions offer variable interest rates on home mortgages to reflect current market conditions. Any contract can be written to adjust dollar amounts over time as the rate of inflation changes.

4.a. **Types of Inflation**

demand-pull inflation:
inflation caused by increasing demand for output

cost-push inflation:
inflation caused by rising costs of production

Economists often classify inflation according to the source of the inflationary pressure. The most straightforward method defines inflation in terms of pressure from the demand side of the market or the supply side of the market. **Demand-pull inflation** is caused by increasing demand for output. Increases in total spending that are not offset by increases in the supply of goods and services cause the average level of prices to rise. **Cost-push inflation** is caused by rising costs of production. Increases in production costs cause firms to raise prices to avoid losses.

Sometimes inflation is blamed on "too many dollars chasing too few goods." This is a roundabout way of saying that the inflation stems from demand pressures. Because demand-pull inflation is a product of increased spending, it is more likely to occur in an economy that is producing at maximum capacity. If resources are fully employed, in the short run it may not be possible to increase output to meet increased demand. The result: Existing goods and services are rationed by rising prices.

Some economists claim that rising prices in the late 1960s were a product of demand-pull inflation. They believe that increased government spending for the Vietnam War caused the level of U.S. prices to rise.

Cost-push inflation can occur in any economy, whatever its output. If prices go up because the costs of resources are rising, the rate of inflation can go up regardless of demand.

For example, some economists argue that the inflation in the United States in the 1970s was largely due to rising oil prices. This means that decreases in the oil supply (a shift to the left in the supply curve) brought about higher oil prices. Because oil is so important in the production of many goods, higher oil prices led to increases in prices throughout the economy. Cost-push inflation stems from changes in the supply side of the market.

Cost-push inflation is sometimes attributed to profit-push or wage-push pressures. *Profit-push pressures* are created by suppliers who want to increase their profit margins by raising prices faster than their costs increase. *Wage-push pressures* are created by labor unions and workers who are able to increase their wages faster than their productivity. There have been times when "greedy" businesses and unions have been blamed for periods of inflation in the United States. The problem with these "theories" is that people have always wanted to improve their economic status and always will. In this sense, people have always been greedy. But inflation has not always been a problem. Were people less greedy in the early 1980s when inflation was low than they were in the late 1970s when inflation was high? Obviously, we have to look to other reasons to explain inflation. We discuss some of those reasons in later chapters.

4.b. The Inflationary Record

Many people today, having always lived with inflation, are surprised to learn that inflation is a relatively new problem for the United States. From 1789, when the U.S. Constitution was ratified, until 1940, there was no particular trend in the general price level. At times prices rose, and at times they fell. The average level of prices in 1940 was approximately the same as it was in the late 18th century.

Since 1940, prices in the United States have gone up markedly. The price level today is eight times what it was in 1940. But the rate of growth has varied. Prices rose rapidly for the first couple of years following World War II and then grew at a relatively slow rate through the 1950s and 1960s. In the early 1970s, the rate of inflation began to accelerate. Prices climbed quickly until the early 1980s, when inflation slowed.

Annual rates of inflation for several industrial and developing nations are shown in Table 11.5. Look at the diversity across countries: Rates range from −0.3 percent in Japan to 8.7 percent in Zambia.

Table 11.5 Rates of Inflation for Selected Countries, 2011

Country	Inflation Rate (Percent)
Selected Industrial	
Canada	2.9
Germany	2.5
Japan	−0.3
United Kingdom	4.5
Selected Developing	
Botswana	8.5
Brazil	6.6
China	5.4
India	8.6
Mexico	3.4
Philippines	4.8
Poland	4.3
South Africa	5.0
Turkey	6.5
Zambia	8.7

Note: Data are average annual percentage changes in the GDP price index as reported by the International Monetary Fund (www.imf.org/external/pubs/weo/2012).

hyperinflation: an extremely high rate of inflation

Hyperinflation is an extremely high rate of inflation. In most cases hyperinflation eventually makes a country's currency worthless and leads to the introduction of a new currency. Argentina experienced hyperinflation in the 1980s. People had to carry large stacks of currency for small purchases. Cash registers and calculators ran out of digits as prices reached ridiculously high levels. After years of high inflation, Argentina replaced the old peso with the peso Argentino in June 1983. The government set the value of 1 peso Argentino equal to 10,000 old pesos (striking four zeros from all prices). A product that sold for 10,000 old pesos before the reform sold for 1 new peso after. But Argentina did not follow up its monetary reform with a noninflationary change in economic policy. In 1984 and 1985, the inflation rate exceeded 600 percent each year. As a result, in June 1985, the government again introduced a new currency, the austral, setting its value at 1,000 pesos Argentino. However, the economic policy associated with the introduction of the austral lowered the inflation rate only temporarily. By 1988, the inflation rate was over 300 percent, and in 1989, the inflation rate was over 3,000 percent. The rapid rise in prices associated with the austral resulted in the introduction of yet another currency, again named peso Argentino, in January 1992, with a value equal to 10,000 australes. This new peso was fixed at a value of 1 peso per 1 U.S. dollar, and this exchange rate lasted for about 10 years due to reasonably stable inflation in Argentina. In late 2001, Argentina experienced another financial crisis due to large government budget deficits, and the fixed rate of exchange between the peso and the dollar ended, but the peso has remained the currency of Argentina.

The most dramatic hyperinflation in recent years, and one of the most dramatic ever, occurred in Zimbabwe in 2007–2008. Although the government has not been forthcoming about inflation data, research[1] indicates that the price index rose from a value of 1.00 in January 2007 to 853,000,000,000,000,000,000,000 by mid-November 2008, when the price level was doubling every 24 hours. As prices rose, the government issued larger and larger units of paper money as people had to carry huge stacks of old currency to buy anything. A 100 trillion Zimbabwe dollar bill was issued in January 2009. Then in the same month, the government sanctioned the use of U.S. dollars as a substitute currency in Zimbabwe as the local currency had become essentially worthless.

Hyperinflation in Zimbabwe caused the government to issue a 100 trillion dollar bill.

DESMOND KWANDE/AFP/GETTY IMAGES

[1] Steve H. Hanke, "R.I.P. Zimbabwe Dollar" (**www.cato.org/zimbabwe**).

In upcoming chapters, we will learn how monetary and fiscal policies of government can create high inflation, and how low and stable inflation results from sound macroeconomic policy. When a central government wants to spend more than it is capable of funding through taxation or borrowing, it simply issues money to finance its budget deficit. As the money supply increases faster than the demand to hold it, spending increases and prices go up.

RECAP

1. Inflation is a sustained rise in the average level of prices.
2. The higher the price level, the lower the real value (purchasing power) of money.
3. Unexpectedly high inflation redistributes income away from those who receive fixed-dollar payments (e.g., creditors) toward those who make fixed-dollar payments (e.g., debtors).
4. The real interest rate is the nominal interest rate minus the rate of inflation.
5. Demand-pull inflation is a product of increased spending; cost-push inflation reflects increased production costs.
6. Hyperinflation is a very high rate of inflation that often results in the introduction of a new currency.

SUMMARY

What is a business cycle?

1. Business cycles are recurring changes in real GDP, in which expansion is followed by contraction.
2. The four stages of the business cycle are expansion (boom), peak, contraction (recession), and trough.
3. Leading, coincident, and lagging indicators are variables that change in relation to changes in output.

How is the unemployment rate defined and measured?

4. The unemployment rate is the percentage of the labor force that is not working.
5. To be in the U.S. labor force, an individual must be working or actively seeking work.
6. Unemployment can be classified as seasonal, frictional, structural, or cyclical.
7. Frictional and structural unemployment are always present in a dynamic economy; cyclical unemployment is a product of recession.

What is the cost of unemployed resources?

8. The GDP gap measures the output lost because of unemployment.

What is inflation?

9. Inflation is a sustained rise in the average level of prices.
10. The higher the level of prices, the lower the purchasing power of money.

Why is inflation a problem?

11. Inflation becomes a problem when income rises at a slower rate than prices.
12. Unexpectedly high inflation hurts those who receive fixed-dollar payments (e.g., creditors) and benefits those who make fixed-dollar payments (e.g., debtors).

13. Inflation can stem from demand-pull or cost-push pressures.
14. Hyperinflation—an extremely high rate of inflation—can force a country to introduce a new currency.

EXERCISES

1. What is the labor force? Do you believe that the U.S. government's definition of the labor force is a good one—that it includes all the people it should include? Explain your answer.
2. Suppose you are able bodied and intelligent, but lazy. You would rather sit home and watch television than work, even though you know you could find an acceptable job if you looked.
   a. Are you officially unemployed?
   b. Are you a discouraged worker?
3. Does the GDP gap measure all of the costs of unemployment? Why or why not?
4. Why do teenagers have the highest unemployment rate in the economy?
5. Write an equation that defines the real interest rate. Use the equation to explain why unexpectedly high inflation redistributes income from creditors to debtors.
6. Many home mortgages in recent years have been made with variable interest rates. Typically, the interest rate is adjusted once a year based on the current rates on government bonds. How do variable interest rate loans protect creditors from the effects of unexpected inflation?
7. The word *cycle* suggests a regular, recurring pattern of activity. Is there a regular pattern in the business cycle? Support your answer by examining the duration (number of months) of each expansion and contraction in Figure 11.1.
8. Suppose 550 people were surveyed, and of those 500, 450 were working full time. Of the 100 not working, 20 were full-time college students, 30 were retired, 10 were under 16 years of age, 15 had stopped looking for work because they believed there were no jobs for them, and 25 were actively looking for work.
   a. How many of the 550 surveyed are in the labor force?
   b. What is the unemployment rate among the 550 surveyed people?
9. Consider the following price information:

	Year 1	Year 2
Cup of coffee	$ .50	$1.00
Glass of milk	$1.00	$2.00

   a. Based on the information given, what was the inflation rate between year 1 and year 2?
   b. What happened to the price of coffee relative to that of milk between year 1 and year 2?
10. Use a supply and demand diagram to illustrate the following conditions:
    a. Cost-push inflation caused by a labor union successfully negotiating for a higher wage
    b. Demand-pull inflation caused by an increase in demand for domestic products from foreign buyers
11. Why can't the nominal interest rate be negative?

STUDY GUIDE FOR CHAPTER 11

Key Term Match

Match each term with its correct definition by placing the appropriate letter next to the corresponding number.

A. business cycle
B. recession
C. depression
D. leading indicator
E. coincident indicator
F. lagging indicator
G. unemployment rate
H. discouraged workers
I. underemployment
J. potential real GDP
K. natural rate of unemployment
L. inflation
M. nominal interest rate
N. real interest rate
O. demand-pull inflation
P. cost-push inflation
Q. hyperinflation

____ 1. a period in which real GDP falls

____ 2. a sustained rise in the average level of prices

____ 3. the nominal interest rate minus the rate of inflation

____ 4. the pattern of rising real GDP followed by falling real GDP

____ 5. a variable that changes before real output changes

____ 6. an extremely high rate of inflation

____ 7. the unemployment rate that would exist in the absence of cyclical unemployment

____ 8. inflation caused by increasing demand for output

____ 9. a severe, prolonged economic contraction

____ 10. the observed interest rate in the market

____ 11. the percentage of the labor force that is not working

____ 12. the output produced at the natural rate of unemployment

____ 13. the employment of workers in jobs that do not utilize their productive potential

____ 14. a variable that changes at the same time that real output changes

____ 15. inflation caused by rising costs of production

____ 16. a variable that changes after real output changes

____ 17. workers who have stopped looking for work because they believe no one will offer them a job

Quick-Check Quiz

1. In correct sequence, the four stages of the business cycle are
   - ☐ a. peak, boom, expansion, and contraction.
   - ☐ b. peak, contraction, trough, and expansion.
   - ☐ c. recession, expansion, peak, and boom.
   - ☐ d. contraction, trough, boom, and expansion.
   - ☐ e. recession, contraction, peak, and boom.

2. To arrive at the number of workers in the U.S. labor force, we subtract all of the following from the number of all U.S. residents *except*
   - ☐ a. residents under 16 years old.
   - ☐ b. institutionalized adults.
   - ☐ c. adults who are not looking for work.
   - ☐ d. unemployed adults.
   - ☐ e. All of the above must be subtracted from the number of U.S. residents to arrive at the number of workers in the labor force.

3. Which of the following cause(s) the unemployment rate to be overstated?
   - ☐ a. discouraged workers
   - ☐ b. underground economic activities
   - ☐ c. part-time employment
   - ☐ d. underemployment
   - ☐ e. students who are not looking for work

4. A person who finds that her skills are no longer needed because she has been replaced by a machine is an example of
   - ☐ a. frictional unemployment.
   - ☐ b. seasonal unemployment.
   - ☐ c. cyclical unemployment.
   - ☐ d. search unemployment.
   - ☐ e. structural unemployment.

5. A steelworker who has been laid off during a recession is an example of
   - ☐ a. frictional unemployment.
   - ☐ b. seasonal unemployment.
   - ☐ c. cyclical unemployment.
   - ☐ d. search unemployment.
   - ☐ e. structural unemployment.

6. Which of the following statements is false?
   - ☐ a. The GDP gap widens during recessions and narrows during expansions.
   - ☐ b. The natural rate of unemployment varies over time and across countries.
   - ☐ c. Men have higher unemployment rates than women because women move out of the labor force to have children.
   - ☐ d. Teenagers have the highest unemployment rates in the economy.
   - ☐ e. Nonwhites have higher unemployment rates than whites.

7. If a college professor's income has increased by 3 percent at the same time that prices have risen by 5 percent, the professor's real income has
   - ☐ a. decreased by 2 percent.
   - ☐ b. increased by 2 percent.
   - ☐ c. increased by 7 percent.
   - ☐ d. decreased by 7 percent.
   - ☐ e. not changed.

8. Which of the following groups benefits from unexpectedly high inflation?
   - ☐ a. creditors
   - ☐ b. retirees on fixed incomes
   - ☐ c. debtors
   - ☐ d. workers whose salaries are tied to the CPI
   - ☐ e. suppliers who have contracted to supply a fixed amount of their product for a fixed price

9. Which of the following statements is true?
   - ☐ a. The higher the price level, the higher the purchasing power of money.
   - ☐ b. Demand-pull inflation can be a result of increased production costs.
   - ☐ c. High rates of inflation are generally caused by rapid growth of the money supply.
   - ☐ d. Unexpectedly high inflation redistributes income away from those who make fixed-dollar payments toward those who receive fixed-dollar payments.
   - ☐ e. The real interest rate increases as the rate of inflation increases.

10. A lender who does not expect any change in the price level is willing to make a mortgage loan at a 10 percent rate of interest. If that same lender anticipates a future inflation rate of 5 percent, she will charge the borrower
    - ☐ a. 5 percent interest.
    - ☐ b. 10 percent interest.
    - ☐ c. 15 percent interest.
    - ☐ d. 2 percent interest.
    - ☐ e. .5 percent interest.

Practice Questions and Problems

1. When real GDP is growing, the economy is in the ______________ phase, or boom period, of the business cycle.
2. The ______________ marks the end of a contraction and the start of a new business cycle.
3. The ______________ marks the end of the expansion phase of a business cycle.
4. Real GDP falls during the contraction, or ______________ phase of the business cycle.
5. Which organization has the responsibility of officially dating recessions in the United States?

   ____
6. ______________ unemployment is a product of business-cycle fluctuations.
7. ______________ unemployment is a product of regular, recurring changes in the hiring needs of certain industries over the months or seasons of the year.
8. ______________ unemployment is a product of short-term movements of workers between jobs and of first-time job seekers.
9. ______________ unemployment is a product of technological change and other changes in the structure of the economy.
10. Potential real GDP minus actual real GDP equals the ______________.
11. The existence of ______________ and ______________ causes the official unemployment rate in the United States to be understated.
12. Economists measure the cost of unemployment in terms of ______________.
13. The higher the price level, the ______________ (higher, lower) the purchasing power of the dollar.
14. Unexpectedly high inflation hurts ______________ (creditors, debtors) and benefits ______________ (creditors, debtors) because it lowers real interest rates.

Exercises and Applications

I In or Out of the Labor Force?

The Department of Labor defines the labor force as all U.S. residents minus residents under 16 years old minus institutionalized adults minus adults who are not looking for work. A person is seeking work if he or she is available to work, has looked for work in the past four weeks, is waiting for a recall after being laid off, or is starting a job within 30 days.

Place an *X* next to the description of those who would be considered part of the labor force.

______________ Per Olsen is a Norwegian citizen who is looking for a job in the United States. He plans to move to the United States to marry his American sweetheart.

______________ Carl Wolcutt is a retired police chief who has recently been offered a position as head of his state's police academy. Mr. Wolcutt is happily raising beagles and has turned down the job.

______________ Blake Stephans has just been laid off from his quality-control job at Boeing. He is waiting for a recall, but the company has just announced it will lay off even more workers.

______________ Thomas Butting is a recent college graduate who quit his part-time job but is taking the summer off before searching for a "real" job.

______________ Joe Shocker, a pitcher on Wichita State University's baseball team, has been selected in the first round of the draft and expects to join the Mets after he finishes playing in the College World Series. In the meantime, he will enjoy the sights and sounds of beautiful downtown Omaha.

II Illustrating the Business Cycle

The horizontal axis measures time, and the vertical axis measures economic activity. Label the points on the following diagram with the appropriate phases of the business cycle.

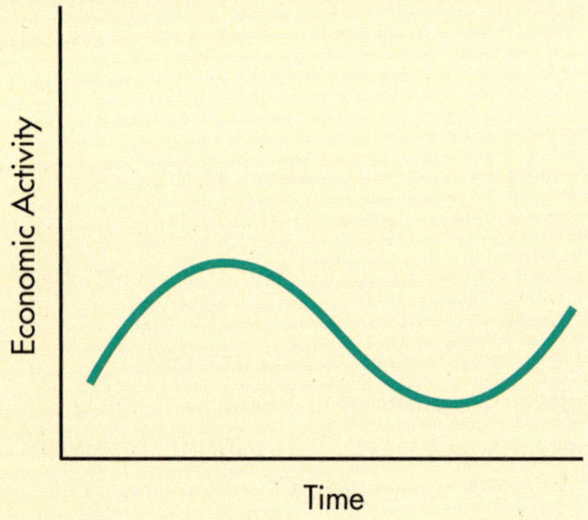

III Economic Reporting

Assume you are a reporter for the *Wall Street Journal*. Respond to the following developments. You should consider whether the indicator in question leads, lags, or moves with the economy.

1. On August 17, 2012, the Conference Board announced that its Leading Economic Index for the U.S. rose 0.4% in July after a 0.4% decrease in June and a 0.3 percent increase in May. A Conference Board economist suggested that the 6-month growth rate of the leading indicators had stabilized at a low level. The Conference Board Coincident Economic Index rose 0.3% in July after increases of 0.2% in June and 0.5% in May. Its Lagging Economic Index also rose 0.3% in May, 0.1% in June and 0.4% in July. What stage of the business cycle do these indicators suggest for the U.S. economy in August 2012?

   ____

   ____

   ____

2. The Bureau of Labor Statistics reported no change in the Consumer Price Index for June or July. What does this news imply about consumers' purchasing power over these months? Did debtors or creditors benefit from price changes during this time?

____

____

____

3. In the first eight months of 2012, the unemployment rate in the United States hovered around 8.3%. What does this unemployment rate suggest about the economy at this time?

____

____

____

4. The Commerce Department reported that U.S. growth slowed to 1.5% in the second quarter of 2012. What measure was released? If upcoming trade figures indicate a higher than expected trade deficit, the measure will be revised. Would the estimate of economic growth be revised upward or downward if the trade deficit is higher than expected?

____

____

____

You can find further practice tests in the Online Quiz at: www.cengagebrain.com

12 Macroeconomic Equilibrium: Aggregate Demand and Supply

FUNDAMENTAL QUESTIONS

1. What is aggregate demand?
2. What causes the aggregate demand curve to shift?
3. What is aggregate supply?
4. Why does the short-run aggregate supply curve become steeper as real GDP increases?
5. Why is the long-run aggregate supply curve vertical?
6. What causes the aggregate supply curve to shift?
7. What determines the equilibrium price level and real GDP?

PREVIEW

Total output and income in the United States have grown over time. Each generation has experienced a higher living standard than the previous generation. Yet, as we learned in Chapter 11, economic growth has not been steady. Economies go through periods of expansion followed by periods of contraction or recession, and such business cycles have major impacts on people's lives, incomes, and living standards.

Economic stagnation and recession throw many people—often those who are already relatively poor—out of their jobs and into real poverty. Economic growth increases the number of jobs and draws people out of poverty and into the mainstream of economic progress. To understand why economies grow and why they go through cycles, we must discover why firms decide to produce more or less and why buyers decide to buy more or less. The approach we take is similar to the approach we followed in the early chapters of the text regarding demand and supply curves. In Chapters 2 and 3, demand and supply curves were derived and used to examine questions involving the equilibrium price and quantities demanded and supplied of a single good or service. This simple yet powerful microeconomic technique of analysis has a macroeconomic counterpart—aggregate demand and aggregate supply, which are used to determine an equilibrium price level and quantity of goods and services produced for the *entire economy*. In this chapter we use aggregate demand and supply curves to illustrate the causes of business cycles and economic growth.

1. AGGREGATE DEMAND, AGGREGATE SUPPLY, AND BUSINESS CYCLES

1

What is aggregate demand?

What causes economic growth and business cycles? We can provide some answers to this important question using aggregate demand (*AD*) and aggregate supply (*AS*) curves. Suppose we represent the economy in a simple demand and supply diagram, as shown in Figure 12.1. Aggregate demand represents the total spending in the economy at alternative price levels. Aggregate supply represents the total output of the economy at alternative price levels. To understand the causes of business cycles and inflation, we must understand how aggregate demand and supply cause the equilibrium price level and real GDP, the nation's output of goods and services, to change. The intersection between the *AD* and *AS* curves defines the equilibrium level of real GDP and level of prices. The equilibrium price level is P_e, and the equilibrium level of real GDP is Y_e. This price and output level represents the level of prices and output for some particular period of time—say, 2011. Once that equilibrium is established, there is no tendency for prices and output to change until changes occur in either the aggregate demand curve or the aggregate supply curve. Let's first consider a change in aggregate demand and then look at a change in aggregate supply.

1.a. Aggregate Demand and Business Cycles

An increase in aggregate demand is illustrated by a shift of the *AD* curve to the right, like the shift from AD_1 to AD_2 in Figure 12.2. This represents a situation in which buyers are buying more at every price level. The shift causes the equilibrium level of real GDP to rise from Y_{e1} to Y_{e2}, illustrating the expansionary phase of the business cycle. As output rises, unemployment decreases. The increase in aggregate demand also leads to a higher price level, as shown by the change in the price level from P_{e1} to P_{e2}. The increase in the price level represents an example of demand-pull inflation, which, you may recall, is inflation caused by increasing demand for output.

If aggregate demand falls, like the shift from AD_1 to AD_3, then there is a lower equilibrium level of real GDP (Y_{e3}). In this case, buyers are buying *less* at every price level. The drop in real GDP caused by lower demand would represent an economic slowdown or a recession, when output falls and unemployment rises.

FIGURE 12.1 Aggregate Demand and Aggregate Supply Equilibrium

The equilibrium price level and real GDP are determined by the intersection of the *AD* and *AS* curves.

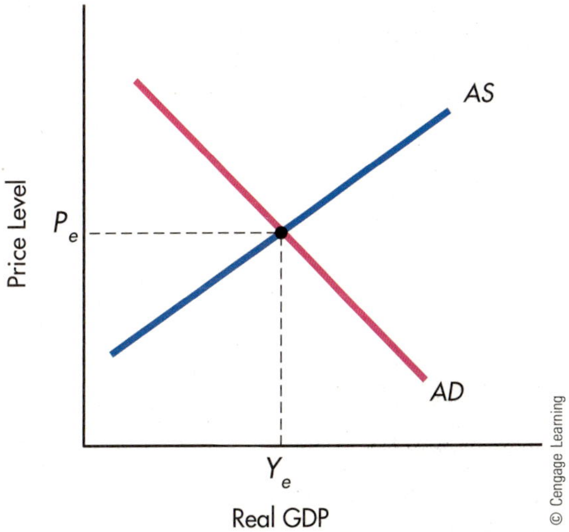

FIGURE 12.2 Effects of a Change in Aggregate Demand

If aggregate demand increases from AD_1 to AD_2, the equilibrium price level increases to P_{e2} and the equilibrium level of real GDP rises to Y_{e2}. If aggregate demand decreases from AD_1 to AD_3, the equilibrium price level falls to P_{e3} and the equilibrium level of real GDP drops to Y_{e3}.

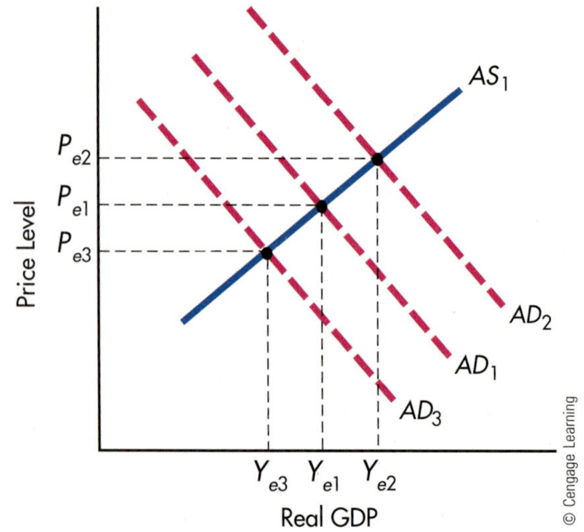

1.b. Aggregate Supply and Business Cycles

Changes in aggregate supply can also cause business cycles. Figure 12.3 illustrates what happens when aggregate supply changes. An increase in aggregate supply is illustrated by the shift from AS_1 to AS_2, leading to an increase in the equilibrium level of real GDP from Y_{e1} to Y_{e2}. An increase in aggregate supply comes about when firms produce more at every price level. Such an increase could result from an improvement in technology or a decrease in costs of production.

If aggregate supply decreased, as in the shift from AS_1 to AS_3, then the equilibrium level of real GDP would fall to Y_{e3}, and the equilibrium price level would increase from P_{e1} to P_{e3}. A decrease in aggregate supply could be caused by higher production costs that lead producers to raise their prices. This is an example of cost-push inflation, where the price level rises due to increased costs of production and the associated decrease in aggregate supply.

FIGURE 12.3 Effects of a Change in Aggregate Supply

If aggregate supply increases from AS_1 to AS_2, the equilibrium price level falls from P_{e1} to P_{e2} and the equilibrium level of real GDP rises to Y_{e2}. If aggregate supply decreases from AS_1 to AS_3, the equilibrium price level rises to P_{e3} and the equilibrium level of real GDP falls to Y_{e3}.

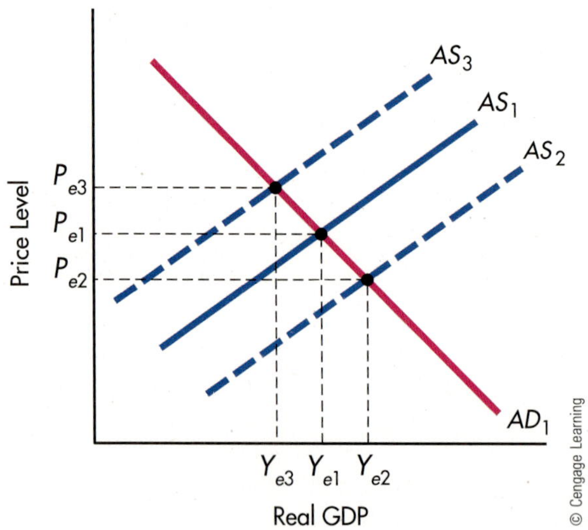

1.c. A Look Ahead

Business cycles result from changes in aggregate demand, from changes in aggregate supply, and from changes in both aggregate demand and aggregate supply. The degree to which real GDP declines during a recession or increases during an expansion depends on the amount by which the *AD* and/or *AS* curves shift. The degree to which an expansion involves output growth or increased inflation depends on the shapes of the *AD* and *AS* curves. We need to consider why the curves have the shapes they do, and what causes them to shift.

The comparison we made earlier, between aggregate demand, aggregate supply, and their microeconomic counterparts, the supply and demand curves, is only superficial. As we examine the aggregate demand and supply curves, you will see that the reasons underlying the shapes and movements of *AD* and *AS* are in fact quite different from those explaining the shapes and movements of the supply and demand curves.

RECAP

1. Aggregate demand (*AD*) represents the total spending in the economy at alternative price levels.
2. Aggregate supply (*AS*) represents the total output of the economy at alternative price levels.
3. The intersection between the *AD* and *AS* curves defines the equilibrium level of real GDP and the level of prices.
4. Business cycles result from changes in *AD* and/or *AS*.

2. FACTORS THAT INFLUENCE AGGREGATE DEMAND

2

What causes the aggregate demand curve to shift?

Aggregate demand is the relation between aggregate expenditures, or total spending, and the price level. Aggregate expenditures are the sum of expenditures of each sector of the economy: households (consumption), business firms (investment), government, and the rest of the world (net exports). Each sector of the economy has different reasons for spending; for instance, household spending depends heavily on household income, whereas business spending depends on the profits businesses expect to earn. Because each sector of the economy has a different reason for the amount of spending it undertakes, aggregate spending depends on all of these reasons. To understand aggregate demand, therefore, we must look at those factors that influence the expenditures of each sector of the economy.

2.a. Consumption

How much households spend depends on their income, wealth, expectations about future prices and incomes, demographics such as the age distribution of the population, and taxes.

- *Income.* If current income rises, households purchase more goods and services.
- *Wealth.* Wealth is different from income. It is the value of assets owned by a household, including homes, cars, bank deposits, stocks, and bonds. An increase in household wealth will increase consumption.
- *Expectations.* Expectations regarding future changes in income or wealth can affect consumption today. If households expect a recession and worry about job loss, consumption tends to fall. On the other hand, if households become more optimistic regarding future increases in income and wealth, consumption rises today.
- *Demographics.* Demographic change can affect consumption in several different ways. Population growth is generally associated with higher consumption for an economy. Younger households and older households

generally consume more and save less than middle-aged households. Therefore, as the age distribution of a nation changes, so will consumption.

- *Taxes.* Higher taxes will lower the disposable income of households and decrease consumption whereas lower taxes will raise disposable income and increase consumption. Government policy may change taxes and thereby bring about a change in consumption.

2.b. **Investment**

Investment is business spending on capital goods and inventories. In general, investment depends on the expected profitability of such spending, so any factor that could affect profitability will be a determinant of investment. Factors affecting the expected profitability of business projects include the interest rate, technology, the cost of capital goods, and capacity utilization.

- *Interest rate.* Investment is negatively related to the interest rate. The interest rate is the cost of borrowed funds. As the cost of borrowing becomes greater, other things being equal, fewer investment projects will offer sufficient profit to be undertaken. As the interest rate falls, investment is stimulated as the cost of financing the investment is lowered.
- *Technology.* New production technology stimulates investment spending as firms are forced to adopt new production methods to stay competitive.
- *Cost of capital goods.* If machines and equipment purchased by firms rise in price, then the higher costs associated with investment will lower profitability and investment will fall.
- *Capacity utilization.* As more excess capacity (i.e., unused capital goods) is available, more firms can expand production without purchasing new capital goods, and investment is lower. As firms approach full capacity, more investment spending is required to expand output further.

2.c. **Government Spending**

Government spending may be set by government authorities independent of current income or other determinants of aggregate expenditures.

2.d. **Net Exports**

Net exports are equal to exports minus imports. We assume exports are determined by conditions such as foreign income, tastes, prices, exchange rates, and government policy in the rest of the world. Imports are determined by similar domestic factors.

- *Income.* As domestic income rises and consumption rises, some of this consumption will include goods produced in other countries. Therefore, as domestic income rises, imports rise, and net exports fall. Similarly, as foreign income rises, foreign residents buy more domestic goods, and net exports rise.
- *Prices.* Other things being equal, higher (lower) foreign prices make domestic goods relatively cheaper (more expensive) and increase (decrease) net exports. Higher (lower) domestic prices make domestic goods relatively more expensive (cheaper) and decrease (increase) net exports.
- *Exchange rates.* Other things being equal, a depreciation of the domestic currency on the foreign exchange market will make domestic goods cheaper to foreign buyers and make foreign goods more expensive to domestic residents, so net exports will rise. An appreciation of the domestic currency will have the opposite effects.
- *Government policy.* Net exports may fall if foreign governments restrict the entry of domestic goods, reducing domestic exports. If the domestic government restricts imports into the domestic economy, net exports may rise.

Exports are determined by conditions such as foreign income, tastes, prices, exchange rates, and government policy.

Faraways/Shutterstock.com

2.e. Aggregate Expenditures

You can see how aggregate expenditures, the sum of all spending on U.S. goods and services, must depend on prices, income, and all of the other determinants discussed in the previous sections. As with the demand curve for a specific good or service, with the aggregate demand curve we want to classify the factors that influence spending into the price and the nonprice determinants for the aggregate demand curves as well. The components of aggregate expenditures that change as the price level changes will lead to movements along the aggregate demand curve—changes in quantity demanded—whereas changes in aggregate expenditures caused by nonprice effects will cause shifts of the aggregate demand curve—changes in aggregate demand.

RECAP

1. Aggregate expenditures are the sum of consumption, investment, government spending, and net exports.
2. Consumption depends on household income, wealth, expectations, demographics, and taxation.
3. Investment depends on the interest rate, technology, the cost of capital goods, and capacity utilization.
4. Government spending is determined independent of current income.
5. Net exports depend on foreign and domestic incomes, prices, government policies, and exchange rates.

3. THE AGGREGATE DEMAND CURVE

When we examined the demand curves in Chapter 2, we divided our study into two parts: the movement along the curves—changes in quantity demanded—and the shifts of the curve—changes in demand. We take the same approach here in examining aggregate demand. We first look at the movements along the aggregate demand curve caused by changes in the price level. We then turn to the nonprice determinants of aggregate demand that cause shifts in the curve.

3.a. Changes in Aggregate Quantity Demanded: Price-Level Effects

Aggregate demand curves are downward sloping just like the demand curves for individual goods that were shown in Chapter 2, although for different reasons. Along the demand curve for an individual good, the price of that good changes while the prices of all other goods remain constant. This means that the good in question becomes relatively more or less expensive compared to all other goods in the economy. Consumers tend to substitute a less expensive good for a more expensive good. The effect of this substitution is an inverse relationship between price and quantity demanded. As the price of a good rises, quantity demanded falls. For the economy as a whole, however, it is not a substitution of a less expensive good for a more expensive good that causes the demand curve to slope down. Instead, aggregate quantity demanded, or total spending, will change as the price level changes due to the wealth effect, the interest rate effect, and the international trade effect of a price-level change on aggregate expenditures.

3.a.1. The Wealth Effect Individuals and businesses own money, bonds, and other financial assets. The purchasing power of these assets is the quantity of goods and services the assets can be exchanged for. When the level of prices falls, the purchasing power of these assets increases, allowing households and businesses to purchase more. When prices go up, the purchasing power of financial assets falls, which causes households and businesses to spend less. This is the **wealth effect** (sometimes called the *real-balance effect*) of a price change: a change in the real value of wealth that causes spending to change when the level of prices changes. *Real values* are values that have been adjusted for price-level changes. Here *real value* means "purchasing power." When the price level changes, the purchasing power of financial assets also changes. When prices rise, the real value of assets and wealth falls, and aggregate expenditures tend to fall. When prices fall, the real value of assets and wealth rises, and aggregate expenditures tend to rise.

wealth effect:
a change in the real value of wealth that causes spending to change when the level of prices changes

3.a.2. The Interest Rate Effect When the price level rises, the purchasing power of each dollar falls, which means more money is required to buy any particular quantity of goods and services (see Figure 12.4). Suppose that a family of three needs $100 each week to buy food. If the price level doubles, the same quantity of food costs $200. The household must have twice as much money to buy the same amount of food. Conversely, when prices fall, the family needs less money to buy food because the purchasing power of each dollar is greater.

When prices go up, people need more money. So they sell their other financial assets, such as bonds, to get that money. The increase in the supply of bonds lowers bond prices and raises interest rates. Since bonds typically pay fixed-dollar interest payments each year, as the price of a bond varies, the interest rate (or yield) will change. For instance, suppose you pay $1,000 for a bond that pays $100 a year in interest. The interest rate on this bond is found by dividing the annual interest payment by the bond price, or $100/$1,000 = 10 percent. If the price of the bond falls to $900, then the interest rate is equal to the annual interest payment (which remains fixed at $100 for the life of the bond) divided by the new price of $900—that is, $100/$900 = 11 percent. When bond prices fall, interest rates rise, and when bond prices rise, interest rates fall.

If people want more money, and they sell some of their bond holdings to raise the money, bond prices will fall, and interest rates will rise. The rise in interest rates is necessary to sell the larger quantity of bonds, but it causes investment expenditures to fall, which causes aggregate expenditures to fall.

When prices fall, people need less money to purchase the same quantity of goods, so they use their money holdings to buy bonds and other financial assets.

FIGURE 12.4 The Interest Rate Effect

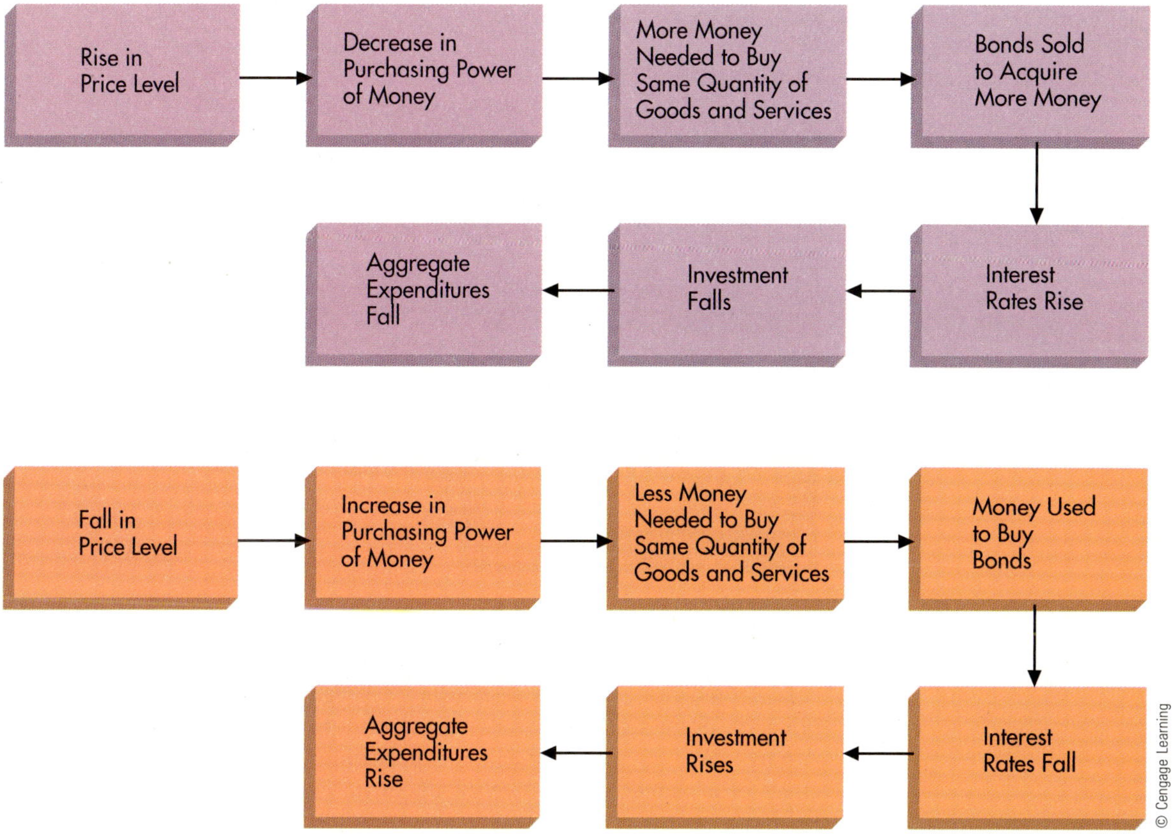

The increased demand for bonds increases bond prices and causes interest rates to fall. Lower interest rates increase investment expenditures, thereby pushing aggregate expenditures up.

interest rate effect: a change in interest rates that causes investment and therefore aggregate expenditures to change as the level of prices changes

Figure 12.4 shows the **interest rate effect**—the relationship among the price level, interest rates, and aggregate expenditures. As the price level rises, interest rates rise, and aggregate expenditures fall. As the price level falls, interest rates fall, and aggregate expenditures rise.

international trade effect: a change in aggregate expenditures resulting from a change in the domestic price level that changes the price of domestic goods in relation to foreign goods

3.a.3. **The International Trade Effect** The third channel through which a price-level change affects the quantity of goods and services demanded is called the **international trade effect**. A change in the level of domestic prices can cause net exports to change. If domestic prices rise while foreign prices and the foreign exchange rate remain constant, domestic goods become more expensive in relation to foreign goods.

Suppose the United States sells oranges to Japan. If the oranges sell for $1 per pound, and the yen–dollar exchange rate is 100 yen = $1, a pound of U.S. oranges costs a Japanese buyer 100 yen. What happens if the level of prices in the United States goes up 10 percent? All prices, including the price of oranges, increase 10 percent. The U.S. oranges sell for $1.10 a pound after the price increase. If the exchange rate is still 100 yen = $1, a pound of oranges now costs the Japanese buyer 110 yen (100 × 1.10). If orange prices in other countries do not change, some Japanese buyers may buy oranges from those countries. The increase in the level of U.S. prices makes U.S. goods more expensive relative to foreign goods and causes U.S. net exports to fall; a decrease in the level of U.S. prices makes U.S. goods cheaper in relation to foreign goods and causes U.S. net exports to rise.

If the price of U.S. oranges increases, countries like Japan may buy oranges from other countries instead of the United States.

When the price of domestic goods increases in relation to the price of foreign goods, net exports fall, causing aggregate expenditures to fall. When the price of domestic goods falls in relation to the price of foreign goods, net exports rise, causing aggregate expenditures to rise. The international trade effect of a change in the level of domestic prices causes aggregate expenditures to change in the opposite direction.

aggregate demand curve: a curve that shows the different levels of expenditures on domestic output at different levels of prices

3.a.4. **The Sum of the Price-Level Effects** The **aggregate demand curve** (*AD*) shows how the equilibrium level of expenditures for the economy's output changes as the price level changes. In other words, the curve shows the amount people spend at different price levels.

Figure 12.5 displays the typical shape of the *AD* curve. The price level is plotted on the vertical axis, and real GDP is plotted on the horizontal axis. Suppose that initially the economy is at point *A* with prices at P_0. At this point, spending

FIGURE 12.5 The Aggregate Demand Curve

The aggregate demand curve (*AD*) shows the level of expenditures at different price levels. At price level P_0, expenditures are \$500; at P_1, \$700; and at P_2, \$300.

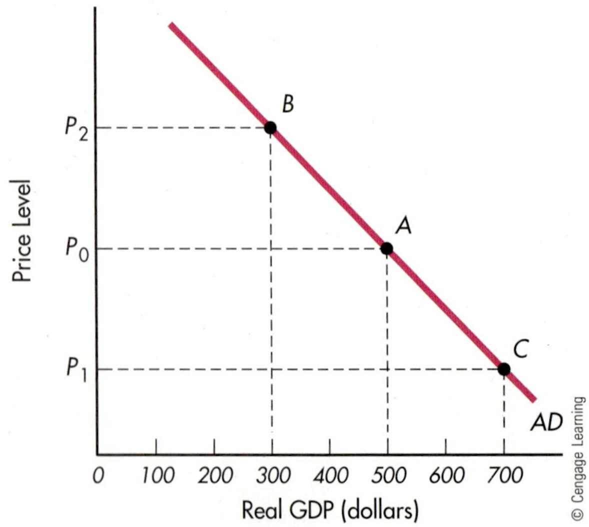

equals $500. If prices fall to P_1, expenditures equal $700, and the economy is at point C. If prices rise from P_0 to P_2, expenditures equal $300 at point B.

Because aggregate expenditures increase when the price level decreases and decrease when the price level increases, the aggregate demand curve slopes down. The aggregate demand curve is drawn with the price level for the *entire economy* on the vertical axis. A price-level change here means that, on average, *all prices in the economy change*; there is no relative price change among domestic goods. The negative slope of the aggregate demand curve is a product of the wealth effect, the interest rate effect, and the international trade effect.

A lower domestic price level increases consumption (the wealth effect), investment (the interest rate effect), and net exports (the international trade effect). As the price level drops, aggregate expenditures rise.

A higher domestic price reduces consumption (the wealth effect), investment (the interest rate effect), and net exports (the international trade effect). As prices rise, aggregate expenditures fall. These price effects are summarized in Figure 12.6.

FIGURE 12.6 Why the Aggregate Demand Curve Slopes Down

(a) Wealth effect (b) Interest rate effect (c) International trade effect

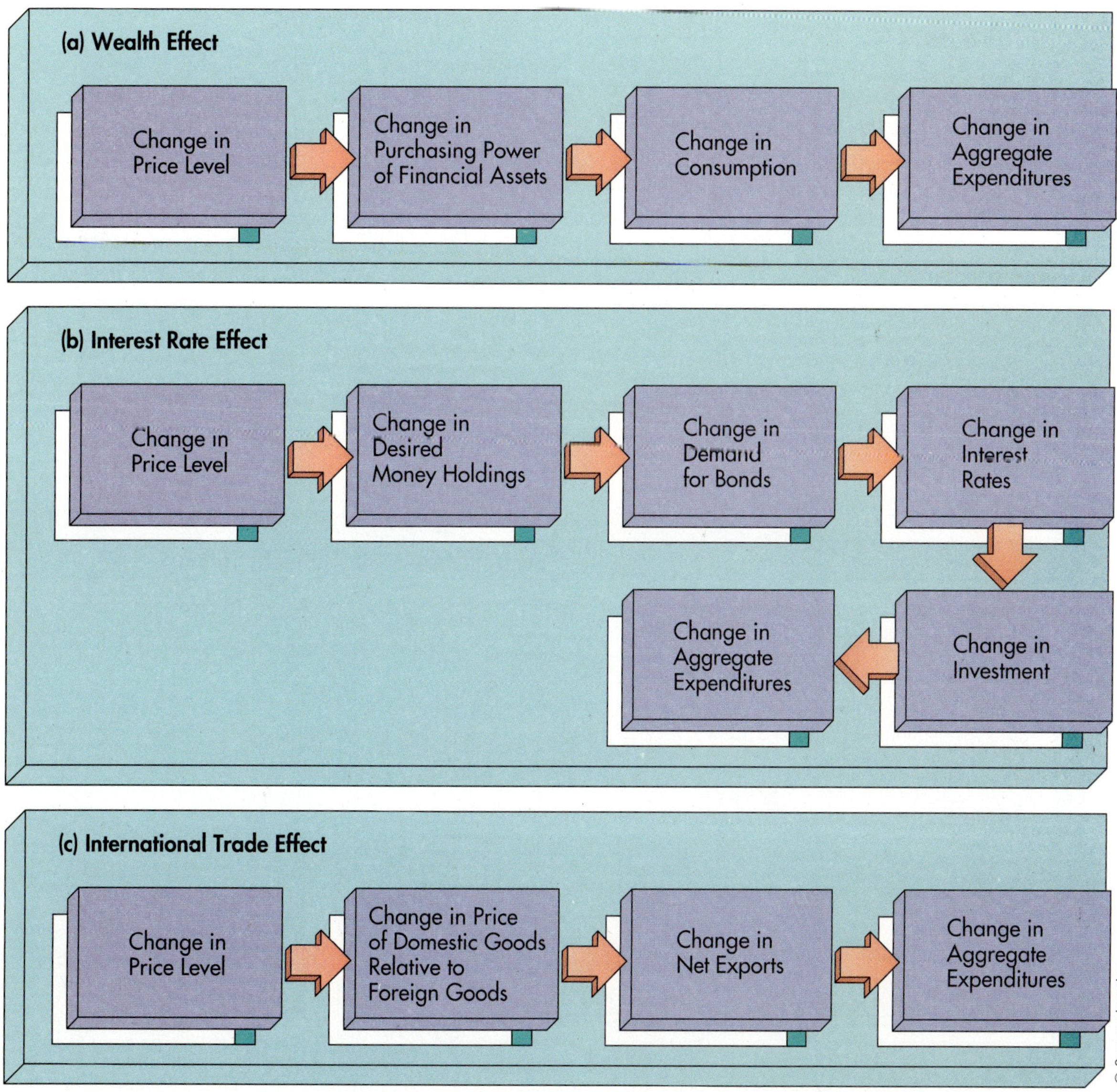

3.b. Changes in Aggregate Demand: Nonprice Determinants

The aggregate demand curve shows the level of aggregate expenditures at alternative price levels. We draw the curve by varying the price level and finding out what the resulting total expenditures are, holding all other things constant. As those "other things"—the nonprice determinants of aggregate demand—change, the aggregate demand curve shifts. The nonprice determinants of aggregate demand include all of the factors covered in the discussion of the components of expenditures—income, wealth, demographics, expectations, taxes, the interest rate (interest rates can change for reasons other than price-level changes), the cost of capital goods, capacity utilization, foreign income and price levels, exchange rates, and government policy. A change in any one of these can cause the *AD* curve to shift. In the discussions that follow, we will focus particularly on the effect of expectations, foreign income levels, and price levels, and we will also mention government policy, which will be examined in detail in Chapter 13. Figure 12.7 summarizes these effects, which are discussed next.

FIGURE 12.7 Nonprice Determinants: Changes in Aggregate Demand

(a) Expectations (b) Foreign income and price levels (c) Government policy

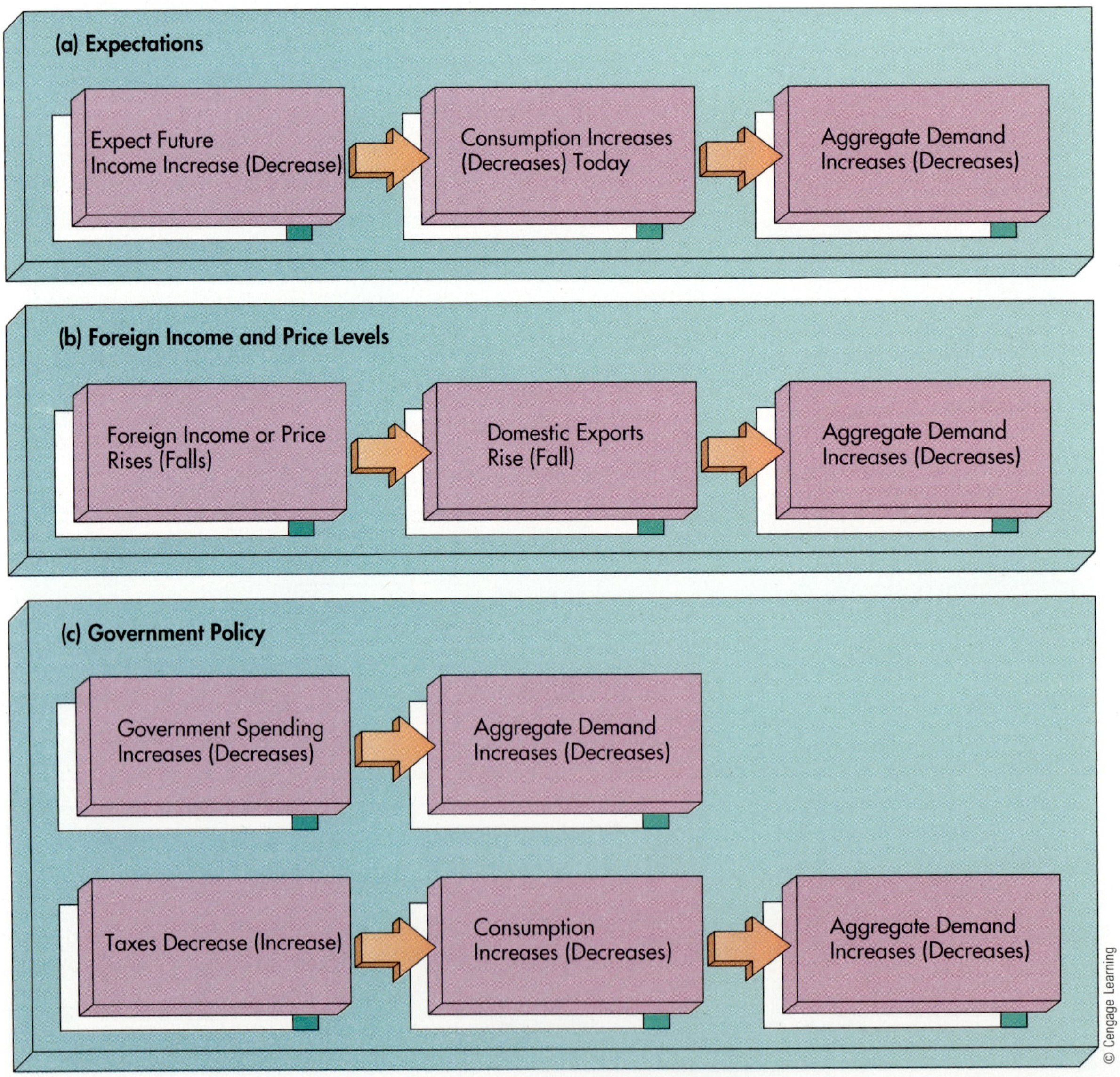

3.b.1. **Expectations** Consumption and business spending are affected by expectations. Consumption is sensitive to people's expectations of future income, prices, and wealth. For example, when people expect the economy to do well in the future, they increase consumption today at every price level. This is reflected in a shift of the aggregate demand curve to the right, from AD_0 to AD_1, as shown in Figure 12.8. When aggregate demand increases, aggregate expenditures increase at every price level.

On the other hand, if people expect a recession in the near future, they tend to reduce consumption and increase saving in order to protect themselves against a greater likelihood of losing a job or a forced cutback in hours worked. As consumption drops, aggregate demand decreases. The *AD* curve shifts to the left, from AD_0 to AD_2. At every price level along AD_2, planned expenditures are less than they are along AD_0.

Expectations also play an important role in investment decisions. Before undertaking a particular project, businesses forecast the likely revenues and costs associated with that project. When the profit outlook is good—say, a tax cut is on the horizon—investment and therefore aggregate demand increase. When profits are expected to fall, investment and aggregate demand decrease.

3.b.2. **Foreign Income and Price Levels** When foreign income increases, so does foreign spending. Some of this increased spending is for goods produced in the domestic economy. As domestic exports increase, aggregate demand rises. Lower foreign income has just the opposite effect. As foreign income falls, foreign spending falls, including foreign spending on the exports of the domestic economy. Lower foreign income, then, causes domestic net exports and domestic aggregate demand to fall.

If foreign prices rise in relation to domestic prices, domestic goods become less expensive relative to foreign goods, and domestic net exports increase. This means that aggregate demand rises, or the aggregate demand curve shifts up, as the level of foreign prices rises. Conversely, when the level of foreign prices falls, domestic goods become more expensive relative to foreign goods, causing domestic net exports and aggregate demand to fall.

FIGURE 12.8 Shifting the Aggregate Demand Curve

As aggregate demand increases, the *AD* curve shifts to the right, like the shift from AD_0 to AD_1. At every price level, the quantity of output demanded increases. As aggregate demand falls, the *AD* curve shifts to the left, like the shift from AD_0 to AD_2. At every price level, the quantity of output demanded falls.

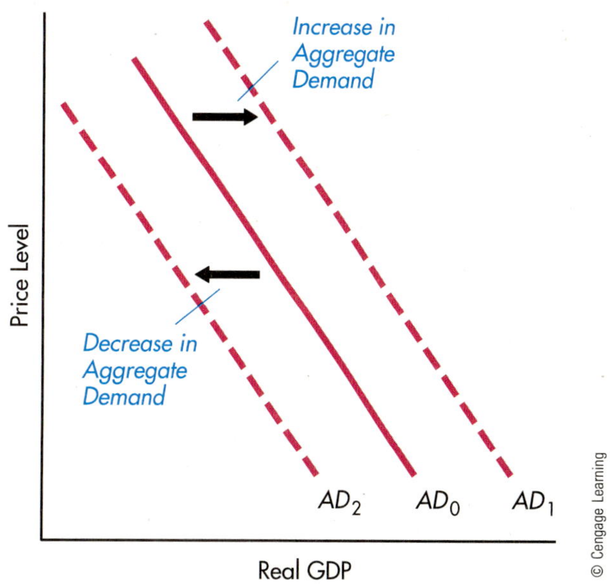

Let's go back to the market for oranges. Suppose U.S. growers compete with Brazilian growers for the Japanese orange market. If the level of prices in Brazil rises while the level of prices in the United States remains stable, the price of Brazilian oranges to the Japanese buyer rises in relation to the price of U.S. oranges. What happens? U.S. exports of oranges to Japan should rise while Brazilian exports of oranges to Japan fall.

3.b.3. **Government Policy** One of the goals of macroeconomic policy is to achieve economic growth without inflation. For GDP to increase, either *AD* or *AS* would have to change. Government economic policy can cause the aggregate demand curve to shift. An increase in government spending or a decrease in taxes will increase aggregate demand; a decrease in government spending or an increase in taxes will decrease aggregate demand. We devote Chapter 13, "Fiscal Policy," to an examination of the effect of taxes and government spending on aggregate demand. In Chapter 15, "Monetary Policy," we describe how changes in the money supply can cause the aggregate demand curve to shift.

RECAP

1. The aggregate demand curve shows the level of aggregate expenditures at different levels of price.
2. Aggregate expenditures are the sum of consumption, investment, government spending, and net exports.
3. The wealth effect, the interest rate effect, and the international trade effect are three reasons why aggregate demand slopes down. These effects explain movements along a given *AD* curve.
4. The aggregate demand curve shifts with changes in the nonprice determinants of aggregate demand: expectations, foreign income and price levels, and government policy.

4. AGGREGATE SUPPLY

3 What is aggregate supply?

aggregate supply curve: a curve that shows the amount of real GDP produced at different price levels

The **aggregate supply curve** shows the quantity of real GDP produced at different price levels. The aggregate supply curve looks like the supply curve for an individual good, but, as with aggregate demand and the microeconomic demand curve, different factors are at work. The positive relationship between price and quantity supplied of an individual good is based on the price of that good's changing in relation to the prices of all other goods. As the price of a single good rises relative to the prices of other goods, sellers are willing to offer more of the good for sale. With aggregate supply, on the other hand, we are analyzing how the amount of all goods and services produced changes as the level of prices changes. The direct relationship between prices and national output is explained by the effect of changing prices on profits, not by relative price changes.

4.a. Changes in Aggregate Quantity Supplied: Price-Level Effects

Along the aggregate supply curve, everything is held fixed except the price level and output. The price level is the price of output. The prices of resources—that is, the costs of production (wages, rent, and interest)—are assumed to be constant, at least for a short time following a change in the price level.

If the price level rises while the costs of production remain fixed, business profits go up. As profits rise, firms are willing to produce more output. As the price level rises, then, the quantity of output firms are willing to supply

FIGURE 12.9 Aggregate Supply

The aggregate supply curve shows the amount of real GDP produced at different price levels. The *AS* curve slopes up, indicating that the higher the price level, the greater the quantity of output produced.

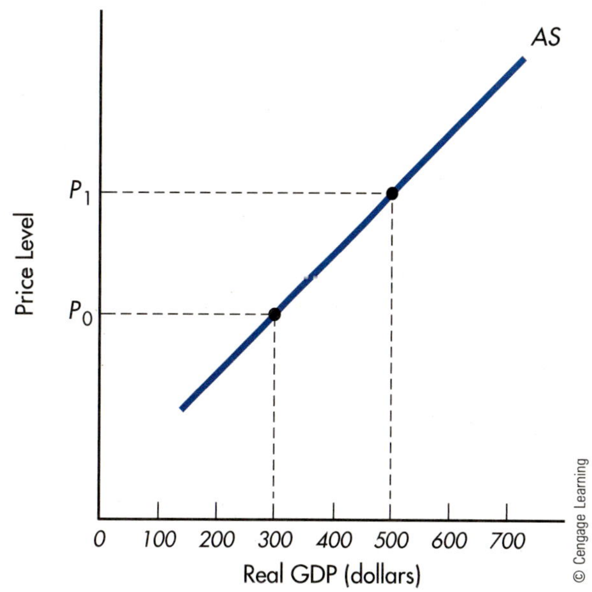

increases. The result is the positively sloped aggregate supply curve shown in Figure 12.9.

As the price level rises from P_0 to P_1 in Figure 12.9, real GDP increases from \$300 to \$500. The higher the price level, the higher the profits, everything else held constant, and the greater the quantity of output produced in the economy. Conversely, as the price level falls, the quantity of output produced falls.

4.b. Short-Run Versus Long-Run Aggregate Supply

The curve in Figure 12.9 is a *short-run* aggregate supply curve because the costs of production are held constant. Although production costs may not rise immediately when the price level rises, eventually they will. Labor will demand higher wages to compensate for the higher cost of living; suppliers will charge more for materials. The positive slope of the *AS* curve, then, is a short-run phenomenon. How short is the short run? It is the period of time over which production costs remain constant. (In the long run, all costs change or are variable.) For the economy as a whole, the short run can be months or, at most, a few years.

4

Why does the short-run aggregate supply curve become steeper as real GDP increases?

4.b.1. Short-Run Aggregate Supply Curve

Figure 12.9 represents the general shape of the short-run aggregate supply curve. In Figure 12.10, you see a more realistic version of the same curve; its steepness varies. The steepness of the aggregate supply curve depends on the ability and willingness of producers to respond to price-level changes in the short run. Figure 12.10 shows the typical shape of the short-run aggregate supply curve.

Notice that as the level of real GDP increases in Figure 12.10, the *AS* curve becomes steeper. This is because each increase in output requires firms to hire more and more resources until eventually full capacity is reached in some areas of the economy, resources are fully employed, and some firms reach maximum output. At this point, increases in the price level bring about smaller and smaller increases in output from firms as a whole. The short-run aggregate supply curve becomes increasingly steep as the economy approaches maximum output.

FIGURE 12.10 The Shape of the Short-Run Aggregate Supply Curve

The upward-sloping aggregate supply curve occurs when the price level must rise to induce further increases in output. The curve gets steeper as real GDP increases since the closer the economy comes to the capacity level of output, the less output will rise in response to higher prices as more and more firms reach their maximum level of output in the short run.

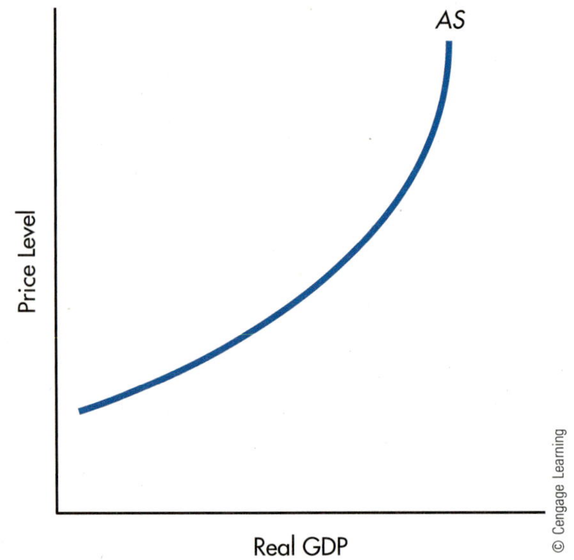

FIGURE 12.11 The Shape of the Long-Run Aggregate Supply Curve

In the long run, the *AS* curve is a vertical line at the potential level of real GDP. This indicates that there is no relationship between price-level changes and the quantity of output produced.

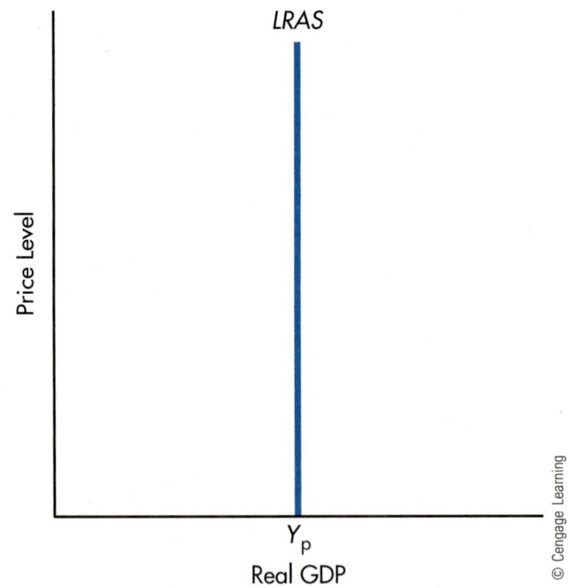

5

Why is the long-run aggregate supply curve vertical?

4.b.2. **Long-Run Aggregate Supply Curve** Aggregate supply in the short run is different from aggregate supply in the long run (see Figure 12.11). That difference stems from the fact that quantities and costs of resources are not fixed in the long run. Over time, contracts expire and wages and other resource costs adjust to current conditions. The increased flexibility of resource costs in the long run has costs rising and falling with the price level and changes the shape of the aggregate supply curve. Lack of information about economic conditions in the short run also contributes to the inflexibility of resource prices as compared to the long run.

long-run aggregate supply curve (*LRAS*):
a vertical line at the potential level of national income

The **long-run aggregate supply curve (*LRAS*)** is viewed by most economists as a vertical line at the potential level of real GDP or output (*Yp*), as shown in Figure 12.11. Remember that the potential level of real GDP is the income level that is produced in the absence of any cyclical unemployment, or when the natural rate of unemployment exists. In the long run, wages and other resource costs fully adjust to price changes. The short-run *AS* curve slopes up because we assume that the costs of production, particularly wages, do not change to offset changing prices. In the short run, then, higher prices increase producers' profits and stimulate production. In the long run, because the costs of production adjust completely to the change in prices, neither profits nor production will increase. What we find here are higher wages and other costs of production to match the higher level of prices.

6 What causes the aggregate supply curve to shift?

4.c. Changes in Aggregate Supply: Nonprice Determinants

The aggregate supply curve is drawn with everything but the price level and real GDP held constant. There are several things that can change and cause the aggregate supply curve to shift. The shift from AS_0 to AS_1 in Figure 12.12 represents an increase in aggregate supply. The AS_1 curve lies to the right of AS_0; this means that at every price level, production is higher on AS_1 than on AS_0. The shift from AS_0 to AS_2 represents a decrease in aggregate supply. The AS_2 curve lies to the left of AS_0; this means that at every price level, production along AS_2 is less than production along AS_0. The nonprice determinants of aggregate supply are resource prices, technology, and expectations. Figure 12.13 summarizes the nonprice determinants of aggregate supply.

4.c.1. Resource Prices

When the price of output changes, the costs of production do not change immediately. At first, then, a change in profits induces a change in production. Costs eventually change in response to the change in prices and production, and when they do, the aggregate supply curve shifts. When the cost of resources (labor, capital goods, materials) falls, the aggregate supply curve shifts to the right, from AS_0 to AS_1 in Figure 12.12. This means firms are willing to produce more output at any given price level. When the cost of resources goes up, profits fall, and the aggregate supply curve shifts to the left, from AS_0 to AS_2. Here, at any given level of price, firms produce less output.

FIGURE 12.12 Changes in Aggregate Supply

The aggregate supply curve shifts with changes in resource prices, technology, and expectations. When aggregate supply increases, the curve shifts to the right, like the shift from AS_0 to AS_1, so that at every price level more is being produced. When aggregate supply falls, the curve shifts to the left, like the shift from AS_0 to AS_2, so that at every price level less is being produced.

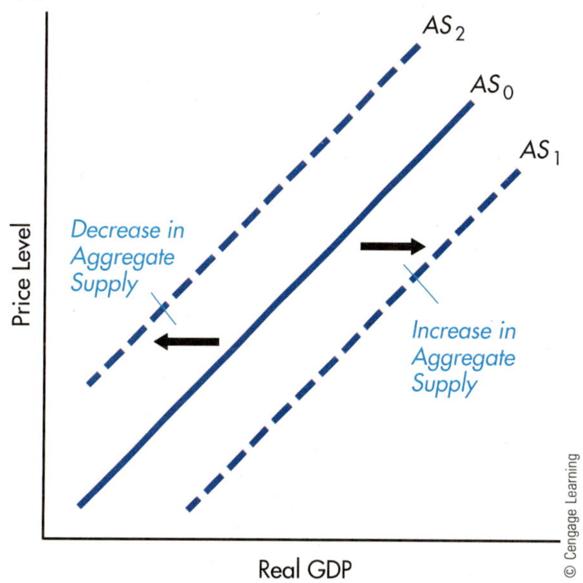

FIGURE 12.13 Determinants of Aggregate Supply

(a) Resource prices (b) Technology (c) Expectations

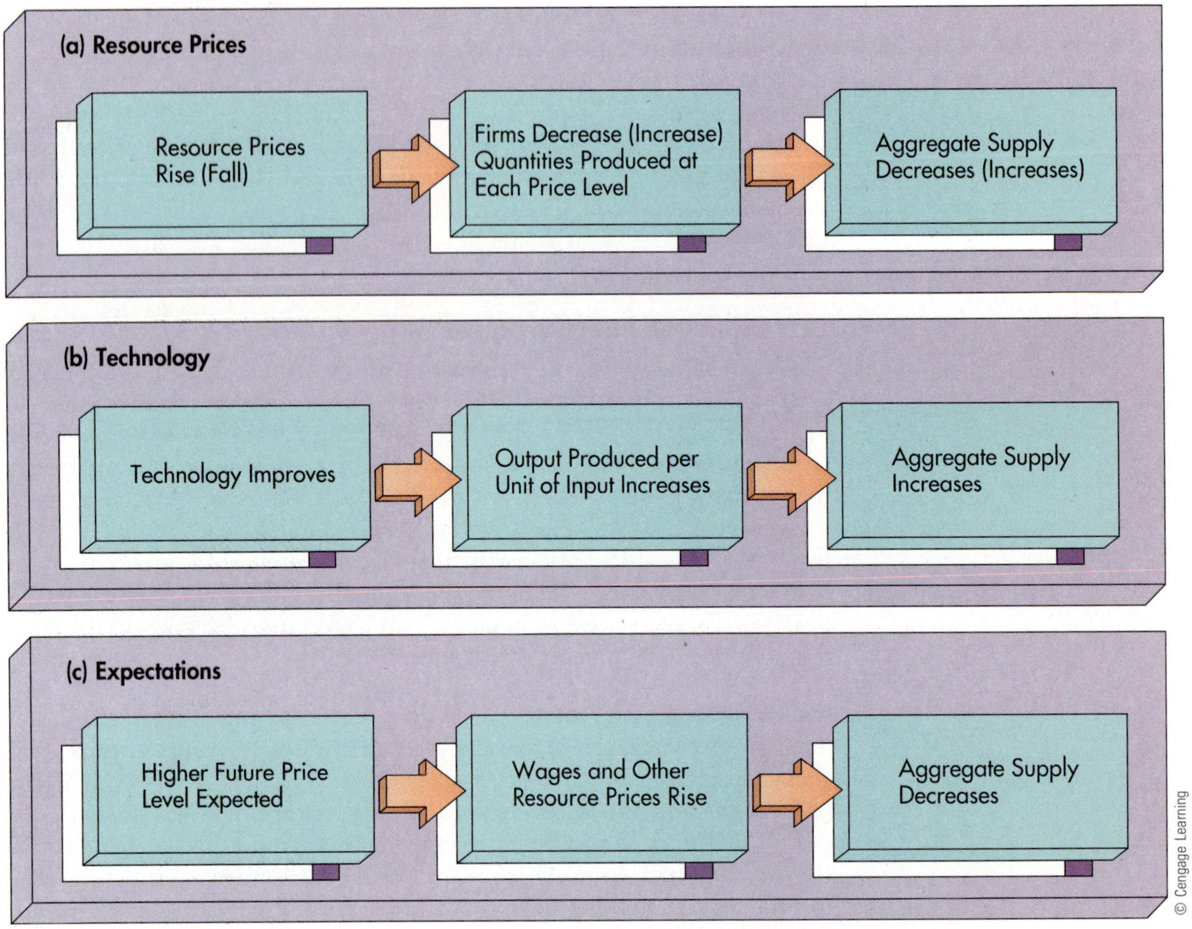

Remember that the vertical axis of the aggregate supply graph plots the price level for all goods and services produced in the economy. Only those changes in resource prices that raise the costs of production across the economy have an impact on the aggregate supply curve. For example, oil is an important raw material. If a new source of oil is discovered, the price of oil falls, and aggregate supply increases. However, if oil-exporting countries restrict oil supplies and the price of oil increases substantially, aggregate supply decreases—a situation that occurred when OPEC reduced the supply of oil in the 1970s (see the Global Business Insight "OPEC and Aggregate Supply"). If the price of only one minor resource changed, then aggregate supply would be unlikely to change. For instance, if the price of land increased in Las Cruces, New Mexico, we would not expect the U.S. aggregate supply curve to be affected.

4.c.2. **Technology** Technological innovations allow businesses to increase the productivity of their existing resources. As new technology is adopted, the amount of output that can be produced by each unit of input increases, moving the aggregate supply curve to the right. For example, personal computers and word-processing software have allowed secretaries to produce much more output in a day than typewriters allowed.

4.c.3. **Expectations** To understand how expectations can affect aggregate supply, consider the case of labor contracts. Manufacturing workers typically contract for a nominal wage on the basis of what they and their employers expect the future level of prices to be. Because wages typically are set for at least a year, any unexpected increase in the price level during the year lowers real wages. Firms receive higher prices for their output, but the cost of labor stays the same. So profits and production go up.

If wages rise in anticipation of higher prices but prices do not go up, the cost of labor rises. Higher real wages caused by expectations of higher prices reduce current profits and production, moving the aggregate supply curve to the left. Other things being equal, anticipated higher prices cause aggregate supply to decrease; conversely, anticipated lower prices cause aggregate supply to

GLOBAL BUSINESS INSIGHT

OPEC and Aggregate Supply

In the late winter of 2003, there was much talk about high oil prices leading to a fall in GDP for oil-importing countries. At the same time that the Bush administration was planning to invade Iraq, a move which would disrupt oil supplies from the Mideast, a strike by Venezuelan oil workers interrupted oil supplies from the world's fifth-largest producer. Oil prices rose dramatically, and the price of gasoline rose from about $1.60 per gallon to more than $2 per gallon. The higher the oil prices rose, the more talk there was about recession. What is the link between oil prices and real GDP? A look back to recent history can help develop our understanding of this link.

In 1973 and 1974, and again in 1979 and 1980, the Organization of Petroleum Exporting Countries (OPEC) reduced the supply of oil, driving the price of oil up dramatically. For example, the price of Saudi Arabian crude oil more than tripled between 1973 and 1974, and more than doubled between 1979 and 1980. Researchers estimate that the rapid jump in oil prices reduced output by 17 percent in Japan, by 7 percent in the United States, and by 1.9 percent in Germany.[*]

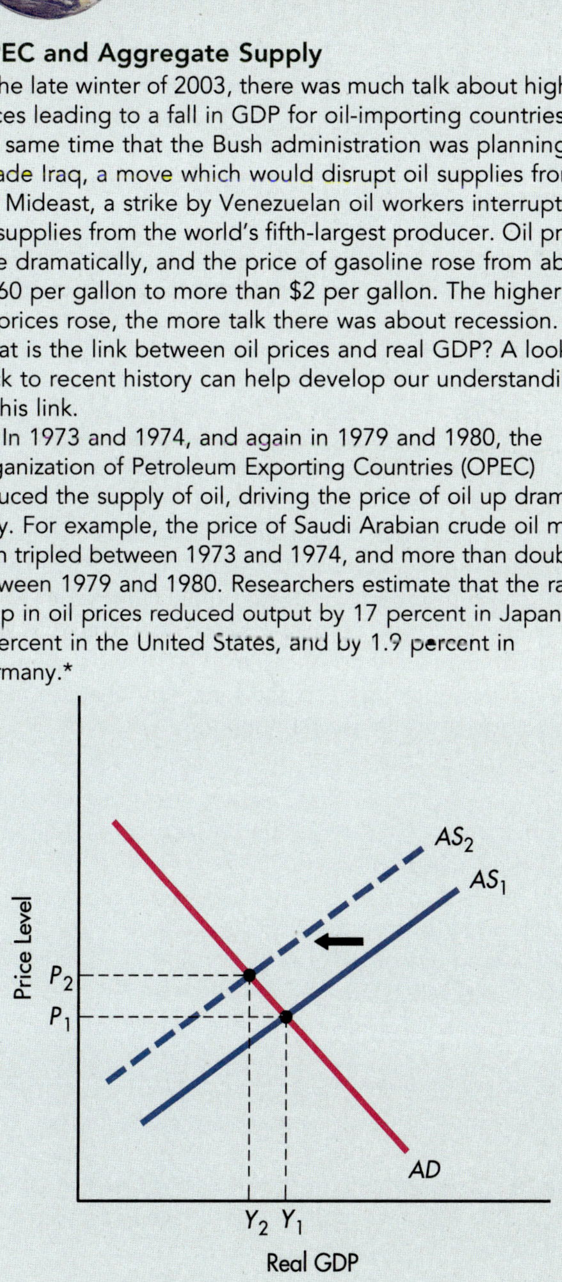

Oil is an important resource in many industries. When the price of oil increases due to restricted oil output, aggregate supply falls. You can see this in the graph. When the price of oil goes up, the aggregate supply curve falls from AS_1 to AS_2. When aggregate supply falls, the equilibrium level of real GDP (the intersection of the *AS* curve and the *AD* curve) falls from Y_1 to Y_2.

Higher oil prices due to restricted oil output would decrease not only short-run aggregate supply and current equilibrium real GDP, as shown in the figure, but also potential equilibrium income at the natural rate of unemployment. Unless other factors change to contribute to economic growth, the higher resource (oil) price reduces the productive capacity of the economy.

There is evidence that fluctuations in oil prices have less effect on the economy today than in the past.[†] The amount of energy that goes into producing a dollar of GDP has declined over time so that oil plays a less important role as a determinant of aggregate supply today than in the 1970s and earlier. This means that any given change in oil prices today will be associated with smaller shifts in the *AS* curve than it would have been in earlier decades.

Although we have focused on the *AS* curve and oil prices, more recently the *AD* curve has entered the discussion. Unlike earlier episodes, where oil price rises were the result of restricting the supply of oil, in the mid-2000s the price of oil was being driven higher by rising demand—particularly from China and the United States.[‡] The recession of 2008 showed that oil prices can drop just as dramatically due to demand shifts as in the earlier supply-driven episodes once supply increased. As spending fell during the recession, oil prices fell sharply from over $140 per barrel in July 2008 to $90 by September, and then to less than $40 by December.

*These estimates were taken from Robert H. Rasche and John A. Tatom, "Energy Price Shocks, Aggregate Supply, and Monetary Policy: The Theory and the International Evidence," in *Carnegie-Rochester Conference Series on Public Policy* (Karl Brunner and Allan H. Meltzer, eds.), no. 14, Spring 1981, pp. 9–93.

†See Stephen P. A. Brown and Mine K. Yücel, "Oil Prices and the Economy," in *Southwest Economy,* Federal Reserve Bank of Dallas, July–August 2000 or Olivier Blanchard and Jordi Galí. "The Macroeconomic Effects of Oil Price Shocks: Why are the 2000s so Different from the 1970s?" *International Dimensions of Monetary Policy.* 2007 ed. Jordi Galí and Mark Gertler.

‡See Christopher J. Neely, "Will Oil Prices Choke Growth?" Federal Reserve Bank of St. Louis, *International Economic Trends,* July 2004.

FIGURE 12.14 Shifting the Long-Run Aggregate Supply Curve

Changes in technology and the availability and quality of resources can shift the *LRAS* curve. For instance, a new technology that increases productivity would move the curve to the right, from *LRAS* to *LRAS*₁.

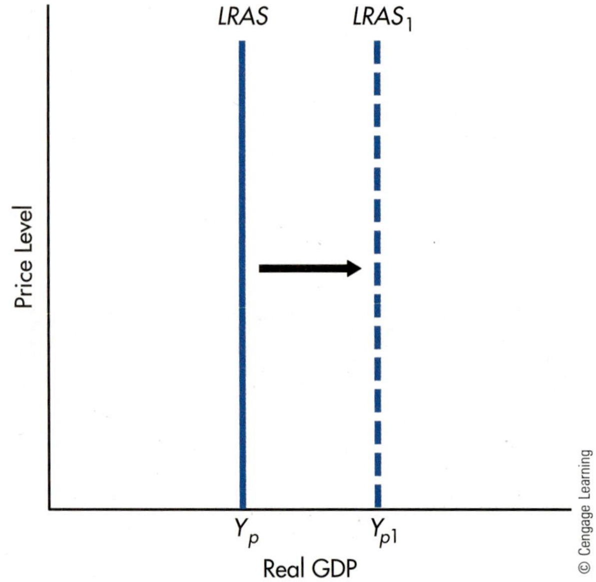

increase. In this sense, expectations of price-level changes that shift aggregate supply bring about price-level changes.

4.c.4. Economic Growth: Long-Run Aggregate Supply Shifts The vertical long-run aggregate supply curve, as shown in Figure 12.11, does not mean that the economy is forever fixed at the current level of potential real GDP. Over time, as new technologies are developed and the quantity and quality of resources increase, potential output also increases, shifting both the short- and long-run aggregate supply curves to the right. Figure 12.14 shows long-run economic growth by the shift in the aggregate supply curve from *LRAS* to $LRAS_1$. The movement of the long-run aggregate supply curve to the right reflects the increase in potential real GDP from Y_p to Y_{p1}. Even though the price level has no effect on the level of output in the long run, changes in the determinants of the supply of real output in the economy do.

RECAP

1. The aggregate supply curve shows the quantity of output (real GDP) produced at different price levels.
2. The aggregate supply curve slopes up because, everything else held constant, higher prices increase producers' profits, creating an incentive to increase output.
3. The aggregate supply curve shifts with changes in resource prices, technology, and expectations. These are nonprice determinants of aggregate supply.
4. The short-run aggregate supply curve is upward sloping, showing that increases in production are accompanied by higher prices.
5. The long-run aggregate supply curve is vertical at potential real GDP because, eventually, wages and the costs of other resources adjust fully to price-level changes.

5. AGGREGATE DEMAND AND SUPPLY EQUILIBRIUM

7

What determines the equilibrium price level and real GDP?

Now that we have defined the aggregate demand and aggregate supply curves separately, we can put them together to determine the equilibrium level of price and real GDP.

5.a. Short-Run Equilibrium

Figure 12.15 shows the level of equilibrium in a hypothetical economy. Initially, the economy is in equilibrium at point 1, where AD_1 and AS_1 intersect. At this point, the equilibrium price is P_1 and the equilibrium real GDP is \$500. At price P_1, the amount of output demanded is equal to the amount supplied. Suppose aggregate demand increases from AD_1 to AD_2. In the short run, aggregate supply does not change, so the new equilibrium is at the intersection of the new aggregate demand curve AD_2 and the same aggregate supply curve AS_1, at point 2. The new equilibrium price is P_2, and the new equilibrium real GDP is \$600. Note that in the short run, the equilibrium point on the short-run aggregate supply curve can lie to the right of the *LRAS*. This is because the *LRAS* curve represents the potential level of real GDP, not the capacity level. It is possible to produce more than the potential level of real GDP in the short run when the unemployment rate falls below the natural rate of unemployment.

NOW YOU TRY IT

What will happen to the equilibrium price level and real GDP when

1. foreign price levels rise?
2. foreign incomes fall?
3. taxes rise?
4. the use of new computers increases productivity?

5.b. Long-Run Equilibrium

Point 2 is not a permanent equilibrium because aggregate supply decreases to AS_2 once the costs of production rise in response to higher prices. Final equilibrium is at point 3, where the price level is P_3 and real GDP is \$500. Notice that

FIGURE 12.15 Aggregate Demand and Supply Equilibrium

The equilibrium level of price and real GDP is at the intersection of the *AD* and *AS* curves. Initially, equilibrium occurs at point 1, where the AD_1 and AS_1 curves intersect. Here the price level is P_1 and real GDP is \$500. If aggregate demand increases, moving from AD_1 to AD_2, in the short run there is a new equilibrium at point 2, where AD_2 intersects AS_1. The price level rises to P_2, and the equilibrium level of real GDP increases to \$600. Over time, as the costs of wages and other resources rise in response to higher prices, aggregate supply falls, moving AS_1 to AS_2. Final equilibrium occurs at point 3, where the AS_2 curve intersects the AD_2 curve. The price level rises to P_3, but the equilibrium level of real GDP returns to its initial level, \$500. In the long run, there is no relationship between prices and the equilibrium level of real GDP because the costs of resources adjust to changes in the level of prices.

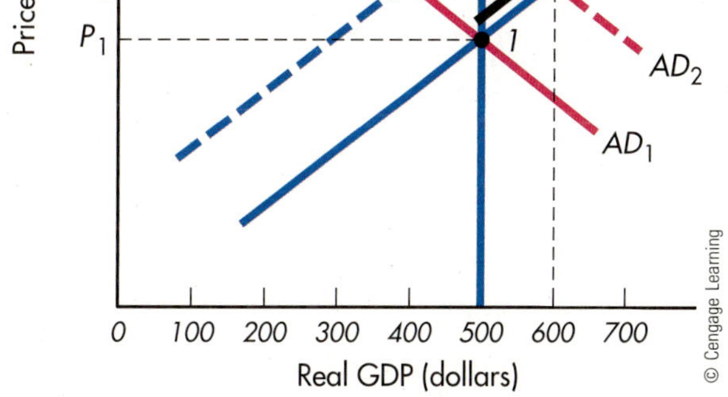

equilibrium here is the same as the initial equilibrium at point 1. Points 1 and 3 both lie along the *LRAS*. The initial shock to or change in the economy was an increase in aggregate demand. The change in aggregate expenditures initially led to higher output and higher prices. Over time, however, as resource costs rise and profit falls, output falls back to its original value.

We are not saying that the level of output never changes. The long-run aggregate supply curve shifts as technology changes and new supplies of resources are obtained. But the output change that results from a change in aggregate demand is a temporary, or short-run, phenomenon. The price level eventually adjusts, and output eventually returns to the potential level.

RECAP

1. The equilibrium level of price and real GDP is at the point where the aggregate demand and aggregate supply curves intersect.
2. In the short run, a shift in aggregate demand establishes a temporary equilibrium along the short-run aggregate supply curve.
3. In the long run, the short-run aggregate supply curve shifts so that changes in aggregate demand only affect the price level, not the equilibrium level of output or real GDP.

SUMMARY

What is aggregate demand?

1. Aggregate demand is the relation between aggregate expenditures and the price level.
2. Aggregate demand is the sum of consumption, investment, government spending, and net exports at alternative price levels.
3. Aggregate expenditures change with changes in the price level because of the wealth effect, the interest rate effect, and the international trade effect. These cause a movement along the *AD* curve.

What causes the aggregate demand curve to shift?

4. The aggregate demand (*AD*) curve shows the level of expenditures for real GDP at different price levels.
5. Because expenditures and prices move in opposite directions, the *AD* curve is negatively sloped.
6. The nonprice determinants of aggregate demand include expectations, foreign income and price levels, and government policy.

What is aggregate supply?

7. Aggregate supply is the relation between the quantity of real GDP produced and the price level.

Why does the short-run aggregate supply curve become steeper as real GDP increases?

8. As real GDP rises and the economy pushes closer to capacity output, the level of prices must rise to induce increased production.

Why is the long-run aggregate supply curve vertical?

9. The long-run aggregate supply curve is vertical at the potential level of real GDP because there is no effect of higher prices on output when an economy is producing at potential real GDP.

☐ d. An increase in long-run aggregate supply will decrease the equilibrium price level.
☐ e. A decrease in long-run aggregate supply will decrease the equilibrium level of real GDP.

8. Which of the following will increase aggregate supply?
   ☐ a. Oil prices increase as Saudi Arabia decreases its production.
   ☐ b. A change in computer chip technology increases productivity.
   ☐ c. The Consumer Price Index rises.
   ☐ d. The price level decreases.
   ☐ e. Consumers anticipate higher prices.

9. In September 2008, the U.S. unemployment rate rose to 10% while inflation declined sharply. This decline in inflation coupled with the huge increase in unemployment can only result from a(n)
   ☐ a. increase in aggregate demand.
   ☐ b. decrease in aggregate demand.
   ☐ c. increase in aggregate supply.
   ☐ d. decrease in aggregate supply.
   ☐ e. decrease in government spending.

10. Which of the following statements is true?
   ☐ a. In the long run, the short-run aggregate demand curve shifts so that changes in aggregate supply determine the price level, not the equilibrium level of income.
   ☐ b. In the long run, the short-run aggregate demand curve shifts so that changes in aggregate supply determine the equilibrium level of income, not the price level.
   ☐ c. In the long run, the equilibrium level of output never changes.
   ☐ d. In the long run, there is a positive relationship between the level of prices and the level of output.
   ☐ e. In the long run, the short-run aggregate supply curve shifts so that changes in aggregate demand determine the price level, not the equilibrium level of income.

Practice Questions and Problems

1. ____________ inflation is inflation caused by increasing demand for output.
2. If aggregate demand falls, the equilibrium level of income ____________ (rises, falls), unemployment ____________ (rises, falls), and the price level ____________ (rises, falls).
3. A(n) ____________ (increase, decrease) in aggregate supply leads to an increase in the equilibrium level of national income, a(n) ____________ (increase, decrease) in unemployment, and a(n) ____________ (increase, decrease) in the price level.
4. ____________ inflation is an increase in the price level caused by increased costs of production.
5. If wealth decreases, consumption (spending by households) ____________.
6. As foreign income rises, net exports ____________.
7. If a new trade agreement with Japan succeeds in opening Japanese markets to U.S. goods, net exports will ____________.
8. ____________ equal exports minus imports.
9. All other things being equal, economists expect consumption to ____________ (rise, fall, not change) as the population increases.
10. As taxation increases, consumption ____________ (rises, falls, does not change).
11. ____________ is business spending on capital goods and inventories.
12. As household wealth increases, consumption ____________ (increases, decreases).
13. List the five determinants of consumption.
    ____
    ____
    ____
    ____
    ____
14. As the cost of capital goods rises, the amount of investment ____________ (rises, falls).
15. When capacity utilization is high, investment tends to ____________ (rise, fall).
16. List the four determinants of investment.
    ____
    ____
    ____
    ____
17. When the domestic currency depreciates, imports ____________ (rise, fall).
18. The higher the domestic income, the ____________ (higher, lower) the net exports.
19. List the four determinants of net exports.
    ____
    ____
    ____
    ____
20. As the level of prices increases, the purchasing power of money ____________ (increases, decreases), and the real value of assets ____________ (increases, decreases). The ____________ effect, or real-balance effect, predicts that the real value of aggregate expenditures will then ____________ (rise, fall).
21. If domestic prices rise while foreign prices and foreign exchange rates remain constant, domestic goods will become ____________ (less expensive, more expensive) for foreigners. Net exports will ____________ (rise, fall), causing aggregate expenditures to ____________ (rise, fall).
22. If foreign prices fall, foreign goods become ____________ (less expensive, more expensive),

which causes ____________ (a movement along the aggregate demand curve, a shift to the left of the aggregate demand curve).

23. A fall in the domestic price level causes ____________ (a movement along the aggregate demand curve, a shift in aggregate demand to the left).
24. Positive expectations about the economy increase ____________ and ____________, which in turn ____________ (increases, decreases) aggregate demand.
25. Higher foreign incomes cause ____________ to rise, causing ____________ (a movement along the aggregate demand curve, a shift in aggregate demand to the right).
26. If the prices of output increase while all other prices remain unchanged, business profits will ____________ (increase, decrease) and producers will produce ____________ (more, less) output.
27. List the three nonprice determinants of short-run aggregate supply.

    ____

    ____

    ____
28. When the prices of resources fall, the short-run aggregate supply curve shifts to the ____________.
29. In the long run, there ____________ (is, is not) a relationship between the level of prices and the level of output.

Exercises and Applications

I Aggregate Demand and Its Determinants

Now that you have finished this chapter, you should be able to predict the effect on aggregate demand when one of its determinants changes. In the following exercise, decide which of the spending components each event affects, whether it increased or decreased the component, and whether it increased or decreased aggregate demand. Remember the determinants of each component of aggregate demand:

Consumption: income, wealth, expectations, demographics, taxes

Investment: interest rate, cost of capital goods, technology, capacity utilization

Government spending: set by government authorities

Net exports: foreign and domestic income and prices, exchange rates, government policy

The first answer is provided for you as an example.

1. The Federal Reserve, fearing future weakness in the economy, decreases interest rates.
2. In the wake of the Euro zone debt crisis, the dollar appreciates against the euro.
3. Consumer spending increases in the first five months of the year.
4. Foreign incomes rise.
5. The population increases more quickly.
6. Factories note a decline in the rate of capacity utilization.
7. Congress imposes a nationwide sales tax on retail goods and services.
8. The cost of capital goods decreases.

Component	Effect on Component	Effect on Aggregate Demand
1. Investment	Increase	Increase
2. ________	________	________
3. ________	________	________
4. ________	________	________
5. ________	________	________
6. ________	________	________
7. ________	________	________
8. ________	________	________

II A Long-Run Analysis of the Effects of a Slump in Productivity

Many people have been concerned about the slower growth of productivity in recent years. Suppose that the growth of productivity in the United States not only slows but actually decreases. This could result from declines in workers' basic skills that some educators believe are due to a lack of students' adequate preparation in the nation's high schools. What will happen to the equilibrium price level and real GDP in the long run? Use a graph to analyze this problem. Be sure to label your axes.

You can find further practice tests in the Online Quiz at: www.cengagebrain.com

financed by tax increases are moderated. The actual magnitude of the effect is the subject of debate among economists. Most argue that the evidence in the United States indicates that tax increases have a fairly small effect on aggregate supply.

1.d. Government Spending Financed by Borrowing

The standard multiplier analysis of government spending does not differentiate among the different methods of financing that spending. Yet you just saw how taxation can offset at least part of the expansionary effect of higher government spending. Borrowing to finance government spending can also limit the increase in aggregate demand.

A government borrows funds by selling bonds to the public. These bonds represent debt that must be repaid at a future date. Debt is, in a way, a kind of substitute for current taxes. Instead of increasing current taxes to finance higher spending, the government borrows the savings of households and businesses. Of course, the debt will mature and have to be repaid. This means that taxes will have to be higher in the future in order to provide the government with the funds to pay off the debt.

Current government borrowing, then, implies higher future taxes. This can limit the expansionary effect of increased government spending. If households and businesses take higher future taxes into account, they tend to save more today so that they will be able to pay those taxes in the future. And as saving today increases, consumption today falls.

1.e. Crowding Out

crowding out: a drop in consumption or investment spending caused by government spending

Expansionary fiscal policy can crowd out private-sector spending; that is, an increase in government spending can reduce consumption and investment. **Crowding out** is usually discussed in the context of government spending financed by borrowing rather than by taxing. Though we have just seen how future taxes can cause consumption to fall today, investment can also be affected. Increases in government borrowing drive up interest rates. As interest rates go up, investment falls. This sort of indirect crowding out works through the bond market. The U.S. government borrows by selling Treasury bonds or bills. Because the government is not a profit-making institution, it does not

These Canadian savings bonds represent a debt that must be repaid at a future date.

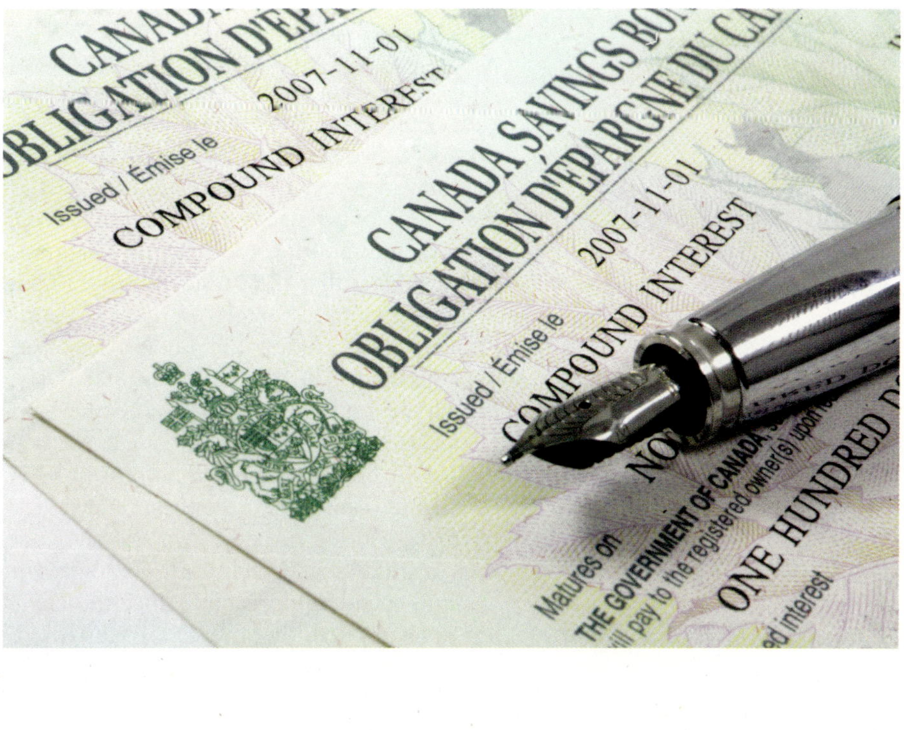

V. J. Matthew/Shutterstock.com

have to earn a profitable return from the money it raises by selling bonds. A corporation does, however. When interest rates rise, fewer corporations offer new bonds to raise investment funds because the cost of repaying the bond debt may exceed the rate of return on the investment.

Crowding out is important in principle, but economists have never demonstrated conclusively that its effects can substantially alter spending in the private sector. Still, you should be aware of the possibility to understand the potential shortcomings of changes in government spending and taxation.

RECAP

1. Fiscal policy refers to government spending and taxation.
2. By increasing spending or cutting taxes, a government can close the GDP gap.
3. If government spending and taxes increase by the same amount, equilibrium real GDP rises.
4. If a tax increase affects aggregate supply, then a balanced-budget change in fiscal policy will have a smaller expansionary effect on equilibrium real GDP than otherwise.
5. Current government borrowing reduces current spending in the private sector if people increase current saving in order to pay future tax liabilities.
6. Increased government borrowing can crowd private borrowers out of the bond market so that investment falls.

2. FISCAL POLICY IN THE UNITED STATES

Our discussion of fiscal policy assumes that policy is made at the federal level. In the modern economy this is a reasonable assumption. This was not the case before the 1930s, however. Before the Depression, the federal government limited its activities largely to national defense and foreign policy and left other areas of government policy to the individual states. With the growth of the importance of the federal government in fiscal policy has come a growth in the role of the federal budget process.

2.a. The Budget Process

Fiscal policy in the United States is the product of a complex process that involves both the executive and legislative branches of government (see Figure 13.3). The fiscal year for the U.S. government begins October 1 of one year and ends September 30 of the next. The budget process begins each spring when the president directs the federal agencies to prepare their budgets for the fiscal year that starts almost 18 months later. The agencies submit their budget requests to the Office of Management and Budget (OMB) by early September. The OMB reviews and modifies each agency's request and consolidates all of the proposals into a budget that the president presents to Congress in January.

Once Congress receives the president's budget, the Congressional Budget Office (CBO) studies the budget and committees modify it before funds are appropriated. The budget is evaluated in Budget Committee hearings in both the House of Representatives and the Senate. In addition, the CBO reports to Congress on the validity of the economic assumptions made in the president's budget. A budget resolution is passed by April 15 that sets out major expenditures and estimated revenues. (Revenues are estimated because future tax payments can never be known exactly.) The resolution is followed by *reconciliation*, a process in which each committee of Congress must coordinate relevant tax and spending decisions. Once the reconciliation process is completed, funds are appropriated. The process is supposed to end before Congress recesses for the summer, at the end of June. When talking about the federal budget, the

FIGURE 13.3 The Making of U.S. Fiscal Policy

The flow chart shows the policy-making process. Start with the president and follow the arrows in order. Although the dates are approximate, the process of setting the federal budget involves these stages and participants.

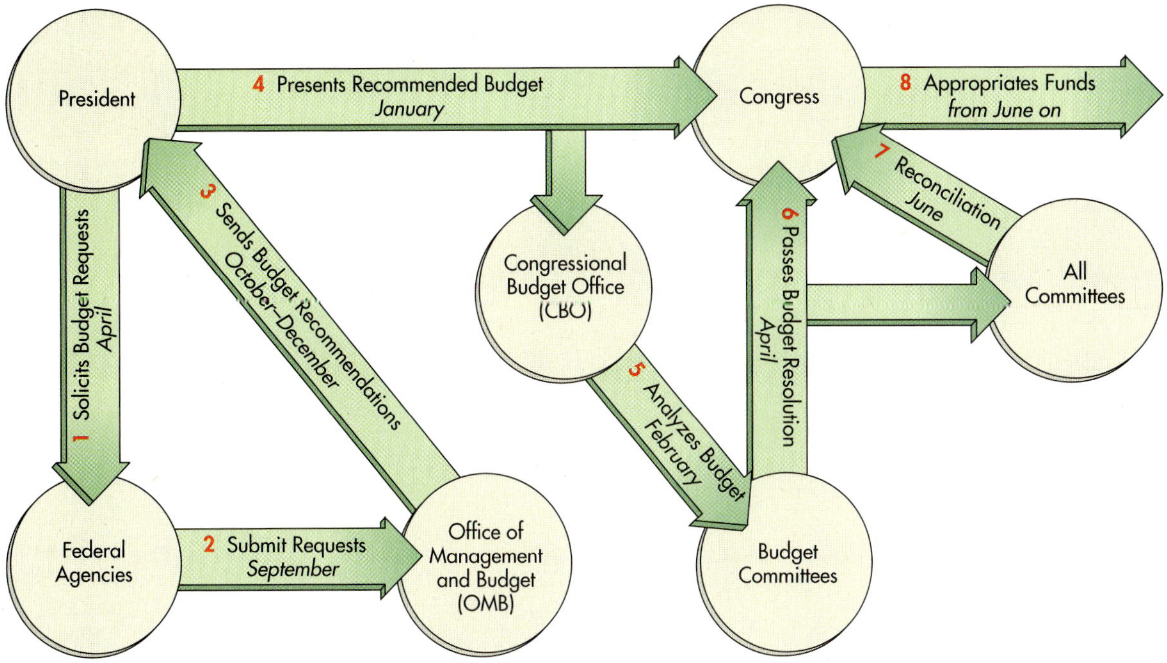

monetary amounts of various categories of expenditures are so huge that they are often difficult to comprehend. But if you were to divide up the annual budget by the number of individual taxpayers, you would come up with an average individual statement that might make more sense, as shown in the Economic Insight "The Taxpayer's Federal Government Credit Card Statement" (see page 283).

The federal budget is determined as much by politics as by economics. Politicians respond to different groups of voters by supporting different government programs regardless of the needed fiscal policy. It is the political response to constituents that tends to drive up federal budget deficits (the difference between government expenditures and tax revenues), not the need for expansionary fiscal policy. As a result, deficits have become commonplace.

2

How has U.S. fiscal policy changed over time?

2.b. The Historical Record

The U.S. government has grown dramatically since the early part of the century. Figure 13.4 shows federal revenues and expenditures over time. Figure 13.5 places the growth of government in perspective by plotting U.S. government spending as a percentage of GDP over time. Before the Great Depression, federal spending was approximately 3 percent of the GDP; by the end of the Depression, it had risen to almost 10 percent. The ratio of spending to GDP reached its peak during World War II, when federal spending hit 45 percent of the GDP. After the war, the ratio fell dramatically and then slowly increased to about 25 percent today.

discretionary fiscal policy: changes in government spending and taxation aimed at achieving a policy goal

automatic stabilizer: an element of fiscal policy that changes automatically as income changes

Fiscal policy has two components: discretionary fiscal policy and automatic stabilizers. **Discretionary fiscal policy** refers to changes in government spending and taxation aimed at achieving a policy goal. **Automatic stabilizers** are elements of fiscal policy that automatically change in value as national income changes. Figures 13.4 and 13.5 suggest that government spending is dominated by growth over time. But there is no indication here of discretionary changes in

FIGURE 13.4 U.S. Government Revenues and Expenditures

Revenues are total revenues of the U.S. government in each fiscal year. Expenditures are total spending of the U.S. government in each fiscal year. The difference between the two curves equals the U.S. budget deficit (when expenditures exceed revenues) or surplus (when revenues exceed expenditures).

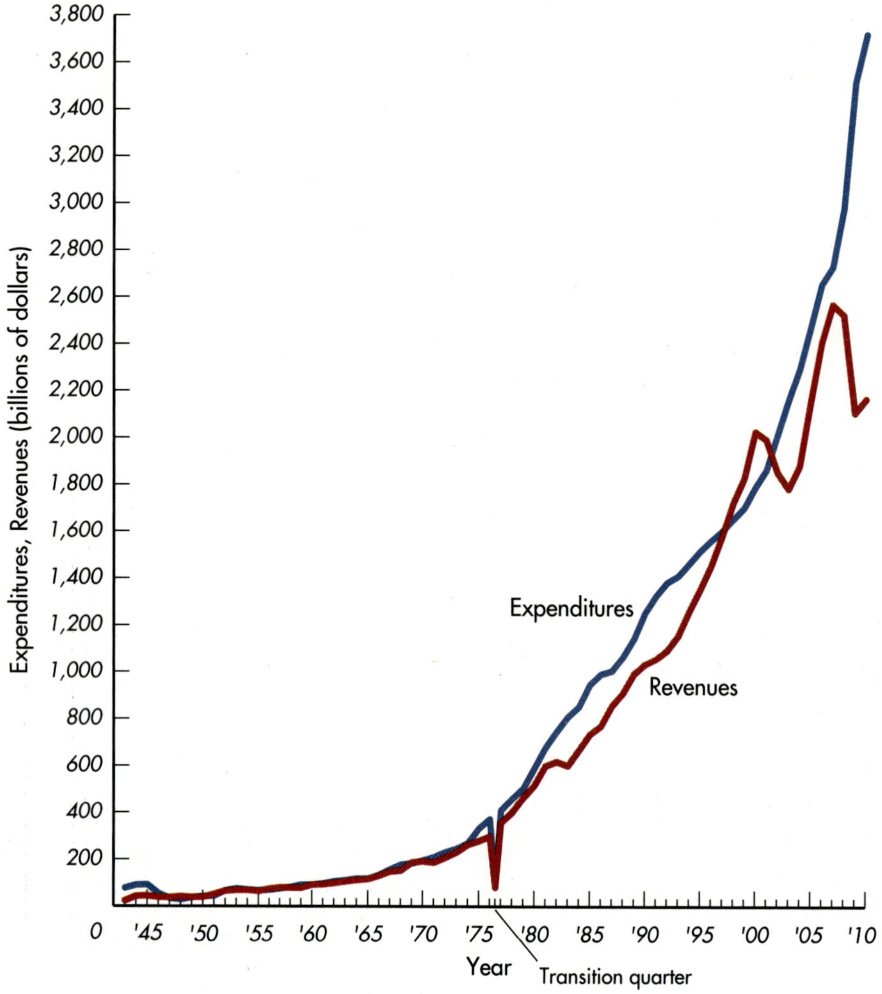

Source: Data are drawn from *Statistical Abstract of the United States*, 2012.

fiscal policy—that is, changes in government spending and taxation aimed at meeting specific policy goals. Perhaps a better way to evaluate the fiscal policy record is in terms of the budget deficit. Government expenditures can rise, but the effect on aggregate demand could be offset by a simultaneous increase in taxes so that there is no expansionary effect on the equilibrium level of national income. By looking at the deficit, we see the combined spending and tax policy results that are missing if only government expenditures are considered.

Figure 13.6 illustrates the pattern of the U.S. federal deficit and the deficit as a percentage of GDP over time. Figure 13.6(a) shows that the United States ran close to a balanced budget for much of the 1950s and 1960s. There were large deficits associated with financing World War II and then large deficits resulting from fiscal policy decisions in the 1970s, 1980s, and 1990s. By 1998, however, the first surplus since 1969 was recorded. However, by 2002, budget deficits had returned. Figure 13.6(b) shows that the deficit as a percentage of GDP was much larger during World War II than in recent years.

The deficit increase in the mid-1970s was a product of a recession that cut the growth of tax revenues. Historically, aside from wartime, budget deficits

FIGURE 13.5 U.S. Government Expenditures as a Percentage of Gross Domestic Product

The U.S. federal government spending as a percentage of the GDP reached a high of 44 percent in 1943 and 1944. Discounting wartime spending and cutbacks after the war, you can see the upward trend in U.S. government spending, which constituted a larger and larger share of the GDP until the early 1980s. More recently, government spending has grown as a fraction of GDP due to spending associated with the financial crisis and recession beginning in 2007.

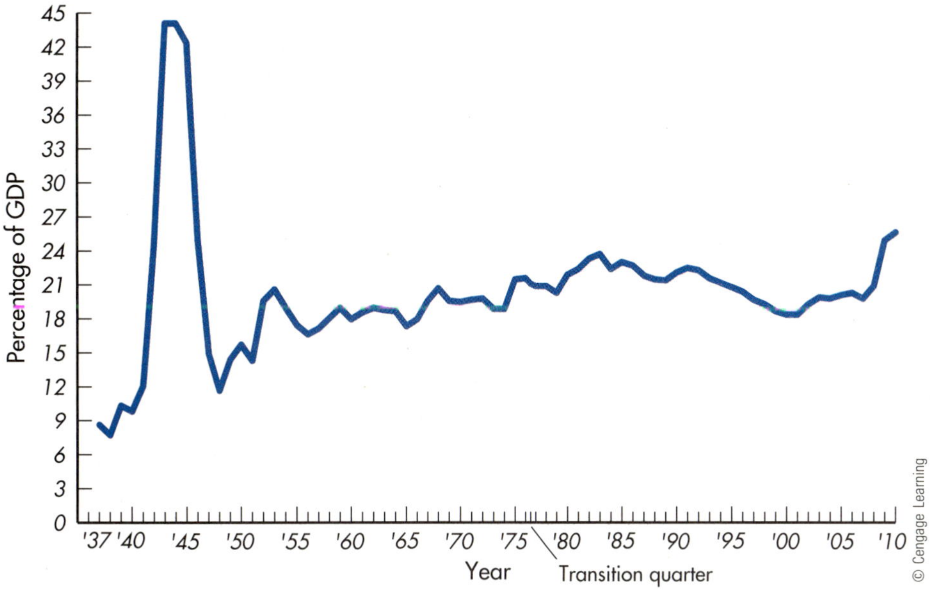

ECONOMIC INSIGHT

The Taxpayer's Federal Government Credit Card Statement

Suppose the U.S. government's expenditures and revenues were accounted for annually to each individual income taxpayer like a credit card statement. For 2011, the statement would look like the one at the right.

Statement for 2011 Budget Year	
Previous balance	$42,508.48
New purchases	
Defense	$5,178.58
Social Security	$5,166.76
Medicare	$3,844.68
Medicaid	$1,913.89
Other	$9,078.98
Total spending	$25,182.93
Payments received	
Individual income and social security taxes	$9,672.49
Corporate income taxes	$2,569.03
Other	$9,069.70
Total payments	$21,311.23
Finance charge	$2,101.32
New balance due	$48,988.89

FIGURE 13.6 The U.S. Deficit

As part (a) shows, since 1940, the U.S. government has rarely shown a surplus. For much of the 1950s and 1960s, the United States was close to a balanced budget. Part (b) shows the federal deficit as a percentage of GDP. The deficits during the 1950s and 1960s generally were small. The early 1980s were a time of rapid growth in the federal budget deficit, and this is reflected in the growth of the deficit as a percentage of GDP. From the late 1990s into the 2000s, there was a brief period of budget surpluses.

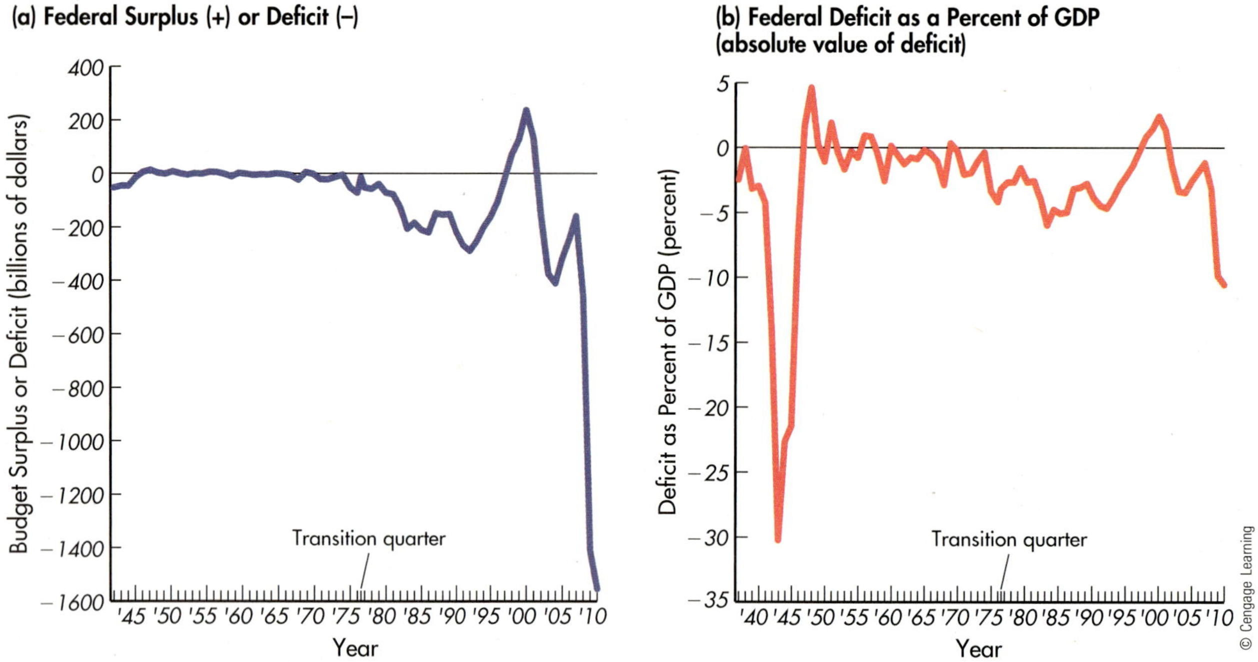

increase the most during recessions. When real GDP falls, tax revenues go down, and government spending on unemployment and welfare benefits goes up. These are examples of automatic stabilizers in action. As income falls, taxes fall and personal benefit payments rise to partially offset the effect of the drop in income. The rapid growth of the deficit in the 1980s involved more than the recessions in 1980 and 1982, however. The economy grew rapidly after the 1982 recession ended, but so did the fiscal deficit. The increase in the deficit was the product of a rapid increase in government spending to fund new programs and enlarge existing programs while taxes were held constant. The reduction in the deficit in the late 1990s was the result of strong economic growth that generated surprisingly large tax revenue gains combined with only moderate government spending increases. However, with the recession of 2001, the country soon returned to deficits. The recession that began at the end of 2007, which was associated with the financial crisis, resulted in dramatic increases in government spending that led to the highest deficits since the 1940s.

2.c. Deficits and the National Debt

3

What are the effects of budget deficits?

The large federal deficits of the 1980s and 1990s led many observers to question whether a deficit can harm the economy. Figure 13.6 shows how the fiscal deficit has changed over time. One major implication of a large deficit is the resulting increase in the national debt—that is, the total stock of government bonds outstanding. Table 13.1 lists data on the debt of the United States. The total debt more than doubled between 1980 and 1986. Column 3 shows debt as a percentage of GDP. During World War II, the debt was greater than the GDP for five years. Despite the talk of "unprecedented" federal deficits in the 1980s and 1990s, clearly the ratio of the debt to GDP was by no means unprecedented.

Table 13.1 Debt of the U.S. Government (dollar amounts in billions)

(1) Year	(2) Total Debt	(3) Debt/GDP (percent)	(4) Net Interest	(5) Interest/Government Spending (percent)
1958	$ 279.7	63	$ 5.6	6.8
1960	290.5	57	6.9	7.5
1962	302.9	55	6.9	6.5
1964	316.1	50	8.2	6.9
1966	328.5	44	9.4	7.0
1968	368.7	43	11.1	6.2
1970	380.9	39	14.4	7.4
1972	435.9	38	15.5	6.7
1974	483.9	34	21.4	8.0
1976	629.0	37	26.7	7.3
1978	776.6	36	35.4	7.9
1980	909.1	34	52.5	9.1
1982	1,137.3	36	85.0	11.6
1984	1,564.7	42	111.1	13.2
1986	2,120.6	50	136.0	13.7
1988	2,601.3	54	151.8	14.3
1990	3,206.6	59	184.2	14.7
1992	4,002.1	68	199.4	14.4
1994	4,643.7	70	203.0	13.9
1996	5,181.9	69	241.1	15.5
1998	5,478.7	63	241.2	14.6
2000	5,629.0	57	223.0	12.5
2002	6,198.4	60	171.0	8.5
2004	7,354.7	64	160.2	7.0
2006	8,451.4	65	226.6	8.5
2008	9,986.1	69	252.8	8.5
2010	13,786.6	94	187.8	5.0
2011	15,476.2	102	206.7	5.4

We have not yet answered the question of whether deficits are bad. To do so, we have to consider their potential effects.

2.c.1. **Deficits, Interest Rates, and Investment** Because government deficits mean government borrowing and debt, many economists argue that deficits raise interest rates as lenders require a higher interest rate to induce them to hold more government debt. Increased government borrowing raises interest rates, which in turn can depress investment. (Remember that as interest rates rise, the rate of return on investment drops, along with the incentive to invest.) What happens when government borrowing crowds out private investment? Lower investment means fewer capital goods in the future, so deficits lower the level of output in the economy both today and in the future. In this sense, deficits are potentially bad.

2.c.2. **Deficits and International Trade** If government deficits raise real interest rates (the nominal interest rate minus the expected inflation rate), they also may have an effect on international trade. A higher real return on

U.S. securities makes those securities more attractive to foreign investors. As the foreign demand for U.S. securities increases, so does the demand for U.S. dollars in exchange for Japanese yen, British pounds, and other foreign currencies. As the demand for dollars increases, the dollar *appreciates* in value on the foreign exchange market. This means that the dollar becomes more expensive to foreigners while foreign currency becomes cheaper to U.S. residents. This kind of change in the exchange rate encourages U.S. residents to buy more foreign goods and foreign residents to buy fewer U.S. goods. Ultimately, then, as deficits and government debt increase, U.S. net exports fall. Such foreign trade effects are another potentially bad effect of deficits.

2.c.3. **Interest Payments on the National Debt** The national debt is the stock of government bonds outstanding. It is the product of past and current budget deficits. As the size of the debt increases, the interest that must be paid on the debt tends to rise. Column 4 of Table 13.1 lists the amount of interest paid on the debt; column 5 lists the interest as a percentage of government expenditures. The numbers in both columns have risen steadily over time and only recently experienced a brief fall before rising again. The decrease shown for 2010 was a result of much lower interest rates that existed at the time, but the interest cost of the debt started to grow again in 2011 and may return to much higher levels when the interest rate rises.

The steady increase in the interest cost of the national debt is an aspect of fiscal deficits that worries some people. However, to the extent that U.S. citizens hold government bonds, we owe the debt to ourselves. The tax liability of funding the interest payments is offset by the interest income bondholders earn. In this case, there is no net change in national wealth when the national debt changes.

Of course, we do not owe the national debt just to ourselves. Over time, the share of U.S. debt held by foreigners has grown. The United States is the world's largest national financial market, and many U.S. securities, including government bonds, are held by foreign residents. In 1965, foreign holdings of the U.S. national debt amounted to about 5 percent of the outstanding debt. Today, this figure has risen to about 32 percent. Because the tax liability for paying the interest on the debt falls on U.S. taxpayers, the greater the payments made to foreigners, the lower the wealth of U.S. residents, other things being equal.

Other things are not equal, however. To understand the real impact of foreign holdings on the economy, we must evaluate what the economy would have been like if the debt had not been sold to foreign investors. If the foreign savings placed in U.S. bonds allowed the United States to increase investment and its productive capacity beyond what would have been possible in the absence of foreign lending, then the country could very well be better off for selling government bonds to foreigners. The presence of foreign funds may keep interest rates lower than they would otherwise be, preventing the substantial crowding out associated with an increase in the national debt.

So while deficits are potentially bad due to the crowding out of investment, larger trade deficits with the rest of the world, and greater interest costs of the debt, we cannot generally say that all deficits are bad. It depends on what benefit the deficit provides. If the deficit spending allowed for greater productivity than would have occurred otherwise, the benefits may outweigh the costs. The financial crisis of 2008 is a prime example of an occasion when the fiscal policy of governments around the world involved a dramatic increase in spending, with the result that budget deficits also increased substantially. However, the rationale of these governments was that the cost of not stimulating the economy would have been a much worse recession with greater unemployment and even lower incomes. The benefits of deficit spending were widely thought to outweigh the costs.

2.d. Automatic Stabilizers

The discussion thus far has focused largely on discretionary fiscal policy, or the changes in government spending and taxing that policymakers make consciously. *Automatic stabilizers* are the elements of fiscal policy that change automatically as income changes. Automatic stabilizers partially offset changes in income: As income falls, automatic stabilizers increase spending; as income rises, automatic stabilizers decrease spending. Any program that responds to fluctuations in the business cycle in a way that moderates the effects of those fluctuations is an automatic stabilizer. Examples are progressive income taxes and transfer payments.

In our examples of tax changes, we have been using *lump-sum taxes*—taxes that are a flat dollar amount regardless of income. However, income taxes are determined as a percentage of income. In the United States, the federal income tax is a **progressive tax:** As income rises, so does the rate of taxation. A person with a very low income pays no income tax, whereas a person with a high income can pay more than a third of that income in taxes. Countries use different rates of taxation on income. Taxes can be **regressive** (the tax rate falls as income rises) or **proportional** (the tax rate is constant as income rises). But most countries, including the United States, use a progressive tax, with the percentage of income paid as taxes rising with taxable income.

progressive tax:
a tax whose rate rises as income rises

regressive tax:
a tax whose rate falls as income rises

proportional tax:
a tax whose rate is constant as income rises

Progressive income taxes act as an automatic stabilizer. As income falls, so does the average tax rate. Suppose a household earning \$60,000 must pay 30 percent of its income (\$18,000) in taxes, leaving 70 percent of its income (\$42,000) for spending. If that household's income drops to \$40,000, and the tax rate falls to 25 percent, the household has 75 percent of its income (\$30,000) available for spending. But if the tax rate is 30 percent at all levels of income, the household earning \$40,000 would have only 70 percent of its income (\$28,000) to spend. By allowing a greater percentage of earned income to be spent, progressive taxes help offset the effect of lower income on spending.

Industrial countries all have progressive federal income tax systems. For instance, the tax rate in Japan starts at 5 percent for low-income households and rises to a maximum of 40 percent for high-income households. U.S. individual income taxes start at 0 percent and rise to a maximum of 35 percent. The United Kingdom's tax system ranges from 0 to 50 percent, whereas taxes in Germany rise from 0 to 45 percent and in France from 0 to 50 percent.

Recall that a transfer payment is a payment to one person that is funded by taxing others. Food stamps, welfare benefits, and unemployment benefits are all government transfer payments: Current taxpayers provide the funds to pay those who qualify for the programs. Transfer payments that use income to establish eligibility act as automatic stabilizers. In a recession, as income falls, more people qualify for food stamps or welfare benefits, raising the level of transfer payments.

Unemployment insurance is also an automatic stabilizer. As unemployment rises, more workers receive unemployment benefits. Unemployment benefits tend to rise in a recession and fall during an expansion. This countercyclical pattern of benefit payments offsets the effect of business cycle fluctuations on consumption.

RECAP

1. Fiscal policy in the United States is a product of the budget process.
2. Federal spending in the United States has grown rapidly over time, from just 3 percent of the GDP before the Great Depression to approximately 18 percent of the GDP today.
3. Government budget deficits can hurt the economy through their effects on interest rates and private investment, net exports, and the tax burden on current and future taxpayers.
4. Automatic stabilizers are government programs that are already in place and that respond automatically to fluctuations in the business cycle, moderating the effect of those fluctuations.

3. FISCAL POLICY IN DIFFERENT COUNTRIES

4

How does fiscal policy differ across countries?

A country's fiscal policy reflects its philosophy toward government spending and taxation. In this section, we present comparative data that demonstrate the variety of fiscal policies in the world.

3.a. Government Spending

Our discussion to this point has centered on U.S. fiscal policy. But fiscal policy and the role of government in the economy can be very different across countries. Government has played an increasingly larger role in the major industrial countries over time. Table 13.2 shows how government spending has gone up as a percentage of output in five industrial nations. In every case, government spending accounted for a larger percentage of output in 2008 than it did more than 100 years earlier. For instance, in 1880, government spending was only 6 percent of the GNP in Sweden. By 1929, it had risen to 8 percent, and by 2010, to 53 percent. In all of the countries in the table, the government spending share increased from 2007, the start of the financial crisis, to 2010. This could reflect the combination of two factors: a decline in the growth rate of overall output, and an increase in government spending as a part of stimulus and/or bailout efforts.

Table 13.2 Share of Government Spending in Output in Selected Industrial Countries, 1880, 1929, and 2010 (percent)

Year	France	Germany	Sweden	United Kingdom	United States
1880	15	10*	6	10	8
1929	19	31	8	24	10
2010	56	47	53	51	42

*1881.

Source: Data from World Bank, *World Development Report*, Washington, DC, various issues and OECD Stat Extracts.

Tony Metaxas/Asia Images/Getty Images

China spends 31 percent of its budget on social services like education—substantially more than most developing countries.

Historically in industrial countries, the growth of government spending has been matched by growth in revenues. But in the 1960s, government spending began to grow faster than revenues, creating increasingly larger debts for national governments.

Developing countries have not shown the uniform growth in government spending found in industrial countries. In fact, in some developing countries (e.g., Chile, the Dominican Republic, and Peru), government spending is a smaller percentage of GDP today than it was 20 years ago. And we find a greater variation in the role of government in developing countries.

One important difference between the typical developed country and the typical developing country is that government plays a larger role in investment spending in the developing country. One reason for this difference is that state-owned enterprises account for a larger percentage of economic activity in developing countries than they do in developed countries. Also, developing countries usually rely more on government than the private sector to build their infrastructure—schools, roads, hospitals—than do developed countries.

GLOBAL BUSINESS INSIGHT

Value-Added Tax

A value-added tax (VAT) is a tax levied on all sales of goods and services at each stage of production. As implied by the name, the tax applies only to the value added at each stage, and so a firm that pays VATs will pay tax only on the value that it added to the good or service that it sells. If a firm sells melons at a fruit stand, the VAT it pays is based on the difference between the cost the firm paid for the melons and the sales price it charges to its customers who buy the fruit. Of course, the customers bear the cost of the VAT, as it is built into the price they must pay.

As the accompanying map indicates, VATs are very popular around the world. Many countries adopted VATs in the 1990s. It is clear that there are more countries that use VATs than do not. Such a tax has its advantages. One important consideration is that a VAT is a tax on consumption. Anyone who buys goods and services will contribute to the government's VAT revenue. Thus, VATs are very powerful revenue generators. Those individuals who evade income taxes and pay less than their legal obligation will not escape the VAT. For instance, a criminal who earns income illegally and pays no tax on that income will be taxed on all legal goods and services that he or she purchases. In this sense, there is a certain attractiveness to taxing consumption rather than income. But a VAT also acts as a regressive tax in that a poor person would tend to pay a higher fraction of income as VAT than a rich person. It is important to realize that no country relies strictly on a VAT for government revenue. VATs are part of an overall government tax policy that attempts to incorporate fairness along with a need to raise sufficient revenue to finance public expenditures.

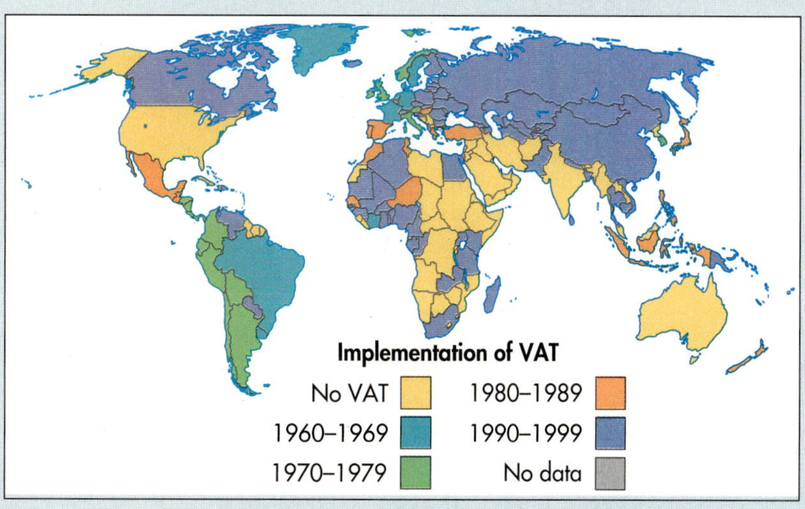

Source: From IMF Survey, *International Monetary Fund*, Vol. 29, No. 9, May 8, 2000, p. 156. Reprinted with permission of International Monetary Fund.

How a government spends its money is a function of its income. Here, we find differences not only between industrial and developing countries but also among developing countries. Consider an industrial country, the United States, and a low-income developing country, China. Although standards of living are lowest in the poorest countries, these countries do not have the resources to spend on social services (e.g., education, health, housing, social security, welfare). The United States spends 43 percent of its budget on social security, health, and education programs. China spends 31 percent of its budget on these programs, and that is substantially more than most developing countries.

3.b. Taxation

There are two different types of taxes: *direct taxes* (on individuals and firms) and *indirect taxes* (on goods and services). Personal income taxes are much more important in industrial countries than in developing countries. Why? Because personal taxes are hard to collect in agricultural nations, where a large percentage of household production is for personal consumption. Taxes on businesses are easier to collect, and thus are more important in developing countries.

That industrial countries are better able to afford social programs is reflected in the great disparity in social security taxes between industrial countries and developing countries. With so many workers living near the subsistence level in the poorest countries, their governments simply cannot tax workers for retirement and health security programs.

Taxes on international trade are very important in developing countries. Because goods arriving or leaving a country must pass through customs inspection, export and import taxes are relatively easy to collect in comparison with income taxes. In general, developing countries depend more heavily on indirect taxes on goods and services than do developed countries.

value-added tax (VAT): a general sales tax collected at each stage of production

Many countries have "goods and services" taxes. Of these, 65 percent are value-added taxes in industrial countries, whereas 61 percent of developing country goods and services taxes come from value-added taxes. A **value-added tax (VAT)** is an indirect tax imposed on each sale at each stage of production. Each seller from the first stage of production onward collects the VAT from the buyer and then deducts any VATs it has paid in buying its inputs. The difference is remitted to the government. See the Global Business Insight, "Value-Added Tax," for additional details. From time to time, Congress has debated the merits of a VAT in the United States, but it has never approved this kind of tax.

RECAP

1. Over time, government spending has become more important in industrial countries.
2. Governments in developing countries typically play a larger role in investment spending in their economies than do the governments of developed countries.
3. Developing countries depend more on indirect taxes on goods and services as a source of revenue than on direct taxes on individuals and businesses.
4. Value-added taxes are general sales taxes that are collected at every stage of production.

SUMMARY

How can fiscal policy eliminate a GDP gap?

1. A GDP gap can be closed by increasing government spending or by cutting taxes.
2. Government spending affects aggregate expenditures directly; taxes affect aggregate expenditures indirectly through their effect on consumption.
3. Aggregate expenditures must rise to bring equilibrium real GDP up to potential real GDP—to eliminate the GDP gap.
4. An increase in government spending matched by an increase in taxes raises equilibrium spending and real GDP.
5. If the public expects to pay higher taxes as a result of government borrowing, then the expansionary effects of government deficits may be reduced.
6. Government borrowing can crowd out private spending by raising interest rates and reducing investments.

How has U.S. fiscal policy changed over time?

7. Fiscal policy in the United States is a product of the budget process.
8. Federal government spending in the United States has increased from just 3 percent of the GDP before the Great Depression to about 18 percent of the GDP today.
9. Fiscal policy has two components: discretionary fiscal policy and automatic stabilizers.

What are the effects of budget deficits?

10. Budget deficits, through their effects on interest rates, international trade, and the national debt, can reduce investment, output, net exports, and national wealth.
11. Progressive taxes and transfer payments are automatic stabilizers, or elements of fiscal policy that change automatically as national income changes.

How does fiscal policy differ across countries?

12. Industrial countries spend a much larger percentage of their government budget for social programs than do developing countries.
13. Industrial countries depend more on direct taxes and less on indirect taxes than do developing countries.

EXERCISES

1. What is the role of aggregate demand in eliminating the GDP gap? How does the slope of the *AS* curve affect the fiscal policy actions necessary to eliminate the GDP gap?
2. Briefly describe the process of setting the federal budget in the United States. What is the time lag between the start of the process and the point at which the money is actually spent?
3. In what ways are government deficits harmful to the economy?
4. Define and give three examples of automatic stabilizers.
5. Briefly describe the major differences between fiscal policy in industrial countries and that in developing countries.
6. Why will real GDP tend to rise when government spending and taxes rise by the same amount?
7. How can a larger government fiscal deficit cause a larger international trade deficit?
8. Why do government budget deficits grow during recessions?
9. Taxes can be progressive, regressive, or proportional. Define each and briefly offer an argument for why income taxes are usually progressive.

STUDY GUIDE FOR CHAPTER 13

Key Term Match

Match each term with its corresponding definition by placing the appropriate letter next to the corresponding number.

A. crowding out
B. discretionary fiscal policy
C. automatic stabilizer
D. progressive tax
E. regressive tax
F. proportional tax
G. value-added tax

____ 1. a tax whose rate rises as income rises

____ 2. a drop in consumption or investment spending caused by government spending

____ 3. a tax whose rate falls as income rises

____ 4. an element of fiscal policy that changes automatically as income changes

____ 5. changes in government spending and taxation aimed at achieving a policy goal

____ 6. a general sales tax collected at each stage of production

____ 7. a tax whose rate is constant as income rises

Quick-Check Quiz

1. Taxes affect the level of aggregate demand primarily through changing the level of ____________, which alters ____________.
   - ☐ a. disposable income; consumption
   - ☐ b. disposable income; investment
   - ☐ c. disposable income; government spending
   - ☐ d. government spending; consumption
   - ☐ e. government spending; investment

2. A(n) ____________ in government spending or a(n) ____________ in taxes lowers the level of expenditures at every price and shifts the aggregate demand curve to the ____________.
   - ☐ a. decrease; increase; right
   - ☐ b. decrease; increase; left
   - ☐ c. increase; decrease; right
   - ☐ d. increase; decrease; left
   - ☐ e. decrease; decrease; left

3. A decrease in taxes may cause aggregate supply to shift to the ____________, causing the level of prices to ____________ and the level of national income to ____________.
   - ☐ a. right; fall; rise
   - ☐ b. right; fall; fall
   - ☐ c. right; rise; rise
   - ☐ d. left; fall; rise
   - ☐ e. left; rise; fall

4. Increases in government spending financed by ____________ may drive interest rates ____________ and decrease ____________.
   - ☐ a. taxes; up; consumption
   - ☐ b. taxes; down; consumption
   - ☐ c. borrowing; down; investment
   - ☐ d. borrowing; up; investment
   - ☐ e. borrowing; down; net exports

5. Expansionary fiscal policy refers to
   - ☐ a. decreasing government spending and decreasing taxes.
   - ☐ b. decreasing government spending and increasing taxes.
   - ☐ c. increasing government spending and increasing taxes.
   - ☐ d. increasing government spending and decreasing taxes.
   - ☐ e. increasing government spending and increasing the money supply.

6. Discretionary fiscal policy refers to
   - ☐ a. government spending at the discretion of the president.
   - ☐ b. government spending at the discretion of the Congress.
   - ☐ c. elements of fiscal policy that automatically change in value as national income changes.
   - ☐ d. government spending at the discretion of the president and the Congress.
   - ☐ e. changes in government spending and taxation aimed at achieving an economic policy goal.

7. Which of the following is *not* a harmful effect of government deficits?
   - ☐ a. lower private investment as a result of crowding out
   - ☐ b. lower net exports as a result of the appreciation of the dollar
   - ☐ c. increased investment caused by foreign savings placed in U.S. bonds
   - ☐ d. an increase in saving caused by anticipated future increases in taxes
   - ☐ e. an increase in imports

8. Which of the following is *not* an example of an automatic stabilizer?
   - ☐ a. unemployment insurance
   - ☐ b. lump-sum taxes
   - ☐ c. progressive taxes
   - ☐ d. food stamps
   - ☐ e. welfare benefits

9. Which of the following statements is true?
   - ☐ a. Developing countries rely more heavily on direct taxes than do developed countries.
   - ☐ b. Developing countries rely more heavily on indirect taxes than do developed countries.
   - ☐ c. Developing countries rely more heavily on personal income taxes than do developed countries.
   - ☐ d. Developing countries rely more heavily on social security taxes than do developed countries.
   - ☐ e. Developed countries rely more heavily on import and export taxes than do developing countries.

10. Which of the following statements is true?
    - ☐ a. The United States imposes value-added taxes.
    - ☐ b. An export tax is an example of a direct tax.
    - ☐ c. Developing countries spend more on social programs than industrial nations because their needs are greater.
    - ☐ d. Personal taxes are hard to collect in low-income, developing countries.
    - ☐ e. Personal income taxes are indirect taxes.

Practice Questions and Problems

1. Fiscal policy is changing ______________ and ______________.
2. Taxes affect aggregate expenditures indirectly by changing ______________. This change alters ______________.
3. Increases in government spending may drive interest rates ______________ (up, down), thereby ______________ (increasing, decreasing) investment.
4. If government spending increases by the same amount as taxes, the effect is ______________ (expansionary, contractionary).
5. A decrease in government spending or an increase in taxes causes the aggregate demand curve to shift to the ______________.
6. List the three ways in which government spending may be financed.

   ____

   ____

   ____

7. An increase in taxes may shift aggregate supply to the ______________, causing unemployment to ______________ (increase, decrease) and the price level to ______________ rise, fall).
8. A government borrows funds by ______________ (buying bonds from, selling bonds to) the public.
9. Fiscal policy in the United States is a product of the budget process, which involves the ______________ and ______________ branches of government.
10. As part of the budget process, federal agencies submit their budgets to the ______________, which reviews and modifies each agency's requests and consolidates all of the proposals into a single budget.
11. The ______________ reports to Congress on the validity of the economic assumptions made in the president's budget.
12. List the two kinds of fiscal policy.

    ____

    ____

13. As income falls, automatic stabilizers ______________ spending.
14. ______________ are taxes that are a flat dollar amount regardless of income.
15. Look at the following tax payment schedules. Which is progressive? ______________
    Regressive? ______________
    Proportional? ______________

	A	B	C
Income	Tax Payment	Tax Payment	Tax Payment
$100	$ 10	$ 50	$ 10
200	20	80	30
300	30	90	60
400	40	100	100

16. ______________ taxes are an example of an automatic stabilizer.
17. Government plays a bigger role in investment spending in ______________ (developing, industrial) countries. Give two reasons why this should be so.

    ____

    ____

18. Low-income countries ______________ (do, do not) spend a greater percentage of their budgets on social programs as compared with industrialized countries.
19. In general, developing countries rely more heavily on ______________ (direct, indirect) taxes than do developed countries.

Exercises and Applications

I Reducing the Deficit

Your text discusses the possible harmful effects of budget deficits. Since a budget deficit results from government spending that is greater than tax revenues, reducing the deficit implies reducing government spending, increasing taxes, or both. But to quote Publius Syrus, "There are some remedies worse than the disease" (Maxim 301). Since reducing government spending and increasing taxes reduce aggregate demand, the economy might be thrown into a recession if spending cuts and tax increases are adopted.

1. Consider the following graph, in which the economy is at equilibrium at P_1 and Y_1. Show what will happen if spending cuts and tax increases are implemented.

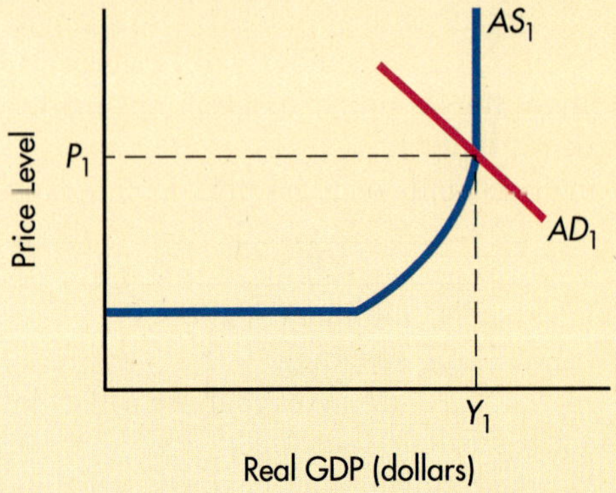

What will happen to equilibrium real GDP and price level?

____

____

2. Now consider an economy operating in the vertical region of the aggregate supply curve. Can you draw a curve that illustrates tax increases and spending cuts but does *not* throw the economy into a recession?

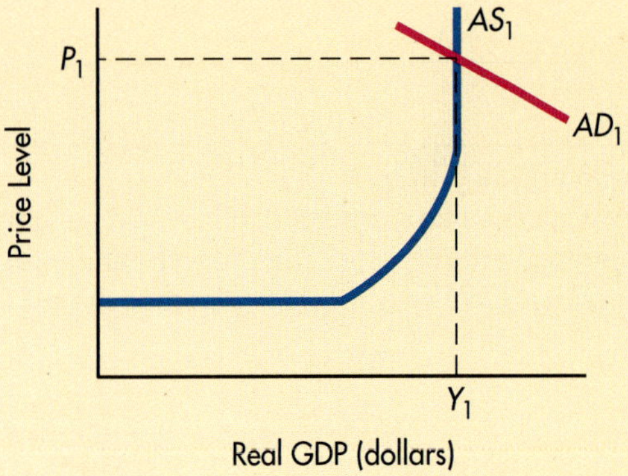

Explain:

____

____

II Obama's Fiscal Policy

1. President Obama's 2013 budget contains spending cuts and tax increases designed to decrease the trillion dollar-plus budget deficits to $901 billion. Reducing government spending and increasing taxes is __________(expansionary, contactionary) fiscal policy.
2. The president proposed these measures when the economy was in a weak recovery, and the unemployment rate was still very high, at about 9%. However, decreases in the federal budget deficit would be expected to __________ (increases, decrease) interest rates. __________ (Higher, Lower) interest rates would __________ (increase, decrease) which component of aggregate? __________ What effect would that change have on real GDP? __________

   ____
3. After the budget had been submitted, newly released economic data suggested that the economy might be performing better than administration officials predicted when drawing up the budget. If the economy did improve, tax revenues would __________ (increase, decrease) and __________(narrow, widen) the budget deficit more than expected.

You can find further practice tests in the Online Quiz at: www.cengagebrain.com

14 Money and Banking

FUNDAMENTAL QUESTIONS

1. What is money?
2. How is the U.S. money supply defined?
3. How do countries pay for international transactions?
4. Why are banks considered intermediaries?
5. How does international banking differ from domestic banking?
6. How do banks create money?

PREVIEW

Up to this point, we have been talking about aggregate expenditures, aggregate demand and supply, and fiscal policy without explicitly discussing money. Yet money is used by every sector of the economy in all nations and plays a crucial role in every economy. In this chapter we discuss what money is, how the quantity of money is determined, and the role of banks in determining this quantity. In Chapter 15, we examine the role of money in the aggregate demand and supply model.

As you will see in Chapters 15 and 16, the quantity of money has a major impact on interest rates, inflation, and the amount of spending in the economy. Money is, then, important for macroeconomic policy making, and government officials use both monetary and fiscal policy to influence the equilibrium level of real GDP and prices.

Banks and the banking system also play key roles, both at home and abroad, in the determination of the amount of money in circulation and the movement of money between nations. After we define *money* and its functions, we look at the banking system. We begin with banking in the United States and then discuss international banking. Someone once joked that banks follow the rule of 3–6–3. They borrow at 3 percent interest, lend at 6 percent interest, and close at 3 p.m. If those days ever existed, clearly they do not today. The banking industry in the United States and the rest of the world has undergone tremendous change in recent years. After decades where new technology and government deregulation were allowing banks to respond to changing economic conditions in ways that were unthinkable only a few years ago, the financial crisis of 2007–2008 resulted in new interest in regulating banks to restrict their activities and limit their ability to create new financial products in order to reduce risk taking.

1. WHAT IS MONEY?

money:
anything that is generally acceptable to sellers in exchange for goods and services

Money is anything that is generally acceptable to sellers in exchange for goods and services. The cash in your wallet can be used to buy groceries or a movie ticket. You simply present your cash to the cashier, who readily accepts it. If you want to use your car to buy groceries or a movie ticket, the exchange is more complicated. You would probably have to sell the car before you could use it to buy other goods and services. Cars are seldom exchanged directly for goods and services (except for other cars). Because cars are not a generally acceptable means of paying for other goods and services, we don't consider them to be money.

liquid asset:
an asset that can easily be exchanged for goods and services

Money is the most liquid asset. A **liquid asset** is an asset that can easily be exchanged for goods and services. Cash is a liquid asset; a car is not. How liquid must an asset be before we consider it money? To answer this question, we must first consider the functions of money.

1 What is money?

1.a. Functions of Money

Money serves four basic functions: It is a *medium of exchange*, a *unit of account*, a *store of value*, and a *standard of deferred payment*. Not all monies serve all of these functions equally well, as will be apparent in the following discussion. But to be money, an item must perform enough of these functions to induce people to use it.

1.a.1. Medium of Exchange Money is a medium of exchange; it is used in exchange for goods and services. Sellers willingly accept money in payment for the products and services they produce. Without money, we would have to resort to *barter*, the direct exchange of goods and services for other goods and services.

For a barter system to work, there must be a *double coincidence of wants*. Suppose Bill is a carpenter and Jane is a plumber. In a monetary economy, when Bill needs plumbing repairs in his home, he simply pays Jane for the repairs using money. Because everyone wants money, money is an acceptable means of payment. In a barter economy, Bill must offer his services as a carpenter in exchange for Jane's work. If Jane does not want any carpentry work done, Bill and Jane cannot enter into a mutually beneficial transaction. Bill has to find a person who can do what he wants and also wants what he can do; there must be a double coincidence of wants.

The example of Bill and Jane illustrates the fact that barter is a lot less efficient than using money. This means that the cost of a transaction in a barter economy is higher than the cost of a transaction in a monetary economy. The use of money as a medium of exchange lowers transaction costs.

The people of Yap Island highly value and thus accept as a medium of exchange giant stones. But in most cultures, in order to be an effective medium of exchange, money must be portable—a property the stone money of Yap Island clearly lacks. Another important property of money is *divisibility*. Money must be measurable in both small units (for low-value goods and services) and large units (for high-value goods and services). Yap stone money is not divisible, so it is not a good medium of exchange for the majority of goods bought and sold.

1.a.2. Unit of Account Money is a unit of account; we price goods and services in terms of money. This common unit of measurement allows us to compare relative values easily. If whole wheat bread sells for a dollar a loaf and white bread sells for 50 cents, we know that whole wheat bread is twice as expensive as white bread.

On Yap Island, giant stones are an accepted medium of exchange, despite their lack of portability.

Using money as a unit of account is efficient. It reduces the costs of gathering information on what things are worth. The use of money as a unit of account lowers information costs relative to barter. In a barter economy, people constantly have to evaluate the worth of the goods and services being offered. When money prices are placed on goods and services, their relative value is obvious.

1.a.3. **Store of Value** Money functions as a store of value or purchasing power. If you are paid today, you do not have to hurry out to spend your money. It will still have value next week or next month. Some monies retain their value better than others. In colonial New England, fish and furs both served as money. But because fish does not store as well as furs, its usefulness as a store of value was limited. An important property of a money is its *durability*, its ability to retain its value over time.

Inflation plays a major role in determining the effectiveness of a money as a store of value. The higher the rate of inflation, the faster the purchasing power of money falls. In high-inflation countries, workers spend their pay as fast as possible because the purchasing power of their money is falling rapidly. It makes no sense to hold on to a money that is quickly losing value. In countries where the domestic currency does not serve as a good store of value, it ceases to fulfill this function of money, and people begin to use something else as money, such as the currency of another nation. For instance, U.S. dollars have long been a favorite store of value in Latin American countries that have experienced high inflation. This phenomenon—**currency substitution**—has been documented in Argentina, Bolivia, Mexico, and other countries during times of high inflation.

currency substitution: the use of foreign money as a substitute for domestic money when the domestic economy has a high rate of inflation

1.a.4. **Standard of Deferred Payment** Finally, money is a standard of deferred payment. Debt obligations are written in terms of money values. If you have a credit card bill that is due in 90 days, the value you owe is stated in monetary units—for example, dollars in the United States and yen in Japan. We use money values to state amounts of debt and use money to pay our debts.

credit: available savings that are lent to borrowers to spend

We should make a distinction here between money and credit. Money is what we use to pay for goods and services. **Credit** is available savings that are lent to borrowers to spend. If you use your Visa or MasterCard to buy a shirt, you are not buying the shirt with your money. You are taking out a loan from the bank that issued the credit card in order to buy the shirt. Credit and money are different. Money is an *asset*, something you own. Credit is *debt*, something you owe.

1.b. The U.S. Money Supply

2 How is the U.S. money supply defined?

The quantity of money available for spending is an important determinant of many key macroeconomic variables since changes in the money supply affect interest rates, inflation, and other indicators of economic health. When economists measure the money supply, they measure spendable assets. Identifying those assets, however, can be difficult. Although it would seem that *all* bank deposits are money, some bank deposits are held for spending while others are held for saving. In defining the money supply, then, economists must differentiate among assets on the basis of their liquidity and the likelihood of their being used for spending.

The problem of distinguishing among assets has produced more than one definition of the money supply. Today in the United States, the Federal Reserve uses M1 and M2.[1] Although economists have tried to identify a single measure that best influences the business cycle and changes in interest rates and inflation, research indicates that different definitions work better to explain changes in macroeconomic variables at different times.

M1 money supply: financial assets that are the most liquid

transactions account: a checking account at a bank or other financial institution that can be drawn on to make payments

1.b.1. M1 Money Supply

The narrowest and most liquid measure of the money supply is the **M1 money supply**, the financial assets that are immediately available for spending. This definition emphasizes the use of money as a medium of exchange. The M1 money supply consists of currency, travelers' checks, demand deposits, and other checkable deposits. Demand and other checkable deposits are **transactions accounts**; they can be used to make direct payments to a third party.

Currency Currency includes coins and paper money in circulation (in the hands of the public). In 2011, currency represented 48 percent of the M1 money supply. A common misconception about currency today is that it is backed by gold or silver. This is not true. There is nothing backing the U.S. dollar except the confidence of the public. This kind of monetary system is called a *fiduciary monetary system*. Fiduciary comes from the Latin *fiducia*, which means "trust." Our monetary system is based on trust. As long as we believe that our money is an acceptable form of payment for goods and services, the system works. It is not necessary for money to be backed by any precious object. As long as people believe that a money has value, it will serve as money.

The United States has not always operated under a fiduciary monetary system. At one time, the U.S. government issued gold and silver coins and paper money that could be exchanged for silver. In 1967, Congress authorized the U.S. Treasury to stop redeeming "silver certificate" paper money for silver. Coins with an intrinsic value are known as *commodity money*; they have value as a commodity in addition to their face value. The problem with commodity money is that as the value of the commodity increases, the money stops being circulated. People hoard coins when their commodity value exceeds their face value. For

[1] Until March 2006, the Federal Reserve also published a broader measure of the money supply known as M3.

example, no one would take an old $20 gold piece to the grocery store to buy $20 worth of groceries because the gold is worth much more than $20 today.

Travelers' Checks Outstanding U.S. dollar-denominated travelers' checks issued by nonbank institutions are counted as part of the M1 money supply. There are several nonbank issuers, among them American Express and Cook's. (Travelers' checks issued by banks are included in demand deposits. When a bank issues its own travelers' checks, it deposits the amount paid by the purchaser in a special account that is used to redeem the checks. Because this amount is counted as part of demand deposits, it is not counted again as part of outstanding travelers' checks.) Travelers' checks account for less than 1 percent of the M1 money supply.

Demand Deposits Demand deposits are checking account deposits at a commercial bank. These deposits pay no interest. They are called *demand deposits* because the bank must pay the amount of the check immediately on the demand of the depositor. Demand deposits accounted for 32 percent of the M1 money supply in 2011.

Other Checkable Deposits Until the 1980s, demand deposits were the only kind of checking account. Today there are many different kinds of checking accounts, known as *other checkable deposits (OCDs)*. The OCDs are accounts at financial institutions that pay interest and give the depositor check-writing privileges. Among the OCDs included in the M1 money supply are the following:

- **Negotiable orders of withdrawal (NOW) accounts** These are interest-bearing checking accounts offered by savings and loan institutions.
- **Automatic transfer system (ATS) accounts** These are accounts at commercial banks that combine an interest-bearing savings account with a non–interest-bearing checking account. The depositor keeps a small balance in the checking account; any time the checking account balance is overdrawn, funds are automatically transferred from the savings account.
- **Credit union share draft accounts** Credit unions offer their members interest-bearing checking accounts called *share drafts*.
- **Demand deposits at mutual savings banks** Mutual savings banks are non-profit savings and loan organizations. Any profits after operating expenses have been paid may be distributed to depositors.

1.b.2. **M2 Money Supply** The components of the M1 money supply are the most liquid assets, the assets most likely to be used for transactions. M2 is a broader definition of the money supply that includes assets in somewhat less liquid forms. The M2 money supply includes the M1 money supply plus the following:

- **Savings deposits** Savings deposits are accounts at banks and savings and loan associations that earn interest but offer check-writing privileges.
- **Small-denomination time deposits** These deposits are often called *certificates of deposit*. Funds in these accounts must be deposited for a specified period of time. (*Small* means less than $100,000.)
- **Retail money market mutual fund balances** These money market mutual funds combine the deposits of many individuals and invest them in government Treasury bills and other short-term securities. Many money market mutual funds grant check-writing privileges but limit the size and number of checks.

Figure 14.1 summarizes the two definitions of the money supply.

FIGURE 14.1 The U.S. Money Supply: M1 and M2 (billions of dollars)

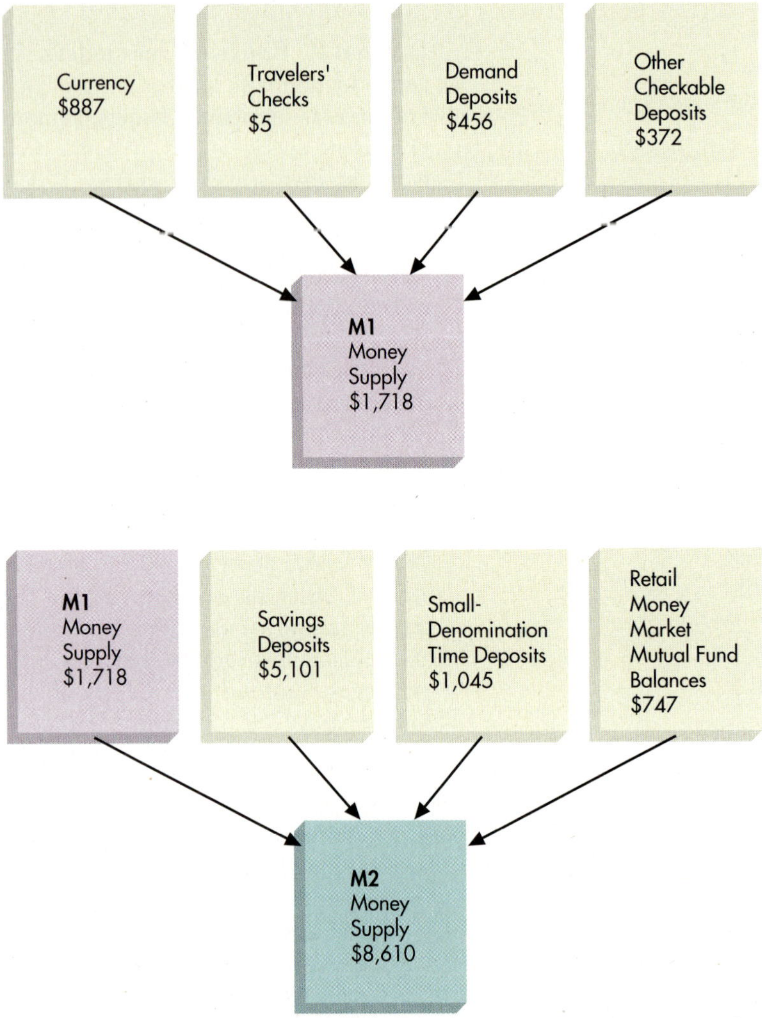

Source: Data are drawn from the Federal Reserve Board 2011 (www.federalreserve.gov/releases/).

3

How do countries pay for international transactions?

1.c. Global Money

So far we have discussed the money supply in a domestic context. Just as the United States uses dollars as its domestic money, every nation has its own monetary unit of account. Japan has the yen, Mexico the peso, Canada the Canadian dollar, and so on. Since each nation uses a different money, how do countries pay for transactions that involve residents of other countries? As you saw in Chapter 10, the foreign exchange market links national monies together so that transactions can be made across national borders. If Sears in the United States buys a home entertainment system from Sony in Japan, Sears can exchange dollars for yen in order to pay Sony in yen. The exchange rate between the dollar and yen determines how many dollars are needed to purchase the required number of yen (¥). For instance, if Sony wants ¥1,000,000 for the component and the exchange rate is ¥100 = $1, Sears needs $10,000 (1,000,000/100) to buy the yen.

Sales contracts between developed countries usually are written (invoiced) in the national currency of the exporter. To complete the transaction, the importer buys the exporter's currency on the foreign exchange market. Trade between developing and developed nations typically is invoiced in the currency of the developed country, whether the developed country is the exporter or importer,

Table 14.1 International Reserve Currencies (percentage shares of national currencies in total official holdings of foreign exchange)

Year	U.S. Dollar	Pound Sterling	Deutsche Mark	French Franc	Japanese Yen	Swiss Franc	Netherlands Guilder	Euro	Unspecified Currencies
1976	78.8	1.0	8.7	1.5	1.9	2.1	0.8	–	5.2
2011	62.1	3.9	–	–	3.7	0.1	–	25.0	5.1

Source: Data from International Monetary Fund Currency Composition of Official Foreign Exchange Reserves (COFER) Database (http://www.imf.org/external/np/sta/cofer/eng/).

because the currency of the developed country is usually more stable and more widely traded on the foreign exchange market than the currency of the developing country. As a result, the currencies of the major developed countries tend to dominate the international medium-of-exchange and unit-of-account functions of money.

international reserve asset: an asset used to settle debts between governments

international reserve currency: a currency held by a government to settle international debts

1.c.1. **International Reserve Currencies** Governments hold monies as a temporary store of value until money is needed to settle international debts. At one time gold was the primary **international reserve asset**, an asset used to settle debts between governments. Although gold still serves as an international reserve asset, its role is unimportant relative to that of currencies. Today national currencies function as international reserves. The currencies that are held for this purpose are called **international reserve currencies**.

Table 14.1 shows the importance of the major international reserve currencies over time. In the mid-1970s, the U.S. dollar made up almost 80 percent of international reserve holdings. By 1990, its share had fallen to less than 50 percent, but its share has risen again recently to more than 60 percent, as shown in Table 14.1.

Prior to the actual introduction of the euro, there was much discussion about its potential popularity as a reserve currency. In fact, some analysts were asserting that we should expect the euro to replace the U.S. dollar as the world's dominant currency. As Table 14.1 shows, the euro is now the second most popular reserve currency, but it has much lower use than the dollar. The dominant world currency evolves over time as business firms and individuals find one currency more useful than another. Prior to the dominance of the dollar, the British pound was the world's most important reserve currency. As the U.S. economy grew in importance and U.S. financial markets developed to the huge size they now have, the growing use of the dollar naturally emerged due to the large volume of financial transactions involving the United States. Perhaps over time, some other currency will someday replace the dollar as the world's dominant money.

RECAP

1. Money is the most liquid asset.
2. Money serves as a medium of exchange, a unit of account, a store of value, and a standard of deferred payment.
3. The use of money lowers transaction and information costs relative to barter.
4. To be used as money, an asset should be portable, divisible, and durable.
5. The M1 money supply is the most liquid definition of money and equals the sum of currency, travelers' checks, demand deposits, and other checkable deposits.
6. The M2 money supply equals the sum of the M1 money supply, savings and small-denomination time deposits, and retail money market mutual fund balances.
7. International reserve currencies are held by governments to settle international debts.

2. BANKING

Commercial banks are financial institutions that offer deposits on which checks can be written. In the United States and most other countries, commercial banks are privately owned. *Thrift institutions* are financial institutions that historically offered just savings accounts, not checking accounts. Savings and loan associations, credit unions, and mutual savings banks are all thrift institutions. Prior to 1980, the differences between commercial banks and thrift institutions were much greater than they are today. For example, only commercial banks could offer checking accounts, and those accounts earned no interest. The law also regulated maximum interest rates. In 1980, Congress passed the Depository Institutions Deregulation and Monetary Control Act, in part to stimulate competition among financial institutions. Now thrift institutions and even brokerage houses offer many of the same services as commercial banks. In 1999, Congress passed the Gramm–Leach–Bliley Act, which allowed commercial banks to expand their business into other areas of finance, including insurance and selling securities. This permitted greater integration of financial products under one umbrella known as a financial holding company. During the financial crisis of 2007–2008, some of these large banks suffered dramatically as a result of very aggressive risk taking in financial products that turned out to be unsuccessful.

4

Why are banks considered intermediaries?

2.a. Financial Intermediaries

Both commercial banks and thrift institutions are *financial intermediaries*, middlemen between savers and borrowers. Banks accept deposits from individuals and firms, and then use those deposits to make loans to individuals and firms. The borrowers are likely to be different individuals or firms from the depositors, although it is not uncommon for a household or business to be both a depositor and a borrower at the same institution. Of course, depositors and borrowers have very different interests. For instance, depositors typically prefer short-term deposits; they don't want to tie their money up for a long time. Borrowers, on the other hand, usually want more time for repayment. Banks typically package short-term deposits into longer-term loans. To function as intermediaries, banks must serve the interests of both depositors and borrowers.

A bank is willing to serve as an intermediary because it hopes to earn a profit from this activity. It pays a lower interest rate on deposits than it charges on loans; the difference is a source of profit for the bank. Islamic banks are prohibited by holy law from charging interest on loans; thus, they use a different system for making a profit (see the Global Business Insight "Islamic Banking" on page 304).

2.b. U.S. Banking

2.b.1. Current Structure Figure 14.2 indicates that there are 7,358 banks and savings institutions in the United States. In addition, there were 83,209 bank branch offices operating in the United States in 2011. Roughly half of the banks were operated by *national banks*, banks chartered by the federal government; the other half, by *state banks*, banks chartered under state laws.

An important change that has taken place in the U.S. bank market is the growth of interstate banking. Historically, banks were allowed to operate in just one state. In some states, banks could operate in only one location. This is known as *unit banking*. Today there are still many unit banks, but these are typically small community banks.

Over time, legal barriers have been reduced so that today almost all states permit entry to banks located out of state. In the future, banking is likely to be done on a national rather than a local scale. The growth of automated teller machines (ATMs) is a big step in this direction. The ATM networks give bank customers access to services over a much wider geographic area than any single

Table 14.2 The Effect on Bank Deposits of an Initial Bank Deposit of $100,000

Bank	New Deposit	Required Reserves	Excess Reserves (New Loans)
First National	$ 100,000	$ 10,000	$ 90,000
Second National	90,000	9,000	81,000
Third National	81,000	8,100	72,900
Fourth National	72,900	7,290	65,610
Fifth National	65,610	6,561	59,049
Sixth National	59,049	5,905	53,144
⋮	⋮	⋮	⋮
TOTAL	$1,000,000	$100,000	$900,000

new deposits, the banking system can increase the money supply only by the multiplier times excess reserves:

Deposit expansion multiplier × excess reserves = maximum increase in money supply

The deposit expansion multiplier indicates the *maximum* possible change in total deposits when a new deposit is made. For the effect to be that large, all excess reserves must be loaned out, and all of the money that is deposited must stay in the banking system.

If banks hold more reserves than the minimum required, they lend a smaller fraction of any new deposits, which reduces the effect of the deposit expansion multiplier. For instance, if the reserve requirement is 10 percent, we know that the deposit expansion multiplier is 10. If a bank chooses to hold 20 percent of its deposits on reserve, the deposit expansion multiplier equals 5 (1/.20).

If money (currency and coin) is withdrawn from the banking system and kept as cash, deposits and bank reserves are smaller, and less money exists to be loaned out. This *currency drain*—removal of money—reduces the deposit expansion multiplier. The greater the currency drain, the smaller the multiplier. There is always some currency drain as people carry currency to pay for day-to-day transactions. However, during historical periods of bank panic when people lost confidence in banks, large currency withdrawals contributed to declines in money supply. In the recent financial crisis, banks have been holding far more reserves than required. Prior to the onset of the recent financial crisis, required reserves were about $40 billion and excess reserves were $1.5 billion. Since then, excess reserves have increased a thousandfold! Banks have over a trillion dollars that they are allowed to lend, but choose to hold as extra reserves instead. This is historically unprecedented.

Remember that the deposit expansion multiplier measures the *maximum* expansion of the money supply by the banking system. Any single bank can lend only its excess reserves, but the whole banking system can expand the money supply by a multiple of the initial excess reserves. Thus, the banking system as a whole can increase the money supply by the deposit expansion multiplier times the excess reserves of the system. The initial bank is limited to its initial loan; the banking system generates loan after loan based on that initial loan. A new deposit can increase the money supply by the deposit expansion multiplier times the new deposit.

NOW YOU TRY IT

What is the deposit expansion multiplier if the reserve requirement is each of the following?

a. 5 percent

b. 25 percent

c. 33 percent

d. 50 percent

RECAP

1. The fractional reserve banking system allows banks to expand the money supply by making loans.

2. Banks must keep a fraction of their deposits on reserve; their excess reserves are available for lending.
3. The deposit expansion multiplier measures the maximum increase in the money supply given a new deposit; it is the reciprocal of the reserve requirement.
4. A single bank increases the money supply by lending its excess reserves.
5. The banking system can increase the money supply by the deposit expansion multiplier times the excess reserves in the banking system.

SUMMARY

What is money?

1. Money is anything that is generally acceptable to sellers in exchange for goods and services.
2. Money serves as a medium of exchange, a unit of account, a store of value, and a standard of deferred payment.
3. Money, because it is more efficient than barter, lowers transaction costs.
4. Money should be portable, divisible, and durable.

How is the U.S. money supply defined?

5. There are two definitions of money based on its liquidity.
6. The M1 money supply equals the sum of currency plus travelers' checks plus demand deposits plus other checkable deposits.
7. The M2 money supply equals the sum of the M1 money supply plus savings and small-denomination time deposits and retail money market mutual fund balances.

How do countries pay for international transactions?

8. Using the foreign exchange market, governments (along with individuals and firms) are able to convert national currencies to pay for trade.
9. The U.S. dollar is the world's major international reserve currency.

Why are banks considered intermediaries?

10. Banks serve as middlemen between savers and borrowers.

How does international banking differ from domestic banking?

11. Domestic banking in most nations is strictly regulated; international banking is not.
12. The Eurocurrency market is the international deposit and loan market.
13. International banking facilities (IBFs) allow U.S. domestic banks to carry on international banking activities on U.S. soil.

How do banks create money?

14. Banks can make loans up to the amount of their excess reserves, their total reserves minus their required reserves.
15. The deposit expansion multiplier is the reciprocal of the reserve requirement.
16. A single bank expands the money supply by lending its excess reserves.
17. The banking system can increase the money supply by the deposit expansion multiplier times the excess reserves in the system.

EXERCISES

1. Describe the four functions of money using the U.S. dollar to provide an example of how dollars serve each function.
2. Discuss how each of the following would serve the functions of money:
   a. Gold
   b. Yap stone money
   c. Cigarettes
   d. Diamonds
3. What is a financial intermediary? Give an example of how your bank or credit union serves as a financial intermediary between you and the rest of the economy.
4. Why are informal financial markets used in developing countries? Give an example of an informal financial market.
5. First Bank has cash reserves of $200,000, loans of $800,000, and deposits of $1,000,000.
   a. Prepare a balance sheet for the bank.
   b. If the bank maintains a reserve requirement of 12 percent, what is the largest loan it can make?
   c. What is the maximum amount the money supply can be increased as a result of First Bank's new loan?
6. Yesterday bank A had no excess reserves. Today it received a new deposit of $6,000.
   a. If the bank maintains a reserve requirement of 2 percent, what is the maximum loan bank A can make?
   b. What is the maximum amount the money supply can be increased as a result of bank A's new loan?
7. The deposit expansion multiplier measures the maximum possible expansion of the money supply in the banking system. What factors could cause the actual expansion of the money supply to differ from that given by the deposit expansion multiplier?
8. What is liquidity? Rank the following assets in order of their liquidity: $10 bill, personal check for $20, savings account with $400 in it, PayPal account with $500 in it, stereo, car, house, travelers' check.

Use the following table on the components of money in a hypothetical economy to do exercises 9 and 10.

Money Component	Amount
Travelers' checks	$100
Currency	2,000
Small-denomination time deposits	3,500
Savings deposits	2,000
Demand deposits	7,000
Other checkable deposits	9,000
U.S. Treasury bonds	25,000
Retail money market mutual funds	7,500

9. What is the value of M1 in the previous table?
10. What is the value of M2 in the previous table?

STUDY GUIDE FOR CHAPTER 14

Key Term Match

Match each term with its correct definition by placing the appropriate letter next to the corresponding number.

A. money
B. liquid asset
C. currency substitution
D. credit
E. M1 money supply
F. transactions account
G. international reserve asset
H. international reserve currency
I. murabaha
J. Federal Deposit Insurance Corporation (FDIC)
K. Eurocurrency market (offshore banking)
L. international banking facility
M. ROSCAS
N. hawala
O. fractional reserve banking system
P. required reserves
Q. excess reserves
R. deposit expansion multiplier
S. shadow banks
T. securitization

____ 1. available savings that are lent to borrowers to spend

____ 2. an asset used to settle debts between governments

____ 3. financial assets that are the most liquid

____ 4. the cash reserves beyond those required, which can be loaned

____ 5. The process of combining, repackaging or restructuring a collection of assets to transform their risk and maturity qualities,

____ 6. a network for transferring money, popular in Muslim countries

____ 7. the use of foreign money as a substitute for domestic money when the domestic economy has a high rate of inflation

____ 8. the reciprocal of the reserve requirement

____ 9. a checking account at a bank or other financial institution that can be drawn on to make payments

____ 10. rotating savings and credit associations

____ 11. a currency held by a government to settle international debts

____ 12. an asset that can easily be exchanged for goods and services

____ 13. a system in which banks keep less than 100 percent of the deposits available for withdrawal

____ 14. a division of a U.S. bank that is allowed to receive deposits from and make loans to nonresidents of the United States without the restrictions that apply to domestic U.S. banks

____ 15. a federal agency that insures deposits in commercial banks

____ 16. anything that is generally acceptable to sellers in exchange for goods and services

____ 17. Financial institutions other than regulated depository institutions, such as mortgage companies, hedge funds, etc.

____ 18. the cash reserves (a percentage of deposits) a bank must keep on hand

____ 19. the market for deposits and loans generally denominated in a currency of a country other than that in which the transaction occurs

____ 20. the most popular instrument for financing Islamic investments

Quick-Check Quiz

1. Which of the following is *not* one of the functions of money?
   - ☐ a. a medium of exchange
   - ☐ b. a unit of account
   - ☐ c. a resource for production
   - ☐ d. a store of value
   - ☐ e. a standard of deferred payment

2. Which of the following is *not* a component of the M1 money supply?
   - ☐ a. demand deposits
   - ☐ b. other checkable deposits
   - ☐ c. currency
   - ☐ d. savings accounts
   - ☐ e. travelers' checks

3. Which of the following is *not* a transactions account?
   - ☐ a. negotiable order of withdrawal
   - ☐ b. credit union share draft account
   - ☐ c. savings account
   - ☐ d. automated transfer system account
   - ☐ e. demand deposit at a commercial bank

4. Which of the following is *not* a component of the M2 money supply?
   - ☐ a. retail money market mutual fund balances
   - ☐ b. small-denomination time deposits
   - ☐ c. currency
   - ☐ d. savings deposits
   - ☐ e. large time deposits

5. Which of the following statements is true?
   - ☐ a. The laws regulating international banks typically are very restrictive whereas domestic banks go relatively unregulated.
   - ☐ b. Offshore banking, called the Eurocurrency market, refers to international banking transactions among the seven Western European industrial powers.
   - ☐ c. Offshore banks are typically able to offer better terms to their customers than domestic banks.
   - ☐ d. Most ATM transactions occur at banks that are not the customer's own bank.
   - ☐ e. U.S. banks that participate in international banking on U.S. soil are subject to the same regulations as domestic banks.

6. Which of the following statements is false?
   - ☐ a. The FDIC does not permit banks to fail for fear of causing a bank panic.
   - ☐ b. Almost all states permit entry to banks located out of state.
   - ☐ c. A Eurodollar is a dollar-denominated deposit outside the U.S. banking industry.
   - ☐ d. International banking facilities are not subject to the same reserve requirements as domestic banks.
   - ☐ e. International banking facilities are not physical entities.

7. The deposit expansion multiplier will be larger the
   - ☐ a. smaller the reserve requirement.
   - ☐ b. greater the currency drain.
   - ☐ c. greater the percentage of excess reserves held by banks.
   - ☐ d. larger the bank.
   - ☐ e. greater the value of the assets held by the bank.

8. Banks increase the money supply by
   - ☐ a. cashing checks.
   - ☐ b. making loans.
   - ☐ c. providing currency.
   - ☐ d. printing money.
   - ☐ e. printing money and coining currency.

9. A bank has $200,000 in deposits and $10,000 in cash. The reserve requirement is 4 percent.

The bank's required reserves are ______________, and its excess reserves are ______________.

- ☐ a. \$400; \$199,600
- ☐ b. \$199,600; \$400
- ☐ c. \$8,000; \$192,000
- ☐ d. \$2,000; \$8,000
- ☐ e. \$8,000; \$2,000

Practice Questions and Problems

1. List the four functions of money.
   ______________ ______________
   ______________ ______________
2. List the four components of the M1 money supply.
   ______________ ______________
   ______________ ______________
3. Credit unions offer their members interest-bearing checking accounts called ______________.
4. ______________ are nonprofit savings and loan institutions.
5. List the four components of the M2 money supply.
   ______________ ______________
   ______________ ______________
6. For a barter system to work, there must be a ______________.
7. ______________ deposits are deposits at banks and at savings and loans that earn interest but offer no check-writing privileges.
8. Small-denomination time deposits are also called __________.
9. True or false? U.S. currency is backed by gold.
10. Thrift institutions include ______________, ______________, and ______________.
11. ______________ (Domestic, Offshore) banks are usually able to offer better terms to their customers.
12. Eurodollar transactions are ______________ (more risky, less risky) than domestic transactions in the United States because of the lack of regulation and deposit insurance.
13. A bank ______________ occurs when depositors, fearing a bank's closing, rush to withdraw their funds.
14. The deposit expansion multiplier equals ______________ (formula).
15. The deposit expansion multiplier tells us the ______________ (maximum, minimum) change in total deposits when a new deposit is made.
16. If people withdraw deposits from banks, ______________ occurs, and the deposit expansion multiplier will be less than the reciprocal of the reserve requirement.
17. Any single bank can lend only up to the amount of its ______________.
18. Banks increase the money supply by ______________.

Exercises and Applications

I How Banks Create Money

The State Bank of Oswald has cash reserves of \$5,000, loans of \$495,000, and deposits of \$500,000. The bank maintains a reserve requirement of 1 percent.

a. Calculate this bank's excess reserves.

____

____

b. The bank receives a new cash deposit of \$100,000. What is the largest loan the bank can make?

____

c. What is the maximum amount the money supply can be increased as a result of the State Bank of Oswald's new loan? ______________

II The Components of the Monetary Aggregates

The following table lists the components of the monetary aggregates in billions of dollars.

Travelers' checks	8.1
Savings deposits	1,135.0
Demand deposits	406.5
Other checkable deposits	420.0
Currency	357.3
Retail money market mutual funds	372.1
Small-denomination time deposits	826.9

Using the previous table, calculate M1 and M2.

M1	M2
______________	______________

You can find further practice tests in the Online Quiz at: www.cengagebrain.com

PART 4
Macroeconomic Policy

CHAPTER 15
Monetary Policy

15-1 What does the Federal Reserve do?

15-2 How is monetary policy set?

15-3 What are the tools of monetary policy?

15-4 What role do central banks play in the foreign exchange market?

15-5 What are the determinants of the demand for money?

15-6 How does monetary policy affect the equilibrium level of real GDP?

15-7 What does the ECB do?

CHAPTER 16
Macroeconomic Policy, Business Cycles, and Growth

16-1 Is there a trade-off between inflation and the unemployment rate?

16-2 How does the trade-off between inflation and the unemployment rate vary from the short to the long run?

16-3 What is the relationship between unexpected inflation and the unemployment rate?

16-4 How are macroeconomic expectations formed?

16-5 Are business cycles related to political elections?

16-6 How do real shocks to the economy affect business cycles?

16-7 How is inflationary monetary policy related to government fiscal policy?

16-8 How are economic growth rates determined?

16-9 What is productivity?

CHAPTER 17
Issues in International Trade and Finance

17-1 What determines the goods a nation will export?

17-2 What are the sources of comparative advantage?

17-3 Why do countries restrict international trade?

17-4 How do countries restrict the entry of foreign goods and promote the export of domestic goods?

17-5 What kinds of exchange rate arrangements exist today?

CHAPTER 18
Globalization

18-1 What is globalization?

18-2 What are the arguments against globalization?

18-3 What are the arguments in support of globalization?

18-4 How has globalization affected economic growth and poverty?

18-5 Can recent financial crises be linked to globalization?

15 Monetary Policy

FUNDAMENTAL QUESTIONS

1. What does the Federal Reserve do?
2. How is monetary policy set?
3. What are the tools of monetary policy?
4. What role do central banks play in the foreign exchange market?
5. What are the determinants of the demand for money?
6. How does monetary policy affect the equilibrium level of real GDP?
7. What does the ECB do?

PREVIEW

In Chapter 14, we saw how banks "create" money by making loans. However, that money must get into the system to begin with. Most of us never think about how money enters the economy. All we worry about is having money available when we need it. But there is a government body that controls the U.S. money supply, and in this chapter we will learn about this agency—the Federal Reserve System and the Board of Governors that oversees monetary policy.

The amount of money available for spending by individuals or businesses affects prices, interest rates, foreign exchange rates, and the level of income in the economy. Thus, having control of the money supply gives the Federal Reserve powerful influence over these important economic variables. As we learned in Chapter 13, fiscal policy, or the control of government spending and taxes, is one of two ways by which government can change the equilibrium level of real GDP. Monetary policy as carried out by the Federal Reserve is the other mechanism through which attempts are made to manage the economy. In this chapter we will also explore the tools of monetary policy and see how changes in the money supply affect the equilibrium level of real GDP.

1. THE FEDERAL RESERVE SYSTEM

The Federal Reserve is the central bank of the United States. A *central bank* performs several functions: accepting deposits from and making loans to commercial banks, acting as a banker for the federal government, and controlling the money supply.

1.a. Structure of the Fed

Congress created the Federal Reserve System in 1913, with the Federal Reserve Act. Bank panics and failures had convinced lawmakers that the United States needed an agency to control the money supply and make loans to commercial banks when those banks found themselves without sufficient reserves. Because Americans tended to distrust large banking interests, Congress called for a decentralized central bank. The Federal Reserve System divides the nation into 12 districts, each with its own Federal Reserve Bank (see Figure 15.1).

1.a.1. Board of Governors Although Congress created a decentralized system so that each district bank would represent the special interests of its own region, in practice the Fed is much more centralized than its creators intended. Monetary policy is largely set by the Board of Governors in Washington, DC. This board is made up of seven members, who are appointed by the president and confirmed by the Senate.

The most visible and powerful member of the board is the chairperson. In fact, the chairperson of the Board of Governors has been called *the second most powerful person in the United States*. This individual serves as a leader and spokesperson for the board and typically exercises more authority in determining the course of monetary policy than do the other governors.

FIGURE 15.1 The Federal Reserve System

The Federal Reserve System divides the country into 12 districts. Each district has its own Federal Reserve bank, headquarters for Fed operations in that district. For example, the first district bank is in Boston; the twelfth is in San Francisco. There are also branch banks in Los Angeles, Miami, and other cities.

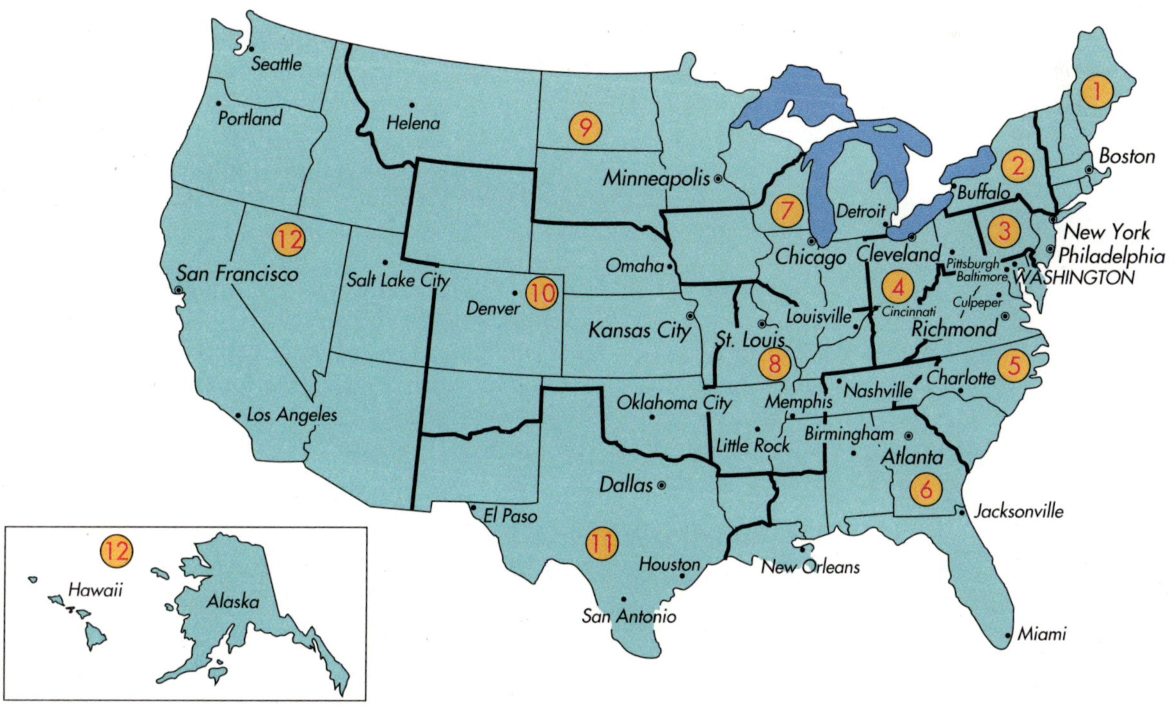

Source: *Federal Reserve Bulletin* (Washington, DC).

Table 15.1 Recent Chairmen of the Federal Reserve Board

Name	Age at Appointment	Term Began	Term Ended	Years of Tenure
William McChesney Martin	44	4/2/51	1/31/70	18.8
Arthur Burns	65	1/31/70	2/1/78	8.0
G. William Miller	52	3/8/78	8/6/79	1.4
Paul Volcker	51	8/6/79	8/5/87	8.0
Alan Greenspan	61	8/11/87	1/31/06	18.4
Ben Bernanke	52	2/1/06		

The chairperson is appointed by the president to a 4-year term. In recent years, most chairs have been reappointed to an additional term (see Table 15.1). The governors serve 14-year terms, the terms being staggered so that every two years a new position comes up for appointment. This system allows continuity in the policymaking process and is intended to place the board above politics. Congress created the Fed as an independent agency: Monetary policy is supposed to be formulated independent of Congress and the president. Of course, this is impossible in practice because the president appoints and the Senate approves the members of the board. But because the governors serve 14-year terms, they outlast the president who appointed them.

1.a.2. **District Banks** Each of the Fed's 12 district banks is formally directed by a nine-person board of directors. Three directors represent commercial banks in the district, and three represent nonbanking business interests. These six individuals are elected by the Federal Reserve System member banks in the district. The three remaining directors are appointed by the Fed's Board of Governors. District bank directors are not involved in the day-to-day operations of the district banks, but they meet regularly to oversee bank operations. They also choose the president of the bank. The president, who is in charge of operations, participates in monetary policymaking with the Board of Governors in Washington, DC.

Federal Open Market Committee (FOMC):
the official policymaking body of the Federal Reserve System

1.a.3. **The Federal Open Market Committee** The **Federal Open Market Committee (FOMC)** is the official policymaking body of the Federal Reserve System. The committee is made up of the 7 members of the Board of Governors plus 5 of the 12 district bank presidents. All of the district bank presidents, except for the president of the Federal Reserve Bank of New York, take turns serving on the FOMC. Because the New York Fed actually carries out monetary policy, that bank's president is always on the committee.

1.a.4. **The Economists** The Federal Reserve maintains a staff of researchers across the nation, who work for the various district banks and produce economic analyses and forecasts. There is a separate research staff for the Board of Governors in Washington, DC, which is organized into the Division of Research and Statistics, the Division of Monetary Affairs, and the Division of International Finance. These groups have approximately 450 staff members, about half with economics PhDs.

1.b. Functions of the Fed

1

What does the Federal Reserve do?

The Federal Reserve System offers banking services to the banking community and the U.S. Treasury, and it supervises the nation's banking system. The Fed also regulates the U.S. money supply.

1.b.1. **Banking Services and Supervision** The Fed provides several basic services to the banking community: It supplies currency to banks, holds their reserves, and clears checks. The Fed supplies U.S. currency (Federal

Reserve notes) to the banking community through its 12 district banks (see the Economic Insight "What's on a 20-Dollar Bill?"). Commercial banks in each district also hold reserves in the form of deposits at their district bank. In addition, the Fed makes loans to banks. In this sense, the Fed is the *bankers' bank*. And the Fed clears checks, transferring funds to the banks where checks are deposited from the banks on which the checks are drawn.

The Fed also supervises the nation's banks, ensuring that they operate in a sound and prudent manner. And it acts as the banker for the U.S. government, selling U.S. government securities for the U.S. Treasury. Working papers, data sets, reports, and forecasts published by the Federal Reserve staff are quite useful to researchers and the public. In fact, if you write a paper for this or a future economics course, you may want to explore the resources available at the Fed website.

1.b.2. **Controlling the Money Supply** All of the functions the Federal Reserve carries out are important, but none is more important than managing the nation's money supply. Before 1913, when the Fed was created, the money supply did not change to meet fluctuations in the demand for money. These fluctuations can stem from changes in income or seasonal patterns of demand. For example, every year during the Christmas season, the demand for currency rises

ECONOMIC INSIGHT

Joshua Roberts/Bloomberg/Getty Images

Women in Economics

By this point in your study of economics, you are hopefully realizing that a large part of economics is thinking about human interactions in insightful ways. Economists and economic policymakers search for creative solutions to complex problems affecting society while carefully considering the many trade-offs they face. Economics thus benefits from diversity—economists from different backgrounds and perspectives will have different insights and ways of thinking about trade-offs. A highly diverse economics profession would likely be more creative and less biased than a more homogenous economics profession.

The economics profession today is still in the process of becoming more diverse, especially in terms of gender. Not one of 27 member states of the European Union has a female governor of its national bank.[*] The General Council of the European Central Bank consists of these 27 men plus a male president and a male vice-president. The United States has never had a female chair of the Board of Governors of the Federal Reserve, and only 12.8% of full professors of economics are female.[†]

The U.S. Federal Reserve does have a female in the second most powerful role. Dr. Janet Yellen took office as vice chair of the Board of Governors on October 4, 2010, for a 4-year term, and simultaneously began a 14-year term as a member of the Board. She previously served as president and CEO of the Federal Reserve Bank of San Francisco and as chairwoman of the President's Council of Economic Advisors. Also a successful academic, Dr. Yellen is professor emeritus at the University of California at Berkeley where she has been a faculty member since 1980. Dr. Yellen is a macroeconomist whose research has focused on unemployment, banking globalization, income inequality, and monetary policy.

"Recent labor market reports and financial developments serve as a reminder that the economy remains vulnerable to setbacks," she said in a speech in Chicago on June 6, 2012. She added that "The deterioration of financial conditions in Europe of late, coupled with notable declines in global equity markets, also serve as a reminder that highly destabilizing outcomes cannot be ruled out." Stock markets jumped at this suggestion that the Fed would pursue accommodative monetary policy, prompting a news headline that read "When Janet Yellen Speaks, Wall Street Listens (and Buys)."[‡]

For more information and resources about women in economics, visit the website of the American Economic Association's Committee on the Status of Women in Economics.[§]

[*]As of July 2012.
[†]2011 Annual Report of the Committee on the Status of Women in the Economics Profession, American Economic Association.
[‡]AEgan, M. June 7, 2012. http://www.foxbusiness.com/investing/2012/06/07/when-janet-yellen-speaks-wall-street-listens-and-buys/
[§]http://www.aeaweb.org/committees/cswep/

because people carry more money to buy gifts. During the holiday season, the Fed increases the supply of currency to meet the demand for cash withdrawals from banks. After the holiday season, the demand for currency drops, and the public deposits currency in banks, which then return the currency to the Fed.

The Fed controls the money supply to achieve the policy goals set by the FOMC. It does this largely through its ability to influence bank reserves and the money-creating power of commercial banks that were discussed in Chapter 14.

RECAP

1. As the central bank of the United States, the Federal Reserve accepts deposits from and makes loans to commercial banks, acts as a banker for the federal government, and controls the money supply.
2. The Federal Reserve System is made up of 12 district banks and the Board of Governors in Washington, DC.
3. The most visible and powerful member of the Board of Governors is the chairperson.
4. The governors are appointed by the president and confirmed by the Senate to serve 14-year terms.
5. Monetary policy is made by the Federal Open Market Committee, whose members include the seven governors and five district bank presidents.
6. The Fed provides currency, holds reserves, clears checks, and supervises commercial banks.
7. The most important function the Fed performs is controlling the U.S. money supply.

2. IMPLEMENTING MONETARY POLICY

2

How is monetary policy set?

Changes in the amount of money in an economy affect the inflation rate, the interest rate, and the equilibrium level of national income. Throughout history, monetary policy has made currencies worthless and toppled governments. This is why controlling the money supply is so important.

2.a. Policy Goals

The ultimate goal of monetary policy is much like that of fiscal policy: economic growth with stable prices. *Economic growth* means greater output; *stable prices* mean a low, steady rate of inflation.

2.a.1. Intermediate Targets The Fed does not control gross domestic product or the price level directly. Instead, it controls the money supply, which in turn affects GDP and the level of prices. The money supply, or the growth of the money supply, is an **intermediate target**, an objective that helps the Fed achieve its ultimate policy objective—economic growth with stable prices.

intermediate target: an objective used to achieve some ultimate policy goal

Using the growth of the money supply as an intermediate target assumes there is a fairly stable relationship among changes in money and changes in income and prices. The bases for this assumption are the equation of exchange and the quantity theory of money. The **equation of exchange** is a definition that relates the quantity of money to nominal GDP:

equation of exchange: an equation that relates the quantity of money to nominal GDP

$$MV = PQ$$

where

M = the quantity of money
V = the velocity of money
P = the price level
Q = the quantity of output, like real income or real GDP

This equation is true by definition: Money times the velocity of money will always be equal to nominal GDP.

velocity of money: the average number of times each dollar is spent on final goods and services in a year

In Chapter 14 we said there are two definitions of the money supply: M1 and M2. The **velocity of money** is the average number of times each dollar is spent on final goods and services in a year. If *P* is the price level and *Q* is real GDP (the quantity of goods and services produced in the economy), then *PQ* equals nominal GDP. If

$$MV = PQ$$

then

$$V = \frac{PQ}{M}$$

Suppose the price level is 2, and real GDP is \$500; *PQ*, or nominal GDP, is \$1,000. If the money supply is \$200, then velocity is 5 (\$1,000/\$200).

ECONOMIC INSIGHT

What's on a 20-Dollar Bill?

The figure shows both sides of a 20-dollar bill. We've numbered several elements for identification.

1. **Watermark** A watermark, created during the paper-making process, depicts the same historical figure as the portrait. It is visible from both sides when held up to a light.
2. **Security thread** An embedded polymer strip, positioned in a unique spot for each denomination, guards against counterfeiting. The thread itself, visible when held up to a bright light, contains microprinting—the letters *USA* and *TWENTY*, and a flag. When viewed under ultraviolet light, the thread glows a distinctive color for each denomination.
3. **Color-shifting ink** The ink used in the numeral in the lower right-hand corner on the front of the bill looks green when viewed straight on but copper when viewed at an angle.
4. **Color background** Background colors of green and peach are used, and the words *TWENTY* and *USA* are printed in blue.
5. **Serial number** No two notes of the same kind, denomination, and series have the same serial number. This fact can be important in detecting counterfeit notes; many counterfeiters make large batches of a particular note with the same number.

   Notes are numbered in lots of 100 million. Each lot has a different suffix letter, beginning with *A* and following in alphabetical order through *Z*, omitting *O* because of its similarity to the numerical zero.

   Serial numbers consist of two prefix letters, eight numerals, and a one-letter suffix. The first letter of the prefix designates the series. The second letter of the prefix designates the Federal Reserve Banks to which the note was issued. *A* designates the first district, or the Boston Fed, and *L*, the twelfth letter in the alphabet, designates the twelfth district, or the San Francisco Fed.
6. **"In God We Trust"** Secretary of the Treasury Salmon P. Chase first authorized the use of "In God We Trust" on U.S. money on the 2-cent coin in 1864. In 1955, Congress mandated the use of this phrase on all currency and coins.
7. **Small yellow 20s are printed on the back of the bill.**

quantity theory of money: with constant velocity, changes in the quantity of money change nominal GDP

NOW YOU TRY IT

If $M = \$100$, $V = 4$, $P = 2$,

a. What is the value of Q?

b. What is the value of nominal GDP?

c. If the central bank raises M to \$105 and V is unchanged, what will happen to the value of nominal GDP?

A velocity of 5 means that each dollar must be spent an average of five times during the year if a money supply of \$200 is going to support the purchase of \$1,000 worth of new goods and services.

The **quantity theory of money** uses the equation of exchange to relate changes in the money supply to changes in prices and output. If the money supply (M) increases, and velocity (V) is constant, then nominal GDP (PQ) must increase. If the economy is operating at maximum capacity (producing at the maximum level of Q), an increase in M causes an increase in P. And if there is substantial unemployment so that Q can increase, the increase in M may mean a higher price level (P) as well as higher real GDP (Q).

The Fed attempts to set money growth targets that are consistent with rising output and low inflation. In terms of the quantity theory of money, the Fed wants to increase M at a rate that supports steadily rising Q with slow and steady increases in P. The assumption that there is a reasonably stable relationship among M, P, and Q is what motivates the Fed to use money supply growth rates as an intermediate target to achieve its ultimate goal—higher Q with slow increases in P.

From the late 1950s to the mid-1970s, the velocity of the M1 money supply grew at a steady pace, from 3.5 in 1959 to 5.5 in 1975. Knowing that V was growing at a steady pace, the Fed was able to set a target growth rate for the M1 money supply, confident that it would produce a fairly predictable growth in nominal GDP. But when velocity is not constant, there can be problems with using money growth rates as an intermediate target. This is exactly what happened in the late 1970s. Although the M2 velocity continued to indicate a stable pattern of growth, M1 velocity behaved erratically. With the breakdown of the relationship between the M1 money supply and GDP, the Fed shifted its emphasis from the M1 money supply, concentrating instead on achieving targeted growth in the M2 money supply. More recently, the velocity of M2 has become less predictable, so the FOMC no longer states explicit targets for money growth.

Economists are still debating the reason for the fluctuations in velocity. Some argue that new deposits and innovations in banking have led to

The velocity of money is the average number of times each dollar is spent on final goods and services in a year.

DAVID YOUNG-WOLFF/PHOTOEDIT

fluctuations in the money held in traditional demand deposits as bank customers switched to different types of financial assets. These unpredictable changes in financial asset holdings affect the various money supplies and their velocities.

In addition to money growth, the Fed monitors other key variables that are used to indicate the future course of the economy. These include commodity prices, interest rates, and foreign exchange rates. The Fed may not set formal targets for all of them, but it considers them in setting policy. The FOMC does set an explicit target for the *federal funds rate* of interest. This is the interest rate banks pay to borrow money overnight from other banks. This rate is now the key intermediate target for Fed monetary policy.

2.a.2. Inflation Targeting

Some countries have moved away from pursuing intermediate targets such as money growth rates and have instead focused on an ultimate goal: a low inflation rate. In part, these countries realize that using monetary policy to support economic growth, low unemployment, and also low inflation has often resulted in an inflationary bias. The public generally likes to see policies such as lower interest rates that support faster economic growth. Fighting inflation may actually involve unpopular higher interest rates and slower growth. Therefore, a central bank may find it politically attractive to stimulate the economy so that inflation takes a secondary position. In addition, if the central bank always considers multiple goals such as maintaining low unemployment and low inflation, the public may not easily be able to understand the central bank's decision-making process. Consequently, there may be great uncertainty regarding monetary policy and more difficulty for business firms and households in making economic plans for the future. Commitment to a target inflation rate greatly reduces that uncertainty.

Inflation targeting has been adopted in several countries, including New Zealand, Canada, the United Kingdom, Australia, Switzerland, Sweden, Chile, Korea, South Africa, and Europe (by the European Central Bank). The Fed recently announced a target of 2 percent inflation as a guide to its policy. It is important to realize that a central bank that follows inflation targeting requires independence from fiscal policy. It is not enough to announce a target for the inflation rate. The central bank must not be in a position of having to help finance government spending. Only with this independence can a central bank truly have a credible inflation target.

2.b. Operating Procedures

The FOMC sets federal funds rate targets and then implements them through the Federal Reserve Bank of New York. The mechanism for translating policy into action is an **FOMC directive**. Each directive outlines the conduct of monetary policy over the six-week period until the FOMC meets again to reconsider its targets and specify policy tools.

FOMC directive: instructions issued by the FOMC to the Federal Reserve Bank of New York to implement monetary policy

Figure 15.2 contains the directive issued by the FOMC meeting of April 24, 2012. The FOMC directed the bond traders at the Federal Reserve Bank of New York to buy or sell government bonds as needed to keep the federal funds rate, or the interest rate that one bank charges another for overnight lending, between 0 and .25 percent. This was during the recovery period following the deepest recession since the Great Depression so the Fed was trying to stimulate the economy with very low interest rates. If the rate starts to rise above .25 percent, then the New York Fed will buy bonds from bond dealers. The dealers are paid with funds drawn on the Federal Reserve, which are then deposited in the dealers' accounts in commercial banks. This will inject money into the banking system. It will increase bank excess reserves (*ER*), giving the banks more money to lend; as a result, the cost of these funds, the federal funds rate, will fall. Nominal interest rates cannot drop below zero, but if the rate reaches zero and

FIGURE 15.2 FOMC Directive and Policy Statement

The FOMC always issues a directive to guide the conduct of monetary policy between meetings. In addition, a press statement at the conclusion of the meeting indicates the Committee's view regarding the likely course of policy in the near future. At the meeting that took place on April 24, 2012, the directive and policy statement shown here were issued.

"The Federal Open Market Committee seeks monetary and financial conditions that will foster price stability and promote sustainable growth in output. To further its long-run objectives, the Committee seeks conditions in reserve markets consistent with federal funds trading in a range from 0 to ¼ percent. The Committee directs the Desk to continue the maturity extension program it began in September to purchase, by the end of June 2012, Treasury securities with remaining maturities of approximately 6 years to 30 years with a total face value of $400 billion, and to sell Treasury securities with remaining maturities of 3 years or less with a total face value of $400 billion. The Committee also directs the Desk to maintain its existing policies of rolling over maturing Treasury securities into new issues and of reinvesting principal payments on all agency debt and agency mortgage-backed securities in the System Open Market Account in agency mortgage-backed securities in order to maintain the total face value of domestic securities at approximately $2.6 trillion. The Committee directs the Desk to engage in dollar roll transactions as necessary to facilitate settlement of the Federal Reserve's agency MBS transactions. The System Open Market Account Manager and the Secretary will keep the Committee informed of ongoing developments regarding the System's balance sheet that could affect the attainment over time of the Committee's objectives of maximum employment and price stability."

POLICY STATEMENT

"Information received since the Federal Open Market Committee met in March suggests that the economy has been expanding moderately. Labor market conditions have improved in recent months; the unemployment rate has declined but remains elevated.

Household spending and business fixed investment have continued to advance. Despite some signs of improvement, the housing sector remains depressed. Inflation has picked up somewhat, mainly reflecting higher prices of crude oil and gasoline. However, longer-term inflation expectations have remained stable.

Consistent with its statutory mandate, the Committee seeks to foster maximum employment and price stability. The Committee expects economic growth to remain moderate over coming quarters then to pick up gradually. Consequently, the Committee anticipates that the unemployment rate will decline gradually toward levels that it judges to be consistent with its dual mandate. Strains in global financial markets continue to pose significant downside risks to the economic outlook. The increase in oil and gasoline prices earlier this year is expected to affect inflation only temporarily, and the Committee anticipates that subsequently inflation will run at or below the rate that it judges most consistent with its dual mandate. To support a stronger economic recovery and to help ensure that inflation, over time, is at the rate most consistent with its dual mandate, the Committee expects to maintain a highly accommodative stance for monetary policy. In particular, the Committee decided today to keep the target range for the federal funds rate at 0 to ¼ percent and currently anticipates that economic conditions—including low rates of resource utilization and a subdued outlook for inflation over the medium run—are likely to warrant exceptionally low levels for the federal funds rate at least through late 2014.

The Committee also decided to continue its program to extend the average maturity of its holdings of securities as announced in September. The Committee is maintaining its existing policies of reinvesting principal payments from its holdings of agency debt and agency mortgage-backed securities in agency mortgage-backed securities and of rolling over maturing Treasury securities at auction. The Committee will regularly review the size and composition of its securities holdings and is prepared to adjust those holdings as appropriate to promote a stronger economic recovery in a context of price stability."

the Fed wants to raise interest rates, then the New York Fed will sell bonds to bond dealers. The dealers pay for the bonds with funds drawn on commercial banks. This drains money from the banking system. Bank excess reserves will fall, and since banks will have less money to lend, the cost of these funds, the federal funds rate, will rise. So the actual federal funds rate fluctuates around the target rate set by the FOMC directive.

At the conclusion of each FOMC meeting, a policy statement is issued to the press. This statement informs the public of the committee's view regarding the likely course of the economy in the near term. It will also indicate the likely course of monetary policy. In Figure 15.2, the policy statement issued at the conclusion of the meeting held on April 24, 2012, is given. The key part of this statement is the following: "... the Committee anticipates that the unemployment rate will decline gradually toward levels that it judges to be consistent with its dual mandate. Strains in global financial markets continue to pose significant downside risks to the economic outlook. The increase in oil and gasoline prices earlier this year is expected to affect inflation only temporarily, and the Committee anticipates that subsequently inflation will run at or below the rate that it judges most consistent with its dual mandate." Remember that the Fed's goals are stable prices and economic growth. If the view was balanced, this would indicate that the FOMC did not clearly see either mounting inflation pressures or recession pressures. However, at this time the FOMC was more concerned with the risk of low growth than with inflation, and kept interest rates very low. Had the Fed been worried about possible rising inflation, then the public would expect that it might raise interest rates at its next meeting.

3

What are the tools of monetary policy?

2.b.1. **Tools of Monetary Policy** The Fed controls the money supply and interest rates by changing bank reserves. There are three tools the Fed can use to change reserves: the *reserve requirement*, the *discount rate*, and *open market operations*. In Chapter 14, you saw that banks can expand the money supply by a multiple of their excess reserves—the deposit expansion multiplier, the reciprocal of the reserve requirement.

Reserve Requirement The Fed requires banks to hold a fraction of their deposits on reserve. This fraction is the reserve requirement. *Transaction deposits* are checking accounts and other deposits that can be used to pay third parties. Large banks hold a greater percentage of deposits in reserve than small banks do (the reserve requirement increases from 0 for the first $11.5 million of deposits to 3 percent for deposits from $11.5 to $71 million, and then to 10 percent for deposits in excess of $71 million).

Remember from Chapter 14 that required reserves are the dollar amount of reserves that a bank must hold to meet its reserve requirement. There are two ways in which required reserves (*RR*) may be held: vault cash at the bank or a deposit in the Fed. The sum of a bank's *vault cash* (coin and currency in the bank's vault) and deposit in the Fed is called its **legal reserves**. When legal reserves (*LR*) equal required reserves, the bank has no excess reserves and can make no new loans. When legal reserves exceed required reserves, the bank has excess reserves available for lending.

legal reserves: the cash a bank holds in its vault plus its deposit in the Fed

As bank excess reserves change, the lending and money-creating potential of the banking system changes. One way the Fed can alter excess reserves is by changing the reserve requirement. If it lowers the reserve requirement, a portion of what was previously required reserves becomes excess reserves, which can be used to make loans and expand the money supply. A lower reserve requirement also increases the deposit expansion multiplier. By raising the reserve requirement, the Fed reduces the money-creating potential of the banking system and tends to reduce the money supply. A higher reserve requirement also lowers the deposit expansion multiplier.

Consider the example in Table 15.2. If First National Bank's balance sheet shows vault cash of $100,000 and a deposit in the Fed of $200,000, the bank has legal reserves of $300,000. The amount of money that the bank can lend is determined by its excess reserves. Excess reserves equal legal reserves minus required reserves:

$$ER = LR - RR$$

If the reserve requirement (r) is 10 percent (.10), the bank must keep 10 percent of its deposits (D) as required reserves:

$$\begin{aligned} RR &= rD \\ &= .10(\$1{,}000{,}000) \\ &= \$100{,}000 \end{aligned}$$

In this case, the bank has excess reserves of $200,000 ($300,000 − $100,000). The bank can make a maximum loan of $200,000. The banking system can expand the money supply by the deposit expansion multiplier ($1/r$) times the excess reserves of the bank, or $2,000,000 ($1/.10 \times \$200{,}000$).

Table 15.2 The Effect of a Change in the Reserve Requirement

Balance Sheet of First National Bank			
Assets		**Liabilities**	
Vault cash	\$100,000	Deposits	\$1,000,000
Deposit in Fed	200,000		
Loans	700,000		
Total	\$1,000,000	Total	\$1,000,000

Legal reserves (*LR*) equal vault cash plus the deposit in the Fed, or \$300,000:

$$\begin{aligned} LR &= \$100{,}000 + \$200{,}000 \\ &= \$300{,}000 \end{aligned}$$

Excess reserves (*ER*) equal legal reserves minus required reserves (*RR*):

$$ER = LR - RR$$

Required reserves equal the reserve requirement (*r*) times deposits (*D*):

$$RR = rD$$

If the reserve requirement is 10 percent:

$$\begin{aligned} RR &= (.10)(\$1{,}000{,}000) \\ &= \$100{,}000 \\ ER &= \$300{,}000 - \$100{,}000 \\ &= \$200{,}000 \end{aligned}$$

First National Bank can make a maximum loan of \$200,000.

The banking system can expand the money supply by the deposit expansion multiplier (1/*r*) times the excess reserves of the bank, or \$2,000,000:

$$\begin{aligned} (1/.10)(\$200{,}000) &= 10(\$200{,}000) \\ &= \$2{,}000{,}000 \end{aligned}$$

If the reserve requirement is 20 percent:

$$\begin{aligned} RR &= (.20)(\$1{,}000{,}000) \\ &= \$200{,}000 \\ ER &= \$300{,}000 - \$200{,}000 \\ &= \$100{,}000 \end{aligned}$$

First National Bank can make a maximum loan of \$100,000.

The banking system can expand the money supply by the deposit expansion multiplier (1/*r*) times the excess reserves of the bank, or \$500,000:

$$\begin{aligned} (1/.20)(\$100{,}000) &= 5(\$100{,}000) \\ &= \$500{,}000 \end{aligned}$$

If the reserve requirement goes up to 20 percent (.20), required reserves are 20 percent of \$1,000,000, or \$200,000. Excess reserves are now \$100,000, which is the maximum loan the bank can make. The banking system can expand the money supply by \$500,000:

$$\begin{aligned} (1/.20)(\$100{,}000) &= 5(\$100{,}000) \\ &= \$500{,}000 \end{aligned}$$

By raising the reserve requirement, the Fed can reduce the money-creating potential of the banking system and the money supply. And by lowering the reserve requirement, the Fed can increase the money-creating potential of the banking system and the money supply.

All this discussion assumes that banks will only hold the minimum required amount of reserves. Usually, this is a good assumption. After all, banks earn money by lending money, not by holding onto it. Lately, however, banks have been holding far more reserves than the Fed requires. In April 2012, banks were required to hold $100.5 billion in reserves, but instead they held $1,586 billion! Reducing the reserve requirement would be ineffective, because banks were holding large quantities of excess reserves due to uncertainty regarding the economic outlook and concerns regarding the credit worthiness of other banks to whom they would usually have lent the excess reserves.

Discount Rate If a bank needs more reserves in order to make new loans, it typically borrows from other banks in the federal funds market. The market is called the *federal funds market* because the funds are being loaned from one commercial bank's excess reserves on deposit with the Federal Reserve to another commercial bank's deposit account at the Fed. For instance, if the First National Bank has excess reserves of $1 million, it can lend the excess to the Second National Bank. When a bank borrows in the federal funds market, it pays a rate of interest called the **federal funds rate**.

federal funds rate: the interest rate a bank charges when it lends excess reserves to another bank

discount rate: the interest rate the Fed charges commercial banks when they borrow from it

At times, however, banks borrow directly from the Fed, although the Fed restricts access to such funds. The **discount rate** is the rate of interest the Fed charges banks. (In other countries, the rate of interest the central bank charges commercial banks is often called the *bank rate*.) Another way the Fed controls the level of bank reserves and the money supply is by changing the discount rate.

When the Fed raises the discount rate, it raises the cost of borrowing reserves, reducing the amount of reserves borrowed. Lower levels of reserves limit bank lending and the expansion of the money supply. When the Fed lowers the discount rate, it lowers the cost of borrowing reserves, increasing the amount of borrowing. As bank reserves increase, so do loans and the money supply.

The discount rate is relatively stable. Although other interest rates can fluctuate daily, the discount rate usually remains fixed for months at a time. Since the late 1970s, the most the rate has been changed in a year has been seven times.

There are actually two different discount rates. The rate on "primary credit" is for loans made to banks in good financial condition and is set above the federal funds target rate. At the time this edition of the text was revised, the interest rate on primary credit was set at half a percentage point above the federal funds rate. Thus, if the FOMC sets the federal funds rate at 2 percent, then the discount rate on primary credit is 2.5 percent. In addition to the rate for primary credit loans, there is another discount rate for "secondary credit." This rate is for banks that are having financial difficulties. At the time of this edition, the secondary credit rate was set at 1 percentage point above the federal funds rate. Thus, if the federal funds target is set at 2 percent, the interest rate on secondary credit is 3 percent. Loans made at these discount rates are for very short terms, typically overnight.

open market operations: the buying and selling of government bonds by the Fed to control bank reserves, the federal funds rate, and the money supply

Open Market Operations The major tool of monetary policy is the Fed's **open market operations**, the buying and selling of U.S. government bonds. Suppose the FOMC wants to increase bank reserves to lower the federal funds rate. The committee issues a directive to the bond-trading desk at the Federal Reserve Bank of New York to change the federal funds rate to a lower level. In order to accomplish this, the Fed must buy bonds. The bonds are purchased from private bond dealers. The dealers are paid with checks drawn on the Federal Reserve, which then are deposited in the dealers' accounts at commercial banks. What happens? As bank deposits and reserves increase, banks have more excess reserves to lend, so the federal funds rate falls. If the higher reserves lead to increased bank lending to the public, then the new loans expand the money supply through the deposit expansion multiplier process.

If the Fed wants to increase the federal funds rate, it sells bonds. Private bond dealers pay for the bonds with checks drawn on commercial banks.

Commercial bank deposits and reserves drop, and as there are fewer reserves to lend, the federal funds rate rises, and the money supply decreases through the deposit expansion multiplier process.

Its open market operations allow the Fed to control the federal funds rate and the money supply. To lower the federal funds rate and increase the money supply, the Fed buys U.S. government bonds. To raise the federal funds rate and decrease the money supply, it sells U.S. government bonds. The effect of selling these bonds, however, varies according to whether there are excess reserves in the banking system. If there are excess reserves, the money supply does not necessarily decrease when the Fed sells bonds. The open market sale may simply reduce the level of excess reserves, reducing the rate at which the money supply increases.

Table 15.3 shows how open market operations change bank reserves and illustrates the money-creating power of the banking system. First National Bank's initial balance sheet shows excess reserves of $100,000 with a 20 percent reserve requirement. Therefore, the bank can make a maximum loan of $100,000. On the basis of the bank's reserve position, the banking system can increase the money supply by a maximum of $500,000.

If the Fed purchases $100,000 worth of bonds from a private dealer, who deposits the $100,000 in an account at First National Bank, the excess reserves

Table 15.3 The Effect of an Open Market Operation

Balance Sheet of First National Bank

Assets		Liabilities	
Vault cash	$100,000	Deposits	$1,000,000
Deposit in Fed	200,000		
Loans	700,000		
Total	$1,000,000	Total	$1,000,000

Initially legal reserves (*LR*) equal vault cash plus the deposit in the Fed, or $300,000:

$$LR = \$100,000 + \$200,000$$
$$= \$300,000$$

If the reserve requirement (*r*) is 20 percent (.20), required reserves (*RR*) equal $200,000:

$$.20(\$1,000,000) = \$200,000$$

Excess reserves (*ER*), then, equal $100,000 ($300,000 − $200,000). The bank can make a maximum loan of $100,000. The banking system can expand the money supply by the deposit expansion multiplier (1/*r*) times the excess reserves of the bank, or $500,000:

$$(1/.20)(\$100,000) = 5(\$100,000)$$
$$= \$500,000$$

Open market purchase:

The Fed purchases $100,000 worth of bonds from a dealer, who deposits the $100,000 in an account at First National. At this point, the bank has legal reserves of $400,000, required reserves of $220,000, and excess reserves of $180,000. It can make a maximum loan of $180,000, which can expand the money supply by $900,000 [(1/.20)($180,000)].

Open market sale:

The Fed sells $100,000 worth of bonds to a dealer, who pays with a check drawn on an account at First National. At this point, the bank has legal reserves of $200,000, required reserves of $180,000 (its deposits now equal $900,000), and excess reserves of $20,000. It can make a maximum loan of $20,000, which can expand the money supply by $100,000 [(1/.20)($20,000)].

of First National Bank increase to $180,000. These reserves can generate a maximum increase in the money supply of $900,000. The open market purchase increases the excess reserves of the banking system, stimulating the growth of money and, eventually, nominal GDP.

What happens when an open market sale takes place? If the Fed sells $100,000 worth of bonds to a private bond dealer, the dealer pays for the bonds using a check drawn on First National Bank. First National's deposits drop from $1,000,000 to $900,000, and its legal reserves drop from $300,000 to $200,000. With excess reserves of $20,000, the banking system can increase the money supply by only $100,000. The open market sale reduces the money-creating potential of the banking system from $500,000 initially to $100,000.

2.b.2. **FOMC Directives** When it sets monetary policy, the FOMC begins with its *ultimate goal*: economic growth at stable prices. It defines that goal in terms of GDP and inflation. As can be seen in Figure 15.3, and as is usually the case in real life, the Fed uses open market operations to achieve its goals. The committee relies on a *short-run operating target* for this information. Both the quantity of excess reserves in the banking system and the federal funds rate can serve as short-run operating targets.

The FOMC carries out its policies through directives to the bond-trading desk at the Federal Reserve Bank of New York, as was discussed at the beginning of section 2.b and illustrated in Figure 15.3. The directives specify a short-run operating target that the trading desk must use in its day-to-day operations. In recent years, the target has been the federal funds rate.

By late 2008, however, the target federal funds rate was between 0 and 0.25 percent—in other words, it could go no lower, and yet the goal of economic growth was still not attained. In such a situation, called a liquidity trap, conventional monetary policies can lose effectiveness. The Fed turned to unconventional tactics. On November 25, 2008, the Federal Open Market Committee announced that the New York Fed would purchase $500 billion of mortgage-backed securities issued by Fannie Mae, Freddie Mac, and Ginnie Mae, in what they called a large-scale asset purchase (LSAP) program.

2.b.3. **Quantitative Easing** The Fed was not the only central bank to engage in nontraditional monetary policy in the period since the financial crisis began. Quantitative easing or "QE" involves increasing the amount of liquidity in the financial system to result in easier credit conditions and lower interest rates on loans made to firms and households. Such policy was also utilized by the Bank of Japan, the Bank of England, and the European Central Bank. These monetary authorities were all dealing with economies where interest rates were very low by historical standards, and the policy rate was close to zero. Given little or no room by which to cut the target rate, like the federal funds rate in the United States, alternative means of stimulating spending were needed and so QE was launched.

FIGURE 15.3 Monetary Policy: Tools, Targets, and Goals

The Fed primarily uses open market operations to implement monetary policy. The decision to buy or sell bonds is based on a short-run operating target, like the federal funds rate. The short-run operating target is set to achieve a certain level of gross domestic product and/or inflation.

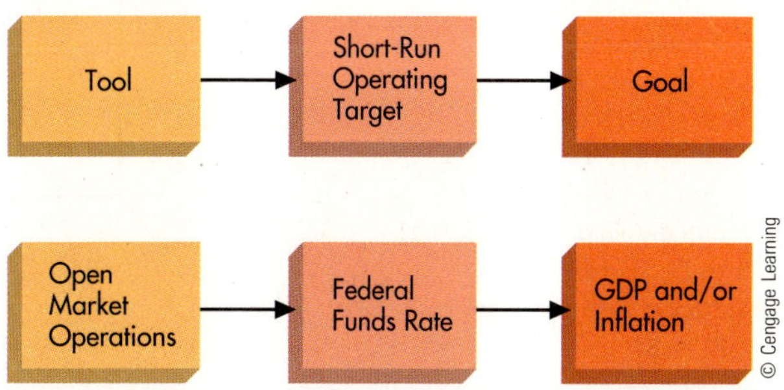

4

What role do central banks play in the foreign exchange market?

2.c. Foreign Exchange Market Intervention

In the mid-1980s, conditions in the foreign exchange market took on a high priority in FOMC directives. There was concern that the value of the dollar in relation to other currencies was contributing to a large U.S. international trade deficit. Furthermore, the governments of the major industrial countries decided to work together to maintain more stable exchange rates. This meant that the Federal Reserve and the central banks of the other developed countries had to devote more attention to maintaining exchange rates within a certain target band of values. Although more recently exchange rates have taken less of a role in FOMC meetings, it is still important to understand how central banks change exchange rates.

foreign exchange market intervention: the buying and selling of foreign exchange by a central bank to move exchange rates up or down to a targeted level

2.c.1. Mechanics of Intervention **Foreign exchange market intervention** is the buying and selling of foreign money by a central bank in order to move exchange rates up or down to a targeted level. We can use a simple supply and demand diagram to illustrate the role of intervention. Figure 15.4 shows the U.S. dollar–Japanese yen exchange market. The demand curve is the demand for dollars produced by the demand for U.S. goods and financial assets. The supply curve is the supply of dollars generated by U.S. residents' demand for the products and financial assets of other countries. Here, the supply of dollars to the dollar–yen market comes from the U.S. demand to buy Japanese products.

The initial equilibrium exchange rate is at point *A*, where the demand curve (D_1) and the supply curve (S_1) intersect. At point *A*, the exchange rate is ¥100 = $1, and Q_1 dollars are exchanged for yen. Suppose that over time, U.S. residents buy more from Japan than Japanese residents buy from the United States. As the supply of dollars increases in relation to the demand for dollars, equilibrium shifts to point *B*. At point *B*, Q_2 dollars are exchanged at a rate of ¥90 = $1. The dollar has *depreciated* against the yen, or, conversely, the yen has *appreciated* against the dollar.

When the dollar depreciates, U.S. goods are cheaper to Japanese buyers (it takes fewer yen to buy each dollar). The depreciated dollar stimulates U.S. exports to Japan. It also raises the price of Japanese goods to U.S. buyers, reducing U.S. imports from Japan. Rather than allow exchange rates to change, with the subsequent changes in trade, central banks often seek to maintain

FIGURE 15.4 The Dollar–Yen Foreign Exchange Market

The demand is the demand for dollars arising out of the Japanese demand for U.S. goods and services. The supply is the supply of dollars arising out of the U.S. demand for Japanese goods and services. Initially, the equilibrium exchange rate is at the intersection of the demand curve (D_1) and the supply curve (S_1), where the exchange rate is ¥100 = $1. An increase in the U.S. demand for Japanese goods increases S_1 to S_2 and pushes the equilibrium exchange rate down to point *B*, where ¥90 = $1. If the Fed's target exchange rate is ¥100 = $1, the Fed must intervene and buy dollars in the foreign exchange market. This increases demand to D_2 and raises the equilibrium exchange rate to point *C*, where ¥100 = $1.

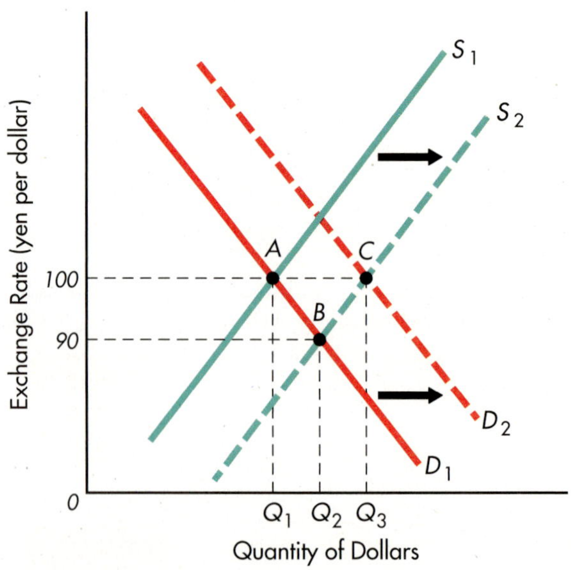

fixed exchange rates because of international agreements or desired trade in goods or financial assets.

Suppose the Fed sets a target range for the dollar at a minimum exchange rate of ¥100 = \$1. If the exchange rate falls below the minimum, the Fed must intervene in the foreign exchange market to increase the value of the dollar. In Figure 15.4, you can see that the only way to increase the dollar's value is to increase the demand for dollars. The Fed intervenes in the foreign exchange market by buying dollars in exchange for yen. It uses its holdings of Japanese yen to purchase $Q_3 - Q_1$ dollars, shifting the demand curve to D_2. Now equilibrium is at point C, where Q_3 dollars are exchanged at the rate of ¥100 = \$1.

The kind of intervention shown in Figure 15.4 is only temporary because the Fed has a limited supply of yen. Under another intervention plan, the Bank of Japan would support the ¥100 = \$1 exchange rate by using yen to buy dollars. The Bank of Japan could carry on this kind of policy indefinitely because it has the power to create yen. A third alternative is *coordinated intervention*, in which both the Fed and the Bank of Japan sell yen in exchange for dollars to support the minimum yen–dollar exchange rate.

2.c.2. **Effects of Intervention** Intervention can be used to shift the demand and supply for currency and thereby change the exchange rate. Foreign exchange market intervention also has effects on the money supply. If the Federal Reserve wanted to increase the dollar price of the euro, it would create dollars to purchase euros. Thus, when foreign exchange market intervention involves the use of domestic currency to buy foreign currency, it increases the domestic money supply. The expansionary effect of this intervention can be offset by a domestic open market operation, in a process called **sterilization**. If the Fed creates dollars to buy euros, for example, it increases the money supply, as we have just seen. To reduce the money supply, the Fed can direct an open market bond sale. The bond sale sterilizes the effect of the intervention on the domestic money supply.

sterilization: the use of domestic open market operations to offset the effects of a foreign exchange market intervention on the domestic money supply

RECAP

1. The ultimate goal of monetary policy is economic growth with stable prices.
2. The Fed controls GDP indirectly through its control of the money supply.
3. The equation of exchange ($MV = PQ$) relates the quantity of money to nominal GDP.
4. The quantity theory of money states that with constant velocity, changes in the quantity of money change nominal GDP.
5. Every six to eight weeks, the Federal Open Market Committee issues a directive to the Federal Reserve Bank of New York that defines the FOMC's monetary targets and policy tools.
6. The Fed controls the nation's money supply by changing banks' excess reserves.
7. The tools of monetary policy are reserve requirements, the discount rate, and open market operations.
8. The money supply tends to increase (decrease) as the reserve requirement falls (rises), the discount rate falls (rises), and the Fed buys (sells) bonds.
9. Each FOMC directive defines its short-run operating target in terms of the federal funds rate.
10. Foreign exchange market intervention is the buying and selling of foreign money by a central bank to achieve a targeted exchange rate.
11. Sterilization is the use of domestic open market operations to offset the money supply effects of foreign exchange market intervention.

3. MONETARY POLICY AND EQUILIBRIUM INCOME

To see how changes in the money supply affect the equilibrium level of real GDP, we incorporate monetary policy into the aggregate demand and supply model. The first step in understanding monetary policy is understanding the demand for money. If you know what determines money demand, you can see how monetary policy is used to shift aggregate demand and change the equilibrium level of real GDP.

3.a. Money Demand

Why do you hold money? What does it do for you? What determines how much money you will hold? These questions are addressed in this section. Wanting to hold more money is not the same as wanting more income. You can decide to carry more cash or keep more dollars in your checking account even though your income has not changed. The quantity of dollars you want to hold is your demand for money. By summing the quantity of money demanded by each individual, we can find the money demand for the entire economy. Once we understand what determines money demand, we can put that demand together with the money supply and examine how money influences the interest rate and the equilibrium level of income.

In Chapter 14, we discussed the functions of money—that is, what money is used for. People use money as a unit of account, a medium of exchange, a store of value, and a standard of deferred payment. These last functions help explain the demand for money.

transactions demand for money: the demand to hold money to buy goods and services

People use money for transactions, to buy goods and services. The **transactions demand for money** is a demand to hold money in order to spend it on goods and services. Holding money in your pocket or checking account is a demand for money. Spending money is not demanding it; by spending it you are getting rid of it.

If your boss paid you the same instant that you wanted to buy something, the timing of your receipts and expenditures would match perfectly. You would not have to hold money for transactions. But because receipts typically occur much less often than expenditures, money is necessary to cover transactions between paychecks.

precautionary demand for money: the demand for money to cover unplanned transactions or emergencies

People also hold money to take care of emergencies. The **precautionary demand for money** exists because emergencies happen. People never know when an unexpected expense will crop up or when actual expenditures will exceed planned expenditures, so they hold money as a precaution.

speculative demand for money: the demand for money created by uncertainty about the value of other assets

Finally, there is a **speculative demand for money**, a demand created by uncertainty about the value of other assets. This demand exists because money is the most liquid store of value. If you want to buy a stock, but you believe the price is going to fall in the next few days, you hold the money until you are ready to buy the stock.

The speculative demand for money is not necessarily tied to a particular use of funds. People hold money because they expect the price of any asset to fall. Holding money is less risky than buying the asset today if the price of the asset seems likely to fall. For example, suppose you buy and sell fine art. The price of art fluctuates over time. You try to buy when prices are low and sell when prices are high. If you expect prices to fall in the short term, you hold money rather than art until the prices do fall. Then you use money to buy art for resale when the prices go up again.

5

What are the determinants of the demand for money?

3.a.1. The Money Demand Function

If you understand why people hold money, you can understand what changes the amount of money they hold. As you've just seen, people hold money in order to (1) carry out transactions (transactions demand), (2) be prepared for emergencies (precautionary demand), and (3) speculate on purchases of various assets (speculative demand).

The interest rate and nominal income (income measured in current dollars) influence how much money people hold in order to carry out these three activities.

The Interest Rate There is an inverse relationship between the interest rate and the quantity of money demanded (see Figure 15.5). The interest rate is the *opportunity cost* of holding money. If you bury \$1,000 bills in your backyard, that currency is earning no interest—you are forgoing the interest. At a low interest rate, the cost of forgone interest is small. At a higher interest rate, however, the cost of holding wealth in the form of money means giving up more interest. The higher the rate of interest, the greater the interest forgone by holding money, so the less money held. The costs of holding money limit the amount of money held.

Some components of the money supply pay interest to the depositor. Here the opportunity cost of holding money is the difference between the interest rate on a bond or some other nonmonetary asset and the interest rate on money. If a bond pays 9 percent interest a year and a bank deposit pays 5 percent, the opportunity cost of holding the deposit is 4 percent.

Figure 15.5 shows a money demand function in which the demand for money depends on the interest rate. The downward slope of the money demand (*Md*) curve shows the inverse relation between the interest rate and the quantity of money demanded. For instance, at an interest rate of 12 percent, the quantity of money demanded is \$400 billion. If the interest rate falls to 9 percent, the quantity of money demanded increases to \$600 billion.

Nominal Income The demand for money also depends on nominal income. Money demand varies directly with nominal income because as income increases, more transactions are carried out, and more money is required for those transactions.

The greater the nominal income, the greater the demand for money. This is true whether the increase in nominal income is a product of a higher price level or an increase in real income. Both generate a greater dollar volume of transactions. If the prices of all goods increase, then more money must be used to purchase goods and services. And as real income increases, more goods and services are being produced and sold, and living standards rise; this means more money is being demanded to execute the higher level of transactions.

FIGURE 15.5 The Money Demand Function

Money demand (*Md*) is a negative function of the rate of interest. The interest rate is the opportunity cost of holding money. The higher the interest rate, the lower the quantity of money demanded. At an interest rate of 9 percent, the quantity of money demanded is \$600 billion. At an interest rate of 12 percent, the quantity of money demanded falls to \$400 billion.

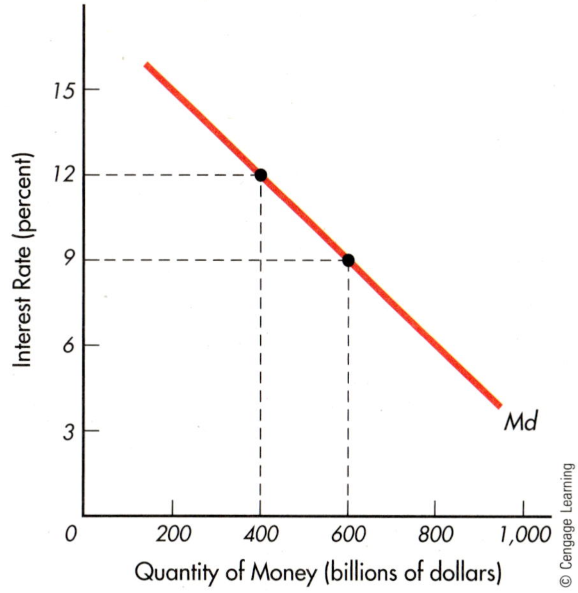

FIGURE 15.6 The Effect of a Change in Income on Money Demand

A change in real GDP, whatever the interest rate, shifts the money demand curve. Initially, real GDP is Y_0; the money demand curve at that level of income is *Md*. At an interest rate of 9 percent, the quantity of money demanded is $600 billion. If income increases to Y_1, the money demand shifts to Md_1. Here $800 billion is demanded at 9 percent. If income falls to Y_2, the money demand curve falls to Md_2, where $400 billion is demanded at 9 percent.

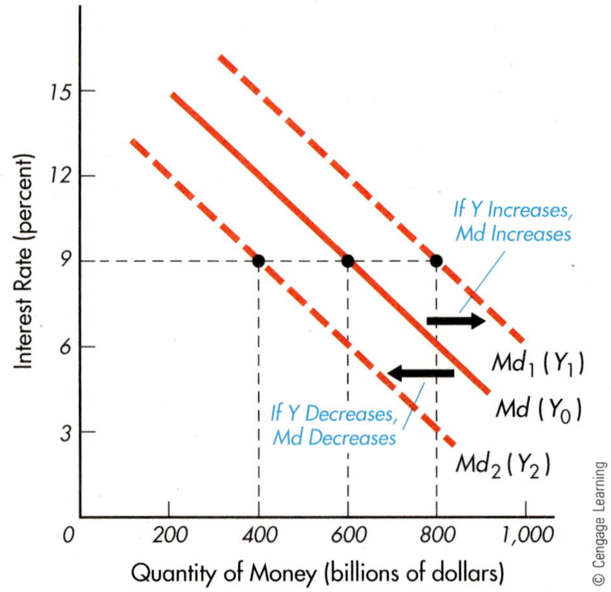

A change in nominal income changes the demand for money at any given interest rate. Figure 15.6 shows the effect of changes in nominal income on the money demand curve. If income rises from Y_0 to Y_1, money demand increases from *Md* to Md_1. If income falls from Y_0 to Y_2, money demand falls from *Md* to Md_2. When the money demand function shifts from *Md* to Md_1, the quantity of money demanded at an interest rate of 9 percent increases from $600 billion to $800 billion. When the money demand function shifts from *Md* to Md_2, the quantity of money demanded at 9 percent interest falls from $600 billion to $400 billion.

6

How does monetary policy affect the equilibrium level of real GDP?

3.a.2. **The Money Supply Function** The Federal Reserve is responsible for setting the money supply. The fact that the Fed can choose the money supply means that the money supply function is independent of the current interest rate and income. Figure 15.7 illustrates the money supply function (*Ms*). In the figure, the money supply is $600 billion at all interest rate levels. If the Fed increases the money supply, the vertical money supply function shifts to the right. If the Fed decreases the money supply, the function shifts to the left.

3.a.3. **Equilibrium in the Money Market** To find the equilibrium interest rate and quantity of money, we have to combine the money demand and money supply functions in one diagram. Figure 15.8 graphs equilibrium in the money market. Equilibrium, point *e*, is at the intersection of the money demand and money supply functions. In the figure, the equilibrium interest rate is 9 percent, and the quantity of money is $600 billion.

What forces work to ensure that the economy tends toward the equilibrium rate of interest? Let's look at Figure 15.8 again to understand what happens if the interest rate is not at equilibrium. If the interest rate falls below 9 percent, there will be an excess demand for money. People will want more money than the Fed is supplying. But because the supply of money does not change, the demand for more money just forces the interest rate to rise. How? Suppose people try to increase their money holdings by converting bonds and other nonmonetary assets into money. As bonds and other nonmonetary assets are sold for money, the interest rate goes up.

FIGURE 15.7 The Money Supply Function

The money supply function is a vertical line. This indicates that the Fed can choose any money supply it wants independent of the interest rate (and real GDP). In the figure, the money supply is set at $600 billion at all interest rates. The Fed can increase or decrease the money supply, shifting the curve to the right or left, but the curve remains vertical.

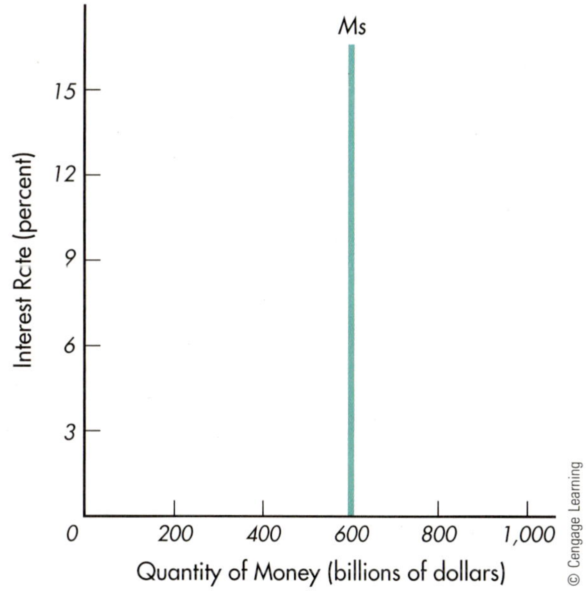

FIGURE 15.8 Equilibrium in the Money Market

Equilibrium is at point e, where the money demand and money supply curves intersect. At equilibrium, the interest rate is 9 percent, and the money supply is $600 billion. An interest rate above 9 percent would create an excess supply of money because the quantity of money demanded falls as the interest rate rises. An interest rate below 9 percent would create an excess demand for money because the quantity of money demanded rises as the interest rate falls.

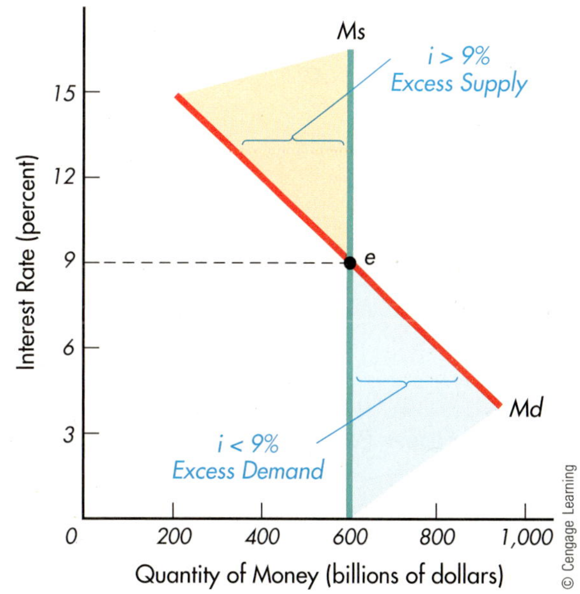

To understand the connection between the rate of interest and buying and selling bonds, you must realize that the current interest rate (yield) on a bond is determined by the bond price:

$$\text{Current interest rate} = \frac{\text{annual interest payment}}{\text{bond price}}$$

The numerator, the annual interest payment, is fixed for the life of the bond. The denominator, the bond price, fluctuates with supply and demand. As the bond price changes, the interest rate also changes.

Suppose a bond pays \$100 a year in interest and sells for \$1,000. The interest rate is 10 percent (\$100/\$1,000). If the supply of bonds increases because people want to convert bonds to money, the price of bonds falls. Suppose the price drops to \$800. At that price the interest rate equals 12.5 percent (\$100/\$800). This is the mechanism by which an excess demand for money changes the interest rate. As the interest rate goes up, the excess demand for money disappears.

Just the opposite occurs at interest rates above equilibrium. In Figure 15.8, any rate of interest above 9 percent creates an excess supply of money. Now people are holding more of their wealth in the form of money than they would like. What happens? They want to convert some of their money balances into nonmonetary assets, such as bonds. As the demand for bonds rises, bond prices increase. And as bond prices go up, interest rates fall. This drop in interest rates restores equilibrium in the money market.

3.b. Money and Equilibrium Income

Now we are ready to relate monetary policy to the equilibrium level of real GDP. We use Figure 15.9 to show how a change in the money supply affects real GDP. In part (a), as the money supply increases from Ms_1 to Ms_2, the equilibrium rate of interest falls from i_1 to i_2.

Remember that investment (business spending on capital goods) declines as the rate of interest increases. The interest rate is the cost of borrowed funds. As the interest rate rises, the return on investment falls and with it the level of investment. As the interest rate falls, the return on investment rises and with it the level of investment. In part (a) of Figure 15.9, the interest rate falls. In part (b) of the figure, you can see the effect of the lower interest rate on investment spending. As the interest rate falls from i_1 to i_2, investment increases from I_1 to I_2.

Figure 15.9(c) is the aggregate demand and supply equilibrium diagram. When investment spending increases, aggregate expenditures are higher at every price level, so the aggregate demand curve shifts to the right, from AD_1 to AD_2. The increase in aggregate demand increases equilibrium income from Y_1 to Y_2.

How does monetary policy affect equilibrium income? As the money supply increases, the equilibrium interest rate falls. As the interest rate falls, the equilibrium level of investment rises. Increased investment increases aggregate demand and equilibrium income. A decrease in the money supply works in reverse: As

FIGURE 15.9 Monetary Policy and Equilibrium Income

The three diagrams show the sequence of events by which a change in the money supply affects the equilibrium level of real GDP. In part (a), the money supply increases, lowering the equilibrium interest rate. In part (b), the lower interest rate pushes the equilibrium level of investment up. In part (c), the increase in investment increases aggregate demand and equilibrium real GDP.

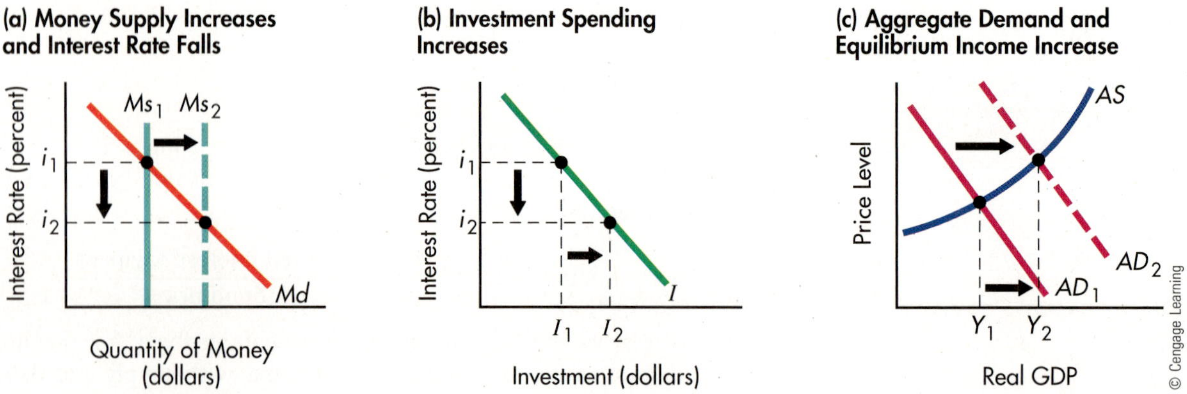

the interest rate rises, investment falls; as investment falls, aggregate demand and equilibrium income go down.

The mechanism we have just described is an oversimplification because the only element of aggregate expenditures that changes in this model is investment. But an excess demand for or supply of money involves more than simply selling or buying bonds. An excess supply of money probably would be reflected in increased consumption as well. If households are holding more money than they want to hold, they buy not only bonds but also goods and services so that consumption increases. If they are holding less money than they want to hold, they will sell bonds and consume less. So the effect of monetary policy on aggregate demand is a product of a change in both investment and consumption.

RECAP

1. The transactions demand for money is the demand to hold money to buy goods and services.
2. The precautionary demand for money exists because all expenditures cannot be planned.
3. The speculative demand for money is created by uncertainty about the value of other assets.
4. There is an inverse relationship between the interest rate and the quantity of money demanded.
5. The greater the nominal income, the greater the demand for money.
6. Because the Federal Reserve sets the money supply, the money supply function is independent of the interest rate and nominal income.
7. The current yield on a bond equals the annual interest payment divided by the price of the bond.
8. An increase in the money supply lowers the interest rate. This raises the level of investment, and this in turn increases aggregate demand and equilibrium income. A decrease in the money supply works in reverse.

The European Central Bank is headquartered in Frankfurt, Germany.

Petronilo G. Dangoy Jr/Shutterstock.com

4. THE EUROPEAN CENTRAL BANK

Traditionally, each country's central bank managed money and credit conditions in that country. This has typically meant control of that nation's money. However, with the agreement of 17 European countries to adopt a new money, the euro, and eliminate the 17 individual national monies, a new central bank, the European Central Bank, or ECB, was founded. We will provide a brief overview of the setup and responsibilities of the ECB.

4.a. The Need for a European Central Bank

7

What does the ECB do?

On January 1, 1999, the ECB assumed responsibility for the monetary policy of the euro nations. Table 15.4 lists the participating nations and the "legacy" currencies that have been replaced by the euro. In the third column of Table 15.4, the exchange rate of each of the former monies against the euro is given. When the euro was introduced, it was worth 13.7603 Austrian schillings, 40.3399 Belgian francs, and so on, as listed in Table 15.4. Once the various national monies were replaced by the euro, the national central banks could no longer control their national money supplies. The ECB determined monetary policy, including the money supply and interest rates for the whole region.

It is not possible for one money to have several different central banks determining how much money should circulate and related policy issues. Although each euro nation has a central bank, like the Bank of France or the German Bundesbank, these national central banks now function much like one of the regional district banks of the Federal Reserve System. Although the Federal Reserve Bank of Dallas does not determine the amount of money in circulation or the federal funds interest rate for the United States, it does have the responsibility for taking care of banking needs, such as regulating banks and distributing cash to banks, in that region. It also represents the special needs of that district at the Federal Reserve Board and FOMC meetings. Similarly, the national central banks of the euro nations handle local banking issues such as

Table 15.4 Countries and Former Currencies of the Euro Region

Country	Former Currency	Amount of Former Currency per Euro
Austria	Schilling	13.7603
Belgium	Franc	40.3399
Cyprus	pound	0.585274
Estonia	kroon	15.6466
Finland	Markka	5.94573
France	Franc	6.55957
Germany	Mark	1.95583
Greece	Drachma	340.750
Ireland	Pound	0.787564
Italy	Lira	1936.27
Malta	lira	0.4293
Luxembourg	Franc	40.3399
The Netherlands	Guilder	2.20371
Portugal	Escudo	200.482
Slovakia	koruna	30.1260
Slovenia	Tolar	239.640
Spain	Peseta	166.386

regulation and cash dispersal while representing the local interests of the national economy at the ECB meetings.

4.b. The Structure of the ECB

The ECB is located in Frankfurt, Germany, and is supervised by a six-member Executive Board. The board members are appointed by the common agreement of heads of state of the participating nations. Each member serves an eight-year nonrenewable term. The president of the ECB is one of the six board members and is chosen by the European Council made up of representatives of the member countries of the European Union. At the time this book was revised, the president was Mario Draghi of Italy.

The policy of the ECB is formulated by the 23-member Governing Council, which includes the 6 executive board members plus the 17 central bank governors of the euro nations. The ECB president chairs the Governing Council meetings and is the chief spokesperson for the Council, assuming a role much like that of the chair of the Federal Reserve Board in the United States.

The Governing Council meets every two weeks to review economic conditions and decide if any change in policy is required. The meetings begin with a review of economic conditions presented by the chief economist of the ECB, who also sits on the executive board. Then each member of the Governing Council has an opportunity to speak. The ECB president then summarizes the discussion, and if there is a majority sentiment to change policy, he suggests that action be taken. Policy change is generally a change in interest rates, similar to the federal funds rate changes in the United States.

4.c. ECB Policy

The main policy target of the ECB is to keep inflation below 2 percent per year. The official position of the ECB is that stable prices should be their most important goal, and any other goals are clearly secondary in importance. The public cannot judge how much debate exists regarding other goals, as the ECB policy meetings are secret and no record of Governing Council votes or discussion are made public. This has been a frequent source of criticism in the early years of the ECB. Since many other central banks, including the Federal Reserve, publish a record of each policy meeting, including votes taken on changing policy, there have been frequent calls for the ECB to make its policy discussions more transparent to the public also. The ECB position is that its Governing Council members are better insulated from political and special interest pressures in their home country if they can have an anonymous debate and voice their opinions more with a view toward the economic well-being of the entire eurozone rather than of one particular country. The rules of the Governing Council are that no members are to receive instructions from their home country but should think only in terms of the common good when voting on interest rate or exchange rate policies.

RECAP

1. The European Central Bank or ECB conducts monetary policy for the 17 nations adopting the euro as their currency.
2. The national central banks of the euro region take care of local banking and business needs but no longer have any monetary policymaking functions.
3. The ECB is governed by a six-member executive board, of which one board member serves as president.
4. Policymaking is done by the Governing Council made up of the 6 board members plus the 17 governors of the national central banks of the euro region.
5. The main target of ECB policy is to keep the inflation rate below 2 percent per year.

SUMMARY

What does the Federal Reserve do?

1. The Federal Reserve is the central bank of the United States.
2. The Federal Reserve System is operated by 12 district banks and a Board of Governors in Washington, DC.
3. The Fed services and supervises the banking system, acts as the banker of the U.S. Treasury, and controls the money supply.

How is monetary policy set?

4. The Fed controls nominal GDP indirectly by controlling the quantity of money in the nation's economy.
5. The Fed uses the federal funds rate as a short-run operating target to help it achieve its ultimate goal—economic growth with stable prices.

What are the tools of monetary policy?

6. The three tools of monetary policy are the reserve requirement, the discount rate, and open market operations.
7. The Fed buys bonds to increase the money supply and sells bonds to decrease the money supply.
8. The Federal Open Market Committee (FOMC) issues directives to the Federal Reserve Bank of New York outlining the conduct of monetary policy.

What role do central banks play in the foreign exchange market?

9. Central banks intervene in the foreign exchange market when it is necessary to maintain a targeted exchange rate.

What are the determinants of the demand for money?

10. The demand for money stems from the need to buy goods and services, to prepare for emergencies, and to retain a store of value.
11. There is an inverse relationship between the quantity of money demanded and the interest rate.
12. The greater the nominal income, the greater the demand for money.
13. Because the Fed sets the money supply, the money supply function is independent of the interest rate and real GDP.

How does monetary policy affect the equilibrium level of real GDP?

14. By altering the money supply, the Fed changes the interest rate and the level of investment, shifting aggregate demand and the equilibrium level of real GDP.

What does the ECB do?

15. The ECB is the central bank of the 17 nations adopting the euro as their national currency.
16. The ECB conducts monetary policy for the euro region.
17. The policy of the ECB is made by a Governing Council composed of the 6 executive board members and the 17 governors of the euro area national central banks.

EXERCISES

1. The Federal Reserve System divides the nation into 12 districts.
   a. List the 12 cities where the district banks are located.
   b. Which Federal Reserve district do you live in?
2. Briefly describe the functions the Fed performs for the banking community. In what sense is the Fed the bankers' bank?
3. Draw a graph showing equilibrium in the money market. Carefully label all curves and

axes and explain why the curves have the slopes they do.

4. Using the graph you prepared for exercise 3, illustrate and explain what happens when the Fed decreases the money supply.
5. When the Fed decreases the money supply, the equilibrium level of income changes. Illustrate and explain how.
6. Describe the quantity theory of money, defining each variable. Explain how changes in the money supply can affect real GDP and the price level. Under what circumstances could an increase in the money supply have *no* effect on nominal GDP?
7. There are several tools the Fed uses to implement monetary policy.
   a. Briefly describe these tools.
   b. Explain how the Fed would use each tool in order to increase the money supply.
8. First Bank has total deposits of $2,000,000 and legal reserves of $220,000.
   a. If the reserve requirement is 10 percent, what is the maximum loan that First Bank can make, and what is the maximum increase in the money supply based on First Bank's reserve position?
   b. If the reserve requirement is changed to 5 percent, how much can First Bank lend, and how much can the money supply be expanded?
9. Suppose you are a member of the FOMC, and the U.S. economy is entering a recession. Write a directive to the New York Fed about the conduct of monetary policy over the next two months. Your directive should address targets for the federal funds rate. You may refer to the *Federal Reserve Bulletin* for examples since this publication reports FOMC directives.
10. Suppose the Fed has a target range for the yen–dollar exchange rate. How would it keep the exchange rate within the target range if free market forces push the exchange rate out of the range? Use a graph to help explain your answer.
11. Why do you demand money? What determines how much money you keep in your pocket, purse, or bank accounts?
12. What is the current yield on a bond? Why do interest rates change when bond prices change?
13. If the Fed increases the money supply, what will happen to each of the following (other things being equal)?
    a. Interest rates
    b. Money demand
    c. Investment spending
    d. Aggregate demand
    e. The equilibrium level of national income
14. Suppose the banking system has vault cash of $1,000, deposits at the Fed of $2,000, and demand deposits of $10,000.
    a. If the reserve requirement is 20 percent, what is the maximum potential increase in the money supply given the banks' reserve position?
    b. If the Fed now purchases $500 worth of government bonds from private bond dealers, what are excess reserves of the banking system? (Assume that the bond dealers deposit the $500 in demand deposits.) How much can the banking system increase the money supply given the new reserve position?
15. Which countries have their monetary policy made by the ECB?
16. How is the ECB different from the Federal Reserve?
17. Visit the Federal Reserve Economic Data website maintained by the St. Louis Fed at research.stlouisfed.org/fred2. Make a graph of the excess reserves of depository institutions from 1959 to the present.

STUDY GUIDE FOR CHAPTER 15

Key Term Match

Match each term with its correct definition by placing the appropriate letter next to the corresponding number.

A. Federal Open Market Committee (FOMC)
B. intermediate target
C. equation of exchange
D. velocity of money
E. quantity theory of money
F. FOMC directive
G. legal reserves
H. federal funds rate
I. discount rate
J. open market operations
K. foreign exchange market intervention
L. sterilization
M. transactions demand for money
N. precautionary demand for money
O. speculative demand for money

____ 1. the buying and selling of government bonds by the Fed to control bank reserves, the federal funds rate, and the money supply

____ 2. the demand to hold money to buy goods and services

____ 3. the official policymaking body of the Federal Reserve System

____ 4. the interest rate a bank charges when it lends excess reserves to another bank

____ 5. the buying and selling of foreign exchange by a central bank to move exchange rates up or down to a targeted level

____ 6. an objective used to achieve some ultimate policy goal

____ 7. the cash a bank holds in its vault plus its deposit in the Fed

____ 8. an equation that relates the quantity of money to nominal GDP

____ 9. the interest rate the Fed charges commercial banks when they borrow from it

____ 10. instructions issued by the FOMC to the Federal Reserve Bank of New York to implement monetary policy

____ 11. the use of domestic open market operations to offset the effects of a foreign exchange market intervention on the domestic money supply

____ 12. the demand for money to cover unplanned transactions or emergencies

____ 13. the demand for money created by uncertainty about the value of other assets

____ 14. the average number of times each dollar is spent on final goods and services in a year

____ 15. with constant velocity, changes in the quantity of money change nominal GDP

Quick-Check Quiz

1. The Fed's most important function is to
   - ☐ a. provide services to the banking community.
   - ☐ b. control the money supply.
   - ☐ c. supervise the banking community.
   - ☐ d. clear checks.
   - ☐ e. hold bank reserves.

2. According to the equation of exchange,
   - ☐ a. if the money supply increases, and velocity is constant, real GDP must rise.
   - ☐ b. if the money supply increases, and velocity is constant, nominal GDP must rise.
   - ☐ c. an increase in the money supply causes an increase in the price level.
   - ☐ d. an increase in the money supply causes an increase in real GDP and higher prices.
   - ☐ e. if the money supply increases, nominal GDP must rise.

3. To increase the money supply, the Fed would
   - ☐ a. increase the reserve requirement, increase the discount rate, and sell bonds.
   - ☐ b. increase the reserve requirement, increase the discount rate, and buy bonds.
   - ☐ c. decrease the reserve requirement, increase the discount rate, and sell bonds.
   - ☐ d. decrease the reserve requirement, decrease the discount rate, and buy bonds.
   - ☐ e. increase the reserve requirement, decrease the discount rate, and buy bonds.

4. If the Fed intervened in the foreign currency market to buy another currency, the domestic money supply would ____________, and the Fed might ____________ bonds to offset its foreign currency operations. This process is called____________.
   - ☐ a. decrease; buy; sterilization
   - ☐ b. decrease; sell; sterilization
   - ☐ c. increase; sell; sterilization
   - ☐ d. increase; buy; sterilization
   - ☐ e. increase; sell; depreciation

5. In recent years, the Fed's short-run operating target has been
   - ☐ a. M1.
   - ☐ b. M2.
   - ☐ c. GDP.
   - ☐ d. the federal funds rate.
   - ☐ e. the level of reserves held by commercial banks.

6. If the money supply is $500, the price level is 3.0, and the velocity of money is equal to 6, Q will be ____________, and nominal GDP will be ____________.
   - ☐ a. 250; $1,500
   - ☐ b. 3,000; $9,000
   - ☐ c. 18; $54
   - ☐ d. 1,000; $3,000
   - ☐ e. 100; $3,000

7. An increase in the interest rate will cause a(n)
   - ☐ a. increase in the demand for money.
   - ☐ b. increase in the quantity demanded of money.
   - ☐ c. decrease in the demand for money.
   - ☐ d. decrease in the quantity demanded of money.
   - ☐ e. increase in the supply of money.

8. The supply of money is
   - ☐ a. a positive function of interest rates.
   - ☐ b. a negative function of interest rates.
   - ☐ c. a positive function of income.
   - ☐ d. a negative function of income.
   - ☐ e. independent of income and interest rates.

9. If the interest rate is above the equilibrium rate, there is an excess ____________ of money. People will ____________ bonds, and the interest rate will ____________.
   - ☐ a. demand; sell; rise
   - ☐ b. demand; sell; drop
   - ☐ c. demand; buy; drop
   - ☐ d. supply; buy; drop
   - ☐ e. supply; sell; rise

10. If the Fed wants to increase equilibrium income, it should ____________ the supply of money, which will ____________ interest rates. The change in interest rates will ____________ consumption and

investment, causing aggregate demand to ______________.

- ☐ a. decrease; increase; decrease; decrease
- ☐ b. decrease; decrease; increase; increase
- ☐ c. increase; decrease; increase; increase
- ☐ d. increase; increase; decrease; decrease
- ☐ e. increase; increase; increase; increase

Practice Questions and Problems

1. The Federal Reserve System was intended to be a ______________ (centralized, decentralized) system.
2. What is the Fed's target inflation rate? ______________.
3. The chairperson of the Federal Reserve Board of Governors is appointed by the ______________ and serves a ______________-year term. Governors serve ______________-year terms.
4. The most important function of the Fed is ______________.
5. The ______________ has been called the second most powerful person in the United States.
6. Write the formula for the equation of exchange: ______________
7. What is LSAP? ______________ ______________
8. The ______________ states that if the money supply increases, and the velocity of money is constant, nominal GDP must rise.
9. List the three tools the Fed uses to change reserves: ______________ ______________ ______________
10. The Fed can reduce the money-creating potential of the banking system by ______________ (raising, lowering) the reserve requirement.
11. The ______________ rate is the rate of interest the Fed charges banks. In other countries, this rate is often called the ______________ rate.
12. If the Fed wants to increase the money supply, it ______________ (raises, lowers) the discount rate.
13. To increase the money supply, the Fed ______________ (buys, sells) bonds.
14. If the Fed wants the dollar to appreciate against the yen, it will buy ______________ (dollars, yen).
15. If the Fed wishes to support a foreign currency, it ______________ (increases, decreases) the domestic money supply unless offsetting operations are undertaken.
16. The demand for money depends on ______________ and ______________.
17. There is a(n) ______________ relationship between the interest rate and the quantity of money demanded.
18. The Fed's traditional tools-the reserve requirement, discount rate, and open market operations- may not have much effect in stimulating the economy if banks do not ______________.
19. The supply of money ______________ (does, does not) depend on interest rates and nominal income.
20. Norm and Debbie keep 1.5 months' income in a NOW account for emergencies. This is an example of the ______________ demand for money.
21. A young couple cashes in a bond to buy a crib and changing table to prepare for the birth of their first child. This is an example of the ______________ demand for money.
22. If nominal income increases, the demand for money ______________ (shifts to the left, does not change, shifts to the right).
23. You read in the *Wall Street Journal* that the bond markets rallied yesterday (bond prices increased). Interest rates must have ______________ (increased, decreased).
24. A decrease in the money supply causes interest rates to ______________ (rise, fall), which causes consumption and investment to ______________ (rise, fall). The changes in consumption and investment cause aggregate demand to ______________ (increase, decrease), which causes equilibrium income to ______________ (rise, fall). Use the following graphs to illustrate the sequence of events following a decrease in the money supply.

(a)

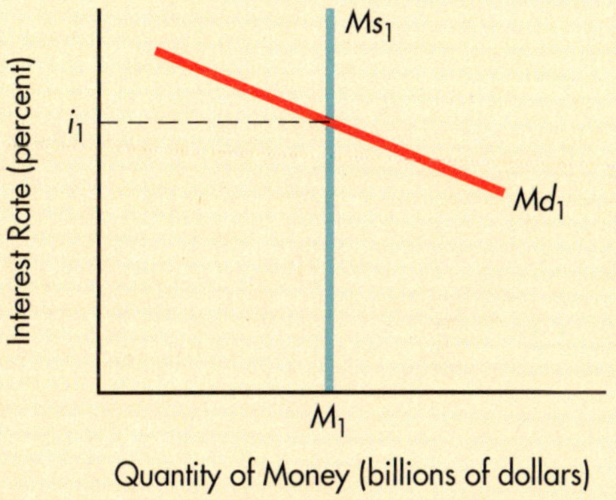

(b)

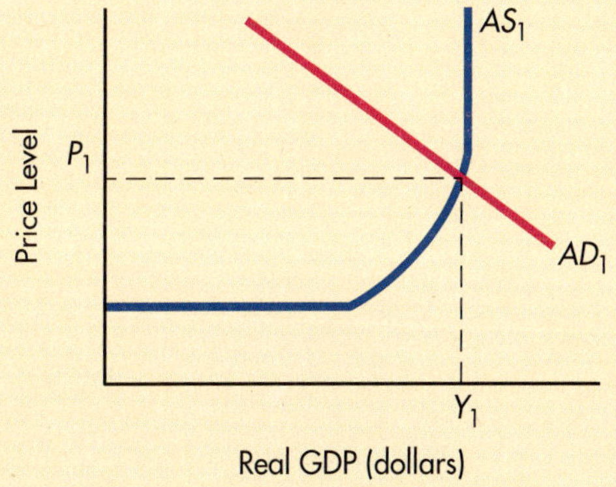

Exercises and Applications

I More on Foreign Exchange Market Intervention

If the Fed feels that the price of the dollar in terms of U.K. pounds is unacceptably high, it may choose to intervene directly in the foreign exchange markets. To bolster the pound, the Fed will ____________(buy, sell) pounds. In the process, the domestic money supply will ____________ (increase, decrease).

In the absence of any sterilization actions by the Fed, domestic interest rates will ____________ (increase, decrease) as a result of the change in the money supply. The change in domestic interest rates will ____________ (increase, decrease) the demand for U.S. securities. The dollar will (appreciate, depreciate) in value. The effect of the change in the money supply has ____________ (reinforced, opposed) the Fed's actions in the foreign exchange market.

II Bond Prices and Interest Rates

Fill in the gaps in these typical quotations from articles from the *Wall Street Journal.*

a. "The benchmark 10-year Treasury bond rose more than 1/4 point to 106, a gain of more than $2.50 for a bond with a $1,000 face amount. Its yield, which moves in the ____________ (same, opposite) direction from the price, ____________ (rose, fell) to 6.65 percent …"
b. "More investors and economists are beginning to believe that interest rates are headed higher, although many think long-term bond yields won't move as fast as short-term rates.... Mr. Olsen … believes there will be a significant sell-off in the bond market."

Why would higher interest rates precipitate a significant sell-off in the bond market?

____

____

____

____

____

16 Macroeconomic Policy, Business Cycles, and Growth

FUNDAMENTAL QUESTIONS

1. Is there a trade-off between inflation and the unemployment rate?
2. How does the trade-off between inflation and the unemployment rate vary from the short to the long run?
3. What is the relationship between unexpected inflation and the unemployment rate?
4. How are macroeconomic expectations formed?
5. Are business cycles related to political elections?
6. How do real shocks to the economy affect business cycles?
7. How is inflationary monetary policy related to government fiscal policy?
8. How are economic growth rates determined?
9. What is productivity?

PREVIEW

Macroeconomics is a dynamic discipline. Monetary and fiscal policies change over time, and so does our understanding of those policies. Economists debate the nature of business cycles and economic growth, and what, if anything, government can do about them. Some economists argue that policies that lower the unemployment rate tend to raise the rate of inflation. Others insist that only unexpected inflation can influence real GDP and employment. If the latter economists are right, does government always have to surprise the public in order to improve economic conditions?

Some economists claim that politicians manipulate the business cycle to increase their chances of reelection. If they are right, we should expect economic growth just before national elections. But what happens after the elections? What are the long-term effects of political business cycles? Because of these issues, the material in this chapter should be considered somewhat controversial.

1. THE PHILLIPS CURVE

In 1958, a New Zealand economist, A. W. Phillips, published a study of the relationship between the unemployment rate and the rate of change in wages in England. He found that over the period from 1826 to 1957, there had been an inverse relationship between the unemployment rate and the rate of change in wages: The unemployment rate fell in years when there were relatively large increases in wages and rose in years when wages increased relatively little. Phillips's study started other economists searching for similar relationships in other countries. In those studies, it became common to substitute the rate of inflation for the rate of change in wages.

Phillips curve: a graph that illustrates the relationship between inflation and the unemployment rate

Early studies in the United States found an inverse relationship between inflation and the unemployment rate. The graph that illustrates this relationship is called a **Phillips curve**. Figure 16.1 shows a Phillips curve for the United States in the 1960s. Over this period, lower inflation rates were associated with higher unemployment rates, as shown by the downward-sloping curve.

The slope of the curve in Figure 16.1 depicts an inverse relationship between the rate of inflation and the unemployment rate: As the inflation rate falls, the unemployment rate rises. In 1969, the inflation rate was relatively high, at 5.5 percent, whereas the unemployment rate was relatively low, at 3.5 percent. In 1967, an inflation rate of 3.1 percent was consistent with an unemployment rate of 3.8 percent; and in 1961, 1 percent inflation occurred with 6.7 percent unemployment.

The downward-sloping Phillips curve seems to indicate a trade-off between unemployment and inflation. A country could have a lower unemployment rate by accepting higher inflation, or a lower rate of inflation by accepting higher unemployment. Certainly this was the case in the United States in the 1960s. But is the curve depicted in Figure 16.1 representative of the trade-off over long periods of time?

1 Is there a trade-off between inflation and the unemployment rate?

1.a. An Inflation–Unemployment Trade-off?

Figure 16.2 shows unemployment and inflation rates in the United States for several years from 1955 to 2010. The points in the figure do not lie along a downward-sloping curve like the one shown in Figure 16.1. For example, in

FIGURE 16.1 A Phillips Curve, United States, 1961–1969

In the 1960s, as the rate of inflation rose, the unemployment rate fell. This inverse relationship suggests a trade-off between the rate of inflation and the unemployment rate.

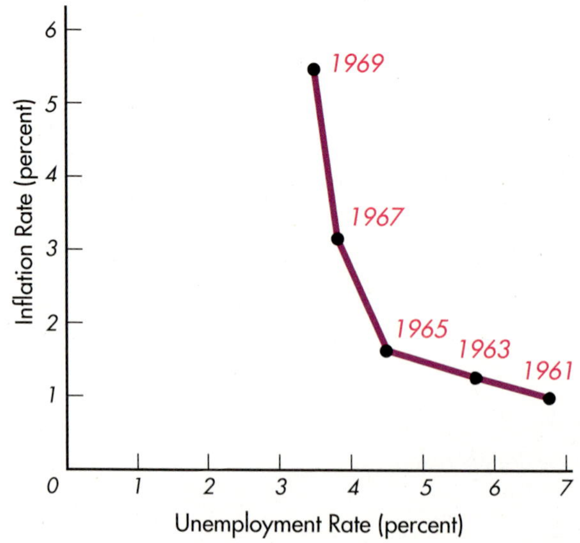

Source: Data from *Economic Report of the President, 1995* (Washington, DC: U.S. Government Printing Office, 1995).

FIGURE 16.2 Unemployment and Inflation in the United States, 1955–2010

The data on inflation and unemployment rates in the United States between 1955 and 2010 show no particular relationship between inflation and unemployment over the long run. There is no evidence here of a downward-sloping Phillips curve.

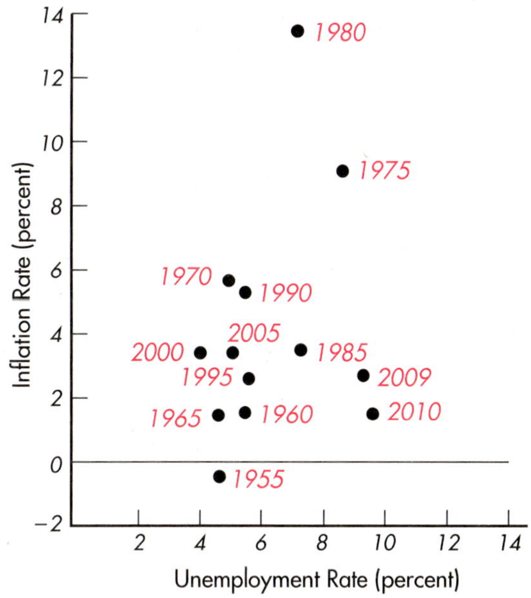

Source: Data from *Economic Report of the President, 2012.*

1955, the unemployment rate was 4.4 percent, and the inflation rate was 20.4 percent. In 1960, the unemployment rate was 5.5 percent, and the inflation rate was 1.7 percent. Both unemployment and inflation rates had increased since 1955. Moving through time, you can see that the inflation rate tended to increase along with the unemployment rate through the 1960s and 1970s. By 1980, the unemployment rate was 7.1 percent, and the inflation rate was 13.5 percent. Following the financial crisis and recession of 2007–2010, in 2010 the inflation rate was 1.5 percent with an unemployment rate of 9.6 percent.

The scattered points in Figure 16.2 show no evidence of a trade-off between unemployment and inflation. A downward-sloping Phillips curve does not seem to exist over the long term.

2

How does the trade-off between inflation and the unemployment rate vary from the short to the long run?

1.b. Short-Run Versus Long-Run Trade-offs

Most economists believe that the downward-sloping Phillips curve and the trade-off it implies between inflation and unemployment are short-term phenomena. Think of a series of Phillips curves, one for each of the points in Figure 16.2. From 1955 to 1980, the curves shifted out to the right. In the early 1980s, they shifted in to the left.

Figure 16.3 shows a series of Phillips curves that could account for the data in Figure 16.2. At any point in time, a downward-sloping Phillips curve indicates a trade-off between inflation and unemployment. Many economists believe that this kind of trade-off is just a short-term phenomenon. Over time, the Phillips curve shifts so that the short-run trade-off between inflation and unemployment disappears in the long run.

On the early 1960s curve in Figure 16.3, 5 percent unemployment is consistent with 2 percent inflation. By the early 1970s, the curve had shifted up. Here 5 percent unemployment is associated with 6 percent inflation. On the late 1970s curve, 5 percent unemployment is consistent with 10 percent inflation. For more than two decades, the trade-off between inflation and unemployment worsened as the Phillips curves shifted up so that higher and higher inflation rates were associated with any given level of unemployment. Then, in the

FIGURE 16.3 The Shifting Phillips Curve

We can reconcile the long-run data on unemployment and inflation with the downward-sloping Phillips curve by using a series of Phillips curves. (In effect, we treat the long-run as a series of short-run curves.) The Phillips curve for the early 1960s shows 5 percent unemployment and 2 percent inflation. Over time, the short-run curve shifted out to the right. The early 1970s curve shows 5 percent unemployment and 6 percent inflation. And the short-run curve for the late 1970s shows 5 percent unemployment and 10 percent inflation. In the early 1980s, the short-run Phillips curve began to shift down toward the origin. By the late 1980s, 5 percent unemployment was consistent with 4 percent inflation.

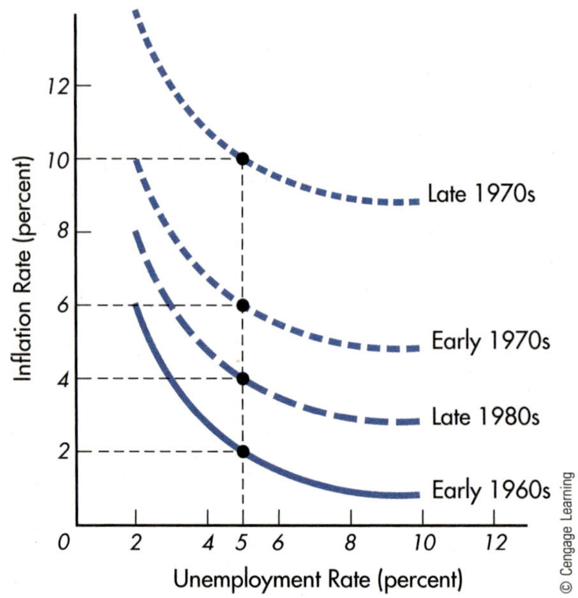

1980s, the trade-off seemed to improve as the Phillips curve shifted down. On the late 1980s curve, 5 percent unemployment is consistent with 4 percent inflation.

The Phillips curves in Figure 16.3 represent changes that took place over time in the United States. We cannot be sure of the actual shape of a Phillips curve at any time, but an outward shift of the curve in the 1960s and 1970s and an inward shift during the 1980s are consistent with the data. Later in this chapter, we describe how changing government policy and the public's expectations about that policy may have shifted aggregate demand and aggregate supply and produced these shifts in the Phillips curves.

1.b.1. **In the Short Run** Figure 16.4 uses aggregate demand and supply analysis to explain the Phillips curve. Initially, the economy is operating at point 1 in both diagrams. In part (a), the aggregate demand curve (AD_1) and aggregate supply curve (AS_1) intersect at price level P_1 and real GDP level Y_p, the level of potential real GDP. Remember that potential real GDP is the level of income and output generated at the natural rate of unemployment, the unemployment rate that exists in the absence of cyclical unemployment. In part (b), point 1 lies on Phillips curve I, where the inflation rate is 3 percent and the unemployment rate is 5 percent. We assume that the 5 percent unemployment rate at the level of potential real GDP is the natural rate of unemployment (U_n).

What happens when aggregate demand goes up from AD_1 to AD_2? A new equilibrium is established along the short-run aggregate supply curve (AS_1) at point 2. Here the price level (P_2) is higher, as is the level of real GDP (Y_2). In part (b), the increase in price and income is reflected in the movement along Phillips curve I to point 2. At point 2, the inflation rate is 6 percent, and the unemployment rate is 3 percent. The increase in expenditures raises the inflation rate and lowers the unemployment rate (because national output has surpassed potential output).

Notice that there appears to be a trade-off between inflation and unemployment on Phillips curve I. The increase in spending increases output and stimulates employment so that the unemployment rate falls. And the higher spending

FIGURE 16.4 Aggregate Demand and Supply and the Phillips Curve

The movement from point 1 to point 2 to point 3 traces the adjustment of the economy to an increase in aggregate demand. Point 1 is initial equilibrium in both diagrams. At this point potential real GDP is Y_p and the price level is P_1 in the aggregate demand and supply diagram, and the inflation rate is 3 percent with an unemployment rate of 5 percent (the natural rate) along short-run curve 1 in the Phillips curve diagram.

If the aggregate demand curve shifts from AD_1 to AD_2, equilibrium real GDP goes up to Y_2 and the price level rises to P_2 in the aggregate demand and supply diagram. The increase in aggregate demand pushes the inflation rate up to 6 percent and the unemployment rate down to 3 percent along Phillips curve I. The movement from point 1 to point 2 along the curve indicates a trade-off between inflation and the unemployment rate.

Over time, the *AS* curve shifts in response to rising production costs at the higher rate of inflation. Along AS_2, equilibrium is at point 3, where real GDP falls back to Y_p and the price level rises to P_3. As we move from point 2 to point 3 in part (b), we shift to short-run Phillips curve II. Here the inflation rate remains high (at 6 percent) while the unemployment rate goes back up to 5 percent, the rate consistent with production at Y_p. In the long run, then, there is no trade-off between inflation and unemployment. The vertical long-run aggregate supply curve at the potential level of real GDP is associated with the vertical long-run Phillips curve at the natural rate of unemployment.

(a) Aggregate Demand and Supply **(b) Phillips Curve**

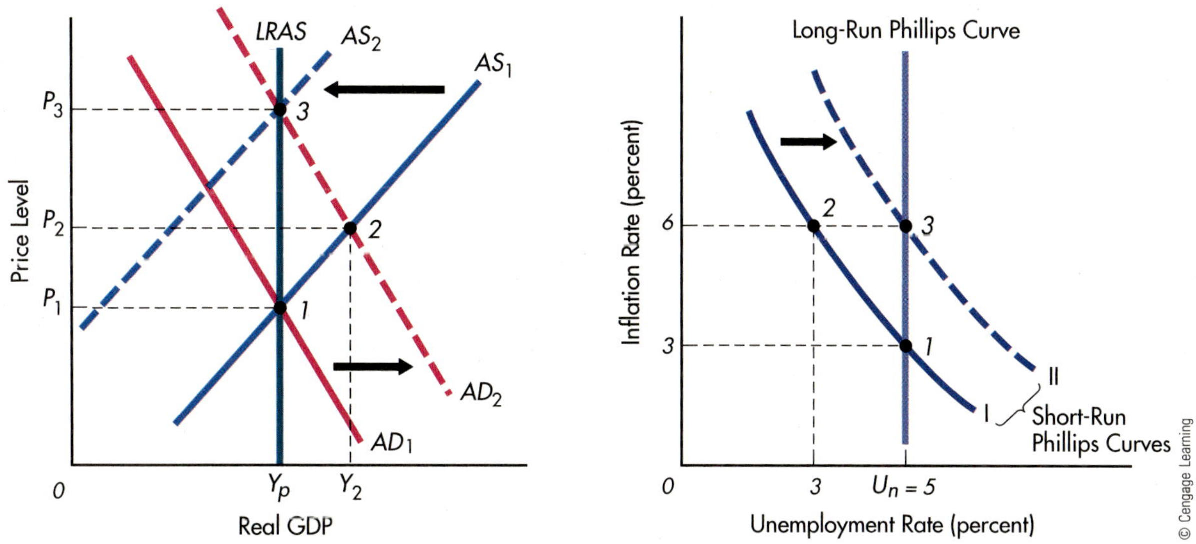

pushes the rate of inflation up. But this trade-off is only temporary. Point 2 in both diagrams is only a short-run equilibrium.

1.b.2. **In the Long Run** As we discussed in Chapter 12, the short-run aggregate supply curve shifts over time as production costs rise in response to higher prices. Once the aggregate supply curve shifts to AS_2, long-run equilibrium occurs at point 3, where AS_2 intersects AD_2. Here, the price level is P_3, and real GDP returns to its potential level Y_p.

The shift in aggregate supply lowers real GDP. As income falls, the unemployment rate goes up. The decrease in aggregate supply is reflected in the movement from point 2 on Phillips curve I to point 3 on Phillips curve II. As real GDP returns to its potential level (Y_p), unemployment returns to the natural rate (U_n), 5 percent. In the long run, as the economy adjusts to an increase in aggregate demand, and expectations adjust to the new inflation rate, there is a period in which real GDP falls and the price level rises.

Over time, there is no relationship between the price level and the level of real GDP. You can see this in the aggregate demand and supply diagram. Points 1 and 3 both lie along the long-run aggregate supply curve (*LRAS*) at potential real GDP. The *LRAS* curve has its analogue in the long-run Phillips curve, a vertical line at the natural rate of unemployment. Points 1 and 3 both lie along this curve.

RECAP

1. The Phillips curve shows an inverse relationship between inflation and unemployment.
2. The downward slope of the Phillips curve indicates a trade-off between inflation and unemployment.
3. Over the long run that trade-off disappears.
4. The long-run Phillips curve is a vertical line at the natural rate of unemployment, analogous to the long-run aggregate supply curve at potential real GDP.

2. THE ROLE OF EXPECTATIONS

The data and analysis in the previous section indicate that there is no long-run trade-off between inflation and unemployment. But they do not explain the movement of the Phillips curve in the 1960s, 1970s, and 1980s. To understand why the short-run curve shifts, you must understand the role that unexpected inflation plays in the economy.

3 What is the relationship between unexpected inflation and the unemployment rate?

2.a. Expected Versus Unexpected Inflation

Figure 16.5 shows two short-run Phillips curves like those in Figure 16.4. Each curve is drawn for a particular expected rate of inflation. Curve I shows the trade-off between inflation and unemployment when the inflation rate is expected to be 3 percent. If the actual rate of inflation (measured along the vertical axis) is 3 percent, the economy is operating at point 1, with an unemployment rate of 5 percent (the natural rate). If the inflation rate unexpectedly increases to 6 percent, the economy moves from point 1 to point 2 along Phillips curve I. Obviously, unexpected inflation can affect the unemployment rate. There are three factors at work here: wage expectations, inventory fluctuations, and wage contracts.

2.a.1. Wage Expectations and Unemployment

reservation wage: the minimum wage a worker is willing to accept

Unemployed workers who are looking for a job choose a **reservation wage**, the minimum wage they are willing to accept. They continue to look for work until they receive an offer that equals or exceeds their reservation wage.

FIGURE 16.5 Expectations and the Phillips Curve

Short-run Phillips curve I shows the trade-off between inflation and the unemployment rate as long as people expect 3 percent inflation. When the actual rate of inflation is 3 percent, the rate of unemployment (U_n) is 5 percent (point 1). Short-run Phillips curve II shows the trade-off as long as people expect 6 percent inflation. When the actual rate of inflation is 6 percent, the unemployment rate is 5 percent (point 3).

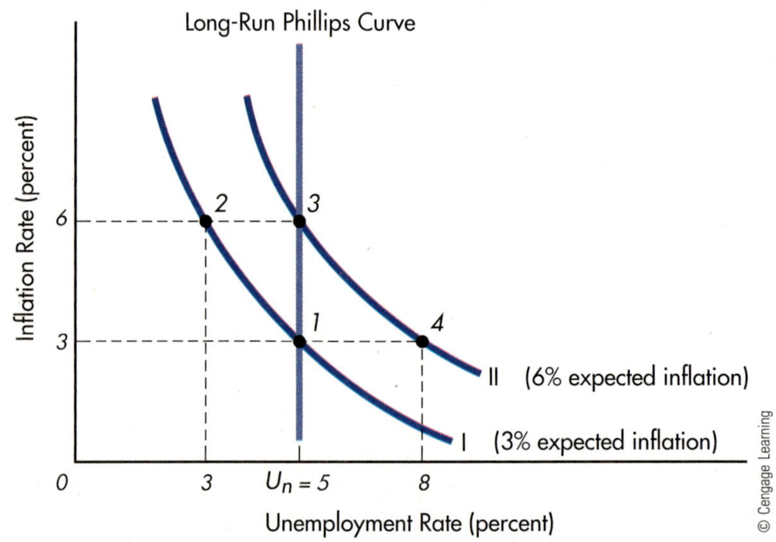

Wages are not the only factor that workers take into consideration before accepting a job offer. A firm that offers good working conditions and fringe benefits can pay a lower wage than a firm that does not offer these advantages. But other things being equal, workers choose higher wages over lower wages. We simplify our analysis here by assuming that the only variable that affects the unemployed worker who is looking for a job is the reservation wage.

The link between unexpected inflation and the unemployment rate stems from the fact that wage offers are surprisingly high when the rate of inflation is surprisingly high. An unexpected increase in inflation means that prices are higher than anticipated, as are nominal income and wages. If aggregate demand increases unexpectedly, then, prices, output, employment, and wages go up. Unemployed workers with a constant reservation wage find it easier to obtain a satisfactory wage offer during a period when wages are rising faster than the workers expected. This means that more unemployed workers find jobs, and they find those jobs more quickly than they do in a period when the rate of inflation is expected. So the unemployment rate falls during a period of unexpectedly high inflation (see Figure 16.6).

In Figure 16.5, an expected increase in inflation moves us from point 1 on curve I to point 3 on curve II. When increased inflation is expected, the reservation wage reflects the higher rate of inflation, and there is no trade-off between inflation and the unemployment rate. Instead, the economy moves along the long-run Phillips curve, with unemployment at its natural rate. The clockwise movement from point 1 to point 2 to point 3 is the pattern that follows an unexpected increase in aggregate demand.

What if the inflation rate is lower than expected? Here we find a reservation wage that reflects higher expected inflation. This means that those people who are looking for jobs are going to have a difficult time finding acceptable wage offers, the number of unemployed workers is going to increase, and the unemployment rate is going to rise. This sequence is shown in Figure 16.5, as the economy moves from point 3 to point 4. When the actual inflation rate is 6 percent and the expected inflation rate is also 6 percent, the economy is operating at the natural rate of unemployment. When the inflation rate falls to 3 percent but workers still expect 6 percent inflation, the unemployment rate rises (at point 4 along curve II). Eventually, if the inflation rate remains at 3 percent, workers adjust their expectations to the lower rate, and the economy moves to point 1 on curve I. The short-run effect of unexpected *disinflation* is rising unemployment. Over time, the short-run increase in the unemployment rate is eliminated.

As long as the actual rate of inflation equals the expected rate, the economy remains at the natural rate of unemployment. The trade-off between inflation and the unemployment rate comes from unexpected inflation.

FIGURE 16.6 Inflation, Unemployment, and Wage Expectations

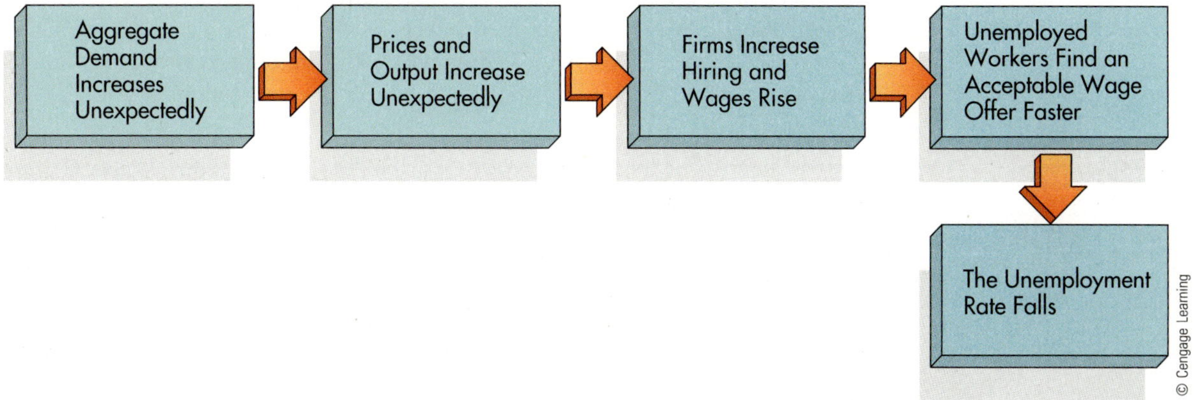

2.a.2. **Inventory Fluctuations and Unemployment** Businesses hold inventories based on what they expect their sales to be. When aggregate demand is greater than expected, inventories fall below targeted levels. To restore inventories to the levels wanted, production is increased. Increased production leads to increased employment. If aggregate demand is lower than expected, inventories rise above targeted levels. To reduce inventories, production is cut back, and workers are laid off from their jobs until sales have lowered unwanted inventories. Once production increases, employment rises again.

Inventory, production, and employment all play a part in the Phillips curve analysis (see Figure 16.7). Expected sales and inventory levels are based on an expected level of aggregate demand. If aggregate demand is greater than expected, inventories fall and prices rise on the remaining goods in stock. With the unexpected increase in inflation, the unemployment rate falls as businesses hire more workers to increase output to offset falling inventories. This sequence represents movement along a short-run Phillips curve because there is a trade-off between inflation and the unemployment rate. We find the same trade-off if aggregate demand is lower than expected. Here inventories increase, and prices are lower than anticipated. With the unexpected decrease in inflation, the unemployment rate goes up as workers are laid off to reduce output until inventory levels fall.

2.a.3. **Wage Contracts and Unemployment** Another factor that explains the short-run trade-off between inflation and unemployment is labor contracts that fix wages for an extended period of time. When an existing contract expires, management must renegotiate with labor. A firm facing lower demand for its products may negotiate lower wages in order to keep as many workers employed as before. If the demand for a firm's products falls while a wage contract is in force, the firm must maintain wages, which means it is going to have to lay off workers.

In the national economy, wage contracts are staggered; they expire at different times. Each year only 30 to 40 percent of all contracts expire across the entire economy. As economic conditions change, firms with expiring wage contracts can adjust *wages* to those conditions; firms with existing contracts must adjust *employment* to those conditions.

How do long-term wage contracts tie in with the Phillips curve analysis? The expected rate of inflation is based on expected aggregate demand and reflected in the wage that is agreed on in the contract. When the actual rate of inflation equals the expected rate, businesses retain the same number of workers they had planned on when they signed the contract. For the economy overall, when actual and expected inflation rates are the same, the economy is operating at the natural rate of unemployment. That is, businesses are not hiring new workers because of an unexpected increase in aggregate demand, and they are not laying off workers because of an unexpected decrease in aggregate demand.

When aggregate demand is higher than expected, those firms with unexpired wage contracts hire more workers at the fixed wage, reducing unemployment (see Figure 16.8). Those firms with expiring contracts have to offer higher wages in order to maintain the existing level of employment at the new demand

FIGURE 16.7 Inflation, Unemployment, and Inventories

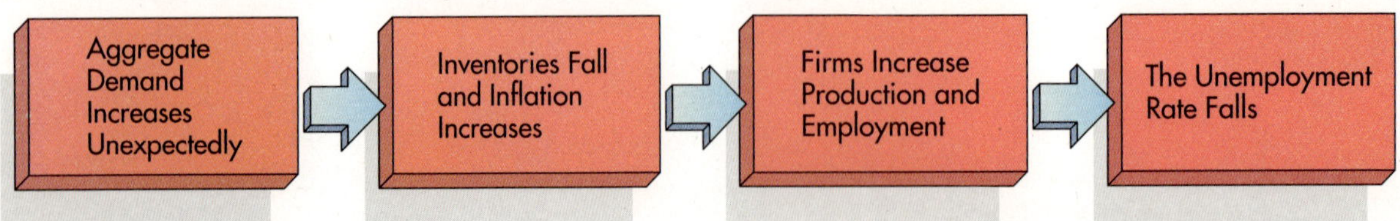

FIGURE 16.8 Inflation, Unemployment, and Wage Controls

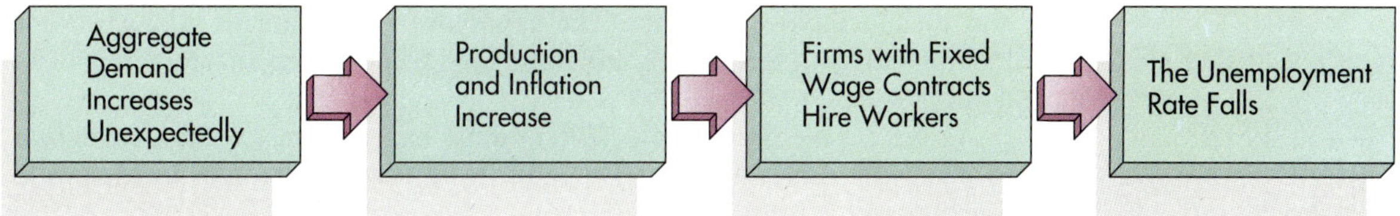

condition. When aggregate demand is lower than expected, those firms with unexpired contracts have to lay off workers because they cannot lower the wage, and those firms with expiring contracts negotiate lower wages in order to keep their workers.

If wages were always flexible, unexpected changes in aggregate demand might be reflected largely in *wage* rather than in *employment* adjustments. Wage contracts force businesses to adjust employment when aggregate demand changes unexpectedly. The Global Business Insight "Why Wages Don't Fall in Recessions" addresses this issue further (see page 356).

2.b. **Forming Expectations**

4

How are macroeconomic expectations formed?

Expectations play a key role in explaining the short-run Phillips curve, the trade-off between inflation and the unemployment rate. How are these expectations formed?

adaptive expectations: expectations formed on the basis of information collected in the past

2.b.1. **Adaptive Expectations**

Expectations can be formed solely on the basis of experience. **Adaptive expectations** are expectations that are determined by what has happened in the recent past.

People learn from their experiences. For example, suppose the inflation rate has been 3 percent for the past few years. On the basis of past experience, then, people expect the inflation rate in the future to remain at 3 percent. If the Federal Reserve increases the growth of the money supply to a rate that produces 6 percent inflation, the public will be surprised by the higher rate of inflation. This unexpected inflation creates a short-run trade-off between inflation and the unemployment rate along a short-run Phillips curve. Over time, if the inflation rate remains at 6 percent, the public will learn that the 3 percent rate is too low and will adapt its expectations to the actual, higher inflation rate. Once public expectations have adapted to the new rate of inflation, the economy returns to the natural rate of unemployment along the long-run Phillips curve.

rational expectations: expectations formed by using all available relevant information

2.b.2. **Rational Expectations**

Many economists believe that adaptive expectations are too narrow. If people look only at past information, they are ignoring what could be important information in the current period. **Rational expectations** are based on all available relevant information.

We are not saying that people have to know everything in order to form expectations. Rational expectations require only that people consider the information they believe to be relevant. This information includes past experience along with what is currently happening and what is expected to happen in the future. For instance, in forming expectations about inflation, people consider rates in the recent past, current policy, and anticipated shifts in aggregate demand and supply that could affect the future rate of inflation.

If the inflation rate has been 3 percent over the past few years, adaptive expectations suggest that the future inflation rate will be 3 percent. No other information is considered. Rational expectations are based on more than the historical rate. Suppose the Fed announces a new policy that everyone believes will increase inflation in the future. With rational expectations the effect of this announcement will be considered. Here, when the actual rate of inflation turns out to be more than 3 percent, there is no short-run trade-off between inflation and the unemployment rate. The economy moves directly along the long-run Phillips curve to the higher inflation rate while unemployment remains at the natural rate.

If we believe that people have rational expectations, we do not expect them to make the same mistakes over and over. We expect them to learn and react quickly to new information.

RECAP

1. Wage expectations, inventory fluctuations, and wage contracts help explain the short-run trade-off between inflation and the unemployment rate.
2. The reservation wage is the minimum wage a worker is willing to accept.
3. Because wage expectations reflect expected inflation, when the inflation rate is surprisingly high, unemployed workers find jobs faster, and the unemployment rate falls.
4. Unexpected increases in aggregate demand lower inventories and raise prices. To increase output (to replenish shrinking inventories), businesses hire more workers, which reduces the unemployment rate.
5. When aggregate demand is higher than expected, those businesses that have wage contracts hire more workers at the fixed wage and thereby lower unemployment.
6. If wages were always flexible, unexpected changes in aggregate demand would be reflected in wage adjustments rather than in employment adjustments.
7. Adaptive expectations are formed on the basis of information about the past.
8. Rational expectations are formed using all available relevant information.

GLOBAL BUSINESS INSIGHT

Why Wages Don't Fall in Recessions

A look at macroeconomic data across countries reveals that when economies experience recessions, unemployment rates rise, but wages fall very little, if at all. If we think of a supply and demand diagram for labor, we would think that as demand for labor falls in a recession, the equilibrium quantity of labor would fall as well as the equilibrium price, the wage rate. We do see the quantity effect as workers lose their jobs and the unemployment rate rises. Why don't we see wages also falling?

The text discusses long-term labor contracts as one reason that wages may be relatively inflexible over time. Beyond the presence of contracts, recent research points to human behavior as a contributing factor.* Surveys of firms and workers indicate that worker morale is a major reason that wages are not reduced during recessions. Workers would view a wage cut as an indication that the firm does not value their work as much, and they may, as a result, suffer lower morale and expend less effort. When some workers are laid off, these workers suffer from the job loss, but they are no longer at the firm and cannot harm others' morale and work effort. Only in the case in which the very survival of the firm is clearly at stake do wage cuts appear to be acceptable to workers.

Thus, wages are "sticky downwards" because this strategy promotes good worker effort and ensures that workers and firms share the same goals of efficient production and profit maximization. Rather than keeping all workers when demand falls by paying lower wages to all, it may be better for the firm to lay off some workers and keep paying the remaining employees the same wage as before.

*Source: Truman F. Bewley, Why Wages Don't Fall During a Recession (Cambridge, MA: Harvard University Press, 1999); Peter Howitt, "Looking Inside the Labor Market: A Review Article," *Journal of Economic Literature XL* (March 2002): 125–138.

3. SOURCES OF BUSINESS CYCLES

In Chapter 13, we examined the effect of fiscal policy on the equilibrium level of real GDP. Changes in government spending and taxes can expand or contract the economy. In Chapter 15, we described how monetary policy affects the equilibrium level of real GDP. Changes in the money supply also produce booms and recessions. Besides the policy-induced sources of business cycles covered in earlier chapters, there are other sources of economic fluctuations that economists have studied. One is the election campaign of incumbent politicians; when a business cycle results from this action, it is called a *political business cycle*. Macroeconomic policy may be used to promote the reelection of incumbent politicians. We also examine another source of business cycles that is not related to discretionary policy actions, the *real business cycle*.

5

Are business cycles related to political elections?

3.a. The Political Business Cycle

If a short-run trade-off exists between inflation and unemployment, an incumbent administration could stimulate the economy just before an election to lower the unemployment rate, making voters happy and increasing the probability of reelection. Of course, after the election, the long-run adjustment to the expansionary policy would lead to higher inflation and move unemployment back to the natural rate.

Figure 16.9 illustrates the pattern. Before the election, the economy is initially at point 1 in parts (a) and (b). The incumbent administration stimulates the economy by increasing government spending or increasing the growth of the money supply. Aggregate demand shifts from AD_1 to AD_2 in part (a). In the short run, the increase in aggregate demand is unexpected, so the economy moves along the initial aggregate supply curve (AS_1) to point 2. This movement is reflected in part (b) of the figure, in the movement from point 1 to point 2 along short-run Phillips curve I. The preelection expansionary policy increases real GDP and lowers the unemployment rate. Once the public adjusts its expectations to the higher inflation rate, the economy experiences a recession. Real GDP falls back to its potential level (Y_p), and the unemployment rate goes back up to the natural rate (U_n), as shown by the movement from point 2 to point 3 in both parts of the figure.

An unexpected increase in government spending or money growth temporarily stimulates the economy. If an election comes during the period of expansion, higher incomes and lower unemployment may increase support for the incumbent administration. The long-run adjustment back to potential real GDP and the natural rate of unemployment comes after the election.

Economists do not agree on whether a political business cycle exists in the United States. But they do agree that an effort to exploit the short-run trade-off between inflation and the unemployment rate would shift the short-run Phillips curve out as shown in part (b) of Figure 16.9.

6

How do real shocks to the economy affect business cycles?

shock:
an unexpected change in a variable

3.b. Real Business Cycles

In recent years, economists have paid increasing attention to real **shocks**—unexpected changes—in the economy as a source of business cycles. Many believe that it is not only fiscal or monetary policy that triggers expansion or contraction in the economy but also technological change, change in tastes, labor strikes, weather, war and terrorism, or other real changes. A real business cycle is one that is generated by a change in a real variable.

Interest in the real business cycle was stimulated by the oil price shocks in the early 1970s and the important role they played in triggering the recession of 1973–1975. At that time, many economists were focusing on the role of unexpected changes in monetary policy in generating business cycles. They argued that these kinds of policy changes (changes in a nominal variable, the money supply) were responsible for the shifts in aggregate demand that led to

FIGURE 16.9 The Political Business Cycle

Before the election, the government stimulates the economy, unexpectedly increasing aggregate demand. The economy moves from point 1 to point 2, pushing equilibrium real GDP above Y_p (part [a]) and the unemployment rate below U_n (part [b]). The incumbent politicians hope that rising incomes and lower unemployment will translate into votes. After the election comes adjustment to the higher aggregate demand as the economy moves from point 2 to point 3. The aggregate supply curve shifts to the left, and equilibrium real GDP falls back to Y_p. Unemployment goes back up to U_n, and the rate of inflation rises.

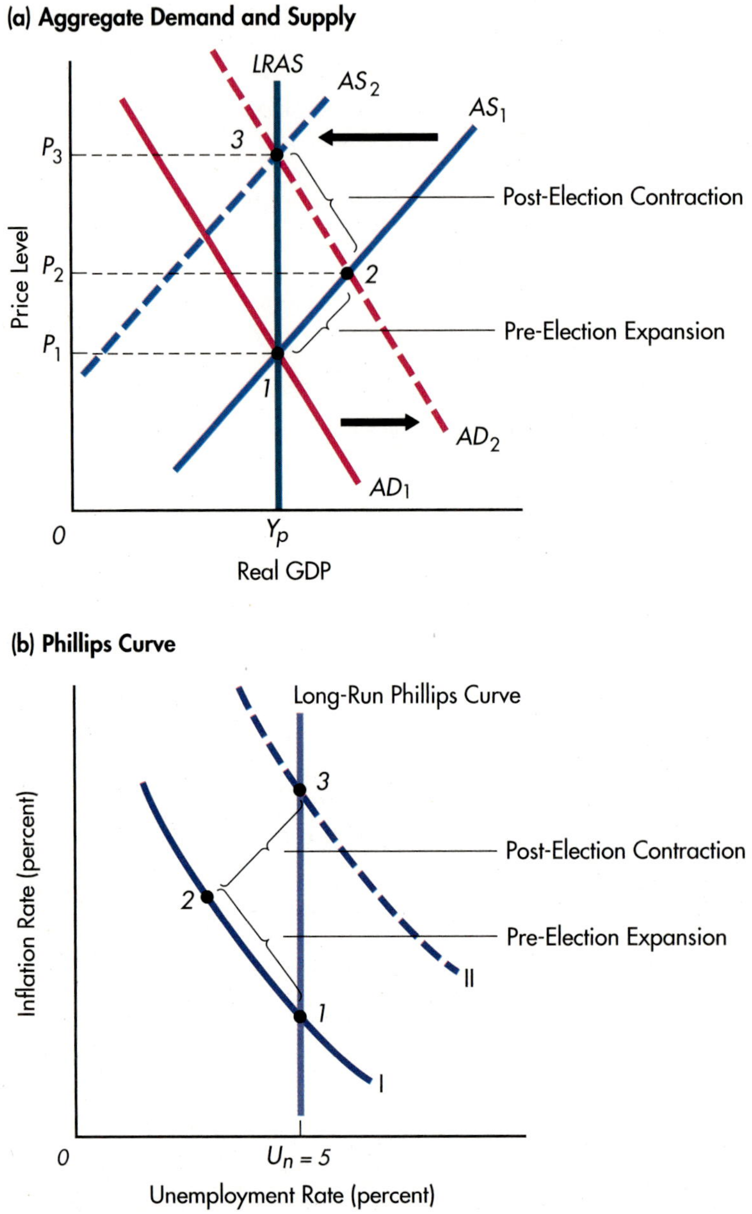

expansions and contractions. When the oil-exporting countries' cartel, OPEC, restricted the supply of oil, leading to higher oil prices, it caused major shifts in aggregate supply. Higher oil prices in 1973 and 1974, and in 1979 and 1980, reduced aggregate supply, pushing the equilibrium level of real GDP down. Lower oil prices in 1986 raised aggregate supply and equilibrium real GDP.

An economy-wide real shock, such as a substantial change in the price of oil, can affect output and employment across all sectors of the economy. Even an industry-specific shock can generate a recession or expansion in the entire economy if the industry produces a product used by a substantial number of other industries. For example, a labor strike in the steel industry would have major recessionary implications for the economy as a whole. If the output of steel fell, the price of steel would be bid up by all the industries that use steel as an input. This would shift the short-run aggregate supply curve to the left, as shown in part (a) of Figure 16.10, and would move equilibrium real GDP from Y_1 down to Y_2.

FIGURE 16.10 The Impact of Real Shocks on Equilibrium Real GDP

A labor strike in a key industry can shift the aggregate supply curve to the left, like the shift from AS_1 to AS_2. This pushes equilibrium real GDP down from Y_1 to Y_2.

If good weather leads to a banner harvest, the aggregate supply curve shifts to the right, like the shift from AS_1 to AS_2, raising equilibrium real GDP from Y_1 to Y_2.

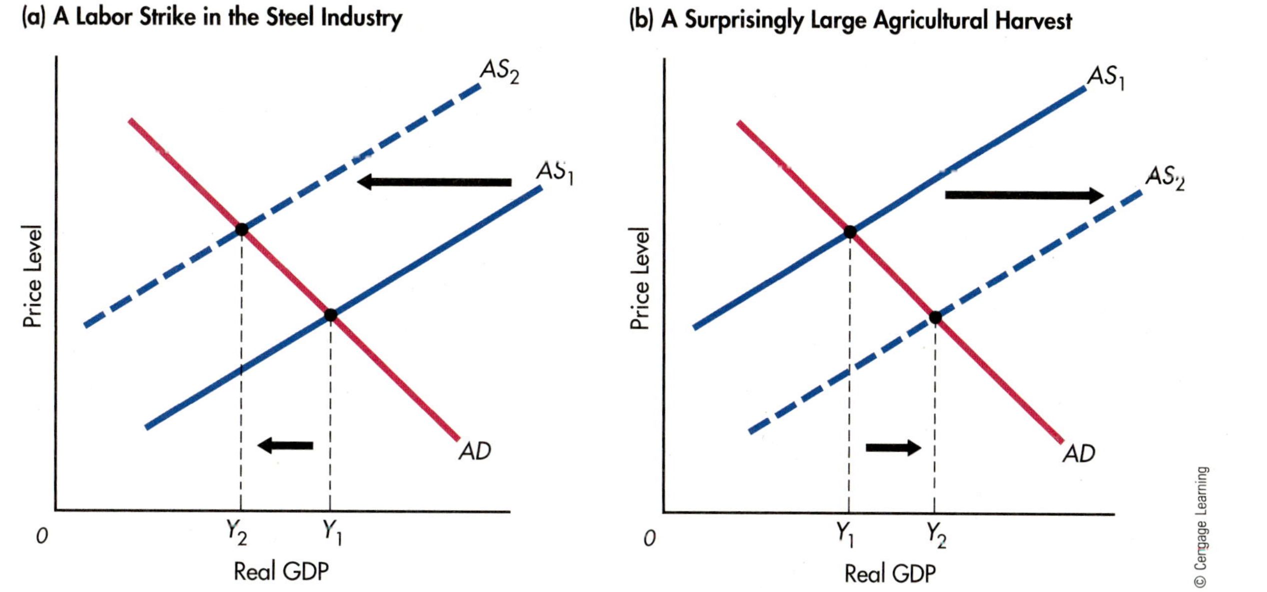

Real shocks can also have expansionary effects on the economy. Suppose that the weather is particularly good one year and that harvests are surprisingly large. What happens? The price of food, cotton, and other agricultural output tends to fall, and the short-run aggregate supply curve shifts to the right, as shown in Figure 16.10(b), raising equilibrium real GDP from Y_1 to Y_2.

Real business cycles explain why national output can expand or contract in the absence of a discretionary macroeconomic policy that would shift aggregate demand. To fully understand business cycles, we must consider both policy-induced changes in real GDP, as covered in Chapters 13 and 15, and real shocks that occur independent of government actions.

RECAP

1. The political business cycle is a short-term expansion stimulated by an administration before an election to earn votes. After the election comes the long-term adjustment (rising unemployment and inflation).
2. A real business cycle is an expansion and contraction caused by a change in tastes or technology, strikes, weather, war and terrorism, or other real factors.

4. THE LINK BETWEEN MONETARY AND FISCAL POLICIES

In earlier chapters we have described how monetary and fiscal policies determine the equilibrium level of prices and national income. In our discussions, we have talked about monetary policy and fiscal policy individually. Here we consider the relationship between them.

In some countries, monetary and fiscal policies are carried out by a single central authority. Even in the United States, where the Federal Reserve was created as an independent agency, monetary policy and fiscal policy are always related. The actions of the central bank have an impact on the proper role for fiscal policy, and the actions of fiscal policymakers have an impact on the proper role for monetary policy.

For example, suppose the central bank follows a monetary policy that raises interest rates. That policy raises the interest cost of new government debt, and in the process also increases government expenditures. On the other hand, a fiscal policy that generates large fiscal deficits could contribute to higher interest rates. If the central bank has targeted an interest rate that lies below the current rate, the central bank could be drawn into an expansionary monetary policy. This interdependence between monetary and fiscal policy is important to policymakers as well as to business people and others who seek to understand current economic developments.

The *government budget constraint* clarifies the relationship between monetary and fiscal policies:

$$G = T + B + \triangle M$$

where

G = government spending
T = tax revenue
B = government borrowing
$\triangle M$ = the change in the money supply[1]

The government budget constraint always holds because there are only three ways for the government to finance its spending: by taxing, by borrowing, and by creating money.

We can rewrite the government budget constraint with the change in M on the left-hand side of the equation:

$$\triangle M = (G - T) - B$$

7 How is inflationary monetary policy related to government fiscal policy?

In this form, you can see that the change in government-issued money equals the government fiscal deficit $(G - T)$ minus borrowing. This equation is always true as an accounting identity. But the President or Congress cannot cause a change in the money supply by changing government spending, only the central bank, the Federal Reserve, can do that. So if government spending went up, and there was no change in the money supply, then either taxes or borrowing would have to also rise to finance the increased government spending. A government that has the ability to borrow at reasonable costs will not have the incentive to create rapid money growth and the consequent inflation that results in order to finance its budget deficit.

In the United States and other industrial nations, monetary and fiscal policies are conducted by separate, independent agencies. Fiscal authorities (Congress and the president in the United States) cannot impose monetary policy on the central bank. But in typical developing countries, monetary and fiscal policies are controlled by a central political authority. Here monetary policy is often an extension of fiscal policy. Fiscal policy can impose an inflationary burden on monetary policy. If a country is running a large fiscal deficit, and much of this deficit cannot be financed by government borrowing, monetary authorities must create money to finance the deficit.

RECAP

1. The government budget constraint ($G = T + B + \triangle M$) defines the relationship between fiscal and monetary policies.
2. The implications of fiscal policy for the growth of the money supply can be seen by rewriting the government budget constraint as $\triangle M = (G - T) - B$.

[1] The M in the government budget constraint is government-issued money (usually called *base money*, or *high-powered money*). It is easiest to think of this kind of money as currency, although in practice base money includes more than currency.

5. ECONOMIC GROWTH

Although much of macroeconomics is aimed at understanding business cycles—recurring periods of prosperity and recession—the fact is that over the long run, most economies do grow wealthier. The long-run trend of real GDP in the United States and most other countries is positive. Yet the rate at which real GDP grows is very different across countries. In this section we examine the determinants of economic growth to understand what accounts for the different rates of growth across countries.

8

How are economic growth rates determined?

5.a. The Determinants of Growth

The long-run aggregate supply curve is a vertical line at the potential level of real GDP (Y_{p1}). As the economy grows, the potential output of the economy rises. Figure 16.11 shows the increase in potential output as a rightward shift in the long-run aggregate supply curve. The higher the rate of growth, the farther the aggregate supply curve moves to the right. To illustrate several years' growth, we would show several curves shifting to the right.

To find the determinants of economic growth, we must turn to the determinants of aggregate supply. In Chapter 12, we identified three determinants of aggregate supply: resource prices, technology, and expectations. Changes in expectations can shift the aggregate supply curve, but changing expectations are not a basis for long-run growth in the sense of continuous rightward movements in aggregate supply. The long-run growth of the economy rests on growth in productive resources (labor, capital, and land) and technological advances.

5.a.1. Labor Economic growth depends on the size and quality of the labor force. The size of the labor force is a function of the size of the working-age population (16 and older in the United States) and the percentage of that population in the labor force. The labor force typically grows more rapidly in developing countries than in industrial countries because birthrates are higher in

FIGURE 16.11 Economic Growth

As the economy grows, the long-run aggregate supply curve shifts to the right. This represents an increase in the potential level of real GDP.

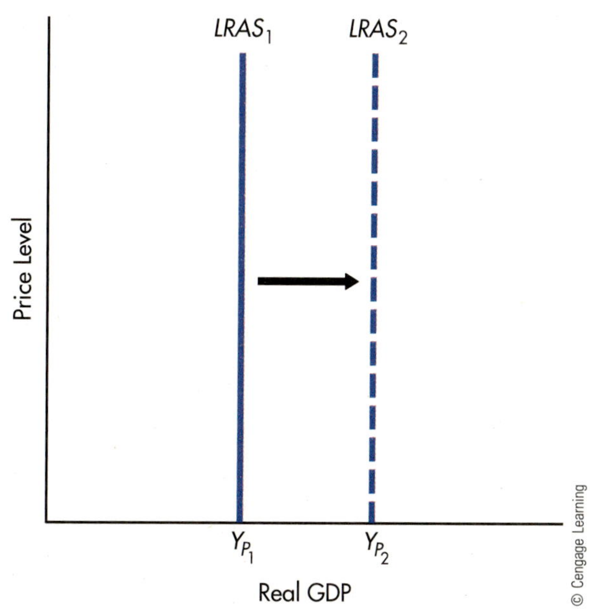

developing countries. Between 2000 and 2010, the population grew at a rate of 26.1 percent in Africa and 10.4 percent in North America.

Solely on the basis of growth in the labor force, it seems that developing countries are growing faster than industrial countries. But the size of the labor force is not all that matters; changes in productivity can compensate for lower growth in the labor force, as we discuss in section 5.b.

5.a.2. **Capital** Labor is combined with capital to produce goods and services. A rapidly growing labor force by itself is no guarantee of economic growth. Workers need machines, tools, and factories to work. If a country has lots of workers but few machines, then the typical worker cannot be very productive. Capital is a critical resource in growing economies.

The ability of a country to invest in capital goods is tied to its ability to save. A lack of current saving can be offset by borrowing, but the availability of borrowing is limited by the prospects for future saving. Debt incurred today must be repaid by not consuming all output in the future. If lenders believe that a nation is going to consume all of its output in the future, they do not make loans today.

The lower the standard of living in a country, the harder it is to forgo current consumption in order to save. It is difficult for a population living at or near subsistence level to do without current consumption. This in large part explains the low level of saving in the poorest countries.

5.a.3. **Land** Land surface, water, forests, minerals, and other natural resources are called *land*. Land can be combined with labor and capital to produce goods and services. Abundant natural resources can contribute to economic growth, but natural resources alone do not generate growth. Several developing countries, such as Argentina and Brazil, are relatively rich in natural resources but have not been very successful in exploiting these resources to produce goods and services. Japan, on the other hand, has relatively few natural resources but showed dramatic economic growth for decades until a recession in the 1990s. The experience of Japan makes it clear that abundant natural resources are not a necessary condition for economic growth.

Argentina is relatively rich in natural resources but has had limited success in exploiting those resources to produce goods and services.

Diego Levy/Bloomberg/Getty Images

technology:
ways of combining resources to produce output

5.a.4. Technology

A key determinant of economic growth is **technology**, ways of combining resources to produce goods and services. New management techniques, scientific discoveries, and other innovations improve technology. Technological advances allow the production of more output from a given amount of resources. This means that technological progress accelerates economic growth for any given rate of growth in the labor force and the capital stock.

Technological change depends on the scientific community. The more educated a population is, the greater its potential for technological advances will be. Industrial countries have better-educated populations than developing countries do. Education gives industrial countries a substantial advantage over developing countries in creating and implementing innovations. In addition, the richest industrial countries traditionally have spent 2 to 3 percent of their GNP on research and development, an investment developing countries cannot afford. The greater the funding for research and development, the greater the likelihood of technological advances.

Impeded by low levels of education and limited funds for research and development, the developing countries lag behind the industrial countries in developing and implementing new technology. Typically these countries follow the lead of the industrial world, adopting new technology developed in that world once it is affordable and feasible, given their capital and labor resources.

5.a.5. Institutions

A country's political, legal, economic, and social institutions help determine its ability to grow. Think of institutions as the rules that economic participants must follow. For example, are private citizens allowed to own property? Is there a court system to protect their property rights? Are contracts and copyrights enforced? Are civil rights granted to all people? What kinds of regulations are imposed on the market?

In the Soviet Union, for example, the economy was based on a system of state ownership of the means of production. Joseph Stalin's First Five-Year Plan, launched in 1928, entailed a major focus on heavy industry. The plan set output targets to direct industrial production, and in 1929 collectivized agriculture. From 1928 to 1970, output grew in excess of 5 percent per year, a very impressive rate, mostly due to the rapid state-directed industrialization and capital accumulation. Output growth did not mean that everyone was better off. Millions of people died in a famine following agricultural collectivization, and the costs of repression and terror are impossible to measure. Output growth eventually deteriorated after the returns to more capital diminished. Mikhail Gorbachev introduced a program of economic, political, and social restructuring called perestroika in 1986, aimed at reforming institutions to improve the economic and social conditions. Ultimately, the Soviet Union collapsed in 1991, and subsequently Russia adopted more market-oriented institutions.

It is good to remember that institutions that promote growth may or may not promote other things a society values, such as freedom or equal distribution of wealth. So countries may create institutions with more than growth maximization in order to address other societal and economic concerns. Finally, it is often the case that a country's institutions change as what works well in one time or place may not work well in another.

5.b. Productivity

9

What is productivity?

total factor productivity (TFP):
the ratio of the economy's output to its stock of labor and capital

One way to assess the contribution a resource makes to output is its productivity. *Productivity* is the ratio of output produced to the amount of input. We could measure the productivity of a single resource—say, labor or capital—or the overall productivity of all resources. **Total factor productivity (TFP)** is the term economists use to describe the overall productivity of an economy. It is the ratio of the economy's output to its stock of labor and capital.

5.b.1. **Productivity and Economic Growth** Economic growth depends on both the growth of resources and technological progress. Advances in technology allow resources to be more productive. If the quantity of resources is growing, and each resource is more productive, then output grows even faster than the quantity of resources. Economic growth, then, is the sum of the growth rate of TFP and the growth rate of resources:

$$\text{Economic growth} = \text{growth rate of TFP} + \text{growth rate of resources}$$

The amount that output grows because the labor force is growing depends on how much labor contributes to the production of output. Similarly, the amount that output grows because capital is growing depends on how much capital contributes to the production of output. To relate the growth of labor and capital to the growth of output (we assume no change in natural resources), then, the growth of labor and the growth of capital must be multiplied by their relative contributions to the production of output. The most straightforward way to measure those contributions is to use the share of real GDP received by each resource. For instance, in the United States, labor receives about 70 percent (.70) of real GDP, and capital receives about 30 percent (.30). Therefore, we can determine the growth of output by using this formula:

$$\%\triangle Y = \%\triangle \text{TFP} + .70(\%\triangle L) + .30(\%\triangle K)$$

where

$$\begin{aligned} \%\triangle &= \text{percentage change in} \\ Y &= \text{real GDP} \\ \text{TFP} &= \text{total factor productivity} \\ L &= \text{size of the labor force} \\ K &= \text{capital stock} \end{aligned}$$

The equation shows how economic growth depends on changes in productivity ($\%\triangle$TFP) as well as changes in resources ($\%\triangle L$ and $\%\triangle K$). Even if labor (L) and capital stock (K) are constant, technological innovation would generate economic growth through changes in TFP.

For example, suppose TFP is growing at a rate of 2 percent a year. Then, even with labor and capital stock held constant, the economy grows at a rate of 2 percent a year. If labor and capital stock also grow at a rate of 2 percent a year, output grows by the sum of the growth rates of all three components (TFP, .70 times labor growth, and .30 times the capital stock growth), or 4 percent.

How do we account for differences in growth rates across countries? Because almost all countries have experienced growth in the labor force, percentage increases in labor forces have generally supported economic growth. But growth in the capital stock has been steadier in the industrial countries than in the developing countries, so differences in capital growth rates may explain some of the differences in economic growth across countries. Yet differences in resource growth rates alone cannot explain the major differences we find across countries. In recent years, those differences seem to be related to productivity.

NOW YOU TRY IT

What is the growth rate of real GDP for an economy in which TFP grows at a rate of 4 percent, the labor force grows at a rate of 1 percent, the capital stock has zero growth, labor receives 70 percent of output, and capital receives 30 percent?

RECAP

1. Economic growth raises the potential level of real GDP, shifting the long-run aggregate supply curve to the right.
2. The long-run growth of the economy is a product of growth in labor, capital, and natural resources and advances in technology.
3. Technology is the way that resources are combined to produce output.
4. Hampered by low levels of education and limited financial resources, developing countries lag behind the industrial nations in developing and implementing new technology.
5. Productivity is the ratio of output produced to the amount of input.

6. Total factor productivity is equal to a nation's real GDP (output) divided by its stock of labor and capital.
7. Economic growth is the sum of the growth of total factor productivity and the growth rate of resources (labor and capital).

SUMMARY

Is there a trade-off between inflation and the unemployment rate?

1. The Phillips curve shows the relationship between inflation and the unemployment rate.

How does the trade-off between inflation and the unemployment rate vary from the short to the long run?

2. In the long run, there is no trade-off between inflation and the unemployment rate.
3. The long-run Phillips curve is a vertical line at the natural rate of unemployment.

What is the relationship between unexpected inflation and the unemployment rate?

4. Unexpected inflation can affect the unemployment rate through wage expectations, inventory fluctuations, and wage contracts.

How are macroeconomic expectations formed?

5. Adaptive expectations are formed on the basis of past experience; rational expectations are formed on the basis of all available relevant information.

Are business cycles related to political elections?

6. A political business cycle is created by politicians who want to improve their chances of reelection by stimulating the economy just before an election.

How do real shocks to the economy affect business cycles?

7. Real business cycles are a product of unexpected change in technology, weather, war and terrorism, or some other real variable.

How is inflationary monetary policy related to government fiscal policy?

8. The government budget constraint defines the relationship between monetary and fiscal policies.
9. When government-issued money is used to finance fiscal deficits, inflationary monetary policy can be a product of fiscal policy.

How are economic growth rates determined?

10. The growth of the economy is tied to the growth of productive resources and technological advances.
11. Because their populations tend to grow more rapidly, developing countries typically experience faster growth in the labor force than do industrial countries.
12. The inability to save limits the growth of capital stock in developing countries.
13. Abundant natural resources are not necessary for rapid economic growth.
14. Technology defines the ways in which resources can be combined to produce goods and services.

What is productivity?

15. Productivity is the ratio of output produced to the amount of input.
16. Total factor productivity is the overall productivity of an economy.
17. The percentage change in real GDP equals the percentage change in total factor productivity plus the percentage changes in labor and capital multiplied by the share of GDP taken by labor and capital.

EXERCISES

1. What is the difference between the short-run Phillips curve and the long-run Phillips curve? Use an aggregate supply and demand diagram to explain why there is a difference between them.
2. Give two reasons why there may be a short-run trade-off between unexpected inflation and the unemployment rate.
3. Economists have identified two kinds of macroeconomic expectations.
   a. Define them.
   b. What are the implications for macroeconomic policy of these two forms of expectations?
4. Write down the government budget constraint and explain how it can be used to understand the relationship between fiscal and monetary policies.
5. If tax revenues equal $100 billion, government spending equals $135 billion, and the government borrows $25 billion, how much do you expect the money supply to increase given the government budget constraint?
6. If the government budget deficit equals $240 billion and the money supply increases by $100 billion, how much must the government borrow?
7. Discuss how each of the following sources of real business cycles would affect the economy:
   a. Farmers go on strike for six months.
   b. Oil prices fall substantially.
   c. Particularly favorable weather increases agricultural output nationwide.
8. Using an aggregate demand and aggregate supply diagram, illustrate and explain how a political business cycle is created.
9. Suppose labor's share of GDP is 70 percent and capital's is 30 percent, real GDP is growing at a rate of 4 percent a year, the labor force is growing at 2 percent, and the capital stock is growing at 3 percent. What is the growth rate of total factor productivity?
10. Suppose labor's share of GDP is 70 percent and capital's is 30 percent, total factor productivity is growing at an annual rate of 2 percent, the labor force is growing at a rate of 1 percent, and the capital stock is growing at a rate of 3 percent. What is the annual growth rate of real GDP?
11. Is the following statement true or false? Explain your answer. "Abundant natural resources are a necessary condition for economic growth."
12. What is the growth rate for an economy in which there is no growth of resources but TFP grows at a rate of 1 percent per year?
13. What is the growth rate for an economy in which TFP is constant, labor grows at a rate of 1 percent per year, capital grows at a rate of 2 percent per year, labor's share of output equals 60 percent, and capital's share equals 40 percent?
14. What is the growth rate for an economy in which TFP grows at a rate of 3 percent per year, the size of the labor force is unchanged, the capital stock grows at a rate of 2 percent per year, and labor and capital each account for 50 percent of output?

STUDY GUIDE FOR CHAPTER 16

Key Term Match

Match each term with its correct definition by placing the appropriate letter next to the corresponding number.

A. Phillips curve
B. reservation wage
C. adaptive expectations
D. rational expectations
E. shock
F. technology
G. total factor productivity (TFP)

____ 1. ways of combining resources to produce output

____ 2. expectations formed by using all available relevant information

____ 3. the ratio of the economy's output to its stock of labor and capital

____ 4. expectations formed on the basis of information collected in the past

____ 5. an unexpected change in a variable

____ 6. the minimum wage a worker is willing to accept

____ 7. a graph that illustrates the relationship between inflation and the unemployment rate

Quick-Check Quiz

1. Which of the following could *not* cause a movement along the Phillips curve?
   - ☐ a. a change in inflation that is not expected by workers
   - ☐ b. an unexpected increase in inflation that causes inventories to decline
   - ☐ c. wage contracts that did not correctly anticipate the inflation rate
   - ☐ d. an anticipated rise in nominal wages
   - ☐ e. All of the above cause movements along the short-run Phillips curve.

2. Which of the following is an example of rational rather than adaptive expectations?
   - ☐ a. The crowd expects a 95 percent free-throw shooter to sink the free throw to win the state basketball championship.
   - ☐ b. A professor has been 10 minutes late to class three times in a row. Students come to the fourth class 10 minutes late.
   - ☐ c. The fans of a pro football team that had four wins, ten losses, and one tie last year find another team to root for this year.
   - ☐ d. Stockholders of a firm that had losses three years in a row sell off their stocks.
   - ☐ e. A company with a poor earnings record over the past five years finds itself swamped by investors when word of its new superproduct leaks out.

3. Which of the following is false?
   - ☐ a. The short-run effect of unexpected disinflation is rising unemployment.
   - ☐ b. The short-run Phillips curve assumes a constant reservation wage and a constant expected rate of inflation.
   - ☐ c. The tradeoff between inflation and unemployment comes from expected inflation.
   - ☐ d. Inventory fluctuations may cause a movement along the Phillips curve.
   - ☐ e. If wages were flexible, unexpected changes in aggregate demand might be reflected more in wage adjustments than in employment adjustments.

4. Unexpected increases in aggregate demand ______________ inventories and ______________ prices. Unemployment ______________.
   - ☐ a. lower; raise; decreases
   - ☐ b. lower; raise; increases
   - ☐ c. lower; lower; increases
   - ☐ d. raise; lower; increases
   - ☐ e. raise; lower; decreases

5. Which of the following would *not* be a cause of a real business cycle?
   - ☐ a. a decrease in government borrowing
   - ☐ b. a drought in the Midwest
   - ☐ c. oil prices skyrocketing as a result of an accident on the world's largest offshore oil rig
   - ☐ d. a labor strike that cripples the steel industry
   - ☐ e. an improvement in the technology for solar energy that yields a lightweight solar battery that can be used to power cars for long trips

6. The existence of a political business cycle implies that, prior to the election, the incumbent administration would
   - ☐ a. increase aggregate demand by increasing government spending and the money supply.
   - ☐ b. increase aggregate demand by increasing government spending and decreasing the money supply.
   - ☐ c. increase aggregate demand by decreasing government spending and the money supply.
   - ☐ d. decrease aggregate demand by increasing government spending and the money supply.
   - ☐ e. decrease aggregate demand by increasing government spending and decreasing the money supply.

7. A drought in the Midwest would cause ______________ to shift to the ______________, which would ______________ real GDP.
   - ☐ a. aggregate demand; left; decrease
   - ☐ b. aggregate demand; right; increase
   - ☐ c. aggregate supply; left; increase
   - ☐ d. aggregate supply; left; decrease
   - ☐ e. aggregate supply; right; increase

8. Which of the following is false?
   - ☐ a. In most developed countries, monetary and fiscal policies are conducted by separate independent agencies.
   - ☐ b. Fiscal policy can impose an inflationary burden on monetary policy.
   - ☐ c. In typical developing countries, monetary and fiscal policies are controlled by the same central authority.
   - ☐ d. Using money to finance deficits has produced severe deflation in many countries.
   - ☐ e. Monetary control is not possible until fiscal policy is under control.

9. Growth in a country's capital stock is tied to
   - ☐ a. increases in the amounts of natural resources available.
   - ☐ b. current and future saving.
   - ☐ c. improvements in technology.
   - ☐ d. increases in the amount of labor available.
   - ☐ e. decreases in the labor force participation ratio.

10. Which of the following is *not* one of the determinants of economic growth?
   - ☐ a. the size and quality of the labor force
   - ☐ b. the amount of capital goods available
   - ☐ c. technology
   - ☐ d. natural resources
   - ☐ e. the shape of the aggregate demand curve

Practice Questions and Problems

1. A country's social, economic and legal institutions ______________ (affect, do not affect) its ability to grow.
2. The Phillips curve tradeoff between inflation and unemployment ______________ (does, does not) persist over the long run.
3. The downward slope of the short-run Phillips curve is caused by shifts in ______________, with ______________ remaining constant.
4. List the two assumptions underlying the short-run Phillips curve.
   ____
   ____
5. If people's expectations about inflation do not change, the short-run effect of disinflation is rising ______________.
6. Unexpected inflation can affect the employment rate in the following three ways:
   ____
   ____
   ____
7. Your economics professor bases her first exam solely on material from the textbook. Before the second exam, she announces that this exam will be based primarily on lecture material. If you only study the textbook, you are acting on the basis of ______________ expectations.
8. When the inflation rate is unexpectedly high, unemployment ______________.
9. Write the equation for the government budget restraint.
   ____
10. All other things being equal, a country that does not enforce private property rights will have a ______________(higher, lower) rate of economic growth than a country that does enforce private property rights.
11. Economic growth shifts the aggregate ______________ (demand, supply) curve to the ______________ (right, left).
12. The long-run growth of the economy rests on growth in productive resources such as ______________, ______________, ______________, and ______________, and on advances in ______________.
13. The size of a country's labor force is determined by the ______________ and the ______________ of the population in the labor force.
14. The reservation wage of a worker who expects inflation will be ______________(higher, lower) than the reservation wage of a worker who expects constant prices.
15. What are two factors that cause developing countries to lag behind in the development and implementation of new technology?
   ____
   ____
16. Productivity is the ratio of ______________ to the amount of ______________.
17. ______________ is the nation's real GDP divided by its stock of labor and capital.
18. In the United States, labor receives about 70 percent of national income, and capital receives about 30 percent. If total factor productivity increases by 1 percent, labor increases by 1 percent, and capital increases by 3 percent, by what percentage will national income increase?

Exercises and Applications

I War on Inflation

The leader of a developing nation has declared war on inflation by issuing a series of belt-tightening measures. Capital gains taxes will be enforced, lending and deposit rates at banks will be raised, and government spending will be slashed.

Use the government's budget constraint to explain how these measures will affect inflation.

____

____

II Government Policy and Growth

Government policies that hold down interest rates have adverse effects on economic growth in developing countries. Although low interest rates are intended to make it cheaper for local businesses to invest in new capital goods, they have the effect of drying up the supply of savings since savers can get a higher return by taking their money out of the country or by making less productive investments on their own. Similar policies are sometimes followed in other economic sectors, with similarly bad results.

For example, many developing countries require farmers to sell their crops to the government, which resells the food to city dwellers. To keep the city dwellers happy, the prices charged for food are set very low, as are the prices paid to farmers. Think about the farmers' opportunity costs of growing food for sale and predict what is likely to happen to the food supply in countries adopting this policy.

____

____

____

You can find further practice tests in the Online Quiz at: www.cengagebrain.com

17 Issues in International Trade and Finance

FUNDAMENTAL QUESTIONS

1. What determines the goods a nation will export?
2. What are the sources of comparative advantage?
3. Why do countries restrict international trade?
4. How do countries restrict the entry of foreign goods and promote the export of domestic goods?
5. What kinds of exchange rate arrangements exist today?

PREVIEW

The world is a global marketplace, and all nations are interdependent. An understanding of international trade and finance is critical to understanding the modern economy. Earlier chapters have frequently considered international implications of various topics; however, in this chapter we delve more deeply into the global economic linkages.

Besides studying the determinants of international trade and how and why nations restrict such trade, we also will learn about the variety of exchange rate regimes that exist in the world today. Some countries allow the value of their currency to float with the free market forces of supply and demand, whereas other countries choose to fix the value of their currency at some constant value against another currency. Still other countries choose some sort of hybrid exchange rate system. Because exchange rates are the prices that link the currencies of the world, we better understand the interrelationships among countries when we understand the current exchange rate environment.

1. AN OVERVIEW OF WORLD TRADE

1

What determines the goods a nation will export?

Recall from Chapter 1 that trade occurs because it makes people better off. International trade occurs because it makes people better off than they would be if they could consume only domestically produced products. Who trades with whom, and what sorts of goods are traded? The underlying reasons for trade are found in comparative advantage.

1.a. Comparative Advantage

In Chapter 1, you learned that *comparative advantage* is the ability to produce a good or service at a lower opportunity cost than someone else. This is true for countries as well as for individuals. Comparative advantage is found by comparing the relative costs of production in each country. We measure the cost of producing a particular good in two countries in terms of opportunity costs—what other goods must be given up in order to produce more of the good in question.

Table 17.1 presents a hypothetical example of two countries, the United States and India, that both produce two goods, wheat and cloth. The table lists the amount of each good that could be produced by one worker. This example assumes that labor productivity differences alone determine comparative advantage. In the United States, one worker can produce either 8 units of wheat or 4 units of cloth. In India, one worker can produce 4 units of wheat or 3 units of cloth.

absolute advantage: an advantage derived from one country's having a lower absolute input cost of producing a particular good than another country

The United States has an **absolute advantage**—greater productivity—in producing both wheat and cloth. Absolute advantage is determined by comparing the absolute productivity in different countries of producing each good. Since one worker can produce more of either good in the United States than in India, the United States is the more efficient producer of both goods.

It might seem that since the United States is the more efficient producer of both goods, there would be no need for trade with India. But absolute advantage is not the critical consideration. What matters in determining the benefits of international trade is comparative advantage. To find the comparative advantage—the lower opportunity cost—we must compare the opportunity cost of producing each good in each country.

The opportunity cost of producing wheat is what must be given up in cloth using the same resources, such as one worker per day. Look again at Table 17.1 to see the production of wheat and cloth in the two countries. Since one U.S. worker can produce 8 units of wheat or 4 units of cloth, if we take a worker from cloth production and move him to wheat production, we gain 8 units of wheat and lose 4 units of cloth. The opportunity cost of producing wheat equals 4/8, or 1/2, unit of cloth and is represented as follows:

$$\frac{\text{Output of cloth given up}}{\text{Output of wheat gained}} = \text{opportunity cost of producing 1 unit of wheat (in terms of cloth given up)}$$

$$4/8 = 1/2$$

Applying the same thinking to India, we find that one worker can produce 4 units of wheat or 3 units of cloth. The opportunity cost of producing 1 unit of wheat in India is 3/4 unit of cloth.

Table 17.1 An Example of Comparative Advantage

	Output per Worker per Day in Either Wheat or Cloth	
	United States (units)	**India (units)**
Wheat	8	4
Cloth	4	3

A comparison of the domestic opportunity costs in each country will reveal which one has the comparative advantage in producing each good. The U.S. opportunity cost of producing 1 unit of wheat is 1/2 unit of cloth; the Indian opportunity cost is 3/4 unit of cloth. Because the United States has a lower domestic opportunity cost, it has the comparative advantage in wheat production and will export wheat. Since wheat production costs are lower in the United States, India is better off trading for wheat rather than trying to produce it domestically.

The comparative advantage in cloth is found the same way. Taking a worker in the United States from wheat production and putting her in cloth production, we gain 4 units of cloth and lose 8 units of wheat per day. Therefore, the opportunity cost is as follows:

$$\frac{\text{Output of wheat given up}}{\text{Output of cloth gained}} = \begin{array}{l}\text{opportunity cost of producing 1 unit}\\ \text{of cloth (in terms of wheat given up)}\end{array}$$

$$8/4 = 2$$

In India, moving a worker from wheat to cloth production means that we gain 3 units of cloth but lose 4 units of wheat, so the opportunity cost is 4/3, or 1⅓, units of wheat for 1 unit of cloth. Comparing the U.S. opportunity cost of 2 units of wheat with the Indian opportunity cost of 1⅓ units, we see that India has the comparative advantage in cloth production and will therefore export cloth. In this case, the United States is better off trading for cloth than producing it since India's costs of production are lower.

In international trade, as in other areas of economic decision making, it is opportunity cost that matters, and opportunity costs are reflected in comparative advantage. Absolute advantage is irrelevant because knowing the absolute number of labor hours required to produce a good does not tell us if we can benefit from trade. We benefit from trade if we are able to obtain a good from a foreign country by giving up less than we would have to give up to obtain the good at home. Because only opportunity cost can allow us to make such comparisons, international trade proceeds on the basis of comparative advantage.

NOW YOU TRY IT

Suppose a worker in Canada can produce 3 units of corn or 3 units of computers per day whereas a worker in China can produce 2 units of corn or 4 units of computers per day. Which country has the comparative advantage in

a. corn?

b. computers?

1.b. Sources of Comparative Advantage

2

What are the sources of comparative advantage?

We know that countries specialize and trade in accordance with comparative advantage, but what gives a country a comparative advantage? Economists have suggested several theories of the source of comparative advantage. Let us review these theories.

1.b.1. Productivity Differences

The example of comparative advantage showed the United States to have a comparative advantage in wheat production and India to have a comparative advantage in cloth production. Comparative advantage was determined by differences in the labor hours required to produce each good. In this example, differences in the *productivity* of labor accounted for comparative advantage.

For over 200 years, economists have argued that productivity differences account for comparative advantage. In fact, this theory of comparative advantage is often called the *Ricardian model*, after David Ricardo, a 19th-century English economist who explained and analyzed the idea of productivity-based comparative advantage. Variation in the productivity of labor can explain many observed trade patterns in the world.

Although we know that labor productivity differs across countries—and that this can help explain why countries produce the goods they do—there are factors other than labor productivity that determine comparative advantage. Furthermore, even if labor productivity were all that mattered, we would still want to know why some countries have more productive workers than others. The standard interpretation of the Ricardian model is that technological differences between countries account for differences in labor productivity.

The countries with the most advanced technology would have a comparative advantage with regard to those goods that can be produced most efficiently with modern technology.

1.b.2. Factor Abundance Goods differ in terms of the resources, or factors of production, required for their production. Countries differ in terms of the abundance of different factors of production: land, labor, and capital. It seems self-evident that countries would have an advantage in producing those goods that use relatively large amounts of their most abundant factor of production. Certainly countries with a relatively large amount of farmland would have a comparative advantage in agriculture, and countries with a relatively large amount of capital would tend to specialize in the production of manufactured goods.

In many cases, factor abundance has served well as an explanation of observed trade patterns. However, there remain cases in which comparative advantage seems to run counter to the predictions of the factor abundance theory. In response, economists have suggested other explanations for comparative advantage.

1.b.3. Other Theories of Comparative Advantage New theories of comparative advantage have typically come about in an effort to explain the trade pattern in some narrow category of products. They are not intended to serve as general explanations of comparative advantage, as do factor abundance and productivity. These supplementary theories emphasize human skills, product cycles, and preferences.

Human Skills This approach emphasizes differences across countries in the availability of skilled and unskilled labor. The basic idea is that countries with a relatively abundant stock of highly skilled labor will have a comparative advantage in producing goods that require relatively large amounts of skilled labor. This theory is similar to the factor abundance theory except that here the analysis rests on two segments (skilled and unskilled) of the labor factor.

The human skills argument is consistent with the observation that most U.S. exports are produced in high-wage (skilled labor) industries, and most

The United States has a comparative advantage in industries requiring a large amount of skilled labor.

Fuse/Jupiter Images

U.S. imports are products produced in relatively low-wage industries. Since the United States has a well-educated labor force relative to that of many other countries, we would expect the United States to have a comparative advantage in industries requiring a large amount of skilled labor. Developing countries would be expected to have a comparative advantage in industries requiring a relatively large amount of unskilled labor.

Product Life Cycles This theory explains how comparative advantage in a specific good can shift over time from one country to another. This occurs because goods experience a *product life cycle.* At the outset, development and testing are required to conceptualize and design the product. For this reason, the early production will be undertaken by an innovative firm. Over time, however, a successful product tends to become standardized, in the sense that many manufacturers can produce it. The mature product may be produced by firms that do little or no research and development, specializing instead in copying successful products invented and developed by others.

The product life cycle theory is related to international comparative advantage in that a new product will be first produced and exported by the nation in which it was invented. As the product is exported elsewhere and foreign firms become familiar with it, the technology is copied in other countries by foreign firms seeking to produce a competing version. As the product matures, comparative advantage shifts away from the country of origin if other countries have lower manufacturing costs using the now-standardized technology.

The history of color television production shows how comparative advantage can shift over the product life cycle. Color television was invented in the United States, and U.S. firms initially produced and exported color TVs. Over time, as the technology of color television manufacturing became well known, countries like Japan and Taiwan came to dominate the business. Firms in these countries had a comparative advantage over U.S. firms in the manufacture of color televisions. Once the technology is widely available, countries with lower production costs due to lower wages can compete effectively against the higher-wage nation that developed the technology.

Preferences The theories of comparative advantage we have looked at so far have all been based on supply factors. It may be, though, that the demand side of the market can explain some of the patterns observed in international trade. Seldom are different producers' goods exactly identical. Consumers may prefer the goods of one firm to those of another firm. Domestic firms usually produce goods to satisfy domestic consumers. But since different consumers have different preferences, some consumers will prefer goods produced by foreign firms. International trade allows consumers to expand their consumption opportunities.

Consumers who live in countries with similar levels of development can be expected to have similar consumption patterns. The consumption patterns of consumers in countries at much different levels of development are much less similar. This suggests that firms in industrial countries will find a larger market for their goods in other industrial countries than in developing countries.

intraindustry trade: simultaneous import and export of goods in the same industry by a particular country

Another feature of international trade that may be explained by consumer preference is **intraindustry trade**, a circumstance in which a country both exports and imports goods in the same industry. The fact that the United States exports Budweiser beer and imports Heineken beer is not surprising when preferences are taken into account. Supply-side theories of comparative advantage rarely provide an explanation of intraindustry trade since they would expect each country to export only those goods produced in industries in which a comparative advantage exists. Yet the real world is characterized by a great deal of intraindustry trade.

We have discussed several potential sources of comparative advantage: labor productivity, factor abundance, human skills, product cycles, and preferences. Each of these theories, summarized in Figure 17.1, has proven useful in

FIGURE 17.1 Theories of Comparative Advantage

Several theories exist that explain comparative advantage: labor productivity, factor abundance, human skills, product life cycles, and preferences.

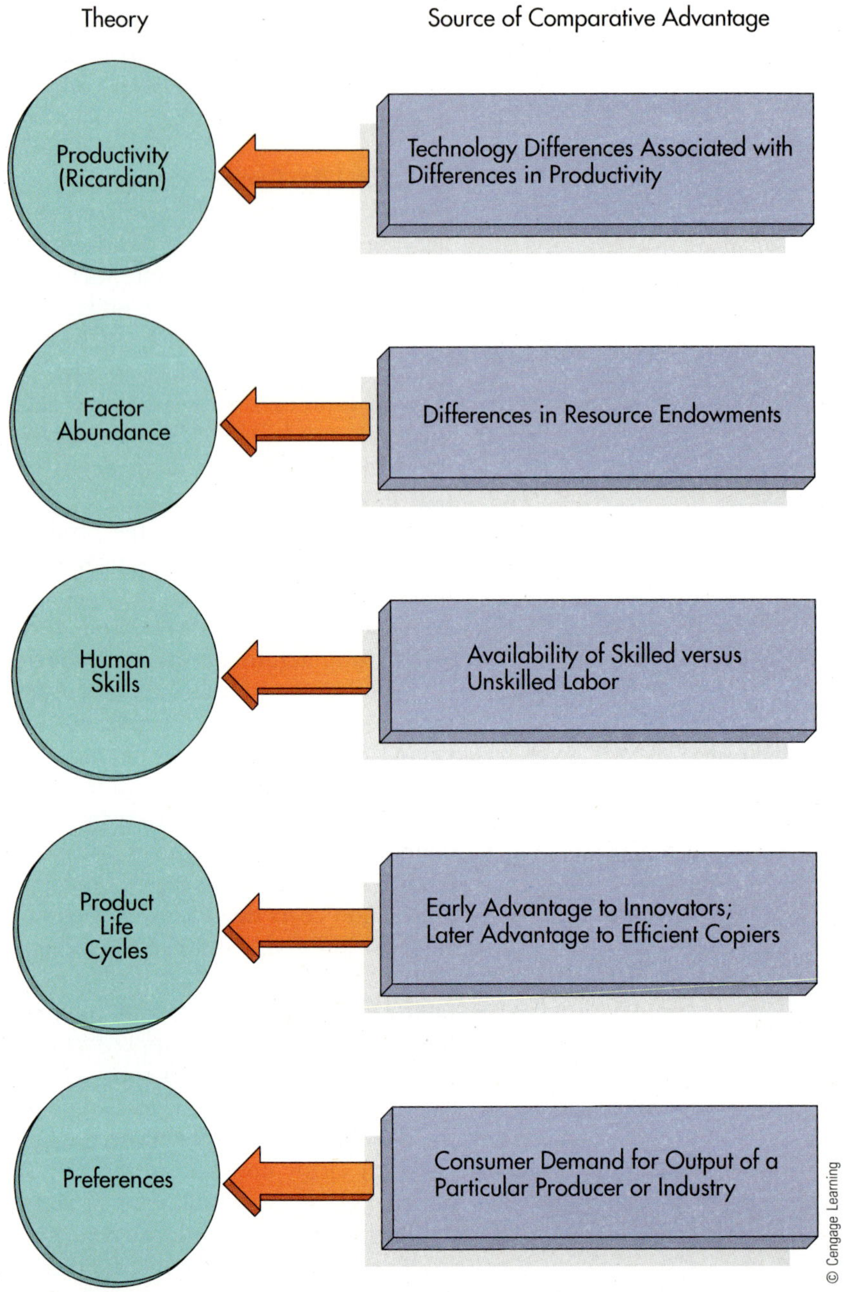

understanding certain trade patterns. Each has also been shown to have limitations as a general theory applicable to all cases. Once again we are reminded that the world is a very complicated place. Theories are simpler than reality. Nevertheless, they help us to understand how comparative advantage arises.

RECAP

1. Comparative advantage can arise because of differences in labor productivity.
2. Countries differ in their resource endowments, and a given country may enjoy a comparative advantage in products that intensively use its most abundant factor of production.

3. Industrial countries may have a comparative advantage in products requiring a large amount of skilled labor. Developing countries may have a comparative advantage in products requiring a large amount of unskilled labor.
4. Comparative advantage in a new good initially resides in the country that invented the good. Over time, other nations learn the technology and may gain a comparative advantage in producing the good.
5. In some industries, consumer preferences for differentiated goods may explain international trade flows, including intraindustry trade.

2. INTERNATIONAL TRADE RESTRICTIONS

3

Why do countries restrict international trade?

commercial policy: government policy that influences international trade flows

International trade is rarely determined solely by comparative advantage and the free market forces of supply and demand. Governments often find that political pressures favor policies that at least partially offset the prevailing comparative advantages. Government policy aimed at influencing international trade flows is called **commercial policy**. This section first examines the arguments in support of commercial policy and then discusses the various tools of commercial policy employed by governments.

2.a. Arguments for Protection

Governments restrict foreign trade to protect domestic producers from foreign competition. In some cases the protection may be justified; in most cases it harms consumers. Of the arguments used to promote such protection, only a few are valid. We will look first at arguments widely considered to have little or no merit and then at those that may sometimes be valid.

International trade on the basis of comparative advantage maximizes world output and allows consumers access to better-quality products at lower prices than would be available in the domestic market alone. If trade is restricted, consumers pay higher prices for lower-quality goods, and world output declines. Protection from foreign competition imposes costs on the domestic economy as well as on foreign producers. When production does not proceed on the basis of comparative advantage, resources are not expended on their most efficient uses. Whenever government restrictions alter the pattern of trade, we should expect someone to benefit and someone else to suffer. Generally speaking, protection from foreign competition benefits domestic producers at the expense of domestic consumers.

2.a.1. Creation of Domestic Jobs If foreign goods are kept out of the domestic economy, it is often argued, jobs will be created at home. This argument holds that domestic firms will produce the goods that otherwise would have been produced abroad, thus employing domestic workers instead of foreign workers. The weakness of this argument is that only the protected industry would benefit in terms of employment. Since domestic consumers will pay higher prices to buy the output of the protected industry, they will have less to spend on other goods and services, which could cause employment in other industries to drop. If other countries retaliate by restricting entry of U.S. exports, the output of U.S. firms that produce for export will fall as well. Typically, restrictions to "save domestic jobs" simply redistribute jobs by creating employment in the protected industry and reducing employment elsewhere.

2.a.2. Creation of a Level Playing Field Special interest groups sometimes claim that other nations that export successfully to the home market have unfair advantages over domestic producers. Fairness, however, is often in the eye of the beholder. People who call for creating a level playing field believe that the domestic government should take steps to offset the perceived advantage of the foreign firm. They often claim that foreign firms have an unfair advantage because foreign workers are willing to work for very low wages. "Fair trade, not free trade" is the cry that this claim generates. But advocates of fair trade are really claiming that production in accordance with comparative advantage is unfair. This is clearly wrong. A country with relatively low wages is typically a country with an abundance of low-skilled labor. Such a country will have a comparative advantage in products that use low-skilled labor most intensively. To create a level playing field by imposing restrictions that eliminate the comparative advantage of foreign firms will make domestic consumers worse off and undermine the basis for specialization and economic efficiency.

Some calls for "fair trade" are based on the notion of reciprocity. If a country imposes import restrictions on goods from a country that does not have similar restrictions, reciprocal tariffs and quotas may be called for in the latter country in order to stimulate a reduction of trade restrictions in the former country. For instance, it has been claimed that U.S. construction firms are discriminated against in Japan because no U.S. firm has had a major construction project in Japan since the 1960s. Yet Japanese construction firms do billions of dollars' worth of business in the United States each year. Advocates of fair trade could argue that U.S. restrictions should be imposed on Japanese construction firms.

One danger of calls for fairness based on reciprocity is that calls for fair trade may be invoked in cases where, in fact, foreign restrictions on U.S. imports do not exist. For instance, suppose the U.S. auto industry wanted to restrict the entry of imported autos to help stimulate sales of domestically produced cars. One strategy might be to point out that U.S. auto sales abroad had fallen and to claim that this was due to unfair treatment of U.S. auto exports in other countries. Of course, there are many other possible reasons why foreign sales of U.S. autos might have fallen. But blaming foreign trade restrictions might win political support for restricting imports of foreign cars into the United States.

2.a.3. **Government Revenue Creation** Tariffs on trade generate government revenue. Industrial countries, which find income taxes easy to collect, rarely justify tariffs on the basis of the revenue they generate for government spending. But many developing countries find income taxes difficult to levy and collect, whereas tariffs are easy to collect. Customs agents can be positioned at ports of entry to examine all goods that enter and leave the country. The observability of trade flows makes tariffs a popular tax in developing countries, whose revenue requirements may provide a valid justification for their existence. Table 17.2 shows that tariffs account for a relatively large fraction of GDP in some developing countries and only a small fraction in industrial countries.

Table 17.2 Tariffs as a Percentage of GDP

Country	Tariffs as Percentage of GDP
United Kingdom	0
United States	0.2
Canada	0.7
Costa Rica	1.2
Lesotho	35.0
Russia Fed	8.5
Vietnam	3.5

Source: International Monetary Fund, *Government Finance Statistics Yearbook* (www.imfstatistics.org/imf/).

2.a.4. **National Defense** It has long been argued that industries crucial to the national defense, such as shipbuilding, should be protected from foreign competition. Even though the United States does not have a comparative advantage in shipbuilding, a domestic shipbuilding industry is necessary since foreign-made ships may not be available during war. This is a valid argument as long as the protected industry is genuinely critical to the national defense. In some industries, such as copper or other basic metals, it might make more sense to import the crucial products during peacetime and store them for use in the event of war; these products do not require domestic production to be useful. Care must be taken to ensure that the national defense argument is not used to protect industries other than those truly crucial to the nation's defense.

2.a.5. **Infant Industries** Nations are often inclined to protect new industries on the basis that the protection will give those industries adequate time to develop. New industries need time to establish themselves and to become efficient enough that their costs are no higher than those of their foreign rivals. An alternative to protecting young and/or critical domestic industries with tariffs and quotas is to subsidize them. Subsidies allow such firms to charge lower prices and to compete with more efficient foreign producers while permitting consumers to pay the world price rather than the higher prices associated with tariffs or quotas on foreign goods.

Protecting an infant industry from foreign competition may make sense but only until the industry matures. Once the industry achieves sufficient size, protection should be withdrawn, and the industry should be made to compete with its foreign counterparts. Unfortunately, such protection is rarely withdrawn because the larger and more successful the industry becomes, the more political power it wields. In fact, if an infant industry truly has a good chance to become competitive and produce profitably once it is well established, it is not at all clear that government should even offer protection to reduce short-run losses. New firms typically incur losses, but they are only temporary if the firm is successful.

strategic trade policy: the use of trade restrictions or subsidies to allow domestic firms with decreasing costs to gain a greater share of the world market

increasing-returns-to-scale industry: an industry in which the costs of producing a unit of output fall as more output is produced

2.a.6. **Strategic Trade Policy** There is another view of international trade that regards as misleading the description of comparative advantage presented earlier. According to this outlook, called **strategic trade policy**, international trade largely involves firms that pursue economies of scale—that is, firms that achieve lower costs per unit of production the more they produce. In contrast to the constant opportunity costs illustrated in the example of wheat and cloth, opportunity costs in some industries may fall with the level of output. Such an **increasing-returns-to-scale industry** will tend to concentrate production in the hands of a few very large firms rather than in many competitive firms. Proponents of strategic trade policy contend that government can use tariffs or subsidies to allow domestic firms with decreasing costs an advantage over their foreign rivals.

A monopoly exists when there is only one producer in an industry and no close substitutes for the product exist. If the average costs of production decline with increases in output, then the larger a firm is, the lower its per-unit costs will be. One large producer will be more efficient than many small ones. A simple example of a natural-monopoly industry will indicate how strategic trade policy can make a country better off. Suppose that the production of buses is an industry characterized by increasing returns to scale and that there are only two firms capable of producing buses: BMW in Germany and General Motors in the United States. If both firms produce buses, their costs will be so high that both will experience losses. If only one of the two produces buses, however, it will be able to sell buses at home and abroad, creating a level of output that allows the firm to earn a profit.

Assume further that a monopoly producer will earn $100 million and that if both firms produce, they will each lose $5 million. Obviously, a firm that doesn't produce earns nothing. Which firm will produce? Because of the decreasing-cost nature of the industry, the firm that is the first to produce will realize lower costs and be able to preclude the other firm from entering the market. But strategic trade policy can alter the market in favor of the domestic firm.

Suppose BMW is the world's only producer of buses. General Motors does not produce them. The U.S. government could offer General Motors an $8 million subsidy to produce buses. General Motors would then enter the bus market since the $8 million subsidy would more than offset the $5 million loss it would suffer by entering the market. BMW would sustain losses of $5 million once General Motors entered. Ultimately, BMW would stop producing buses to avoid the loss, and General Motors would have the entire market and earn $100 million plus the subsidy.

Strategic trade policy is aimed at offsetting the increasing-returns-to-scale advantage enjoyed by foreign producers and at stimulating production in domestic industries capable of realizing decreasing costs. One practical problem for government is the need to understand the technology of different industries and to forecast accurately the subsidy needed to induce domestic firms to produce new products. A second problem is the likelihood of retaliation by the foreign government. If the U.S. government subsidizes General Motors in its attack on the bus market, the German government is likely to subsidize BMW rather than lose the entire bus market to a U.S. producer. As a result, taxpayers in both nations will be subsidizing two firms, each producing too few buses to earn a profit.

2.b. Tools of Policy

4

How do countries restrict the entry of foreign goods and promote the export of domestic goods?

Commercial policy makes use of several tools, including tariffs, quotas, subsidies, and nontariff barriers such as health and safety regulations that restrict the entry of foreign products. Since 1945, barriers to trade have been reduced. Much of the progress toward free trade may be linked to the *General Agreement on Tariffs and Trade*, or *GATT*, which began in 1947. In 1995, the World Trade Organization (WTO) was formed to incorporate the agreements under GATT into a formal permanent international organization that oversees world trade. The WTO has three objectives: help global trade flow as freely as possible, achieve reductions in trade restrictions gradually through negotiation, and provide an impartial means of settling disputes. Nevertheless, restrictions on trade still exist, and this section will review the most commonly used restrictions.

tariff:
a tax on imports and selected exports

2.b.1. Tariffs

In Chapter 3, we defined a **tariff** as a tax on imports—goods and services purchased from foreign suppliers. Every country imposes tariffs on at least some imports. Some countries also impose tariffs on selected *exports* as a means of raising government revenue. Brazil, for instance, taxes coffee exports. The United States does not employ export tariffs, which are forbidden by the U.S. Constitution.

Tariffs are frequently imposed in order to protect domestic producers from foreign competition. The dangers of imposing tariffs are well illustrated in the Economic Insight "Smoot-Hawley Tariff." The effect of a tariff is illustrated in Figure 17.2, which shows the domestic market for oranges. Without international trade, the domestic equilibrium price (P_d) and quantity demanded (Q_d) are determined by the intersection of the domestic demand and supply curves. If the world price (P_w) of oranges is lower than the domestic equilibrium price, this country will import oranges. The quantity imported will be the difference between the quantity Q_1 produced domestically at a price of P_w and the quantity Q_2 demanded domestically at the world price of oranges.

When the world price of the traded good is lower than the domestic equilibrium price without international trade, free trade causes domestic production to fall and domestic consumption to rise. The domestic shortage at the world price is met by imports. Domestic consumers are better off since they can buy more at

FIGURE 17.2 The Effects of a Tariff

The domestic equilibrium price and quantity with no trade are P_d and Q_d, respectively. The world price is P_w. With free trade, therefore, imports will equal $Q_2 - Q_1$. A tariff added to the world price reduces imports to $Q_4 - Q_3$.

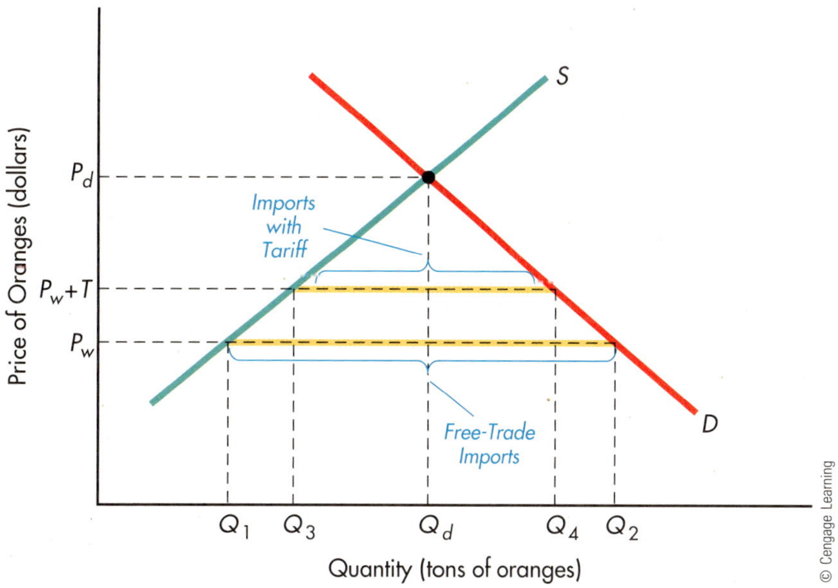

a lower price. But domestic producers are worse off since they now sell fewer oranges and receive a lower price.

Suppose a tariff of T (the dollar value of the tariff) is imposed on orange imports. The price paid by consumers is now $P_w + T$, rather than P_w. At this higher price, domestic producers will produce Q_3, and domestic consumers will purchase Q_4. The tariff has the effect of increasing domestic production and reducing domestic consumption, relative to the free trade equilibrium. Imports fall accordingly, from $Q_2 - Q_1$ to $Q_4 - Q_3$.

ECONOMIC INSIGHT

Smoot-Hawley Tariff

Many economists believe that the Great Depression of the 1930s was at least partly due to the Smoot-Hawley Tariff Act, signed into law by President Herbert Hoover in 1930. Hoover had promised that, if elected, he would raise tariffs on agricultural products to raise U.S. farm income. Congress began work on the tariff increases in 1928. Congressman Willis Hawley and Senator Reed Smoot conducted the hearings.

In testimony before Congress, manufacturers and other special interest groups also sought protection from foreign competition. The resulting bill increased tariffs on over 12,000 products. Tariffs reached their highest levels ever, about 60 percent of average import values. Only twice before in U.S. history had tariffs approached the levels of the Smoot-Hawley era.

Before President Hoover signed the bill, 38 foreign governments made formal protests, warning that they would retaliate with high tariffs on U.S. products. A petition signed by 1,028 economists warned of the harmful effects of the bill. Nevertheless, Hoover signed the bill into law.

World trade collapsed as other countries raised their tariffs in response. Between 1930 and 1931, U.S. imports fell 29 percent, but U.S. exports fell 33 percent. By 1933, world trade was about one-third of the 1929 level. As the level of trade fell, so did income and prices. In 1934, in an effort to correct the mistakes of Smoot-Hawley, Congress passed the Reciprocal Trade Agreements Act, which allowed the president to lower U.S. tariffs in return for reductions in foreign tariffs on U.S. goods. This act ushered in the modern era of relatively low tariffs. In the United States today, tariffs are about 5 percent of the average value of imports.

Many economists believe the collapse of world trade and the Depression to be linked by a decrease in real income caused by abandoning production based on comparative advantage. Few economists argue that the Great Depression was caused primarily by the Smoot-Hawley tariff, but the experience serves as a lesson to those who support higher tariffs to protect domestic producers.

Domestic producers are better off since the tariff has increased their sales of oranges and raised the price they receive. Domestic consumers pay higher prices for fewer oranges than they would with free trade, but they are still better off than they would be without trade. If the tariff had raised the price paid by consumers to P_d, there would be no trade, and the domestic equilibrium quantity Q_d would prevail.

The government earns revenue from imports of oranges. If each ton of oranges generates tariff revenue of T, the total tariff revenue to the government is found by multiplying the tariff by the quantity of oranges imported. In Figure 17.2, this amount is $T \times (Q_4 - Q_3)$. As the tariff changes, so does the quantity of imports and the government revenue.

quantity quota:
a limit on the amount of a good that may be produced

value quota:
a limit on the monetary value of a good that may be imported

2.b.2. **Quotas** Quotas are limits on the quantity or value of goods imported and exported. A **quantity quota** restricts the physical amount of a good. For instance, in 2010 the United States allowed only 1.1 million tons of raw cane sugar to be imported and allocated individual country quotas to major sugar-exporting nations. Even though the United States is not a competitive sugar producer in comparison with other nations such as the Dominican Republic or Cuba, the quota allows the United States to be one of the world's largest sugar-producing countries. A **value quota** restricts the monetary value of a good that may be traded. Instead of a physical quota on sugar, the United States could have limited the dollar value of sugar imports.

Quotas are used to protect domestic producers from foreign competition. By restricting the amount of a good that may be imported, they increase its price and allow domestic producers to sell more at a higher price than they would with free trade. Figure 17.3 illustrates the effect of a quota on the domestic orange market. The domestic equilibrium supply and demand curves determine the equilibrium price and quantity without trade to be P_d and 250 tons, respectively. The world price of oranges is P_w. Since P_w lies below P_d, this country will import oranges. The quantity of imports is equal to the amount of the domestic shortage at P_w. The quantity demanded at P_w is 400 tons, and the quantity supplied domestically is 100 tons, so imports will equal 300 tons of oranges. With free trade, domestic producers sell 100 tons at a price of P_w.

FIGURE 17.3 The Effects of a Quota

The domestic equilibrium price with no international trade is P_d. At this price, 250 tons of oranges would be produced and consumed at home. With free trade, the price is P_w, and 300 tons will be imported. An import quota of 100 tons will cause the price to be P_q, where the domestic shortage equals the 100 tons allowed by the quota.

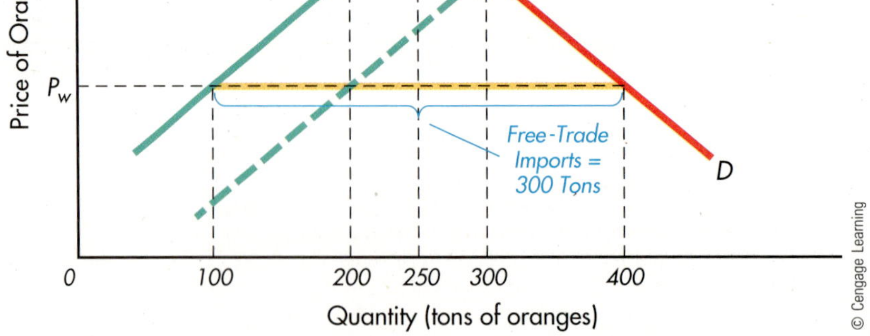

But suppose domestic orange growers convince the government to restrict orange imports. The government then imposes a quota of 100 tons on imported oranges. The effect of the quota on consumers is to shift the supply curve to the right by the amount of the quota, 100 tons. Since the quota is less than the quantity of imports with free trade, the quantity of imports will equal the quota. The domestic equilibrium price with the quota occurs at the point where the domestic shortage equals the quota. At price P_q, the domestic quantity demanded (300 tons) is 100 tons more than the domestic quantity supplied (200 tons).

Quotas benefit domestic producers in the same way that tariffs do. Domestic producers receive a higher price (P_q instead of P_w) for a greater quantity (200 instead of 100) than they do under free trade. The effect on domestic consumers is also similar to that of a tariff: They pay a higher price for a smaller quantity than they would with free trade. A tariff generates government tax revenue; quotas do not (unless the government auctioned off the right to import under the quota). Furthermore, a tariff only raises the price of the product in the domestic market. Foreign producers receive the world price, P_w. With a quota, both domestic and foreign producers receive the higher price, P_q, for the goods sold in the domestic market. So foreign producers are hurt by the reduction in the quantity of imports permitted, but they do receive a higher price for the amount they sell.

2.b.3. **Other Barriers to Trade** Tariffs and quotas are not the only barriers to the free flow of goods across international borders. There are three additional sources of restrictions on free trade: subsidies, government procurement, and health and safety standards. Though these restrictions are often enacted for reasons other than protection from foreign competition, a careful analysis reveals their import-reducing effect.

Before discussing these three types of barriers, let us note the cultural or institutional barriers to trade that also exist in many countries. Such barriers may exist independently of any conscious government policy. For instance, Japan has frequently been criticized by U.S. officials for informal business practices that discriminate against foreigners. Under the Japanese distribution

Japanese law requires a new retail firm to receive permission from other retailers in the area in order to open a business.

Iain Masterton/Alamy

system, goods typically pass through several layers of intermediaries before appearing in a retail store. A foreign firm faces the difficult task of gaining entry to this system to supply goods to the retailer. Furthermore, a foreigner cannot easily open a retail store. Japanese law requires a new retail firm to receive permission from other retailers in the area in order to open a business. A firm that lacks contacts and knowledge of the system cannot penetrate the Japanese market.

subsidies:
a grant of money given to help produce or purchase a specific good or service

Subsidies **Subsidies** are payments by a government to an exporter. Subsidies are paid to stimulate exports by allowing the exporter to charge a lower price. The amount of a subsidy is determined by the international price of a product relative to the domestic price in the absence of trade. Domestic consumers are harmed by subsidies in that their taxes finance the subsidies. Also, since the subsidy diverts resources from the domestic market toward export production, the increase in the supply of export goods could be associated with a decrease in the supply of domestic goods, causing domestic prices to rise.

Subsidies may take forms other than direct cash payments. These forms include tax reductions, low-interest loans, low-cost insurance, government-sponsored research funding, and other devices. The U.S. government subsidizes export activity through the U.S. Export-Import Bank, which provides loans and insurance to help U.S. exporters sell their goods to foreign buyers. Subsidies are more commonplace in Europe than in Japan or the United States.

Government Procurement Governments are often required by law to buy only from local producers. In the United States, a "buy American" act passed in 1933 required U.S. government agencies to buy U.S. goods and services unless the domestic price was more than 12 percent above the foreign price. This kind of policy allows domestic firms to charge the government a higher price for their products than they charge consumers; the taxpayers bear the burden. The United States is by no means alone in the use of such policies. Many other nations also use such policies to create larger markets for domestic goods.

Health and Safety Standards Government serves as a guardian of the public health and welfare by requiring that products offered to the public be safe and fulfill the use for which they are intended. Government standards for products sold in the domestic marketplace can have the effect (intentional or not) of protecting domestic producers from foreign competition. These effects should be considered in evaluating the full impact of such standards.

The government of Japan once threatened to prohibit foreign-made snow skis from entering the country for reasons of safety. Only Japanese-made skis were determined to be suitable for Japanese snow. Several western European nations announced that U.S. beef would not be allowed into Europe because hormones approved by the U.S. government are fed to U.S. beef cattle. In the late 1960s, France required tractors sold there to have a maximum speed of 17 mph; in Germany, the permissible speed was 13 mph; and in the Netherlands it was 10 mph. Tractors produced in one country had to be modified to meet the requirements of the other countries. Such modifications raise the price of goods and discourage international trade.

Product standards may not eliminate foreign competition, but standards different from those of the rest of the world do provide an element of protection to domestic firms.

RECAP

1. Government restrictions on foreign trade are usually aimed at protecting domestic producers from foreign competition.
2. Import restrictions may save domestic jobs, but the costs to consumers may be greater than the benefits to those who retain their jobs.
3. Advocates of "fair trade," or the creation of a level playing field, call for import restrictions as a means of lowering foreign restrictions on markets for domestic exports.
4. The national defense argument in favor of trade restrictions is that protection from foreign competition is necessary to ensure that certain key defense-related industries continue to produce.
5. The infant industries argument in favor of trade restrictions is to allow a new industry a period of time in which to become competitive with its foreign counterparts.
6. Strategic trade policy is intended to provide domestic increasing-returns-to-scale industries an advantage over their foreign competitors.
7. A tariff is a tax on imports or exports. Tariffs protect domestic firms by raising the prices of foreign goods.
8. Tariffs are an important source of revenue in many developing countries.
9. Quotas are government-imposed limits on the quantity or value of an imported good. Quotas protect domestic firms by restricting the entry of foreign products to a level less than the quantity demanded.
10. Subsidies are payments by the government to domestic producers. Subsidies lower the price of domestic goods.
11. Governments are often required by law to buy only domestic products.
12. Health and safety standards can also be used to protect domestic firms.

3. EXCHANGE RATE SYSTEMS AND PRACTICES

5

What kinds of exchange rate arrangements exist today?

The world today consists of some countries with fixed exchange rates, whose governments keep the exchange rates between two or more currencies constant over time; other countries with floating exchange rates, which shift on a daily basis according to the forces of supply and demand; and still others whose exchange rate systems lie somewhere in between. Table 17.3, which lists the exchange rate arrangements of over 180 countries, illustrates the diversity of exchange rate arrangements currently in effect. We provide a brief description of each.

- *Crawling pegs* The exchange rate is adjusted periodically in small amounts at a fixed, preannounced rate or in response to certain indicators (e.g., inflation differentials against major trading partners).
- *Floating* The monetary authority (usually the central bank) influences the exchange rate through active foreign exchange market intervention with no preannounced path for the exchange rate.
- *Free floating* The exchange rate is market determined, and any intervention is aimed at moderating fluctuations rather than determining the level of the exchange rate.

Table 17.3 Exchange Rate Arrangements

Exchange Rate Arrangement (number of countries)	Monetary Policy Framework: Exchange Rate Anchor: U.S. Dollar (66)	Exchange Rate Anchor: Euro (27)	Exchange Rate Anchor: Composite (15)	Exchange Rate Anchor: Other (7)	Monetary Aggregate Target (22)	Inflation Targeting Framework (44)	Other[1] (11)
Exchange arrangement with no separate legal tender (10)	Ecuador El Salvador Marshall Islands Micronesia, Fed. States of Palau Panama Timor-Leste Zimbabwe	Kosovo Montenegro San Marino		Kiribati			
Currency board arrangement (13)	Antigua and Barbuda[2] Djibouti Dominica[2] Grenada[2] ECCU Hong Kong SARSt. Kitts and Nevis[2] St. Lucia[2] St. Vincent and the Grenadines[2]	Bosnia and Herzegovina Bulgaria Estonia[3] Lithuania[3]		Brunei Darussalam			
Other conventional fixed peg arrangement (68)	Aruba Bahamas, The Bahrain Bangladesh Barbados Belize Eritrea Guyana Honduras Jordan Kazakhstan Lebanon Malawi Maldives Mongolia The Netherlands Antilles Oman Qatar Seychelles Sierra Leone Solomon Islands Sri Lanka Suriname Tajikistan Trinidad and Tobago Turkmenistan United Arab Emirates Venezuela, Rep. Bolivariana de Vietnam Yemen, Rep. of	Cameroon[5] Cape Verde Central African Rep.[5] Chad[5] Comoros Congo, Rep. of[5] Côte d'Ivoire[4] Croatia Denmark[3] Equatorial Guinea[5] Gabon[5] Guinea-Bissau[4] Latvia[3] Macedonia, FYR Mali[4] Niger[4] Senegal[4]	Fiji Kuwait Libya Morocco Russian Federation Samoa Tunisia	Bhutan Lesotho Namibia Nepal Swaziland	Argentina Malawi Rwanda Sierra Leone		

(Continued)

Table 17.3 Exchange Rate Arrangements *(Continued)*

	Monetary Policy Framework							
Exchange Rate Arrangement (number of countries)	**Exchange Rate Anchor**					**Monetary Aggregate Target**	**Inflation Targeting Framework**	**Other[1]**
		U.S. Dollar (66)	**Euro (27)**	**Composite (15)**	**Other (7)**	**(22)**	**(44)**	**(11)**
Pegged exchange rate within horizontal bands (3)			Slovak Rep.[3]	Syria Tonga Belarus				
Crawling peg (8)	Bolivia China Ethiopia Nicaragua Uzbekistan			Botswana Iran, I.R. of.				
Crawling band (2)	Costa Rica		Afghanistan, I.R. of Burundi Gambia, The Georgia Guinea Haiti Jamaica Kenya Madagascar	Azerbaijan				
Managed floating with no predetermined path for the exchange rate (44)	Cambodia Kyrgyz Rep. Lao P.D.R. Liberia Mauritania Mauritius Myanmar Ukraine	Algeria Singapore Vanuatu	Moldova Mozambique Nigeria Papua New Guinea São Tomé and Príncipe Sudan Tanzania Uganda	Colombia Ghana Guatemala Indonesia Peru Romania Serbia[6] Thailand Uruguay	Dominican Rep. Egypt India Malaysia Pakistan Paraguay			Armenia[6]

(Continued)

Table 17.3 Exchange Rate Arrangements *(Continued)*

Exchange Rate Arrangement (number of countries)	Monetary Policy Framework						
	Exchange Rate Anchor				Monetary Aggregate Target	Inflation Targeting Framework	Other[1]
	U.S. Dollar (66)	Euro (27)	Composite (15)	Other (7)	(22)	(44)	(11)
Independently floating (40)		Zambia	Albania Australia Austria[7] Belgium[7] Brazil Canada Chile Cyprus[7] Czech Rep. Finland[7] France[7] Germany[7] Greece[7] Hungary Iceland Ireland[7] Israel Italy[7] Korea, Rep. of	Luxembourg[7] Malta[7] Mexico Netherlands[7] New Zealand Norway Philippines Poland Portugal[7] Slovenia[7] South Africa Spain[7] Sweden Turkey United Kingdom	Congo, Dem. Rep. of Japan Somalia[8] Switzerland United States		

[1]Includes countries that have no explicitly stated nominal anchor, but rather monitor various indicators in conducting monetary policy.
[2]The member participates in the Eastern Caribbean Currency Union.
[3]The member participates in the ERM II.
[4]The member participates in the West African Economic and Monetary Union.
[5]The member participates in the Central African Economic and Monetary Community.
[6]The central bank has taken preliminary step toward inflation targeting and is preparing for the transition to full-fledged inflation targeting.
[7]The member participates in the European Economic and Monetary Union.
[8]As of end-December 1989.

Source: IMF, "De Facto Classification of Exchange Rate Arrangements and Monetary Frameworks," 2010, http://www.imf.org/external/pubs/ft/ar/2010/eng/pdf/a2.pdf.

- *No separate legal tender* Either another country's currency circulates as the legal tender, or the country belongs to a monetary union in which the legal tender is shared by the members (e.g., the euro).
- *Currency board* A fixed exchange rate is established by a legislative commitment to exchange domestic currency for a specified foreign currency at a fixed exchange rate. New issues of domestic currency are typically backed in some fixed ratio (e.g., one-to-one) by additional holdings of the key foreign currency.
- *Conventional peg* The exchange rate is fixed against a major currency or some basket of currencies. Active intervention may be required to maintain the target pegged rate.
- *Pegged exchange rate within horizontal bands* The exchange rate fluctuates around a fixed central target rate. Such target zones allow for a moderate amount of exchange rate fluctuation while tying the currency to the target central rate.

The choice of an exchange rate system is seen to range from the extreme of independently floating, in which the market supply and demand largely determine the exchange rate, to the other extreme of using another country's currency (e.g., the U.S. dollar for Ecuador).

RECAP

1. Fixed exchange rates are maintained by government intervention in the foreign exchange market; governments or central banks buy and sell currencies to keep the equilibrium exchange rate steady.
2. Some countries choose floating exchange rates; others peg their currencies to a single currency or a composite or adopt another country's money.

GLOBAL BUSINESS INSIGHT

The IMF and the World Bank

The International Monetary Fund (IMF) and the World Bank were both created at the Bretton Woods conference in 1944. The IMF oversees the international monetary system, promoting stable exchange rates and macroeconomic policies. The World Bank promotes the economic development of the poor nations. Both organizations are owned and directed by their 185 member countries.

The IMF provides loans to nations having trouble repaying their foreign debts. Before the IMF lends any money, however, the borrower must agree to certain conditions. The IMF *conditionality* usually requires that the country meet targets for key macroeconomic variables such as money supply growth, inflation, tax collections, and subsidies. The conditions attached to IMF loans are aimed at promoting stable economic growth. The IMF primarily employs economists to carry out its mission.

The World Bank assists developing countries by providing long-term financing for development projects and programs. The bank also provides expertise in many areas in which poor nations lack expert knowledge: agriculture, medicine, construction, and education, as well as economics.

The diversity of World Bank activities results in the employment of about 10,000 people. The IMF has a staff of approximately 2,400. Both organizations post employees around the world, but most work at the headquarters in Washington, DC.

World Bank funds are largely acquired by borrowing on the international bond market. The IMF receives its funding from member country subscription fees, called *quotas*. A member's quota determines its voting power in setting IMF policies. The United States, whose quota accounts for the largest fraction of the total, has the most votes.

SUMMARY

What determines the goods a nation will export?

1. Comparative advantage is based on the opportunity costs of production.

What are the sources of comparative advantage?

2. The productivity differences and factor abundance theories of comparative advantage are general theories that seek to explain patterns of international trade.
3. Other theories of comparative advantage aimed at explaining trade in particular kinds of goods focus on human skills, product life cycles, and consumer preferences.

Why do countries restrict international trade?

4. Commercial policy is government policy that influences the direction and volume of international trade.
5. Protecting domestic producers from foreign competition usually imposes costs on domestic consumers.
6. Rationales for commercial policy include saving domestic jobs, creating a fair trade relationship with other countries, raising tariff revenue, ensuring a domestic supply of key defense goods, allowing new industries a chance to become internationally competitive, and giving domestic industries with increasing returns to scale an advantage over foreign competitors.

How do countries restrict the entry of foreign goods and promote the export of domestic goods?

7. Tariffs protect domestic industry by increasing the price of foreign goods.
8. Quotas protect domestic industry by limiting the quantity of foreign goods allowed into the country.
9. Subsidies allow relatively inefficient domestic producers to compete with foreign firms.
10. Government procurement practices and health and safety regulations can protect domestic industry from foreign competition.

What kinds of exchange rate arrangements exist today?

11. Today some countries have fixed exchange rates, others have floating exchange rates, and still others have managed floats or other types of systems.

EXERCISES

1. Why must voluntary trade between two countries be mutually beneficial?

Use the following table to do exercises 2–5.

Output per Worker per Day in Beef or Computers

	Canada (units)	Japan (units)
Beef	12	10
Computers	4	8

2. Which country has the absolute advantage in beef production?
3. Which country has the absolute advantage in computer production?
4. Which country has the comparative advantage in beef production?
5. Which country has the comparative advantage in computer production?
6. How would each of the following theories of comparative advantage explain the fact that the United States exports computers?
   a. productivity differences
   b. factor abundance
   c. human skills
   d. product life cycle
   e. preferences
7. Which of the theories of comparative advantage could explain why the United States exports computers to Japan at the same time that it imports them from Japan? Explain.
8. What are the potential benefits and costs of a commercial policy designed to pursue each of the following goals?
   a. save domestic jobs

b. create a level playing field
c. increase government revenue
d. provide a strong national defense
e. protect an infant industry
f. stimulate exports of an industry with increasing returns to scale

9. For each of the goals listed in exercise 8, discuss what the appropriate commercial policy is likely to be (in terms of tariffs, quotas, subsidies, and so on).
10. Tariffs and quotas both raise the price of foreign goods to domestic consumers. What is the difference between the effects of a tariff and the effects of a quota on the following?
    a. the domestic government
    b. foreign producers
    c. domestic producers
11. Draw a graph of the U.S. automobile market in which the domestic equilibrium price without trade is P_d and the equilibrium quantity is Q_d. Use this graph to illustrate and explain the effects of a tariff if the United States were an auto importer with free trade. Then use the graph to illustrate and explain the effects of a quota.
12. How would the effects of international trade on the domestic orange market change if the world price of oranges were above the domestic equilibrium price? Draw a graph to help explain your answer.
13. Suppose the world price of kiwi fruit is $20 per case and the U.S. equilibrium price with no international trade is $30 per case. If the U.S. government had previously banned the import of kiwi fruit but then imposed a tariff of $5 per case and allowed kiwi imports, what would happen to the equilibrium price and quantity of kiwi fruit consumed in the United States?
14. What kinds of exchange rate arrangements do the countries of the world use? What is the most popular exchange rate arrangement for the major industrial countries?

STUDY GUIDE FOR CHAPTER 17

Key Term Match

Match each key term with its correct definition by placing the appropriate letter next to the corresponding number.

A. absolute advantage
B. intraindustry trade
C. commercial policy
D. strategic trade policy
E. increasing-returns-to-scale industry
F. tariff
G. quantity quota
H. value quota
I. subsidy

____ 1. simultaneous import and export of goods in the same industry by a particular country

____ 2. the use of trade restrictions or subsidies to allow domestic firms with decreasing costs to gain a greater share of the world market

____ 3. an advantage derived from one country's having a lower absolute input cost of producing a particular good than another country

____ 4. a tax on imports and selected exports

____ 5. an industry in which the costs of producing a unit of output fall as more output is produced

____ 6. government policy that influences international trade flows

____ 7. a limit on the monetary value of a good that may be imported

____ 8. a limit on the amount of a good that may be imported into a country

____ 9. a grant of money given to help produce or purchase a specific good or service

Quick-Check Quiz

1. A nation has an absolute advantage in producing a good when
   ☐ a. it can produce a good for a lower input cost than other nations can.
   ☐ b. the opportunity cost of producing a good, in terms of the forgone output of other goods, is lower than that of other nations.
   ☐ c. it can produce a good for a higher input cost than other nations can.
   ☐ d. the opportunity cost of producing a good, in terms of the forgone output of other goods, is higher than that of other nations.
   ☐ e. the nation's export supply curve is below its import demand curve.

2. A nation has a comparative advantage in producing a good when
   ☐ a. it can produce a good for a lower input cost than other nations can.
   ☐ b. the opportunity cost of producing a good, in terms of the forgone output of other goods, is lower than that of other nations.
   ☐ c. it can produce a good for a higher input cost than other nations can.
   ☐ d. the opportunity cost of producing a good, in terms of the forgone output of other goods, is higher than that of other nations.
   ☐ e. the nation's export supply curve is below its import demand curve.

3. The productivity differences explanation of comparative advantage stresses
   ☐ a. differences in labor productivity among countries.

- ☐ b. the advantage that comes to a country that is the first to develop and produce a product.
- ☐ c. the relative amounts of skilled and unskilled labor in a country.
- ☐ d. differences in the amounts of resources countries have.
- ☐ e. differences in tastes within a country.

4. The factor abundance explanation of comparative advantage stresses
   - ☐ a. differences in labor productivity among countries.
   - ☐ b. the advantage that comes to a country that is the first to develop and produce a product.
   - ☐ c. the relative amounts of skilled and unskilled labor in a country.
   - ☐ d. differences in the amounts of resources countries have.
   - ☐ e. differences in tastes within a country.

5. The product life cycle explanation of comparative advantages stresses
   - ☐ a. differences in labor productivity among countries.
   - ☐ b. the advantage that comes to a country that is the first to develop and produce a product.
   - ☐ c. the relative amounts of skilled and unskilled labor in a country.
   - ☐ d. differences in the amounts of resources countries have.
   - ☐ e. differences in tastes within a country.

6. The basic objective of commercial policy is to
   - ☐ a. promote free and unrestricted international trade.
   - ☐ b. protect domestic consumers from dangerous, low-quality imports.
   - ☐ c. protect domestic producers from foreign competition.
   - ☐ d. protect foreign producers from domestic consumers.
   - ☐ e. promote the efficient use of scarce resources.

7. Using trade restrictions to save domestic jobs
   - ☐ a. usually forces consumers to pay higher prices.
   - ☐ b. usually redistributes jobs from other industries to the protected industry.
   - ☐ c. may provoke other countries to restrict U.S. exports.
   - ☐ d. does all of the above.
   - ☐ e. does only b and c.

8. Some arguments for trade restrictions have economic validity. Which of the following arguments has *no* economic validity?
   - ☐ a. the infant industry argument
   - ☐ b. the national defense argument
   - ☐ c. the government revenue creation from tariffs argument
   - ☐ d. the creation of domestic jobs argument
   - ☐ e. All of the above have some economic validity.

9. The exchange rate system whereby the central bank fixes the exchange rate against a major currency or some basket of currencies is called a
   - ☐ a. currency board.
   - ☐ b. conventional peg.
   - ☐ c. free floating exchange rate.
   - ☐ d. floating exchange rate.
   - ☐ e. pegged exchange rate within horizontal bands.

10. The exchange rate system used by Austria, Belgium, France, Germany, Greece, Italy and other countries that use the euro is called a
    - ☐ a. pegged exchange rate within horizontal bands.
    - ☐ b. currency board.
    - ☐ c. conventional peg
    - ☐ d. floating.
    - ☐ e. no separate legal tender.

Practice Questions and Problems

1. The following table shows the output per worker per day in either mangoes or papayas in Samoa and in Fiji.

	Samoa	Fiji
Mangoes (in tons)	6	2
Papayas (in tons)	12	6

   a. The country that has an absolute advantage in producing mangoes is ____________.
   b. The country that has an absolute advantage in producing papayas is ____________.
   c. The opportunity cost of 1 ton of papayas in Samoa is ____________.
   d. The opportunity cost of 1 ton of papayas in Fiji is ____________.
   e. The country that has a comparative advantage in papayas is ____________.
   f. The opportunity cost of 1 ton of mangoes in Samoa is ____________.
   g. The opportunity cost of 1 ton of mangoes in Fiji is ____________.
   h. The country that has a comparative advantage in mangoes is ____________.
   i. The lowest price the mango producer would accept for a ton of mangoes is ____________ tons of papayas, and the highest price the papaya producer would pay for a ton of mangoes is ____________ tons of papayas. If the price of a ton of mangoes is not within these bounds, trade will not occur.

2. Name the comparative advantage theory that matches each of the following explanations of comparative advantage.
   a. Differences in labor productivity among countries: ____________

b. The advantage that comes to a country that is the first to develop and produce a product: ______________
c. The relative amounts of skilled and unskilled labor in a country: ______________
d. Differences in the amounts of resources countries have: ______________
e. Differences in tastes within a country: ______________

3. Governments can generate revenues by restricting trade through ______________; this is a common tactic in ______________ (industrial, developing) countries.
4. The argument that new industries should receive temporary protection is known as the ______________ argument.
5. Trade restrictions usually ______________ (create more, redistribute) domestic jobs within the economy.
6. Tariffs are ______________ on imports or exports. In the United States, tariffs on ______________ (imports, exports) are illegal under the Constitution.
7. Tariffs and quotas ______________ (raise, lower) the prices of goods and services for domestic consumers, and ______________ (increase, decrease) the quantity of goods and services consumed by domestic consumers.
8. What type of exchange rate system does the United States use?

Exercises and Applications

I Saving Jobs by Restricting Imports: Is It Worth the Cost?

One area of the U.S. economy that has been protected from international competition is the food and beverage industry. According to a study by the Institute for International Economics in Washington, DC, the cost to U.S. consumers of this protection is about $2,947,000,000 per year that U.S. consumers have paid in higher prices for food and beverages. That's about $10 per person in the United States per year. That might look like a reasonable price to pay to protect jobs, but let's look more closely.

1. The trade restrictions on food and beverages save about 6,039 jobs per year. How much does it cost U.S. consumers every year for each job saved?

   ____

2. Some people who work in the food and beverage industry may make a lot of money, but they don't average almost $500,000 per year! How much money would U.S. consumers save if the United States got rid of the trade restrictions and paid the 6,039 people in the food and beverage industry protected by trade restrictions each $100,000 per year to sit at home and watch TV? ______________
3. If U.S. consumers took the money they would save if the United States removed trade restrictions on food and beverages and instead spent it buying other things, do you think that this spending would create other jobs? ______________________________
4. Instead of paying the 6,039 workers each $100,000 per year to stay home and watch TV, is there something else that the United States could do to help these people that would cost only a small fraction of the almost $3 billion a year currently spent on trade protection in the food and beverage industry? (*Hint:* It's what you are doing in your economics class now.) ______________________________

II Tax Effects of Import Restrictions

According to *Newsweek:*

Lower-income families are hit hardest by trade restrictions, because they spend a far greater share of their earnings at the store. In a recent year, for example, households earning more than $50,000 laid out 3.3 percent of their disposable incomes on clothing, but households in the $20,000–$30,000 bracket spent 4.6 percent—and families earning $10,000 to $15,000 spent 5.4 percent. The quotas and tariffs that force import prices up to protect U.S. apparel jobs don't matter much in Beverly Hills, but they put a big dent in pocketbooks in Watts.*

Let's look more closely at the effects of tariffs and quotas on apparel purchased by different income groups. Assuming that 20 percent of the price of clothing is due to tariffs and quotas, calculate the dollar cost of tariffs and quotas on families making the following incomes. Then calculate the percentage of its income that each family pays because of tariffs and quotas.

1. Family income = $50,000; cost: ______________; percentage of income: ______________.
2. Family income = $25,000; cost: ______________; percentage of income: ______________.
3. Family income = $10,000; cost: ______________; percentage of income: ______________.
4. Do tariffs and quotas hit lower-income families the hardest, as *Newsweek* maintains?

____

* Source: *Newsweek*, July 12, 1993, p. 45.

18 Globalization

FUNDAMENTAL QUESTIONS

1. What is globalization?
2. What are the arguments against globalization?
3. What are the arguments in support of globalization?
4. How has globalization affected economic growth and poverty?
5. Can recent financial crises be linked to globalization?

PREVIEW

In every chapter we have discussed the international aspects of the topics covered. However, we have not yet considered the implications of closer links among economies internationally. The so-called *globalization* of the world's economies has become an issue that is rich in controversy. Thousands have gathered to protest globalization in Washington, DC, and Seattle in the United States; in Johannesburg, South Africa; in Davos, Switzerland; and in many other places. This chapter will provide an introduction to the potential costs and benefits of globalization and offer an analysis of the historical record regarding the effects of globalization.

It is important to recognize that the debate over globalization continues and involves political and social as well as economic dimensions. Intelligent people disagree about the impact of globalization on rich as well as poor countries. The reader should keep in mind that the issue is unsettled and much can change in the coming years.

1. THE MEANING OF GLOBALIZATION

1 What is globalization?

Globalization is characterized by an increased cross-border flow of trade in goods, services, and financial assets, along with an increased international mobility of technology, information, and individuals. As globalization progresses, countries become less isolated, so we can think more in terms of a global economy and its implications for individuals and nations.

1.a. Globalization Is Neither New nor Widespread

Globalization is not new. The forces that drive globalization have existed as long as humans have been around. Everyone has a natural desire to improve his or her well-being, so interest in trade has always existed. As we learned in earlier chapters, trade based on comparative advantage raises living standards. Even primitive societies engaged in trade so that their living standards would be higher than would otherwise have been possible. As circumstances permitted a greater range of travel, trade with more remote regions became possible. International trade is not a new phenomenon. World trade as a fraction of world GDP was about the same at the end of the 19th century as it is today. However, between World War I and World War II, the value of international trade plummeted. Then, in the postwar era, international trade rose substantially. Thus, the view that the growth of world trade is something new is true only in the shortsighted view of the world since the 1950s.

Globalization is not yet a truly global phenomenon. Some countries have remained largely closed to the rest of the world. These are mostly the world's poorest countries. If a government follows policies that work against economic integration with other countries, international trade and investment will not materialize.

The movement of people across international borders is greatly limited by government policies. There was much more immigration in the 19th and early 20th centuries than there is in the present day. Barriers to immigration are high today, and workers generally cannot move freely from country to country. This was not always the case. In 1900, 14 percent of the U.S. population had been born in a foreign country. Today that number is 12 percent. However, there are some multinational agreements that permit international movements of workers. An important example is the European Union (EU). Within the EU,

A multinational agreement, like that of the members of the European Union, can permit international mobility of labor.

David Pearson/Alamy

there is free mobility of labor. Of course, this does not mean that there are widespread relocations of workers from, say, Germany to Italy. Family, language, and customs tie people to particular areas, so the fact that people have the right to move does not mean that large numbers of them will actually do so. This is analogous to the situation of workers in the United States, who have the right to move anywhere in the country, but many of whom choose to stay in a particular area because they have personal ties to the area.

1.b. **The Role of Technological Change**

The pace of globalization has been driven by technological change. International trade and movement of people are facilitated by falling transportation costs. It is estimated that the real cost of ocean freight transport fell by 70 percent between 1920 and 1990.

International communication is enhanced by reductions in the cost of communications. Measured in 2000 U.S. dollars, a three-minute telephone call from New York to London cost $60.42 in 1960 and $.40 in 2000. Today, many people would make such a call for free using a technology like Skype. The reduction in communication costs has made possible global interactions that were at best a dream just a few decades ago.

The development of fast, modern computers allows information to be processed at speeds that were unimaginable just a generation ago. As a result, technology is shared more efficiently, so management of business operations can extend more easily to far-flung locations, and complex transactions can be completed in a fraction of the time that was once required. Technological progress in the computer industry is truly amazing. A computer that would sell for $1,000 today would have cost $1,869,004 in 1960.

The fact that globalization has progressed at an uneven rate over time is due to the uneven pace of technological change, in addition to important events such as war that disrupt relationships among nations.

1.c. **Measuring Globalization**

There are many alternatives for measuring how globalized the world and individual nations are. One useful ranking is provided by *Foreign Policy* magazine. It ranks countries in terms of four broad categories:

- *Political engagement* Number of memberships in international organizations, U.N. Security Council missions in which the country participates, and foreign embassies that the country hosts
- *Technology* Number of Internet users, Internet hosts, and secure servers
- *Personal contact* International travel and tourism, international telephone traffic, and cross-border income transfers
- *Economic integration* International trade, foreign direct investment and portfolio capital flows, and income and receipts

Table 18.1 shows the globalization rankings for several countries. Note that the rankings for economic integration tend to penalize countries with large domestic markets, such as the United States and Japan. For these countries, international trade is a relatively small fraction of GDP. Note also that poor countries tend to rank low in terms of personal contact and technology. These countries have few foreign workers and relatively low amounts of international telephone use. They also have relatively low levels of Internet use since a large segment of the population does not have access to computers or the training to use computers in daily life.

The more globalized an economy, the greater its links with the rest of the world. The aftermath of the terrorist attacks in the United States on September 11, 2001, showed how measures of globalization may be affected by important events. World trade fell after the attacks, as did global foreign direct investment.

Table 18.1 Globalization Rankings

Country	Rankings	Change from 2006	Economic	Dimension Personal	Technological	Political
Singapore	1	0	2	3	15	40
Hong Kong	2	N/A	1	1	17	71
The Netherlands	3	4	4	16	6	8
Switzerland	4	−2	11	2	7	28
Ireland	5	−1	6	4	13	5
Denmark	6	−1	5	13	5	7
United States	7	−4	71	40	1	51
Canada	8	−2	34	11	2	13
Jordan	9	N/A	10	5	50	1
Estonia	10	N/A	3	10	21	25
Sweden	11	−1	15	19	8	10
Britain	12	0	18	21	9	6
Australia	13	−5	26	39	3	41
Austria	14	−5	20	8	14	4
Belgium	15	N/A	7	7	22	16
New Zealand	16	−5	57	23	4	34
Norway	17	−3	35	27	11	26
Finland	18	−5	38	36	10	27
Czech Republic	19	−3	12	6	29	32
Slovenia	20	−3	23	17	23	12
Israel	21	−6	25	12	19	50
Germany	22	−4	45	34	16	19
Malaysia	23	−4	9	20	31	63
Hungary	24	−4	14	26	28	14
France	25	−2	31	29	24	3
Croatia	26	−4	24	9	30	39
Bulgaria	27	N/A	13	31	40	33
Japan	28	0	70	65	12	15
Spain	29	−4	40	30	25	18
Panama	30	−9	8	55	37	43
Portugal	31	−7	54	24	27	9
Slovakia	32	−6	16	54	32	24
Ghana	33	N/A	42	15	69	2
Italy	34	−7	56	38	26	11
South Korea	35	−6	47	52	20	44
Romania	36	−6	29	37	42	35
Taiwan	37	−2	28	25	18	72
Philippines	38	−7	41	14	61	49
Costa Rica	39	N/A	32	44	33	46
Morocco	40	0	30	22	47	61
Poland	41	−8	44	41	36	30
Ukraine	42	−3	17	49	53	55

(Continued)

Table 18.1 Globalization Rankings (*Continued*)

Country	Rankings	Change from 2006	Dimension Economic	Personal	Technological	Political
Chile	43	−9	27	61	34	31
Uganda	44	−8	62	18	70	29
Greece	45	−13	68	33	35	21
Tunisia	46	−9	37	35	55	48
Botswana	47	−9	36	48	66	22
Vietnam	48	N/A	19	50	52	57
Mexico	49	−7	50	45	41	37
Colombia	50	4	22	56	51	56
Senegal	51	−10	59	46	64	17
Saudi Arabia	52	−8	46	28	57	66
Thailand	53	−8	21	57	49	68
Argentina	54	−11	61	63	38	20
Egypt	55	0	33	47	59	67
Sri Lanka	56	−10	55	32	68	60
Nigeria	57	−9	39	58	65	45
Peru	58	−8	60	53	45	47
South Africa	59	−10	58	64	44	36
Kenya	60	−7	64	51	67	38
Tanzania	61	N/A	52	69	71	23
Russia	62	−15	49	60	46	52
Pakistan	63	−7	63	42	60	64
Bangladesh	64	−6	67	43	72	54
Turkey	65	−8	51	66	43	58
China	66	−15	43	67	56	65
Brazil	67	−15	69	71	39	42
Venezuela	68	−9	53	70	48	59
Indonesia	69	−9	48	68	58	62
Algeria	70	N/A	72	62	62	53
India	71	−10	66	59	63	69
Iran	72	−10	65	72	54	70

Source: Data are drawn from www.atkearney.com.

International travel and tourism dropped in 2002 for the first time since 1945. However, political engagement increased as a result of multinational efforts aimed at combating terrorism. The number of countries participating in U.N. peacekeeping missions increased. The volume of international telephone calls increased substantially. The increase in telephone use may partly be due to the drop in international travel. If people choose not to travel for personal or business reasons because of safety concerns, they may be more likely to have telephone conversations with the parties they otherwise would have visited in person. In addition, the number of Internet users grew 22 percent in 2002, with China alone adding 11 million new users. So major events like the terrorist attacks of September 2001 may suppress some measures of globalization while increasing others. This serves as a good reminder to take a broad view when measuring globalization rather than narrowly focusing on one or two measures.

RECAP

1. Globalization is characterized by an increased flow of trade in goods, services, and financial assets across national borders, along with increased international mobility of technology, information, and individuals.
2. The process of globalization is not new, but it accelerated after World War II.
3. Technological advance plays an important role in determining the pace of globalization.
4. Measuring globalization involves measurement of the international movements of goods, services, financial assets, people, ideas, and technology.

2. GLOBALIZATION CONTROVERSY

Globalization has stimulated much controversy in recent years. Massive demonstrations have been held to coincide with meetings of the World Trade Organization (WTO), the International Monetary Fund (IMF), the World Bank, and other gatherings of government and business leaders dealing with the process of developing international trade and investment. Each side sees globalization in a very different light. On the one hand are the critics of globalization, who believe that free international trade in goods and financial assets does more harm than good. On the other hand are the supporters of free international trade, who believe that globalization holds the key to increasing the living standards of all the world's people. We will review the arguments on both sides.

2 What are the arguments against globalization?

2.a. Arguments Against Globalization

Critics view globalization as a vehicle for enriching corporate elites to the detriment of poor people and the environment. In this view, the major international organizations are tools of corporations whose aim is to increase corporate profits at the expense of people and the environment. Rather than being a democratic system in which the majority of people are involved in economic decision making, globalization is seen by critics as a force that reduces the influence of people at the local level, with power being taken by the global elites, represented by rich corporations and their government supporters. A few specific criticisms associated with the antiglobalization movement follow.

"race to the bottom": with globalization, countries compete for international investment by offering low or no environmental regulations or labor standards

2.a.1. "Fair," Not "Free," Trade Critics argue that free trade agreements put people out of jobs. When goods are produced by the lowest-cost producer, people working in that industry in less competitive countries will no longer be employed. If foreign competition were limited, then these jobs would be saved. In addition, free trade may encourage governments to participate in a **"race to the bottom,"** with environmental safeguards and workers' rights being ignored in order to attract the investment and jobs that come from a concentration of production based upon comparative advantage. International trade agreements are seen as roadblocks to democratic decision making at the local level as they transfer power away from local authorities to multinational authorities.

2.a.2. International Organizations Serve Only the Interests of Corporations An example of this argument is the assertion that the WTO is a tool of corporations and that international trade agreements negotiated and enforced through the WTO are used to generate corporate profits against the interests of the citizens of the world. The Global Business Insight "The World Trade Organization" provides background information on the nature of the organization and its duties. International organizations like the WTO are used as platforms for instituting rules for international trade. Thus, an individual who is against free international trade would also be critical of organizations whose aim is the promotion of free trade. The WTO, the IMF, and the World Bank are viewed as undemocratic organizations that have assumed powers over economic decision making that rightly belong to local authorities.

2.a.3. Globalization Occurs at the Cost of Environmental Quality

As stated earlier, critics of globalization fear a "race to the bottom," in which governments block costly regulations related to environmental quality in order to provide a cheaper location for large global firms seeking manufacturing facilities. If the rich countries impose costly regulations on manufacturers, then these firms will shift production to poor countries that are willing to trade environmental degradation for jobs and higher money incomes. Related to this issue is World Bank financing for resource extraction projects such as mining or oil and gas extraction. Such projects are seen as benefiting the corporations that receive contracts for work related to the projects while environmental destruction is a little-considered by-product. World Bank funding for large dams is also seen as harmful as these projects frequently involve the relocation of large numbers of poor people who lose what modest living arrangements they had.

2.a.4. Globalization Encourages Harmful Labor Practices

This argument is based on a belief that multinational corporations will locate where wages are cheapest and workers' rights weakest. In these settings, on-the-job safety is ignored, and workers who are injured or ill are likely to be dismissed without any compensation. Furthermore, critics believe that globalization may result in the worst employment practices, such as child labor or prisoner labor. If such practices are allowed in poor countries, then the industrial countries will suffer follow-on effects as workers in rich countries lose their jobs to workers in countries where there are no regulations associated with worker protection, no minimum wages, and no retirement plans, and where employers must pay nothing more than the minimum necessary to attract an employee.

2.b. Arguments in Favor of Globalization

3
What are the arguments in support of globalization?

Globalization's supporters believe that free trade and international investment result in an increase in living standards in all countries. Of course, some individuals and firms are harmed by the globalization process. Those industries that exist in a country only as a result of protection from foreign competitors will

GLOBAL BUSINESS INSIGHT

The World Trade Organization

The World Trade Organization (WTO) is an international organization with 153 member countries, established in 1995 and headquartered in Geneva, Switzerland. The job of the WTO is to provide a venue for negotiating international trade agreements and then to enforce these global rules of international trade. The WTO trade agreements are negotiated and signed by a large majority of the world's nations. These agreements are contracts for the proper conduct of international trade. An important role of the WTO is the settlement of trade disputes between countries. An example of such a dispute involved bananas and the European Union (EU). The EU restricted banana imports so that only a few countries—countries that were former European colonies—could ship bananas to the EU. As a result, the price paid for bananas in European markets was about twice the price of bananas in the United States. The world's largest banana companies—Dole, Chiquita, and Del Monte, headquartered in the United States—complained that they were being harmed because their bananas, which came from other countries of Central and South America, were excluded from the EU system, which favored a few former colonies. The WTO ruled that the EU restrictions on banana imports were harmful and against the rules of trade to which all nations had agreed. This is but one example of the role of the WTO in promoting fair and free international trade.

suffer when that country's markets are opened to the rest of the world. Yet the few who suffer are small in number relative to the many who benefit from the advantages that globalization provides. This section will consider each of the criticisms mentioned in the prior section and present the alternative view of those who support globalization.

2.b.1. **Free Trade Helps Developing Countries** As just discussed, opening markets to free trade will usually harm some individuals and firms. But supporters of globalization believe that the benefits of globalization for all consumers greatly outweigh the costs of providing a social safety net for those who lose their jobs as a result of opening markets to global competitors. Developing countries have much to gain from free trade. Restrictions on trade in the rich countries are often aimed at products that poor countries can produce most efficiently. For instance, textile imports are restricted by the United States, and this harms many developing countries that could provide clothing and fabrics to the United States at a lower cost than U.S. producers can. The European Union restricts imports of agricultural products in order to increase the incomes of European farmers. If such restrictions were lifted, incomes in poor countries would rise substantially. Supporters of globalization believe that free trade agreements administered by the WTO can offer great benefits to the poor countries.

2.b.2. **International Organizations Represent Governments and People** Globalization supporters argue that international organizations offer all countries a platform for expressing their dissatisfaction with economic and social conditions and provide a mechanism for change. Without organizations like the IMF, World Bank, United Nations, and WTO, there would be no opportunities for representatives of all nations to come together to discuss needed changes in the global economy. These organizations also provide for transfers of funds from rich to poor countries that would not occur in an ongoing manner in the absence of such organizations. International organizations are funded by governments, not corporations. Representatives of the government of each member nation participate in the decision making at each organization. This suggests that if international organizations have followed unwise policies, the most effective path to change would be putting political pressure on national governments to support policies that open markets for the goods of poor countries as well as rich countries.

2.b.3. **The Connection Between Globalization and Environmental Harm Is Weak** Supporters of globalization argue that there is no evidence of a "race to the bottom" in which multinational firms move production to countries with lax environmental standards. Looking at the globalization rankings in Table 18.1, the countries at the top of the list have more stringent environmental regulations than do less open economies. Figure 18.1 plots the globalization rank against a ranking of environmental quality, in which the environmental performance of a country is determined by its rankings in terms of the quality of its air and water, its protection of land, and its impact on climate change through carbon dioxide emissions. The figure plots data for those countries ranked in the top 50 on the environmental quality scale that also have globalization rankings. The lower the number for a country, the better its environmental ranking or the greater its globalization. The figure indicates that, in general, the more globalized countries have better environmental quality. For instance, Switzerland is shown to have the highest ranking in terms of environmental quality and is among the most globalized. Only five of the countries ranked in the bottom 30 on environmental quality have globalization rankings. The scatter of the countries plotted in Figure 18.1 indicates that those five countries with the worst environmental quality are significantly less globalized than the countries with better environmental quality.

FIGURE 18.1 Globalization and Environmental Quality

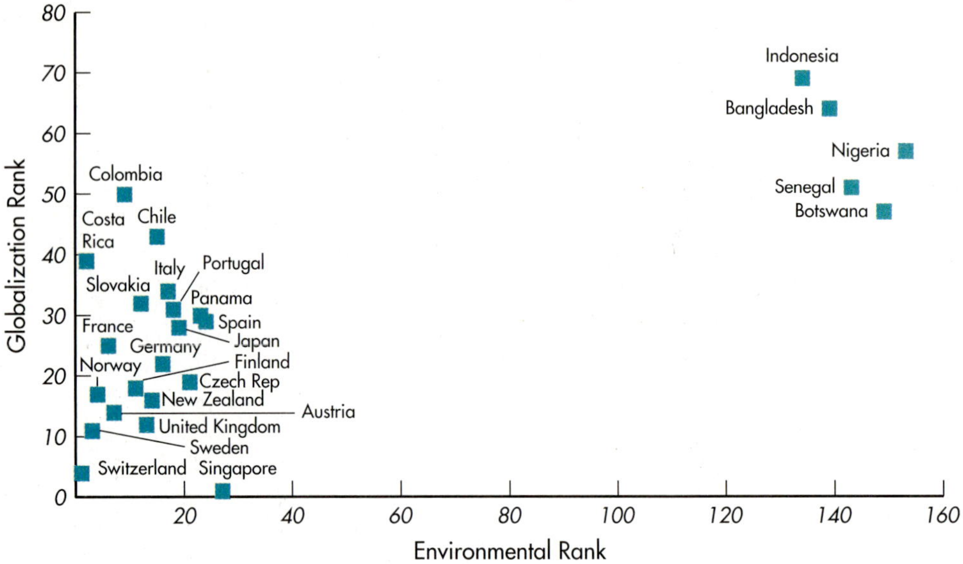

Source: Globalization data are from the A. T. Kearney website (www.atkearney.com). Environmental quality rankings are taken from the Pilot Environmental Performance Index (www.yale.edu/epi).

In addition, there are many cases of environmental degradation associated with countries that are closed to economic relations with the rest of the world. The former communist countries of eastern Europe had governments that displayed the greatest disregard of the environment of any group of nations in modern times. As these nations globalize as part of the transition away from socialism, they are attracting foreign direct investment from rich countries, which has transferred cleaner technology to eastern Europe and improved environmental quality.

One of the major assumptions made by critics of globalization is that multinational firms will locate production units in developing countries, employ local resources, and then sell the products in the rich countries. This may be typical of certain industries, such as the production of shoes or clothing. However, increasingly, multinational firms' production is aimed at supplying local markets. The U.S. Department of Commerce found that more than 60 percent of the production of U.S. firms' subsidiaries in developing countries was sold in the local market where the production occurred. One look at the global firms that have raced to invest in China indicates that the prospect of selling to the massive Chinese market is the attraction for much of the investment. In this setting, governments do not need to offer a lack of environmental standards in order to attract multinational firms.

2.b.4. Does Globalization Encourage Harmful Labor Practices?

Supporters of globalization argue that there is no evidence of a "race to the bottom" in labor standards. In fact, multinational firms tend to pay higher wages than local firms and tend to provide greater benefits for workers than existed in the country prior to globalization. At a basic level, if a worker freely accepts employment, that worker must be better off than with the next best alternative. So even though wages in, for instance, Vietnam may be much lower than those in western Europe or North America, this is not evidence of worker

Fototrav/iStockphoto.com

While wages in this multinational factory in Vietnam may be much lower than wages in countries like France and Canada, they are higher than the wages of many other employment options available to Vietnamese workers.

exploitation. The local wages across the Vietnamese economy are lower than those in, say, France or Canada. The workers who accept employment at a factory in Vietnam operated by a multinational firm prefer such work to working in agriculture at much lower wages. It is common to find long waiting lists of workers who want jobs at multinational firms' factories in developing countries. Rather than exploitation, this suggests that globalization is raising living standards and making people better off.

RECAP

1. Arguments against globalization include a concern that free trade is harmful to people, that international organizations serve only the interests of corporations, and that there is a "race to the bottom," with countries offering lax regulation of environmental quality and labor standards in order to offer multinational firms better opportunities for profit.
2. Supporters of globalization argue that trade based on comparative advantage raises living standards everywhere; that international organizations are funded by governments, not corporations, and provide a formal mechanism for all governments to be represented and to push for change; and that environmental quality and welfare of workers actually improve with globalization.

3. GLOBALIZATION, ECONOMIC GROWTH, AND INCOMES

4

How has globalization affected economic growth and poverty?

The increased integration of the world's economies has been associated with economic growth and reduction of poverty in most countries. The so-called **Asian tigers**—Hong Kong, South Korea, Singapore, and Taiwan—underwent the process of opening their economies in the 1960s and 1970s and experienced rapid growth and dramatic increases in their living standards. Nowadays, these

FIGURE 18.2 NICs and Post-1980 Globalizers

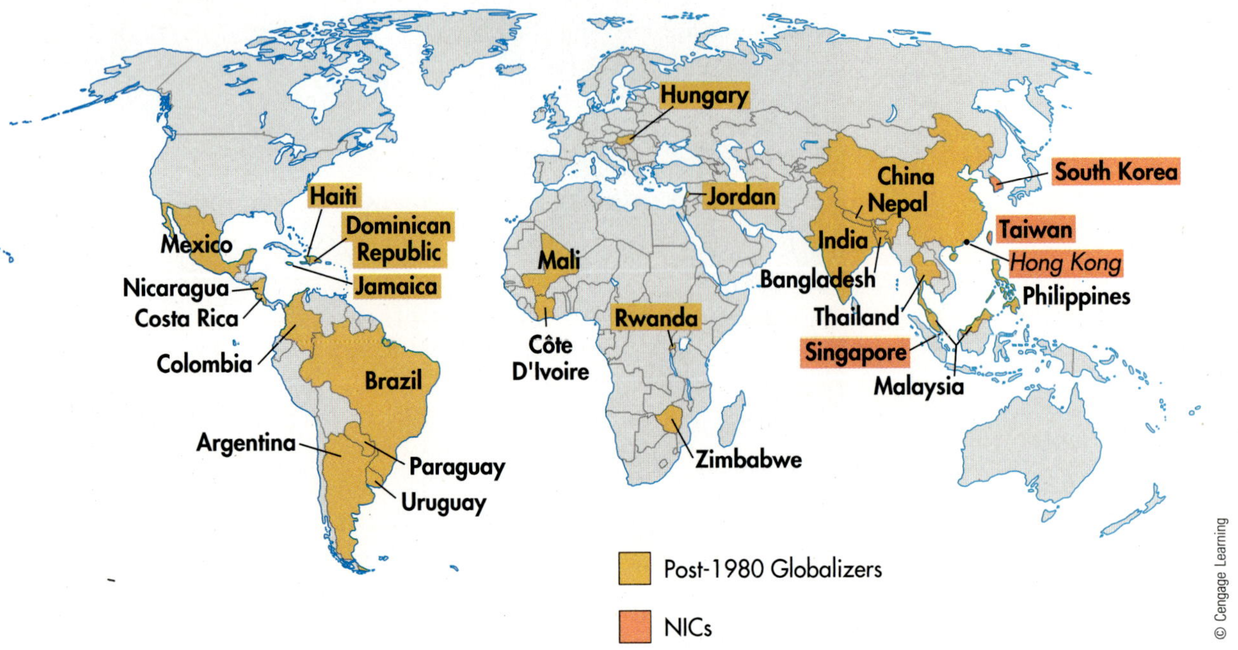

Asian tigers:
Hong Kong, South Korea, Singapore, and Taiwan—countries that globalized in the 1960s and 1970s and experienced fast economic growth

NICs:
newly industrialized countries

countries are sometimes referred to as "newly industrialized countries," or **NICs**. Several other countries have been through the globalization process since 1980. Figure 18.2 shows the NICs and the post-1980 globalizers. The 24 post-1980 globalizers are spread around the world. One World Bank study tracked the performance of all of these countries over time to measure how globalization has affected them.[1] The major conclusions of the study are as follows:

- *Economic growth has increased with globalization.* Average growth of per capita GDP increased from 1.4 percent per year in the 1960s to 2.9 percent in the 1970s to 3.5 percent in the 1980s to 5.0 percent in the 1990s. At the same time that these countries were increasing their growth rates, average annual per capita GDP growth in the rich countries fell from 4.7 percent in the 1960s to 2.2 percent in the 1990s. What makes this even more dramatic is the fact that nonglobalizing developing countries had average annual growth rates of only 1.4 percent during the 1990s.
- *Income inequality has not increased.* The benefits of increased economic growth are widely shared in globalizing countries. An important exception to this finding is China, where income inequality has increased. However, government policies in China that resulted in moving to free markets from socialism while restricting internal migration may have played a much bigger role in causing changes in the Chinese income distribution than globalization did.
- *The gap between rich countries and globalized developing countries has shrunk.* Some of the countries listed in Figure 18.2 were among the poorest countries in the world 25 years ago. The higher growth rates experienced by these countries have allowed them to gain ground on the rich countries.

[1] David Dollar and Aart Kraay, "Trade, Growth, and Poverty," *World Bank Policy Research Department Working Paper No. 2615*, 2001. For additional evidence and discussion, see "Globalization: Threat or Opportunity," *IMF Issues Brief*, January 2002, and the references cited (www.imf.org/external/np/exr/ib/2000/041200.htm).

- *Poverty has been reduced.* The fraction of the very poor, those who live on less than $1 per day, declined in the newly globalized economies. For instance, between the 1980s and the 1990s, the fraction of the population living on less than $1 per day fell from 43 percent to 36 percent in Bangladesh, from 20 percent to 15 percent in China, and from 13 percent to 10 percent in Costa Rica.

The evidence from around the world indicates that the real losers in the globalization of the world economy are those countries that have not participated. They tend to be mired in a low-growth path, with enduring poverty and none of the benefits that globalization has conferred.

RECAP

1. Some studies have shown that globalization increases economic growth without increases in income inequality within nations.
2. Some studies have shown that globalization narrows the income gap between rich and poor nations and reduces poverty.

4. FINANCIAL CRISES AND GLOBALIZATION

5 Can recent financial crises be linked to globalization?

The financial crisis of 2007–2008 was concentrated in the rich countries, led by the United States. However, in the 1990s, there were several dramatic episodes of financial crises in developing countries, in which local businesses as well as investors in those countries were punished with substantial losses. To understand the nature of the crises, we will first look at data that illustrate the severity of the crises. Then we will analyze the reasons for the crises. It will be seen that globalization may have played a contributing role in these recent crises.

4.a. Crises of the 1990s

Table 18.2 provides summary data on some key economic indicators for countries that underwent severe crises. Crises occurred in Mexico in 1994–1995 and in Southeast Asia—Indonesia, South Korea, Malaysia, the Philippines, and Thailand—in 1997. The table shows that in the year prior to the crises, each of these countries except Malaysia owed substantial short-term debt to foreigners. Short-term debt is debt that is due in less than one year. The table lists short-term debt as a fraction of reserves. International reserves were discussed in Chapter 14, where it was stated that these are assets that countries hold that can be used to settle international payments. The primary international reserve asset is foreign currency, mainly U.S. dollars. So except for Malaysia, all the countries affected by these crises owed more short-term debt to foreigners than the value of their international reserves.

Table 18.2 Economic Conditions in Crisis Countries

Country	Short-Term External Debt/ Reserves (year)	Bank Loans/GDP (year)	Stock Market Returns (%)	Exchange Rate	
Mexico	230% (1993)	24% (1993)	−29	3.88 (12/94);	6.71 (3/95)
Indonesia	226% (1996)	55% (1996)	−40	2368 (1/97);	9743 (1/98)
South Korea	300% (1996)	59% (1996)	−26	850 (1/97);	1694 (1/98)
Malaysia	42% (1996)	93% (1996)	−57	2.49 (1/97);	4.38 (1/98)
Philippines	126% (1996)	49% (1996)	−29	26.3 (1/97);	42.7 (1/98)
Thailand	103% (1996)	99% (1996)	−30	25.7 (1/97);	52.6 (1/98)

Note: Data on short-term debt/reserves and bank loans/GDP come from Steven B. Kamin, "The Current International Financial Crisis: How Much Is New?" *Journal of International Money & Finance*, August 1999. Stock market returns and exchange rates are drawn from Yahoo! Finance (www.yahoo.com). Stock market returns are calculated for the six-month period following the onset of the crisis in each country. Exchange rates are price of local currency per 1 U.S. dollar.

Table 18.2 also shows that bank loans were a sizable fraction of GDP in all the crisis countries except Mexico. This becomes a problem when business turns bad. If individuals and business firms have falling incomes, then they will be less able to repay their loans to banks. As a result, the banks will also be in trouble, and the result may be an economic crisis.

In each country, the stock market dropped dramatically. This is seen in Table 18.2 as the percentage change in stock prices over the first six months following the onset of the crisis. Stock prices dropped by an amount ranging from 26 percent in South Korea to 57 percent in Malaysia. Investors in each country lost huge amounts of wealth as a result of the rapid drop in the values of local firms.

Finally, Table 18.2 shows that the exchange rate against the U.S. dollar dropped substantially in each country. Exchange rates played a particularly large role in these financial crises and pointed out a vulnerability of small developing countries to globalization in terms of international capital flows.

4.b. **Exchange Rates and Financial Crises**

Each of the countries in Table 18.2 had a fixed exchange rate prior to the crisis period. Chapter 15 included a discussion of how central banks must intervene in the foreign exchange market to maintain a fixed exchange rate. Here we can apply the same analysis to understand how a fixed exchange rate may contribute to financial crises. Figure 18.3 illustrates the situation for Mexico. The demand in this figure is the demand for dollars arising out of the Mexican demand for U.S. goods, services, and financial assets. The supply is the supply

FIGURE 18.3 Foreign Exchange Market Intervention with a Fixed Exchange Rate

The demand is the demand for dollars arising out of the Mexican demand for U.S. goods, services, and financial assets. The supply is the supply of dollars arising out of the U.S. demand for Mexican goods, services, and financial assets. Initially, the equilibrium is located at point *A*, where the exchange rate is 4 pesos per dollar, and $10 billion are traded for pesos each day. If there is concern that Mexican financial assets will fall in value, then investors will start to sell peso-denominated assets and then will sell their pesos for dollars in order to buy dollar-denominated assets. This shifts the demand curve for dollars from D_1 to D_2. The new equilibrium would then be at point *B*, with a depreciated peso exchange rate of 6 pesos per dollar and $15 billion per day being traded. To maintain a fixed exchange rate of 4 pesos per dollar and avoid private traders' shifting the equilibrium to point *B*, the central bank (Banco de Mexico) must intervene in the foreign exchange market, selling dollars equal to the private market demand for dollars in excess of the amount that would yield an equilibrium at point *A*. In the figure, we see that the new equilibrium with central bank intervention is at point *C*, where the central bank is selling $10 billion per day ($20 − $10 billion) in order to maintain the exchange rate at 4 pesos per dollar.

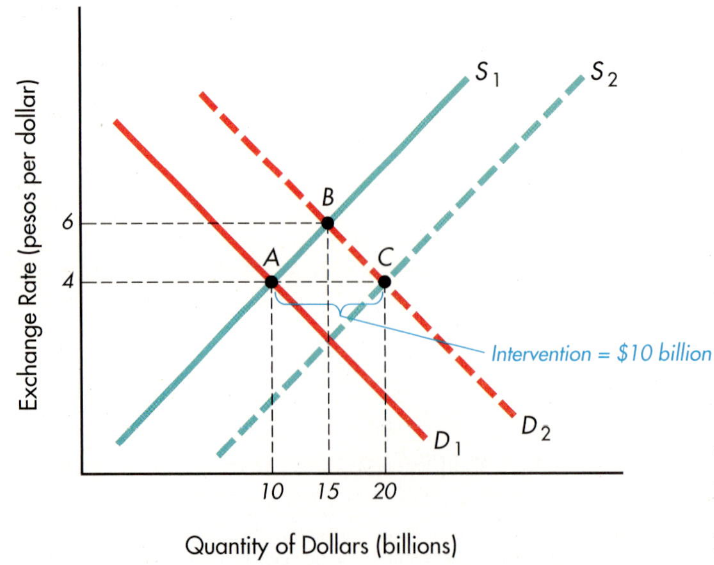

of dollars arising out of the U.S. demand for Mexican goods, services, and financial assets. Initially, the equilibrium is located at point *A*, where the exchange rate is 4 pesos per dollar, and $10 billion are traded for pesos each day. If there is concern that Mexican financial assets will fall in value, then investors will start to sell peso-denominated assets and will then sell their pesos for dollars in order to buy dollar-denominated assets. This shifts the demand curve for dollars from D_1 to D_2. The new equilibrium would then be at point *B*, with a depreciated peso exchange rate of 6 pesos per dollar and $15 billion per day being traded. To maintain a fixed exchange rate of 4 pesos per dollar and keep the private traders from shifting the equilibrium to point *B*, the central bank (Banco de Mexico) must intervene in the foreign exchange market by selling dollars equal to the private market demand for dollars in excess of the amount that would yield equilibrium at point *A*. In the figure, we see that the new equilibrium with central bank intervention is at point *C*, where the central bank is selling $10 billion per day ($20 – $10 billion) in order to maintain the exchange rate at 4 pesos per dollar.

If the shift in private investors' demand from D_1 to D_2 is not a temporary phenomenon, then there is a problem for the Banco de Mexico: It has a limited supply of international reserves, including U.S. dollars. The intervention to support the fixed exchange rate involves selling dollars and buying pesos. Eventually it will exhaust its supply of dollars, and it will then be forced to devalue the currency, letting the exchange rate adjust to the free market equilibrium of 6 pesos per dollar. Once speculators realize that the central bank is losing a substantial fraction of its international reserves, a **speculative attack** occurs. This is the term given to a situation in which private speculators start selling even more pesos for dollars, expecting that the central bank will be forced to devalue the currency. If a speculator sells pesos and buys dollars for a price of 4 pesos per dollar, and then the peso is devalued to 6 pesos per dollar, that speculator can turn around and sell the dollars for pesos, receiving 6 – 4 = 2 pesos in profit for each dollar invested in the speculative activity. Of course, once the speculative attack occurs, the demand for dollars shifts out even further, and the central bank will have to spend even more of its international reserves to defend the fixed exchange rate.

speculative attack: a situation in which private investors sell domestic currency and buy foreign currency, betting that the domestic currency will be devalued

Each of the recent international financial crises has involved a fixed exchange rate. In each case, once it became clear that the domestic currency was overvalued relative to its true free market value, speculative attacks occurred, and the central bank lost a sizable amount of its international reserves. With floating or flexible exchange rates, the exchange rate changes every day with the free market forces of supply and demand, so countries are not forced to intervene and spend their international reserves to maintain a fixed exchange rate. In this situation, a speculative attack cannot occur.

Once the currency has been devalued, it is common for some local business firms to be driven into bankruptcy as a result of the effect of the devaluation on the value of their debt. This is because much borrowing is done in U.S. dollars. In Thailand, for instance, prior to the crisis of 1997, the Thai government had repeatedly stated that there was no way it would ever change the fixed exchange rate. Business firms, believing that the exchange rate between the Thai baht and the U.S. dollar would not change, borrowed in U.S. dollars, expecting that the dollars they borrowed and the dollars they would have to repay would be worth the same amount of baht. Imagine a firm that had a debt of $1 million. Prior to the financial crisis that started in the summer of 1997, the exchange rate was about 25 baht to 1 U.S. dollar. At this exchange rate, it would cost 25 million baht to repay $1 million. By January 1998, the exchange rate was about 52 baht per dollar. So the firm would find that the baht price of repaying $1 million had risen to 52 million baht. The cost of repaying the dollar loan had more than doubled as a result of the currency devaluation. Because of such exchange rate changes, the financial crises of the 1990s had devastating effects on local businesses in each country. As business firms in these countries lost value, foreign investors who had invested in these firms also suffered large losses. The 1990s financial crises imposed huge costs on the global economy.

4.c. What Caused the Crises?

The prior section showed how a fixed exchange rate could contribute to a crisis. The crises of the 1990s taught economists some lessons regarding exchange rates and other factors that increased the vulnerability of countries to crises. Considerable resources have been devoted to understanding the nature and causes of financial crises in hopes of avoiding future crises and forecasting those crises that do occur. Forecasting is always difficult in economics, and it is safe to say that there will always be surprises that no economic forecaster anticipates. Yet there are certain variables that are so obviously related to past crises that they may serve as warning indicators of potential future crises. The list includes the following:

- *Fixed exchange rates.* All of the developing countries involved in the crises of the 1990s and early 2000s, including Mexico in 1993–1994, the southeast Asian countries in 1997, and Argentina in 2002, utilized fixed exchange rates prior to the onset of the crisis. Generally, these countries' macroeconomic policies were inconsistent with the maintenance of the fixed exchange rate, and when large devaluations ultimately occurred, domestic residents holding loans denominated in foreign currency suffered huge losses.
- *Falling international reserves.* The maintenance of fixed exchange rates may be no problem. One way to tell if the exchange rate is no longer an equilibrium rate is to monitor the country's international reserve holdings (largely the foreign currency held by the central bank and the treasury). If the stock of international reserves is falling steadily over time, it is a good indicator that the fixed exchange rate regime is under pressure and that there is likely to be a devaluation.
- *Lack of transparency.* Many crisis countries suffer from a lack of transparency in government activities and a lack of public disclosure of business conditions. Investors need to know the financial situation of firms in order to make informed investment decisions. If accounting rules allow firms to hide the financial impact of actions that would harm investors, then investors may not be able to adequately judge when the risk of investing in a firm rises. In such cases, a financial crisis may come as a surprise to all but the insiders in a troubled firm. Similarly, if the government does not disclose its international reserve position in a timely and informative manner, investors may be taken by surprise when a devaluation occurs. The lack of good information on government and business activities serves as a warning sign of potential future problems.

This short list of warning signs provides an indication of the sorts of variables an international investor must consider when evaluating the risks of investing in a foreign country. This list is also useful to international organizations such as the IMF when monitoring countries and advising them on recommended changes in policy.

So far we have not explicitly considered how globalization may contribute to crises. The analysis of Figure 18.3 provides a hint. If there is free trading in a country's currency, and the country has globalized financial markets so that foreign investors trade domestic financial assets, there is a greater likelihood of a crisis than in a country that is not globalized. The money that comes into the developing country from foreign investors can also flow back out. This points out an additional factor to be considered:

- *Short-term international investment.* The greater the amount of short-term money invested in a country, the greater the potential for a crisis if investors lose confidence in the country. So if foreigners buy large amounts of domestic stocks, bonds, or other financial assets, they can turn around and sell these assets quickly. These asset sales will depress the value of the country's financial markets, and as foreigners sell local currency for foreign currency, such as U.S. dollars, the local currency will also fall in value. Too much short-term foreign investment may serve as another warning sign for a financial crisis.

Of course, a country can always avoid financial crises by not globalizing—keeping its domestic markets closed to foreigners. However, such a policy costs more than it is worth. As discussed earlier in this chapter, globalization has paid off with faster economic growth and reductions in poverty. To avoid globalization in order to avoid financial crises is to remain in poverty as the rest of the world grows richer. We should think of globalization and financial crises in these terms: A closed economy can follow very bad economic policies for a long time, and the rest of the world will have no influence in bringing about change for the better. A country with a globalized economy will be punished for bad economic policy as foreign investors move money out of the country, contributing to financial market crises in that country. It is not globalization that brings about the crisis. Instead, globalization allows the rest of the world to respond to bad economic policies in a way that highlights the bad policy and imposes costs on the country for following such policies. In this sense, globalization acts to discipline countries. A country with sound economic policy and good investment opportunities is rewarded with large flows of savings from the rest of the world to lower the cost of developing the local economy.

RECAP

1. The 1990s saw financial crises in Mexico, Indonesia, South Korea, Malaysia, the Philippines, and Thailand.
2. Fixed exchange rates encouraged speculative attacks and ultimate devaluations of the currencies of the countries involved in these crises.
3. Exchange rate devaluations raised the cost of debts that were denominated in foreign currency and imposed large losses on debtor firms.
4. Factors contributing to the financial crises included fixed exchange rates, falling international reserves, a lack of transparency to investors, and a high level of short-term international investment.

SUMMARY

What is globalization?

1. Globalization involves an increased cross-border flow of trade in goods, services, and financial assets, along with increased international mobility of technology, information, and individuals.
2. The process of globalization has always existed because of its potential to raise living standards.
3. The rapid pace of globalization in recent decades has been made possible by technological advances and by falling transportation costs and tariffs.

What are the arguments against globalization?

4. Free trade increases corporate profits but harms people.

5. International organizations and the agreements they are associated with serve corporate interests and harm people.
6. Globalization occurs at the cost of environmental quality.
7. Globalization encourages harmful labor practices.

What are the arguments in support of globalization?

8. Those who lose their jobs to more efficient producers in other countries will be harmed, but the benefits to all consumers far outweigh the losses of those workers and firms that are harmed by globalization.
9. International organizations are funded by governments, not firms, and such organizations serve the interests of all nations in that they provide a setting where grievances must be heard and policy changes can be implemented.
10. Globalization has not resulted in a "race to the bottom," in which labor practices suffer and environmental decay results.

How has globalization affected economic growth and poverty?

11. Globalizers have faster economic growth and less poverty than nonglobalizers.

Can recent financial crises be linked to globalization?

12. Globalization allows for international financial flows that punish countries that follow bad economic policy.

EXERCISES

1. What is globalization?
2. Comment on the following statement: "Globalization is an event of the 1980s and 1990s. Prior to this time, we never had to worry about globalization and its effects."
3. Write a script for two speakers arguing about globalization and its effects. Give each speaker a name and then write a script for a debate between the two. The debate should be no longer than two pages, double-spaced. Each speaker should make a few key points, and the other speaker should offer a reply to each point the first speaker makes.
4. Why has the pace of globalization quickened since the 1950s?
5. If you wanted to compare countries on the basis of how globalized they are, how could you construct some numerical measures that would allow a cross-country comparison?
6. What are the major arguments against globalization?
7. What are the major arguments in favor of globalization?
8. What is the WTO? Where is it located, and what does it do?
9. Suppose we find that multinational firms are paying much lower wages in some poor countries than they would have to pay in the United States. Would this be sufficient evidence that these firms are exploiting the workers in the poor countries? Why or why not?
10. How can globalization reduce poverty? What does the evidence suggest about globalization and poverty?
11. There were several major international financial crises in the 1990s. What role did globalization play in these crises?
12. What role did globalization play in the financial crisis of 2007–2008?
13. Using a supply and demand diagram, explain how central banks maintain a fixed exchange rate. What can cause an end to the fixed exchange rate regime?
14. Using a supply and demand diagram, explain how speculative attacks occur in the foreign exchange market.
15. If you worked for a major international bank, forecasting the likelihood of a financial crisis, what key variables would you want to monitor for the countries you are studying? Why would you want to monitor these variables?
16. Read the following excerpt from the World Economic Forum's report, "Global Risks 2012."

    "Two dominant issues of concern emerged from the Arab Spring, the 'Occupy' movements worldwide and recent similar incidents of civil discontent: the growing frustration among citizens with the political and economic establishment, and the rapid public mobilization enabled by greater technological connectivity.... Chronic labour market imbalances, chronic fiscal imbalances and severe income disparity ... could lead to a retrenchment from globalization and the emergence of a new type of critical fragile states – formerly wealthy countries that descend into a spiral of decay as they become increasingly unable to meet their social and fiscal obligations. The signs already exist that the world is becoming more fragmented, inconsistent and mistrustful ..."

a. Why are some citizens growing discontented and what does it have to do with globalization?

b. Is it reasonable to blame labor imbalances, fiscal imbalances or income disparity on globalization?

c. Which countries are most likely to retrench from globalization, and what do they stand to gain or lose?

STUDY GUIDE FOR CHAPTER 18

Key Term Match

Match each term with the correct definition by placing the appropriate letter next to the corresponding number.

A. "race to the bottom"
B. Asian tigers
C. NICs
D. speculative attack

____ 1. a situation in which private investors sell domestic currency and buy foreign currency, betting that the domestic currency will be devalued

____ 2. Hong Kong, South Korea, Singapore, and Taiwan—countries that globalized during the 1960s and 1970s and experienced fast economic growth

____ 3. with globalization, countries compete for international investment by offering low or no environmental regulations or labor standards

____ 4. newly industrialized countries

Quick-Check Quiz

1. Which of the following has *not* been a factor in the increased pace of globalization since the 1950s?
   - ☐ a. increased governmental barriers to immigration
   - ☐ b. reduced costs of international communications
   - ☐ c. formation of the European Union
   - ☐ d. reduced costs for information processing
   - ☐ e. the desire to improve living standards

2. Which of the following would be a sign of decreased globalization?
   - ☐ a. Norway, Denmark, and the United Kingdom decide to adopt the euro as their common currency.
   - ☐ b. Out of concern for safety, businesses conduct teleconferences in place of face-to-face meetings.
   - ☐ c. Global foreign direct investment decreases.
   - ☐ d. Poor countries, enraged by U.S. farm subsidies, stall trade negotiations at the World Trade Organization meetings.
   - ☐ e. The number of countries participating in U.N. peacekeeping missions declines.

3. Which of the following is an argument against globalization?
   - ☐ a. Poor countries compete for multinational firms by allowing lax environmental standards.
   - ☐ b. Multinational firms tend to pay higher wages than local firms.
   - ☐ c. The benefits of globalization to all consumers greatly outweigh the loss of jobs to international competition.
   - ☐ d. Removal of restrictions against agricultural products would increase incomes in poor countries.
   - ☐ e. The increased integration of the world's economies has been associated with economic growth in most countries.

4. Which of the following is an argument in favor of globalization?
   - ☐ a. There is evidence of a "race to the bottom" in labor standards as multinational firms search the world for the lowest labor costs.
   - ☐ b. Multinational firms produce goods for international markets at the expense of local markets.
   - ☐ c. Multinational firms are attracted by the prospects of consumer markets in developing countries.
   - ☐ d. World organizations provide a forum for corporate elites to secure legislation that will benefit them.
   - ☐ e. Poor countries compete for multinational corporations by permitting lax labor standards.

5. Which of the following is true?
   - ☐ a. Some individuals and firms are harmed by free trade agreements.
   - ☐ b. There is widespread evidence of a "race to the bottom" by which multinational firms move production to countries with lax environmental standards.
   - ☐ c. Multinational companies usually locate production units in developing countries, exploit the local labor supply, and then sell the products in rich countries.
   - ☐ d. The fact that wages are lower in developing countries than they are for the same work in western countries is evidence of worker exploitation.
   - ☐ e. International organizations are funded by corporations and are tools of those corporations.

6. The World Bank tracked the performance of countries that had undergone varying degrees of globalization since the 1960s. Which of the following was *not* a conclusion of the study?

- ☐ a. The process of globalization widened the gap between rich countries and poor countries.
- ☐ b. The growth rates of globalizing countries were higher than the growth rates of nonglobalizers.
- ☐ c. The fraction of the very poor declined in newly globalized economies.
- ☐ d. Except for China, globalization did not increase income inequality.
- ☐ e. Poverty has been reduced in newly globalized countries.

7. Which of the following was characteristic of the Asian tigers after they globalized in the 1960s and 1970s?
   - ☐ a. They experienced annual growth rates of 1.4 percent.
   - ☐ b. Environmental standards declined.
   - ☐ c. Unemployment rose as workers lost their jobs because lower-cost imports displaced domestic products.
   - ☐ d. Worker safety regulations were relaxed.
   - ☐ e. Living standards increased dramatically.

8. A speculative attack
   - ☐ a. cannot occur if central banks maintain a fixed exchange rate.
   - ☐ b. cannot occur if exchange rates are allowed to float.
   - ☐ c. is more likely to occur if the domestic currency is appreciating in value.
   - ☐ d. can force a central bank to revalue its currency.
   - ☐ e. can be precipitated by an unprecedented increase in the demand for domestic goods and services.

9. Which of the following is an indicator of a potential financial crisis?
   - ☐ a. floating exchange rates
   - ☐ b. falling international reserves
   - ☐ c. transparency in government activities
   - ☐ d. a high level of long-term international investment
   - ☐ e. bank loans as a small percentage of GDP

10. Which of the following statements is an accurate characterization of the relationship between financial crises and globalization?
    - ☐ a. A country with a globalized economy is more vulnerable to financial crises than a country with a closed economy.
    - ☐ b. The greater the amount of short-term money invested in a country, the greater the potential for a crisis if investors lose confidence in the country.
    - ☐ c. An open economy will be punished for bad economic policy as foreign investors move money out of the country.
    - ☐ d. A globalized country with sound economic policies will be rewarded with large flows of savings from the rest of the world.
    - ☐ e. All these statements are accurate characterizations of the relationship between financial crises and globalization.

Practice Questions and Problems

1. True or false? The growth of international trade is a new phenomenon ____________.
2. World trade as a fraction of world GDP is ____________ (larger than, smaller than, about the same as) it was at the end of the 19th century.
3. Barriers to immigration ____________ (increase, decrease) globalization.
4. List the four broad categories used by *Foreign Policy* magazine to measure the degree of globalization in individual nations.

   ____

   ____
5. ____________ plays an important role in determining the pace of globalization.
6. ____________ (Rising, Constant, Falling) transportation costs increase the pace of globalization.
7. Critics view international organizations such as ____________, ____________, and ____________ as undemocratic organizations that have usurped economic decision-making powers that rightly belong to local authorities.
8. The ____________ comes under criticism for funding resource extraction projects and dams, which critics say benefit the corporations that do the work while also destroying the environment.
9. The role of the ____________ is to provide a venue for negotiating international trade agreements and to enforce international trade rules.
10. List three arguments against globalization.

    ____

    ____

    ____
11. List three arguments in favor of globalization.

    ____

    ____

    ____
12. International organizations such as the WTO are funded by ____________, not corporations.
13. List the four Asian tigers that opened their economies in the 1960s and 1970s and experienced rapid growth and dramatic increases in their living standards.

    ____

    ____
14. The increased globalization of the world's economies has been associated with economic ____________ (growth, stagnation) and ____________ (growth, reduction) of poverty in most countries.
15. Globalizing countries find that income inequality ____________ (does, does not) increase as the pace of globalization increases.

16. The gap between rich countries and globalized developing countries has ____________ (shrunk, widened).
17. Each of the recent international financial crises has involved ____________ exchange rates.
18. A speculative attack cannot occur in countries with ____________ exchange rates.
19. List four factors that may serve as indicators of potential financial crises.

____

____

____

____

20. The greater the amount of short-term money invested in a country, the ____________ (greater, less) potential for a crisis if investors lose confidence in the country.

Exercises and Applications

I China's Currency Manipulation

Senator Sherrod Brown (D-Ohio) says his Currency Exchange Rate Oversight Reform Act of 2011, which has already passed the Senate, "would ensure a fair and level playing field for American manufacturers." Under the bill, the U.S. Treasury Department would be responsible for identifying countries with undervalued currencies, and then the Commerce Department would impose tariffs on imports from those countries. China argues that its currency has appreciated against the dollar.

Source: The Hill's Congress Blog: http://thehill.com/blogs/congress-blog/economy-a-budget/237423-currency-manipulation-gives-chinese-an-unfair-advantage.

a. China has resisted letting its currency rise against the dollar. Why?

____

____

____

b. Senator Brown argues that Chinese currency manipulation acts as a tariff against American exports, and that American jobs are lost as a result. Do his arguments have merit? Explain.

____

____

____

c. How might China react if the Commerce Department imposes tariffs against Chinese goods and services?

____

____

____

d. Is China vulnerable to a speculative attack because of its currency manipulation?

____

____

____

II U.S. Tariffs Against Chinese Solar Panels

In May 2012, the Obama administration imposed stiff tariffs on solar panel imports from China. Local firms had appealed to the U.S. Commerce Department, which ruled that Chinese companies were dumping the solar panels in U.S. markets below cost. Chinese importers receive low cost loans from state-run banks. In campaign speeches, President Obama promised to crack down on unfair competition from Chinese imports.

a. Which anti-globalization arguments, described in this chapter, might U.S. firms have used to convince the Commerce Department to impose the tariffs?

____

b. As a result of the tariffs, what is likely to happen to the prices that American consumers pay for solar panels?

____

c. What might China do in retaliation against the tariff on solar panels?

____

You can find further practice tests in the Online Quiz at: www.cengagebrain.com

ANSWERS FOR NOW YOU TRY IT

Chapter 1, page 6

With ownership, people can invest in their property. They can gain from appreciation of their property value. As a result, these owners may be able to afford to send their children to school. For the people without ownership, their children may work to help support the family.

Chapter 1, page 16

Specializing, Maria produces economics problems and Able math problems. Maria produces 10 economics and Able 10 math. Then, trading 1 math = 3/4 economics means Maria can trade 3 economics and get back 4 math. Able would trade 4 math and get 3 economics. In this case Maria gains 1 math since she could produce 7 economics and 3 math on her own; Able gains 1 math and .5 economics since he could produce 5 math and 2.5 economics on his own.

	Maria		Able	
	Econ	Math	Econ	Math
Pre Trade	7	3	2.5	5
Specialize	10			10
Trade	7	4	3	6
Gain		1	.5	1

Chapter 2, page 38

Price	Market Demand
10	8
8	11
6	14
4	16

Chapter 2, page 49

$P = 1000$, $Q = 800$

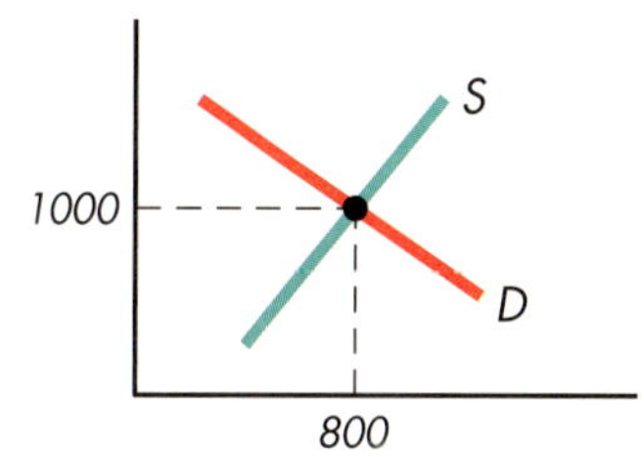

Chapter 2, page 50

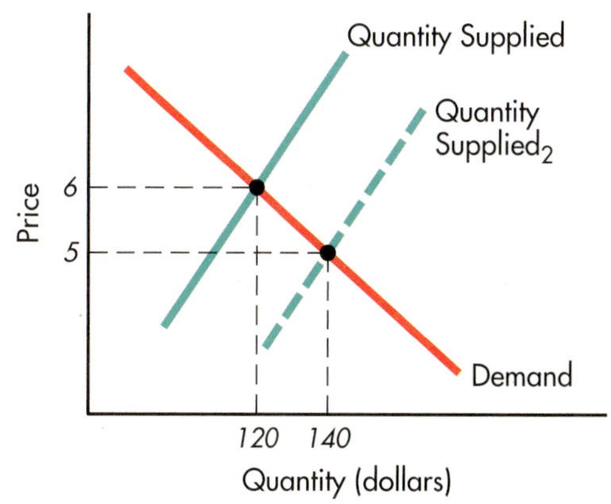

Chapter 3, page 64

The training necessary to become a physician far exceeds that to become a PA. Thus, fewer people become physicians relative to the demand for physicians than is the case for PAs.

Chapter 3, page 70

At $3, quantity demanded is 40 and quantity supplied is 15, a shortage of 25.

At $7, quantity demanded is 20 and quantity supplied is 35, a surplus of 15. This means the price would drop to equilibrium; the price ceiling is not effective.

Chapter 3, page 72

Illustrate what would happen to the price of sugar in the US if the quota was decreased.

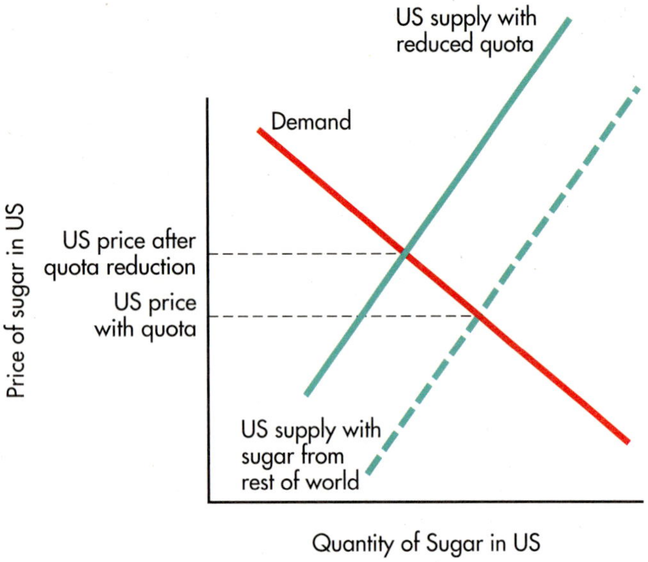

With less sent to US more is available in world so world price decreases.

Chapter 4, page 82

$10 and $10

Chapter 4, page 85

.25; 4.

Chapter 4, page 86

The theater could think about increasing the price, but if it does, it will find that revenue falls. For example, if the theater increases the price by 10 percent, the quantity demanded declines by 14 percent. Revenue declines. The theater has to reduce price to increase revenue.

Chapter 4, page 87

The reason for the different prices to tourists and residents is that the price elasticity of demand is different for tourists and residents. Tourists have fewer options than the residents; tourists are at the golf resort only for a short period. This means the price elasticity of demand for tourists is more inelastic than that for residents.

Demand is greater during the good weather months than it is during the bad weather months. The greater demand will drive prices up.

Chapter 5, page 96

ATC	20	14.5	12.3	11	10	10.3
MC	—	9	8	7	6	12

Chapter 5, page 98

The automobile is the fixed resource, the airbag is the variable resource, and safety is the output. The first airbag, placed in the driver front, increases safety a great deal. The second, placed in the passenger front, increases safety but not as much as the first airbag. The third airbag, placed on the driver side, increases safety but not as much as the second or the first; the fourth, placed on the passenger side, increases safety but not as much as the previous ones. This is the law of diminishing marginal returns.

Chapter 5, page 101

A constant $800 price would mean that revenue is $Q \times$ $800; marginal revenue is $800. $MR = MC$ at $800, which is an output level of 7. While 6 has the same profit level as 7, selecting 7 or in general where $MR = MC$ is never wrong.

Chapter 5, page 103

MR	2300	2100	1900	1700	1500

MC is the same as in Figure 2.

Chapter 6, page 117

The result is a U-shaped *LRATC* with a downward slope until 1 million and an upward slope thereafter.

Chapter 7, page 135

Monopoly is the market structure in which a firm is the sole supplier of a good or service. Monopolization refers to the case where a firm attempts to become the sole supplier when there are other suppliers in existence. It not only attempts to become the sole supplier, but does so in an "anticompetitive" way. The courts determine what "anticompetitive" means in this case.

Chapter 7, page 144

Some people may argue that the infection is an externality that needs to be corrected. Others may argue that the government policy is an infringement of private property rights.

Chapter 7, page 146

Based on the value of a human life at $10 million, only the grain dust regulation would benefit society more than not regulating grain dust.

Chapter 8, page 173

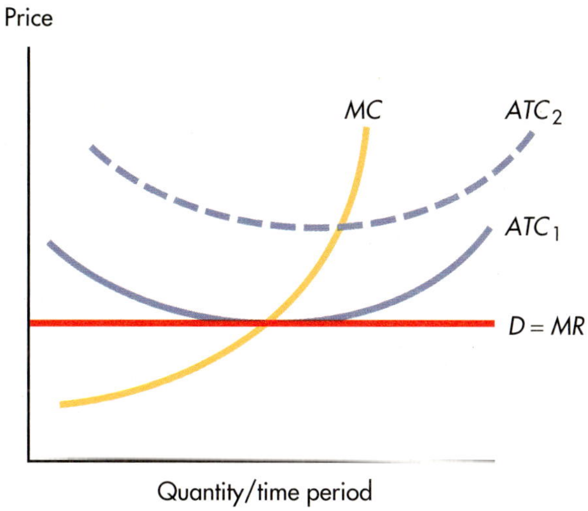

Chapter 10, page 210

a. GDP = $C + I + G + X$ = $1,000
b. GNP = GDP + receipts of factor income from the rest of the world – payments of factor income to the rest of the world = $1,000
c. NNP – GNP – capital consumption allowance = $770
d. NI = NNP – indirect business taxes = $680
e. PI = NI – income earned but not received + income received but not earned = $690
f. DPI = PI – personal taxes = $490

Chapter 11, page 231

1. 850
2. 5.9%

Chapter 12, page 269

1. price level and real GDP increase
2. price level and real GDP fall
3. price level and real GDP fall
4. price level falls and real GDP rises

Chapter 14, page 311

a. 20
b. 4
c. 3
d. 2

Chapter 15, page 324

a. 200
b. $400
c. nominal GDP increases by $20 from $400 to $420

Chapter 16, page 364

0.047 or 4.7%

Chapter 17, page 371

a. Canada has the comparative advantage in corn.
b. China has the comparative advantage in computers.

ANSWERS FOR STUDY GUIDE EXERCISES

CHAPTER 1

Key Term Match

1. k **2.** g **3.** e **4.** h **5.** b **6.** i **7.** f **8.** c **9.** j **10.** d **11.** a **12.** l

Quick-Check Quiz

1. e **2.** c **3.** a **4.** a **5.** c **6.** c **7.** b **8.** a **9.** e **10.** a **11.** a **12.** a

Practice Questions and Problems

1. Yes. Absolute advantage is not the basis for trade. If Canada has a comparative advantage over the U.S. in making a good or service, it will benefit the U.S. to trade with Canada **2.** $10 and 90 minutes. The 30 minutes for the snack isn't an opportunity cost of the ticket. **3.** everyone involved **4.** lowest **5.** higher **6. a.** five **b.** two **c.** gains from trade **7. a.** 4 ties **b.** 1/4 shirt **c.** 3 ties (6 ties divided by 2 shirts) **d.** 1/3 shirt **e.** Harry (He has a lower opportunity cost—3 ties—than Joe—4 ties.) **f.** Joe (He has a lower opportunity cost—1/4 shirt—than Harry—1/3 shirt.) **g.** Joe (He has a comparative advantage in ties.) **h.** Harry (He has a comparative advantage in shirts.)

Exercises and Applications

I. **Scarce Parking in Wichita?** Parking *is* scarce. If there is not enough of an item to satisfy everyone that wants it at a zero price, then an item is scarce. If people want parking at the front door of wherever they are going and have to walk—on average, about a block—parking is scarce.

II. **Resource and Income Flows**

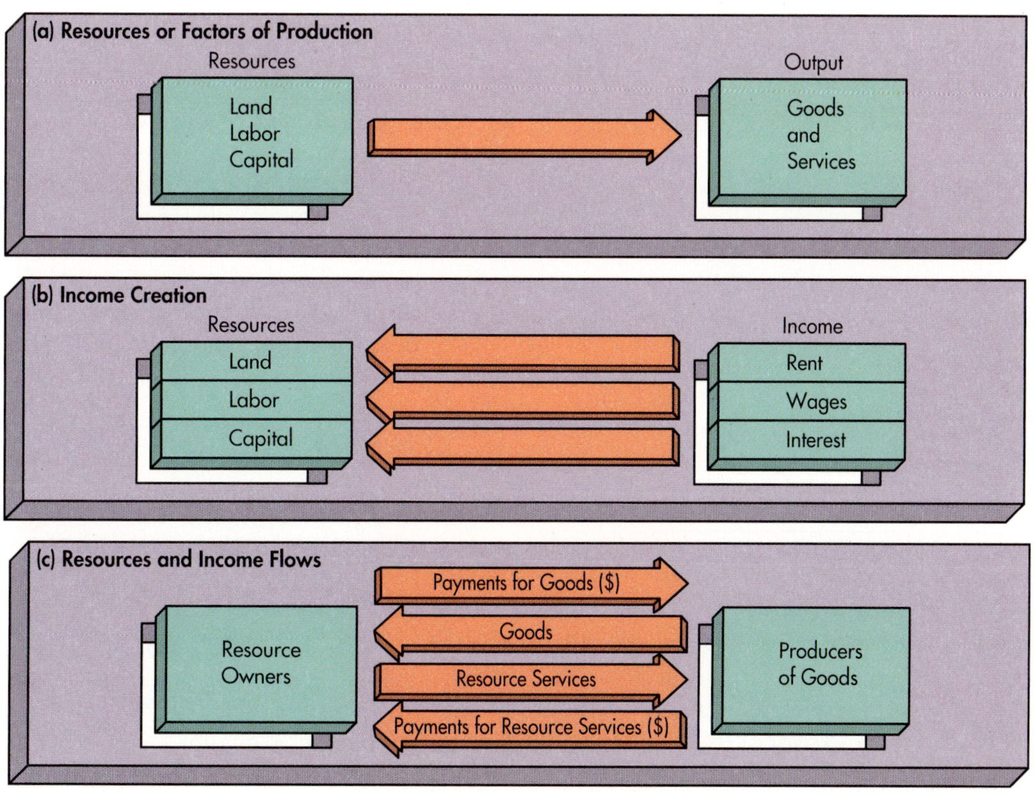

III. Opportunity Costs The opportunity cost for Mr. Safi to cut his grass is $200 an hour; that is what he would make in his next-best use of time. It is better for him to spend his hour consulting and pay the neighbor's child to cut the grass—unless the neighbor's child charges $200 an hour!

CHAPTER 2

Key Term Match

1. e **2.** i **3.** k **4.** o **5.** b **6.** p **7.** c **8.** l **9.** h **10.** n **11.** j **12.** q **13.** d **14.** f **15.** r **16.** m **17.** a **18.** g

Quick-Check Quiz

1. d (If the price of a resource used to make a good increases, the cost to make the good increases. Less will be offered at every price, which is a decrease in supply) **2.** e (Item a causes a change in quantity demanded—not a change in demand. Items b and c cause the demand for eggs to *decrease*. Item d affects supply.) **3.** b (The price of barley affects the supply of beer.) **4.** b (The Nook e-reader and the Kindle are substitutes in consumption. When the price of the Nook e-reader drops, people substitute Nook e-readers for Kindles. They buy fewer Kindles at every price, so the demand for Kindles decreases.) **5.** d **6.** c **7.** c **8.** b **9.** c **10.** c

Practice Questions and Problems

1. random allocation; market allocation; government allocation; first-come, first-served allocation **2.** income; tastes; prices of related goods or services; consumers' expectations; number of buyers **3.** increases; demand **4.** decreased; demand; increased; demand **5.** increase **6.** increase **7.** prices of resources; technology and productivity; expectations of producers; number of producers; prices of related goods or services **8.** supply; decreased

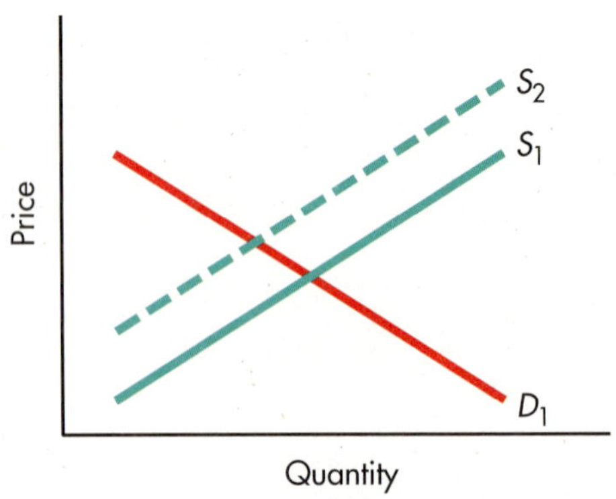

9. supply; decrease **10.** increase; shift to the right **11.** notebook paper; decrease **12.** increases; decrease **13.** decreases; increase **14.** supply of; increase; decrease; increase **15.** $10; 12; 8; 16; surplus; 8; decrease; increase; 18; 6; shortage; 12; increase; decrease **16.** $4 **17.** 8 **18.** shortage; 12; increase **19.** surplus; 6; decrease

Exercises and Applications

I. The Market for Battery-Operated Dancing Flowers

	Demand	Supply	Price	Quantity
a.	decrease	no change	decrease	decrease
b.	no change	increase	decrease	increase
c.	no change	increase	decrease	increase
d.	increase	no change	increase	increase
e.	increase	no change	increase	increase
f.	no change	decrease	increase	decrease
g.	no change	decrease	increase	decrease
h.	decrease	no change	decrease	decrease

CHAPTER 3

Key Term Match

1. c **2.** a **3.** e **4.** b **5.** d **6.** f **7.** g

Quick-Check Quiz

1. c **2.** d **3.** a **4.** c **5.** b **6.** e **7.** c **8.** d **9.** e

Practice Questions and Problems

1. consumer **2.** compensating wage differential **3.** a profit **4.** low; high **5.** demand; supply **6.** Business firms **7.** Households **8.** down; less **9.** up; more **10.** demand; supply **11.** Medicare; Medicaid **12.** demand; increase **13.** subsidies **14.** below **15.** above **16.** above or equal to **17.** limit; quantity; reducing; supply of **18.** increase; decrease; supply; increasing; decreasing **19.** decreasing; increasing

Exercises and Applications

I. Price Controls and Medical Care
1. price ceiling
2. Shortages would occur. There would probably be long waits to obtain these procedures.

II. A Solution for High Gas Prices
a. price ceiling
b. If the legislation passes, a gas shortage will develop. People will not be able to get gas for their cars, so they will need bicycles.

CHAPTER 4

Key Term Match

1. c **2.** e **3.** a **4.** g **5.** i **6.** f **7.** b **8.** j **9.** h **10.** d

Quick-Check Quiz

1. b **2.** c **3.** a **4.** c **5.** d **6.** a **7.** a **8.** b **9.** a

Practice Questions and Problems

1. $P \times Q$ (price times quantity) **2.** TR/Q (total revenue divided by quantity) **3.** change in TR/change in Q

4. marginal revenue **5.** price
6.

Price	Quantity	Total Revenue	Average Revenue	Marginal Revenue
$10	1	$10	$10	$10
9	2	18	9	8
8	3	24	8	6
7	4	28	7	4

(Total revenue = price × quantity; average revenue = total revenue/quantity; marginal revenue = change in total revenue/change in quantity.)
7. quantity demanded; price
8.

Price	Quantity	Total Revenue	Average Revenue	Marginal Revenue
$5	1	$ 5	$5	$5
5	2	10	5	5
5	3	15	5	5
5	4	20	5	5

Calculations use the same formulas as problem 6. In problem 6, when price goes down, marginal revenue goes down faster. In problem 8, price stays the same, and marginal revenue is the same as the price.

9.

Price	Quantity	Total Revenue	Average Revenue	Marginal Revenue
$20	100	$2,000	$20	$20
18	200	3,600	18	16
16	300	4,800	16	12
14	400	5,600	14	8

(Marginal revenue is the change in total revenue divided by the change in quantity. In this problem, the change in quantity between different prices is 100, not 1.)

10. 2; elastic (Remember the equation for the price elasticity of demand:

$$e_d = \frac{\text{percentage change in quantity demanded}}{\text{percentage change in price}}.$$ The change in quantity demanded is 10 percent, and the change in price is 5 percent, so $e_d = 10/5 = 2$. This is more than 1, so demand must be elastic.) **11.** 0.5; inelastic (Refer to the previous equation for the price elasticity of demand. In this problem, the change in quantity demanded is 3 percent, and the change in price is 6 percent, so $e_d = 3/6 = 0.5$. This is less than 1, so demand must be inelastic.) **12.** 1; unit elastic (Refer to the previous equation for the price elasticity of demand. In this problem, the change in quantity demanded is 2 percent, and the change in price is 2 percent, so $e_d = 2/2 = 1$. Therefore, demand must be unit elastic.) **13.** 0; perfectly inelastic (refer to the previous equation for the price elasticity of demand. In this problem, the percentage change in quantity demanded is 0 percent, and the change in price is 5 percent, so $e_d = 0/5 = 0$. Therefore, demand must be perfectly inelastic.)
14.

Demand Elasticity	Price Change	Effect on Total Revenue (Increase, Decrease, Unchanged)
Elastic	Increase	Decrease
Elastic	Decrease	Increase
Inelastic	Increase	Increase
Inelastic	Decrease	Decrease
Unit elastic	Increase	Unchanged
Unit elastic	Decrease	Unchanged

15. many; few **16.** less (For most people, there are many good substitutes for Chevrolets: Fords, Chryslers, Toyotas, Volkswagens, and so on. The demand for a particular brand of a product is usually more elastic than the demand for the product itself.) **17.** large; small **18.** long; short

Exercises and Applications

I. Taxing Gasoline to Reduce Pollution

1. 0.68 (The price elasticity of demand for gas is 3%/4.4% = 0.6818 or .68.); inelastic (Because the price elasticity of demand is less than 1, demand is inelastic.)
2. There aren't many good substitutes for gasoline. Most people view gasoline as a necessity. Gasoline consumption is usually a small part of the consumer's budget. In the short run, consumers cannot immediately buy more gas–efficient vehicles or change their driving habits in response to price increases. In the long run, when consumers can make these adjustments, the price of gas becomes more elastic.
3. No

II. Price Discrimination in Airline Fares

1. Elastic. The people who are sensitive to price will download the ap. People who don't care so much about the price will not bother.
2. Southwest thinks vacation travelers have a higher elasticity of demand than business travelers, who usually do not have much choice about when they travel.
3. Vacation travelers. Business travelers do not have much choice about when they travel, so their demand is less elastic.

CHAPTER 5

Key Term Match

1. h **2.** k **3.** a **4.** f **5.** b **6.** c **7.** h **8.** g or j
9. l **10.** e **11.** d **12.** i

Quick-Check Quiz

1. a **2.** d **3.** e **4.** d **5.** e (Miss Andrea must make at least $30 per class, since she can get $30 by renting the studio to the ballroom dancing instructor during that class time)

Practice Questions and Problems

1. change in total costs/change in quantity of output **2.** at least one; fixed **3.** quantity; fixed resources
4.

Burgers	TC	ATC	MC
0	$5.50		
1	9.00	$9.00	$3.50
2	10.00	5.00	1.00
3	10.50	3.50	.50
4	11.50	2.88	1.00
5	13.00	2.60	1.50
6	15.00	2.50	2.00
7	17.50	2.50	2.50
8	20.50	2.56	3.00
9	24.00	2.67	3.50
10	28.00	2.80	4.00

$ATC = TC/Q$
$MC =$ change in TC/change in Q

(a) Total Costs

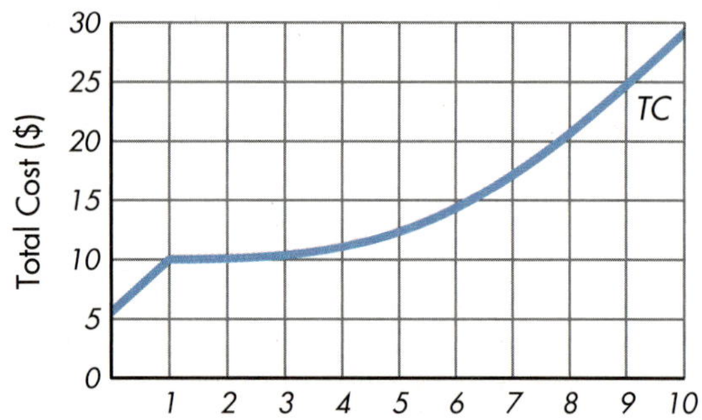

(b) Unit Costs

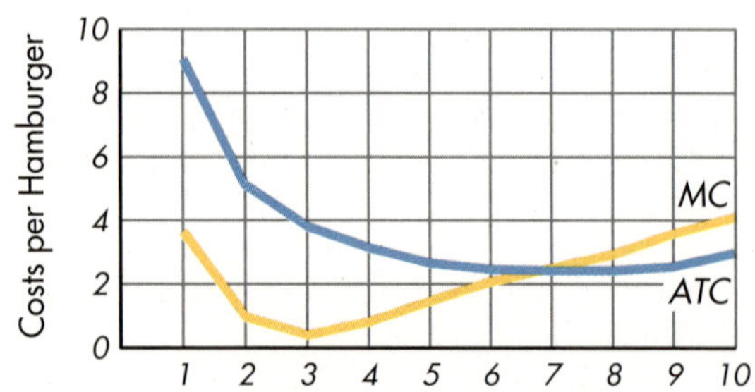

5. U **6.** rise **7. a.** positive **b.** negative or zero **8. a.** –$20,000 ($200,000 – [$140,000 + $10,000 + $20,000 + 50,000]) **b.** negative **c.** unlikely **d.** $20,000. Must have economic profit equal to zero. **9.** more **10.** $.80; zero economic or normal; not decline; positive economic. **11.** want to enter the business; zero; positive; zero; as long as entry does not occur and good or service is valued.

Exercises and Applications

I. Profit Maximization and Pollution Reduction

1. 2

2. For the first 1-ton reduction, people gain $10 million in benefits at a cost of $1 million; the "profit" is $9 million from the first 1-ton reduction.

The second 1-ton reduction gives us $5 million in benefits at a cost of $4 million; we gain an additional $1 million profit from the second 1-ton reduction. After reducing pollution by 2 tons, we have total benefits of $15 million ($10 million + $5 million), and total costs of $5 million ($1 million + $4 million), for a total net gain or profit of $10 million.

If we made the third 1-ton reduction, we would gain $2 million in benefits at a cost of $10 million; we'd "lose" $8 million on the third 1-ton reduction. If we reduced pollution by a total of 3 tons, our total benefits would be $17 million ($10 million + $5 million + $2 million), and our total costs would be $15 million ($1 million + $4 million + $10 million), for a total net gain of $2 million. By the criterion specified for this example, we would be better off with only 2 tons of pollution reduction; we would get more value from spending $10 million on other things than on the third 1-ton reduction of pollution.

(Although making decisions about pollution reduction is much more complex than this simple example, the problem does illustrate the basic concepts involved, including some of the economic principles we've been studying in the last few chapters.)

CHAPTER 6

Key Term Match

1. d **2.** c **3.** p **4.** b **5.** m **6.** q **7.** j **8.** e **9.** k **10.** r **11.** l **12.** a **13.** h **14.** n **15.** s **16.** i **17.** o **18.** g **19.** f

Quick-Check Quiz

1. c **2.** c **3.** c **4.** b **5.** a **6.** c **7.** a **8.** b **9.** e

Practice Questions and Problems

1. Perfect; many; identical; easy **2.** Monopolistic; many; differentiated; easy **3.** perfect competition **4.** do not; do **5.** enter; down; down; normal **6.** exit; up; up; normal **7.** economic losses **8.** smaller

9.

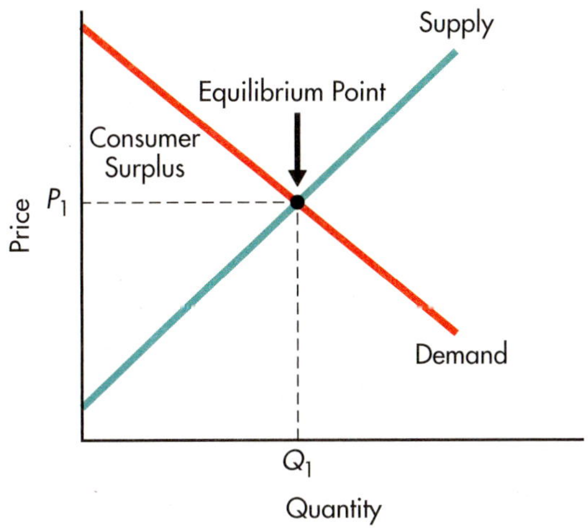

10. lower **11.** product differentiation; licenses; brand names; sunk costs; owning unique resources; economies of scale **12.** Owning all the bauxite in the world gave Alcoa control of a unique resource that was necessary to produce aluminum. Without access to bauxite, other firms could not enter the market for new aluminum. **13.** decrease **14.** increase **15.** A new firm entering the market cannot start out small and then grow larger; to compete with existing large firms, a new firm has to start out large enough to gain all the economies of scale.

Exercises and Applications

I. Is Advertising Profitable?

1. a. 5 (The first 5 hamburgers have $MR > MC$. The sixth hamburger's MR is $2, less than its MC of $3.50, so it is not worth making and selling.)
   b. $8 (This is the price at which consumers will buy 5 hamburgers.)
   c. zero ($P = ATC$)
2. a. 5 (The first 5 hamburgers have $MR > MC$. The sixth hamburger's MR is $2.50, less than its MC of $3.50, so it is not worth making and selling.)
   b. $10 (This is the price at which consumers will buy 5 hamburgers.)
   c. $5 (profit per hamburger = $10 ($P$) − $9 ($ATC$) = $1; $1 profit per hamburger × 5 hamburgers = $5)

II. Away With the Old! In with the New!

a. creative destruction
b. Cassette tapes, 35 mm film, fax machines, encyclopedias and typewriters are just a few examples of creative destruction.

III. The Stability of Cartels

a. The fewer the number of firms in the industry, the easier it is to detect cheaters.
b. If the firms' products are homogenous, member firms would know that a decline in their individual sales is most likely due to a member cheating. If the products are different, the change could be due to consumer tastes changing.
c. If firms have similar cost structures, the cartel is likely to have an easier time deciding on price and quantity restrictions. If cost structures are different, their profit maximizing conditions will be different, and it will be harder to come to an agreement.

CHAPTER 7

Key Term Match

1. e **2.** c **3.** f **4.** a **5.** n **6.** g **7.** h **8.** b **9.** i **10.** o **11.** j **12.** k **13.** d **14.** m **15.** l

Quick-Check Quiz

1. b **2.** e **3.** a **4.** b **5.** c **6.** a **7.** a **8.** c **9.** c

Practice Questions and Problems

1. moral hazard **2.** creative destructive **3.** don't **4.** make profit **5.** reduces, raises **6.** antitrust **7.** economies; more; lower **8.** regulated **9.** negative externality; internalized **10.** private property rights Ronald Coase **11.** no one owns black rhinos **12.** private property rights **13.** regulation; social regulation **14.** costs; benefits **15.** more than $100 million. **16.** too much **17.** too little

Exercises and Applications

I. The Pelzman effect

The Pelzman effect is a variant of moral hazard. Moral hazard refers to a situation in which people have an incentive to engage in more risky behaviors because they will not bear all the costs if things go wrong. If people feel that safety equipment will protect them in the event of an accident, they may be more willing to risk getting into an accident than if they were not protected.

II. Halloween Street

Negative Externality or spillover cost. Your neighbors' Halloween decorations are a negative externality because you are not involved in the production or enjoyment of the decorations, but bear the cost in terms of damage to your lawn and traffic congestion on your street.

CHAPTER 8

Key Term Match

1. a **2.** c **3.** e 4. d **5.** b

Quick-Check Quiz

1. b **2.** b

Practice Questions and Problems

1. Third party payer **2.** too long **3.** property rights **4.** inelastic **5.** tougher **6.** decrease; decrease **7.** supply of **8.** inelastic **9.** costly **10.** easy

Exercises and Applications

I. Creative Destruction

1. a. Q1 P1
   b. Demand falls as spending decreases. The lower demand leads to a lower quantity produced and a lower price. Q2 P2
2. If the economy is left alone, the new equilibrium represents full employment since everyone willing and able to work at the going wage has a job. If more people were willing to work at the lower wages that come with the lower Q2 P2, then they would drive the wage lower still.
   If the government increases spending then what happens depends on whether businesses and consumers reduce spending to compensate for the higher taxes they may pay to finance government spending. In reality both business and consumers react to the higher government spending by reducing their own spending, in most cases. However, if they just retained their current spending, the demand would rise and a new equilibrium would be reached.
3. If wages are set by ensuring that English teachers and math teachers earn the same, then there will be too many English teachers and too few math teachers.

II. Drug Prohibition and Drug Addiction
By making the drugs much more powerful without increasing the size or weight of the drugs, then more value can be shipped for the same cost.

III. Insurance and Health Care Costs

1. Most likely you would have more maintenance and get it more often.
2. The demand for maintenance would rise. The price would rise.

CHAPTER 9

Key Term Match

1. d **2.** e **3.** o **4.** h **5.** l **6.** c **7.** n **8.** g **9.** m **10.** i **11.** r **12.** a **13.** p **14.** b **15.** k **16.** q **17.** f **18.** j

Quick-Check Quiz

1. c **2.** a **3.** a **4.** d **5.** b **6.** e **7.** d **8.** e **9.** c **10.** d

Practice Questions and Problems

1. household or consumer **2.** 35-44; 45-54 **3.** Corporations **4.** World Bank **5.** Investment spending **6.** Developing; industrial **7.** per capita income **8.** provision of police protection; provision of military protection; correction of a problem such as pollution **9.** to show the flow of output and income from one sector of the economy to another **10.** output

Exercises and Applications

I. The Circular Flow Diagram **a.** savings **b.** investments **c.** payments for goods and services **d.** goods and services **e.** taxes **f.** government services **g.** resource services **h.** payments for resource services **i.** taxes **j.** government services **k.** goods and services **l.** payments for goods and services **m.** resource services **n.** payments for resource services **o.** net exports **p.** payments for net exports

CHAPTER 10

Key Term Match

1. d **2.** h **3.** r **4.** e **5.** n **6.** g **7.** i **8.** x **9.** aa **10.** b **11.** q **12.** u **13.** j **14.** y **15.** p **16.** k **17.** bb **18.** z **19.** m **20.** s **21.** a **22.** v **23.** f **24.** cc **25.** c **26.** l **27.** o **28.** t **29.** w

Quick-Check Quiz

1. d **2.** a **3.** c **4.** false **5.** positive; 71% **6.** c **7.** b **8.** d **9. a.** depreciate **b.** more expensive **c.** increase **d.** buy as soon as possible **10.** rise; fall

Practice Questions and Problems

1. land: rent; labor: wages; capital: interest To get GDP, you must add capital consumption allowance and indirect business taxes, and subtract net factor income from abroad.
2. \$69.50 (The lei maker gets \$3.99 for each of her 50 leis, for a total of \$199.50. Since her cost for the flowers was \$130, her value added is \$199.50 – \$130 = \$69.50.)
3. \$5 (The total of the values added is \$300 + \$200 + \$50 = \$550. The 110 ornaments are worth \$550, or \$5 each.)
4. is
5. GDP (as expenditures) = $C + I + G + X$
   GDP (as income) = wages + rent + interest + profits – net factor income from abroad + indirect business taxes + capital consumption allowance
   GNP = GDP + net factor income from abroad
   NNP = GNP – capital consumption allowance
   NI = NNP – indirect business taxes

PI = NI + income received but not earned – income earned but not received DPI = PI – personal taxes

6. GDP = wages + rent + interest + profits (corporate profits + proprietor's income) – net factor income from abroad + indirect business taxes + capital consumption allowance = 1,803 + 6 + 264 + (124 + 248) – 43 + 328 + 273 = 3,003
   GNP = GDP + net factor income from abroad = 3,003 + 43 = 3,046
   NNP = GNP – capital consumption allowance – 3,046 – 328 = 2,718
   NI = NNP – indirect business taxes = 2,718 – 273 = 2,445
7.

Year	Real GDP
1	206/98 × 110 = 210.20
2	216 (this is the base year)
3	228/115 × 100 = 198.26

   a. Year 2. (You can tell because the price index is 100 for that year.)
   b. higher
   c. increased
8. Increases in nominal GDP can come about from a rise in prices, an increase in output, or both. To know if the economy is performing better than before, we need to know if output has increased. Real GDP is a better measure, since it rises only when output has increased.
9. increased; 112
10. a. 1/.86610 = C$1.154601
    b. 1/.8707 = €1.1485
    c. 1/.00677 = ¥147.71048
    d. 1/1.8155 = £.5508124
11. a. $150 × €1.1485/$ = €172.275
    b. $150 × RS21.61/$ = RS3,241.5
    c. $150 × 22.66 pesos/$ = 3,399 pesos

Exercises and Applications

I. Understanding Price Indexes

1. The dollar value of output for year 1 is 1,000(5) + 8,000(6) + 3,000(20) + 5,000(20) = 213,000. For year 2 the value is 1,000(6) + 8,000(6.6) + 3,000(25) + 5,000(18) = 223,800. For year 3 the value is 4,000(7) + 10,000(6.8) + 3,500(25) + 4,900(15) = 257,000.

2. a **3.** c

II. The Balance of Payments as an Indicator

A merchandise deficit may indicate that domestic producers have higher costs than their foreign competitors. Many analysts view the current account deficit as a sign that U.S. manufacturers have lost their competitive edge.

III. The Balance of Payments and Exchange Rates

A capital account surplus means that there are more foreign purchases of U.S. stocks and bonds than U.S. purchases of foreign stocks and bonds. Foreign purchasers therefore need to acquire U.S. dollars, so the dollar will appreciate. U.S. federal budget deficits may signal higher domestic interest rates. Foreign investors will be attracted to the high U.S. interest rates, and the dollar will appreciate.

CHAPTER 11

Key Term Match

1. b **2.** l **3.** n **4.** a **5.** d **6.** q **7.** k **8.** o **9.** c **10.** m **11.** g **12.** j **13.** i **14.** e **15.** p **16.** f **17.** h

Quick-Check Quiz

1. b **2.** d **3.** b **4.** e **5.** c **6.** c **7.** a **8.** c **9.** c **10.** c

Practice Questions and Problems

1. expansion **2.** trough **3.** peak **4.** recession
5. NBER (National Bureau of Economic Research)
6. Cyclical **7.** Seasonal **8.** Frictional (or search)
9. Structural **10.** GDP gap **11.** discouraged workers; underemployment **12.** lost output (or the GDP gap)
13. lower **14.** creditors; debtors

Exercises and Applications

I. In or Out of the Labor Force?

Mr. Olsen is not in the U.S. labor force since he is not a U.S. resident.

Mr. Wolcutt is not looking for work and therefore would not be considered part of the labor force.

X Mr. Stephans was laid off and is waiting for a recall, so he is part of the labor force.

Thomas Butting is not looking for work and therefore would not be considered part of the labor force.

X Joe Shocker will start a new job within 30 days, so he is part of the labor force.

II. Illustrating the Business Cycle

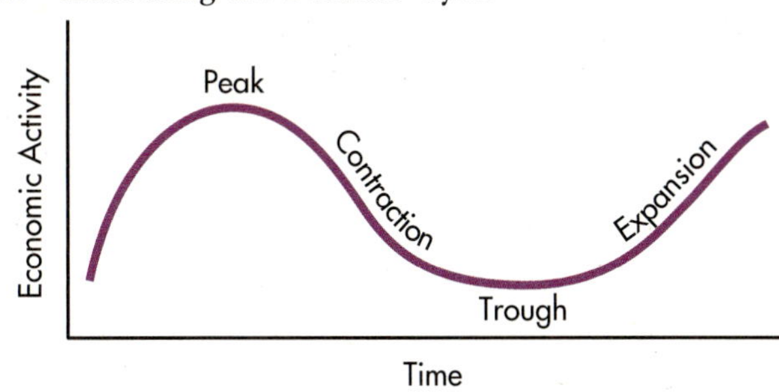

III. Economic Reporting

1. Continued increases in the Lagging Indicators Index and the Coincident Indicators Index suggest the economy was expanding in the past and is currently expanding. If the growth rate in the Leading Indicators Index truly has stabilized, it may point toward continued growth in the future. If the economy was growing in the past and is expected to continue to grow in the future, the U.S. was in the boom/expansion phase during this time.

2. No change in the CPI suggests that consumers neither gained nor lost purchasing power over these two months. Neither creditors nor debtors benefited from price changes.
3. The natural rate of unemployment falls in the range of 4-7%, so living standards during the first 8 months of 2012 were lower than they would have been if the economy had been at the natural rate of unemployment.
4. The GDP is the main measure of the economy's performance. An increase in the trade deficit indicates that net exports decreased. Since GDP = C + *I* + *G* + X; the GDP would be revised downward.

CHAPTER 12

Key Term Match

1. d **2.** f **3.** a **4.** e **5.** b **6.** c

Quick-Check Quiz

1. a **2.** b **3.** d **4.** b **5.** b **6.** e **7.** c **8.** b **9.** b **10.** e

Practice Questions and Problems

1. Demand-pull **2.** falls; rises; falls **3.** increase; decrease; decrease **4.** Cost-push **5.** decreases **6.** increase **7.** increase **8.** Net exports **9.** rise **10.** falls **11.** Investment **12.** increases **13.** income; wealth; expectations; demographics; taxes **14.** falls **15.** rise **16.** interest rate; technology; cost of capital goods; capacity utilization **17.** fall **18.** lower **19.** foreign and domestic income; foreign and domestic prices; exchange rates; government policy **20.** decreases; decreases; wealth; fall **21.** more expensive; fall; fall **22.** less expensive; a shift to the left of the aggregate demand curve **23.** a movement along the aggregate demand curve **24.** consumption; investment; increases **25.** exports; a shift in aggregate demand to the right **26.** increase; more **27.** resource prices; technology; expectations **28.** right **29.** is not

Exercises and Applications

I. Aggregate Demand and Its Determinants

Component	Effect on Component	Effect on Aggregate Demand
1. Investment	Increase	Increase
2. Net exports	Decrease	Decrease
3. Consumption	Increase	Increase
4. Net exports	Increase	Increase
5. Consumption	Increase	Increase
6. Investment	Decrease	Decrease
7. Consumption	Decrease	Decrease
8. Investment	Increase	Increase

II. A Long-Run Analysis of the Effects of a Slump in Productivity A decrease in productivity causes the long-run aggregate supply curve to shift to the left. If aggregate demand does not change, equilibrium real GDP will be lower and the price level will be higher—a very sorry prospect indeed.

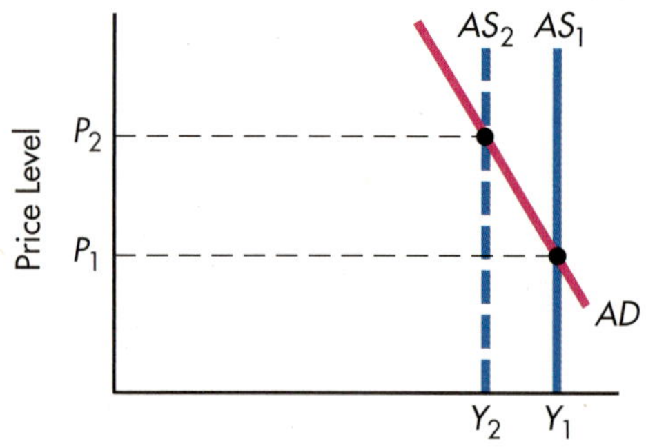

CHAPTER 13

Key Term Match

1. d **2.** a **3.** e **4.** c **5.** b **6.** g **7.** f

Quick-Check Quiz

1. a **2.** b **3.** a **4.** d **5.** d **6.** e **7.** c **8.** b **9.** b **10.** d

Practice Questions and Problems

1. taxation; government spending **2.** disposable income; consumption **3.** up; decreasing **4.** expansionary **5.** left **6.** taxes; changes in government debt (borrowing); changes in the stock of government-issued money **7.** left; increase; rise **8.** selling bonds to **9.** legislative; executive **10.** Office of Management and Budget **11.** Congressional Budget Office **12.** discretionary fiscal policy; automatic stabilizers **13.** increase **14.** Lump-sum taxes **15.** C; B; A

To determine what kind of tax it is, we must first calculate the tax *rate* at each level of income. Since A's tax *rate* is constant at .10, A is a proportional tax schedule. B's tax *rate* decreases with income, so B is a regressive tax. C's tax *rate* increases with income, so C is a progressive tax schedule.

	A		B		C	
Income	Tax Payment	Tax Rate	Tax Payment	Tax Rate	Tax Payment	Tax Rate
$100	$10	.10	$ 50	.50	$ 10	.10
200	20	.10	80	.40	30	.15
300	30	.10	90	.30	60	.20
400	40	.10	100	.25	100	.25

Note: If you look at just the *dollar* amount of taxes paid, all three schedules look "progressive" because the dollar amount of tax payments increases as income increases. But we classify these taxes according to how the tax *rate* changes as income increases.

16. Progressive **17.** developing; State-owned enterprises account for a larger percentage of economic activity in developing countries as compared with industrial countries. Also, developing countries rely on their governments, as opposed to private investment, to build their infrastructure. **18.** do not **19.** indirect

Exercises and Applications

I. Reducing the Deficit

1. Government spending cuts and tax increases both decrease aggregate demand. If the economy is operating in the Keynesian or intermediate regions, decreasing aggregate demand will decrease real GDP. If the economy is in the intermediate range, the price level will decline. If it is in the Keynesian region, there will be no change in the price level. These are the dire results that economic analysts fear.

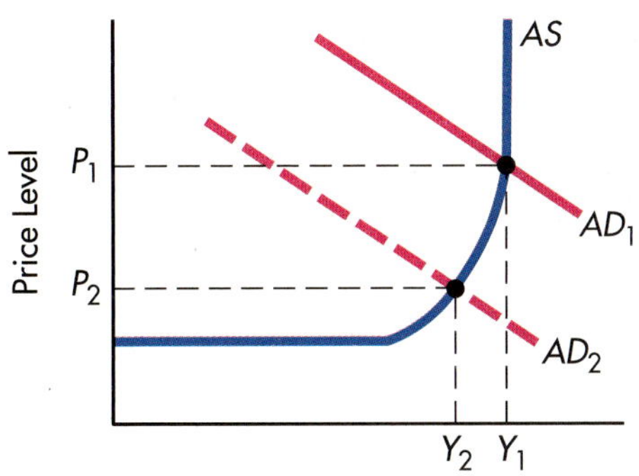

2. If the economy is operating in the vertical region of short-run aggregate supply (above), a decrease in aggregate demand may bring only a decrease in the price level with no decrease in real GDP.

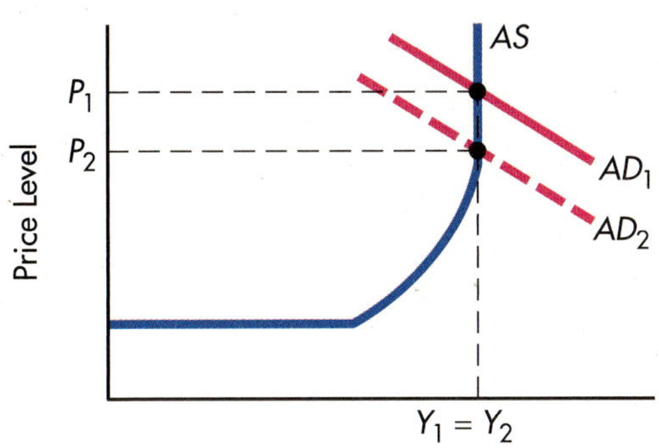

II. Obama's Fiscal Policy

1. conractionary
2. decrease; Lower interest rates would increase investment, thereby increasing aggregate demand and equilibrium real GDP.
3. increase; narrow

CHAPTER 14

Key Term Match

1. d **2.** g **3.** e **4.** q **5.** t 6. n **7.** c **8.** r **9.** f **10.** m **11.** h **12.** b **13** o **14.** l **15.** j **16.** a **17.** s **18.** p **19.** k **20.** i

Quick-Check Quiz

1. c **2.** d **3.** c **4.** e **5.** c **6.** a **7.** a **8.** b **9.** e

Practice Questions and Problems

1. medium of exchange; unit of account; store of value; standard of deferred payment **2.** currency; travelers' checks; demand deposits; other checkable deposits (OCDs) **3.** share drafts **4.** Mutual savings banks **5.** M1; savings deposits; small denominationtime deposits (certificates of deposit, or CDs); retail money market mutual fund balances **6.** double coincidence of wants **7.** Savings **8.** certificates of deposit 9. False 10. savings and loans; mutual savings banks; credit unions **11.** Offshore **12.** more risky **13.** panic **14.** 1/reserve requirement **15.** maximum **16.** currency drain **17.** excess reserves **18.** making loans

Exercises and Applications

I. How Banks Create Money

a. Required reserves = .01 ($500,000) = $5,000. Excess reserves = $5,000 – $5,000 = 0.
b. $99,000 (Cash = $105,000. Deposits = $600,000. Required reserves = .01($600,000) = $6,000. Excess reserves = $105,000 – $6,000 = $99,000.)
c. $9,900,000 (Deposit expansion multiplier = 1/.01 = 100. Maximum amount of money that can be created = deposit expansion multiplier × excess reserves = 100($99,000) = $9,900,000.)

II. The Components of the Monetary Aggregates

M1	= Currency + travelers' checks + demand deposits + other checkable deposits = 357.3 + 8.1 + 406.5 + 420.0 = 1,191.9
M2	= M1 + savings deposits + small-denomination time deposits + retail money market mutual funds = 1,191.9 + 1,135.0 + 826.9 + 372.1 = 3,525.9

CHAPTER 15

Key Term Match

1. j **2.** m **3.** a **4.** h **5.** k **6.** b **7.** g **8.** c **9.** i **10.** f **11.** l **12.** n **13.** o **14.** d **15.** e

Quick-Check Quiz

1. b **2.** b (Answer a is false, and the others are true only if certain assumptions are made. For c to be true, velocity must be constant and the economy must be at full employment, so that *Q* cannot rise. For d to be true, velocity must be constant and there must be some unemployment in the economy. Answer e may be true if velocity is constant.) **3.** d **4.** c **5.** d **6.** d **7.** d **8.** e **9.** d **10.** c

Practice Questions and Problems

1. decentralized **2.** 2% **3.** president; 4; 14 **4.** controlling the money supply **5.** Fed chairperson **6.** $MV = PQ$ **7.** LSAP stands for Large-Scale Asset Purchase. The Fed bought mortgage backed securities, which was not part of traditional monetary policy. **8.** quantity theory of money **9.** reserve requirement; discount rate; open market operations **10.** raising **11.** discount; bank **12.** lowers **13.** buys **14.** dollars **15.** increases **16.** nominal income; interest rates **17.** inverse **18.** make loans **19.** does not **20.** precautionary **21.** transactions **22.** shifts to the right **23.** decreased **24.** rise; fall; decrease; fall

(a)

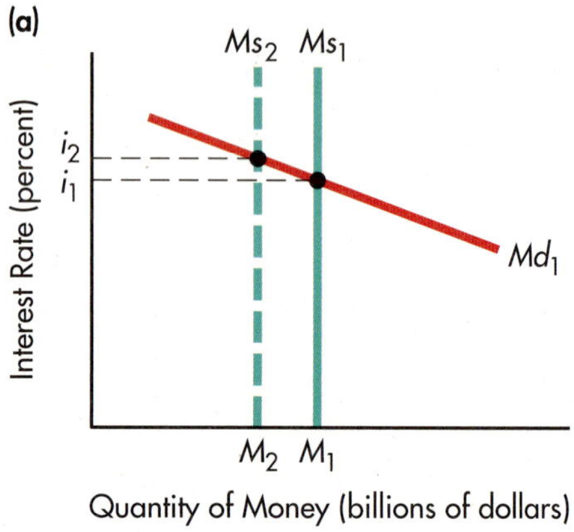

(b)

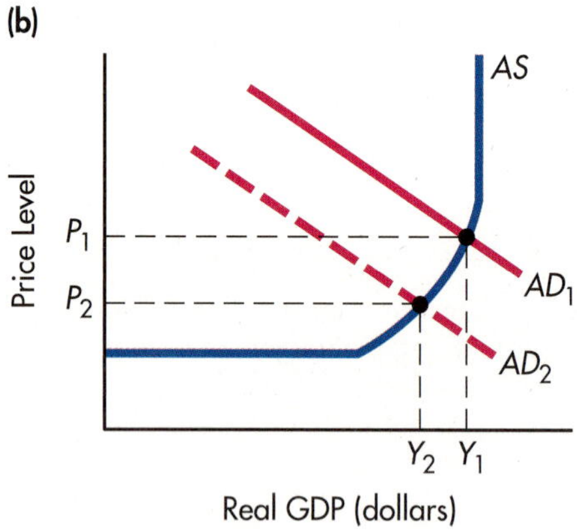

Exercises and Applications

I. More on Foreign Exchange Market Intervention buy; increase; decrease; decrease; depreciate; reinforced

II. Bond Prices and Interest Rates

a. opposite; fell

b. Bond prices drop as interest rates rise. If owners of bonds expect higher interest rates, they will want to sell their bonds before the prices of the bonds decrease.

CHAPTER 16

Key Term Match

1. f **2.** d **3.** g **4.** c **5.** e **6.** b **7.** a

Quick-Check Quiz

1. d (Only unanticipated inflation makes the inflation–unemployment tradeoff possible.) **2.** e **3.** c **4.** a **5.** a **6.** a **7.** d **8.** d **9.** b **10.** e

Practice Questions and Problems

1. affect (For example, the lack of private property rights hampered growth in the former Soviet Union.) **2.** does not **3.** aggregate demand; aggregate supply (Note that aggregate supply does shift in the long run.) **4.** constant expected rate of inflation; constant reservation wage **5.** unemployment **6.** wage expectations; inventory fluctuations; wage contracts **7.** adaptive **8.** decreases **9.** $G = T + B + \Delta M$ **10.** lower. **11.** supply; right **12.** labor; capital; natural resources; technology **13.** working-age population; percentage **14.** higher **15.** low levels of education; limited funds for research and development **16.** output produced; inputs **17.** Total factor productivity **18.** 2.6 percent (Growth is growth in *TFP* plus growth in each resource × that resource's share of national income. For this case, growth = 1 (*TFP* growth) + .7 (1 percent growth in labor × labor's .7 share of national income) + .9 (3 percent growth in capital × capital's .3 share of national income.)

Exercises and Applications

I. War on Inflation $\Delta M = (G - T) - B$. If G is decreased and T is increased, $(G - T)$ will be smaller. If there is no change in government borrowing, the change in the money supply will be negative and inflation will decrease.

II. Government Policy and Growth If the price paid for food crops is low enough, farmers will decide to do something else with their resources than grow food crops. They may switch to cash crops sold for export or just take more leisure, growing only enough to feed themselves and their families. Either way, the amount of food produced for sale to city dwellers will drop substantially. The low prices charged to city dwellers will not help them much when there is no food available for sale.

CHAPTER 17

Key Term Match

1. b **2.** d **3.** a **4.** f **5.** e **6.** c **7.** h **8.** g **9.** i

Quick-Check Quiz

1. a **2.** b **3.** a **4.** d **5.** b **6.** c **7.** d **8.** d **9.** c **10.** e

Practice Questions and Problems

1. a. Samoa (One Samoan worker can produce more mangoes than one worker in Fiji.) **b.** Samoa (One Samoan worker can produce more tons of papayas than one worker in Fiji.) **c.** 1/2 ton of mangoes (6 mangoes = 12 papayas, so 12/12 papayas = 6/12 mangoes) **d.** 1/3 ton of mangoes (2 mangoes = 6 papayas, so 6/6 papayas = 2/6 mangoes) **e.** Fiji (Fiji has the lower opportunity cost; it has to give up only 1/3 ton of mangoes to get a ton of papayas, whereas Samoa has to give up 1/2 ton.) **f.** 2 tons of papayas (6 mangoes = 12 papayas, so 6/6 mangoes = 12/6 papayas) **g.** 3 tons of papayas (2 mangoes = 6 papayas, so 2/2 mangoes = 6/2 papayas) **h.** Samoa (Samoa has the lower opportunity cost; it has to give up only 2 tons of papayas to get a ton of mangoes, whereas Fiji has to give up 3 tons.) **i.** 2; 3 **2. a.** productivity differences **b.** product life cycle **c.** human skills **d.** factor abundance **e.** consumer preferences **3.** tariffs; developing **4.** infant industry **5.** redistribute **6.** taxes; exports **7.** raise; decrease **8.** Independently Floating

Exercises and Applications

I. Saving Jobs by Restricting Imports: Is It Worth the Cost?

1. $487,995 (the $2,947,000,000 total cost divided by the 6,039 jobs saved)
2. $2,343,100,000 (the $2,947,000,000 total cost minus (6,039 × $100,000))
3. yes
4. The U.S. could help these workers get an education by paying for college or a trade school. As you learned in Chapter 3, workers with more skills usually get paid better.

II. Tax Effects of Import Restrictions

1. $330 (3.3 percent of $50,000 = $1,650 spent on clothing; 20 percent of $1,650 = $330); 0.66 percent ($330/$50,000 = .0066 = 0.66 percent)
2. $230 (4.6 percent of $25,000 = $1,150 spent on clothing; 20 percent of $1,150 = $230); 0.92 percent ($230/$25,000 = .0092 = 0.92 percent)
3. $108 (5.4 percent of $10,000 = $540 spent on clothing; 20 percent of $540 = $108); 1.08 percent ($108/$10,000 = .0108 = 1.08 percent)
4. Yes. (The percentage of income paid in the "tax" is highest for low-income families and then decreases for higher-income families.)

CHAPTER 18

Key Term Match

1. d **2.** b **3.** a **4.** c

Quick-Check Quiz

1. a **2.** c **3.** a **4.** c **5.** a **6.** a **7.** e **8.** b **9.** b **10.** e

Practice Questions and Problems

1. false **2.** about the same as **3.** decrease **4.** economic integration; technology; personal contact; political engagement **5.** Technology **6.** Falling **7.** The World Trade Organization; the World Bank; the International Monetary Fund **8.** World Bank **9.** World Trade Organization **10.** Free trade is harmful to people who might lose their jobs if lower-cost foreign producers are permitted to compete with domestic producers. Globalization results in countries competing for international investment by offering little or no environmental regulations or labor standards. International organizations are the tools of multinational corporations, who use them to generate profits without regard for the interests of the citizens of the world. **11.** Free trade based on comparative advantage raises living standards everywhere. International organizations are funded by governments, not corporations; they are tools of governments in achieving international agreements that benefit their people. Environmental quality and wages tend to improve after globalization. **12.** governments **13.** Hong Kong; South Korea; Singapore; Taiwan **14.** growth; reduction **15.** does not **16.** shrunk **17.** fixed **18.** floating **19.** fixed exchange rates; falling international reserves; lack of transparency; short-term international investment **20.** greater

Exercises and Applications

I. China's Currency Manipulation

a. If its currency appreciates against the dollar, Chinese exports will be more expensive for Americans and American imports will be cheaper for Chinese consumers. China is trying to protect its export industries.
b. Yes. If China permits the Yuan to rise, American exports become cheaper, which would increase the number of jobs in American export industries
c. China might retaliate by imposing tariffs against American imports into China.
d. No. To help its export industries, China manipulates its currency to be weak. If China was trying to prop up its currency, it would be vulnerable to a speculative attack.

II. U.S. Steel Tariffs

a. U.S. companies probably argued "Fair," not "Free" trade. Subsidies on loans from state-run banks unfairly lowered costs for Chinese producers. They also may have argued that the competition was unfair because Chinese safety and environmental standards are not as strict as U.S. standards. Another argument might be that higher tariffs are needed to protect U.S. jobs.
b. Prices will increase as a result of the tariff.
c. China might impose tariffs on U.S. exports to China.

GLOSSARY

A

absolute advantage: an advantage derived from one country's having a lower absolute input cost of producing a particular good than another country

adaptive expectations: expectations formed on the basis of information collected in the past

adverse selection: a situation where a lack of information causes low-quality items to dominate a market and high-quality items to be driven out of the market

aggregate demand curve: a curve that shows the different levels of expenditures on domestic output at different levels of prices

aggregate supply curve: a curve that shows the amount of real GDP produced at different price levels

antitrust: laws that restrict large dominant firms from behaving anticompetitively

Asian tigers: Hong Kong, South Korea, Singapore, and Taiwan—countries that globalized in the 1960s and 1970s and experienced fast economic growth

automatic stabilizer: an element of fiscal policy that changes automatically as income changes

average revenue (AR): per-unit revenue, total revenue divided by quantity $AR = TR \div Q = P \times Q \div Q$

average total costs (ATC): per-unit costs, total costs divided by quantity $ATC = TC \div Q$

B

balance of trade: the balance on the merchandise account in a nation's balance of payments

base year: the year against which other years are measured

brand name: a way to differentiate similar products from each other

budget deficit: the shortage that results when government spending is greater than revenue

budget surplus: the excess that results when government spending is less than revenue

business cycle: pattern of rising real GDP followed by falling real GDP

C

capital: the equipment, machines, and buildings used to produce goods and services

capital consumption allowance: the estimated value of depreciation plus the value of accidental damage to capital stock

cartel: an organization of independent firms whose purpose is to control and limit production and maintain or increase prices and profits; an organization of independent producers that dictates the quantities produced by each member of the organization

circular flow diagram: a model showing the flow of output and income from one sector of the economy to another

coincident indicator: a variable that changes at the same time that real output changes

collusion: the practice by rivals to limit competition by agreeing not to lower prices or to work together to limit entry by others

commercial policy: government policy that influences international trade flows

commodity: goods perceived to be identical no matter who supplies them

comparative advantage: the situation where one individual's opportunity cost is relatively lower than another's

compensating wage differential: wage differences due to different risks or job characteristics

consumer price index (CPI): a measure of the average price of goods and services purchased by the typical household

consumer surplus: the difference between what the consumer is willing to pay for a unit of a good and the price that the consumer actually has to pay; the difference between what consumers would be willing to pay and what they have to pay to purchase some item

consumption: household spending

convention: an institution procedure increasing efficiency

cost of living adjustments (COLAs): an increase in wages that is designed to match increases in the prices of items purchased by the typical household

cost-plus or markup pricing: a pricing policy whereby a firm computes its average cost of producing a product and then sets the price at some percentage above this cost; a price set by adding an amount to the per-unit cost of producing and supplying a good or service

cost-push inflation: inflation caused by rising costs of production

creative destruction: the process of competition whereby old, inefficient, or obsolete goods, services, and resources are driven out of business as new or efficient technologies and goods and services arise

credit: available savings that are lent to borrowers to spend

crowding out: a drop in consumption or investment spending caused by government spending

currency substitution: the use of foreign money as a substitute for domestic money when the domestic economy has a high rate of inflation

current account: the sum of the merchandise, services, investment income, and unilateral transfers accounts in the balance of payments

D

deadweight loss: the reduction of consumer surplus without a corresponding increase in monopoly profit when a perfectly competitive firm is monopolized

demand: the amount of a product that people are willing and able to purchase at every possible price

demand curve: a graph showing the law of demand

demand schedule: a table listing the quantity demanded at each price

demand-pull inflation: inflation caused by increasing demand for output

deposit expansion multiplier: the reciprocal of the reserve requirement

depreciation: a reduction in value of capital goods over time due to their use in production

depression: a severe, prolonged economic contraction

determinants of demand: things that influence demand other than the price

determinants of supply: those factors that affect supply other than price

differentiated: a good, service, or firm that consumers believe to be somewhat unique

discount rate: the interest rate the Fed charges commercial banks when they borrow from it

discouraged workers: workers who have stopped looking for work because they believe no one will offer them a job

discretionary fiscal policy: changes in government spending and taxation aimed at achieving a policy goal

discrimination: the practice of treating people differently in a market, based on a characteristic having nothing to do with that market

diseconomies of scale: the increases in per-unit costs when all resources are increased

disequilibrium: a price level at which quantities demanded and supplied are not the same

disposable personal income (DPI): personal income minus personal taxes

dominant strategy: a strategy that produces best results no matter what strategy the opposing firm follows

E

economic freedom: the ability to engage in voluntary trade without interference or restrictions by government or outside parties

economic profit: revenue less all costs, including the opportunity cost of the owner's capital

economies of scale: the decreases in per-unit costs when all resources are increased

efficiency: the measure of how well an allocation system satisfies people's wants and needs

elastic: percent change in quantity demanded greater than percent change in price

equation of exchange: an equation that relates the quantity of money to nominal GDP

equilibrium: the price and quantity at which quantity demanded equals quantity supplied

Eurocurrency market (offshore banking): the market for deposits and loans generally denominated in a currency other than the currency of the country in which the transaction occurs

excess reserves: the cash reserves beyond those required, which can be loaned

exports: products that a country sells to other countries

externalities: a cost or benefit created by a transaction that is not paid for or enjoyed by those carrying out the transaction

F

facilitating practices: actions by oligopolistic firms that can contribute to cooperation and collusion even though the firms do not formally agree to cooperate; actions that lead to cooperation among rivals

federal funds rate: the interest rate a bank charges when it lends excess reserves to another bank

Federal Open Market Committee (FOMC): the official policymaking body of the Federal Reserve System

Federal Reserve: the central bank of the United States

financial account: the record in the balance of payments of the flow of financial assets into and out of a country

financial capital: the funds used to purchase capital

fiscal policy: policy directed toward government spending and taxation

fixed costs: costs of fixed resources; costs that do not change as output changes

FOMC directive: instructions issued by the FOMC to the Federal Reserve Bank of New York to implement monetary policy

foreign exchange: currency and bank deposits that are denominated in foreign money

foreign exchange market: a global market in which people trade one currency for another

foreign exchange market intervention: the buying and selling of foreign exchange by a central bank to move exchange rates to a targeted level

fractional reserve banking system: a system in which banks keep less than100 percent of the deposits available for withdrawal

free rider: a consumer or producer who enjoys a good or service without paying for it

G

gains from trade: the additional amount one can consume by trading

game theory: a description of oligopolistic behavior as a series of strategic moves and countermoves

GDP price index (GDPPI): a broad measure of the prices of goods and services included in the gross domestic product

gross domestic product (GDP): the market value of all final goods and services produced in a year within a country

gross investment: total investment, including investment expenditures required to replace capital goods consumed in current production

gross national product (GNP): gross domestic product plus receipts of factor income from the rest of the world minus payments of factor income to the rest of the world

H

hawala: a network for transferring money, popular in Muslim countries

household: one or more persons who occupy a unit of housing

I

imports: products that a country buys from other countries

increasing-returns-to-scale industry: an industry in which the costs of producing a unit of output fall as more output is produced

indirect business taxes: taxes that are collected by businesses for a government agency

inelastic: percent change in quantity demanded less than percent change in price

inferior goods: as income rises, quantity demandedfalls

inflation: a sustained rise in the average level of prices

interest rate effect: a change in interest rates that causes investment and therefore aggregate expenditures to change as the level of prices changes

intermediate goods: goods that are used as inputs in the production of final goods and services

intermediate target: an objective used to achieve some ultimate policy goal

internalized: a situation when what was an external cost is paid for by the parties creating the cost

international banking facility (IBF): a division of a U.S. bank that is allowed to receive deposits from and make loans to nonresidents of the United States without the restrictions that apply to domestic U.S. banks

international reserve asset: an asset used to settle debts between governments

international reserve currency: a currency held by a government to settle international debts

international trade effect: a change in aggregate expenditures resulting from a change in the domestic price level that changes the price of domestic goods in relation to foreign goods

intraindustry trade: simultaneous import and export of goods in the same industry by a particular country

inventory: the stock of unsold goods held by a firm

investment: spending on capital goods to be used in producing goods and services

L

labor: the general category of resources encompassing all human activity related to the productive process

lagging indicator: a variable that changes after real output changes

land: the general category of resources encompassing all natural resources, land, and water

law of demand: an inverse relationship between price and quantity demanded

law of diminishing marginal returns: as the quantity of a variable resource is increased while fixed resources do not change, output initially rises rapidly, then more slowly, and eventually may decline

leading indicator: a variable that changes before real output changes

legal reserves: the cash a bank holds in its vault plus its deposit in the Fed

liquid asset: an asset that can easily be exchanged for goods and services

logrolling: legislators support one another's projects in order to ensure support for their own

long run: period of time just long enough so that everything can be changed

long-run aggregate supply curve (LRAS): a vertical line at the potential level of national income

M

M1 money supply: financial assets that are the most liquid

marginal costs (MC): incremental costs, change in total costs divided by change in quantity MC = change in $TC \div$ change in Q

marginal revenue (MR): incremental revenue, change in total revenue divided by change in quantity MR =change in $TR \div$ change in Q

market demand: the sum of the individual demands

monetary policy: policy directed toward the control of money and credit

money: anything that is generally acceptable to sellers in exchange for goods and services

monopolistic competition: a market structure characterized by a large number of firms, easy entry, and differentiated products

monopolization of a market: market dominance by one firm gained unfairly

monopoly: a market structure in which there is just one firm, and entry by other firms is not possible. One supplier of a good or service

moral hazard: a situation where imperfect information provides an incentive for a consumer or producer to change behavior after agreeing to a specific behavior

most-favored customer (MFC): a customer who receives a guarantee of the lowest price and all product features for a certain period of time; a commitment that the customer will receive a lower price if anyone else receives a lower price

multinational business: a firm that owns and operates producing units in foreign countries

murabaha: the most popular instrument for financing Islamic investments

N

Nash equilibria: no player can be made better off by changing unilaterally

national income (NI): net national product minus indirect business taxes

national income accounting: the framework that summarizes and categorizes productive activity in an economy over a specific period of time, typically a year

natural monopolies: when economies of scale lead to just one firm

natural rate of unemployment: the unemployment rate that would exist in the absence of cyclical unemployment

negative economic profit: revenue does not pay for all opportunity costs

net investment: gross investment minus capital consumption allowance

net national product (NNP): gross national product minus capital consumption allowance

NICs: newly industrialized countries

nominal GDP: a measure of national output based on the current prices of goods and services

nominal interest rate: the observed interest rate in the market

nonrenewable resources: resources that cannot replenish themselves

normal goods: as income rises, quantity demanded rises

normal profit: zero economic profit

O

open market operations: the buying and selling of government bonds by the Fed to control bank reserves, the federal funds rate, and the money supply

opportunity costs: the highest-valued alternative that must be forgone when a choice is made

P

perfect competition: a market structure characterized by such a large number of firms that no one firm has an effect on the market

perfectly elastic: infinite price elasticity

perfectly inelastic: zero price elasticity

personal income (PI): national income plus income currently received but not earned, minus income currently earned but not received

Phillips curve: a graph that illustrates the relationship between inflation and the unemployment rate

positive economic profit: revenue exceeds all opportunity costs

potential real GDP: the output produced at the natural rate of unemployment

precautionary demand for money: the demand for money to cover unplanned transactions or emergencies

price ceiling: a specific level above which price is not allowed to rise

price discrimination: different prices charged to different customers

price elasticity of demand: the percentage change in quantity demanded divided by the percentage change in price

price floor: a specific level below which price is not allowed to fall

price index: a measure of the average price level in an economy

price law of supply: as the price rises, the quantity supplied rises and vice versa

price taker: a firm in a perfectly competitive market structure

private property rights: ownership; the right to do anything you want with what you own as long as it does not harm the property of others. The right to claim ownership of an item

private sector: households, businesses, and the international sector

producer price index (PPI): a measure of average prices received by producers

production possibilities curve (PPC): a graphical representation showing the maximum quantity of goods and services that can be produced using limited resources to the fullest extent possible; it shows the maximum output that can be produced using resources fully and efficiently

productivity: total output per unit of input

progressive tax: a tax whose rate rises as income rises

proportional tax: a tax whose rate is constant as income rises

public goods: a good that is not excludable and is not rivalrous

public sector: the government

Q

quantity demanded: the amount of a product that people are willing and able to purchase at a specific price

quantity quota: a limit on the amount of a good that may be produced

quantity supplied: the amount supplied at any specific

quantity theory of money: with constant velocity, changes in the quantity of money change nominal GDP

quota: a limit on the amount of a good that may be imported

R

"race to the bottom": with globalization, countries compete for international investment by offering low or no environmental regulations or labor standards

rational expectations: expectations formed by using all available relevant information

real GDP: a measure of the quantity of goods and services produced, adjusted for price changes; a measure of the quantity of final goods and services produced, obtained by eliminating the influence of price changes from the nominal GDP statistics

real interest rate: the nominal interest rate minus the rate of inflation

recession: a period in which real GDP falls

regressive tax: a tax whose rate falls as income rises

regulation: the control of some aspect of business by the government

renewable resources: resources that can renew themselves

required reserves: the cash reserves (a percentage of deposits) a bank must keep on hand

reservation wage: the minimum wage a worker is willing to accept

resources: inputs used to create goods and services

ROSCAS: rotating savings and credit associations

S

scarcity: not everyone can get everything he wants

Shadow bank: non-bank financial institutions that can issue packages of assets, like home mortgages, that may have different risks than the underlying individual mortgages

shock: an unexpected change in a variable

short run: a period of time just short enough so that at least one resource is fixed

shortage: the quantity demanded is greater than the quantity supplied

social regulation: government regulation of health, safety, the environment, and employment policies

speculative attack: a situation in which private investors sell domestic currency and buy foreign currency, betting that the domestic currency will be devalued

speculative demand for money: the demand for money created by uncertainty about the value of other assets

statistically discriminating: using characteristics that apply to a group, although not to all individual members of that group, as an allocation device

sterilization: the use of domestic open market operations to offset the effects of a foreign exchange market intervention on the domestic money supply

strategic trade policy: the use of trade restrictions or subsidies to allow domestic firms with decreasing costs to gain a greater share of the world market

subsidies: a grant of money given to help produce or purchase a specific good or service

substitute goods: items that can be used in place of eachother; as the price of one rises, demand for the other rises

complementary goods: items that are used together; as theprice of one rises, demand for the other falls

sunk cost: cost that cannot be recouped

supply: the quantities suppliers are willing and able to supply at each price

supply curve: a plot of the supply schedule

supply schedule: a list of prices and corresponding quantities supplied

surplus: the quantity demanded is less than the quantity supplied

T

tariff: a tax on imports and selected exports

technology: ways of combining resources to produce output

total factor productivity (TFP): the ratio of the economy's output to its stock of labor and capital

total revenue: price times quantity sold ($P \times Q$)

trade deficit: the situation that exists when imports exceed exports

net exports: the difference between the value of exports and the value of imports

trade surplus: the situation that exists when imports are less than exports

trade-offs: what must be given up to acquire something else

transactions account: a checking account at a bank or other financial institution that can be drawn on to make payments

transactions demand for money: the demand to hold money to buy goods and services

transfer payments: income transferred from one citizen who is earning income to another citizen who may not be

U

underemployment: the employment of workers in jobs that do not utilize their productive potential

unemployment rate: the percentage of the labor force that is not working

unit elastic: price elasticity $= -1$

V

value added: the difference between the value of the output and the value of the intermediate goods used in the production of that output

value quota: a limit on the monetary value of a good that may be imported

value-added tax (VAT): a general sales tax collected at each stage of production

variable costs: costs that vary as output varies

velocity of money: the average number of times each dollar is spent on final goods and services in a year

W

wealth effect: a change in the real value of wealth that causes spending to change when the level of prices changes

Z

zero economic profit: revenue just pays all opportunity costs

INDEX

F

G